FLIGHT

VOLUME SIX

V

Villard Trade Paperbacks • New York

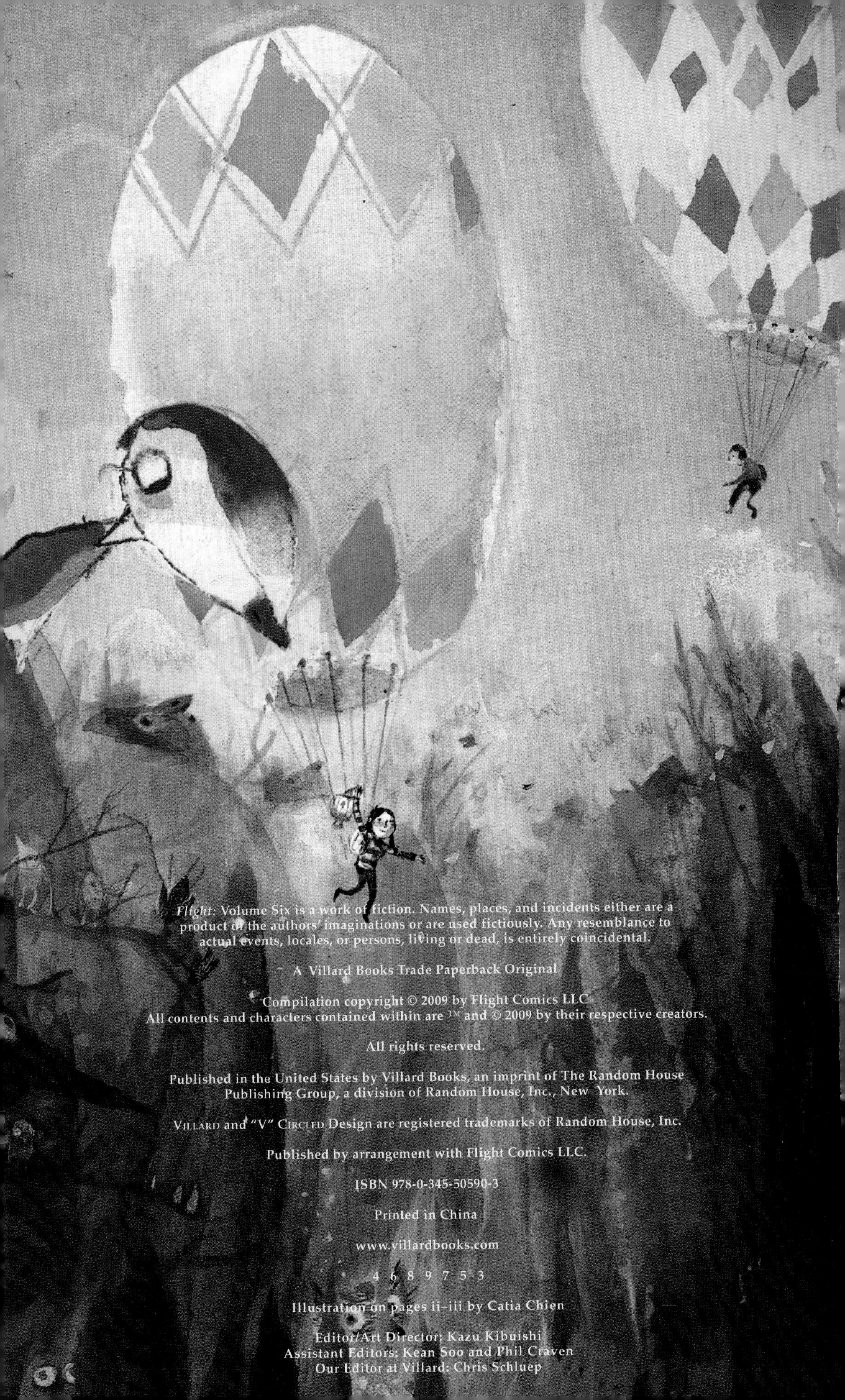

Flight: Volume Six is a work of fiction. Names, places, and incidents either are a product of the authors' imaginations or are used fictiously. Any resemblance to actual events, locales, or persons, living or dead, is entirely coincidental.

A Villard Books Trade Paperback Original

Published in the United States by Villard Books, an imprint of The Random House Publishing Group, a division of Random House, Inc., New York.

Published by arrangement with Flight Comics LLC.

ISBN 978-0-345-50590-3

Printed in China

www.villardbooks.com

4 6 8 9 7 5 3

Illustration on pages ii–iii by Catia Chien

Editor/Art Director: Kazu Kibuishi
Assistant Editors: Kean Soo and Phil Craven
Our Editor at Villard: Chris Schluep

CONTENTS

FLIGHT

VOLUME SIX

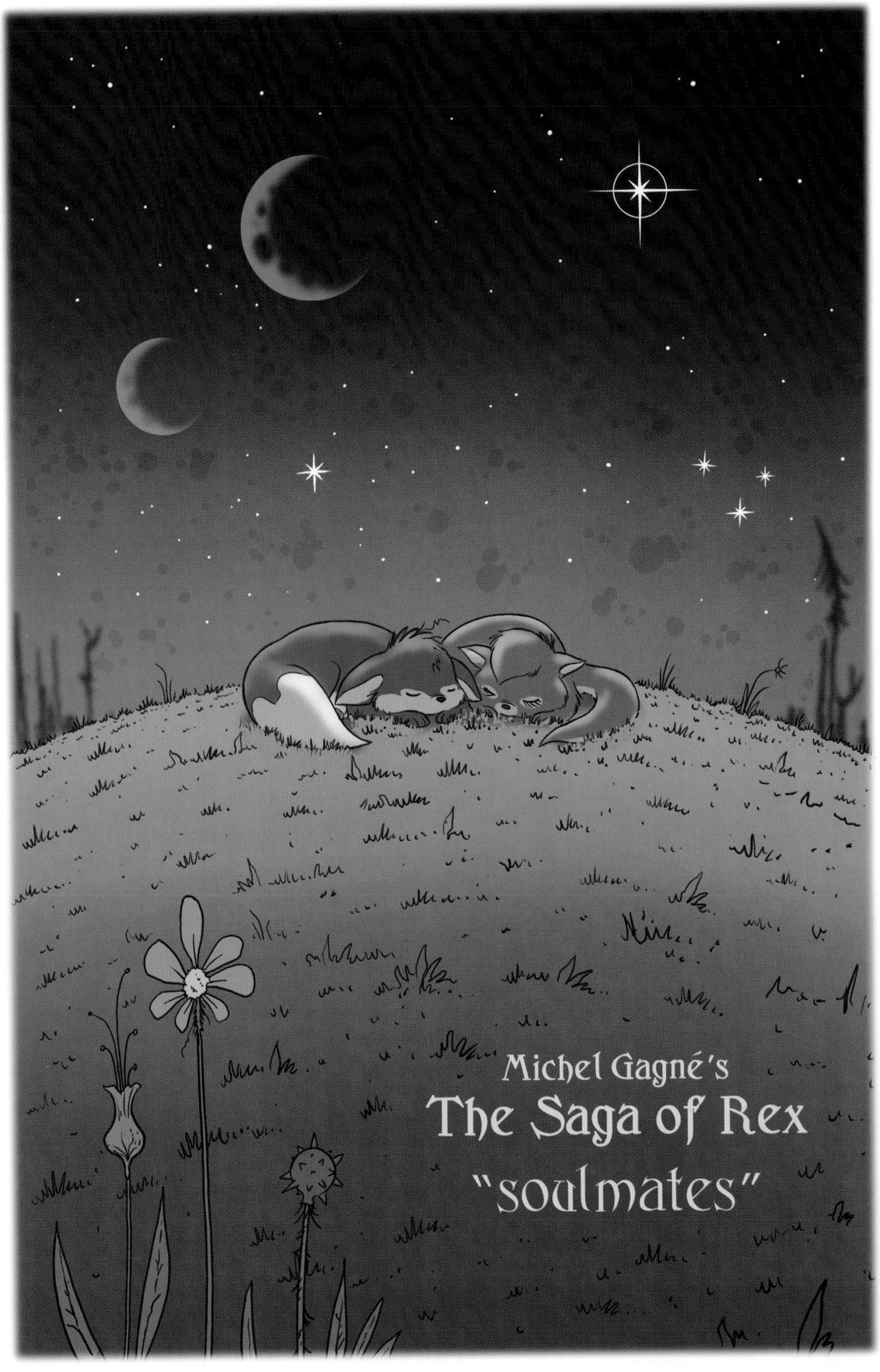
Michel Gagné's
The Saga of Rex
"soulmates"

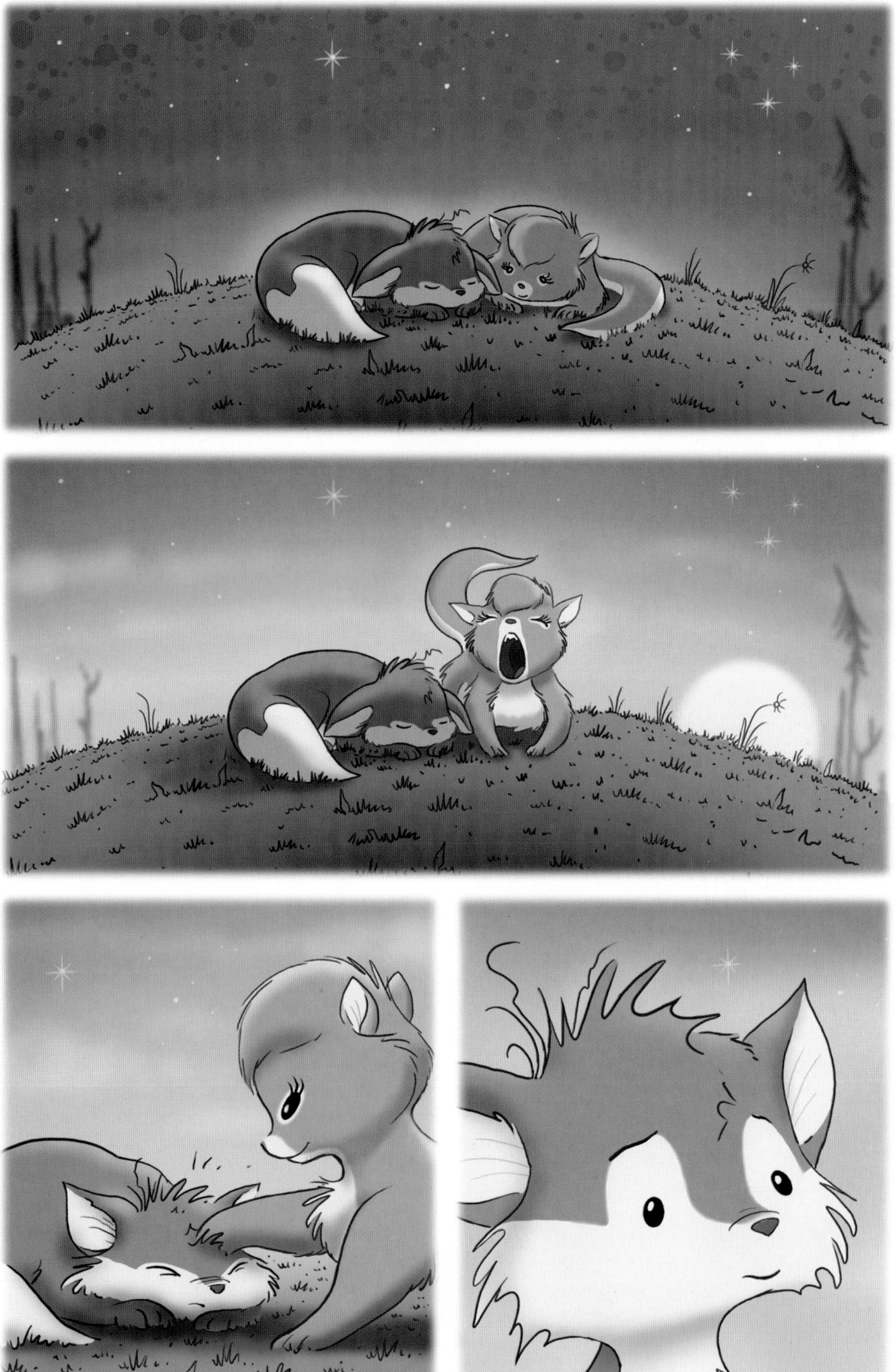

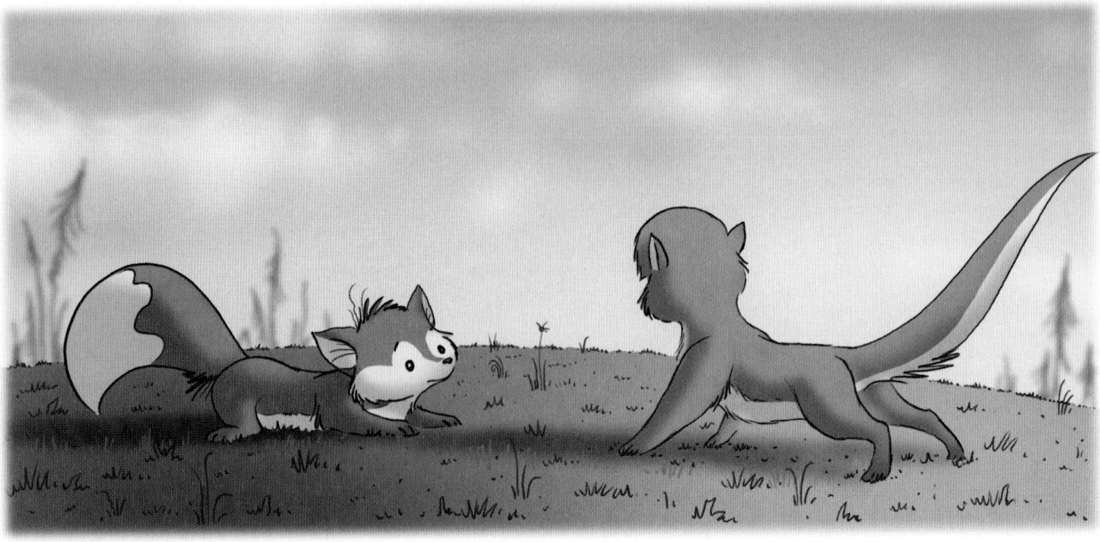

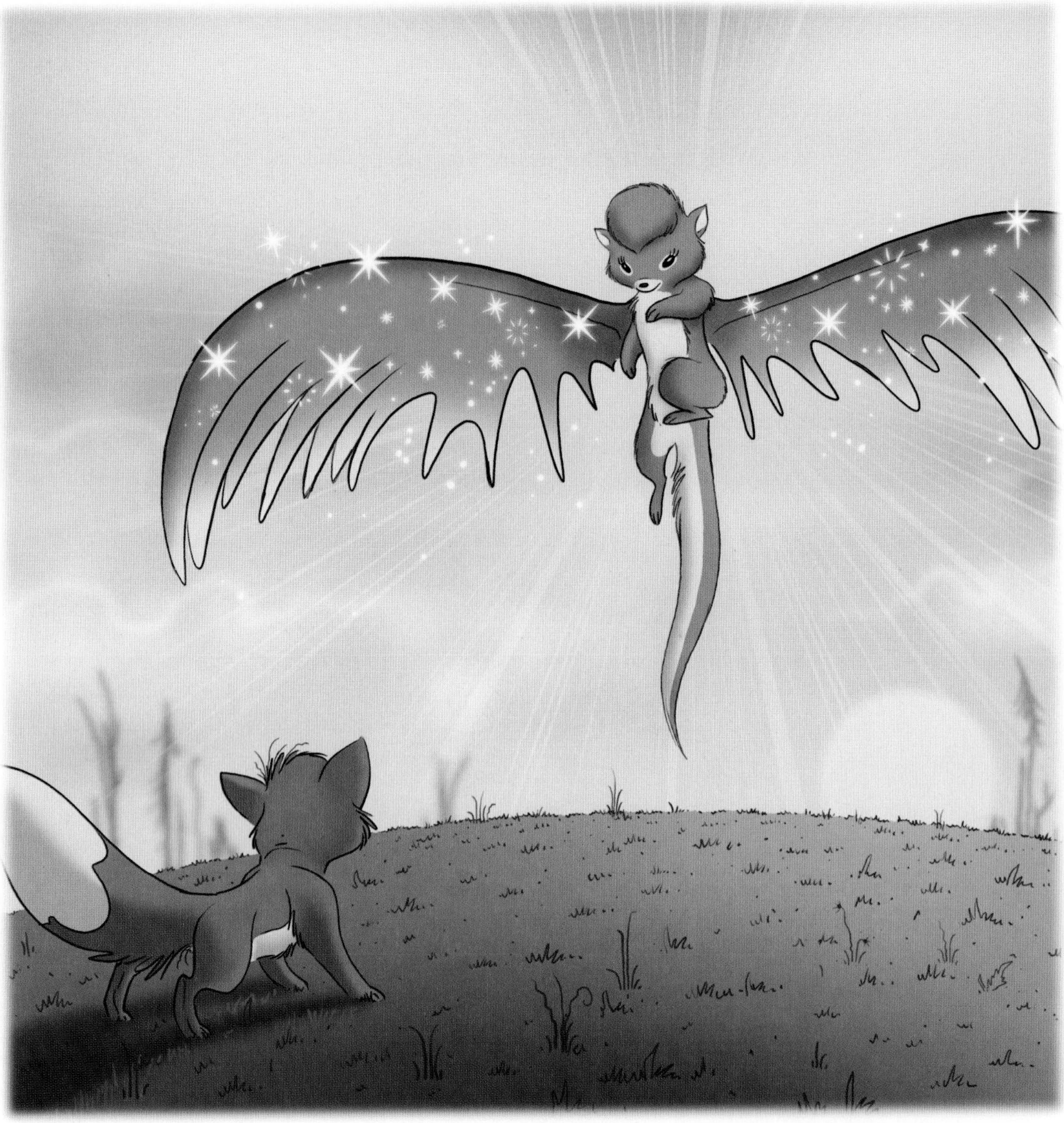

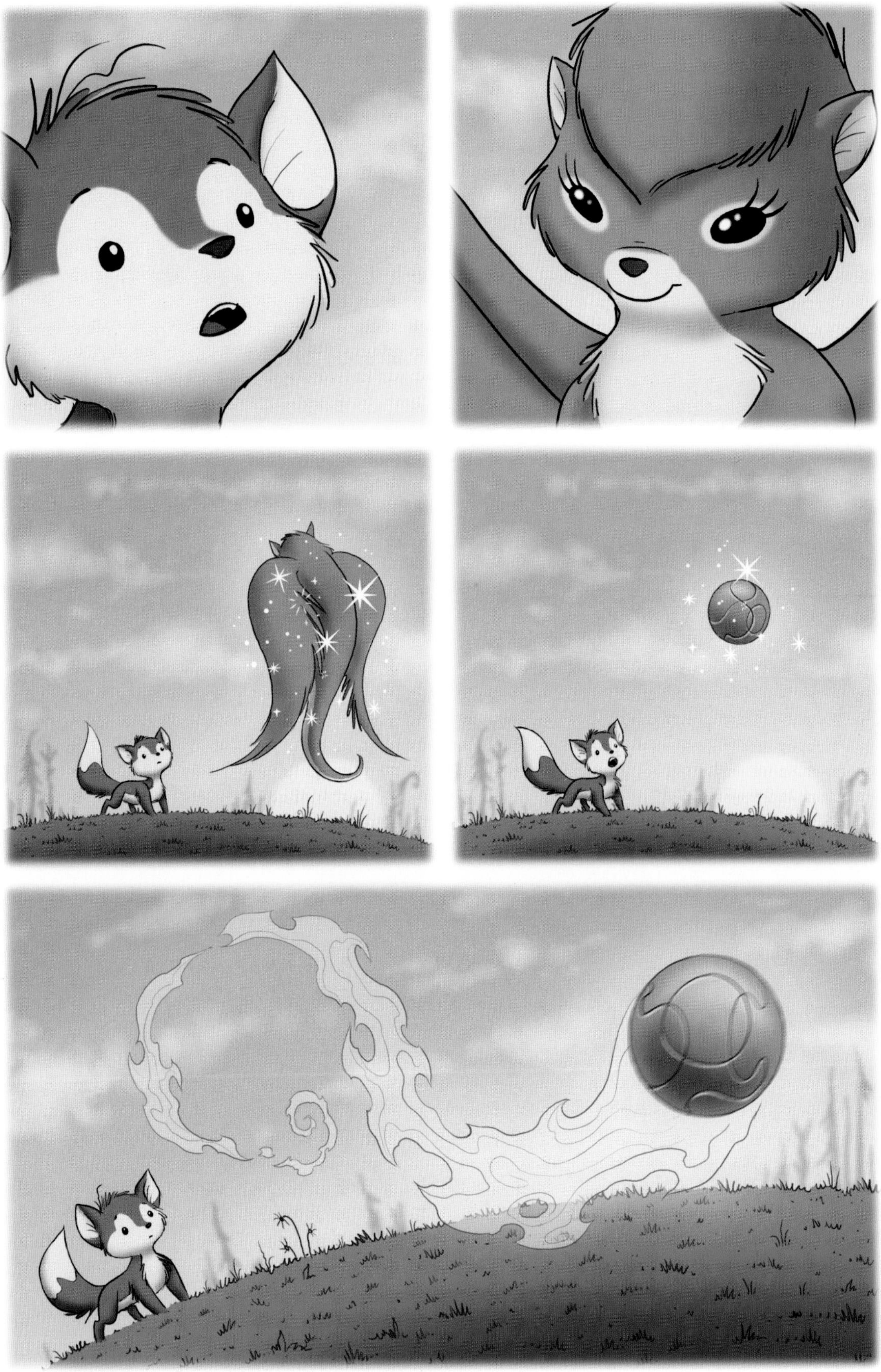

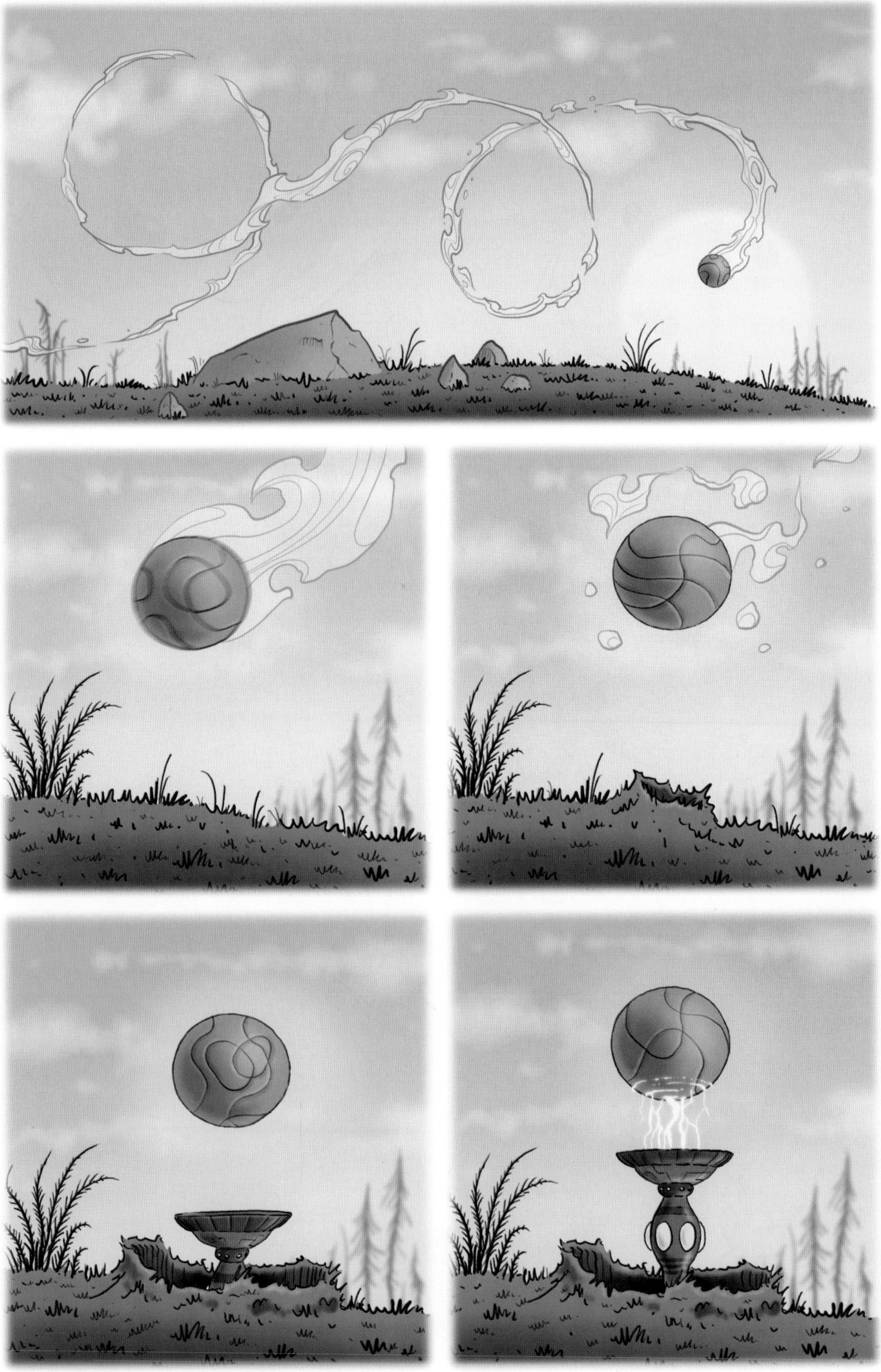

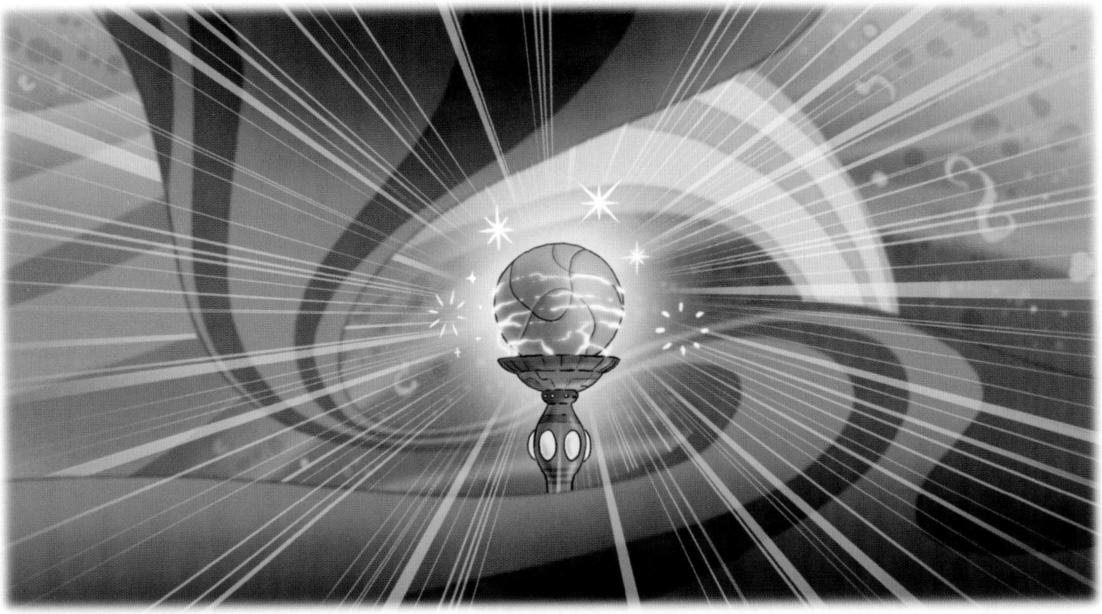

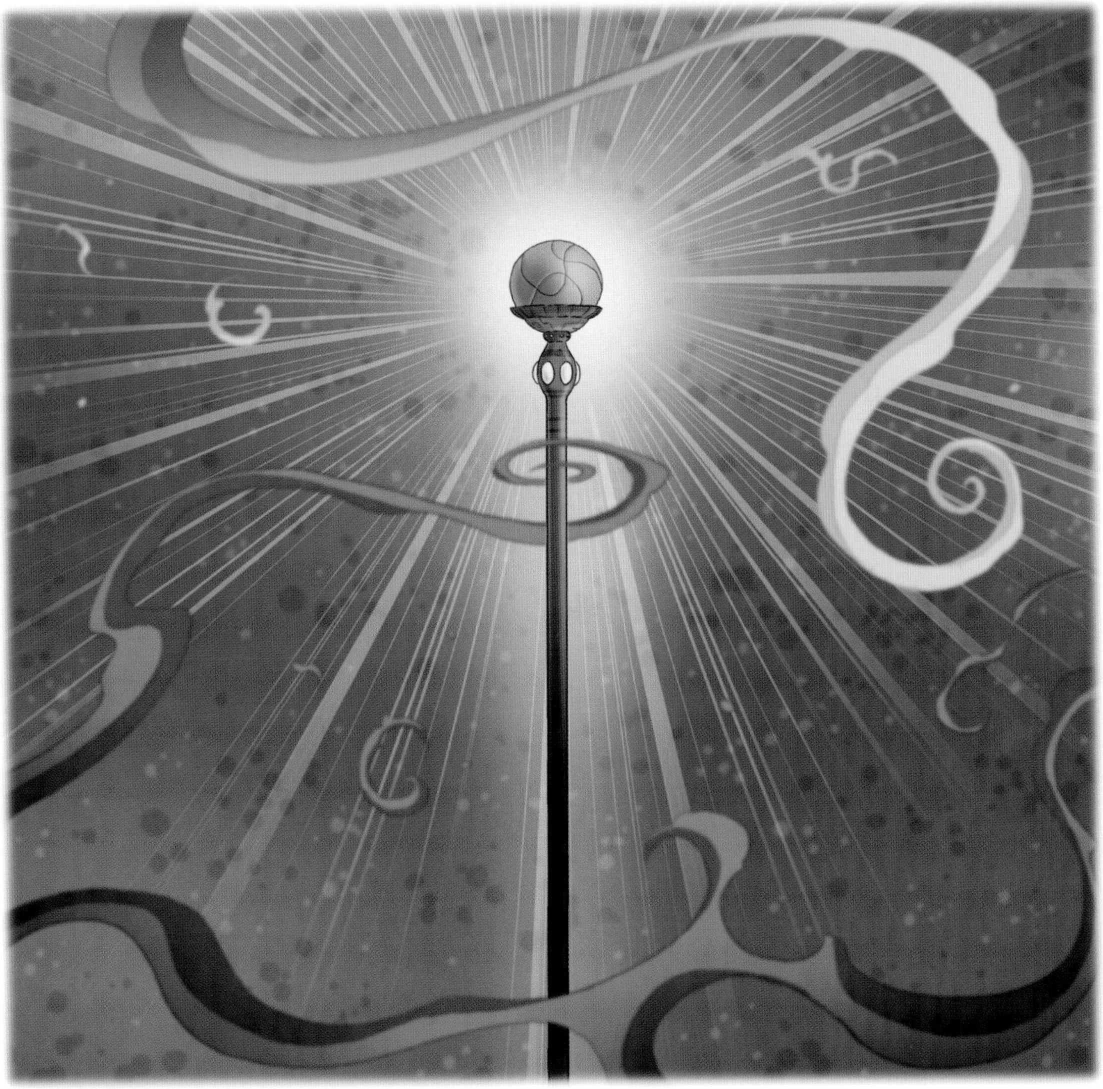

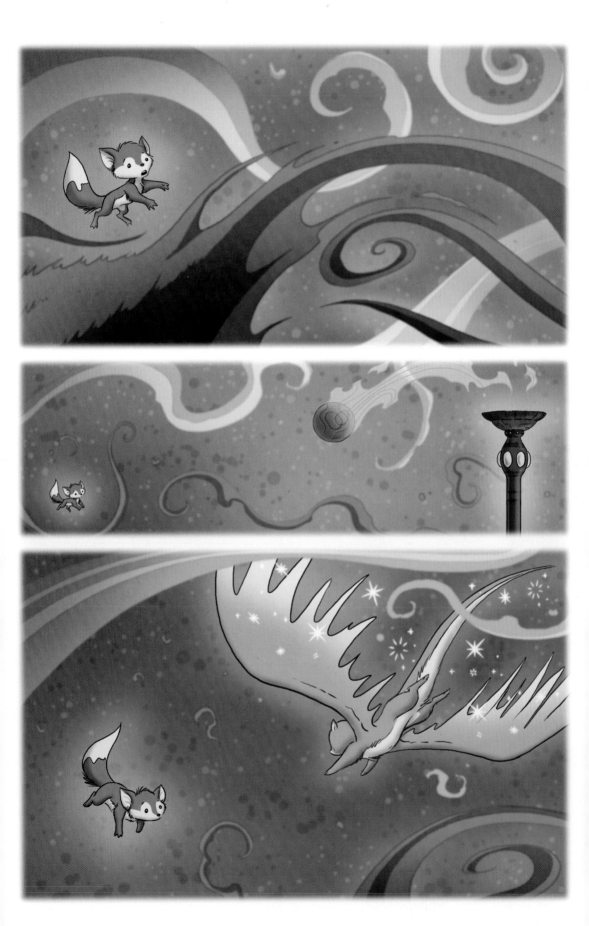

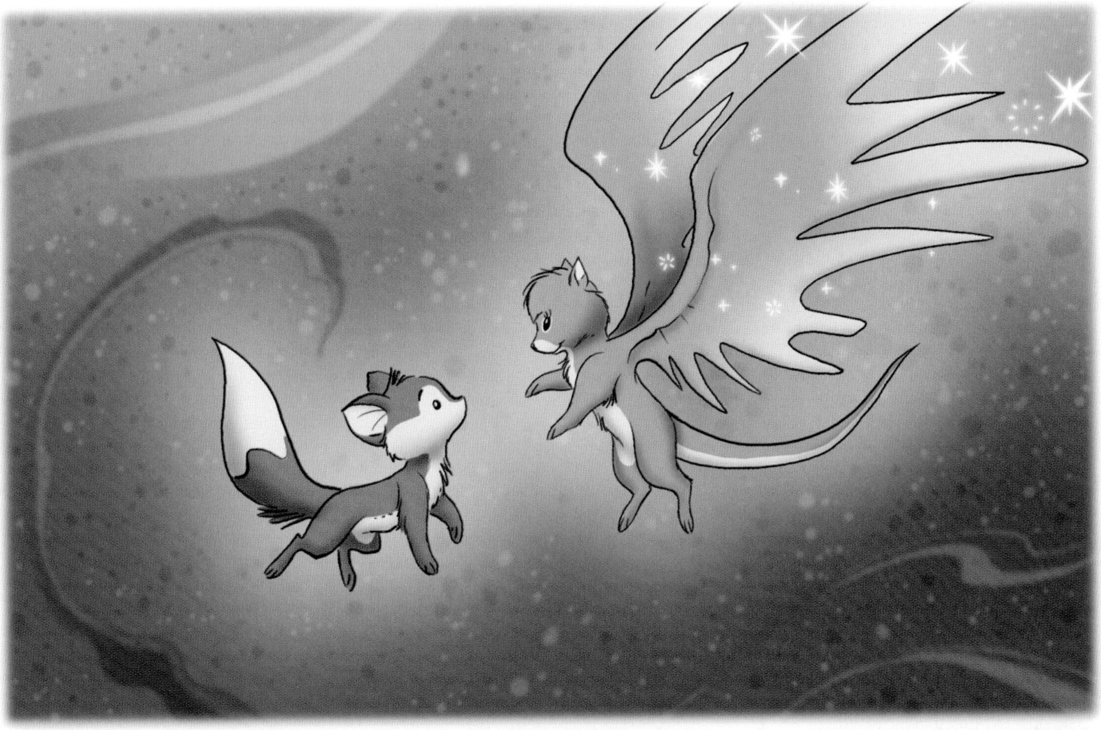

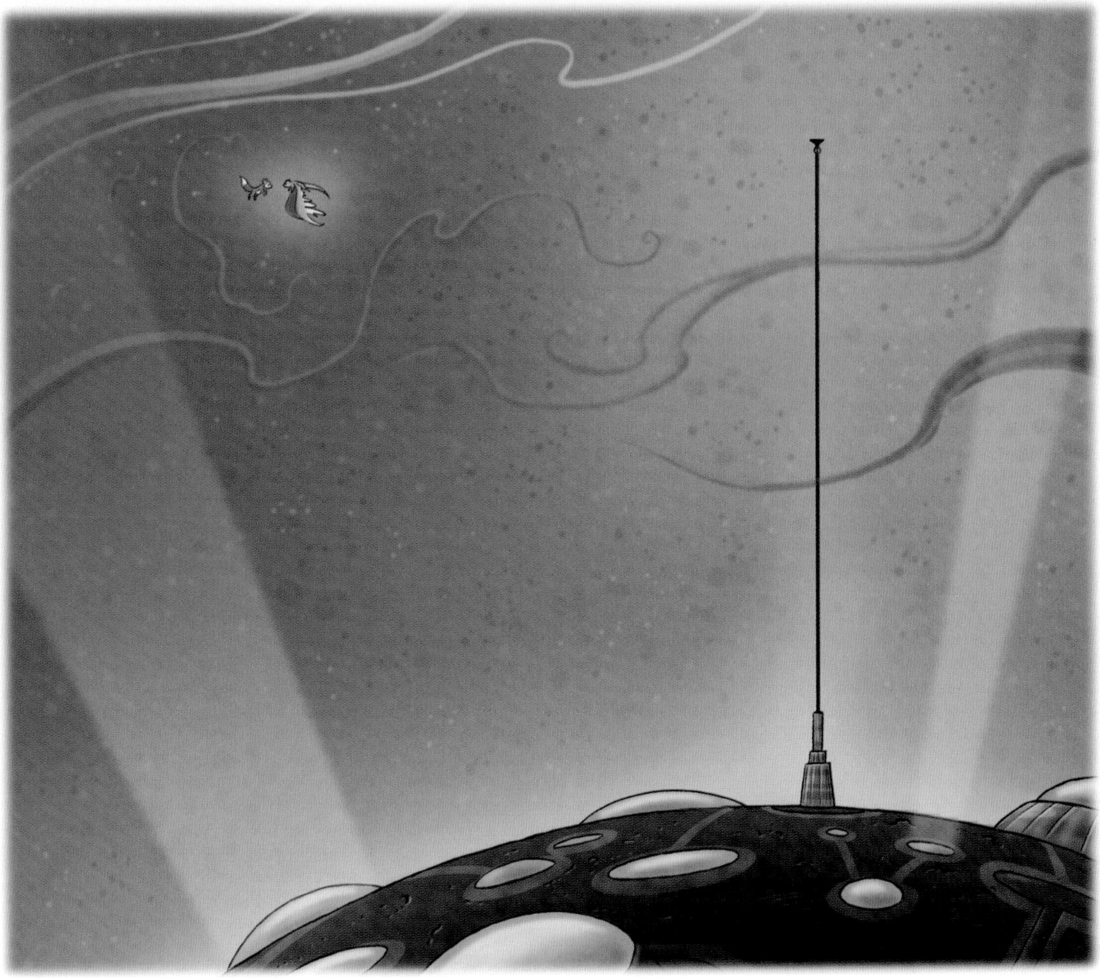

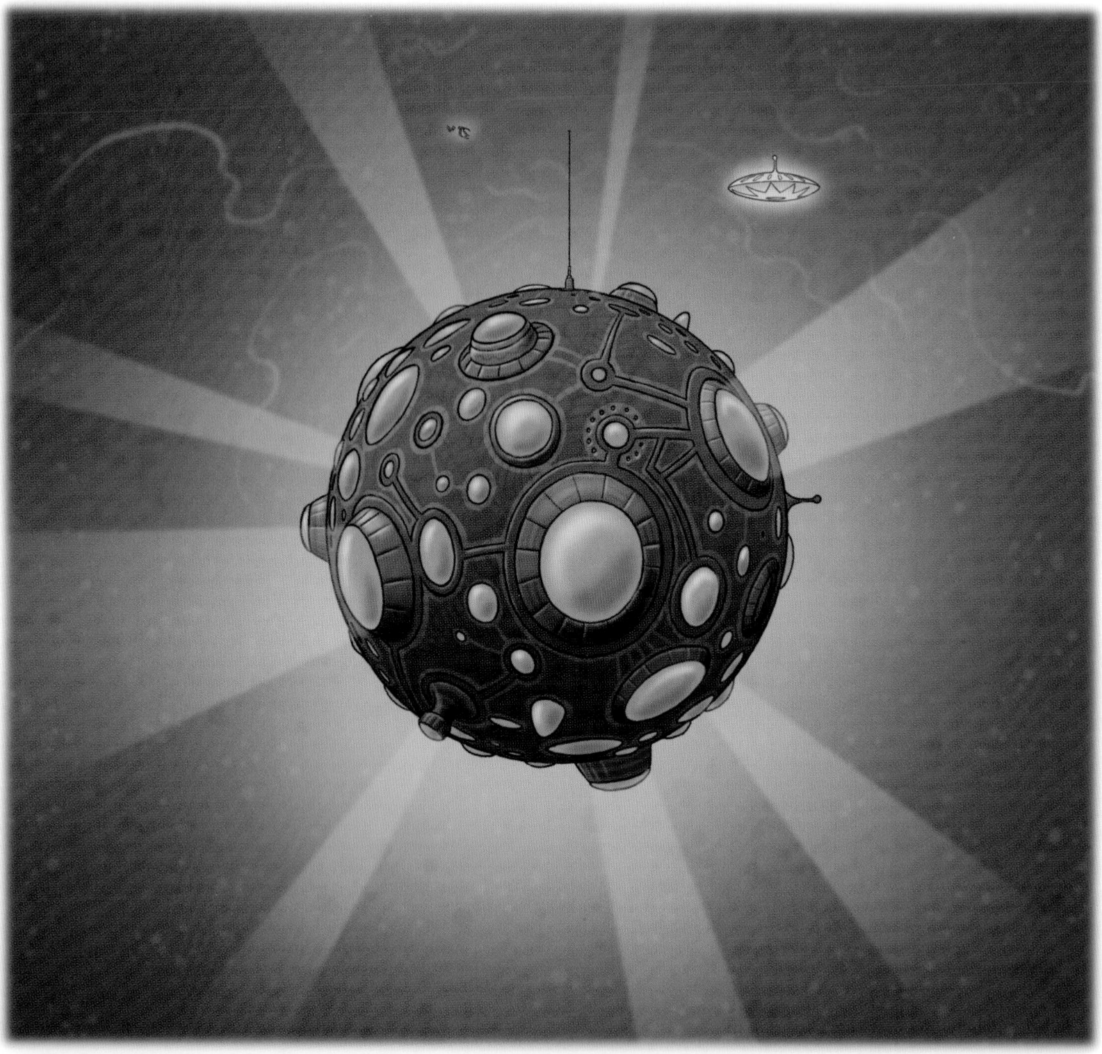

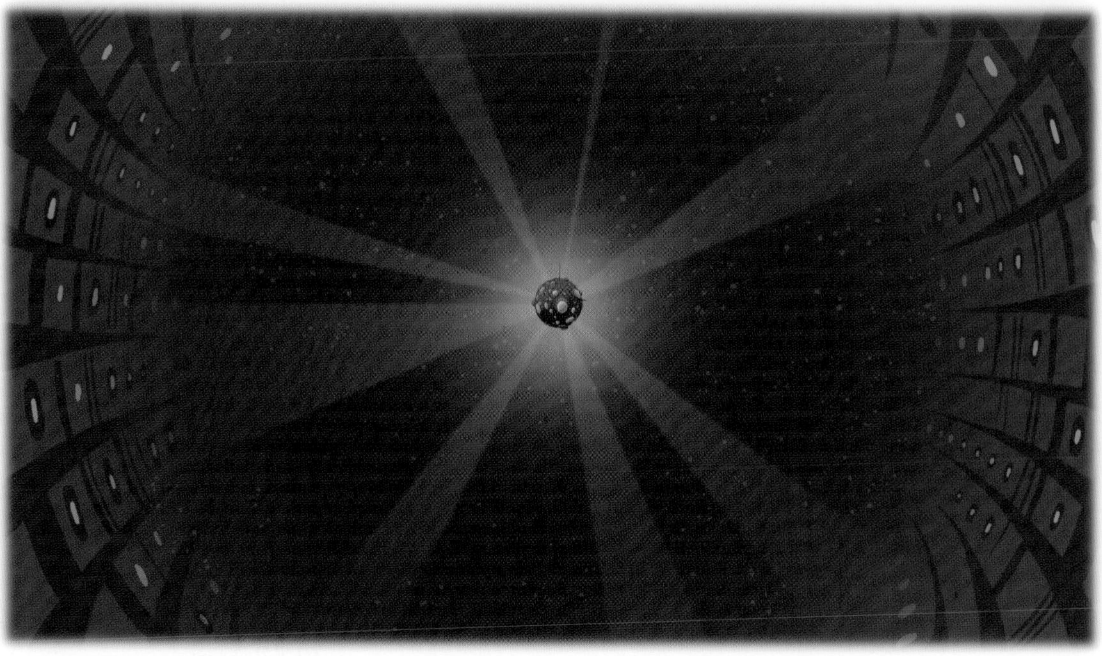

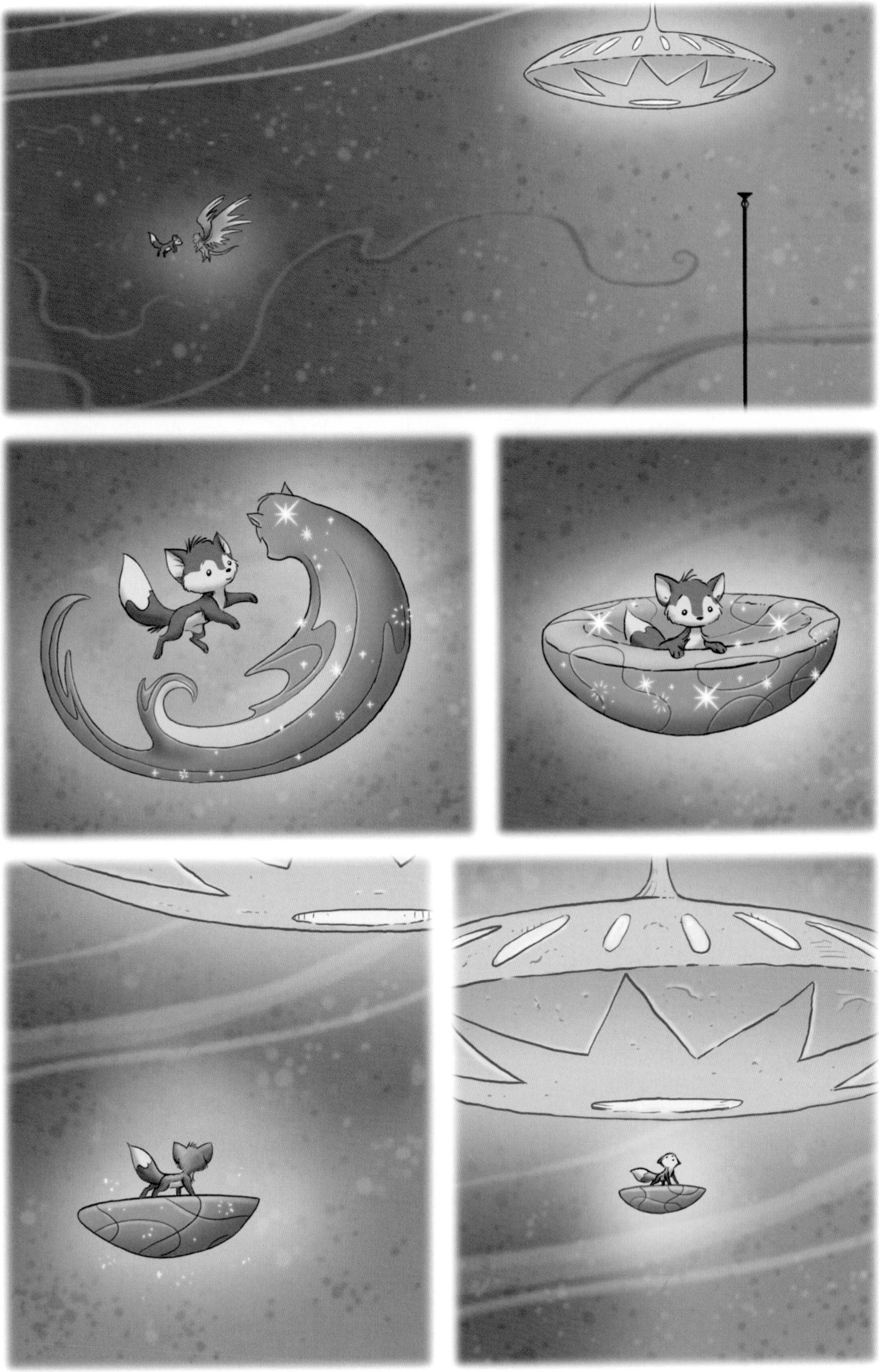

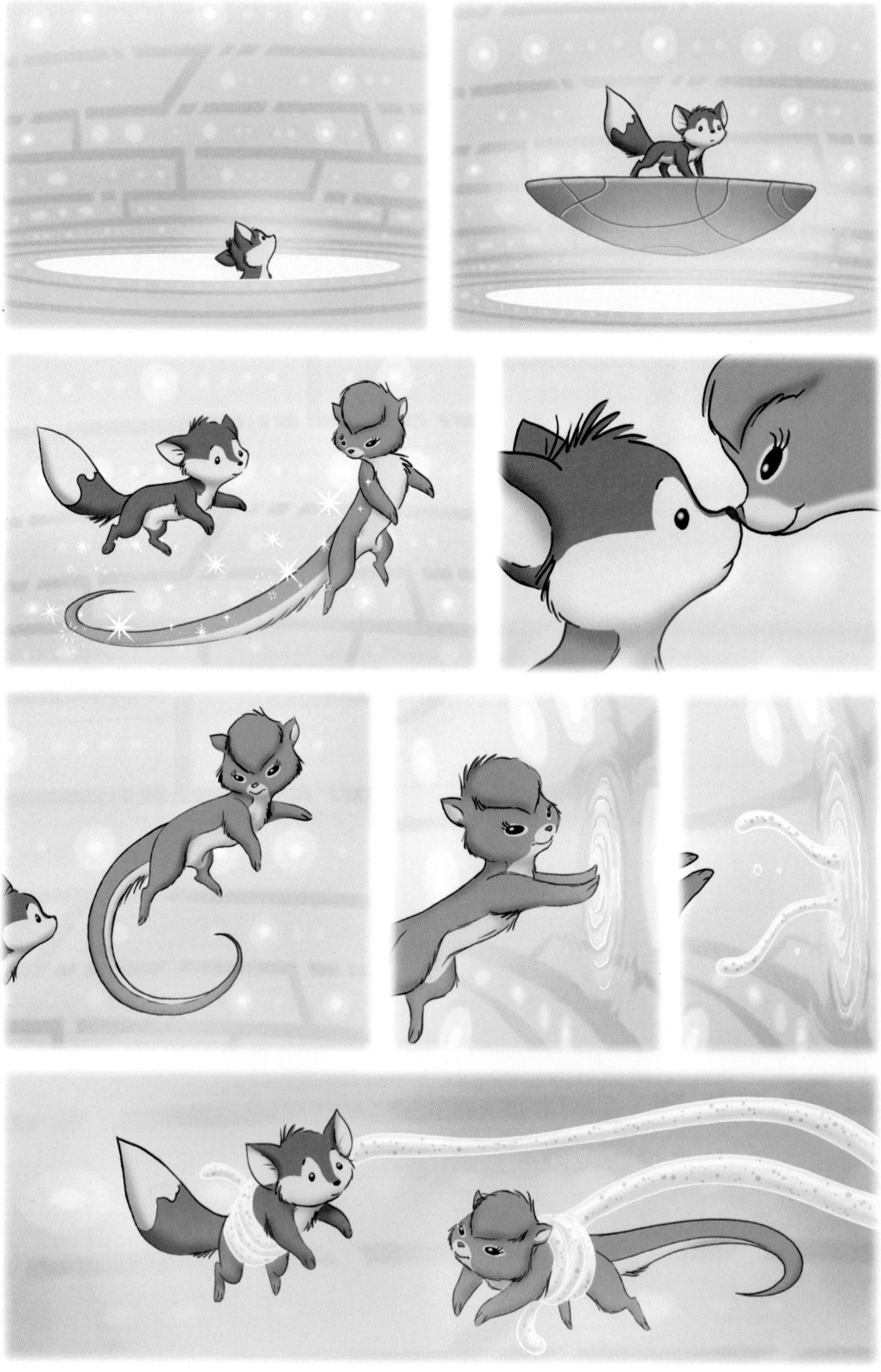

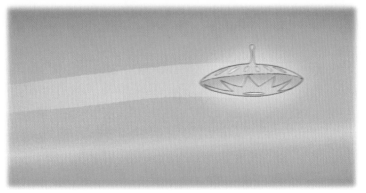

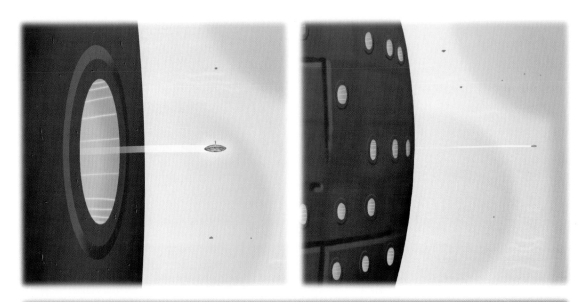

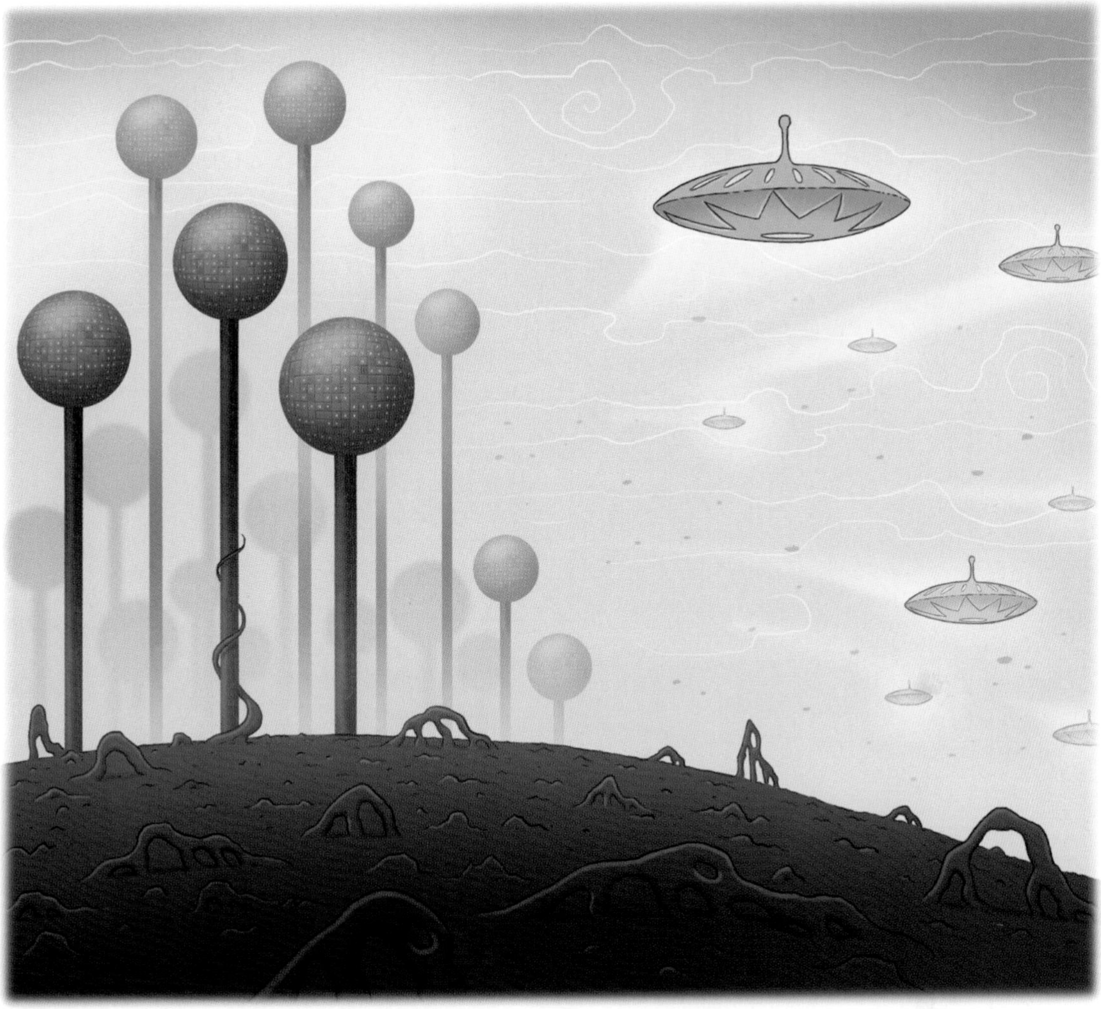

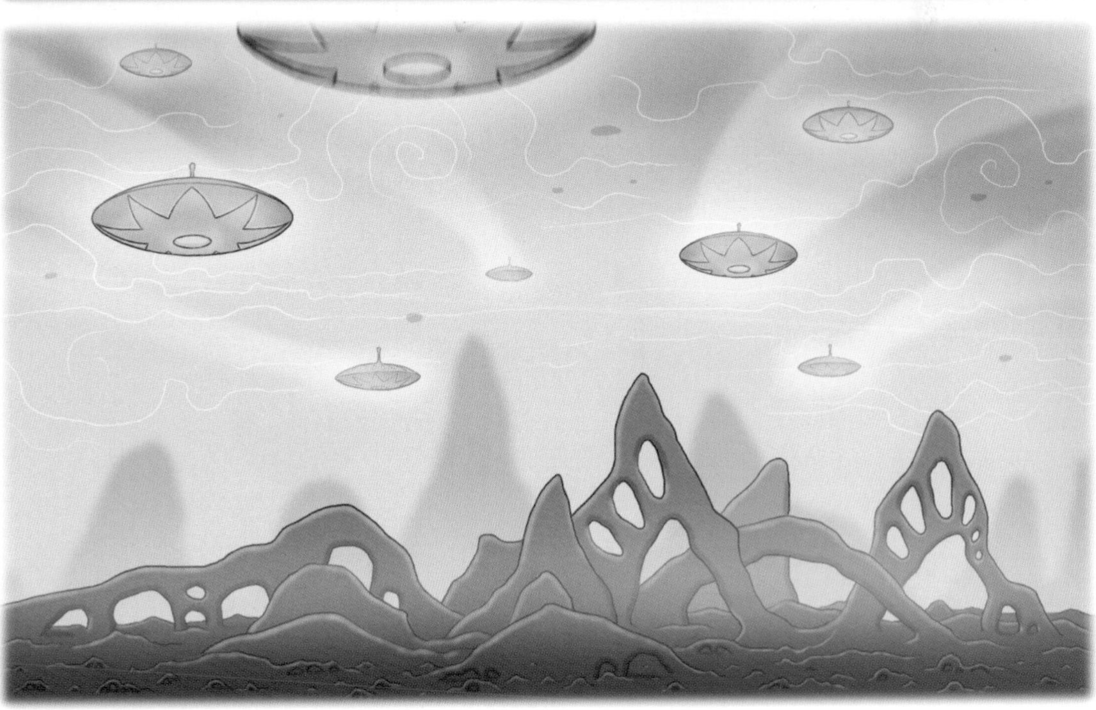

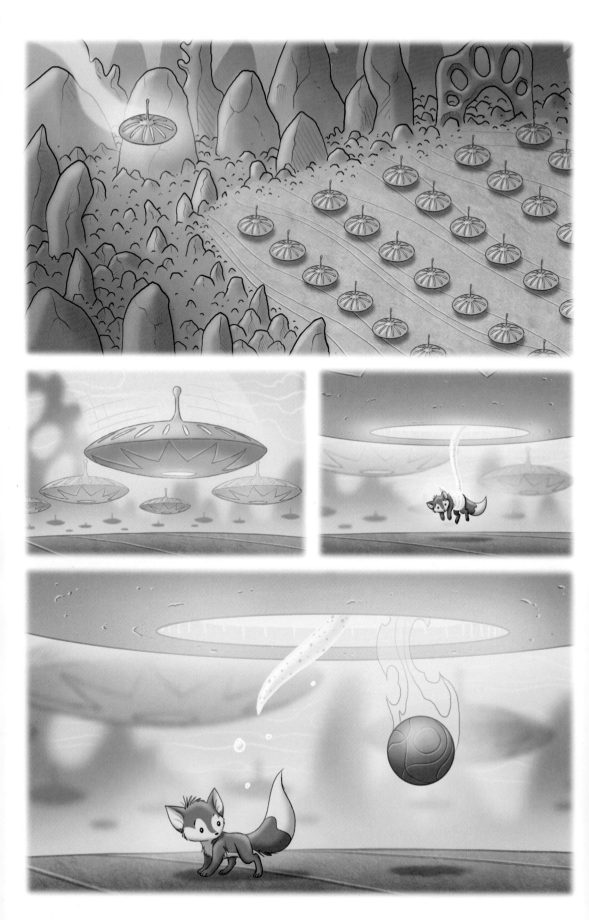

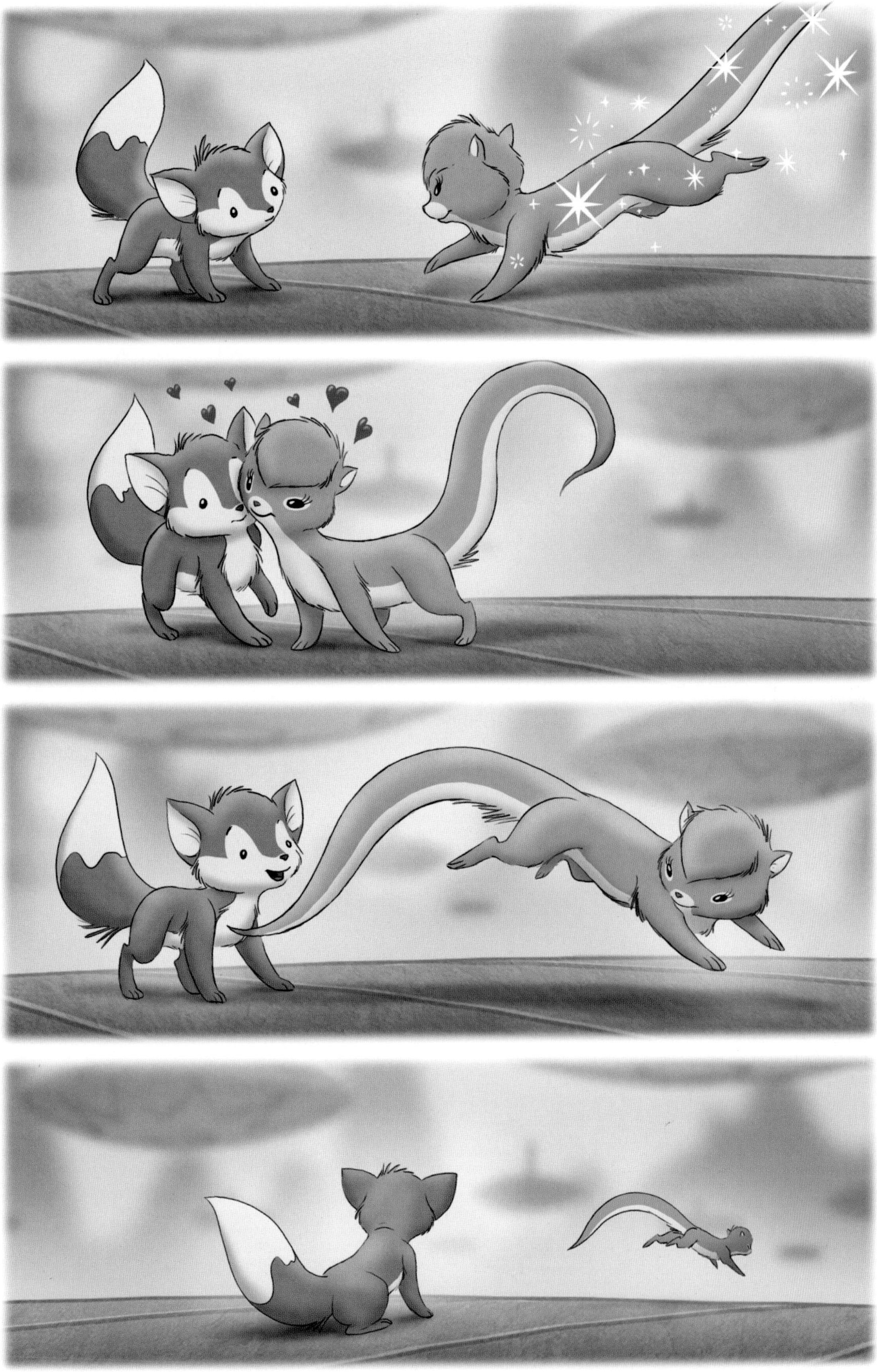

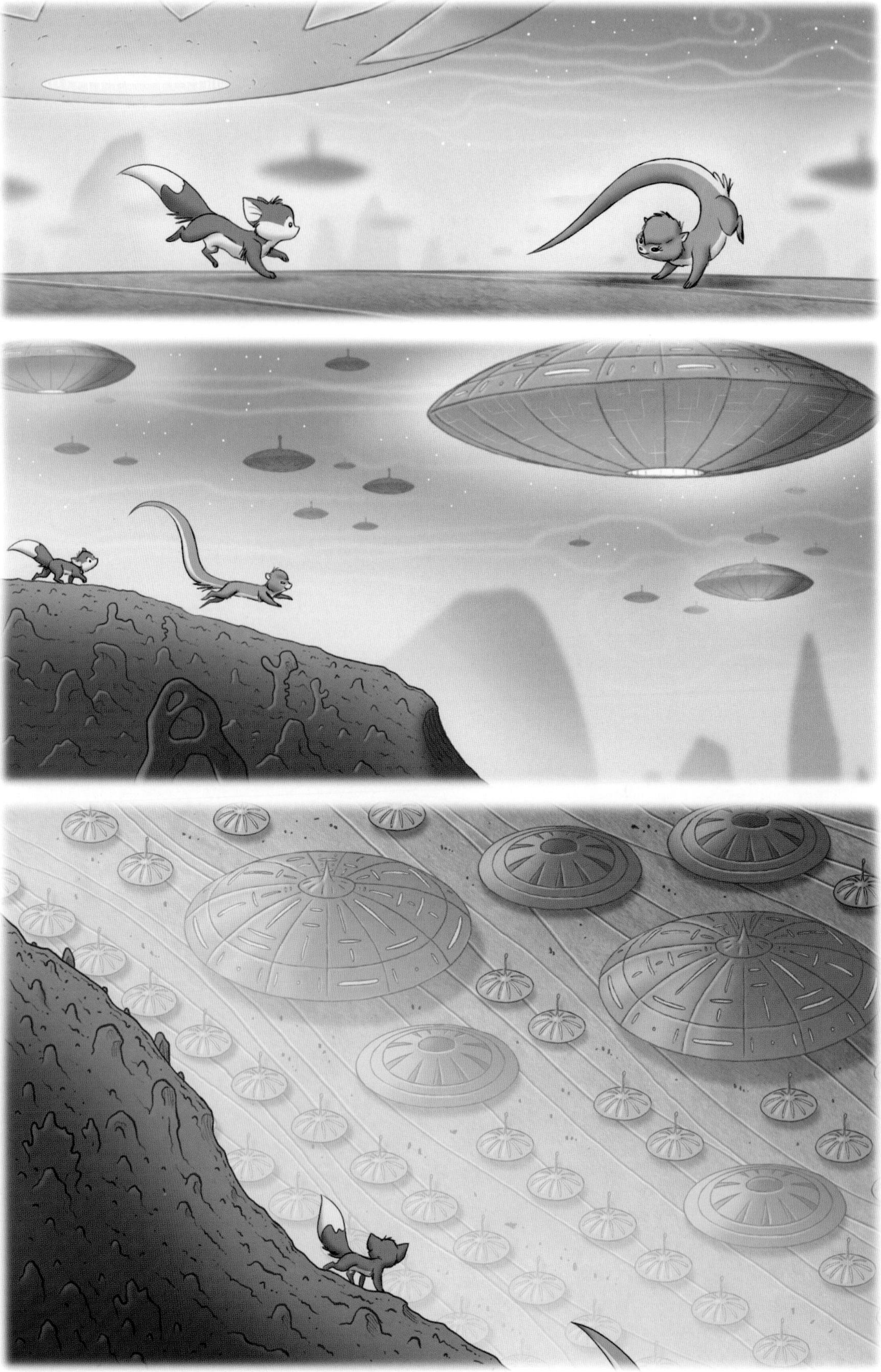

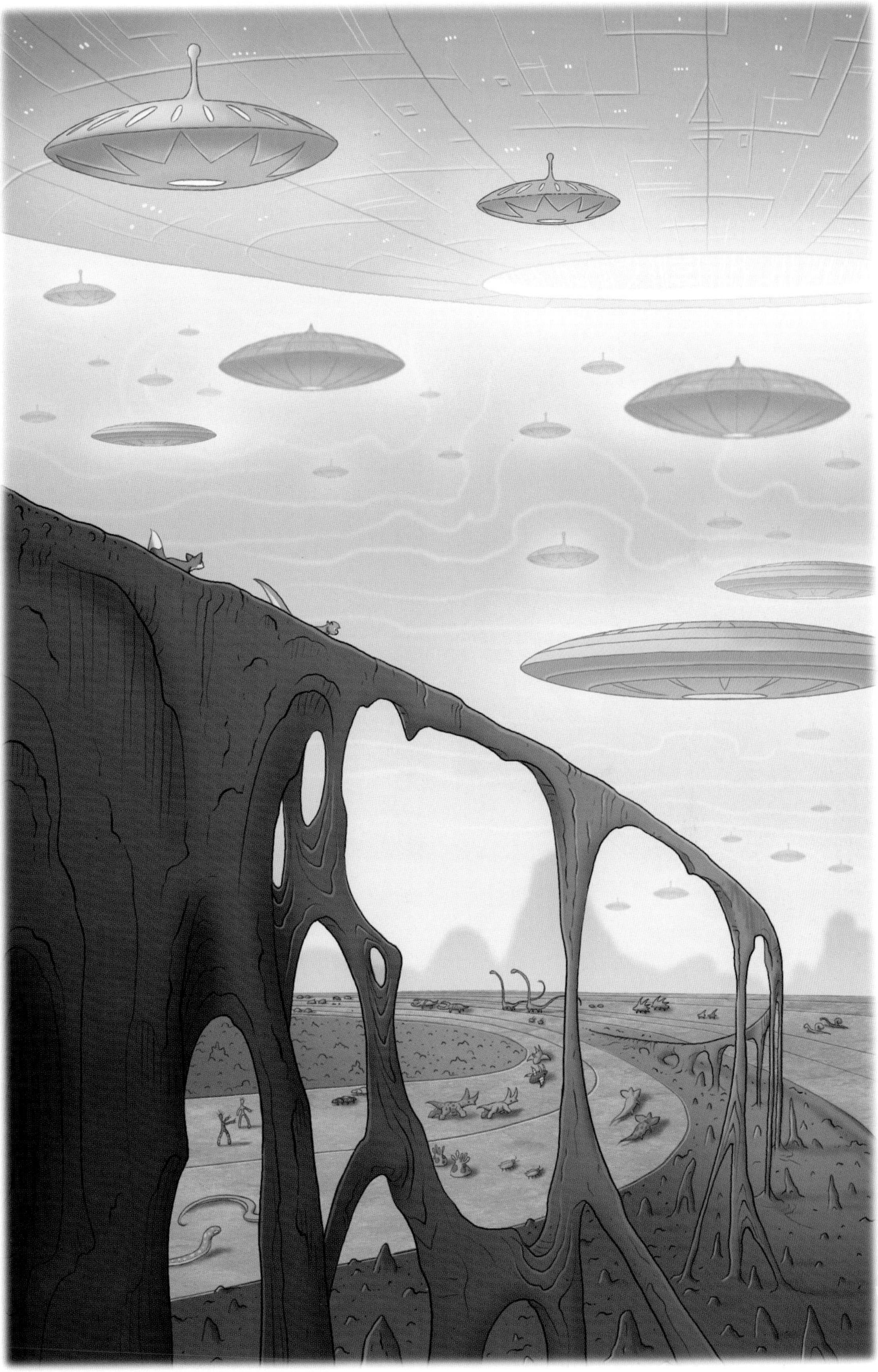

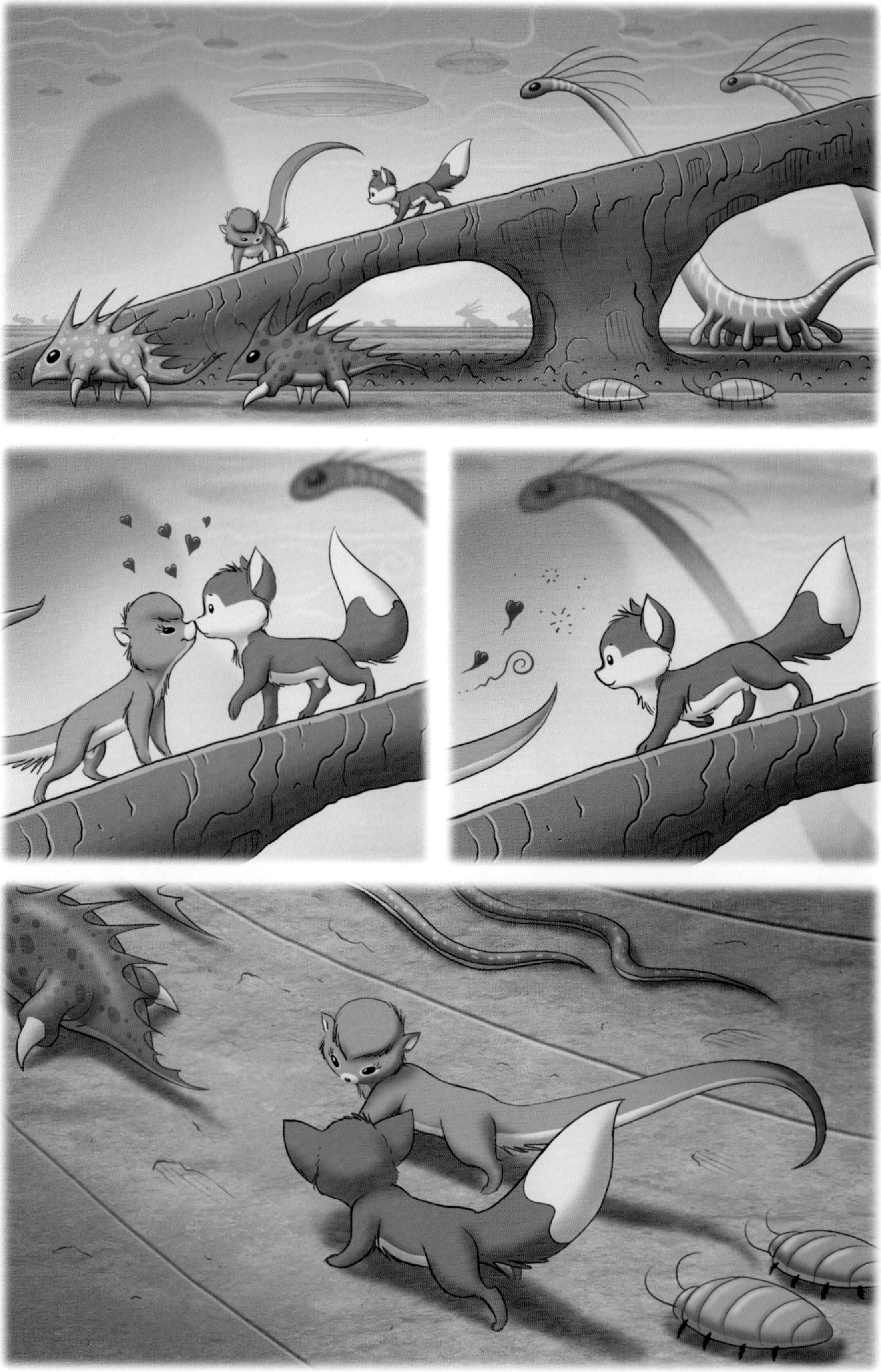

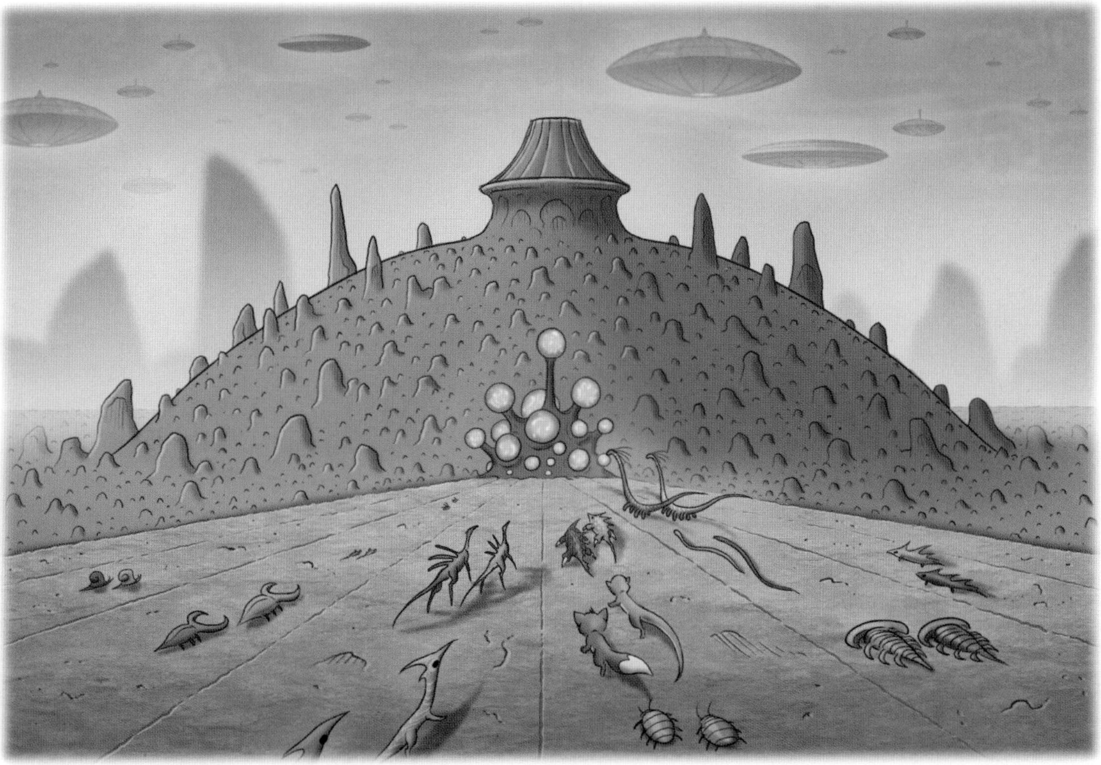

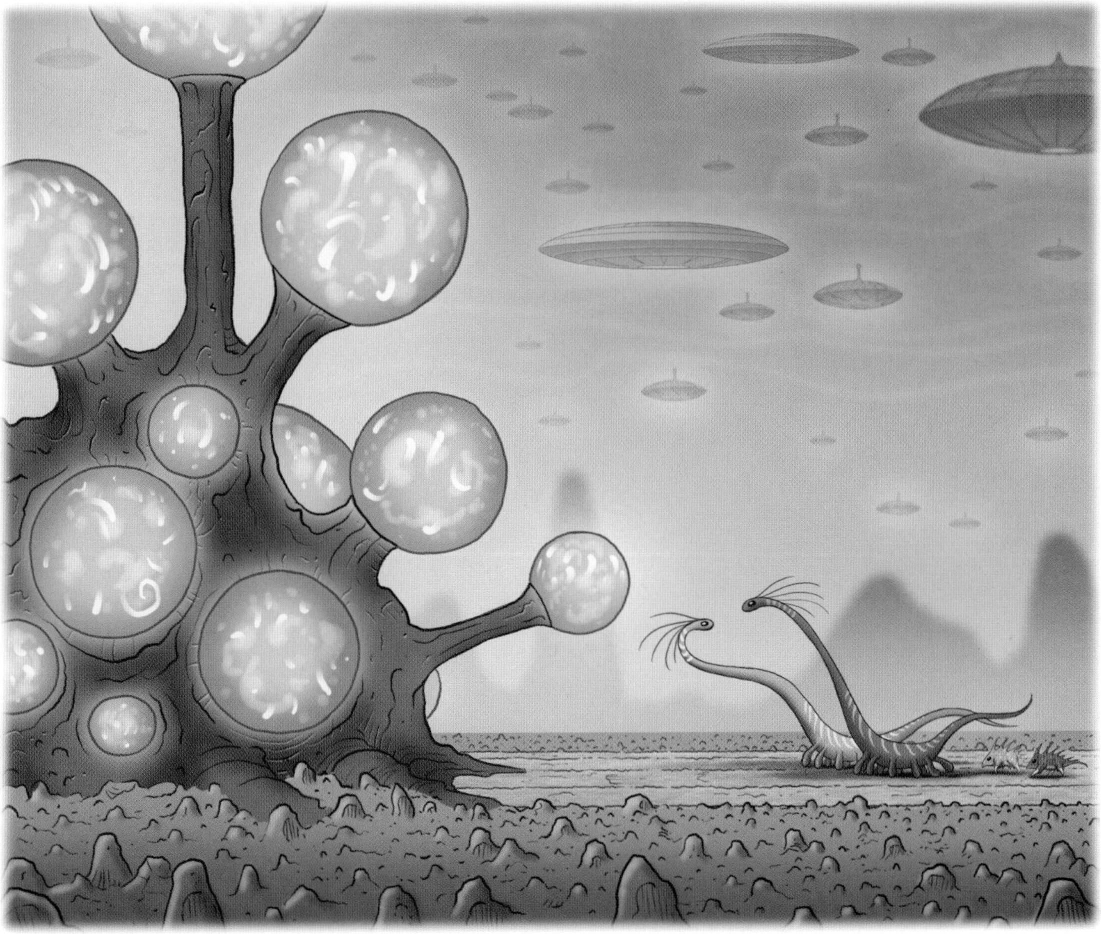

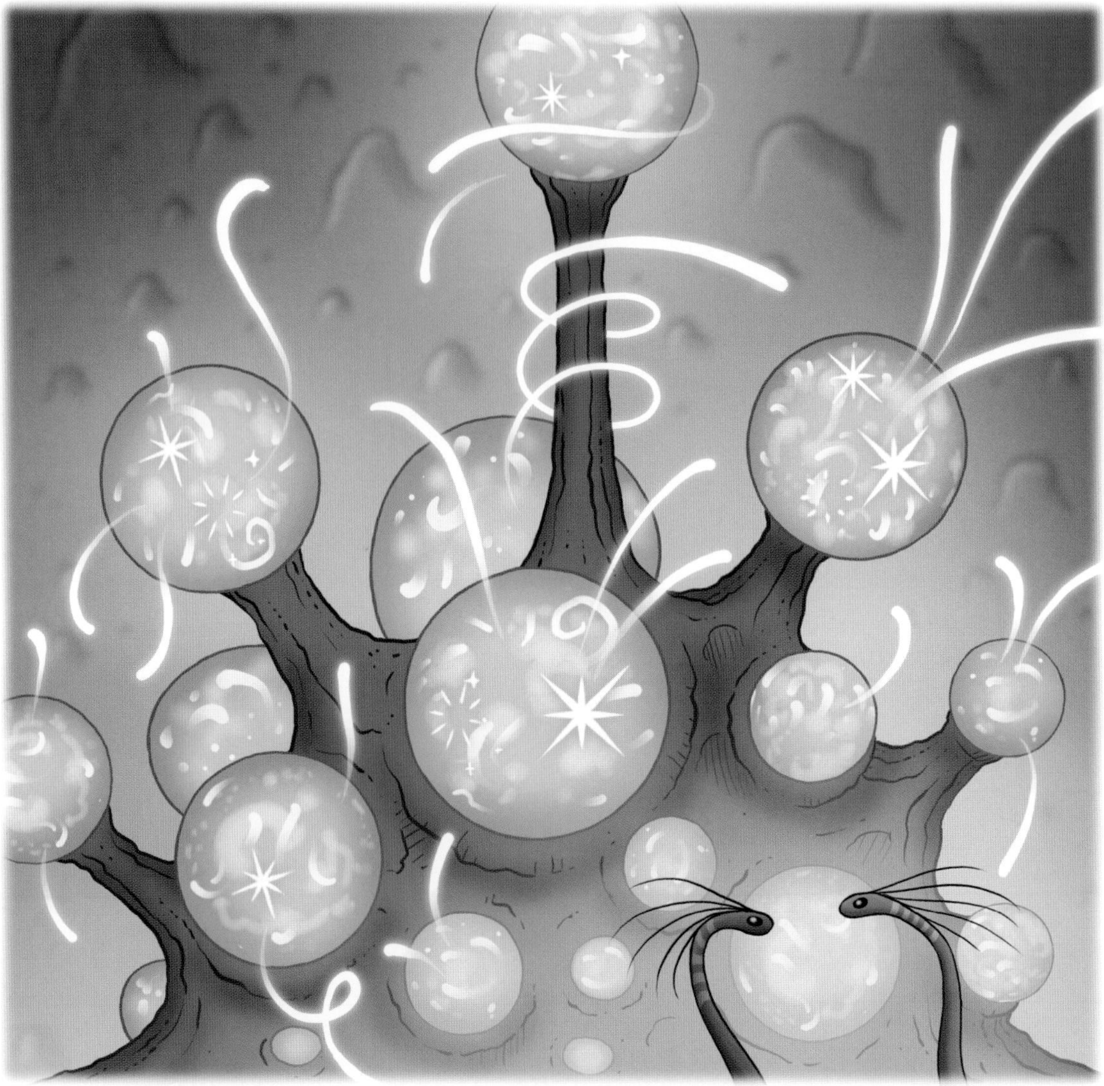

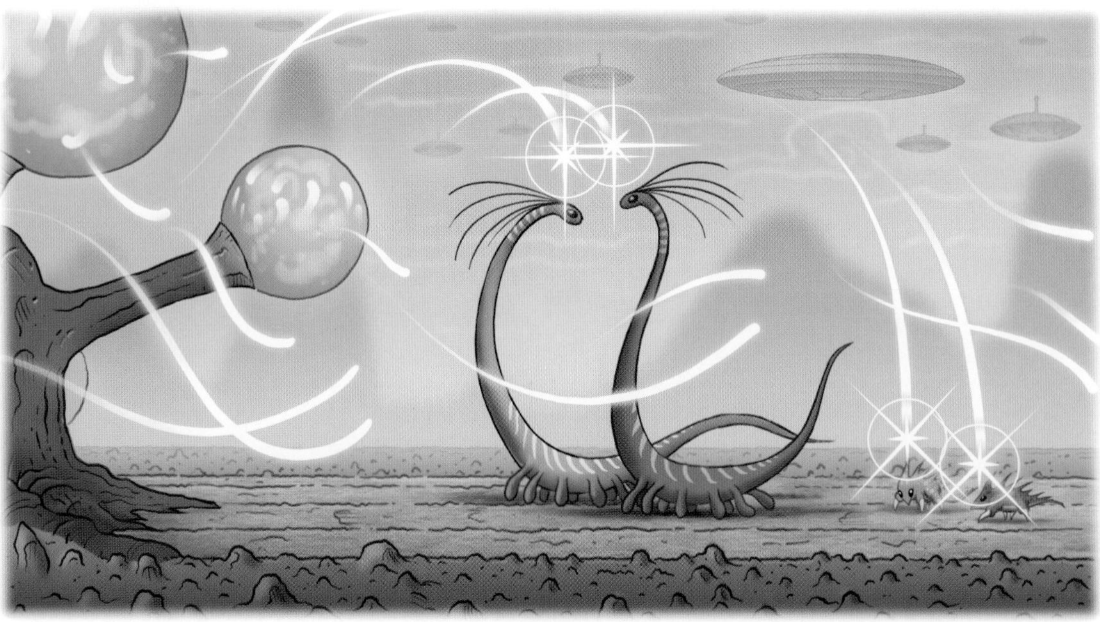

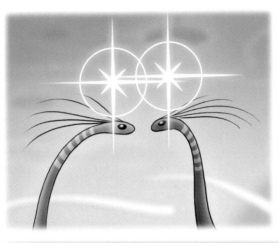

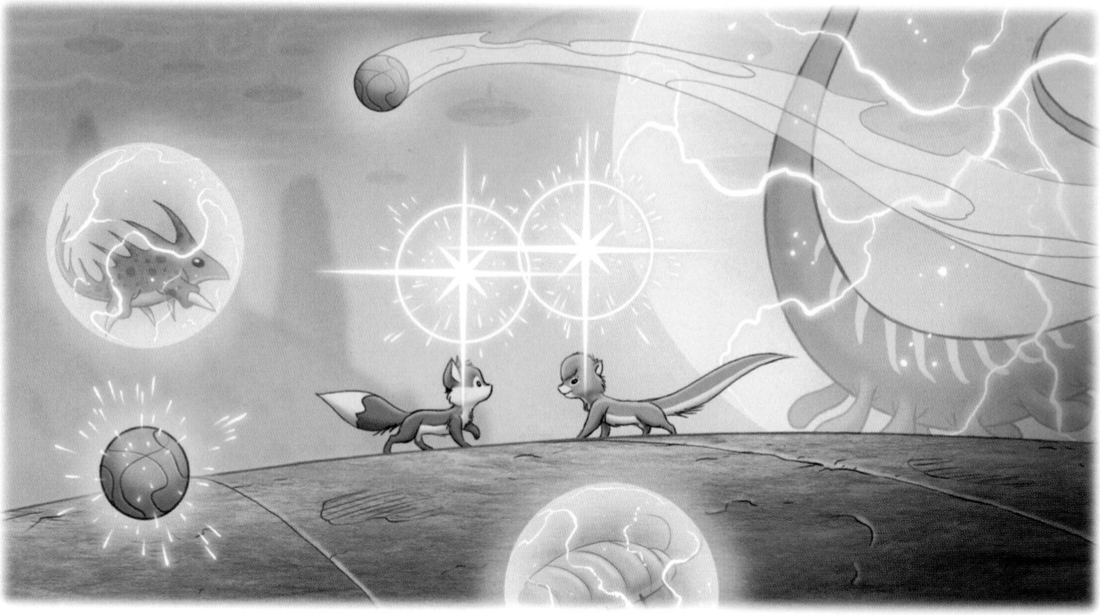

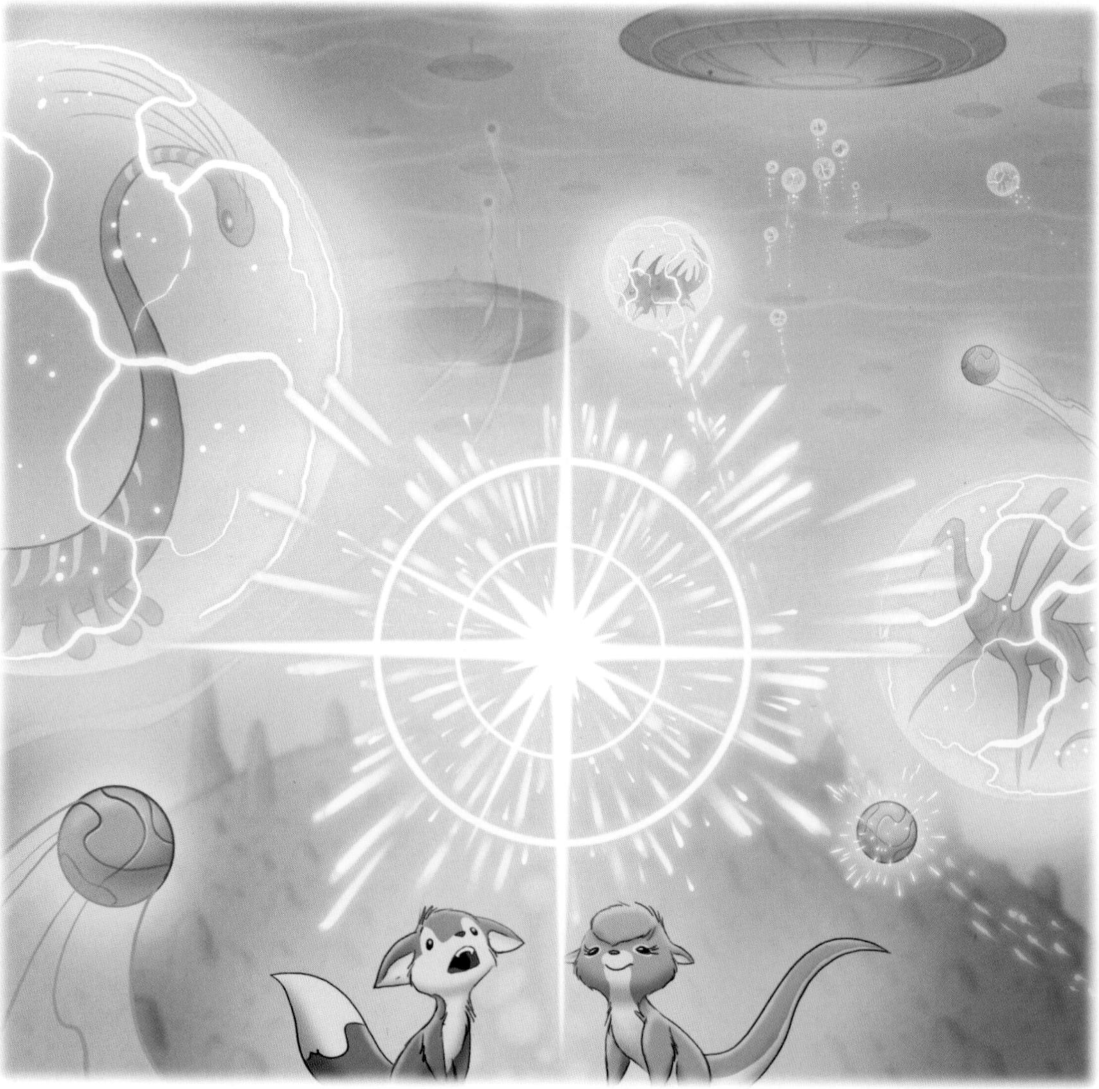

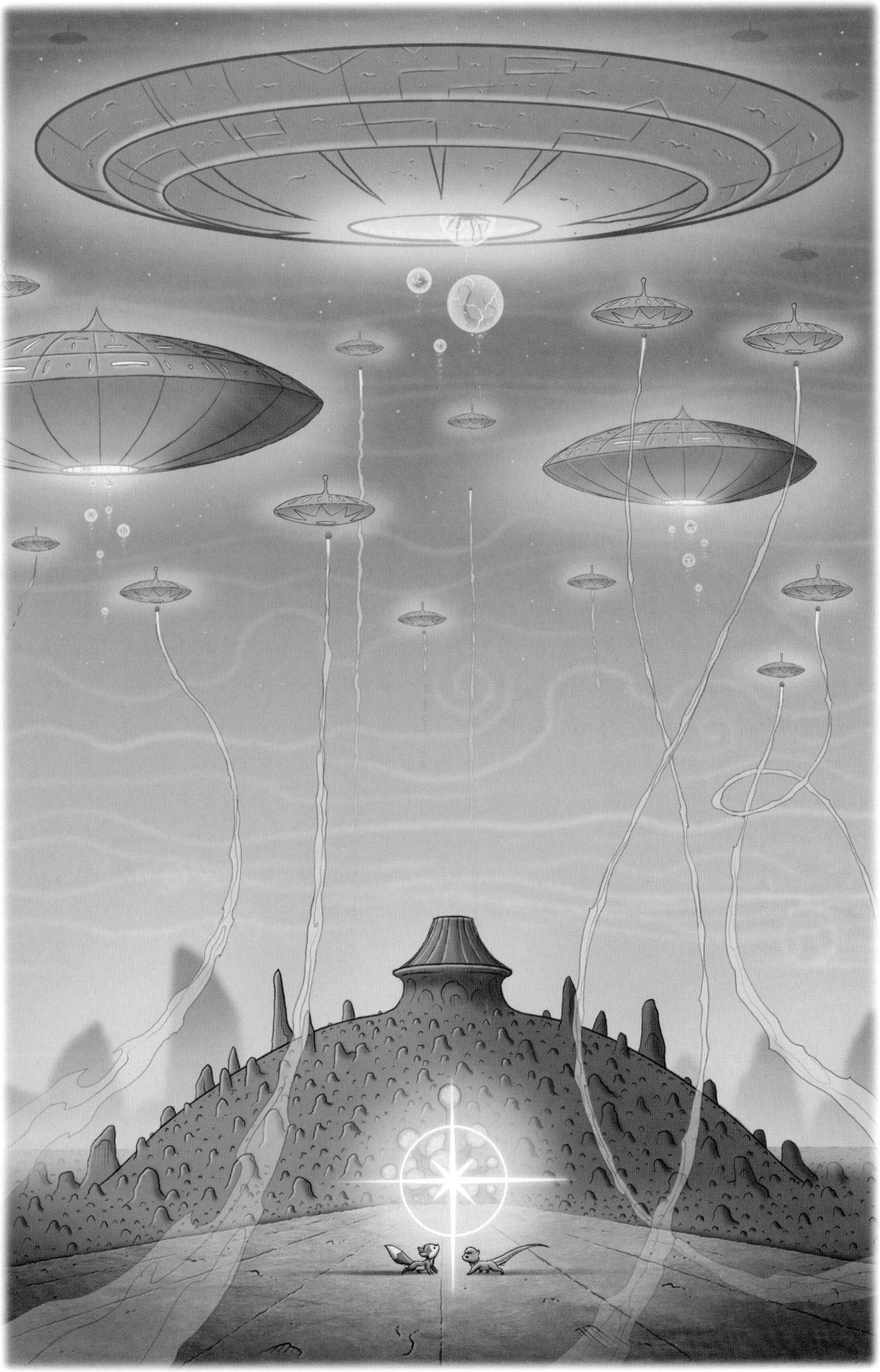

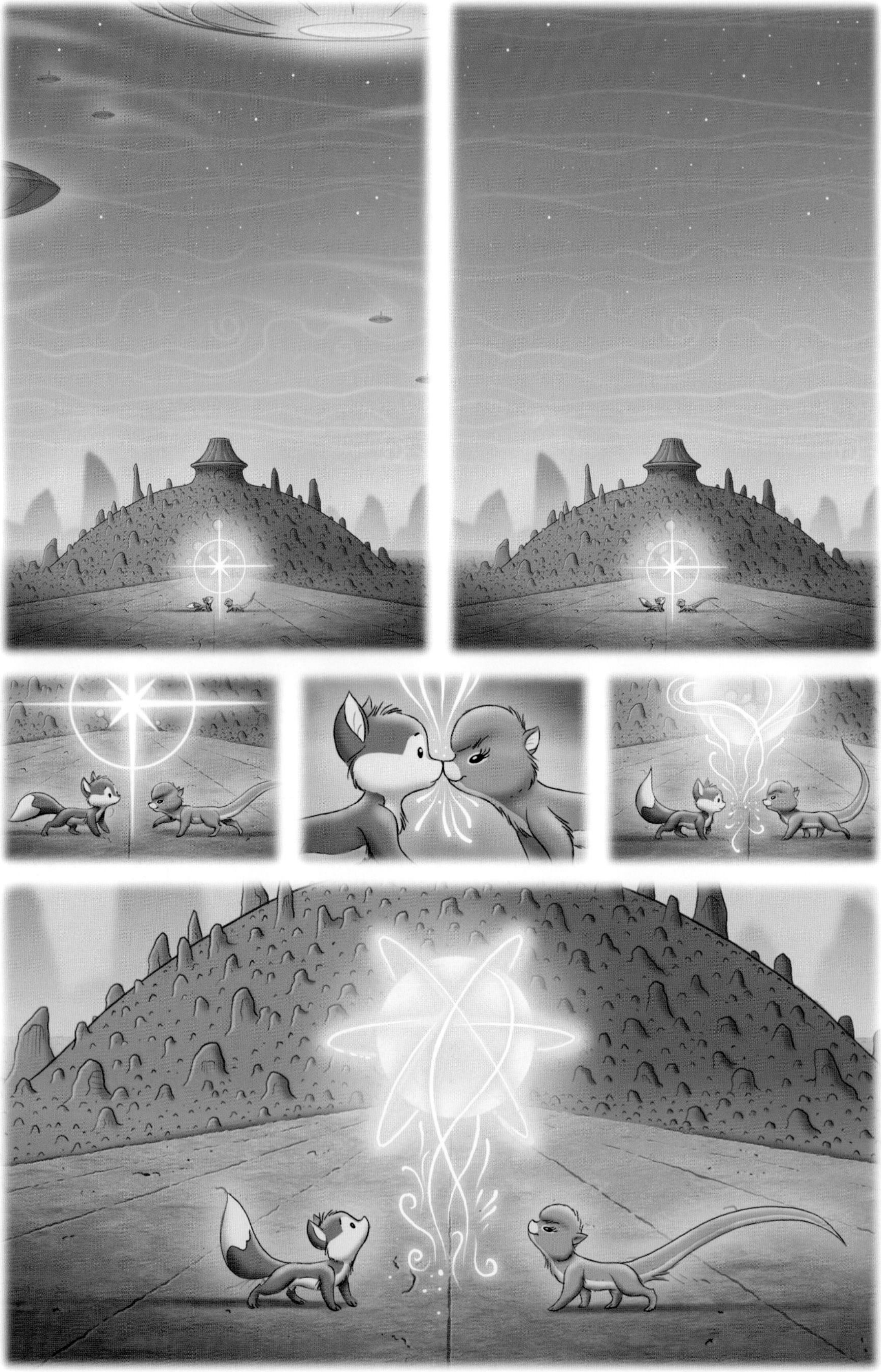

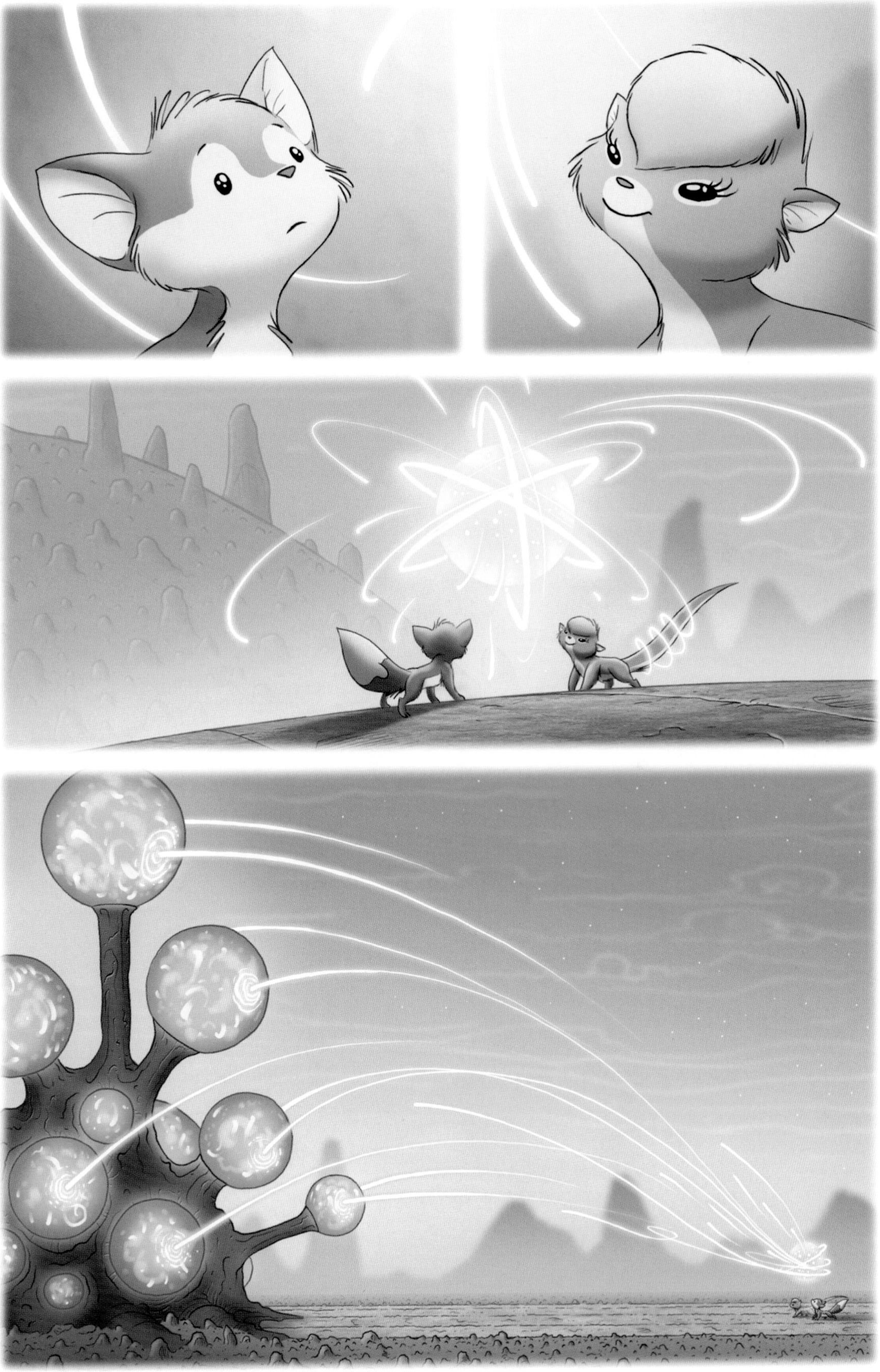

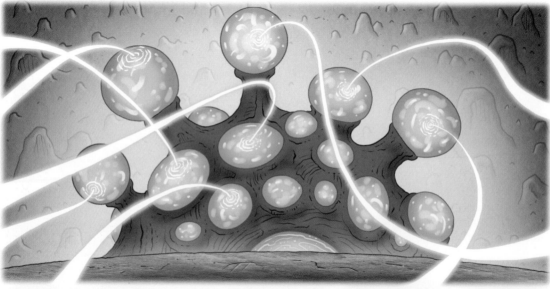

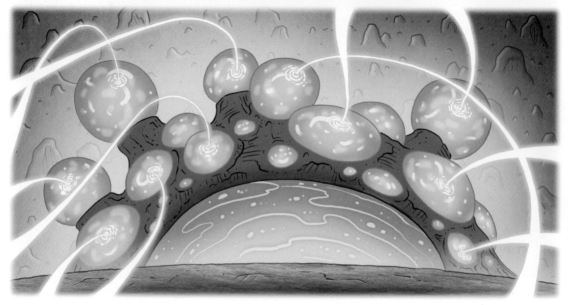

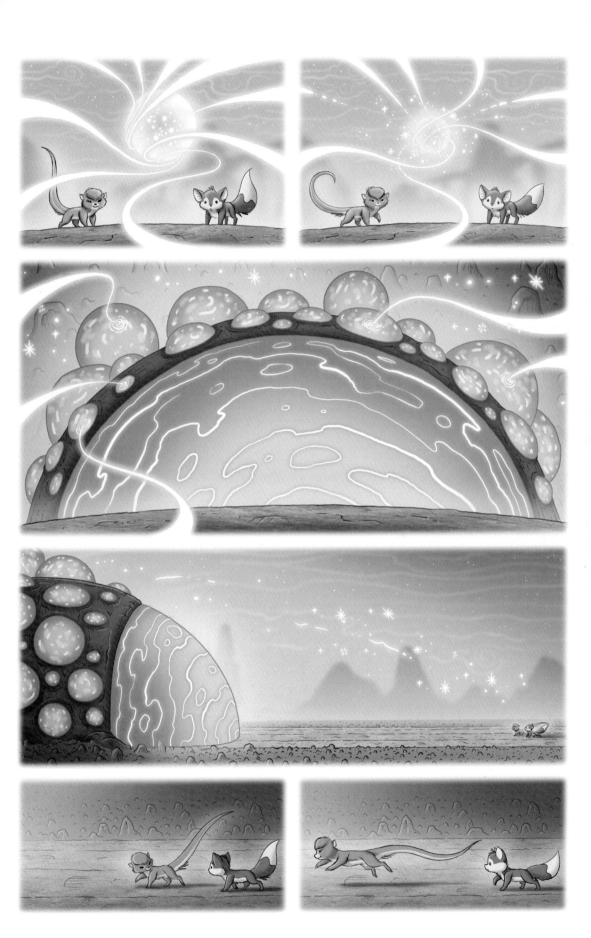

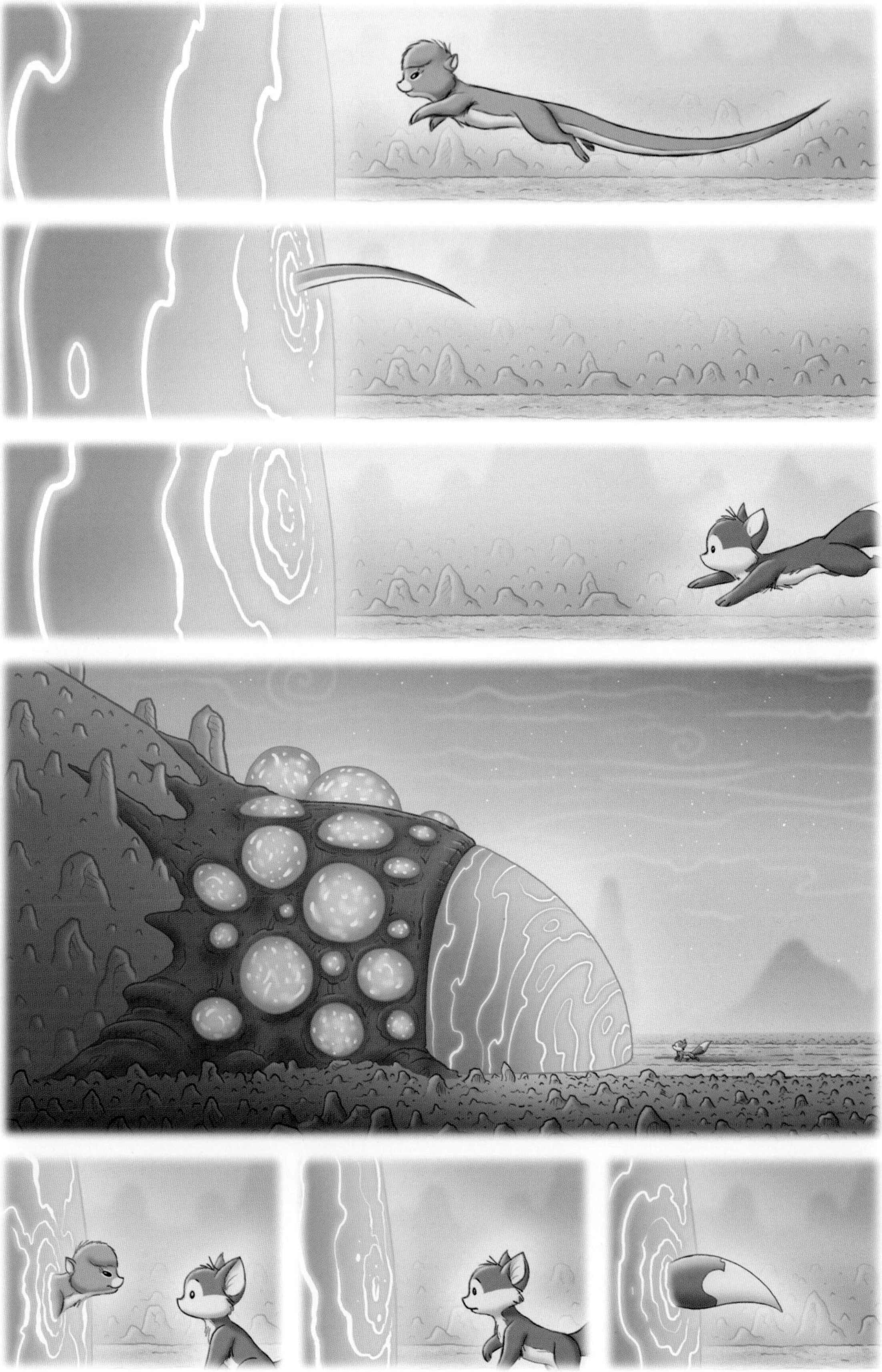

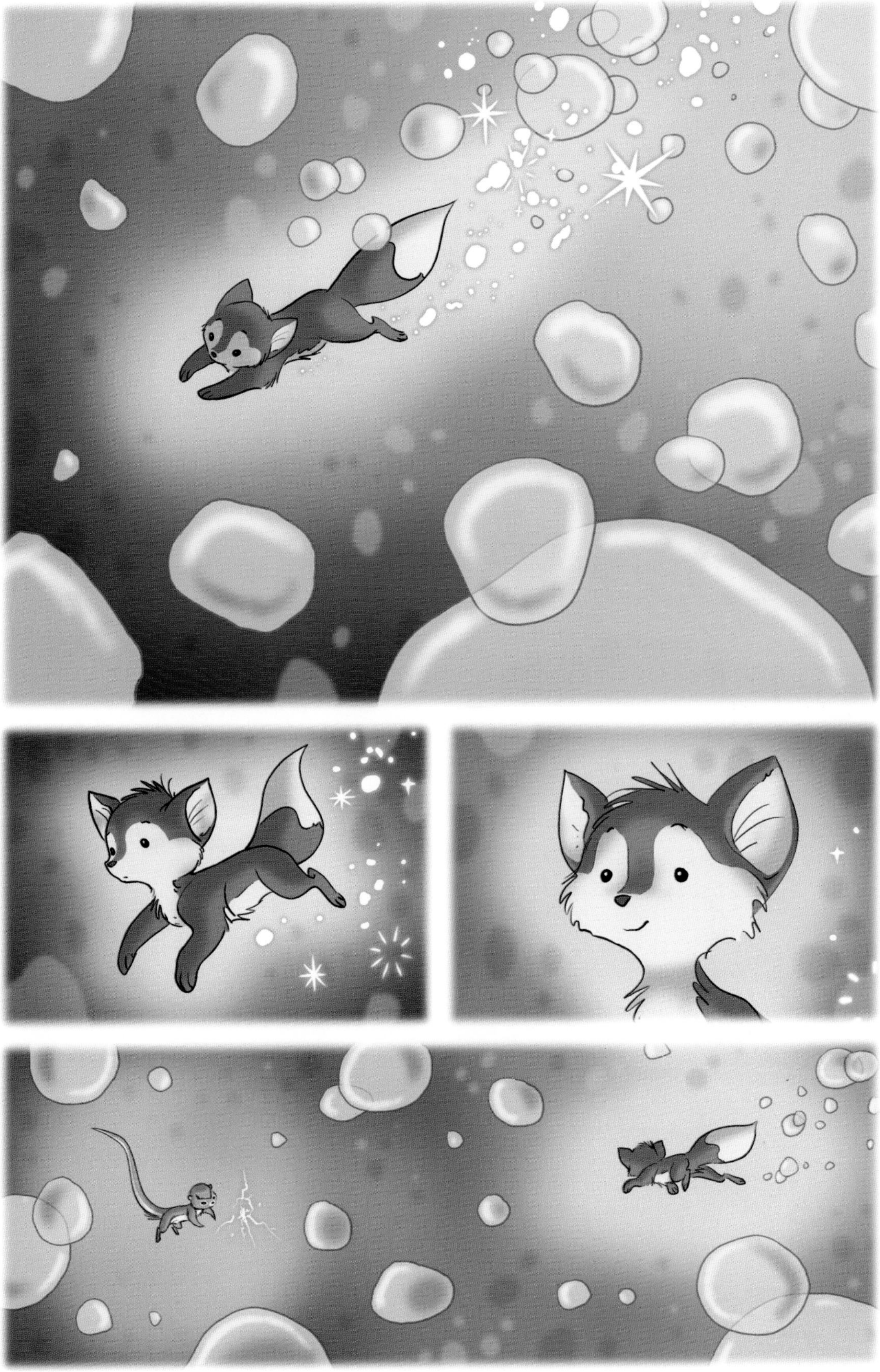

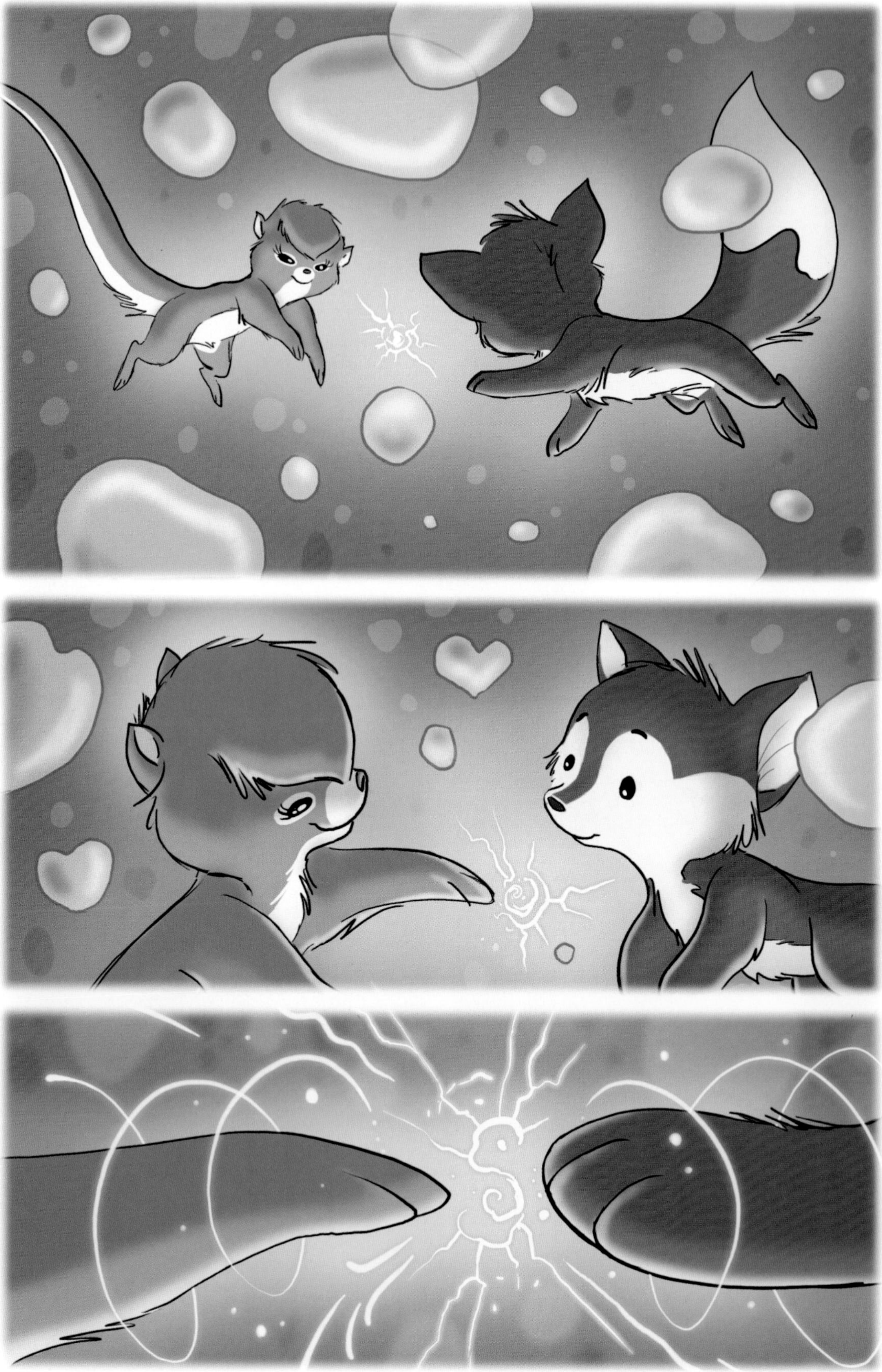

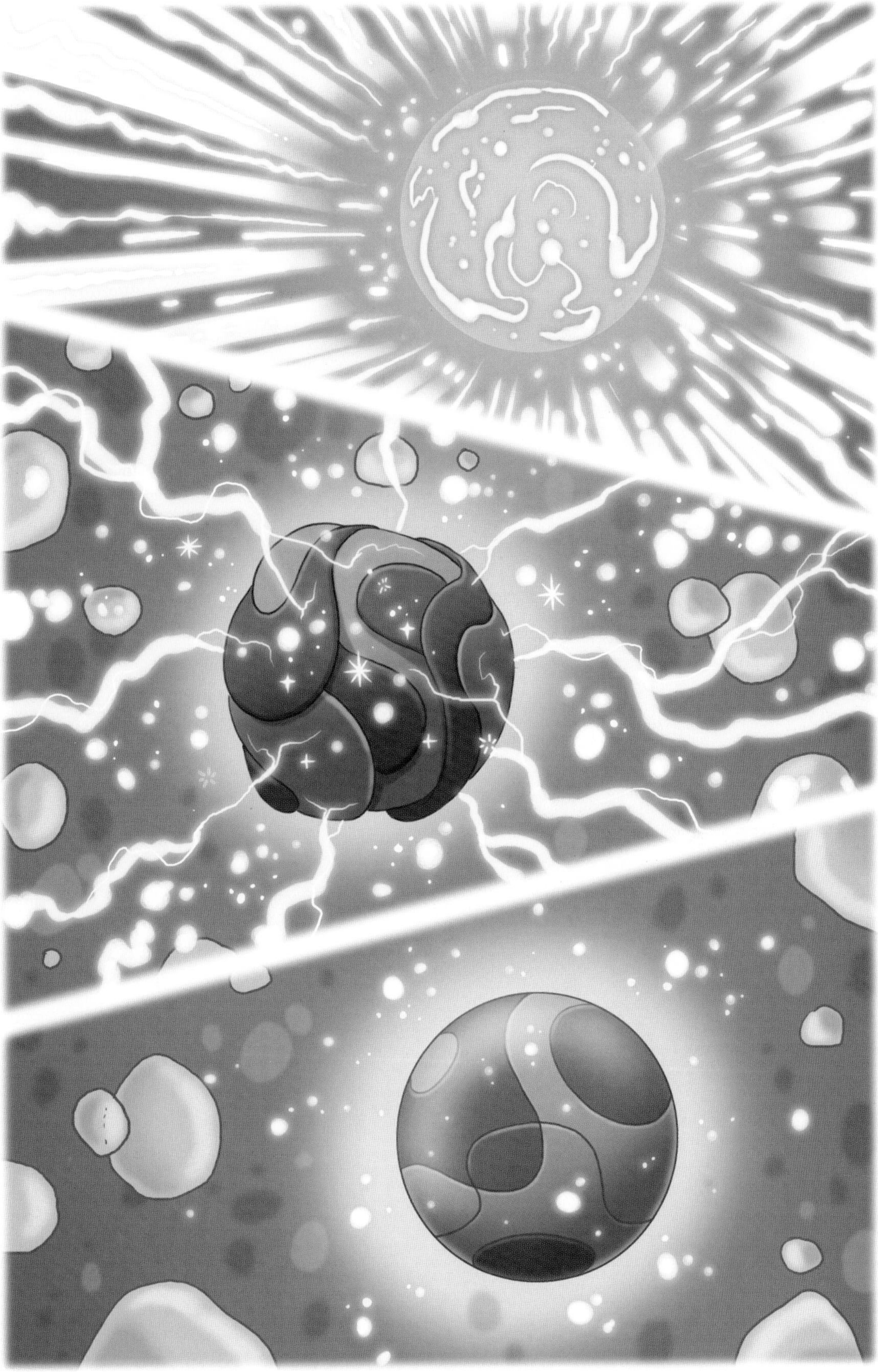

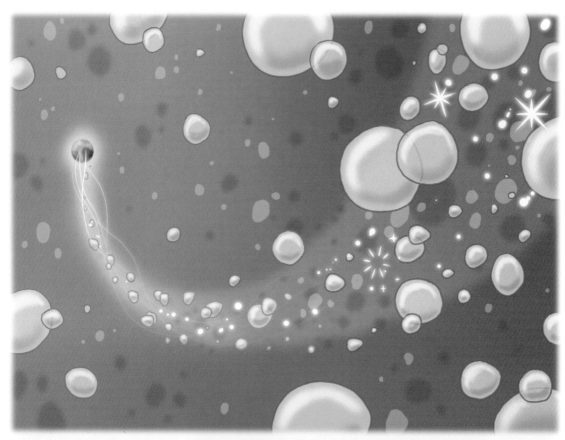

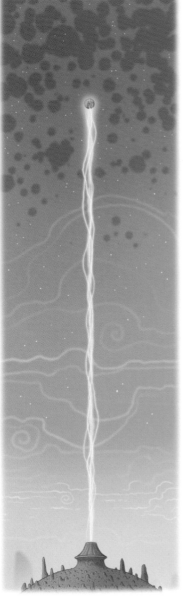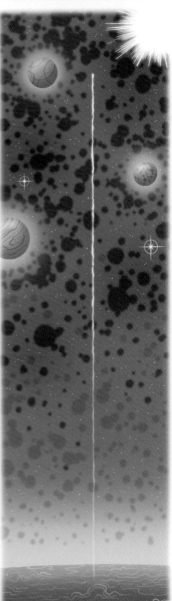

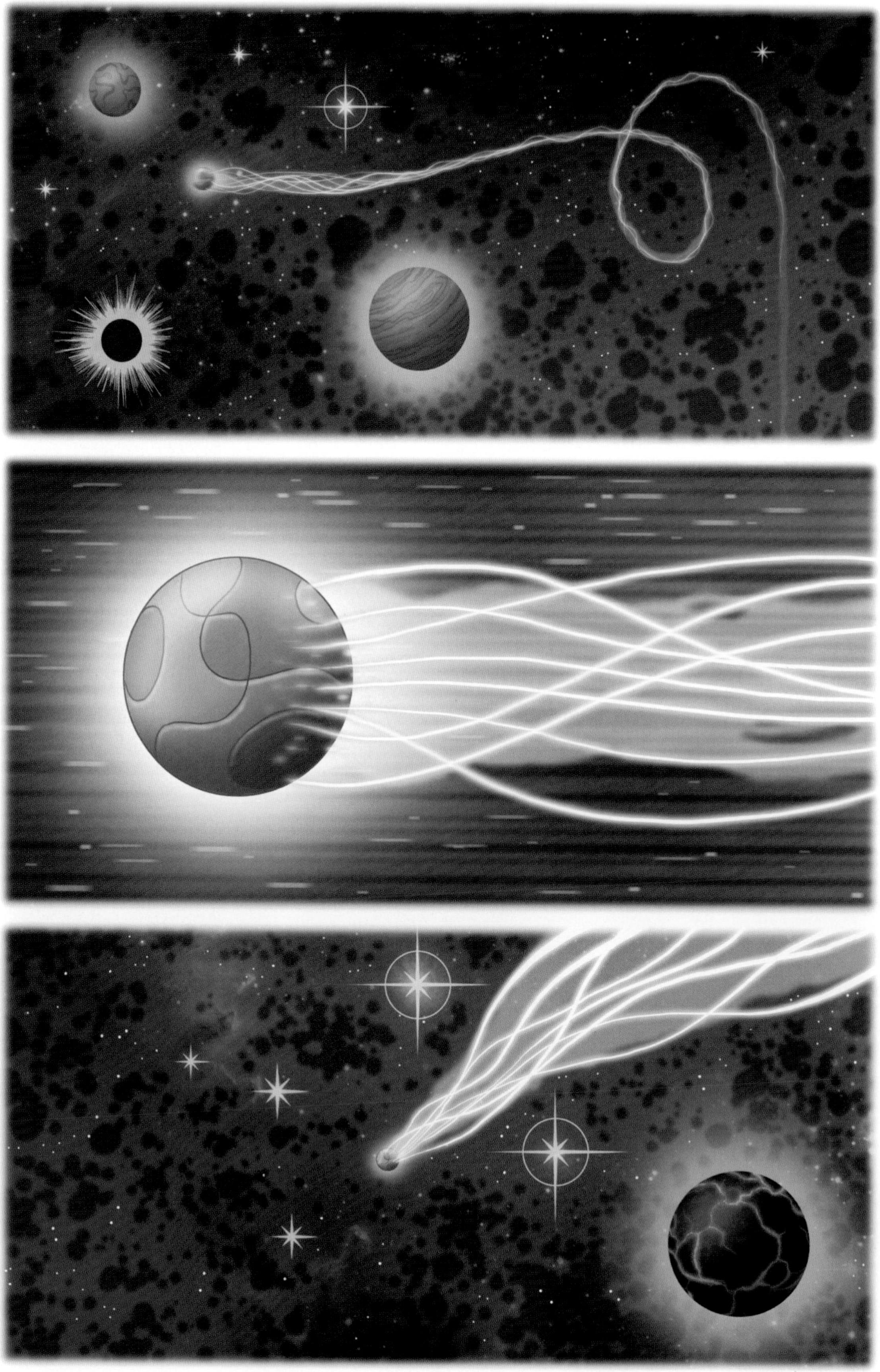

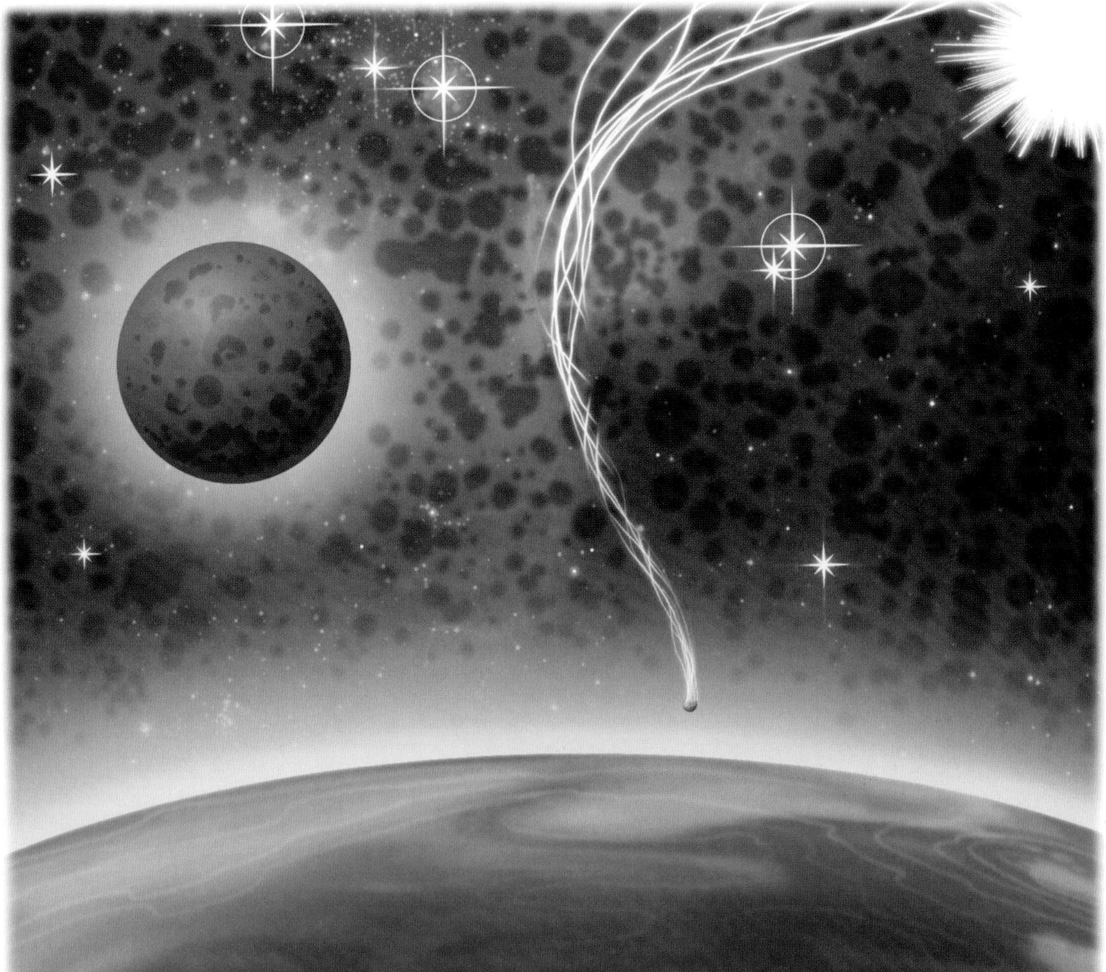

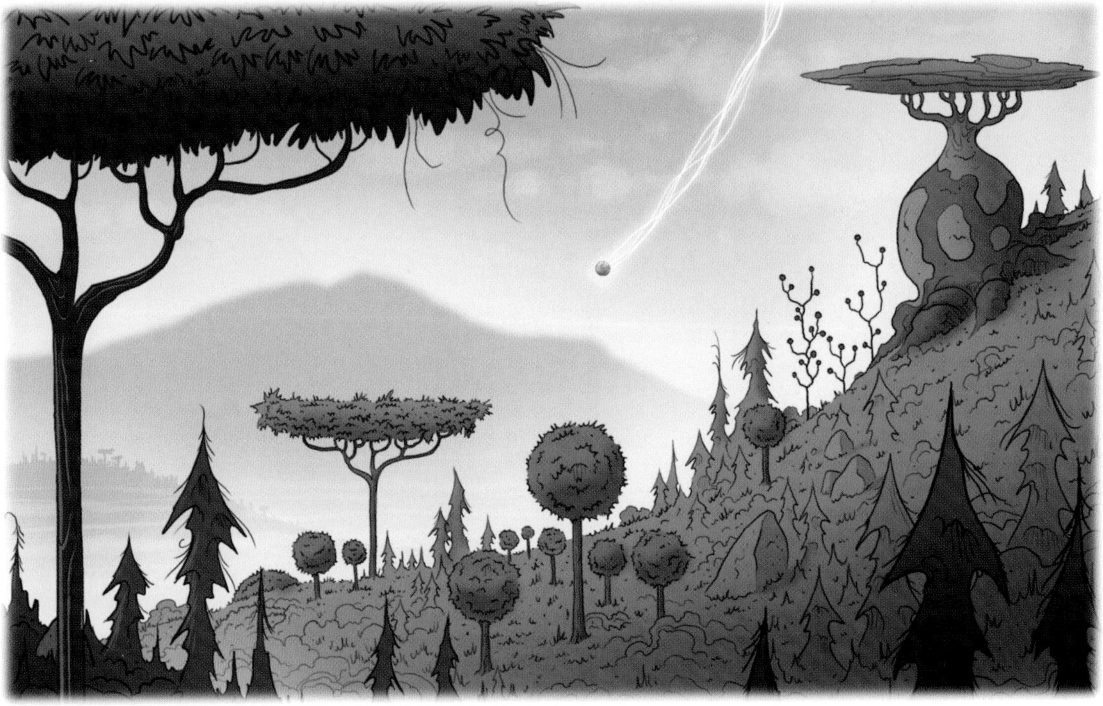

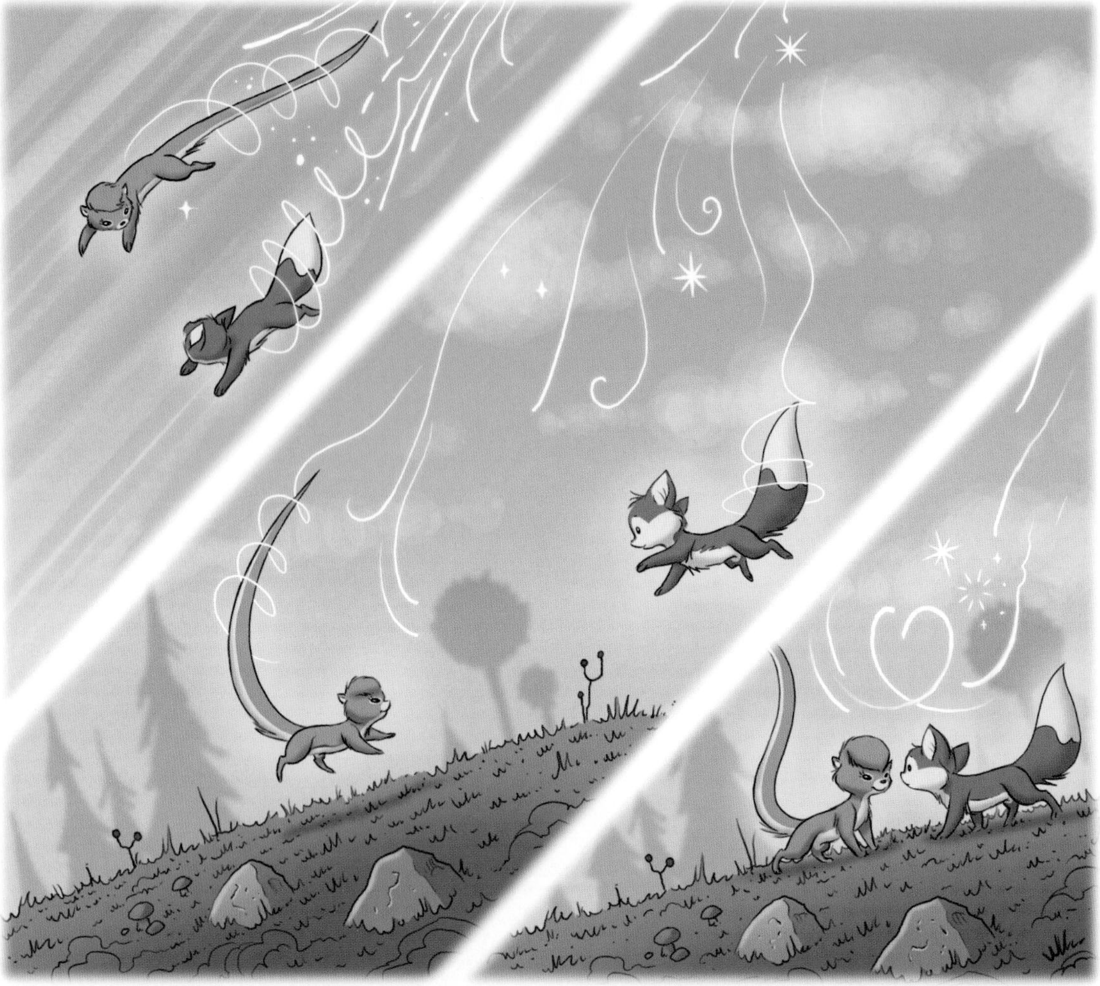

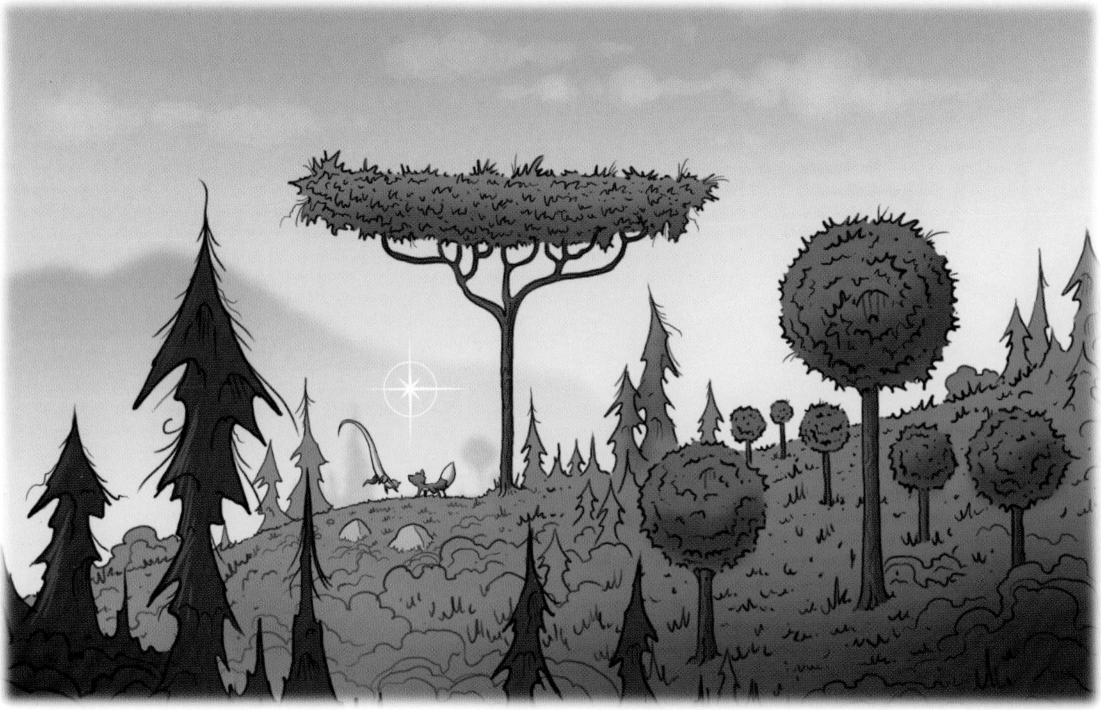

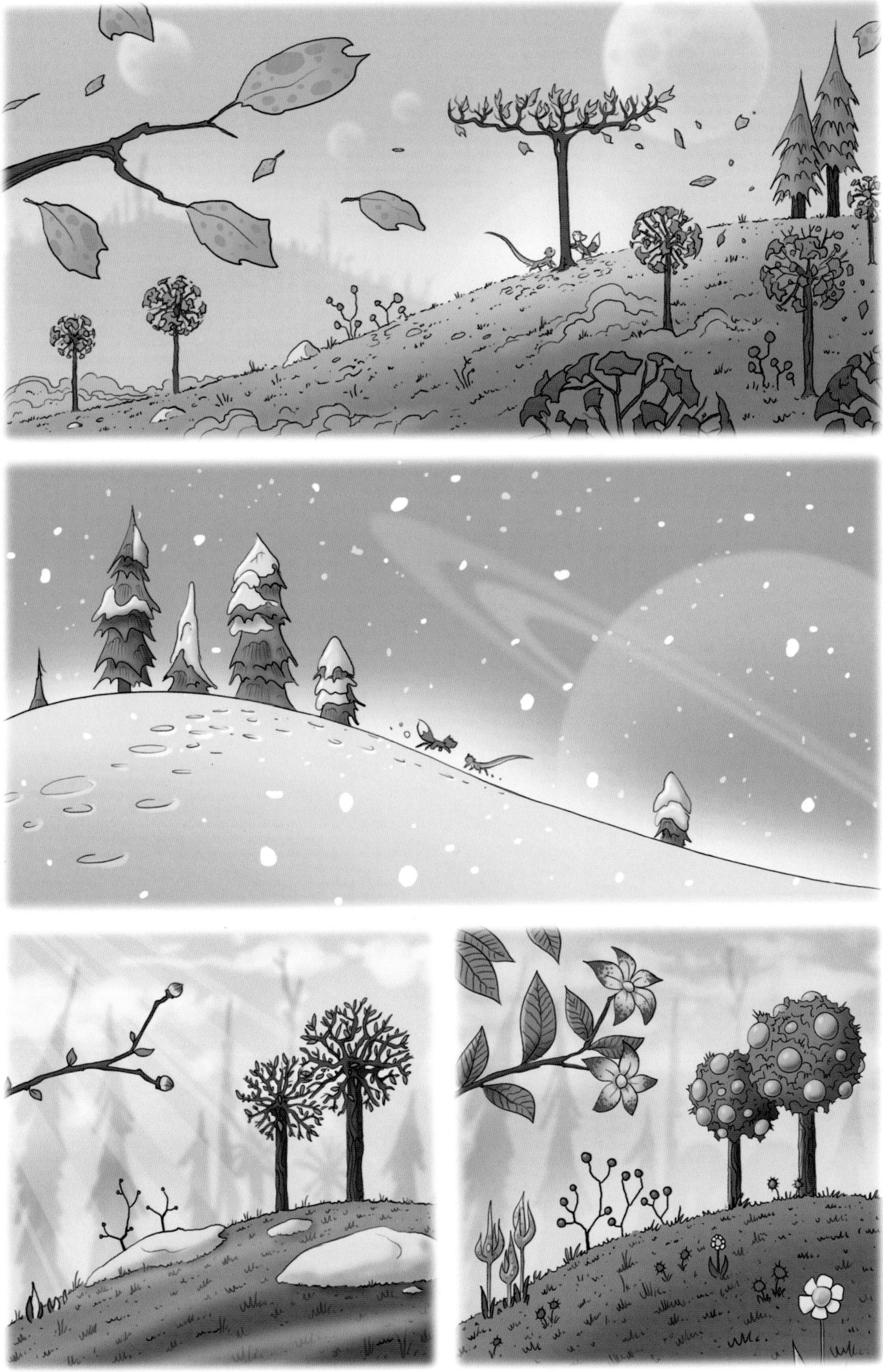

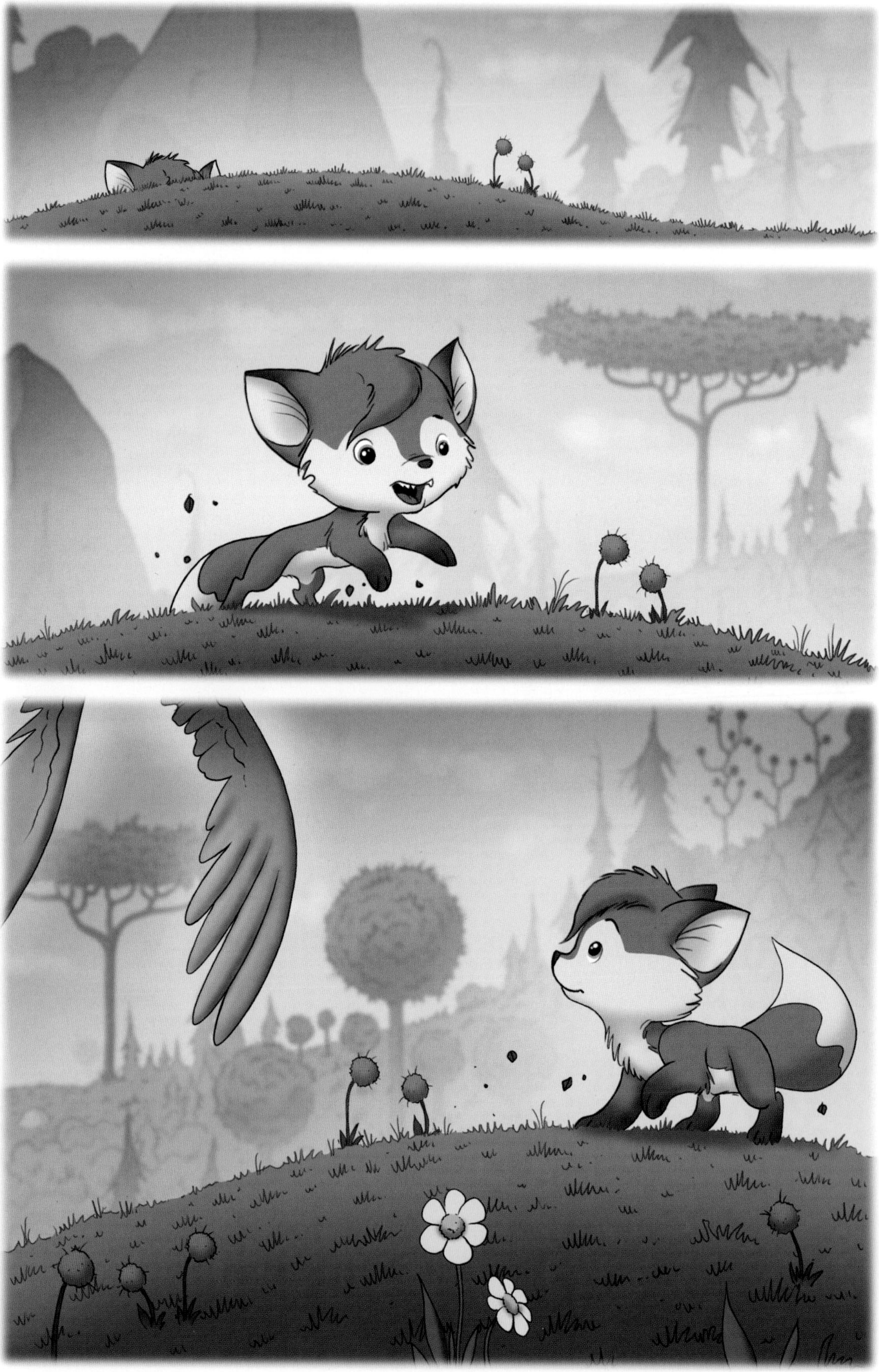

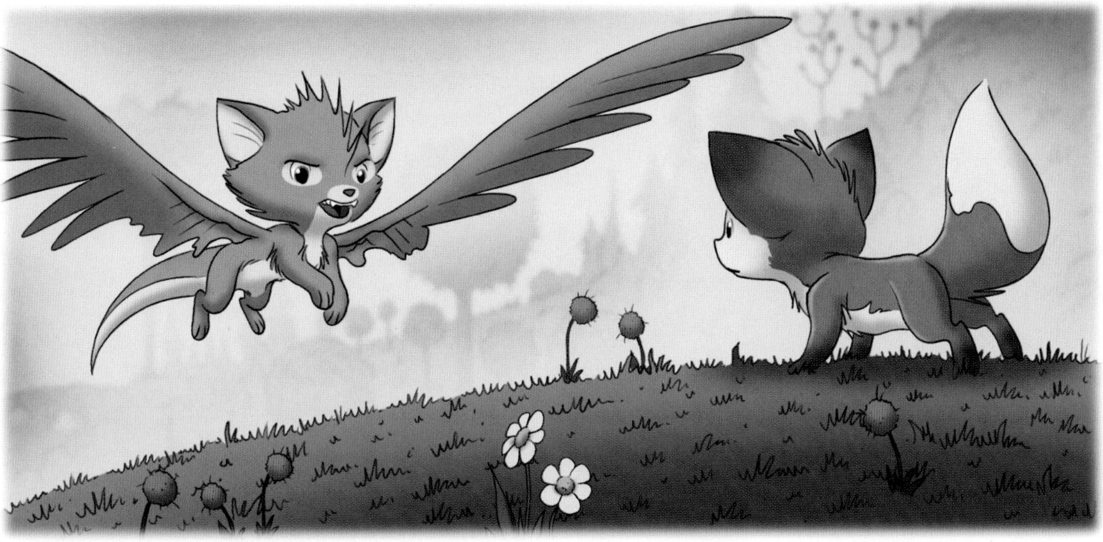

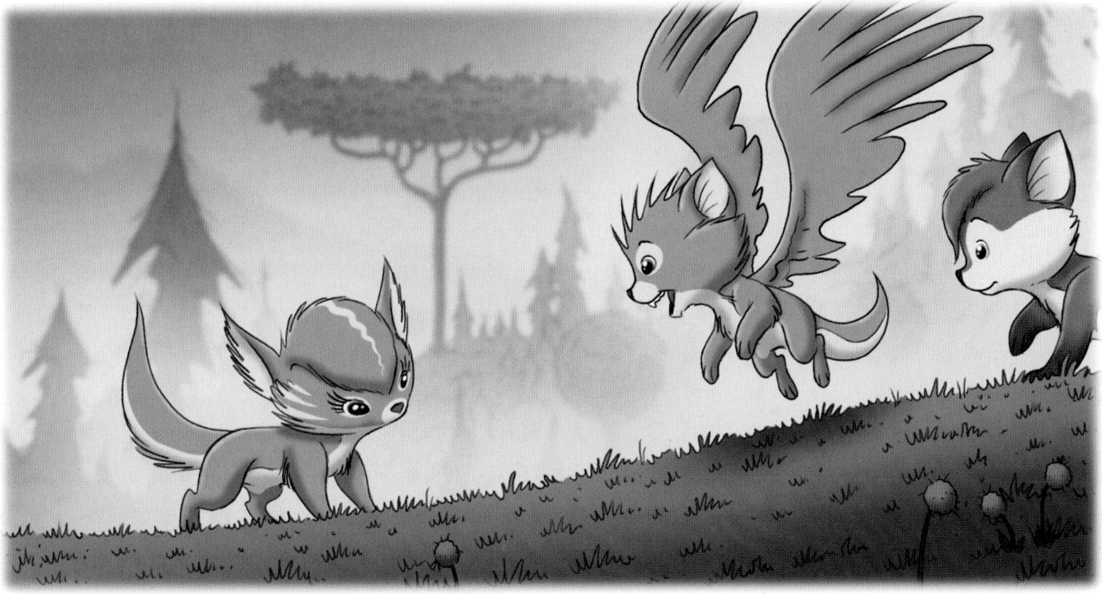

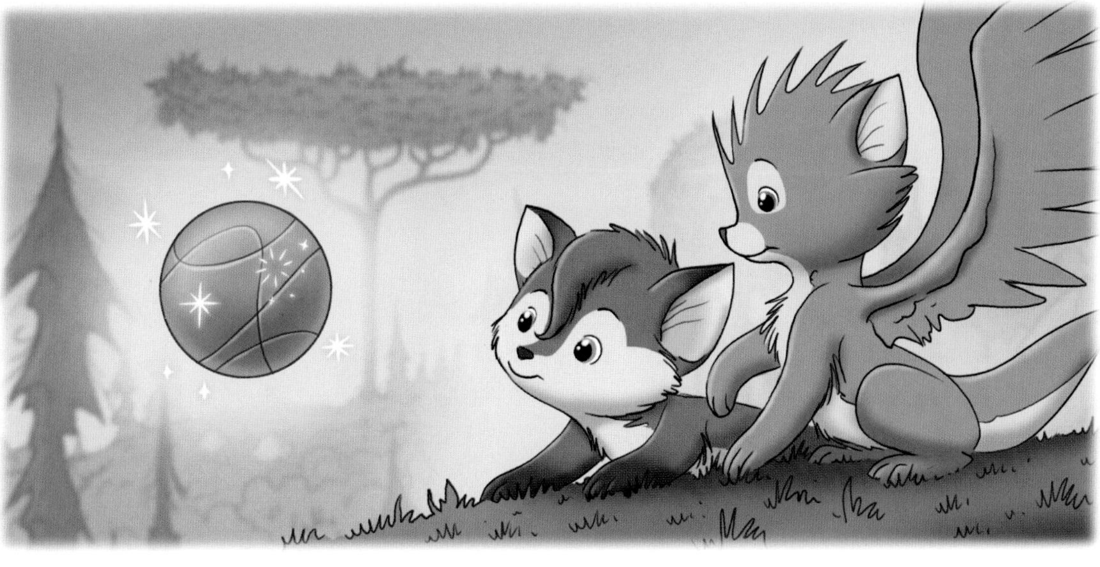

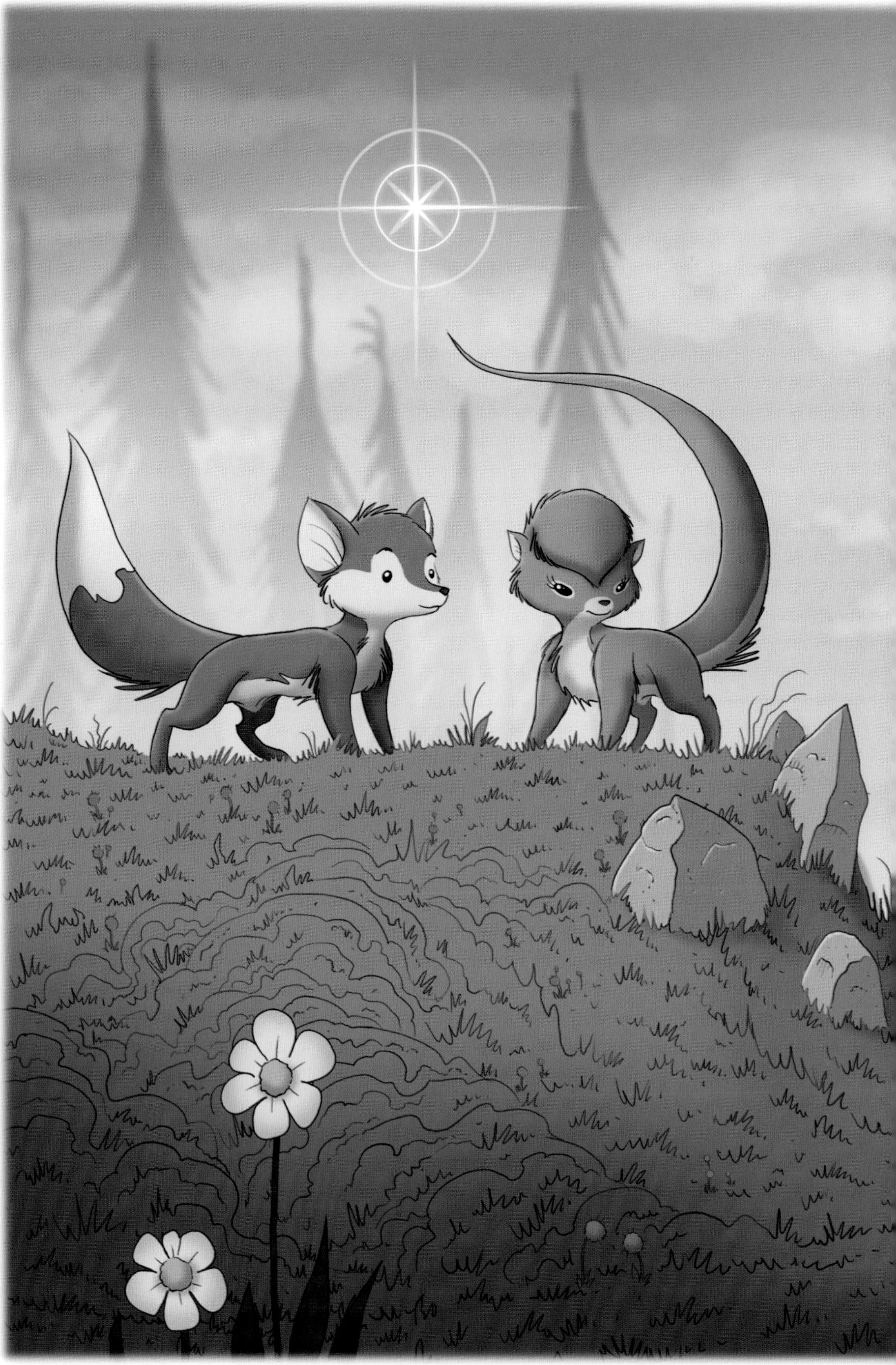

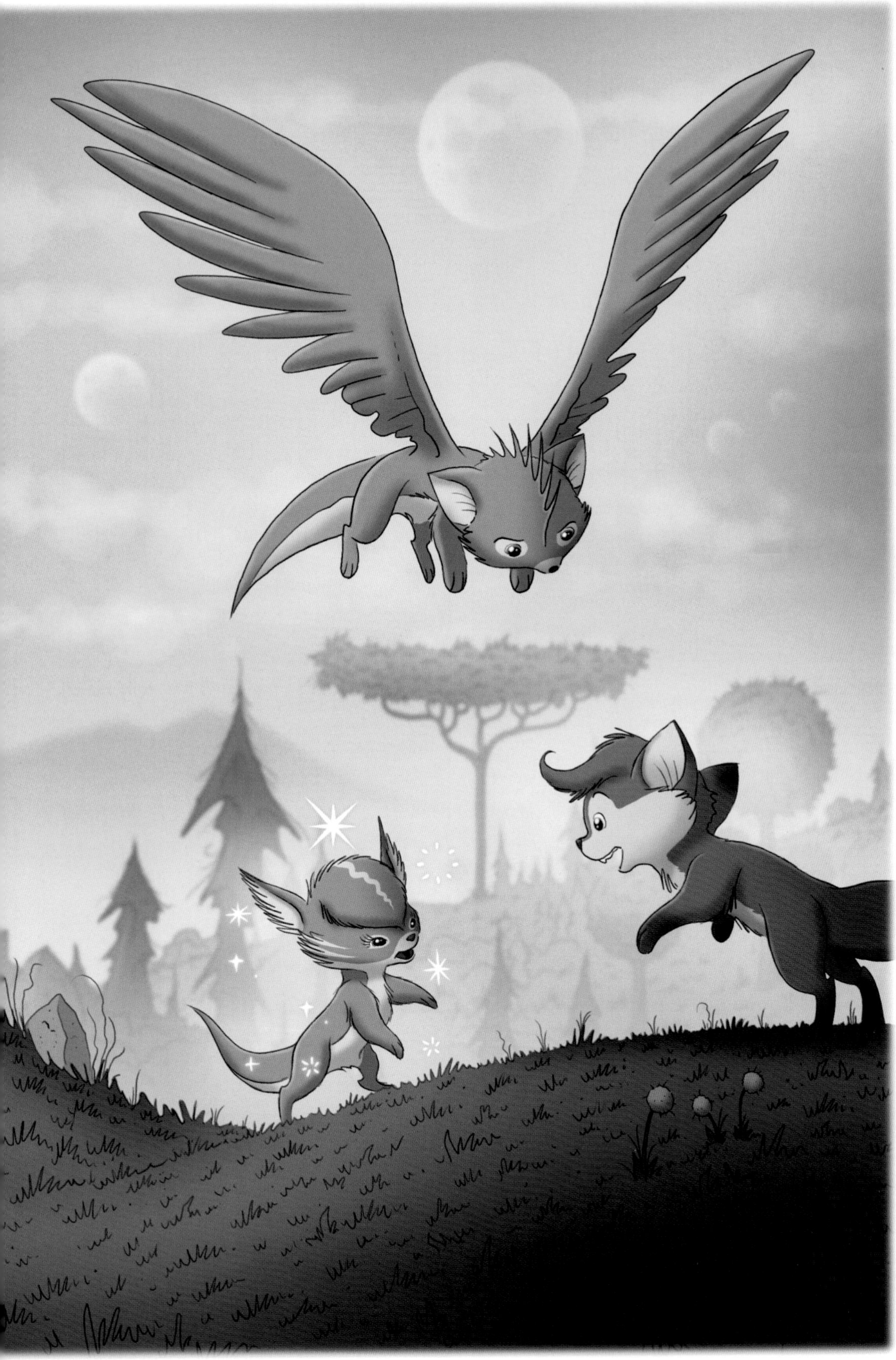

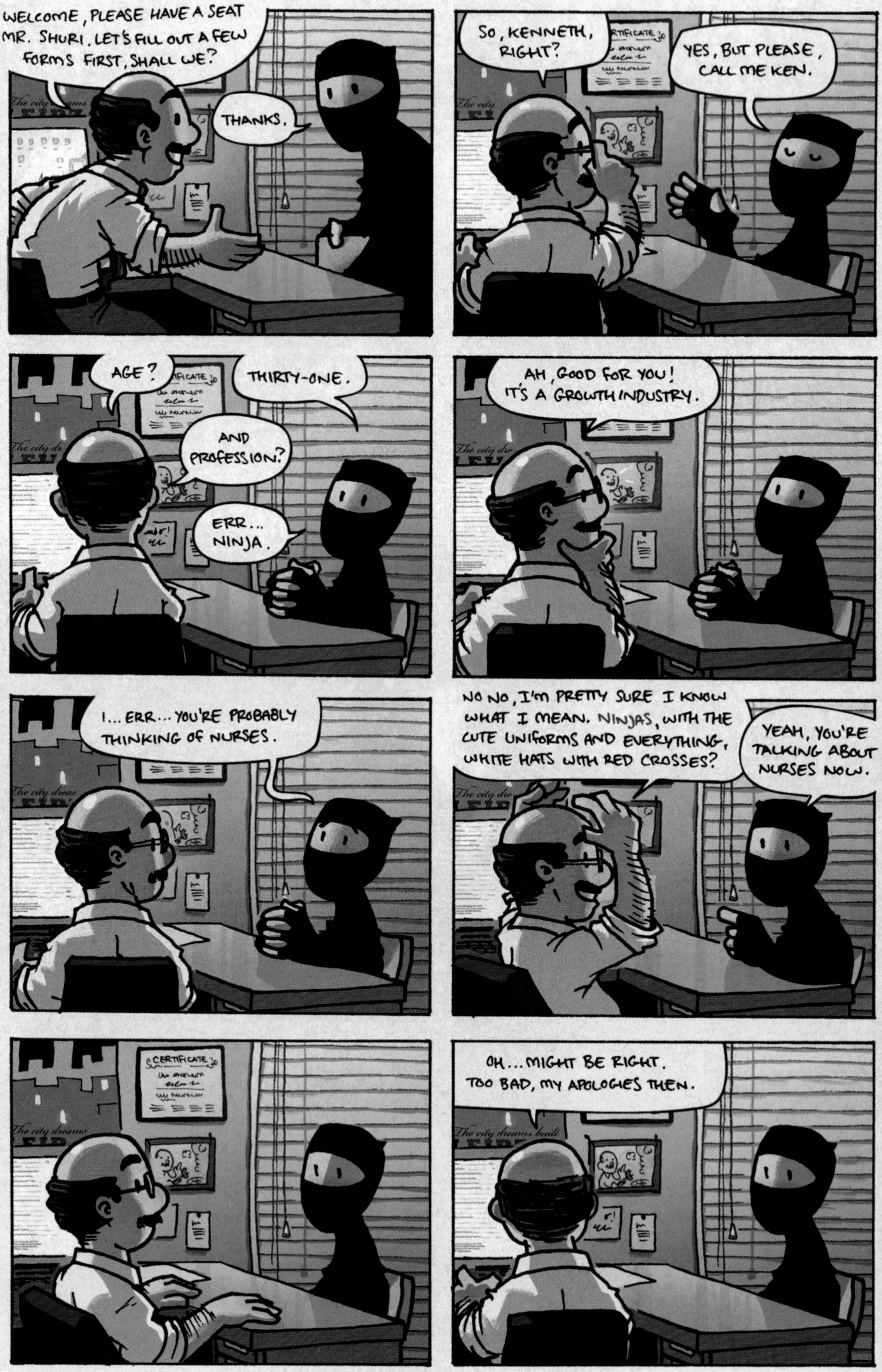
WELCOME, PLEASE HAVE A SEAT MR. SHURI. LET'S FILL OUT A FEW FORMS FIRST, SHALL WE?
THANKS.
SO, KENNETH, RIGHT?
YES, BUT PLEASE, CALL ME KEN.
AGE?
THIRTY-ONE.
AND PROFESSION?
ERR... NINJA.
AH, GOOD FOR YOU! IT'S A GROWTH INDUSTRY.
I... ERR... YOU'RE PROBABLY THINKING OF NURSES.
NO NO, I'M PRETTY SURE I KNOW WHAT I MEAN. NINJAS, WITH THE CUTE UNIFORMS AND EVERYTHING, WHITE HATS WITH RED CROSSES?
YEAH, YOU'RE TALKING ABOUT NURSES NOW.
OH... MIGHT BE RIGHT. TOO BAD, MY APOLOGIES THEN.

DEDICATED TO
Arttu Ahonen

The *Excitingly* *Mundane* Life of KENNETH SHURI

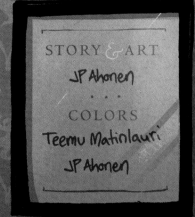

STORY & ART
JP Ahonen
. . .
COLORS
Teemu Matinlauri
JP Ahonen

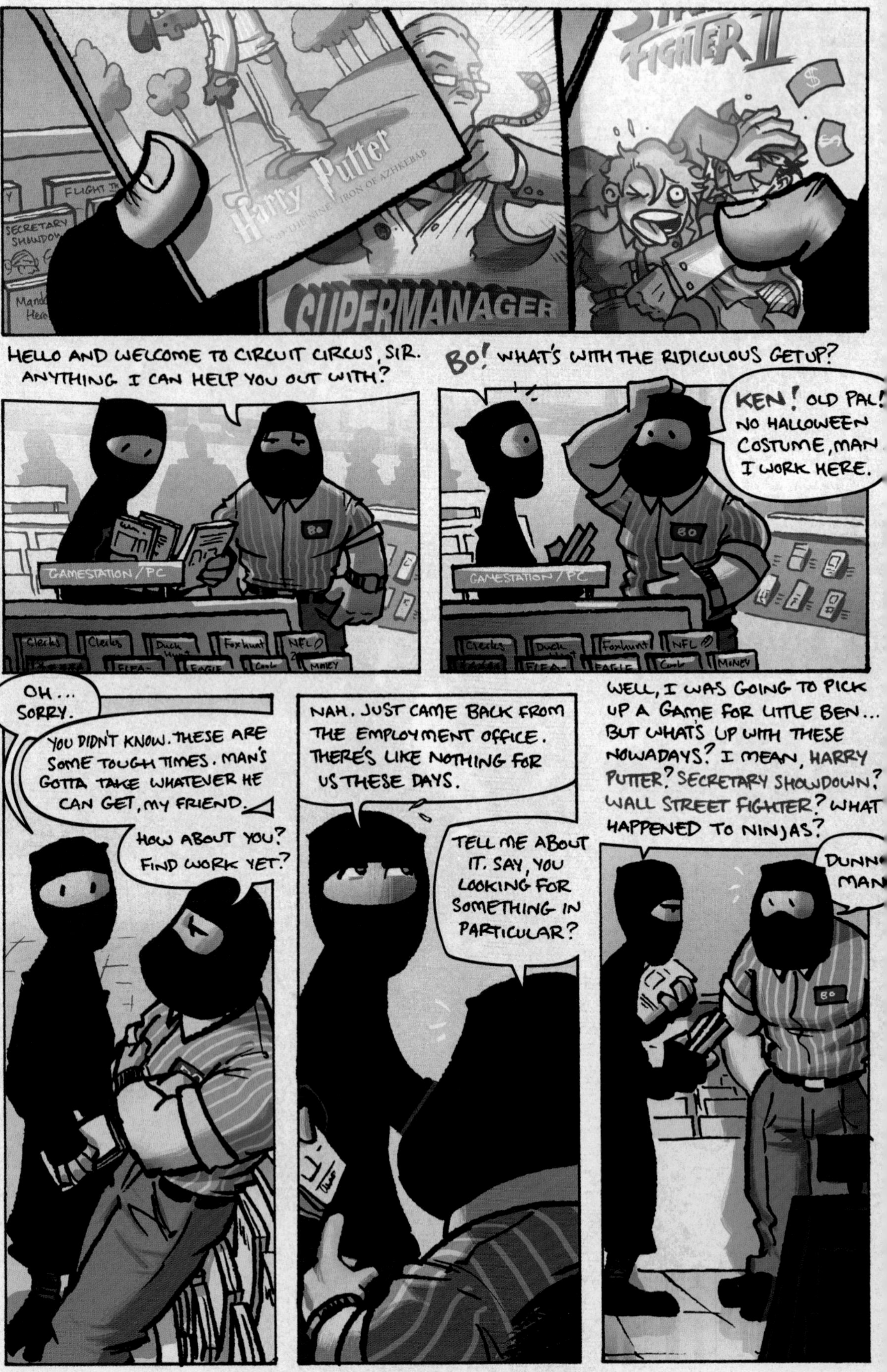
Harry Putter
and the Nine Iron of Azhkebab
Flight
Secretary Showdown
Supermanager
Street Fighter II
HELLO AND WELCOME TO CIRCUIT CIRCUS, SIR. ANYTHING I CAN HELP YOU OUT WITH?
BO! WHAT'S WITH THE RIDICULOUS GETUP?
KEN! OLD PAL! NO HALLOWEEN COSTUME, MAN. I WORK HERE.
GAMESTATION / PC
BO
OH... SORRY.
YOU DIDN'T KNOW. THESE ARE SOME TOUGH TIMES. MAN'S GOTTA TAKE WHATEVER HE CAN GET, MY FRIEND.
HOW ABOUT YOU? FIND WORK YET?
NAH. JUST CAME BACK FROM THE EMPLOYMENT OFFICE. THERE'S LIKE NOTHING FOR US THESE DAYS.
TELL ME ABOUT IT. SAY, YOU LOOKING FOR SOMETHING IN PARTICULAR?
WELL, I WAS GOING TO PICK UP A GAME FOR LITTLE BEN... BUT WHAT'S UP WITH THESE NOWADAYS? I MEAN, HARRY PUTTER? SECRETARY SHOWDOWN? WALL STREET FIGHTER? WHAT HAPPENED TO NINJAS?
DUNN MAN

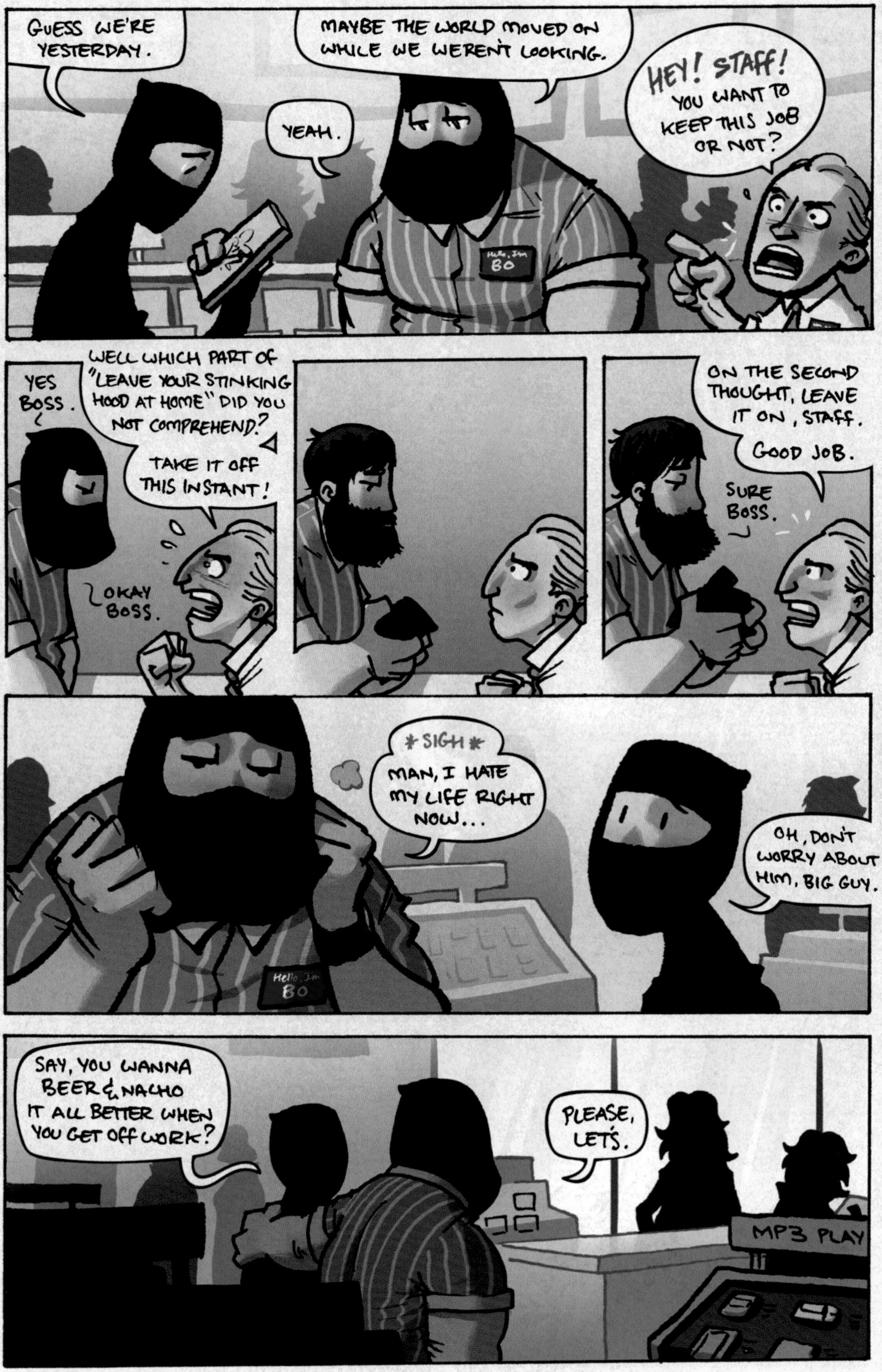
GUESS WE'RE YESTERDAY.
YEAH.
MAYBE THE WORLD MOVED ON WHILE WE WEREN'T LOOKING.
HEY! STAFF! YOU WANT TO KEEP THIS JOB OR NOT?
Hello, I'm BO
YES BOSS.
WELL WHICH PART OF "LEAVE YOUR STINKING HOOD AT HOME" DID YOU NOT COMPREHEND?
TAKE IT OFF THIS INSTANT!
OKAY BOSS.
ON THE SECOND THOUGHT, LEAVE IT ON, STAFF.
GOOD JOB.
SURE BOSS.
SIGH
MAN, I HATE MY LIFE RIGHT NOW...
OH, DON'T WORRY ABOUT HIM, BIG GUY.
Hello, I'm BO
SAY, YOU WANNA BEER & NACHO IT ALL BETTER WHEN YOU GET OFF WORK?
PLEASE, LET'S.
MP3 PLAY

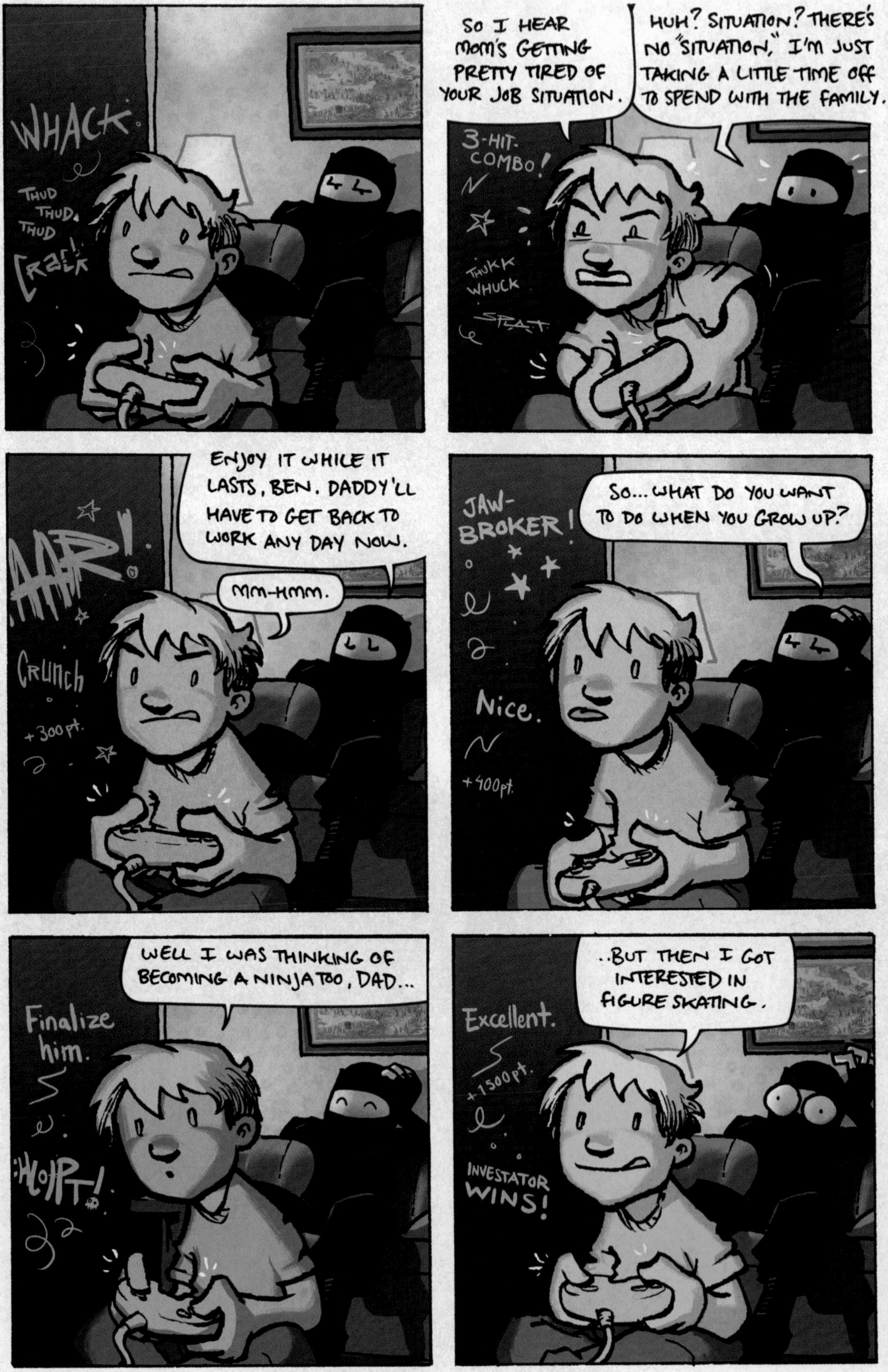
WHACK.
THUD
THUD.
THUD
CRACK
SO I HEAR MOM'S GETTING PRETTY TIRED OF YOUR JOB SITUATION.
HUH? SITUATION? THERE'S NO "SITUATION," I'M JUST TAKING A LITTLE TIME OFF TO SPEND WITH THE FAMILY.
3-HIT-COMBO!
THUKK
WHUCK
SPLAT
ENJOY IT WHILE IT LASTS, BEN. DADDY'LL HAVE TO GET BACK TO WORK ANY DAY NOW.
MM-HMM.
AAR!
Crunch
+300 pt.
SO... WHAT DO YOU WANT TO DO WHEN YOU GROW UP?
JAW-BROKER!
Nice.
+400pt.
WELL I WAS THINKING OF BECOMING A NINJA TOO, DAD...
Finalize him.
..BUT THEN I GOT INTERESTED IN FIGURE SKATING.
Excellent.
+1500 pt.
INVESTATOR WINS!

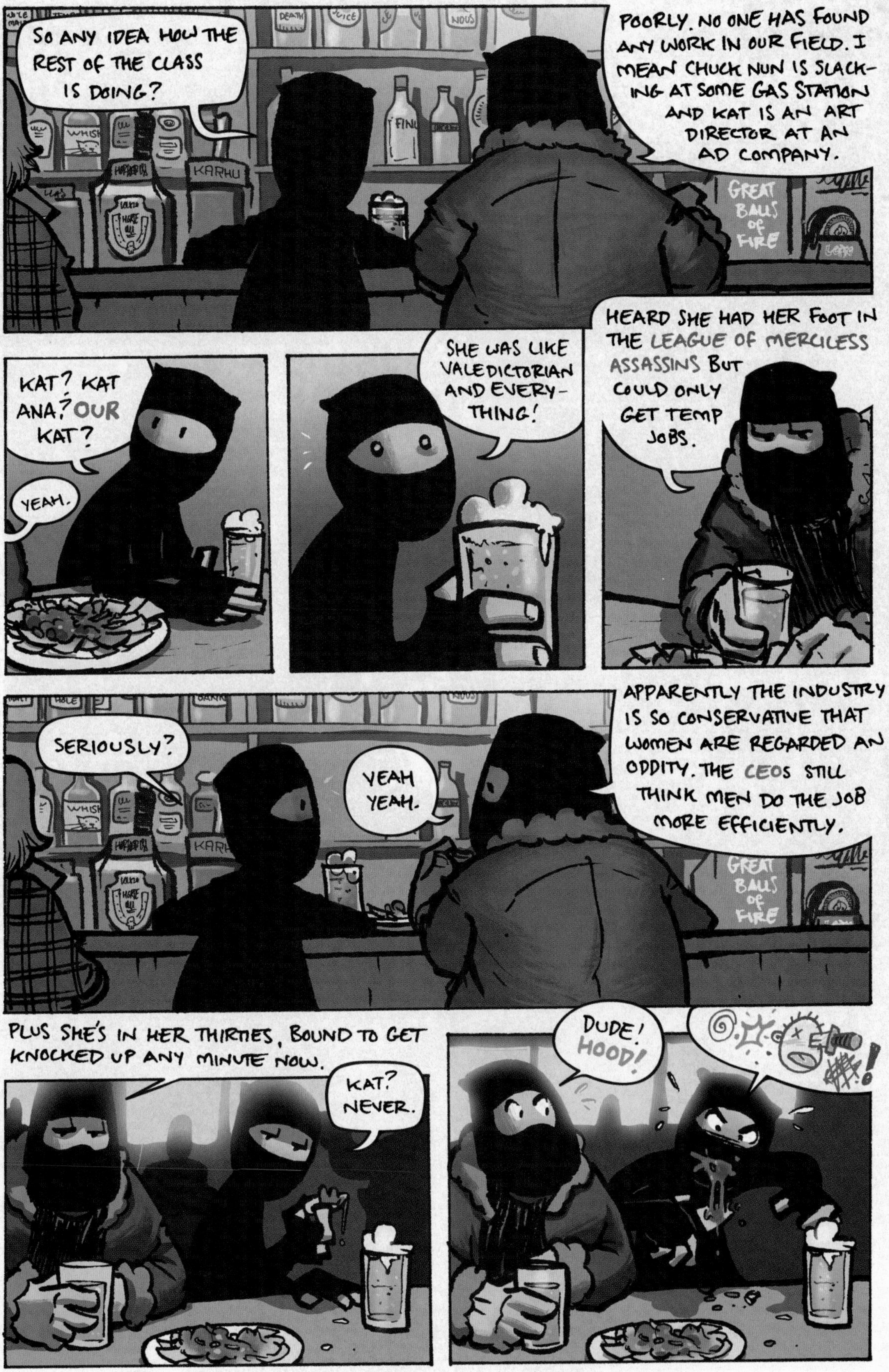
SO ANY IDEA HOW THE REST OF THE CLASS IS DOING?
POORLY. NO ONE HAS FOUND ANY WORK IN OUR FIELD. I MEAN CHUCK NUN IS SLACKING AT SOME GAS STATION AND KAT IS AN ART DIRECTOR AT AN AD COMPANY.
GREAT BALLS of FIRE
KARHU
KAT? KAT ANA? OUR KAT?
YEAH.
SHE WAS LIKE VALEDICTORIAN AND EVERYTHING!
HEARD SHE HAD HER FOOT IN THE LEAGUE OF MERCILESS ASSASSINS BUT COULD ONLY GET TEMP JOBS.
SERIOUSLY?
YEAH YEAH.
APPARENTLY THE INDUSTRY IS SO CONSERVATIVE THAT WOMEN ARE REGARDED AN ODDITY. THE CEOS STILL THINK MEN DO THE JOB MORE EFFICIENTLY.
PLUS SHE'S IN HER THIRTIES, BOUND TO GET KNOCKED UP ANY MINUTE NOW.
KAT? NEVER.
DUDE! HOOD!

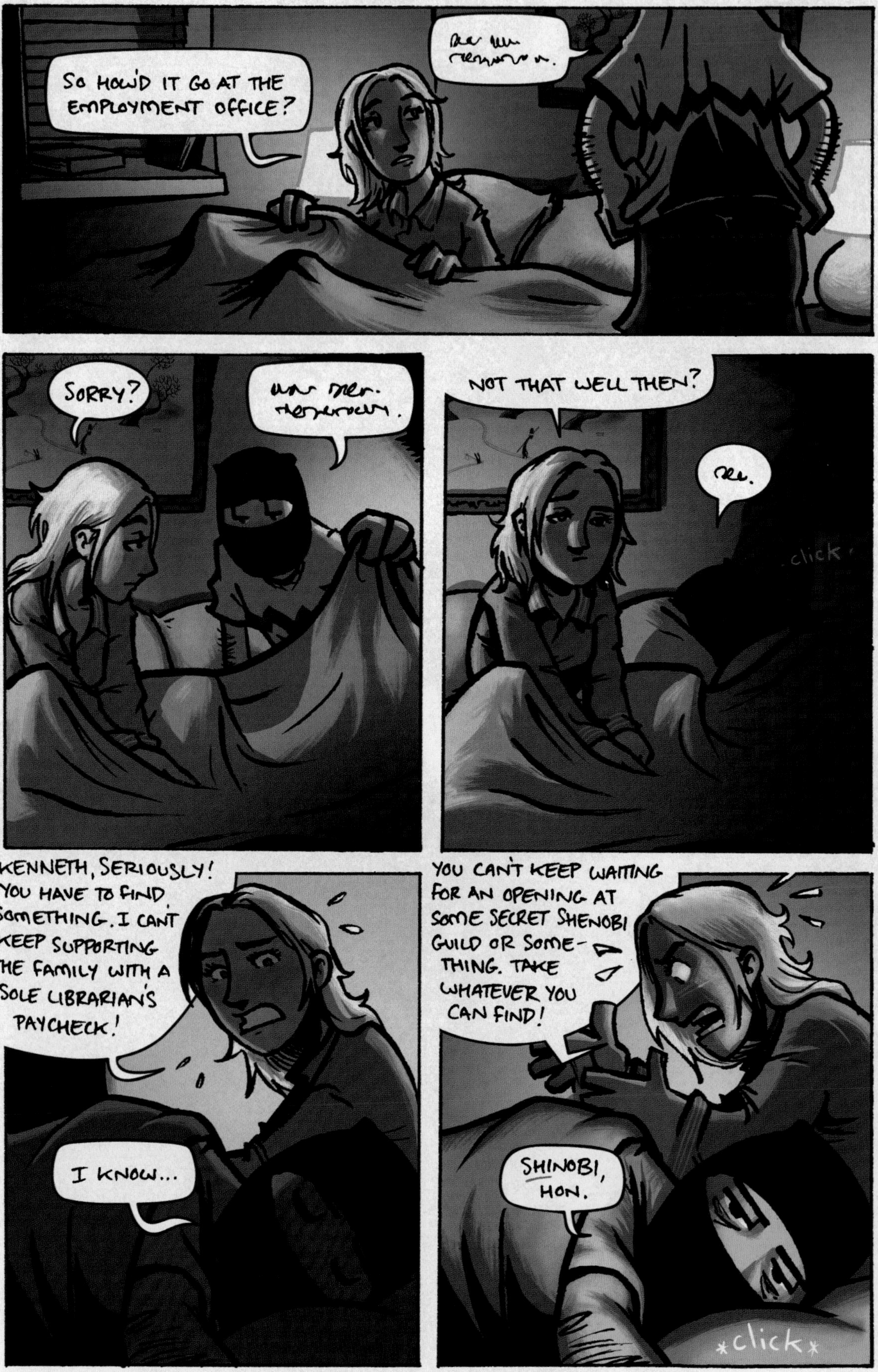
SO HOW'D IT GO AT THE EMPLOYMENT OFFICE?
SORRY?
NOT THAT WELL THEN?
click
KENNETH, SERIOUSLY! YOU HAVE TO FIND SOMETHING. I CAN'T KEEP SUPPORTING THE FAMILY WITH A SOLE LIBRARIAN'S PAYCHECK!
I KNOW...
YOU CAN'T KEEP WAITING FOR AN OPENING AT SOME SECRET SHENOBI GUILD OR SOME-THING. TAKE WHATEVER YOU CAN FIND!
SHINOBI, HON.
click

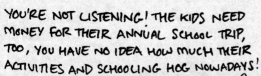
YOU'RE NOT LISTENING! THE KIDS NEED MONEY FOR THEIR ANNUAL SCHOOL TRIP, TOO, YOU HAVE NO IDEA HOW MUCH THEIR ACTIVITIES AND SCHOOLING HOG NOWADAYS!

BARBARA PLEASE! GET OFF MY BACK FOR JUST A SEC!

SHEESH, I TOLD YOU IT'S JUST A PHASE! OUR LINE OF WORK IS THE FIRST THAT GETS CUT WHEN THE ECONOMY TAKES A DIVE!

THAT BEING KILLING EACH OTHER.

WELL...YES. BUT IT'S NOT ALL FUN & GAMES, THERE'S A LOT OF OTHER STUFF TOO.

AND THAT'S ANOTHER THING I DON'T LIKE ABOUT YOUR PROFESSION EITHER.

WHAT?

IT'S TOO DANGEROUS.

OH NOW YOU'VE JUST BEEN LISTENING TOO MUCH TO YOUR MOTHER!

MOMMY, WHY ARE YOU TWO FIGHTING?

OH, WE'RE NOT FIGHTING, DEAR. IF WE WERE FIGHTING, DADDY WOULD BE DEAD BY NOW.

ANYTHING NEW?

SORRY.

HAVE YOU EVER THOUGHT ABOUT FREELANCING?

WELL OBVIOUSLY, BUT I DON'T SEE MYSELF DOING ALL THE PAPERWORK.

HMM...YES. WELL, IS THERE A POSSIBILITY OF MAYBE DOING THE WORK BEFOREHAND AND THEN SELLING IT AFTERWARDS?

I... DON'T QUITE FOLLOW.

WELL, LIKE A LOT OF WRITERS DO, FOR EXAMPLE. THEY WRITE BEFOREHAND AND THEN SELL THEIR SCRIPTS TO PUBLISHERS AND ETC.

SO...I SHOULD ASSASSINATE A RANDOM GUY AND LATER SEE IF SOMEONE WANTED THE POOR BASTARD DEAD ANYHOW?

WHY, YES!

I...I DON'T QUITE SEE HOW THAT COULD WORK, SORRY.

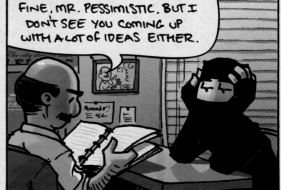

FINE, MR. PESSIMISTIC. BUT I DON'T SEE YOU COMING UP WITH A LOT OF IDEAS EITHER.

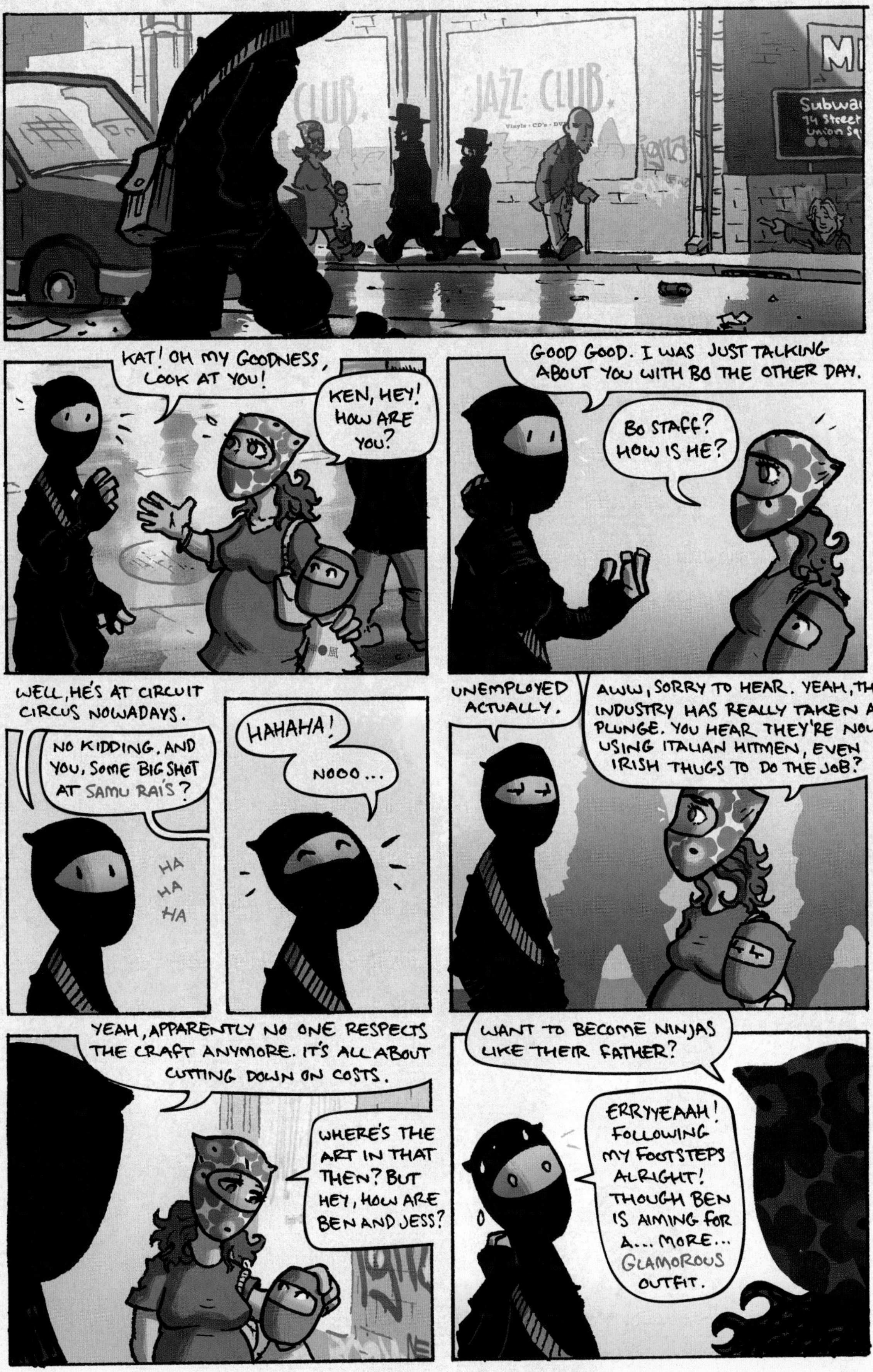

JAZZ CLUB
Vinyls • CD's • DVD
CLUB
Subway
74 Street
Union Sq
KAT! OH MY GOODNESS, LOOK AT YOU!
KEN, HEY! HOW ARE YOU?
GOOD GOOD. I WAS JUST TALKING ABOUT YOU WITH BO THE OTHER DAY.
BO STAFF? HOW IS HE?
WELL, HE'S AT CIRCUIT CIRCUS NOWADAYS.
NO KIDDING. AND YOU, SOME BIG SHOT AT SAMU RAI'S?
HA HA HA
HAHAHA!
NOOO...
UNEMPLOYED ACTUALLY.
AWW, SORRY TO HEAR. YEAH, THE INDUSTRY HAS REALLY TAKEN A PLUNGE. YOU HEAR THEY'RE NOW USING ITALIAN HITMEN, EVEN IRISH THUGS TO DO THE JOB?
YEAH, APPARENTLY NO ONE RESPECTS THE CRAFT ANYMORE. IT'S ALL ABOUT CUTTING DOWN ON COSTS.
WHERE'S THE ART IN THAT THEN? BUT HEY, HOW ARE BEN AND JESS?
WANT TO BECOME NINJAS LIKE THEIR FATHER?
ERRYYEAAH! FOLLOWING MY FOOTSTEPS ALRIGHT! THOUGH BEN IS AIMING FOR A... MORE... GLAMOROUS OUTFIT.

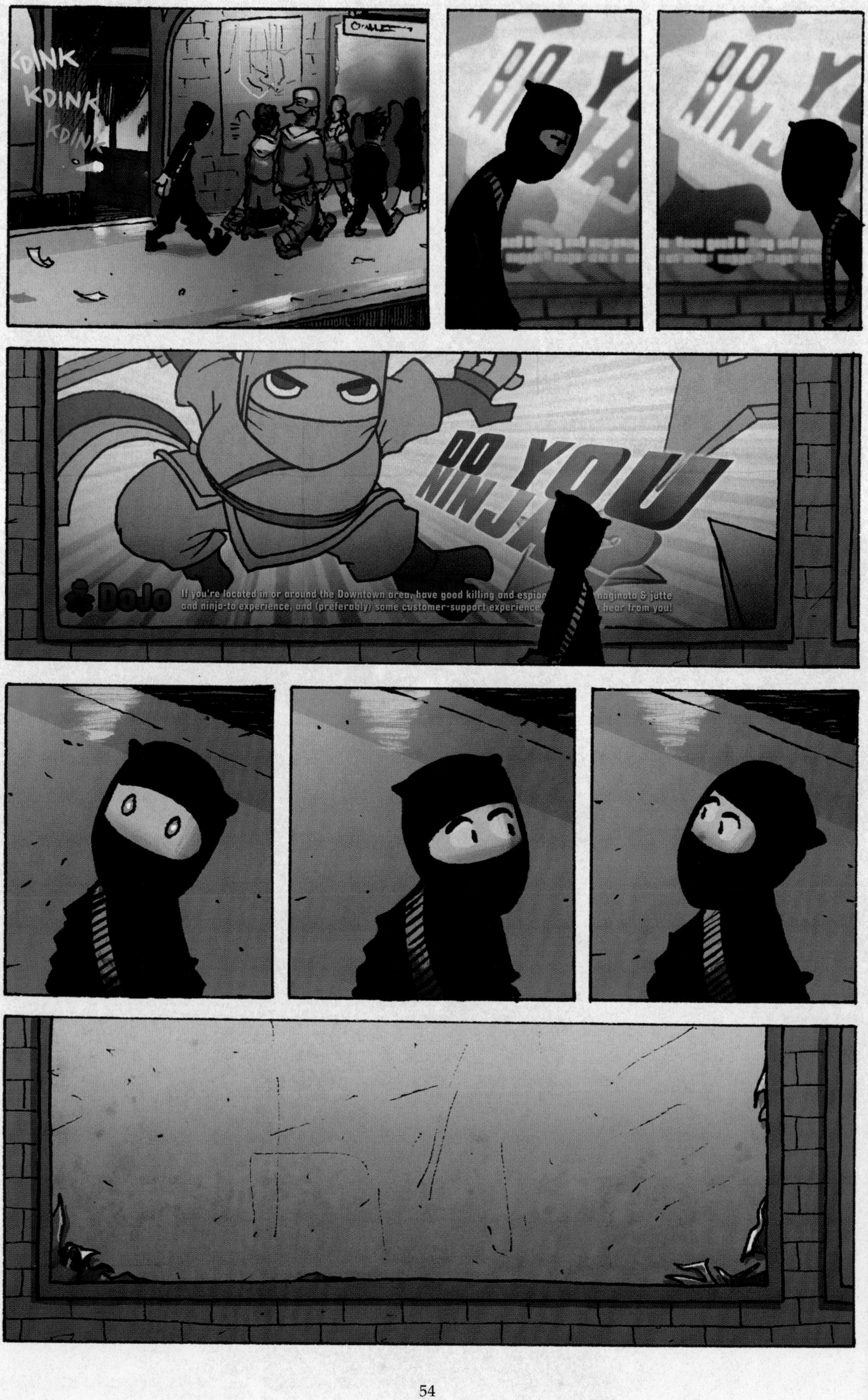
KDINK
KDINK
KDINK
DO YOU NINJA?
DoJo
If you're located in or around the Downtown area, have good killing and espion
naginata & jutte
and ninja-to experience, and (preferably) some customer-support experience
hear from you!

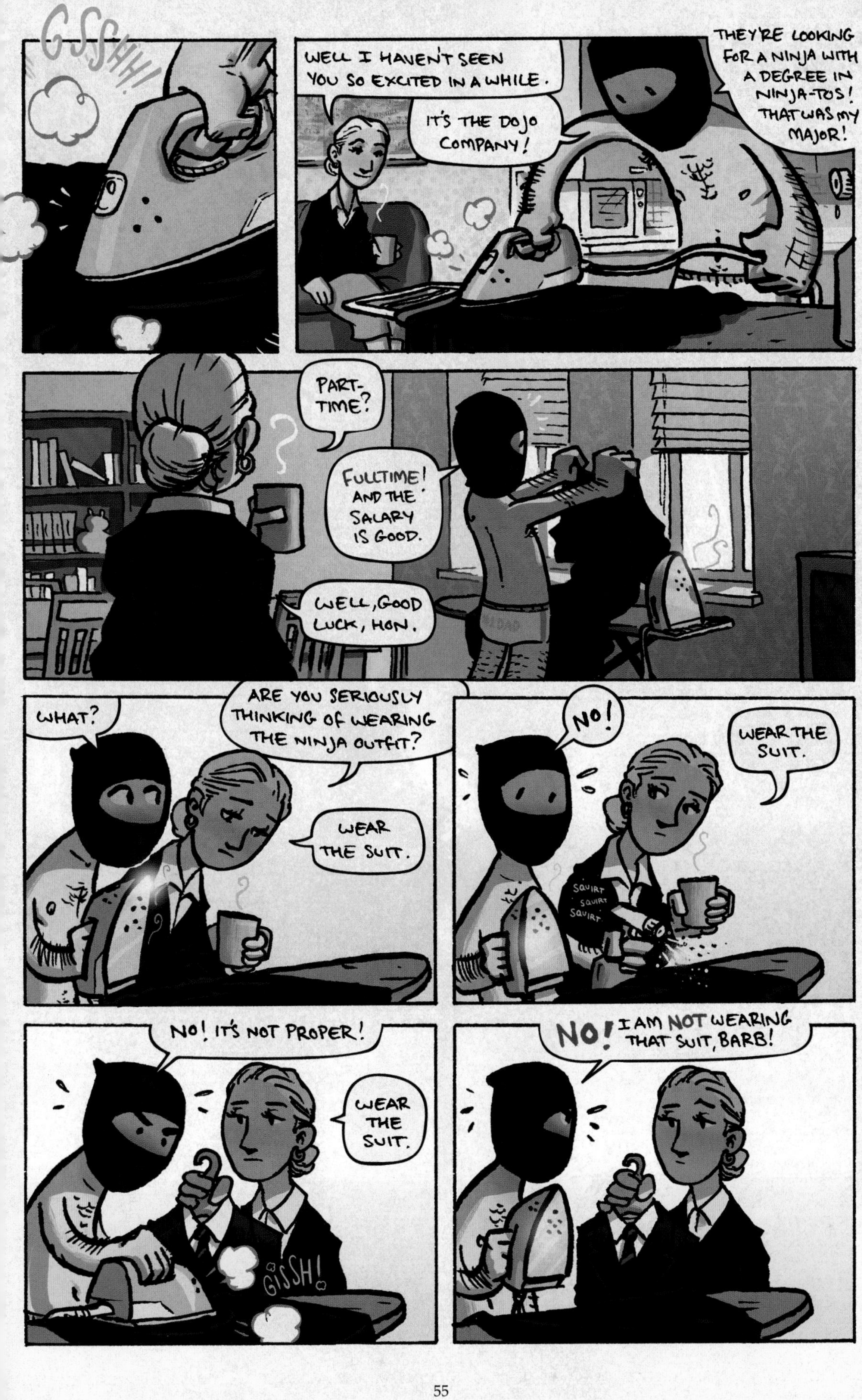
GSSHH!
WELL I HAVEN'T SEEN YOU SO EXCITED IN A WHILE.
IT'S THE DOJO COMPANY!
THEY'RE LOOKING FOR A NINJA WITH A DEGREE IN NINJA-TOS! THAT WAS MY MAJOR!
PART-TIME?
FULLTIME! AND THE SALARY IS GOOD.
WELL, GOOD LUCK, HON.
WHAT?
ARE YOU SERIOUSLY THINKING OF WEARING THE NINJA OUTFIT?
WEAR THE SUIT.
NO!
WEAR THE SUIT.
SQUIRT SQUIRT SQUIRT
NO! IT'S NOT PROPER!
WEAR THE SUIT.
GISSH!
NO! I AM NOT WEARING THAT SUIT, BARB!

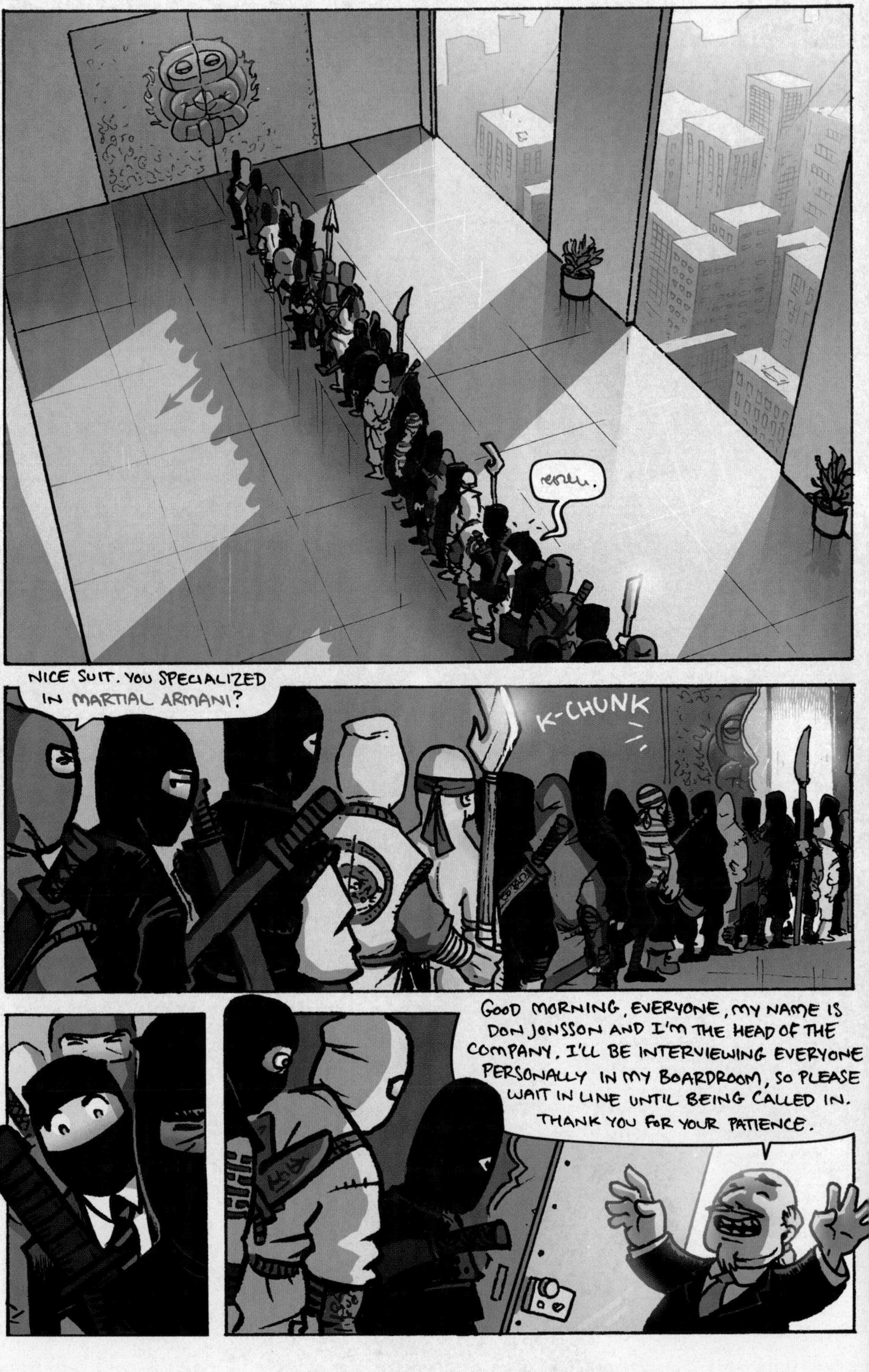
NICE SUIT. YOU SPECIALIZED IN MARTIAL ARMANI?
K-CHUNK
GOOD MORNING, EVERYONE, MY NAME IS DON JONSSON AND I'M THE HEAD OF THE COMPANY. I'LL BE INTERVIEWING EVERYONE PERSONALLY IN MY BOARDROOM, SO PLEASE WAIT IN LINE UNTIL BEING CALLED IN. THANK YOU FOR YOUR PATIENCE.

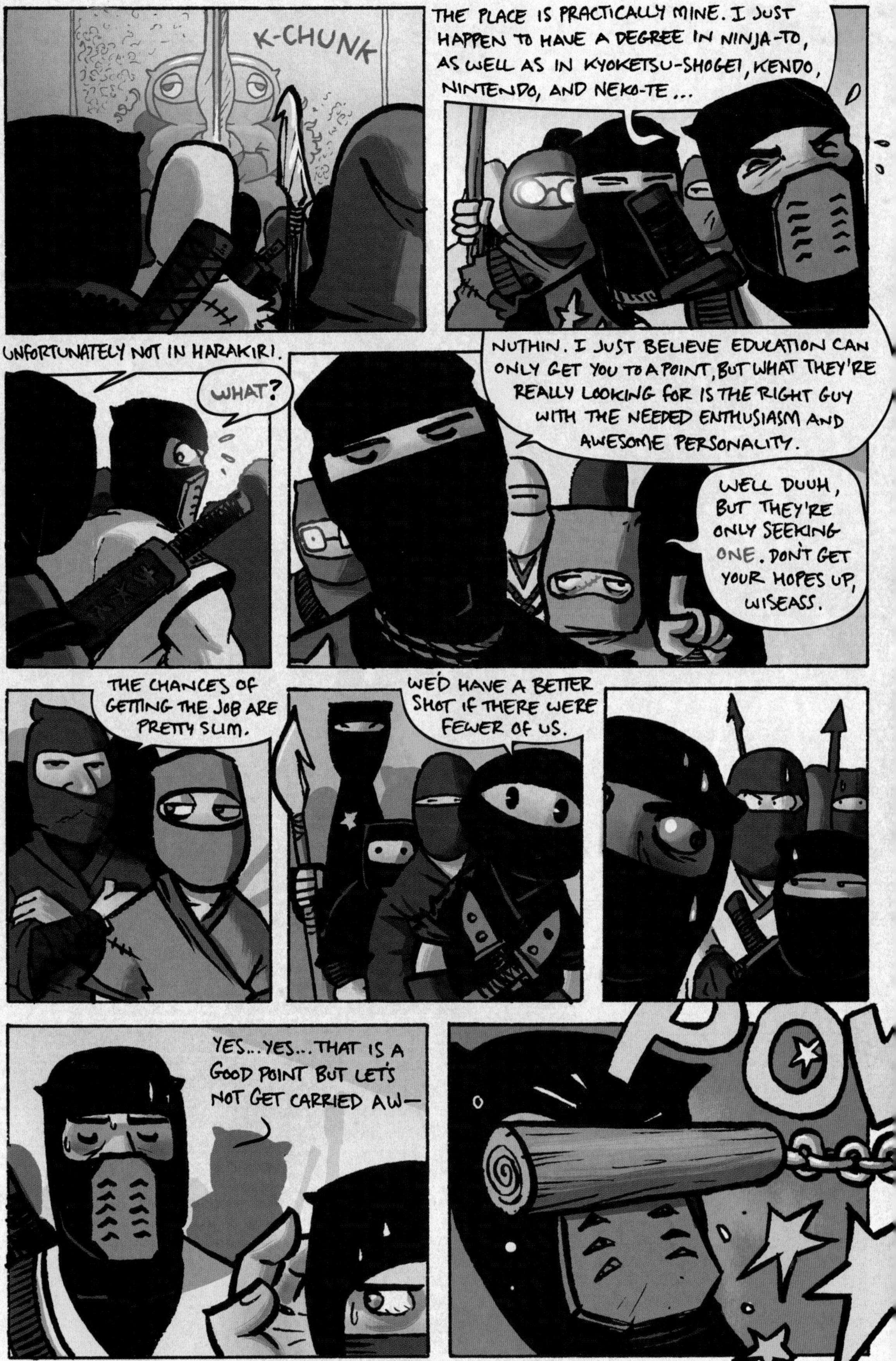

K-CHUNK
THE PLACE IS PRACTICALLY MINE. I JUST HAPPEN TO HAVE A DEGREE IN NINJA-TO, AS WELL AS IN KYOKETSU-SHOGEI, KENDO, NINTENDO, AND NEKO-TE...
UNFORTUNATELY NOT IN HARAKIRI.
WHAT?
NUTHIN. I JUST BELIEVE EDUCATION CAN ONLY GET YOU TO A POINT, BUT WHAT THEY'RE REALLY LOOKING FOR IS THE RIGHT GUY WITH THE NEEDED ENTHUSIASM AND AWESOME PERSONALITY.
WELL DUUH, BUT THEY'RE ONLY SEEKING ONE. DON'T GET YOUR HOPES UP, WISEASS.
THE CHANCES OF GETTING THE JOB ARE PRETTY SLIM.
WE'D HAVE A BETTER SHOT IF THERE WERE FEWER OF US.
YES...YES...THAT IS A GOOD POINT BUT LET'S NOT GET CARRIED AW—
POW

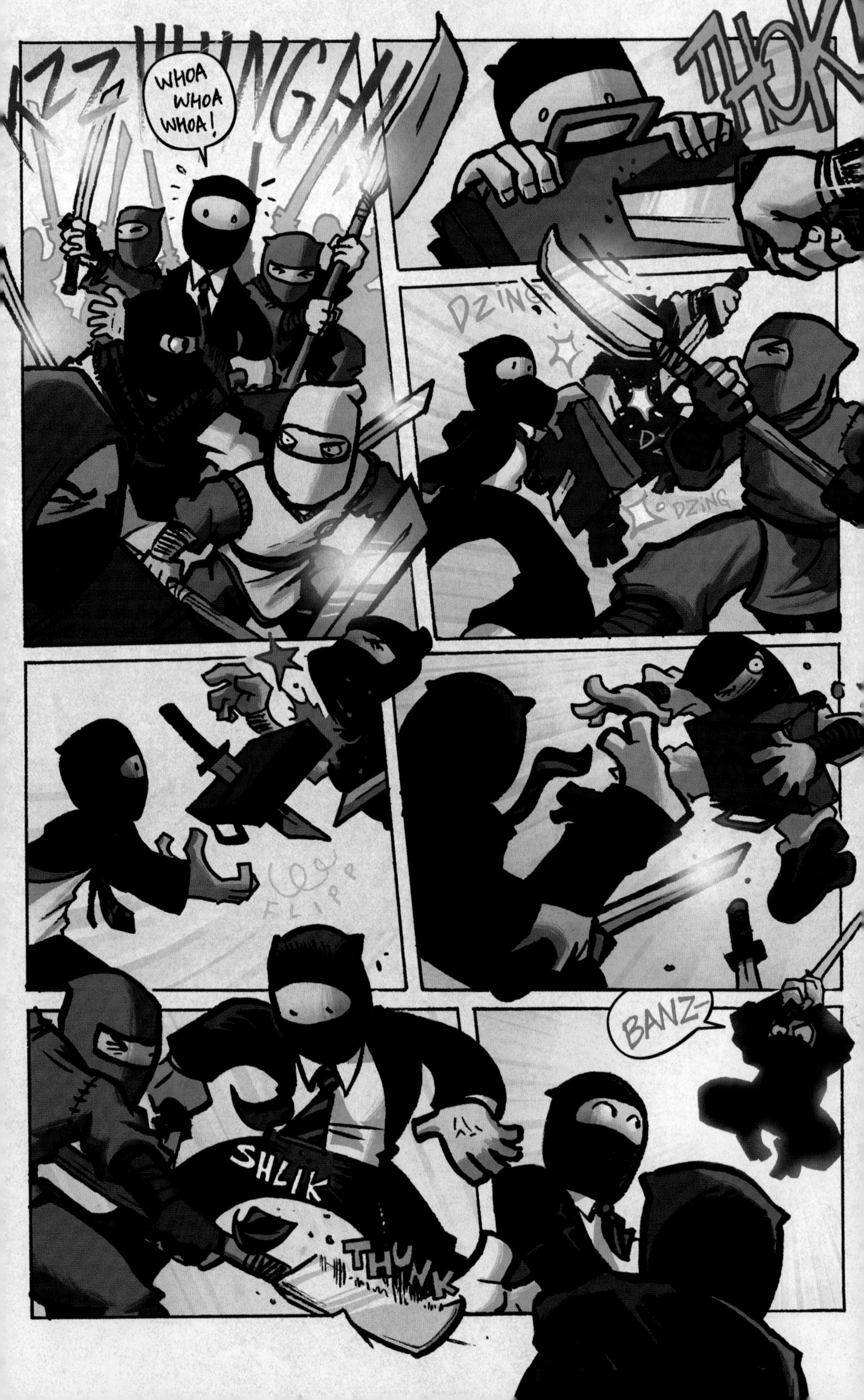
WHOA WHOA WHOA!
THOK!
DZING
DZING
FLIP
BANZ-
SHLIK
THUNK

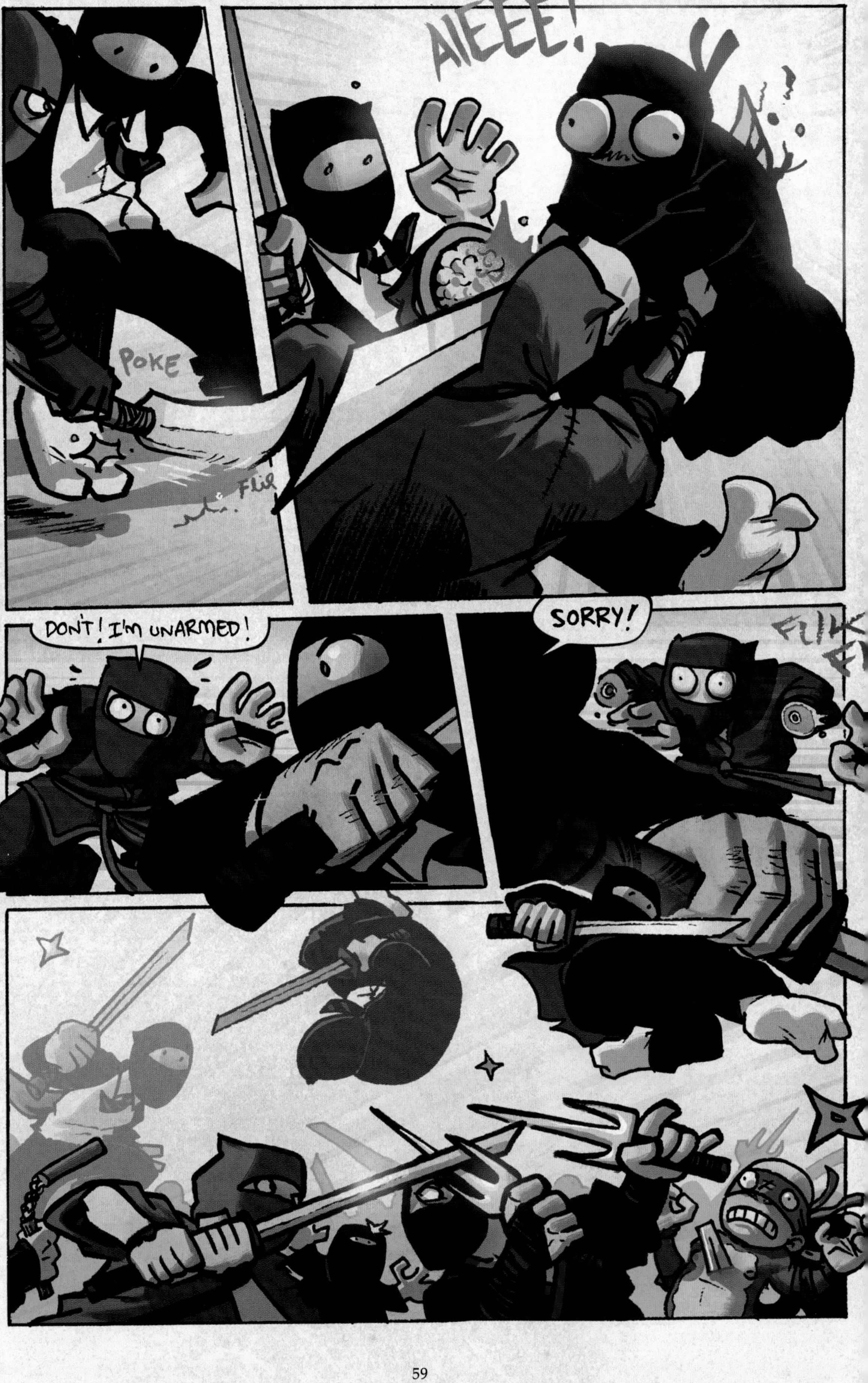
POKE
Flik
AIEEE!
DON'T! I'M UNARMED!
SORRY!

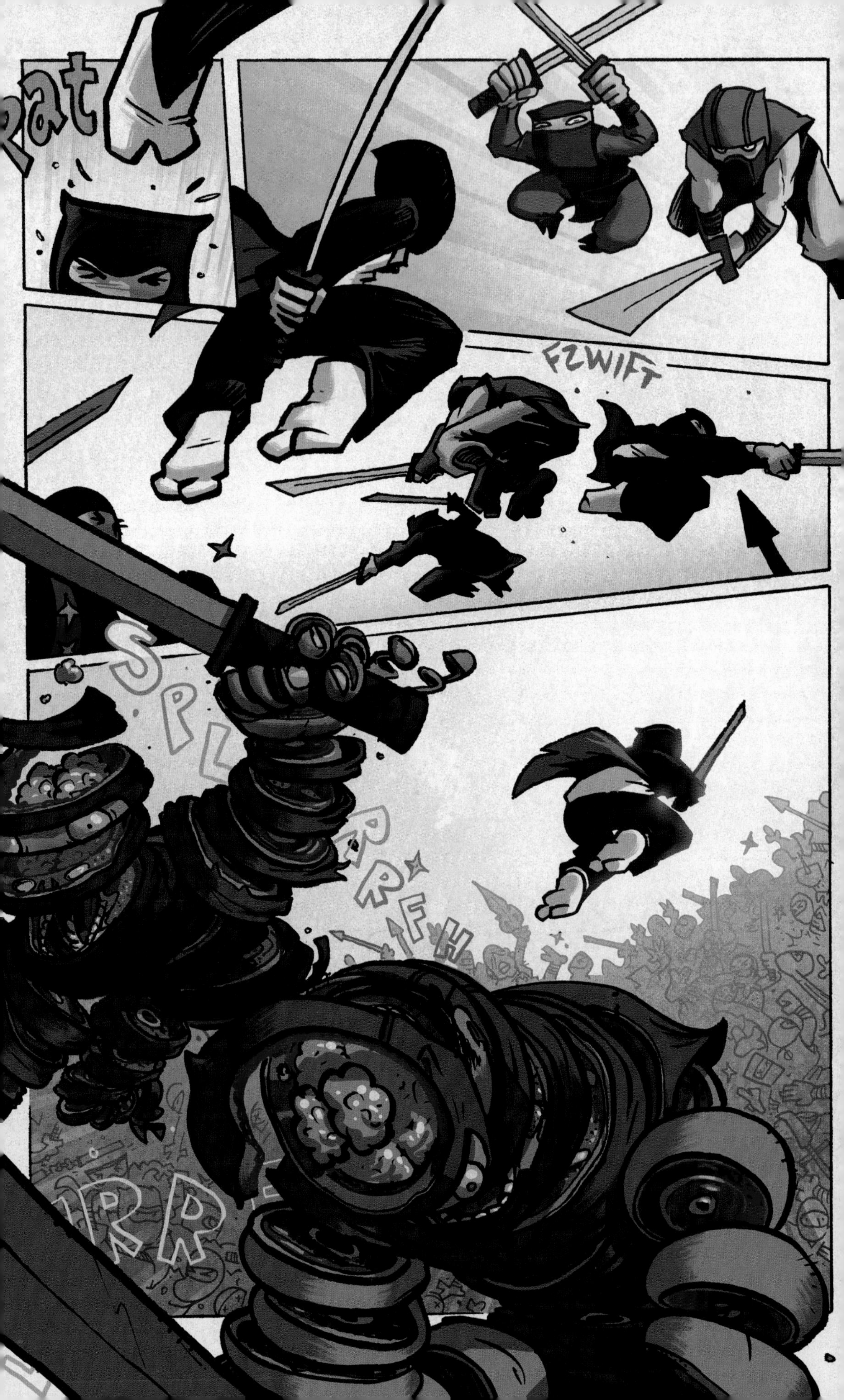
pat
FZWIFT
SPLRRFH
RR

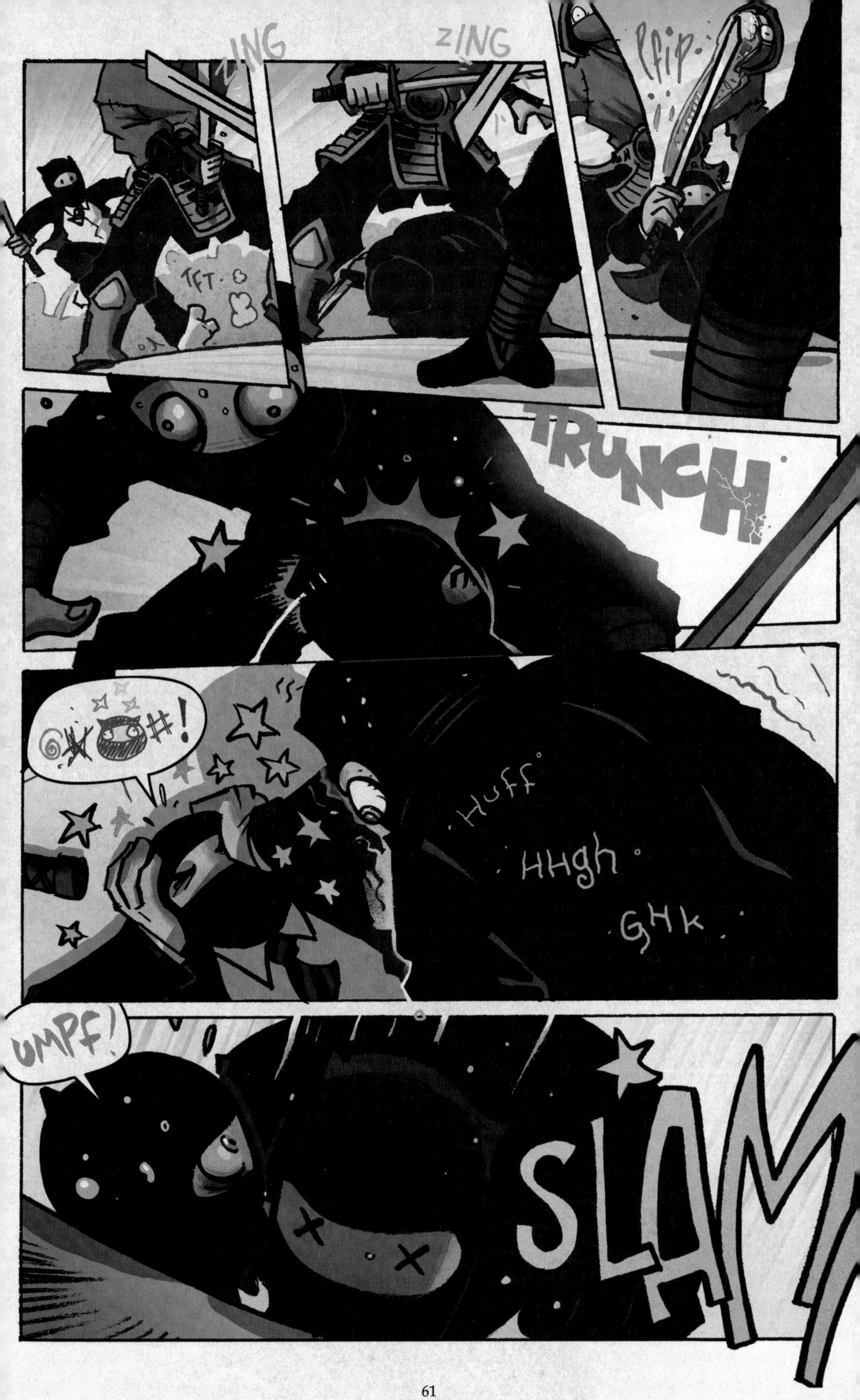
ZING
TFT
ZING
Pfip
TRUNCH
Huff
HHgh
GHk
UMPF!
SLAM

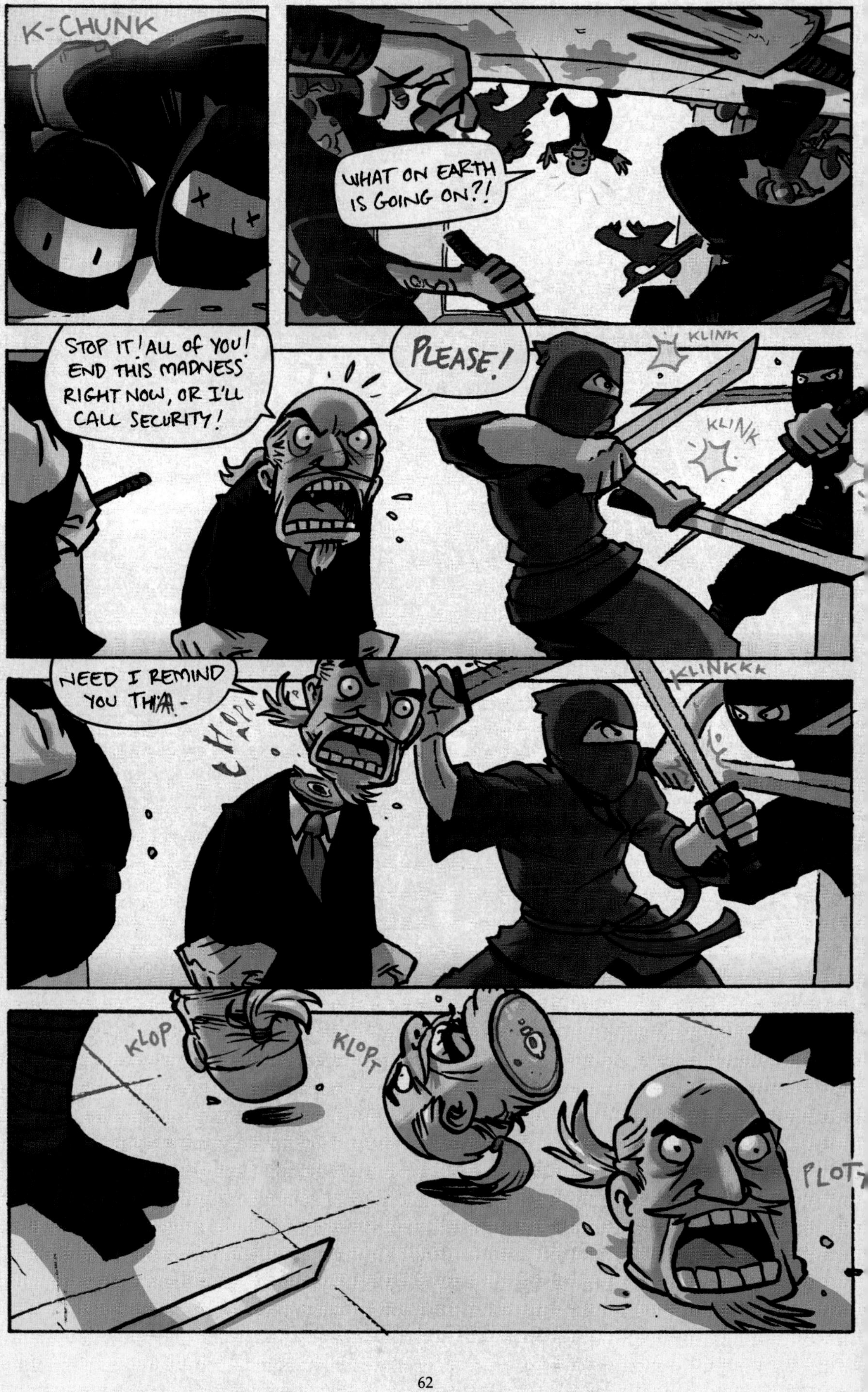
K-CHUNK
WHAT ON EARTH IS GOING ON?!
STOP IT! ALL OF YOU! END THIS MADNESS RIGHT NOW, OR I'LL CALL SECURITY!
PLEASE!
KLINK
KLINK
NEED I REMIND YOU THAA-
KLINKKK
KLOP
KLOPT
PLOT

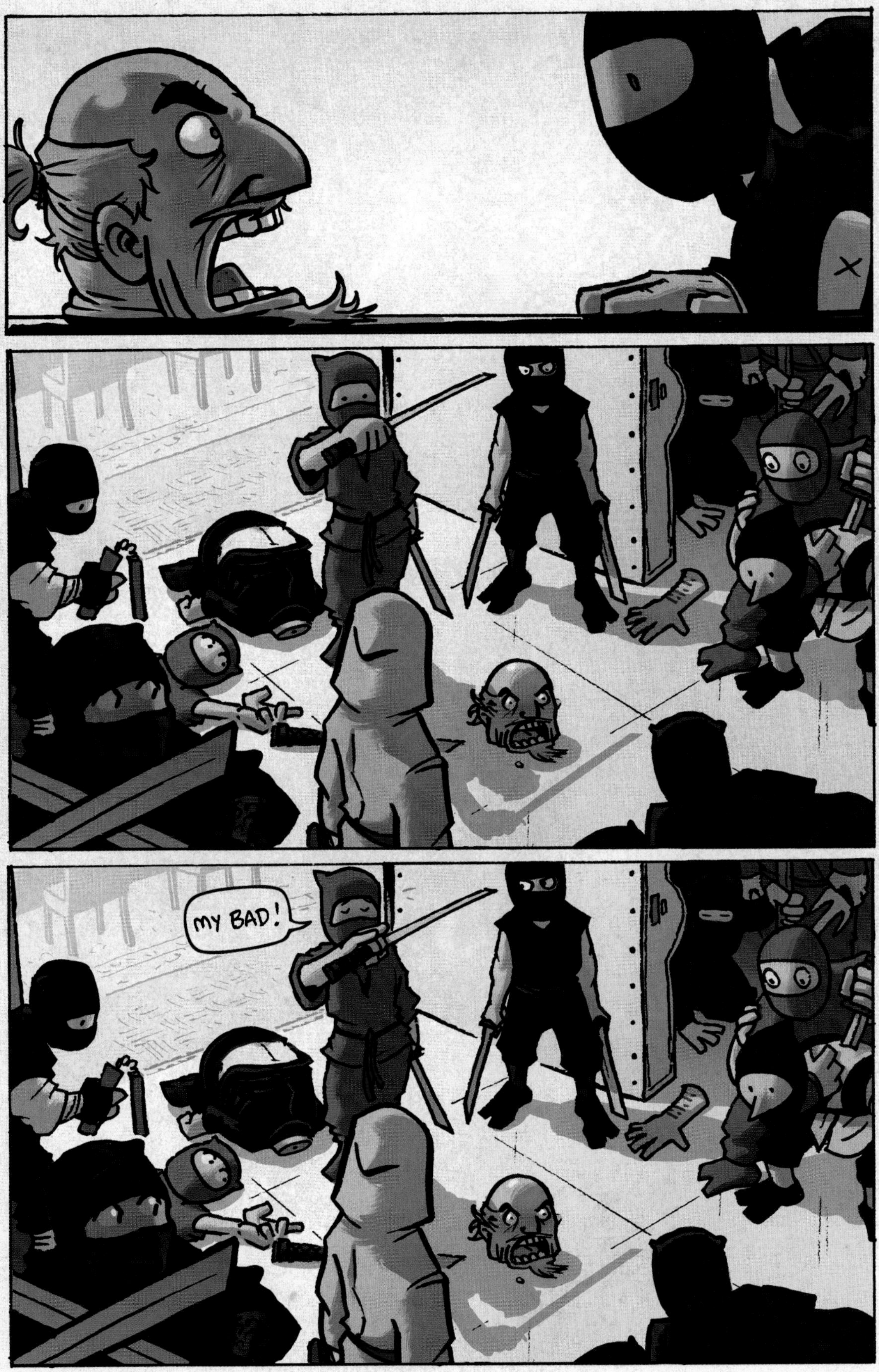
MY BAD!

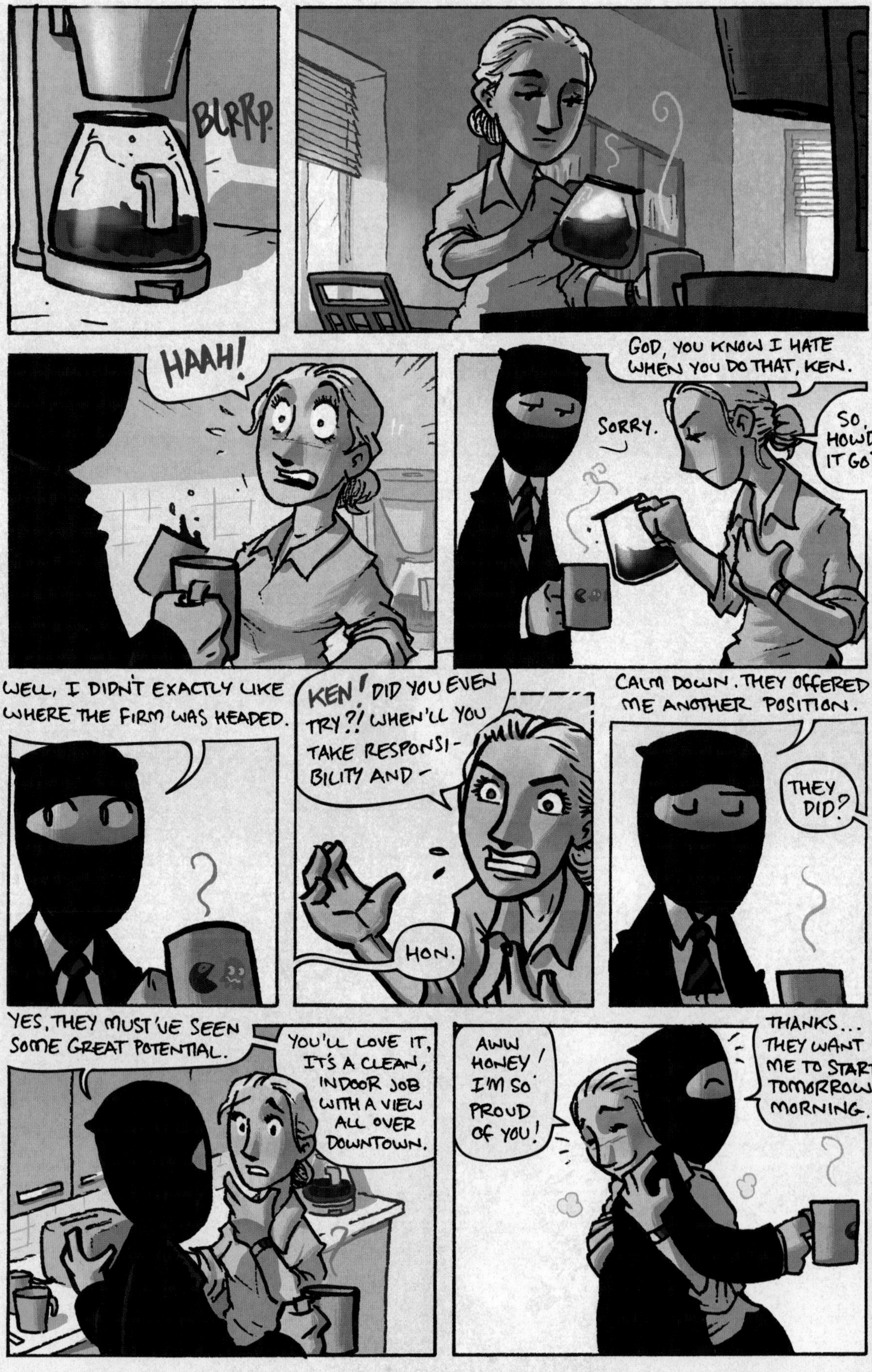
BLRRP.
HAAH!
GOD, YOU KNOW I HATE WHEN YOU DO THAT, KEN.
SORRY.
SO, HOW'D IT GO?
WELL, I DIDN'T EXACTLY LIKE WHERE THE FIRM WAS HEADED.
KEN! DID YOU EVEN TRY?! WHEN'LL YOU TAKE RESPONSI-BILITY AND-
HON.
CALM DOWN. THEY OFFERED ME ANOTHER POSITION.
THEY DID?
YES, THEY MUST'VE SEEN SOME GREAT POTENTIAL.
YOU'LL LOVE IT, IT'S A CLEAN, INDOOR JOB WITH A VIEW ALL OVER DOWNTOWN.
AWW HONEY! I'M SO PROUD OF YOU!
THANKS... THEY WANT ME TO START TOMORROW MORNING.

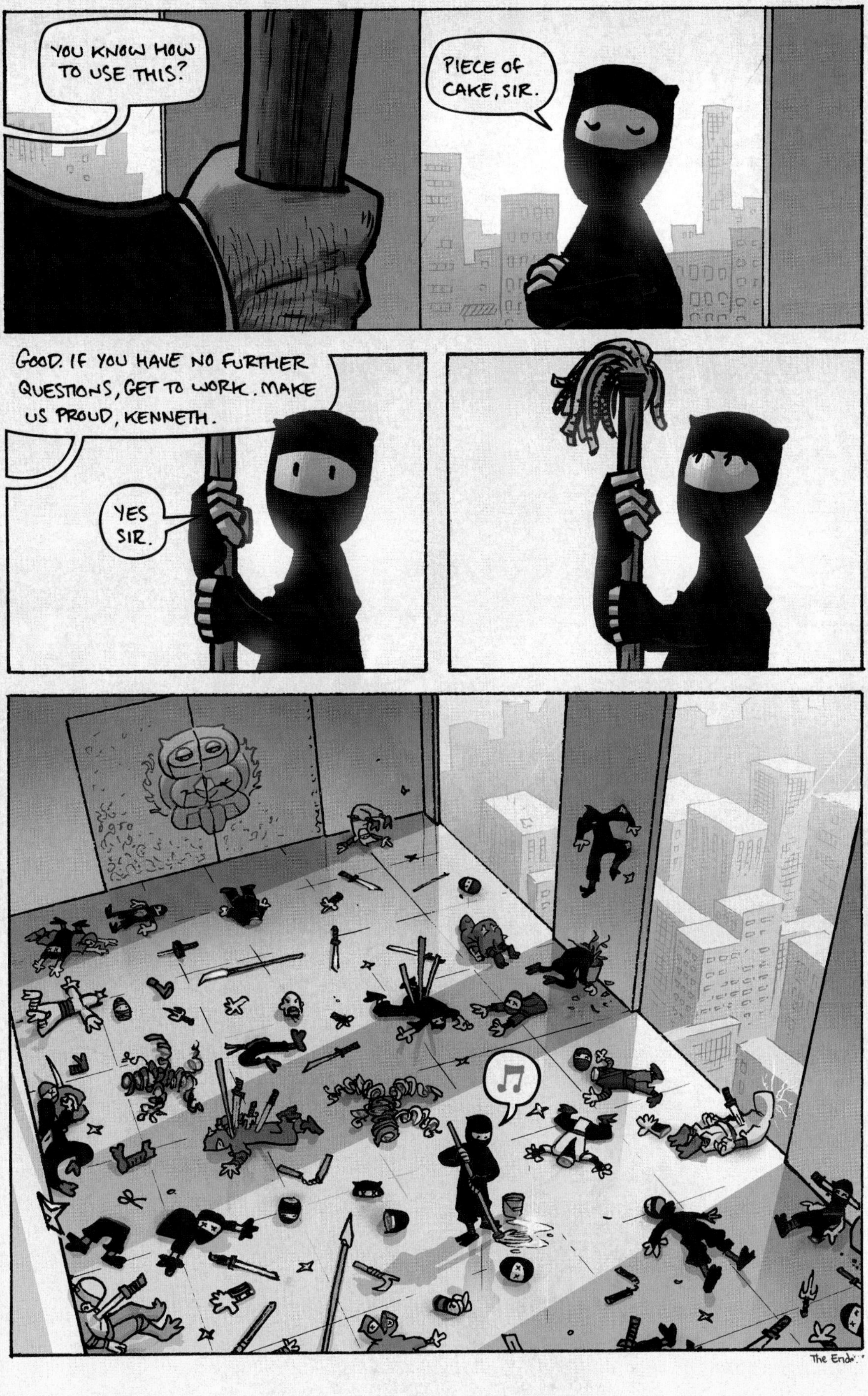
YOU KNOW HOW TO USE THIS?
PIECE OF CAKE, SIR.
GOOD. IF YOU HAVE NO FURTHER QUESTIONS, GET TO WORK. MAKE US PROUD, KENNETH.
YES SIR.
The End...

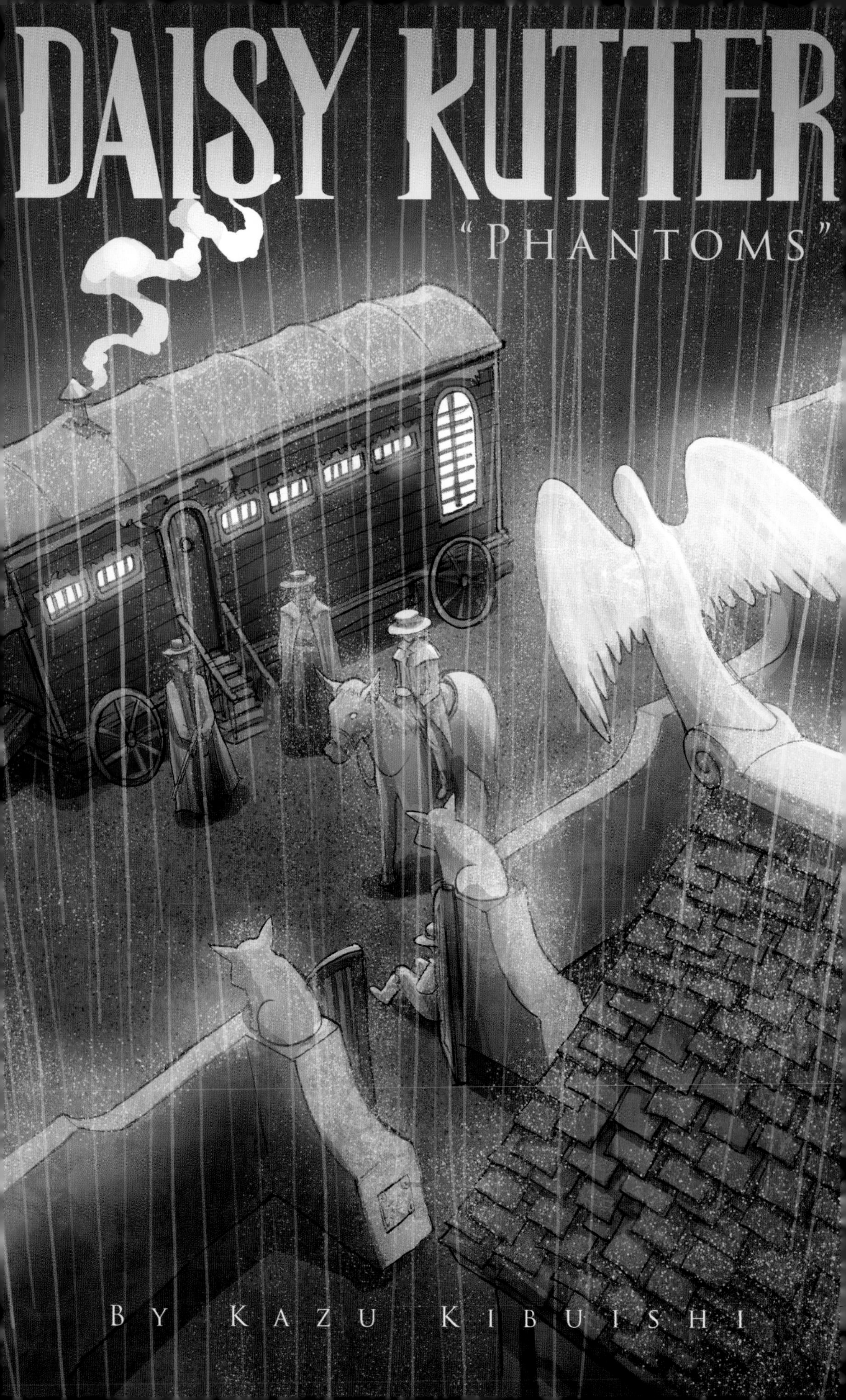
DAISY KUTTER
"PHANTOMS"
BY KAZU KIBUISHI

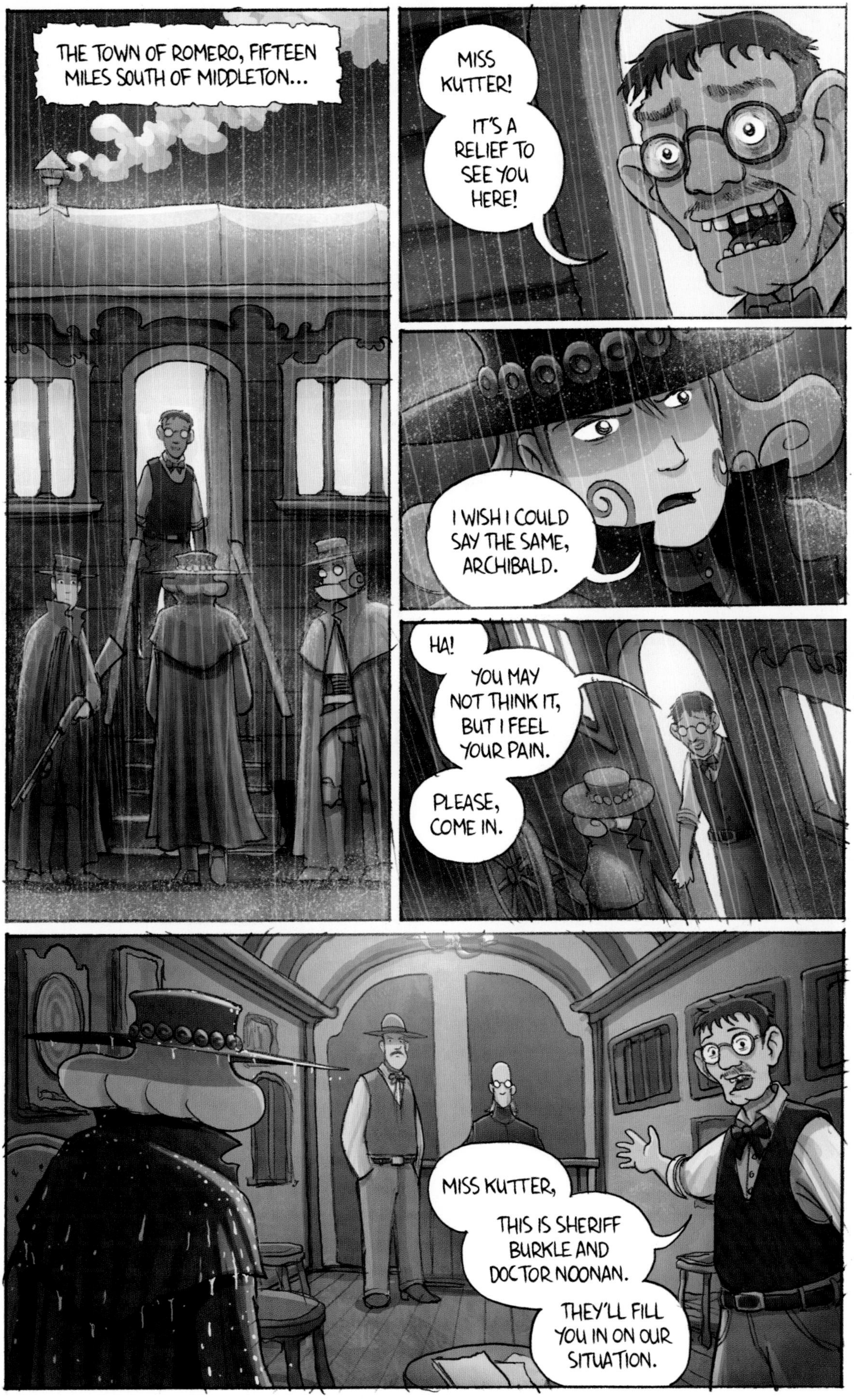
THE TOWN OF ROMERO, FIFTEEN MILES SOUTH OF MIDDLETON...
MISS KUTTER!
IT'S A RELIEF TO SEE YOU HERE!
I WISH I COULD SAY THE SAME, ARCHIBALD.
HA!
YOU MAY NOT THINK IT, BUT I FEEL YOUR PAIN.
PLEASE, COME IN.
MISS KUTTER,
THIS IS SHERIFF BURKLE AND DOCTOR NOONAN.
THEY'LL FILL YOU IN ON OUR SITUATION.

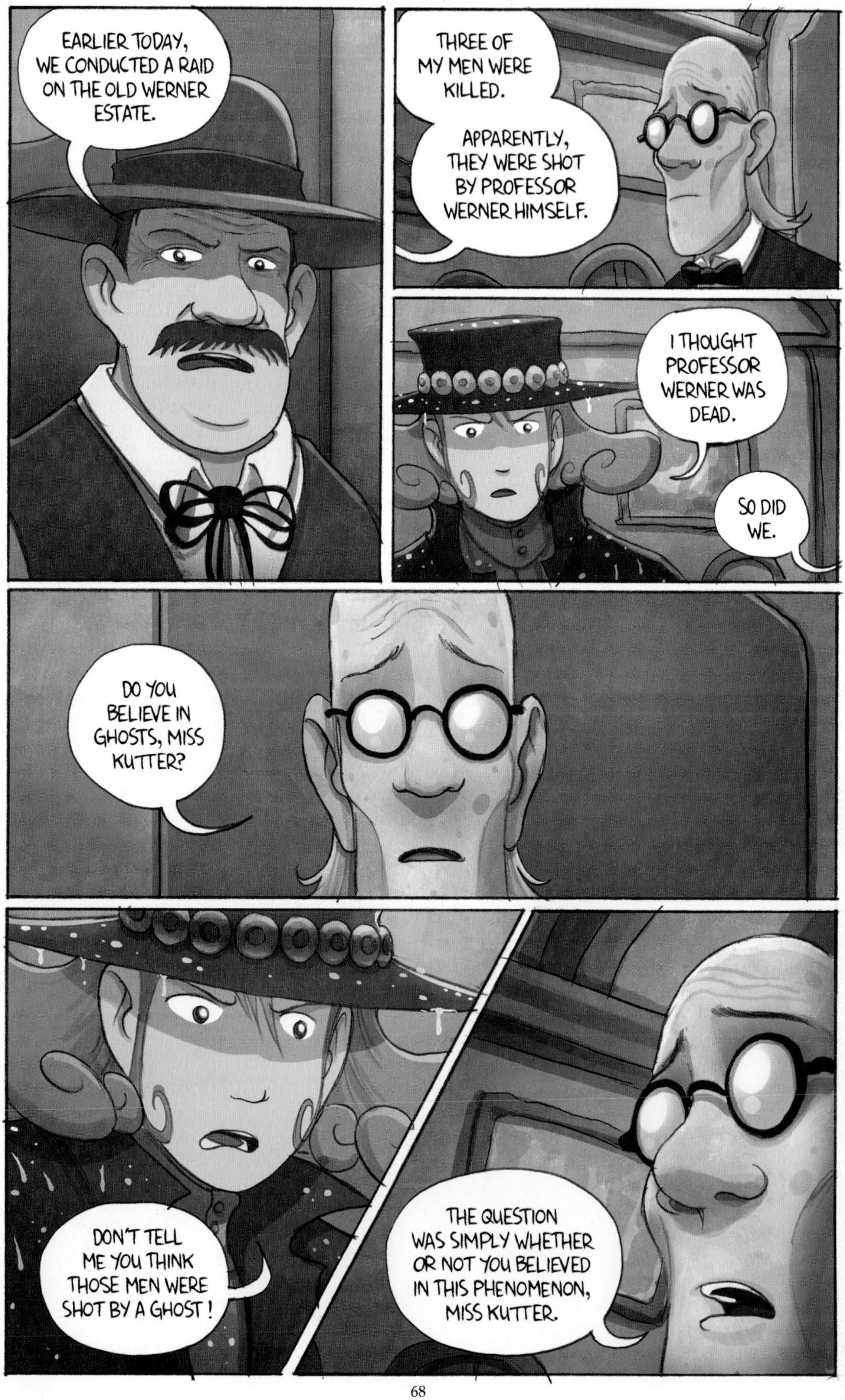
EARLIER TODAY, WE CONDUCTED A RAID ON THE OLD WERNER ESTATE.
THREE OF MY MEN WERE KILLED.
APPARENTLY, THEY WERE SHOT BY PROFESSOR WERNER HIMSELF.
I THOUGHT PROFESSOR WERNER WAS DEAD.
SO DID WE.
DO YOU BELIEVE IN GHOSTS, MISS KUTTER?
DON'T TELL ME YOU THINK THOSE MEN WERE SHOT BY A GHOST!
THE QUESTION WAS SIMPLY WHETHER OR NOT YOU BELIEVED IN THIS PHENOMENON, MISS KUTTER.

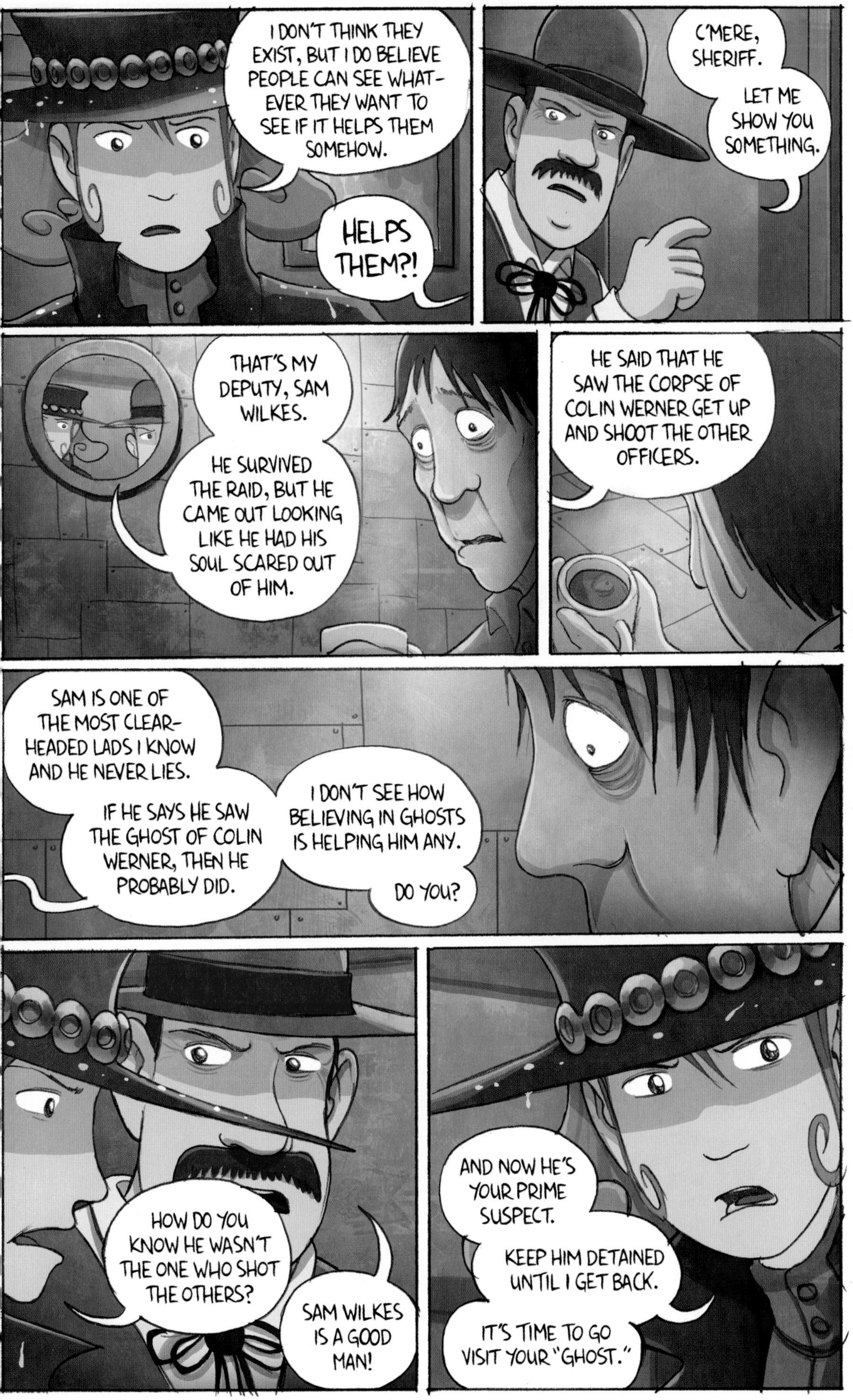
I DON'T THINK THEY EXIST, BUT I DO BELIEVE PEOPLE CAN SEE WHATEVER THEY WANT TO SEE IF IT HELPS THEM SOMEHOW.
HELPS THEM?!
C'MERE, SHERIFF.
LET ME SHOW YOU SOMETHING.
THAT'S MY DEPUTY, SAM WILKES.
HE SURVIVED THE RAID, BUT HE CAME OUT LOOKING LIKE HE HAD HIS SOUL SCARED OUT OF HIM.
HE SAID THAT HE SAW THE CORPSE OF COLIN WERNER GET UP AND SHOOT THE OTHER OFFICERS.
SAM IS ONE OF THE MOST CLEAR-HEADED LADS I KNOW AND HE NEVER LIES.
IF HE SAYS HE SAW THE GHOST OF COLIN WERNER, THEN HE PROBABLY DID.
I DON'T SEE HOW BELIEVING IN GHOSTS IS HELPING HIM ANY.
DO YOU?
HOW DO YOU KNOW HE WASN'T THE ONE WHO SHOT THE OTHERS?
SAM WILKES IS A GOOD MAN!
AND NOW HE'S YOUR PRIME SUSPECT.
KEEP HIM DETAINED UNTIL I GET BACK.
IT'S TIME TO GO VISIT YOUR "GHOST."

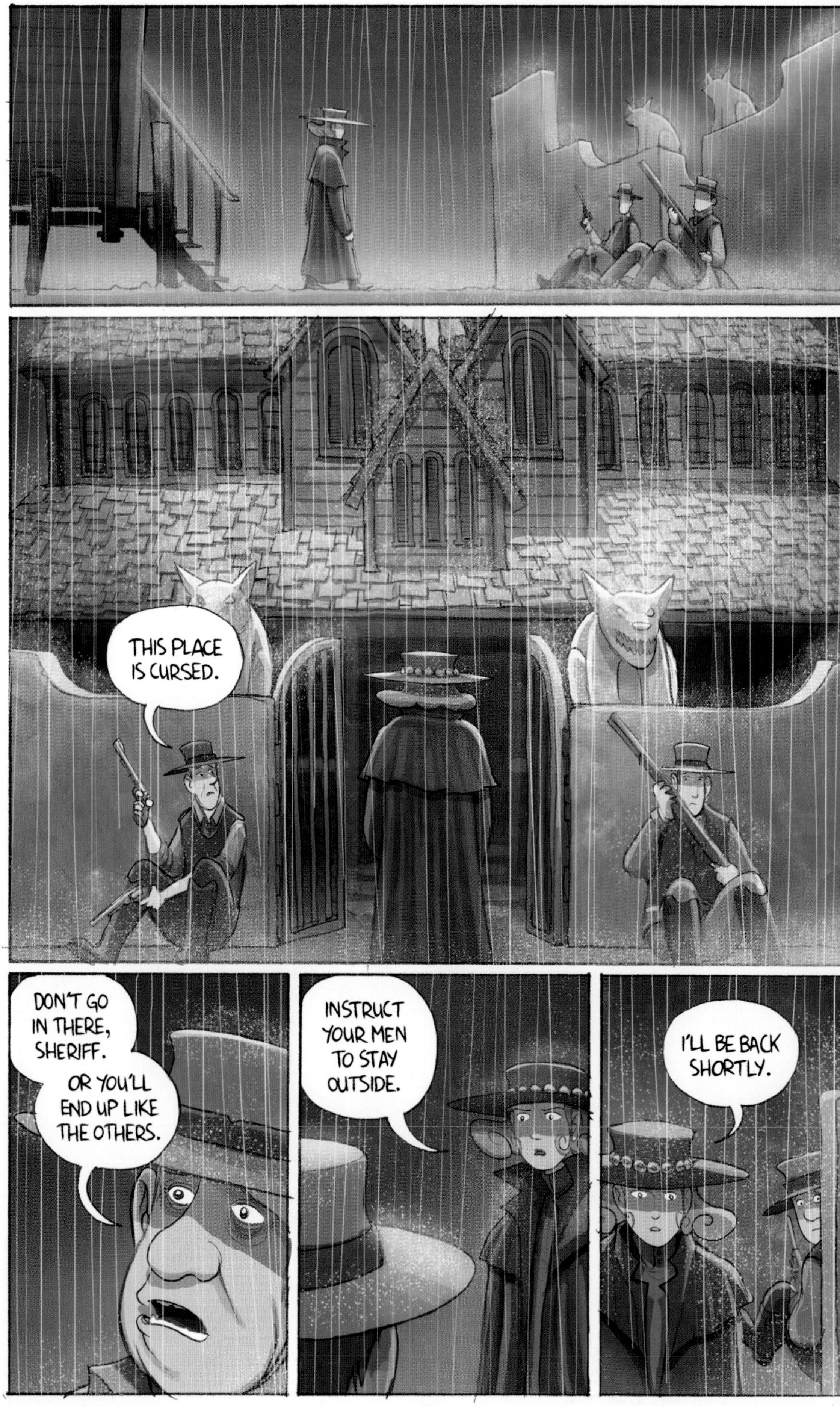
THIS PLACE IS CURSED.
DON'T GO IN THERE, SHERIFF.
OR YOU'LL END UP LIKE THE OTHERS.
INSTRUCT YOUR MEN TO STAY OUTSIDE.
I'LL BE BACK SHORTLY.

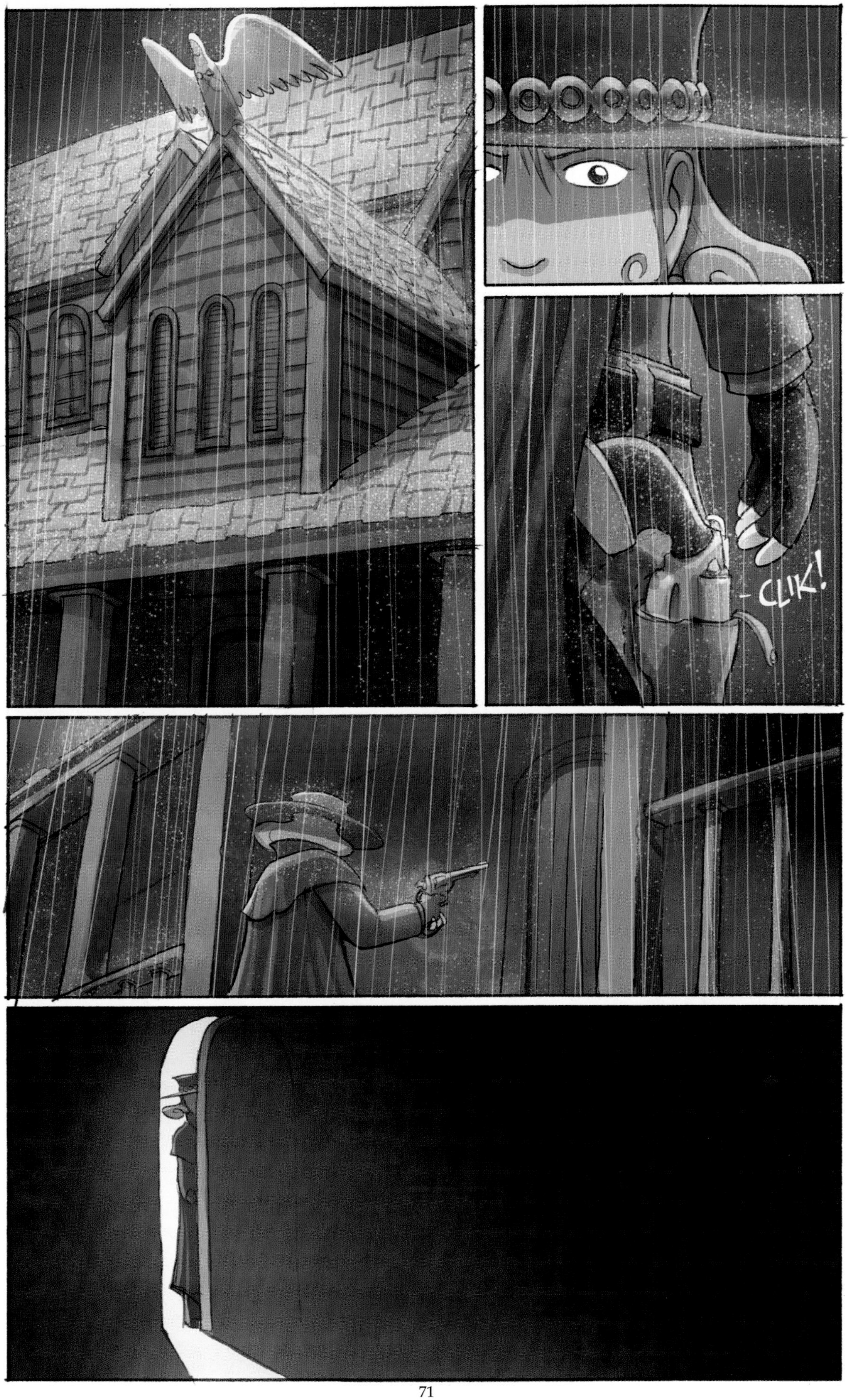
CLIK!

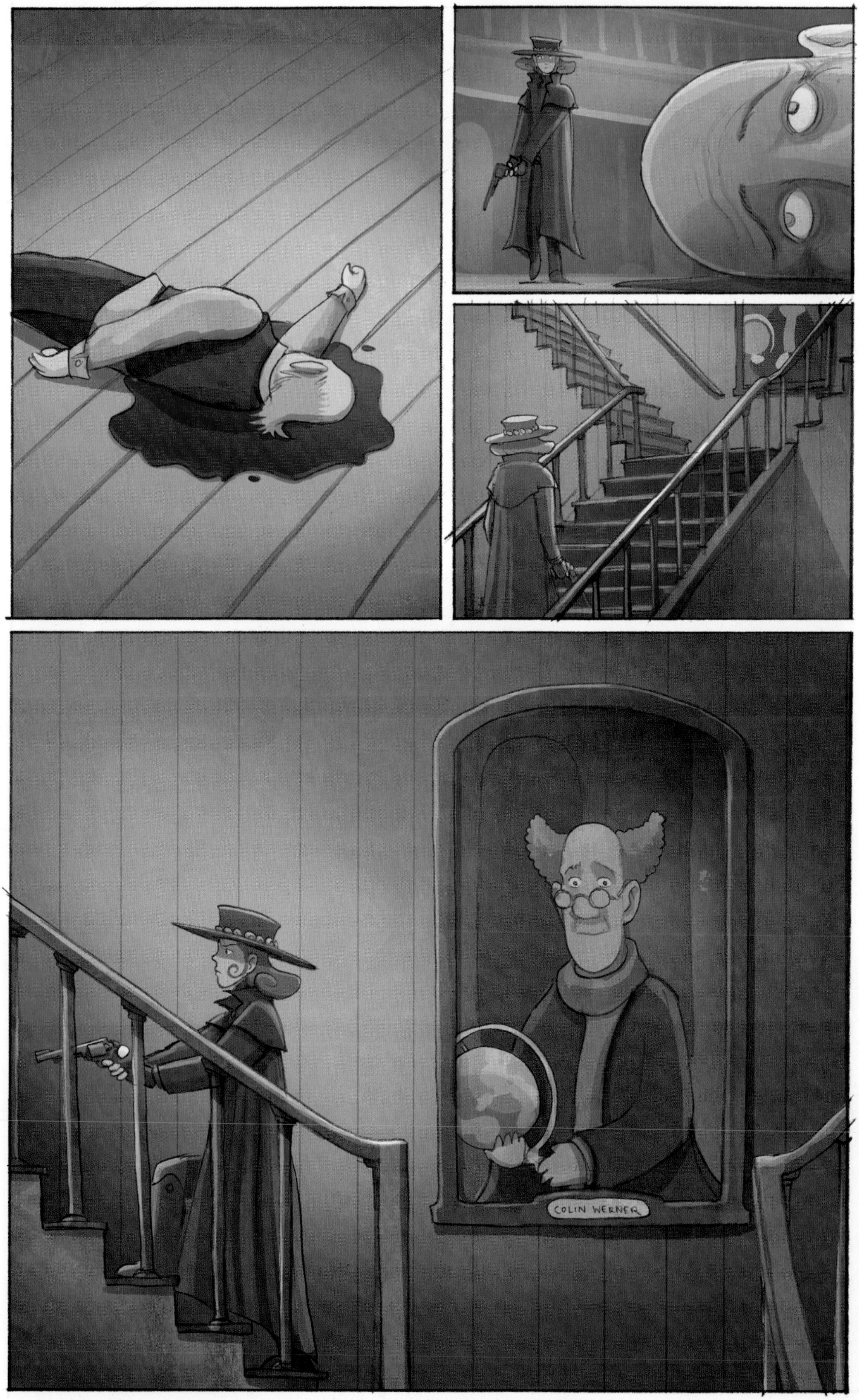
COLIN WERNER

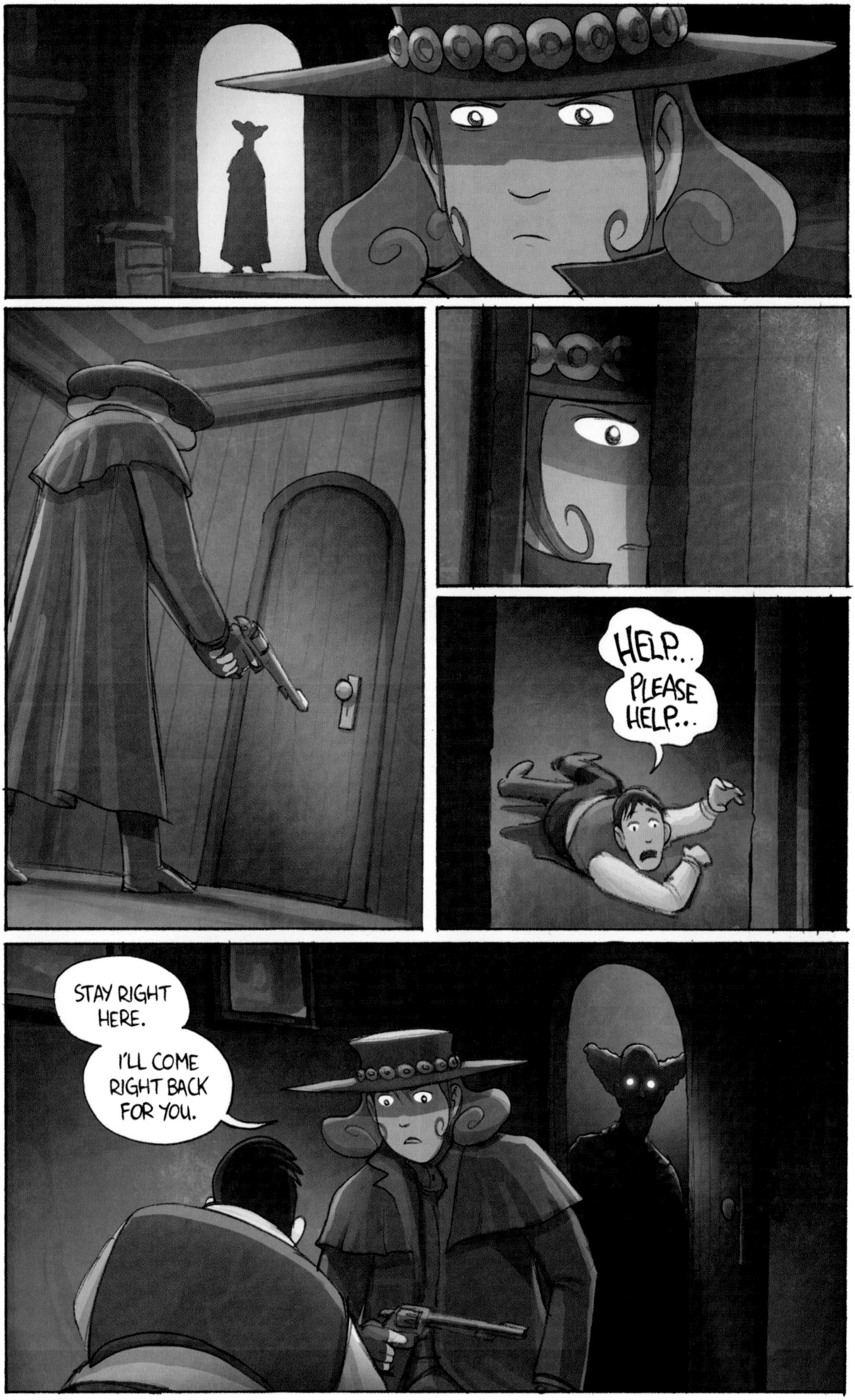
HELP...
PLEASE HELP...
STAY RIGHT HERE.
I'LL COME RIGHT BACK FOR YOU.

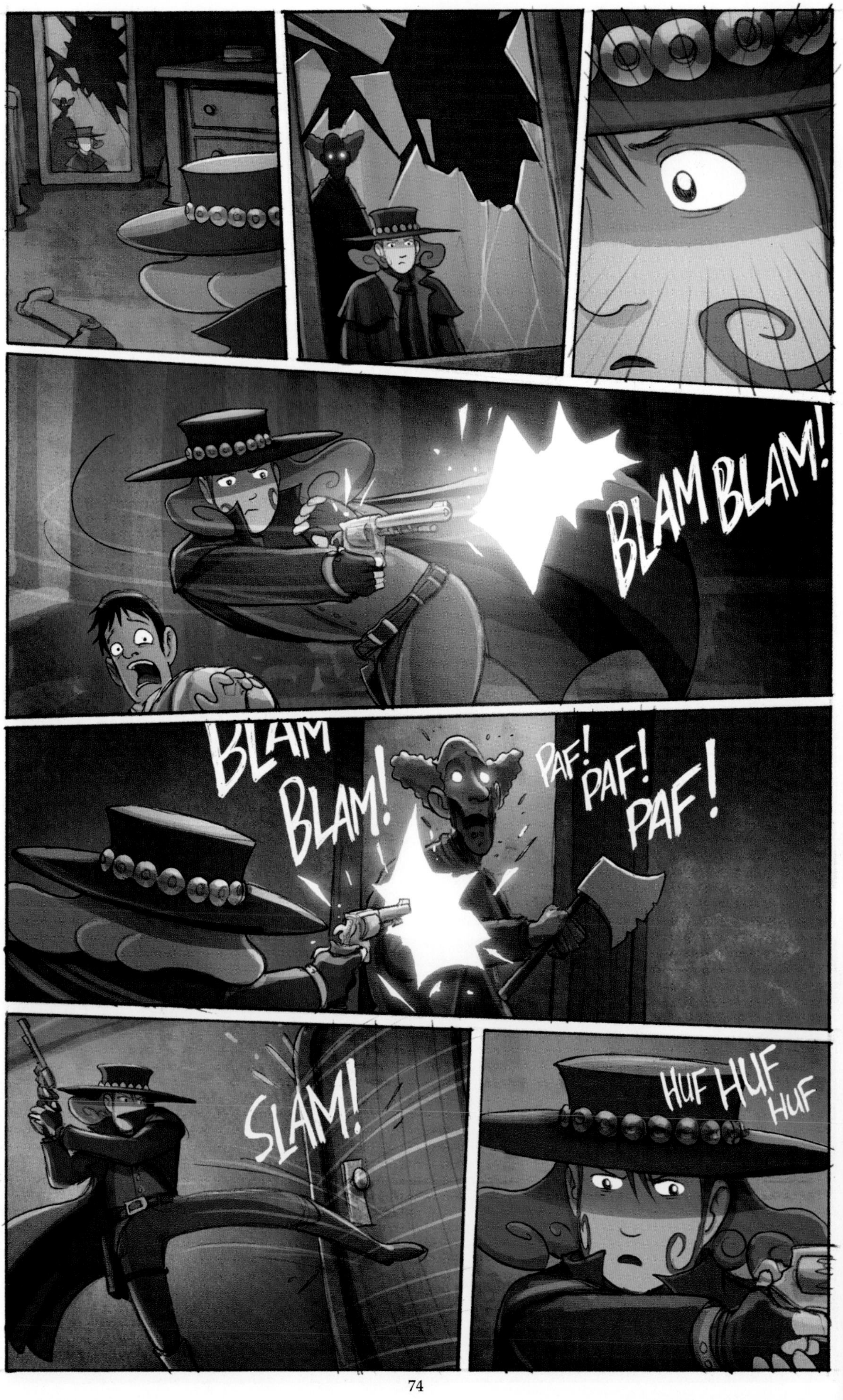
BLAM BLAM!
BLAM BLAM!
PAF! PAF! PAF!
SLAM!
HUF HUF HUF

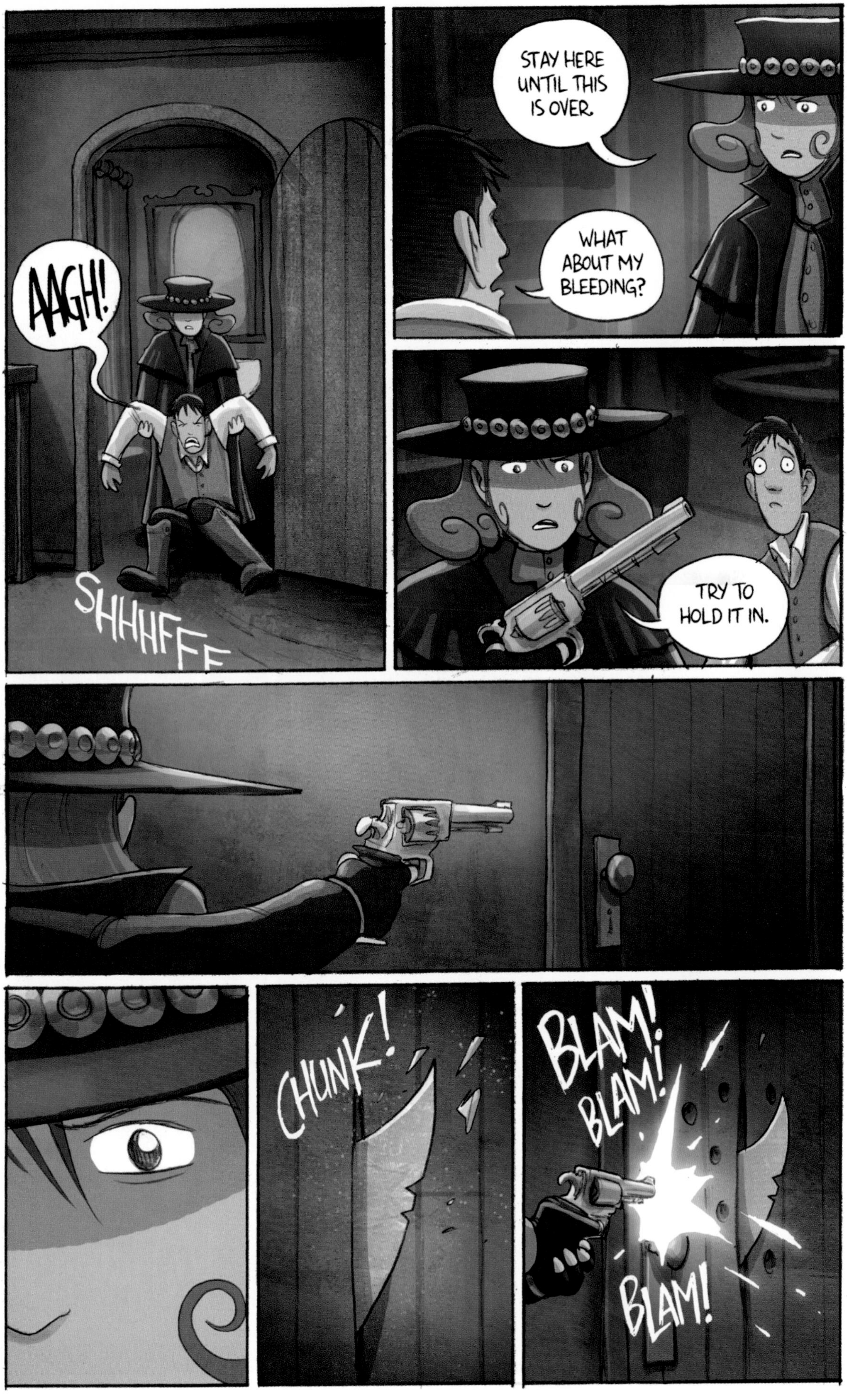
AAGH!
SHHHFFF
STAY HERE UNTIL THIS IS OVER.
WHAT ABOUT MY BLEEDING?
TRY TO HOLD IT IN.
CHUNK!
BLAM!
BLAM!
BLAM!

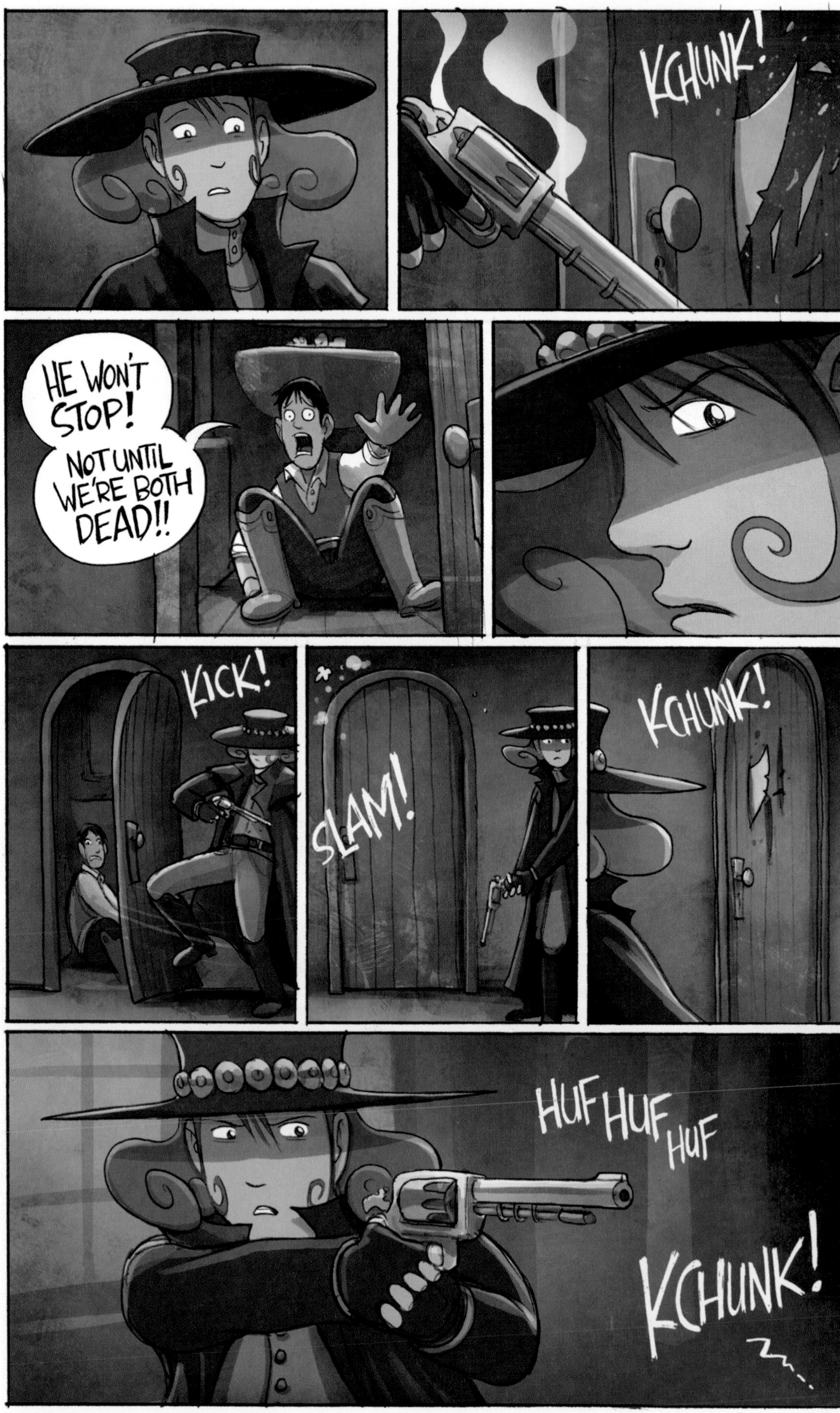
KCHUNK!
HE WON'T STOP!
NOT UNTIL WE'RE BOTH DEAD!!
KICK!
SLAM!
KCHUNK!
HUF HUF HUF
KCHUNK!

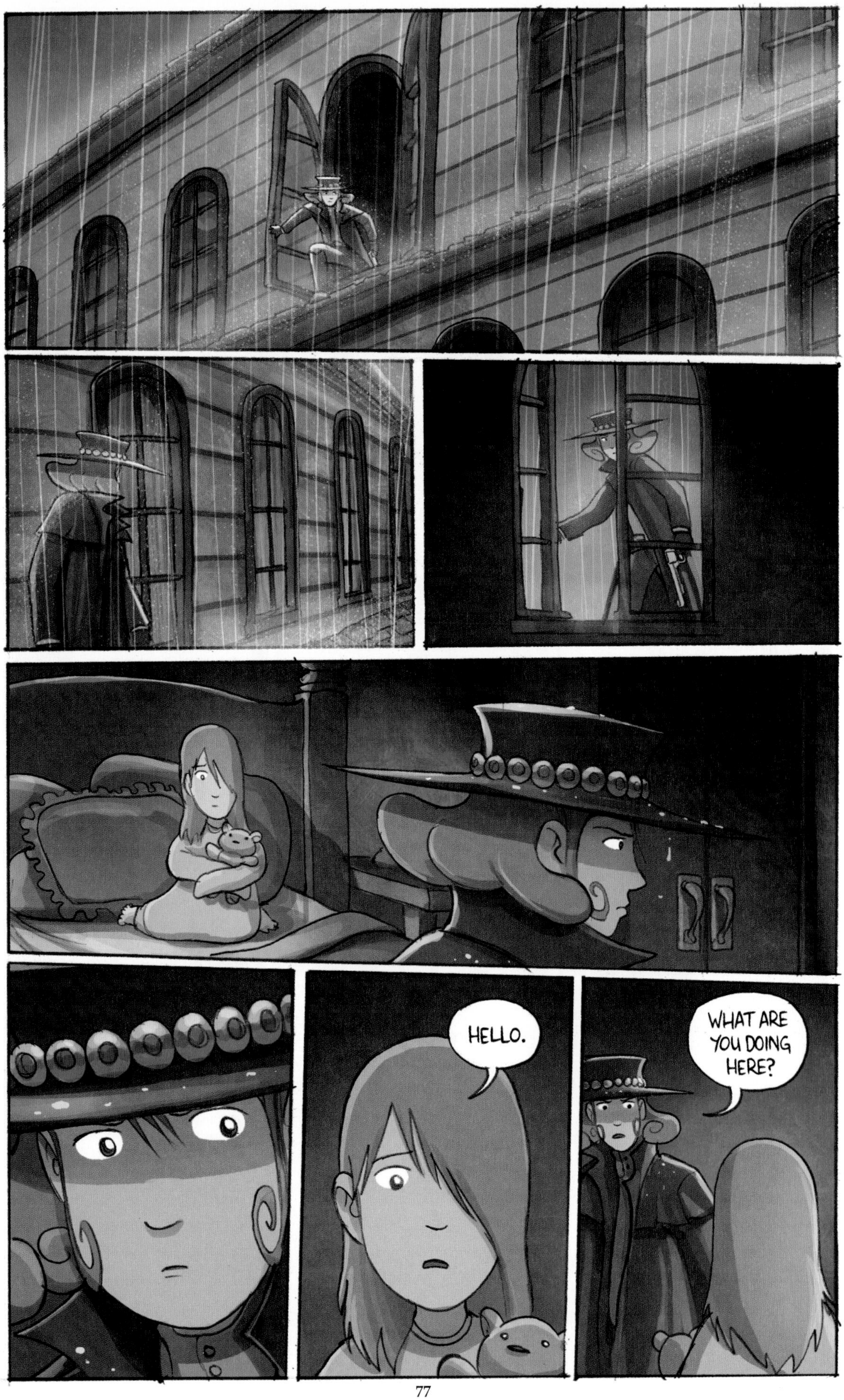
HELLO.
WHAT ARE YOU DOING HERE?

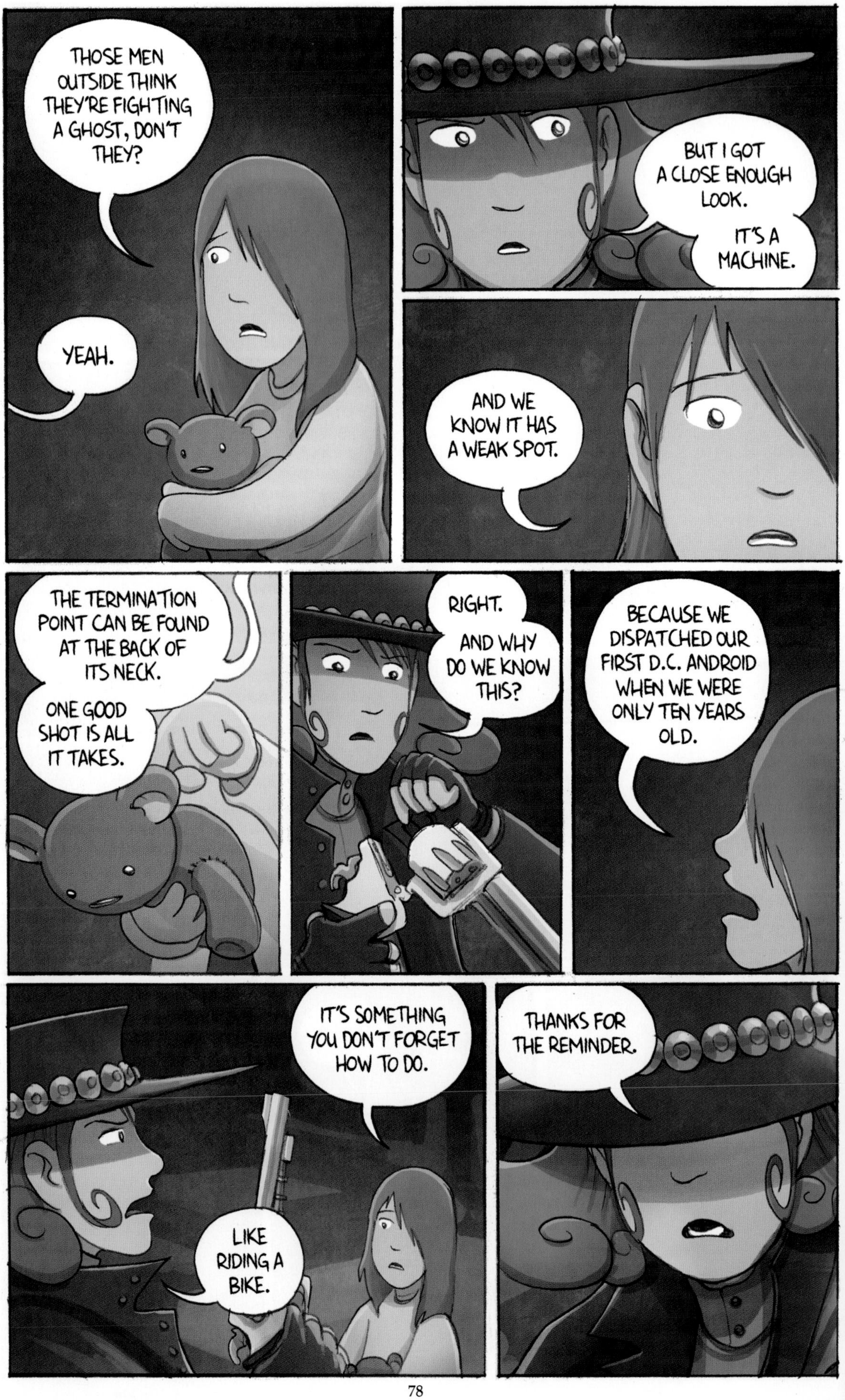
THOSE MEN OUTSIDE THINK THEY'RE FIGHTING A GHOST, DON'T THEY?
YEAH.
BUT I GOT A CLOSE ENOUGH LOOK.
IT'S A MACHINE.
AND WE KNOW IT HAS A WEAK SPOT.
THE TERMINATION POINT CAN BE FOUND AT THE BACK OF ITS NECK.
ONE GOOD SHOT IS ALL IT TAKES.
RIGHT.
AND WHY DO WE KNOW THIS?
BECAUSE WE DISPATCHED OUR FIRST D.C. ANDROID WHEN WE WERE ONLY TEN YEARS OLD.
IT'S SOMETHING YOU DON'T FORGET HOW TO DO.
LIKE RIDING A BIKE.
THANKS FOR THE REMINDER.

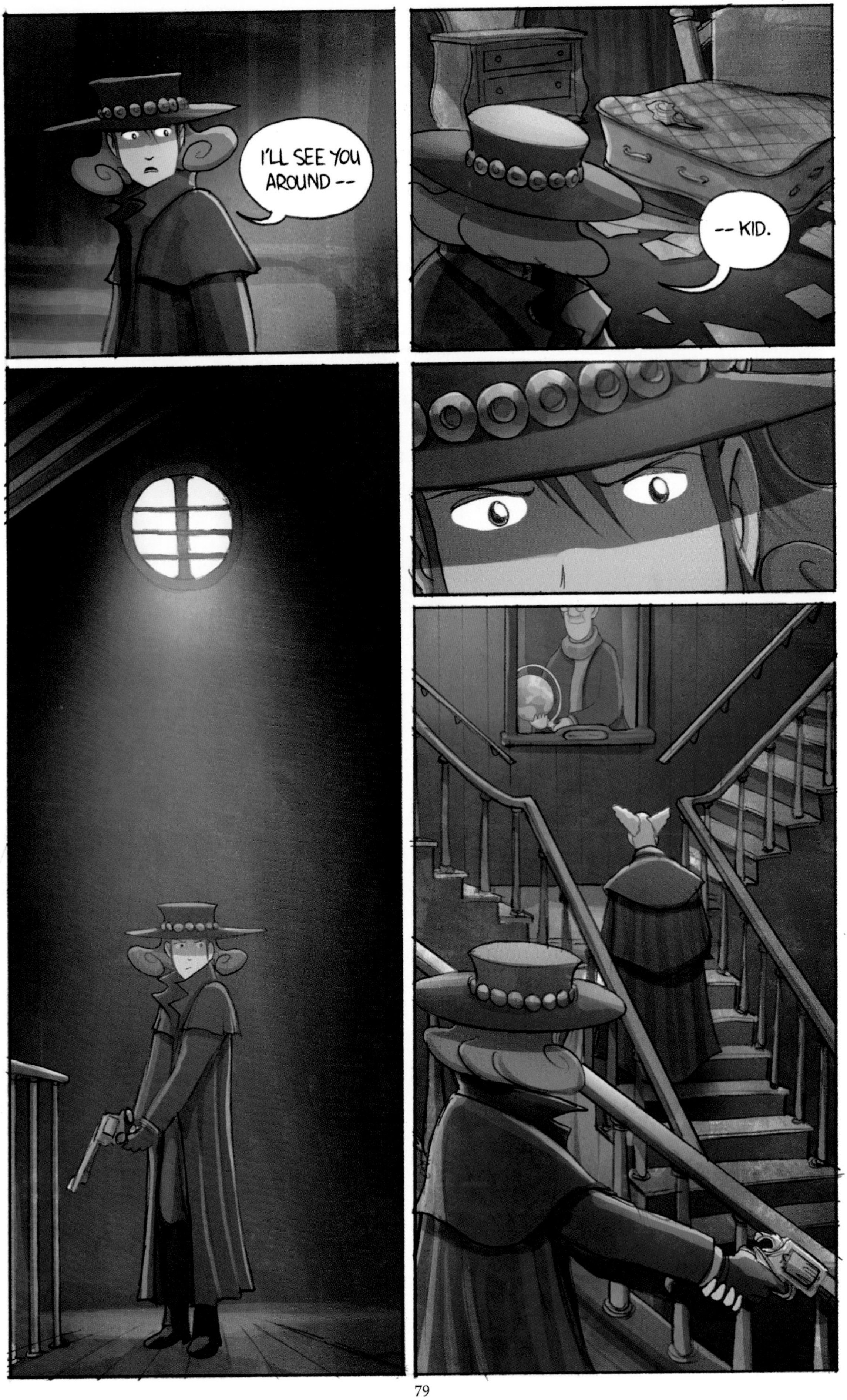
I'LL SEE YOU AROUND --
-- KID.

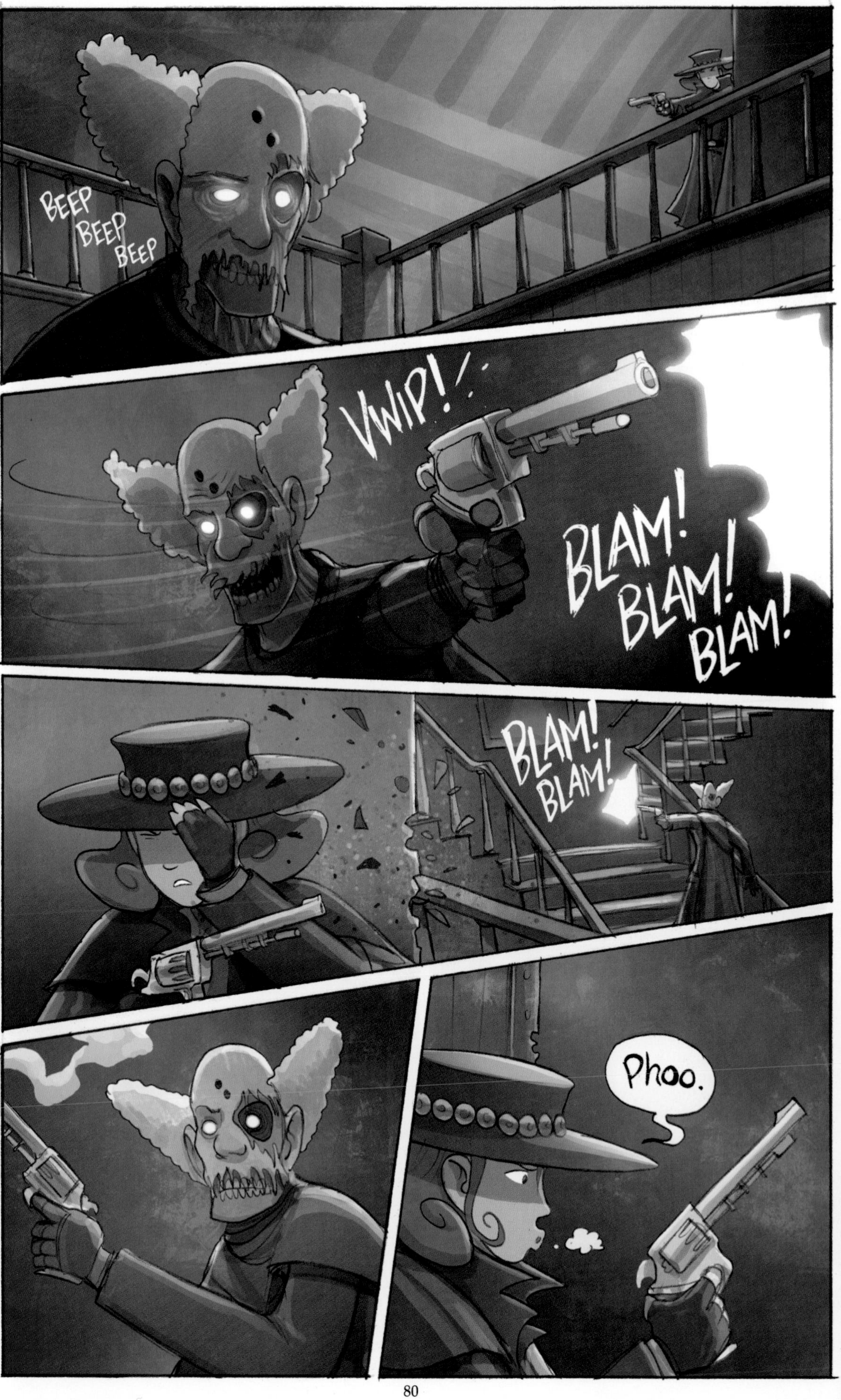
BEEP
BEEP
BEEP
VWIP!
BLAM!
BLAM!
BLAM!
BLAM!
BLAM!
Phoo.

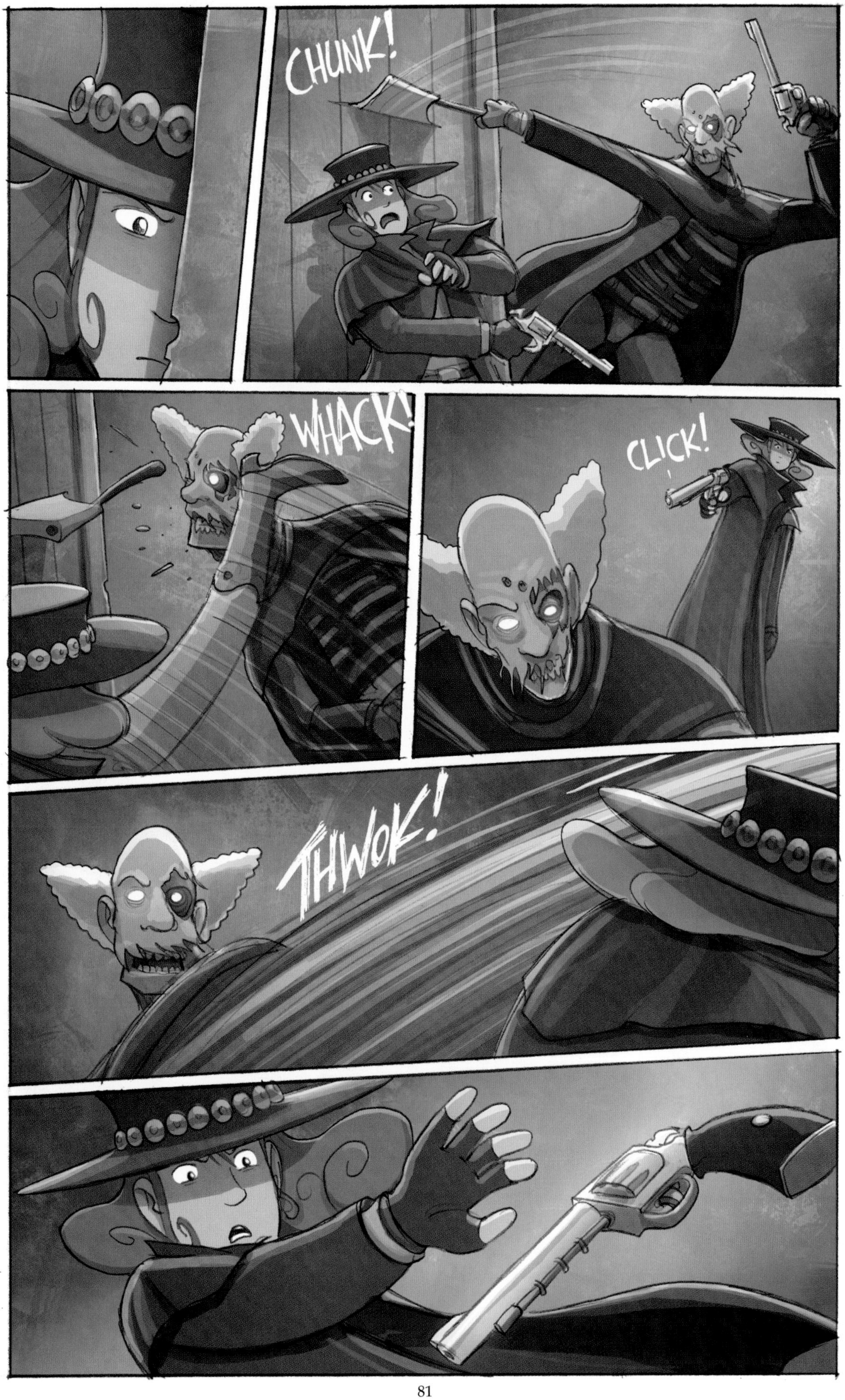
CHUNK!
WHACK!
CLICK!
THWOK!

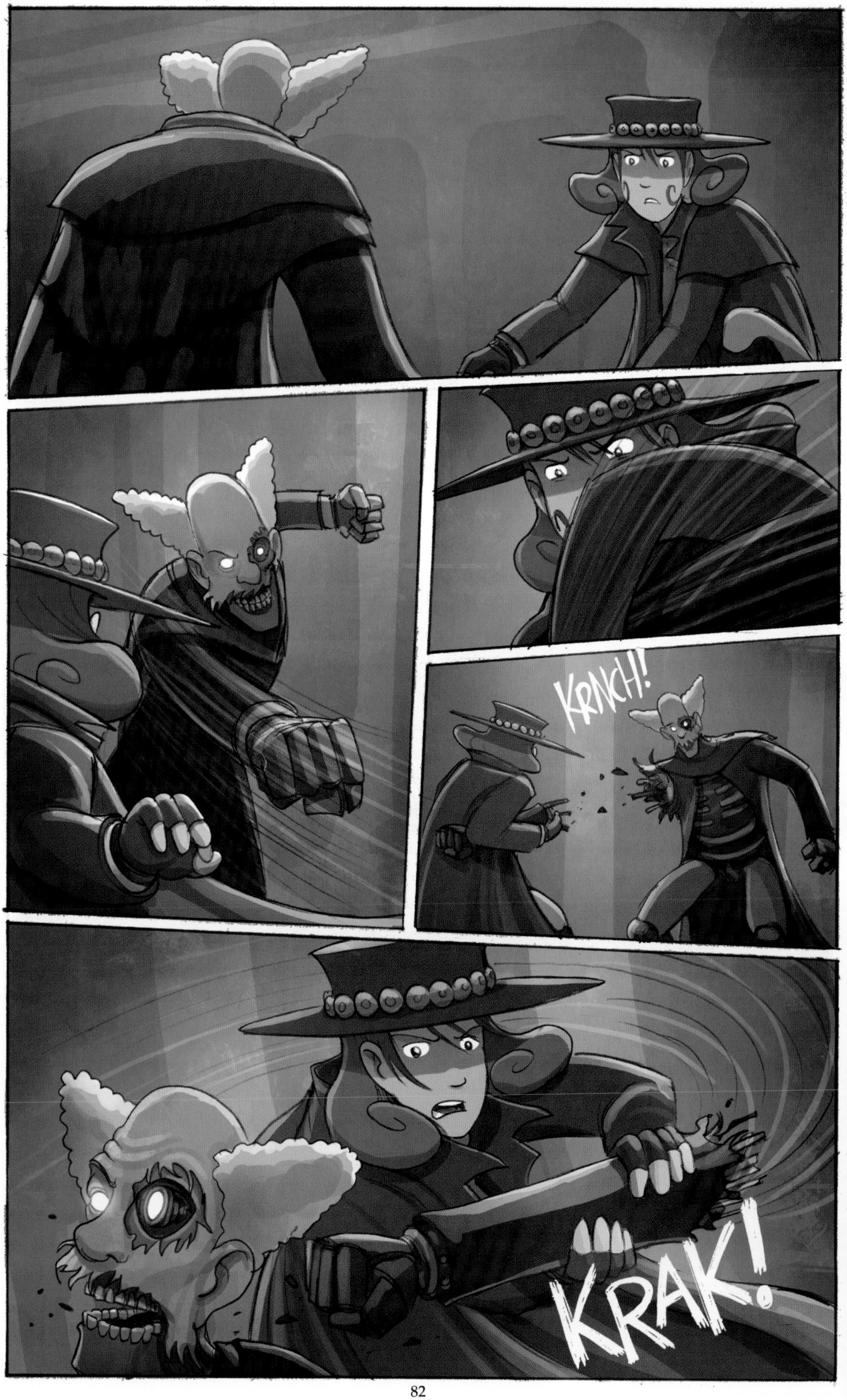
KRNCH!
KRAK!

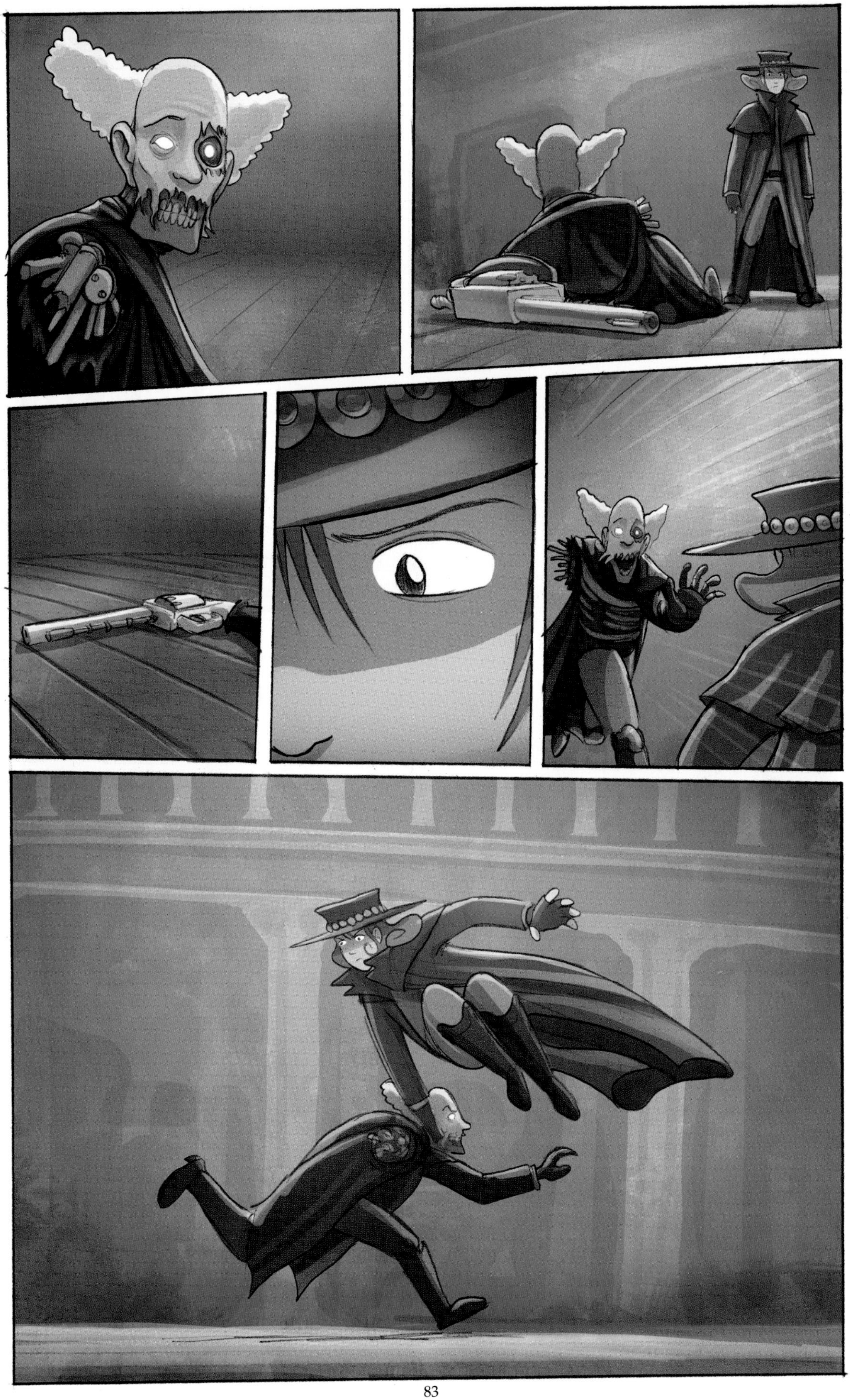

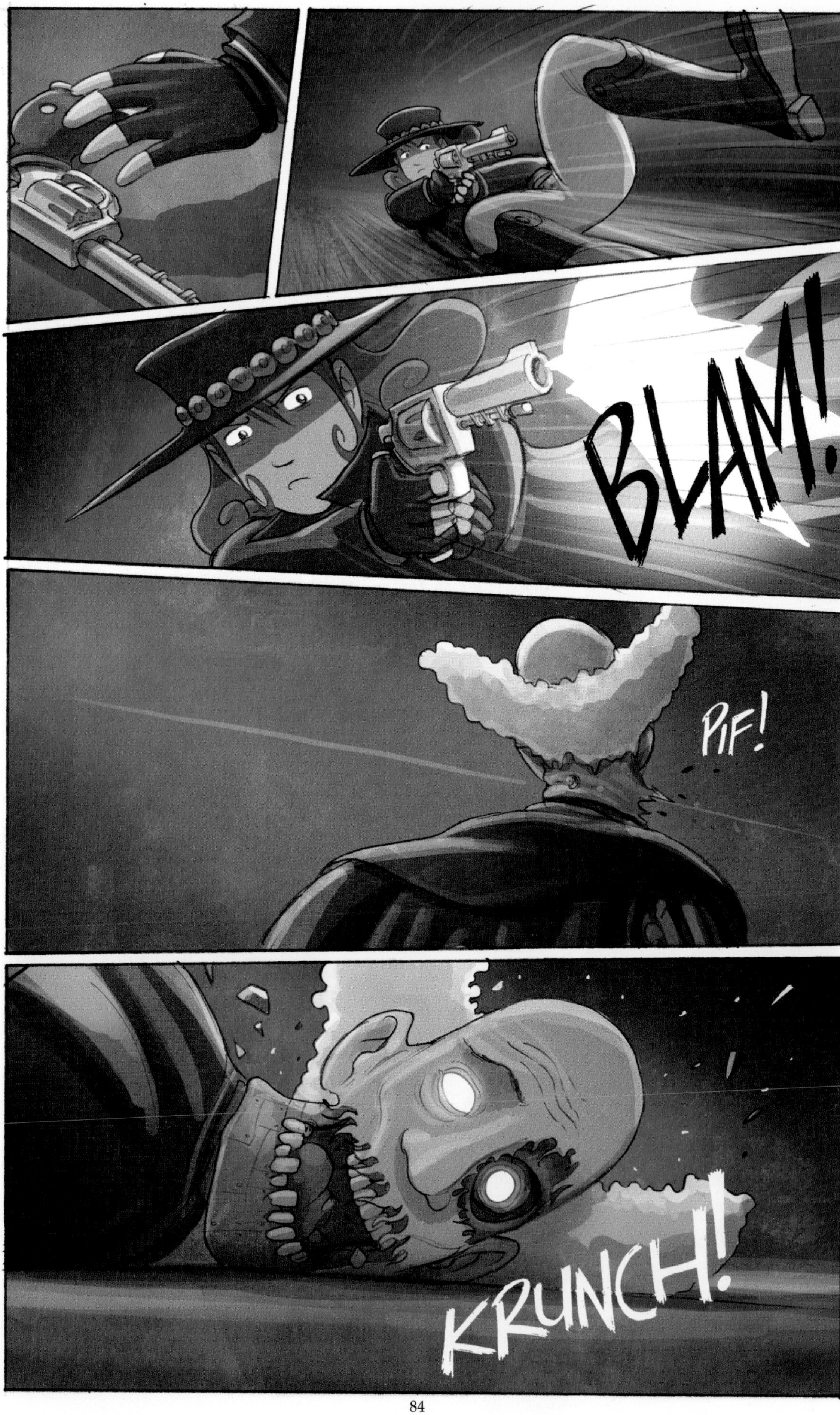
BLAM!
PIF!
KRUNCH!

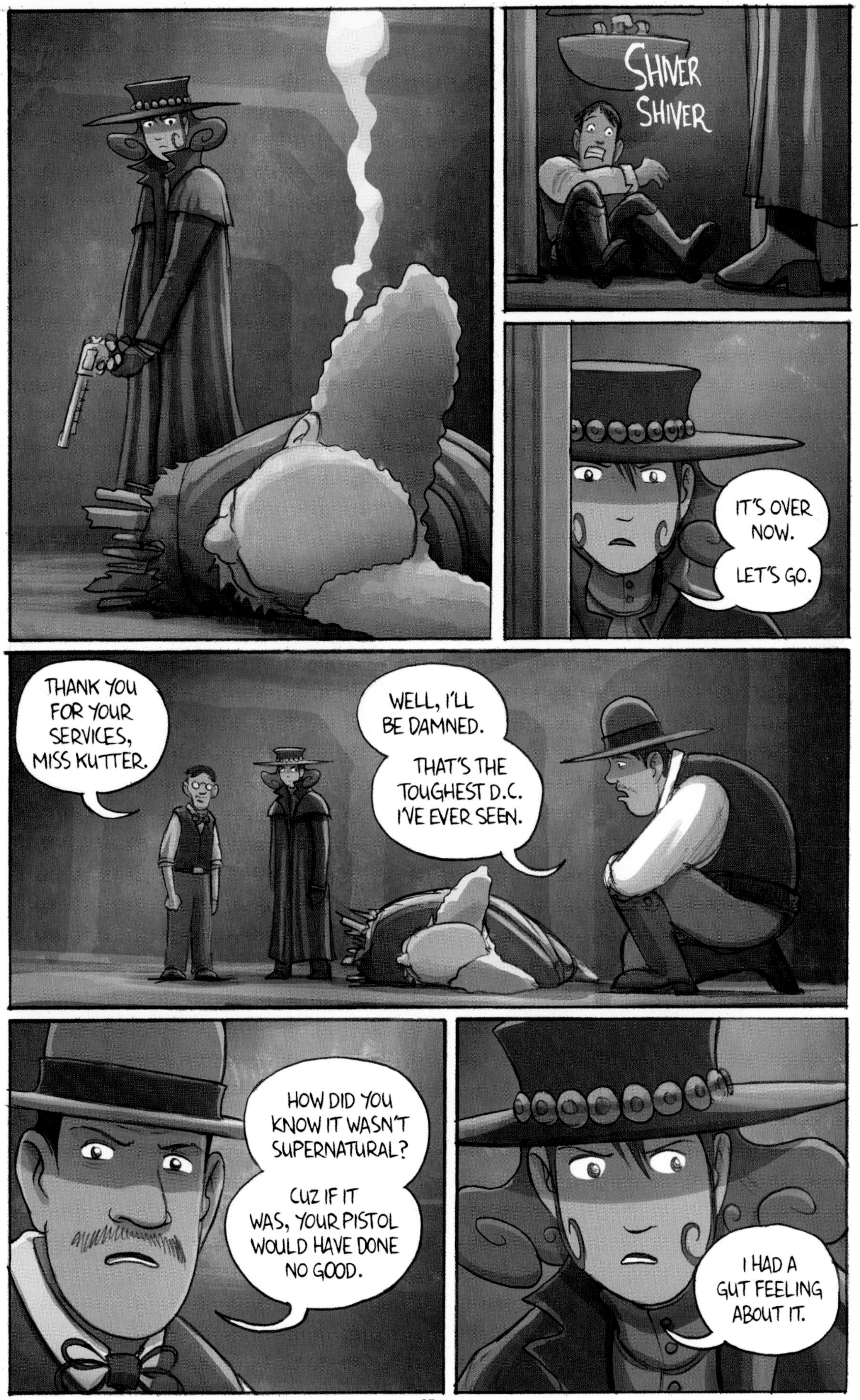
SHIVER
SHIVER
IT'S OVER NOW.
LET'S GO.
THANK YOU FOR YOUR SERVICES, MISS KUTTER.
WELL, I'LL BE DAMNED.
THAT'S THE TOUGHEST D.C. I'VE EVER SEEN.
HOW DID YOU KNOW IT WASN'T SUPERNATURAL?
CUZ IF IT WAS, YOUR PISTOL WOULD HAVE DONE NO GOOD.
I HAD A GUT FEELING ABOUT IT.

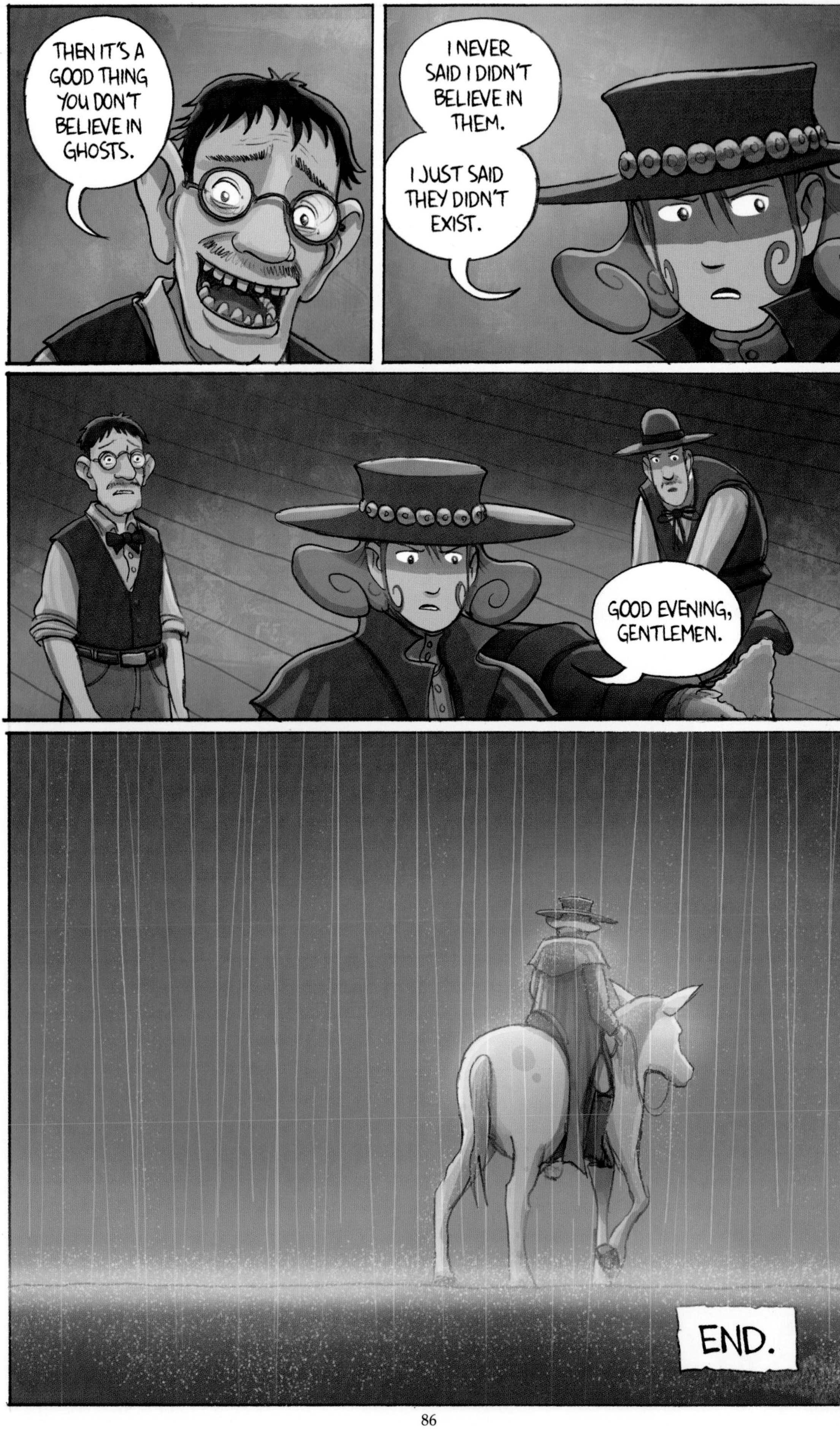
THEN IT'S A GOOD THING YOU DON'T BELIEVE IN GHOSTS.
I NEVER SAID I DIDN'T BELIEVE IN THEM.
I JUST SAID THEY DIDN'T EXIST.
GOOD EVENING, GENTLEMEN.
END.

MAGNUS the MISFIT

a.k.a.

Kanipinikassikew

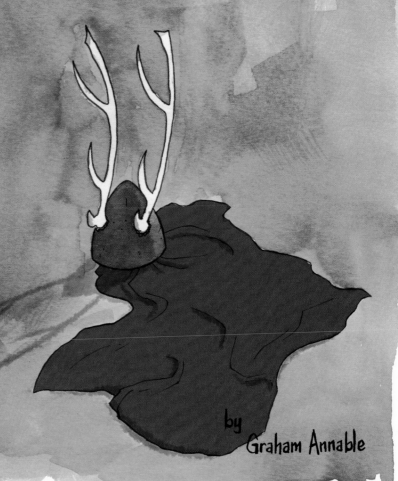

by
Graham Annable

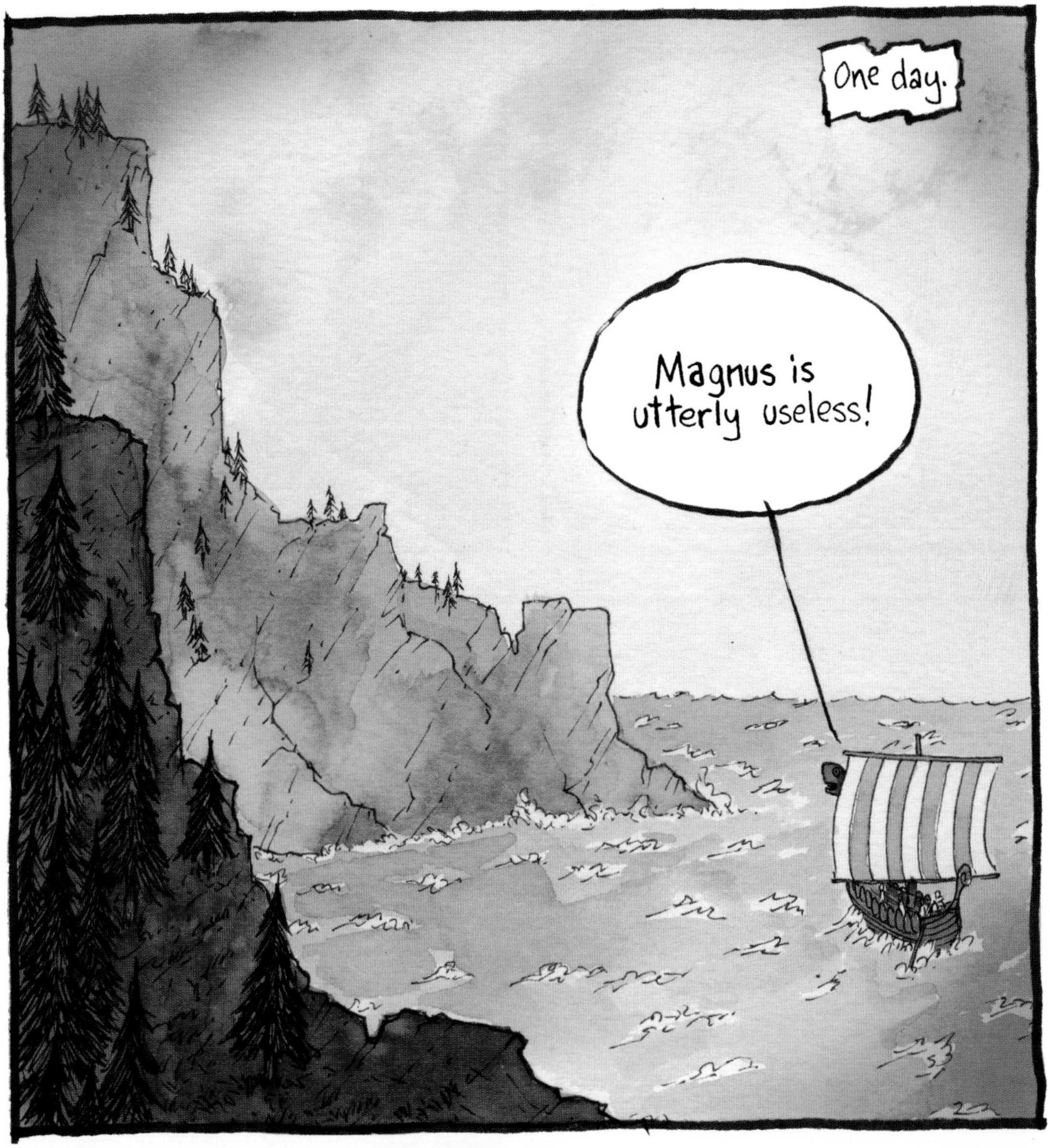
One day.
Magnus is utterly useless!

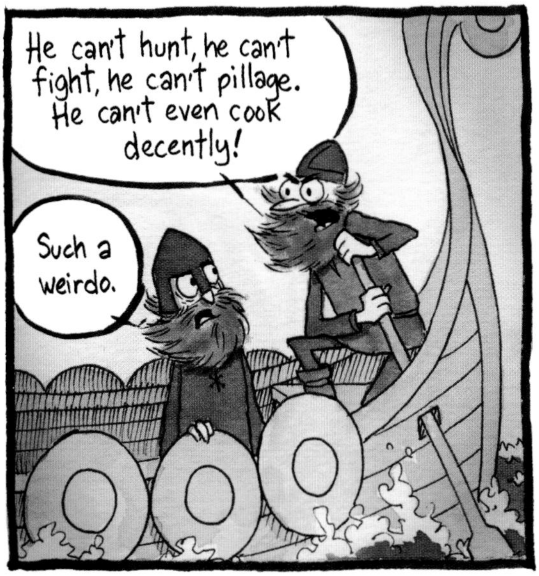
He can't hunt, he can't fight, he can't pillage. He can't even cook decently!
Such a weirdo.

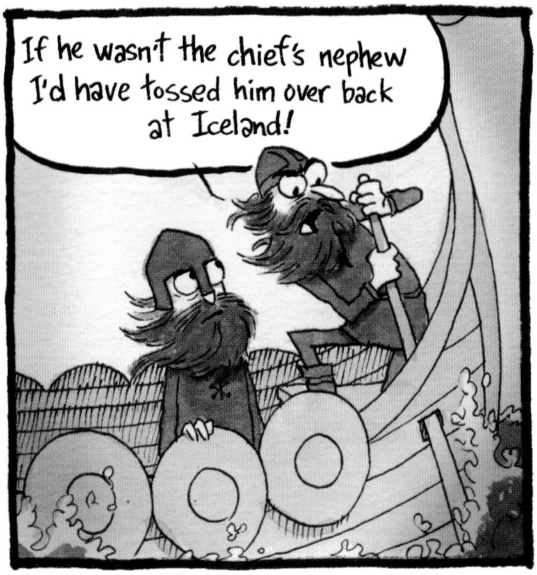
If he wasn't the chief's nephew I'd have tossed him over back at Iceland!

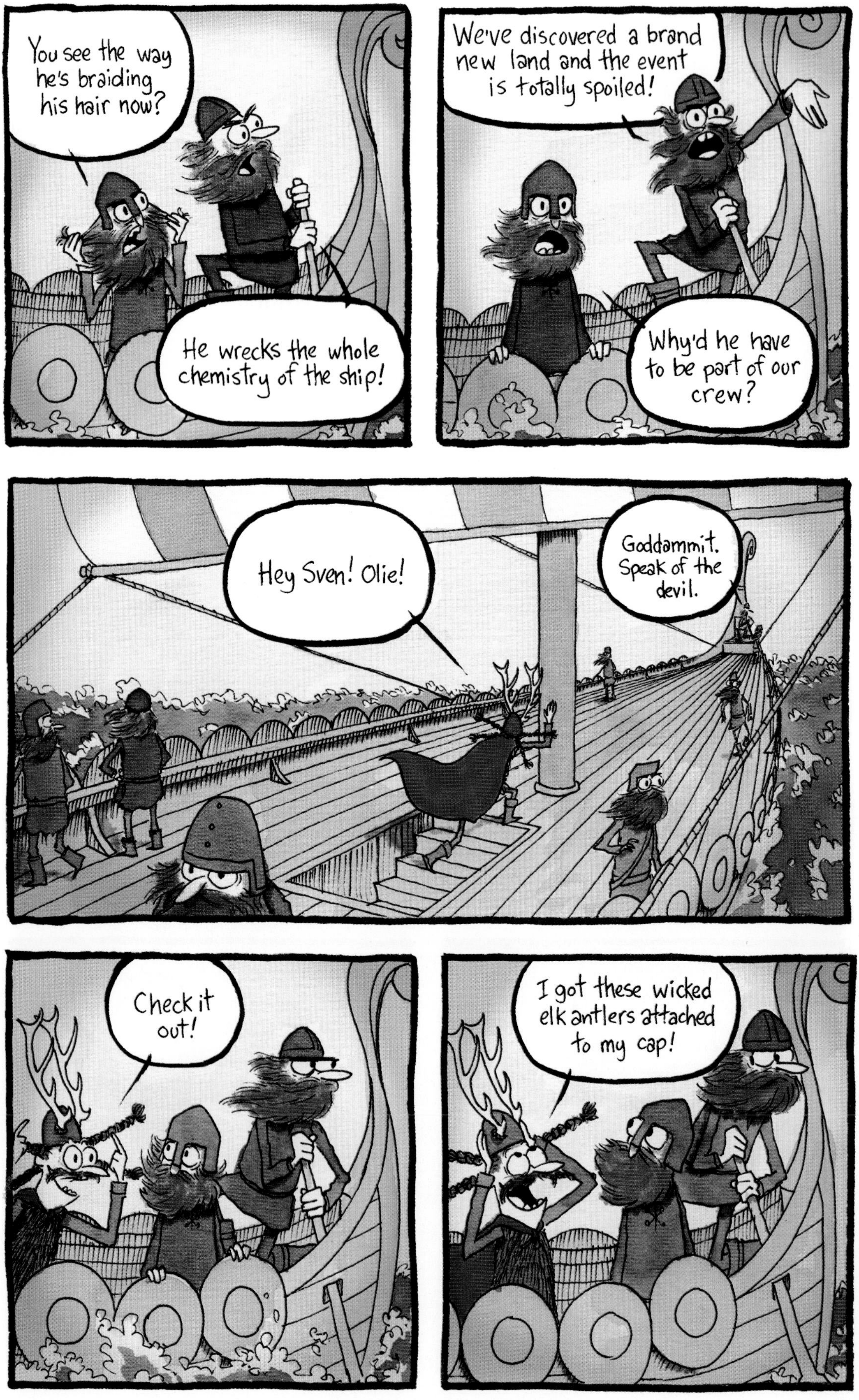
You see the way he's braiding his hair now?
He wrecks the whole chemistry of the ship!
We've discovered a brand new land and the event is totally spoiled!
Why'd he have to be part of our crew?
Hey Sven! Olie!
Goddammit. Speak of the devil.
Check it out!
I got these wicked elk antlers attached to my cap!

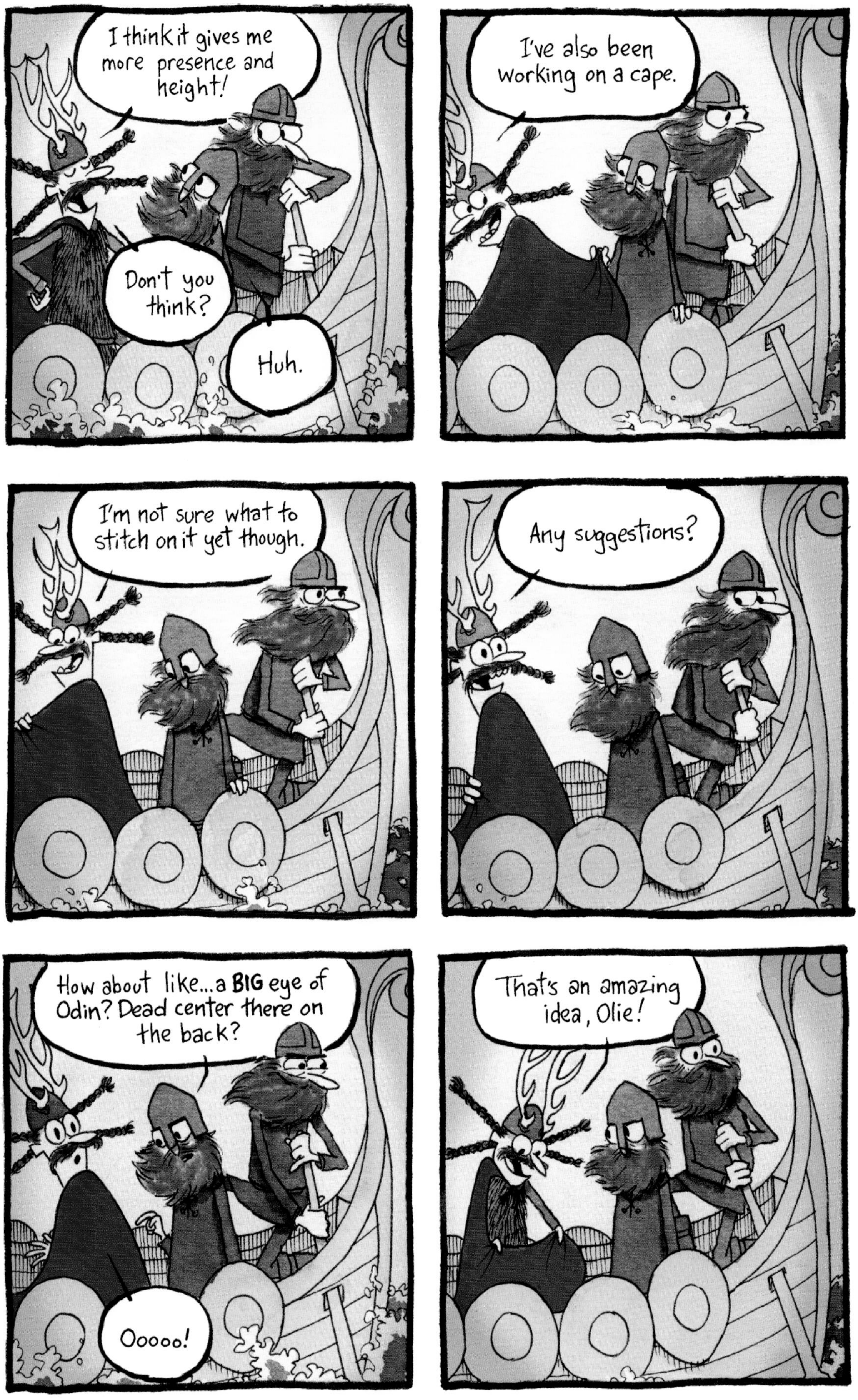
I think it gives me more presence and height!
Don't you think?
Huh.
I've also been working on a cape.
I'm not sure what to stitch on it yet though.
Any suggestions?
How about like... a **BIG** eye of Odin? Dead center there on the back?
Ooooo!
That's an amazing idea, Olie!

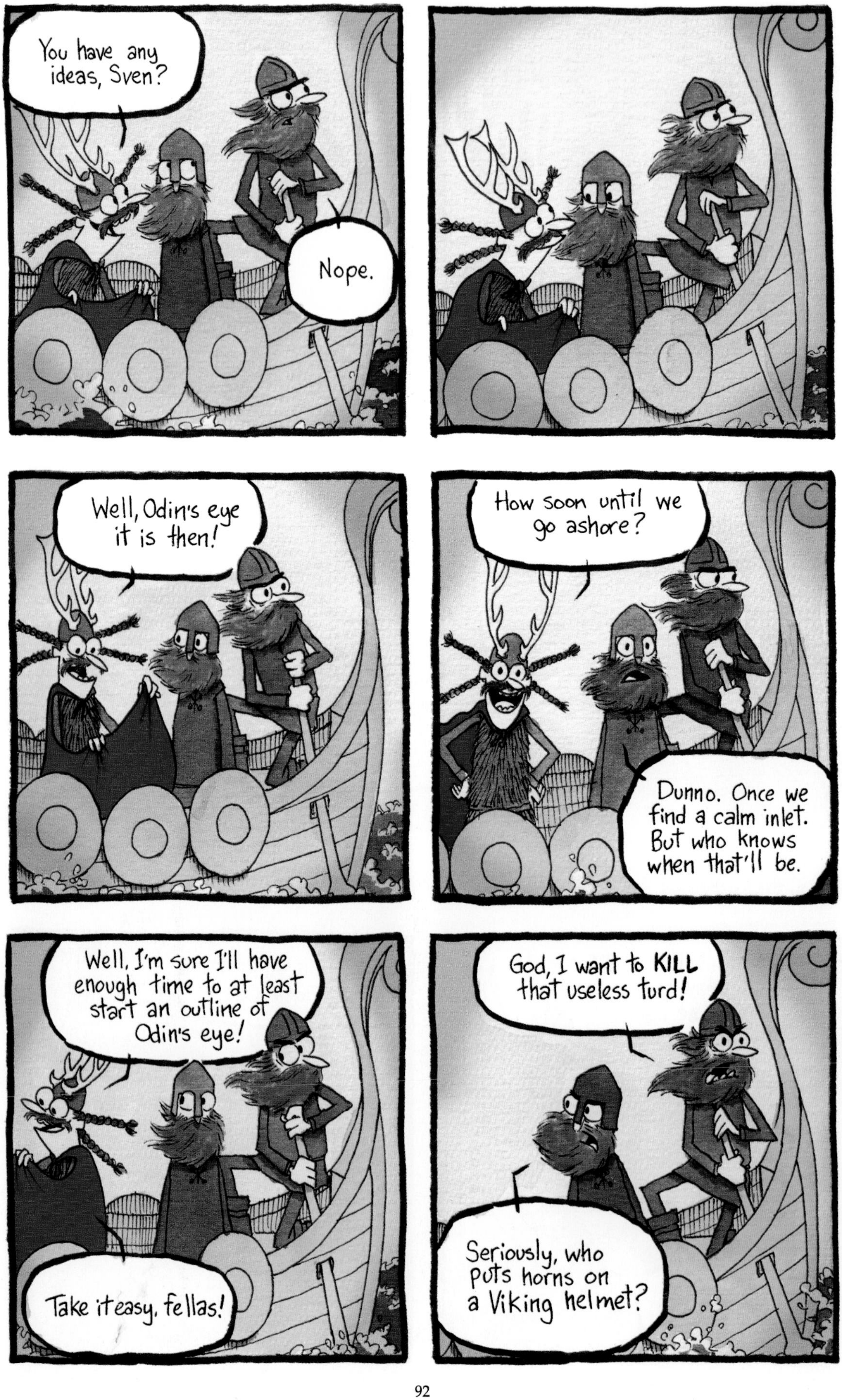

You have any ideas, Sven?
Nope.
Well, Odin's eye it is then!
How soon until we go ashore?
Dunno. Once we find a calm inlet. But who knows when that'll be.
Well, I'm sure I'll have enough time to at least start an outline of Odin's eye!
Take it easy, fellas!
God, I want to **KILL** that useless turd!
Seriously, who puts horns on a Viking helmet?

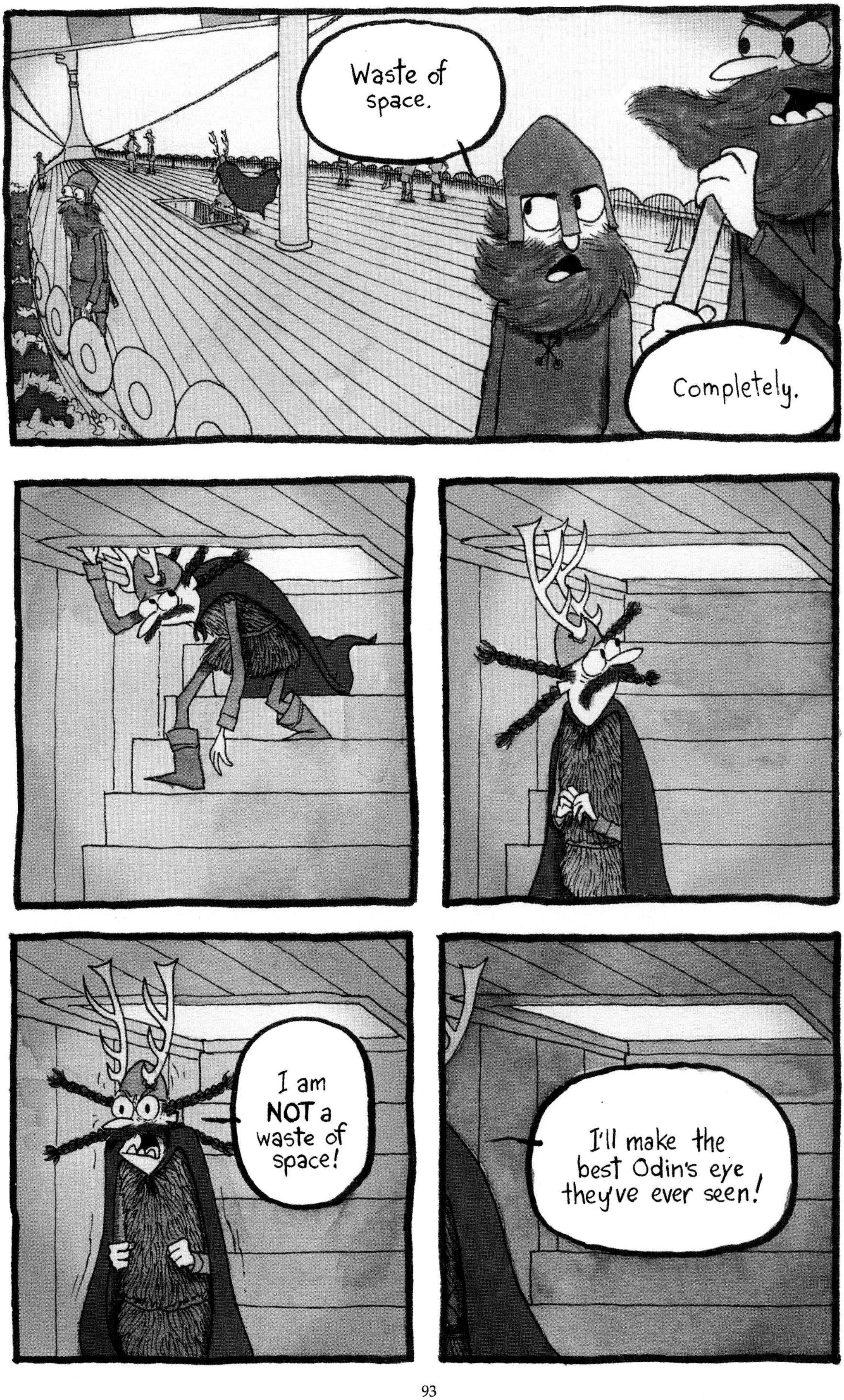
Waste of space.
Completely.
I am NOT a waste of space!
I'll make the best Odin's eye they've ever seen!

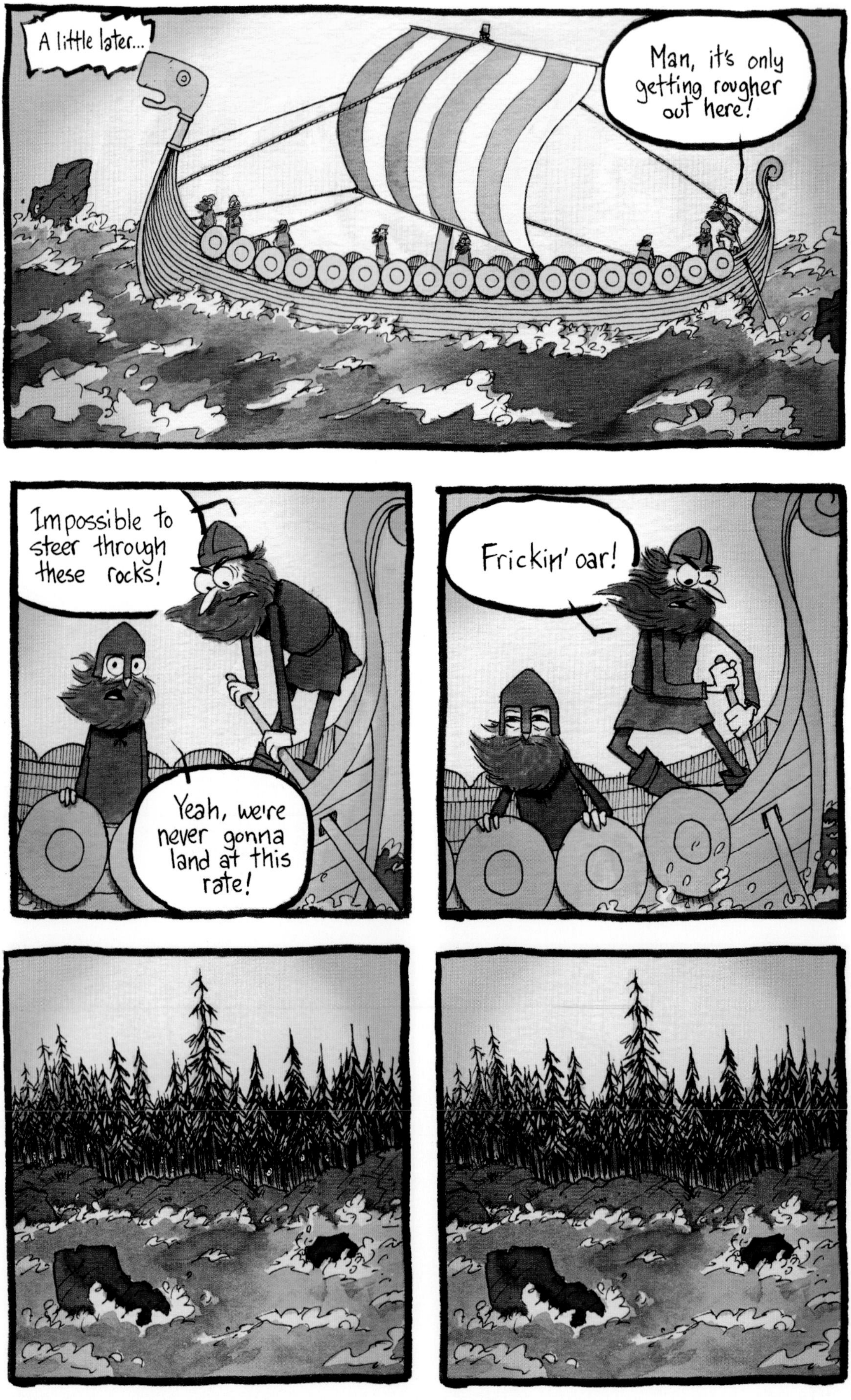
A little later...
Man, it's only getting rougher out here!
Impossible to steer through these rocks!
Yeah, we're never gonna land at this rate!
Frickin' oar!

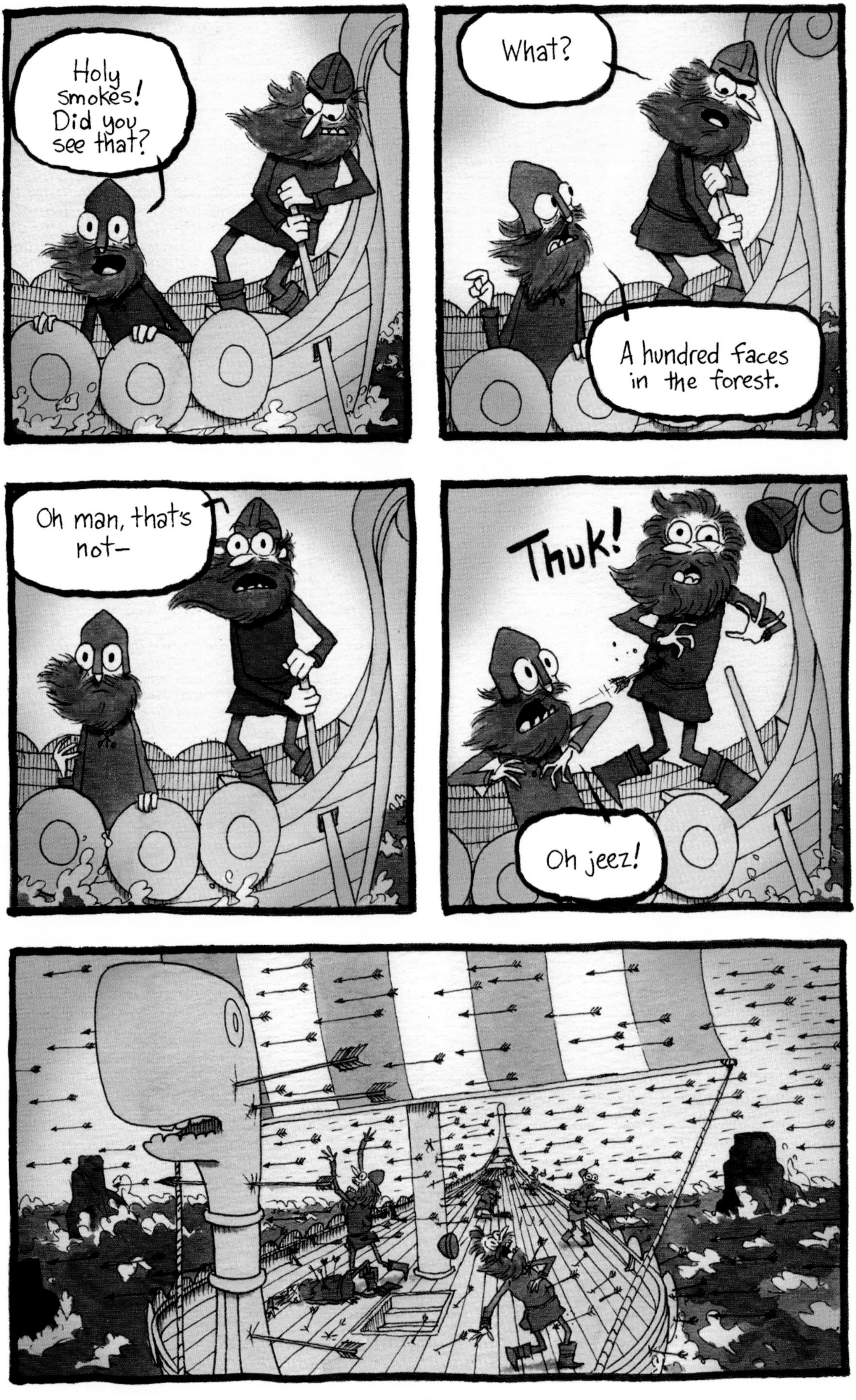
Holy smokes! Did you see that?
What?
A hundred faces in the forest.
Oh man, that's not–
Thuk!
Oh jeez!

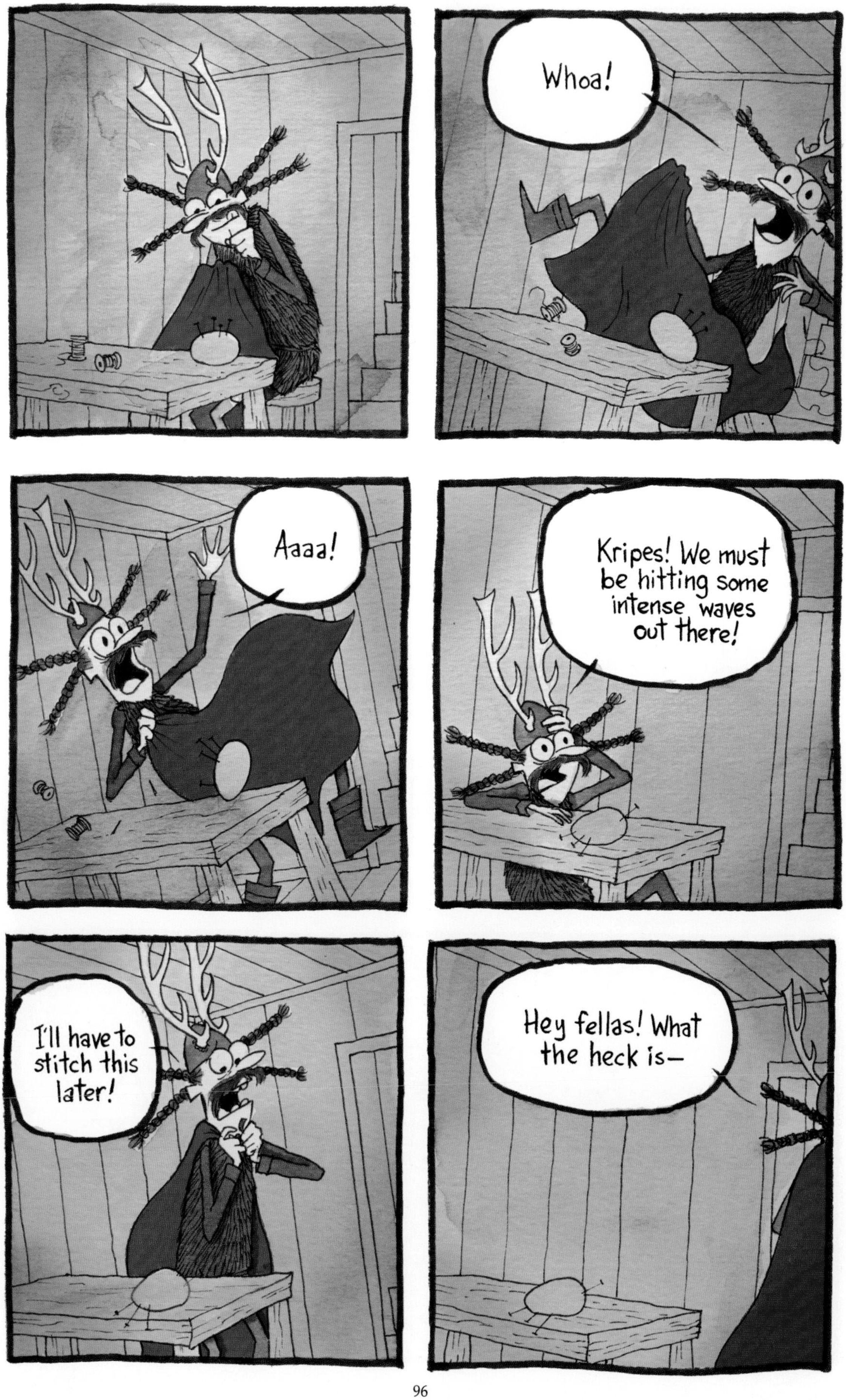
Whoa!
Aaaa!
Kripes! We must be hitting some intense waves out there!
I'll have to stitch this later!
Hey fellas! What the heck is—

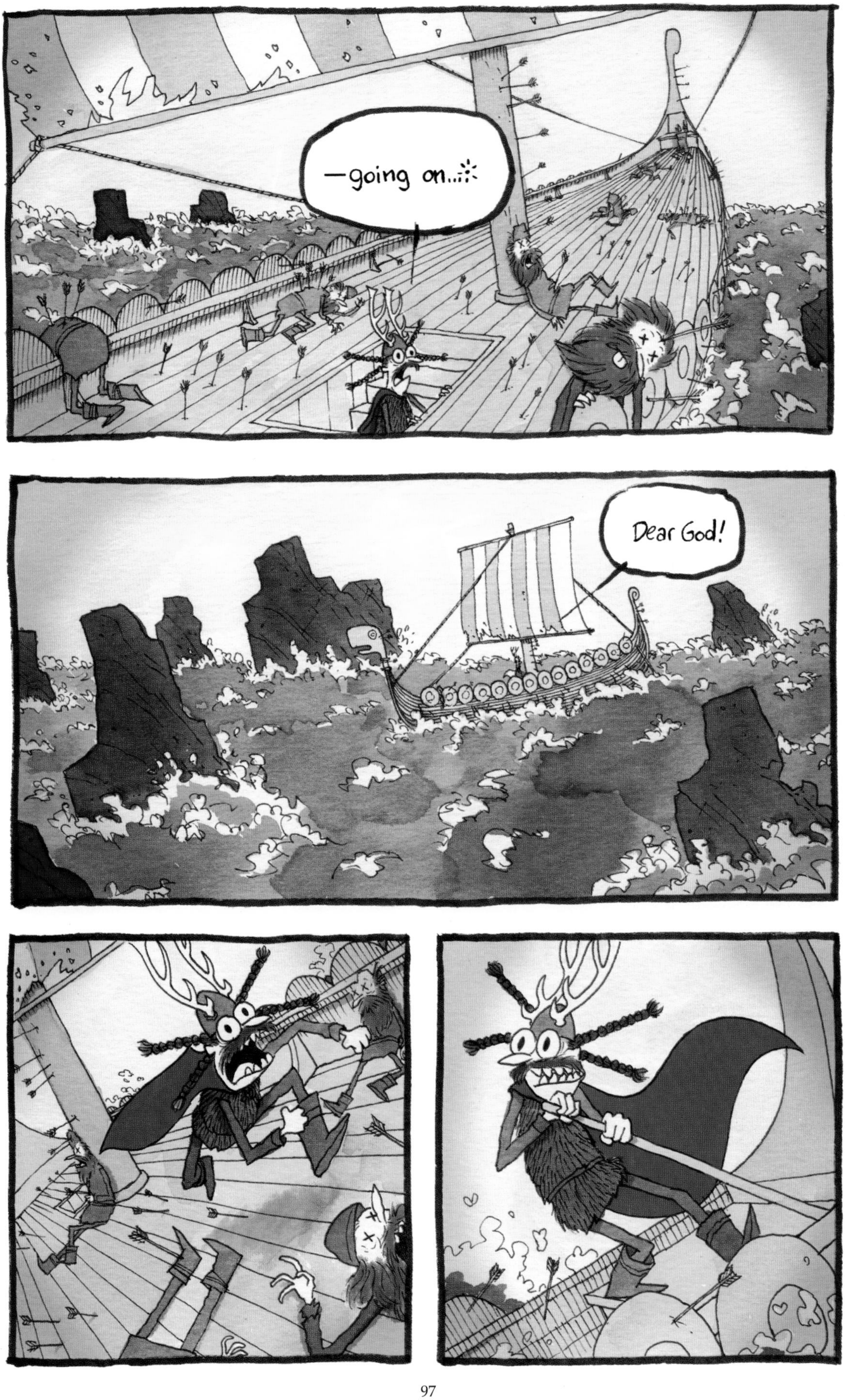
—going on...
Dear God!

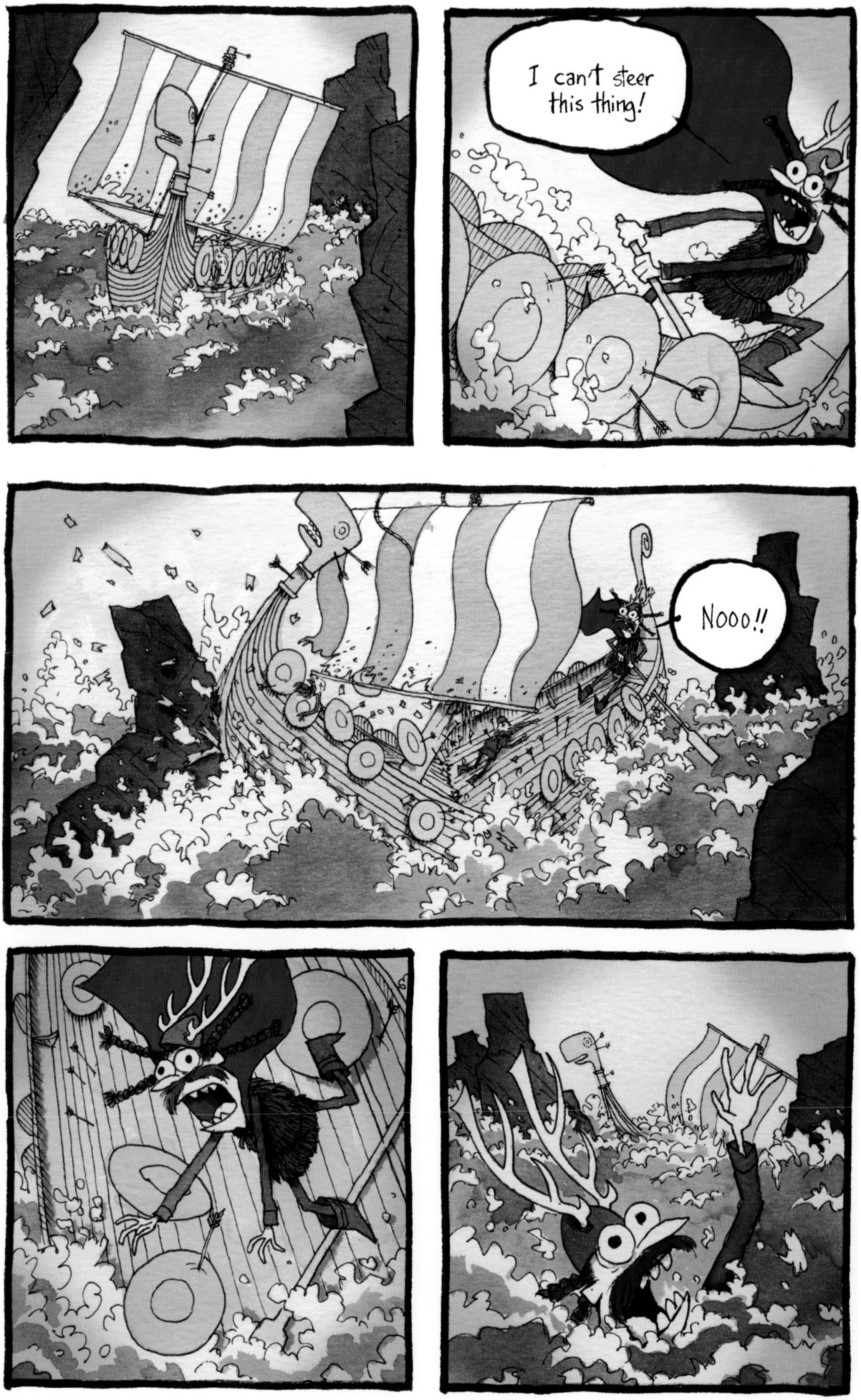
I can't steer this thing!
Nooo!!

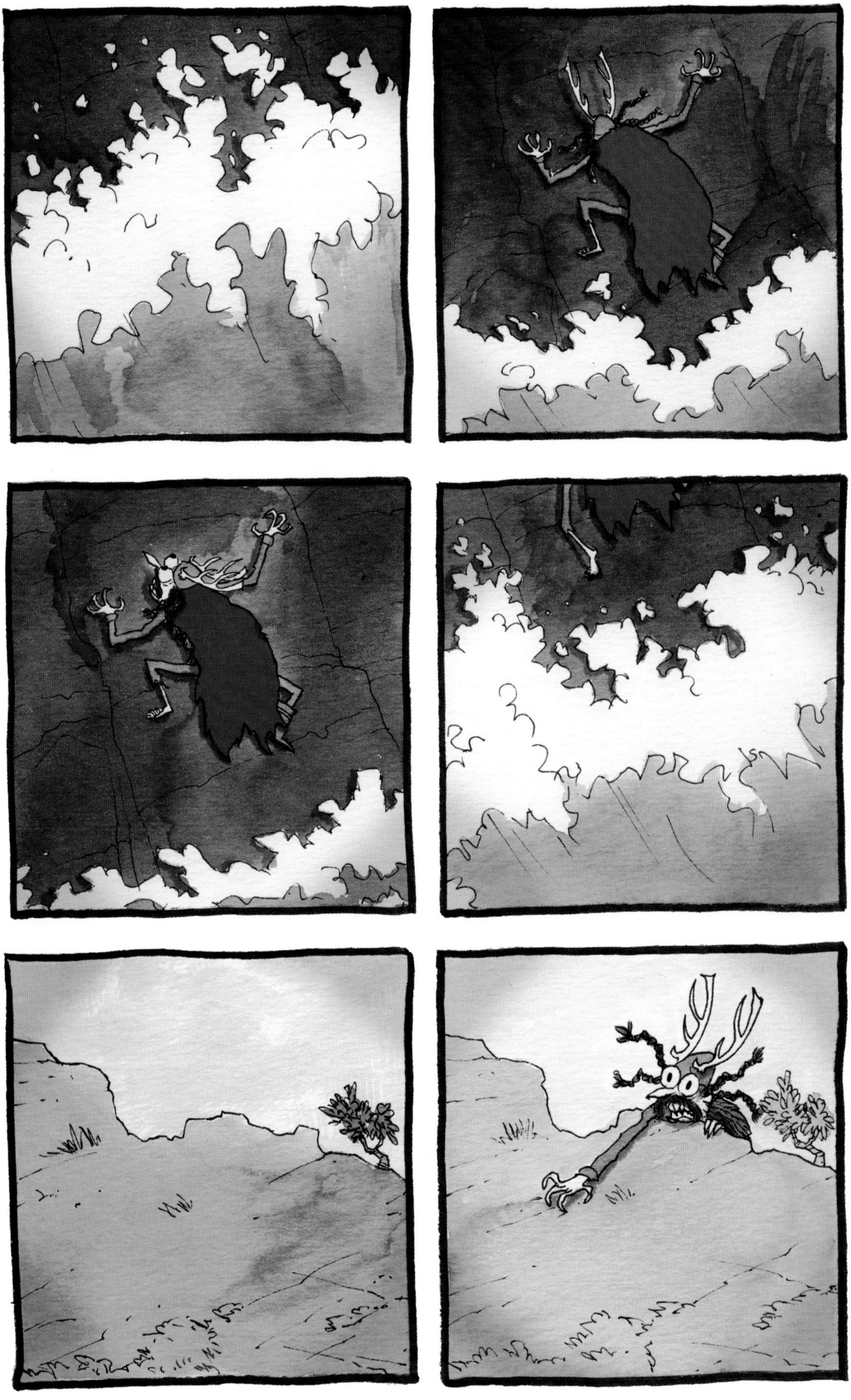

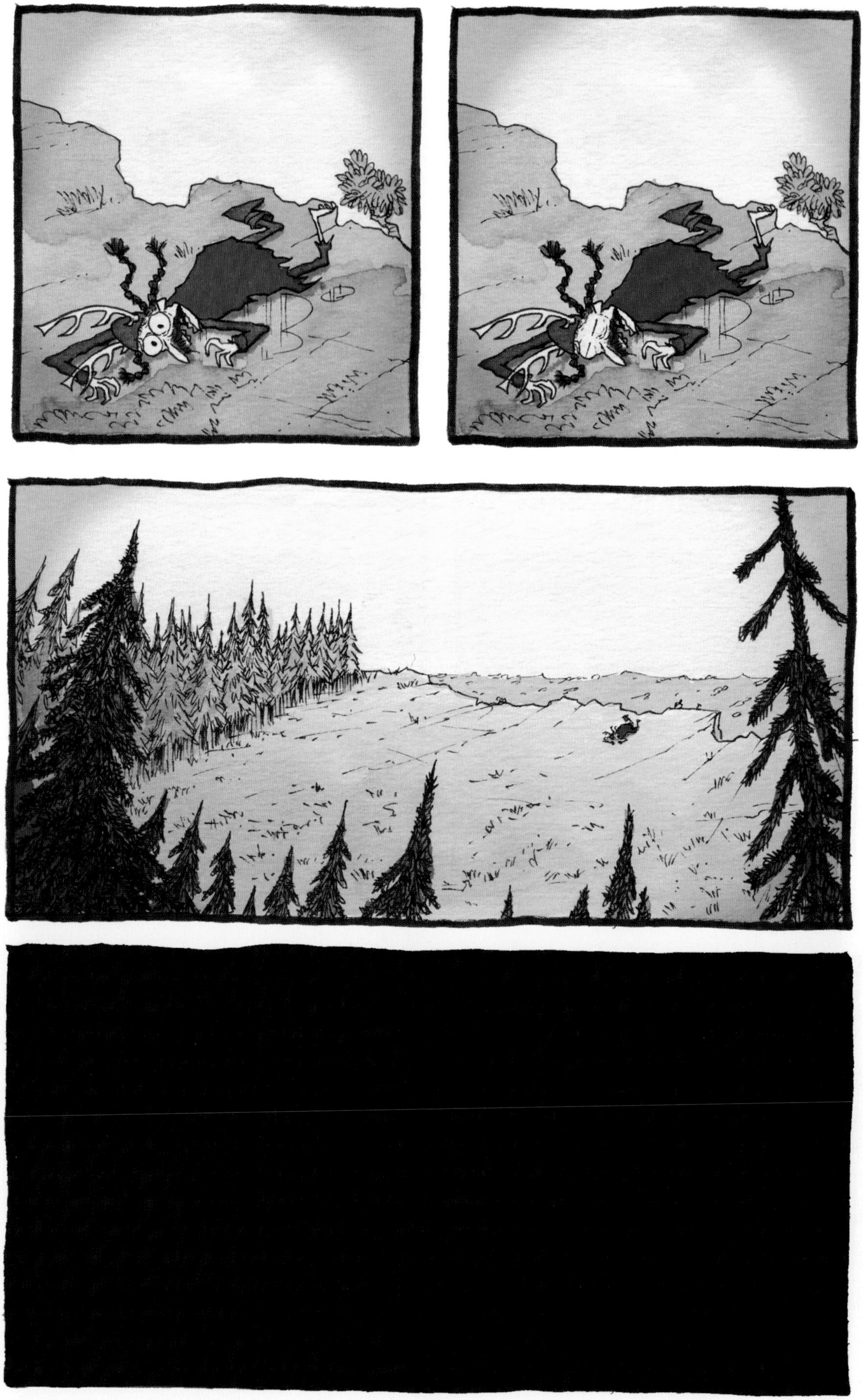

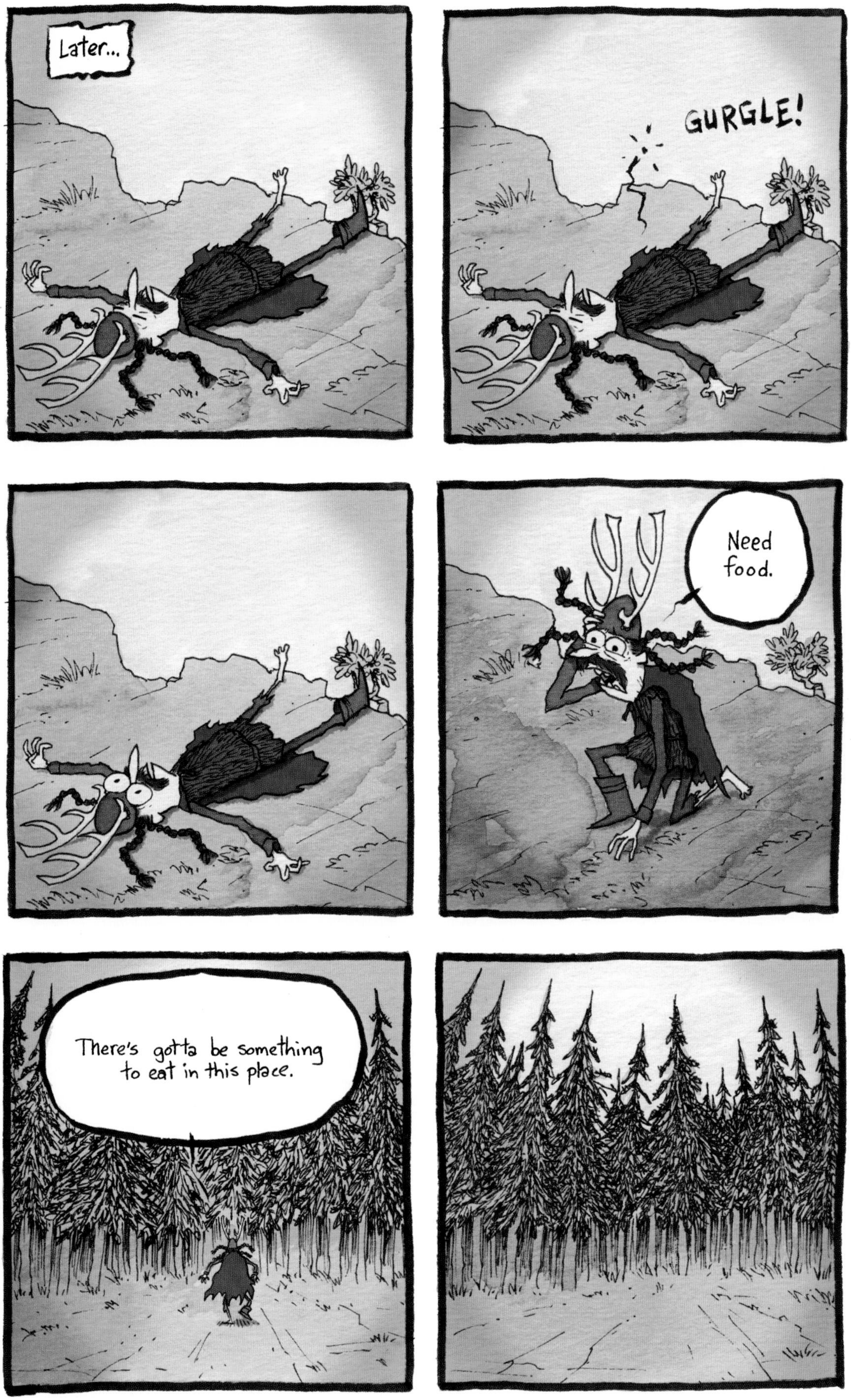
Later...
GURGLE!
Need food.
There's gotta be something to eat in this place.

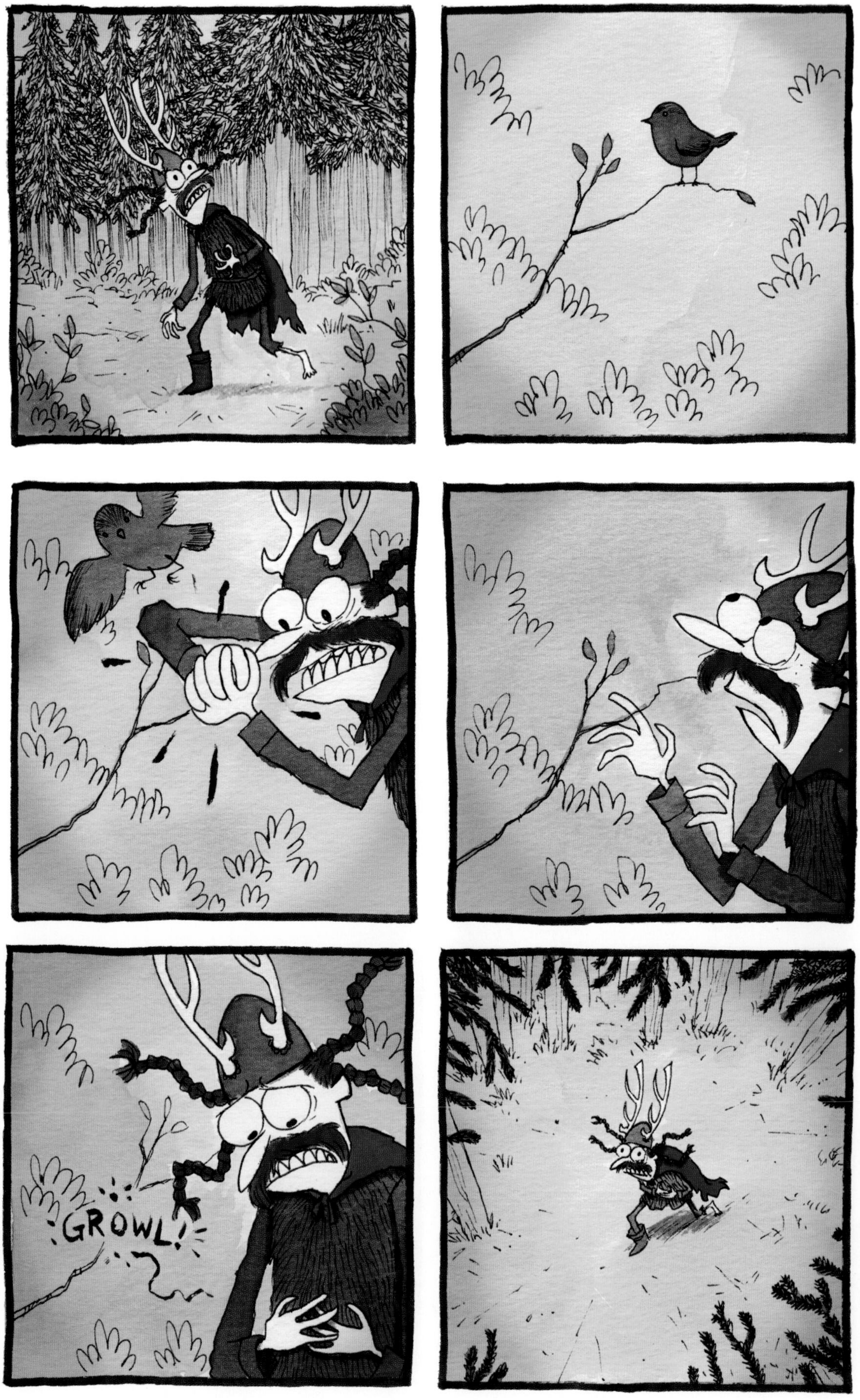
GROWL!

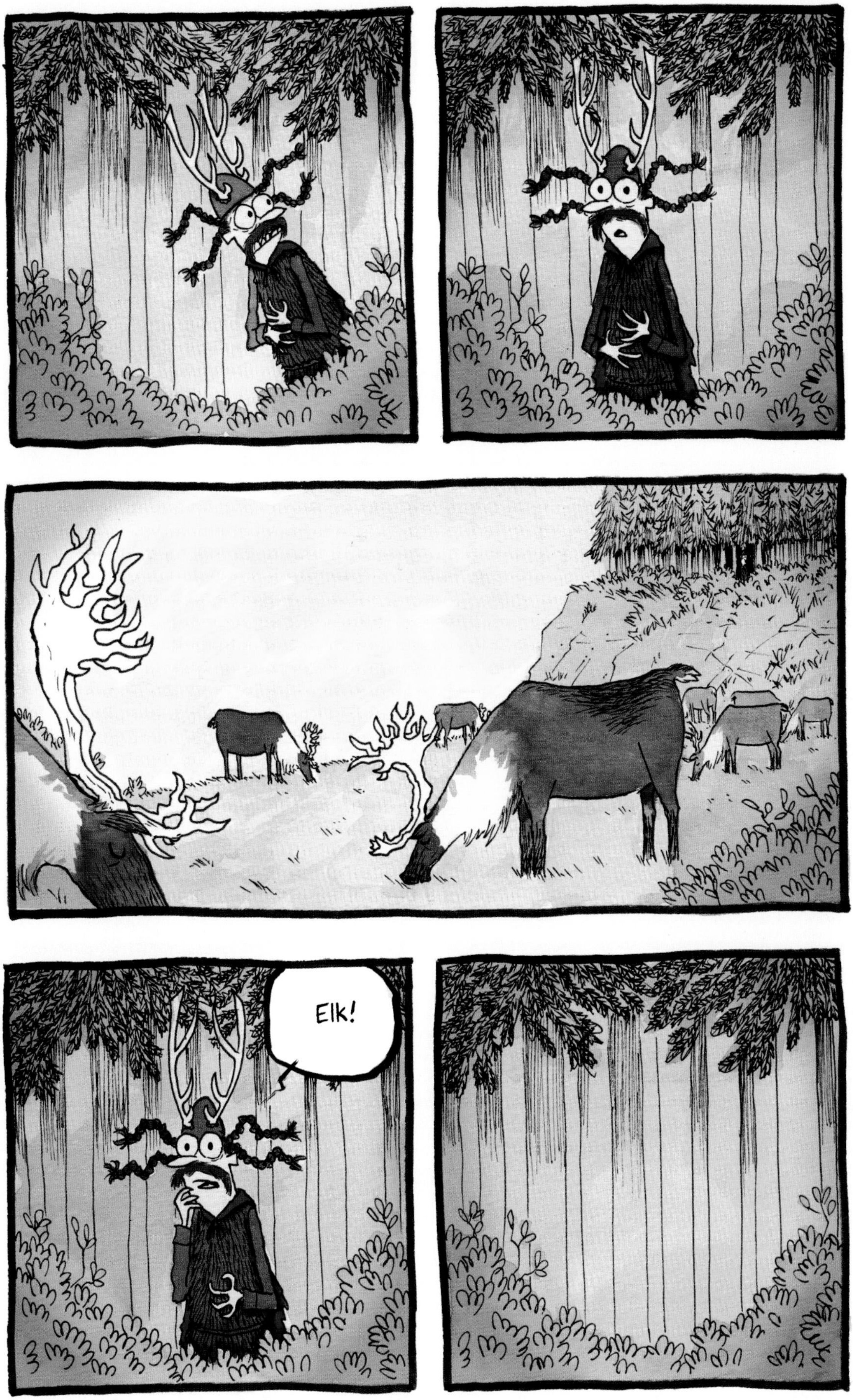
Elk!

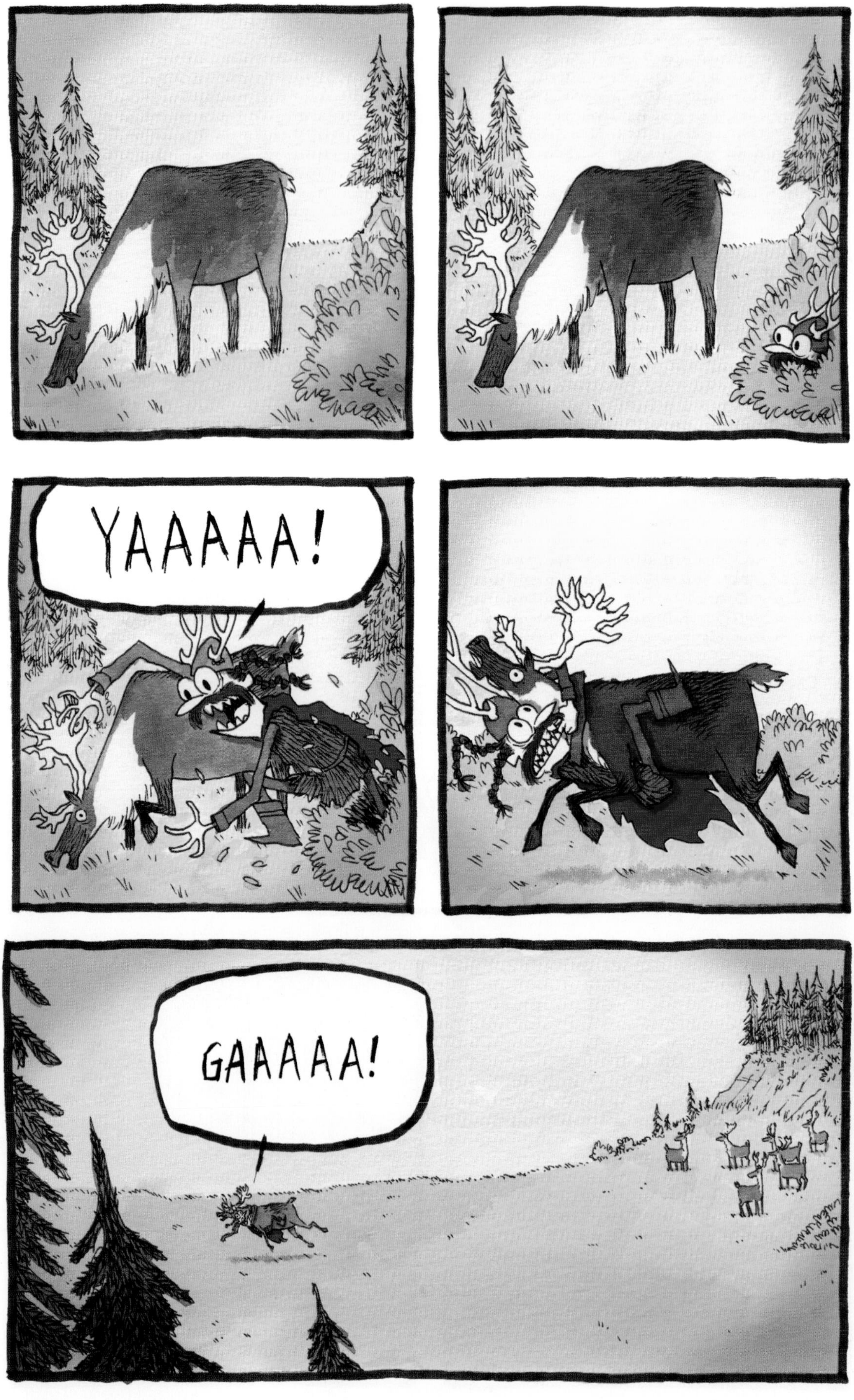
YAAAAA!
GAAAAA!

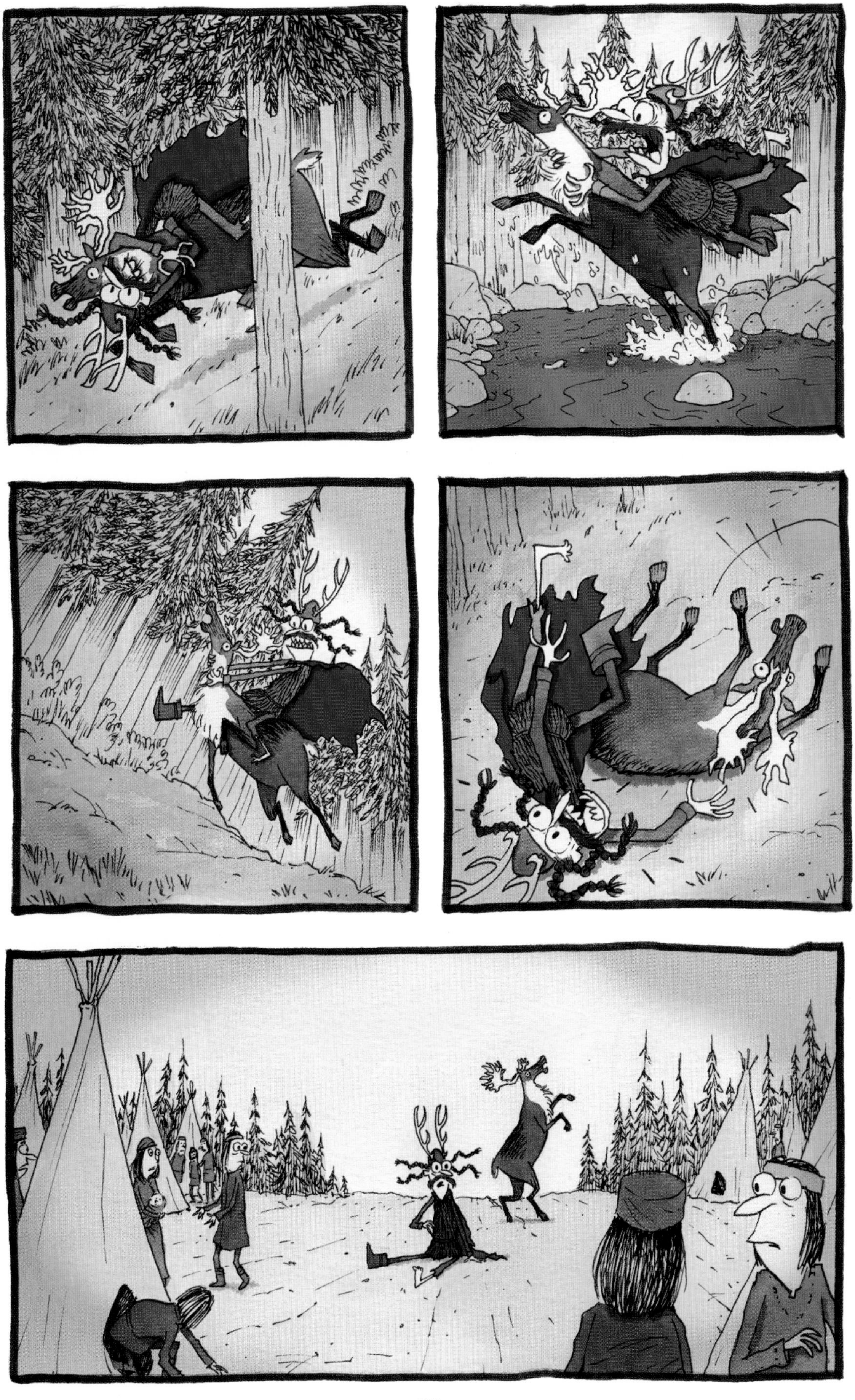

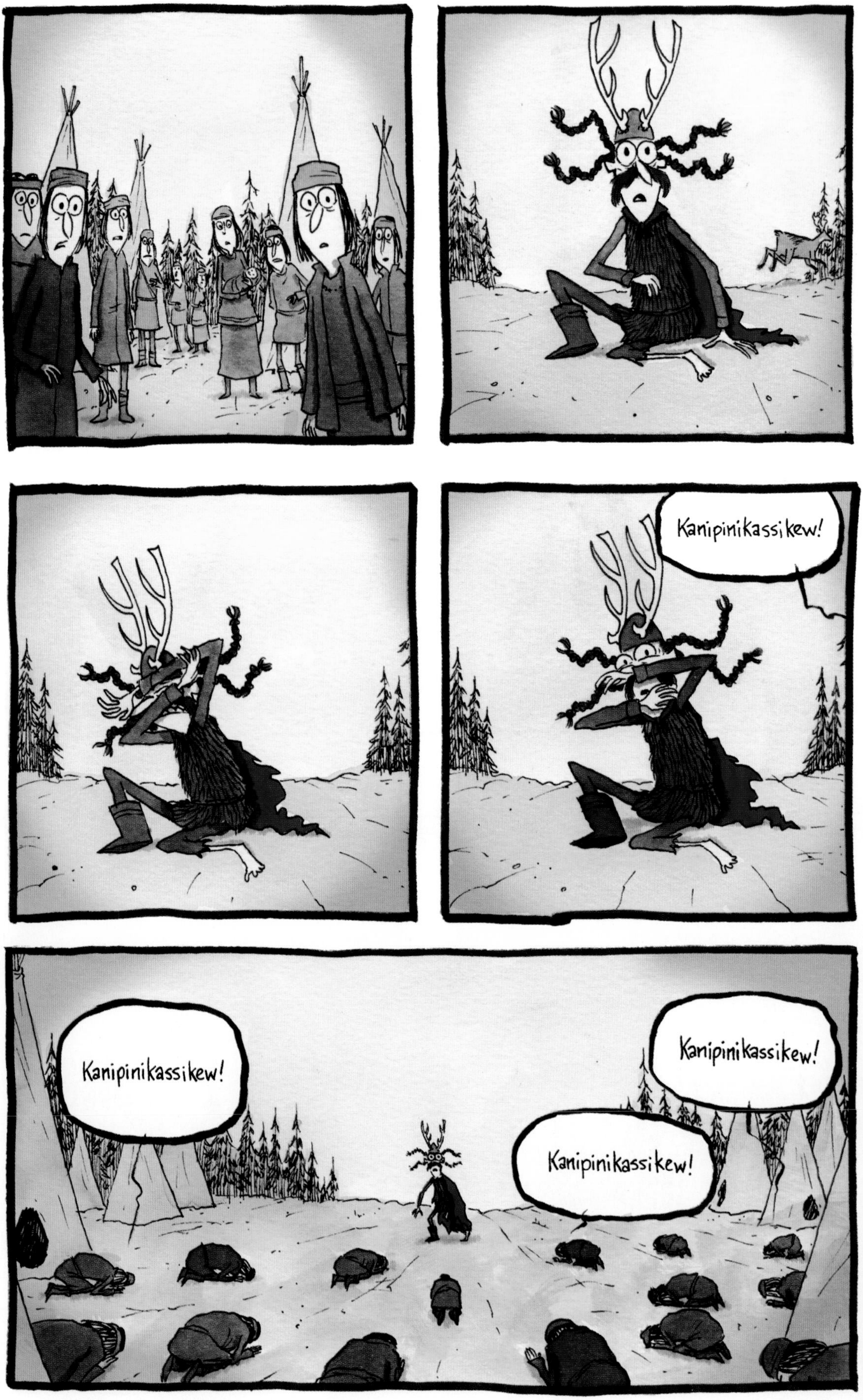
Kanipinikassikew!
Kanipinikassikew!
Kanipinikassikew!
Kanipinikassikew!

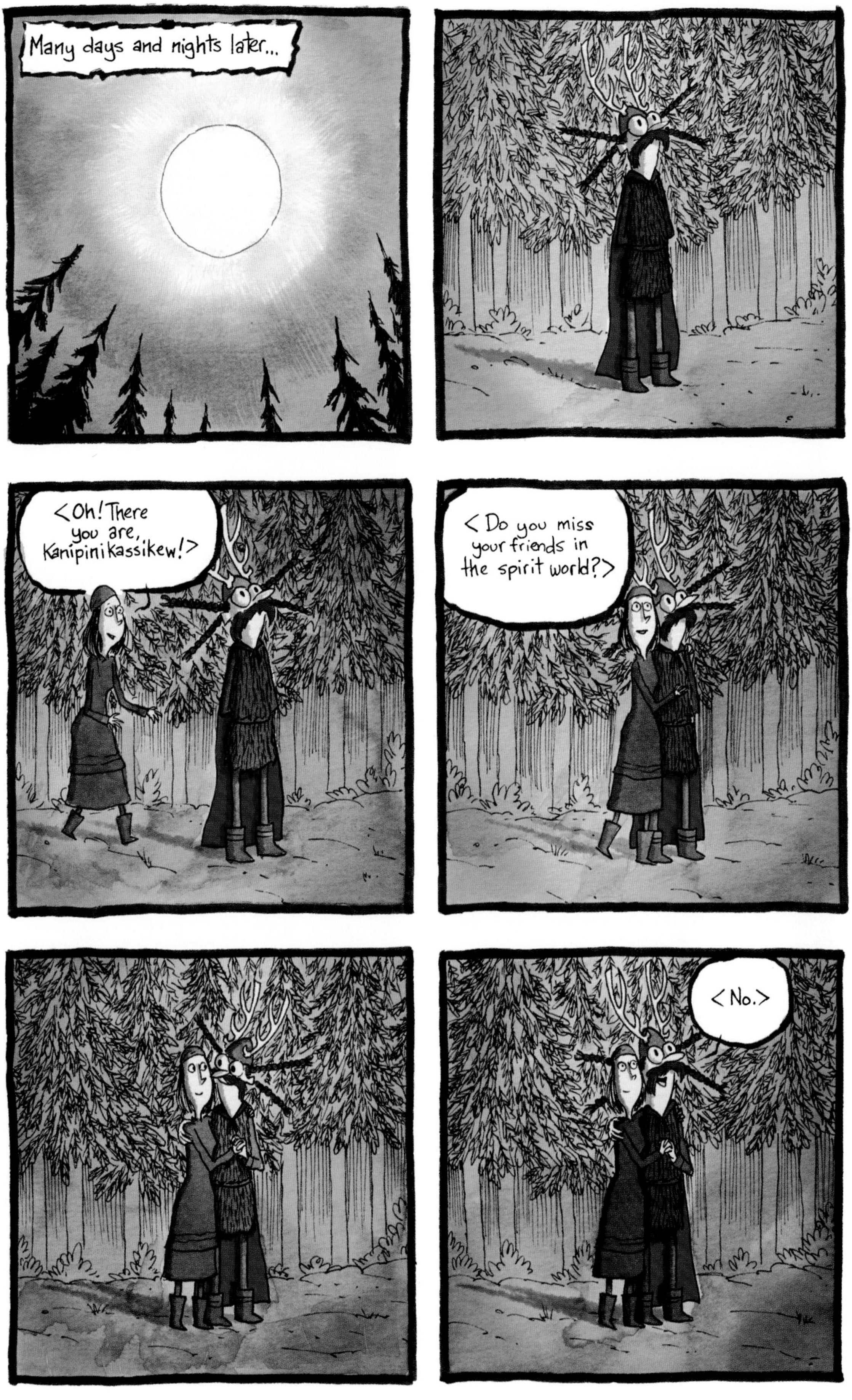
Many days and nights later...
<Oh! There you are, Kanipinikassikew!>
<Do you miss your friends in the spirit world?>
<No.>

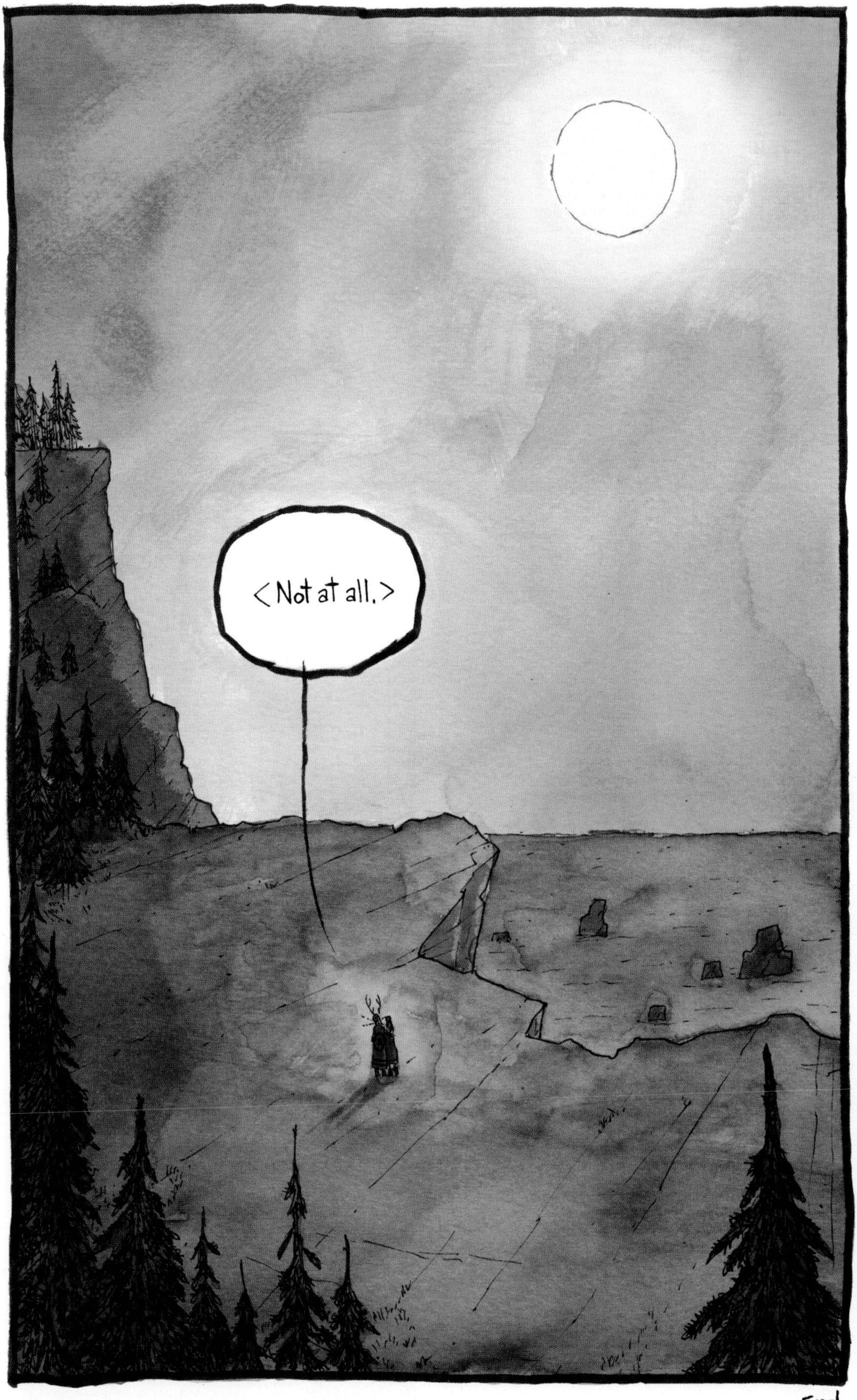
< Not at all. >

End.

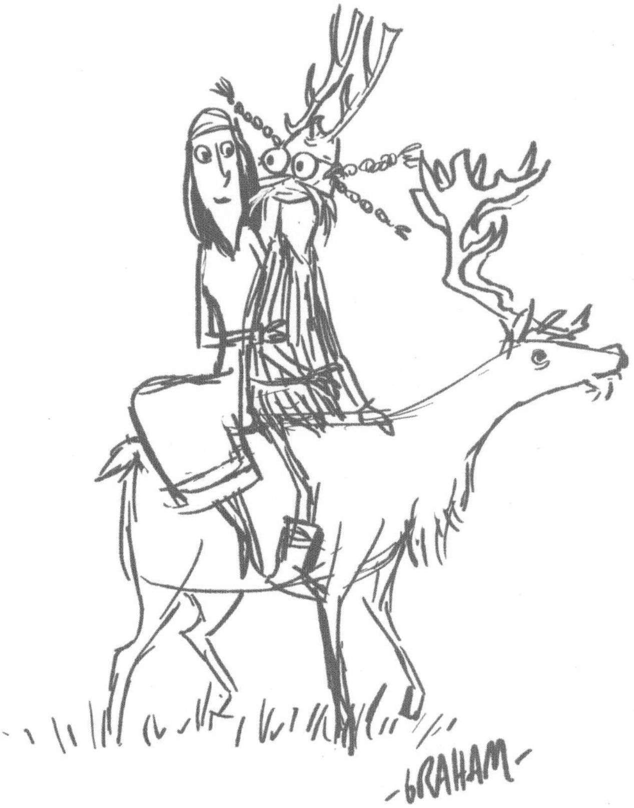
-GRAHAM-

DEAD AT NOON

STORY AND ART BY RODOLPHE GUENODEN

COLOR BY EUAN MACTAVISH

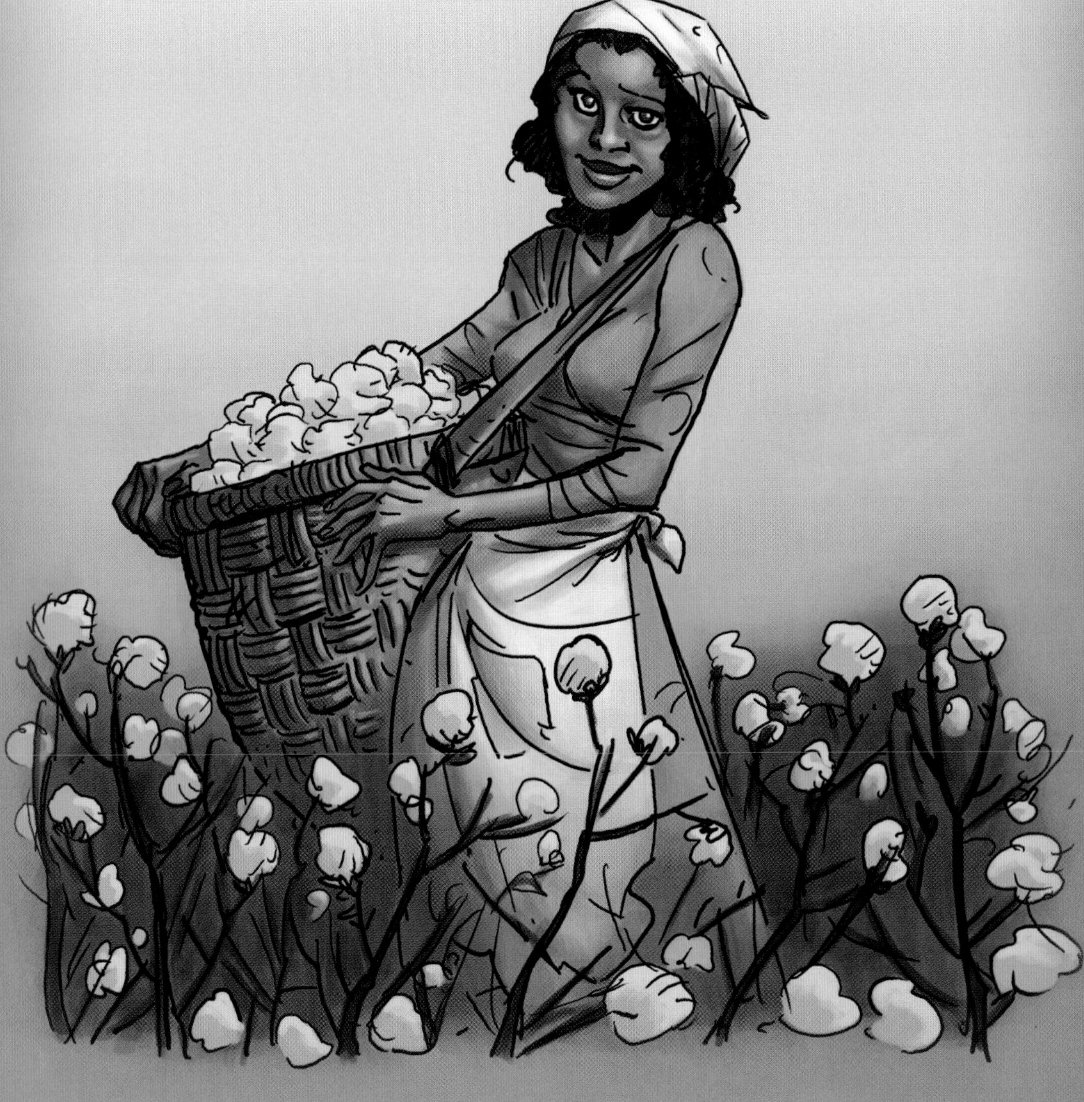

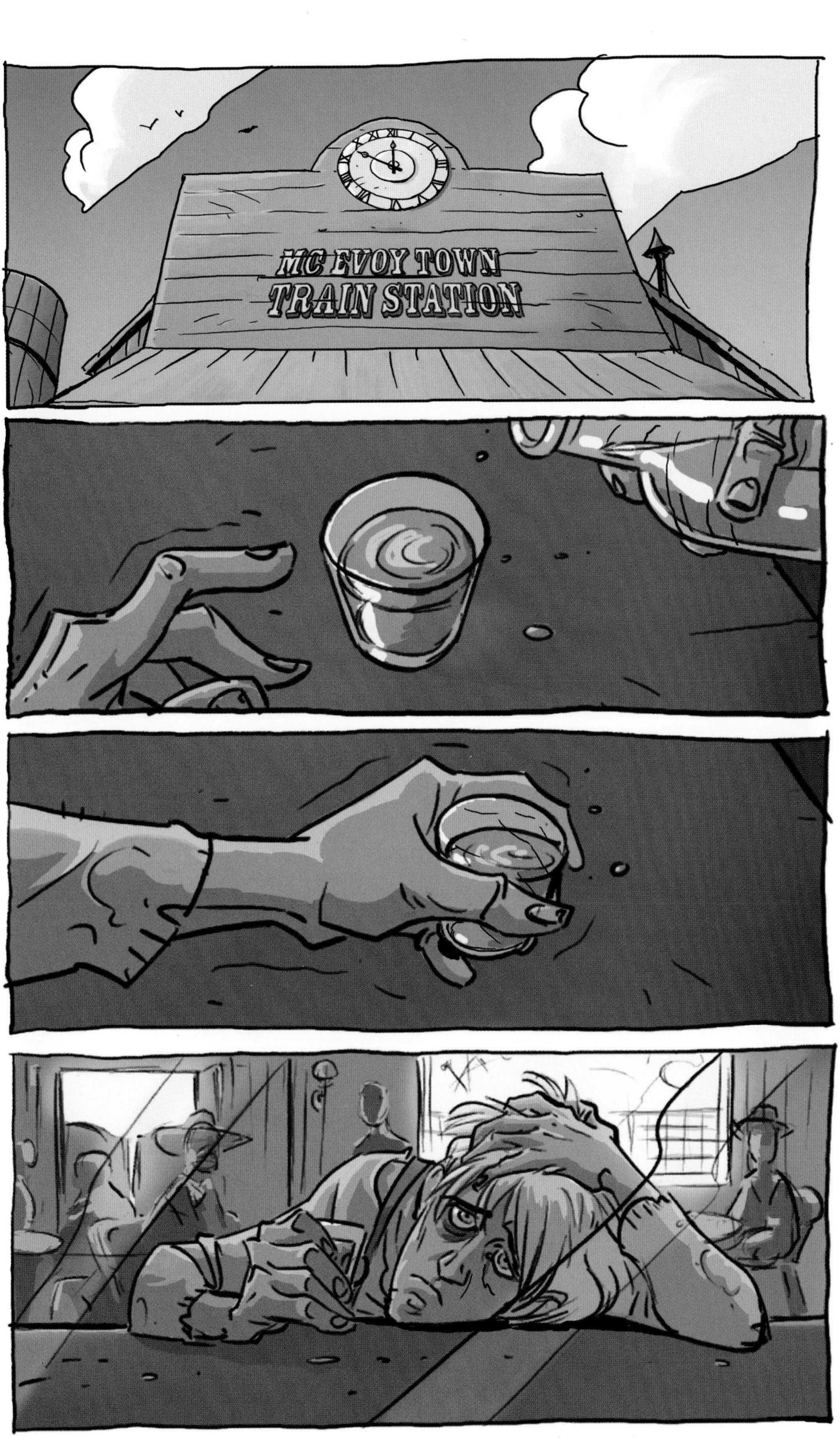
MC EVOY TOWN
TRAIN STATION

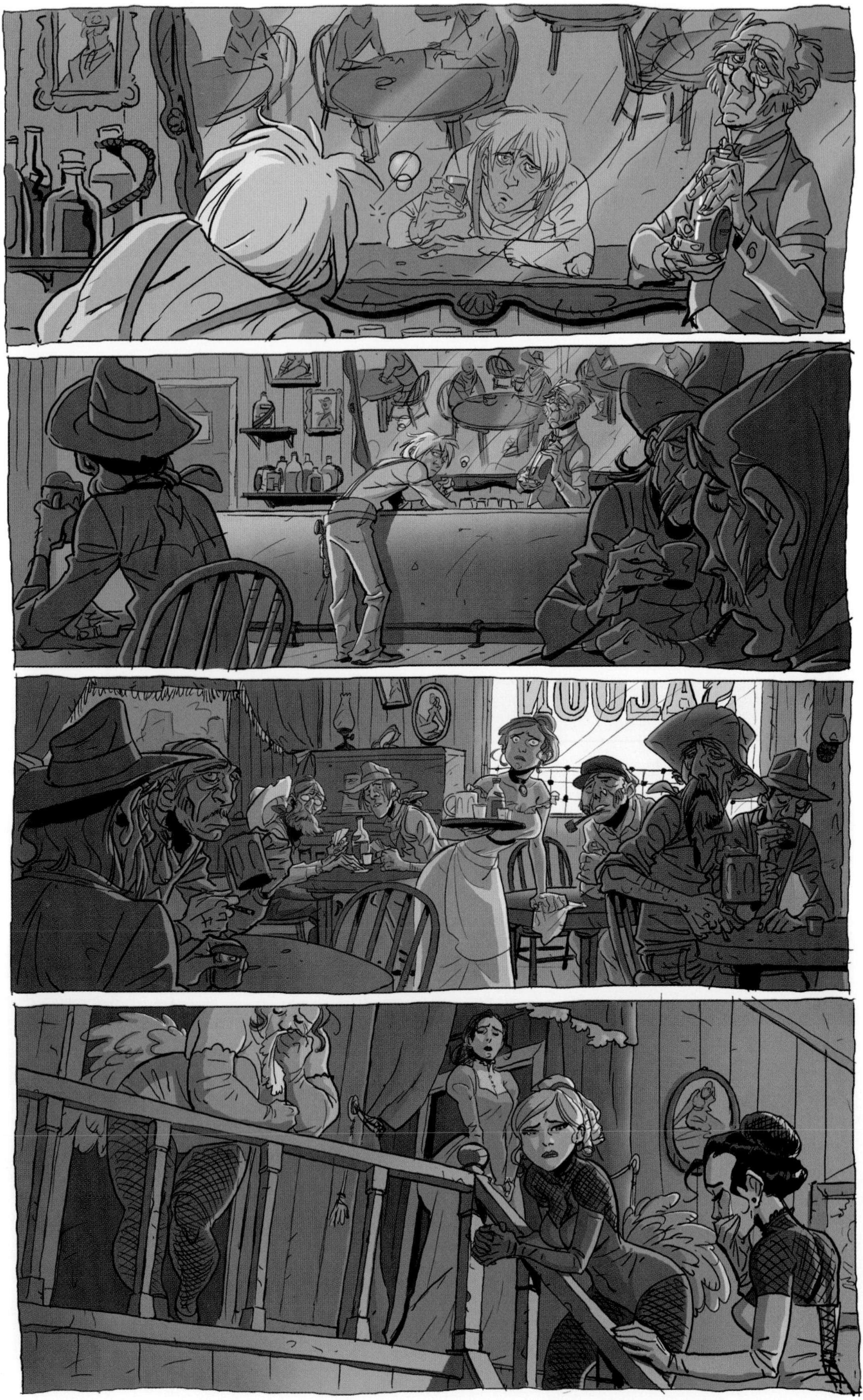

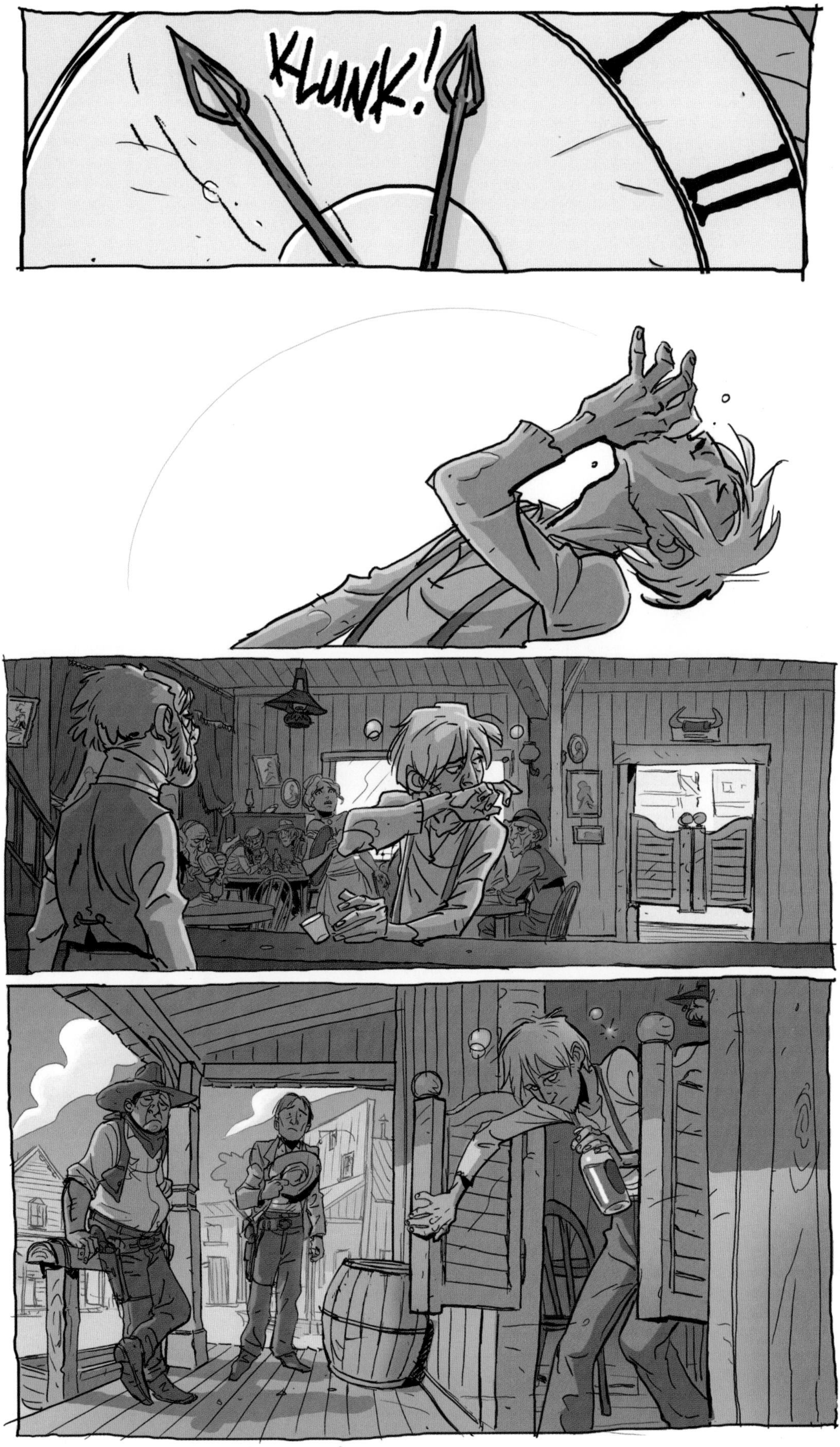
KLUNK!

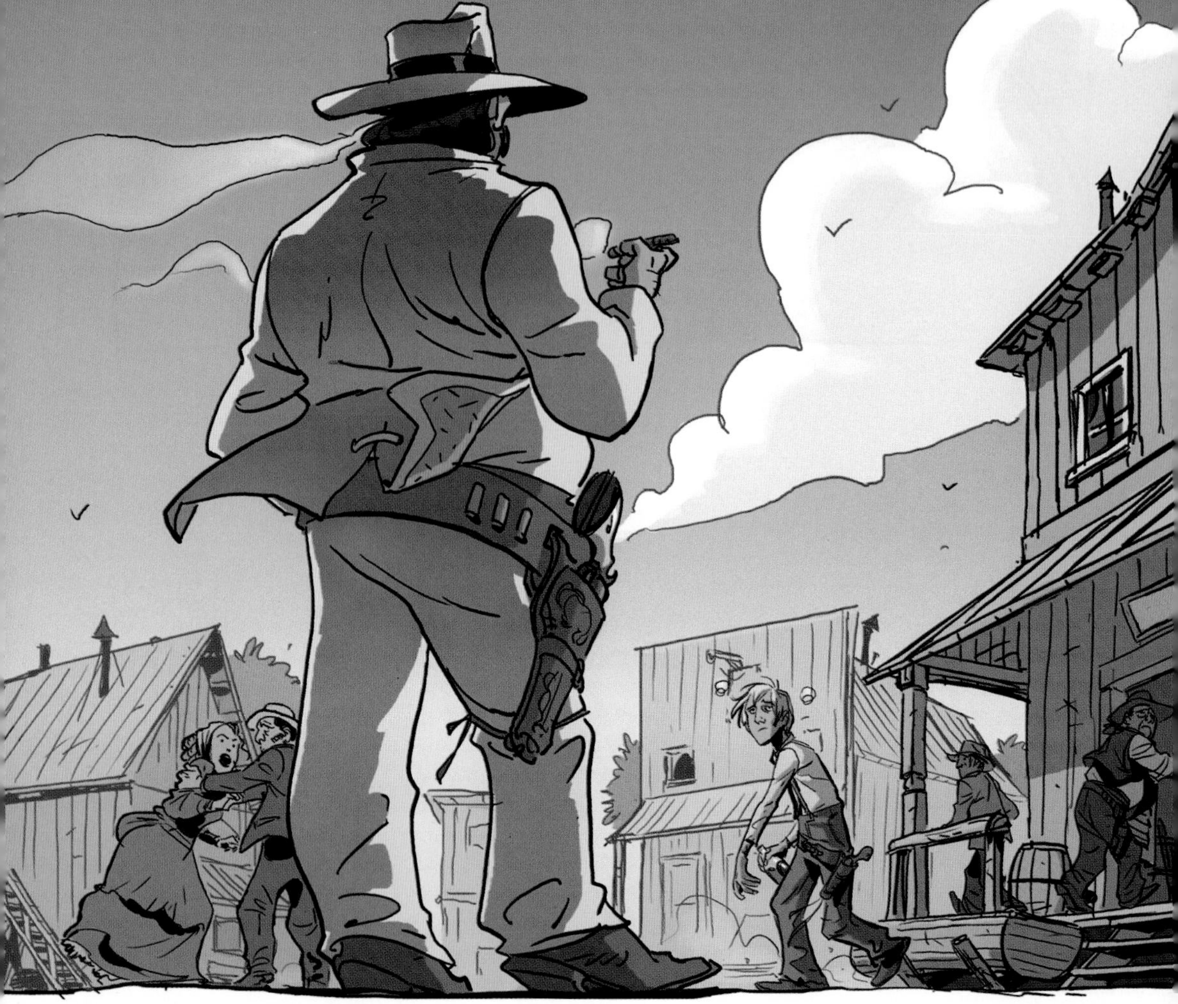

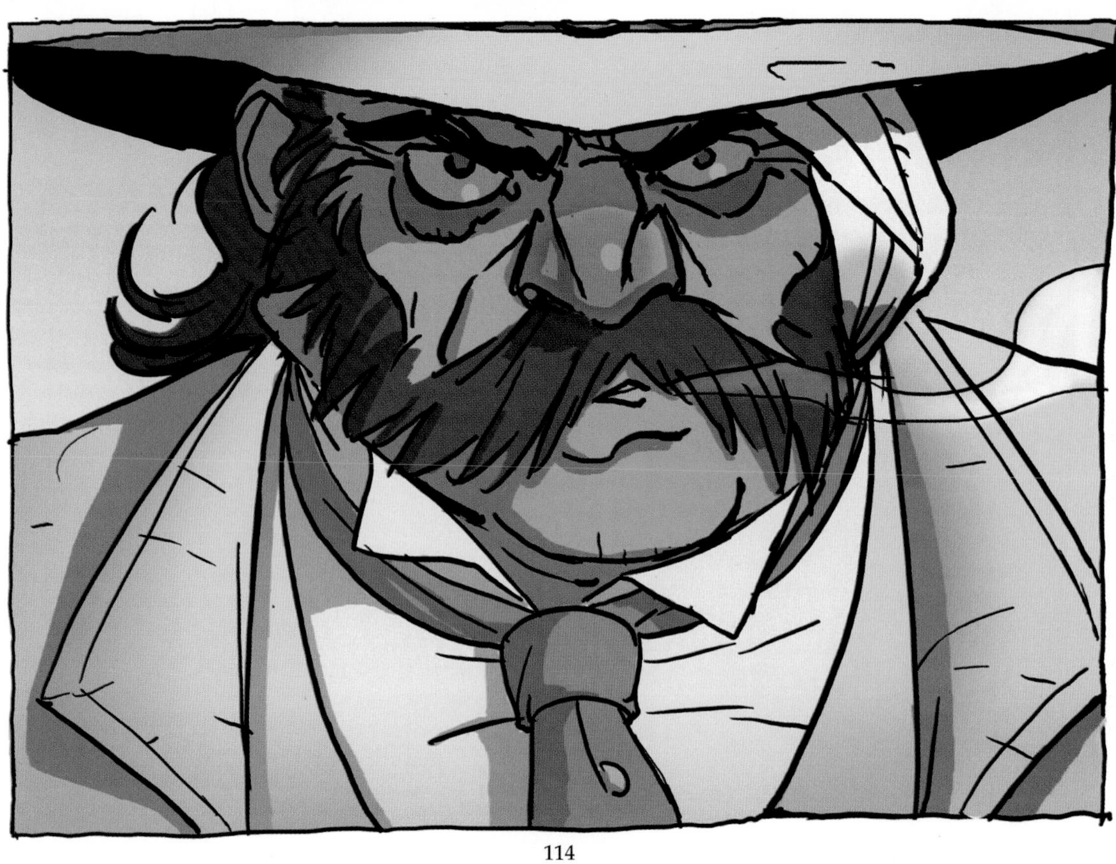

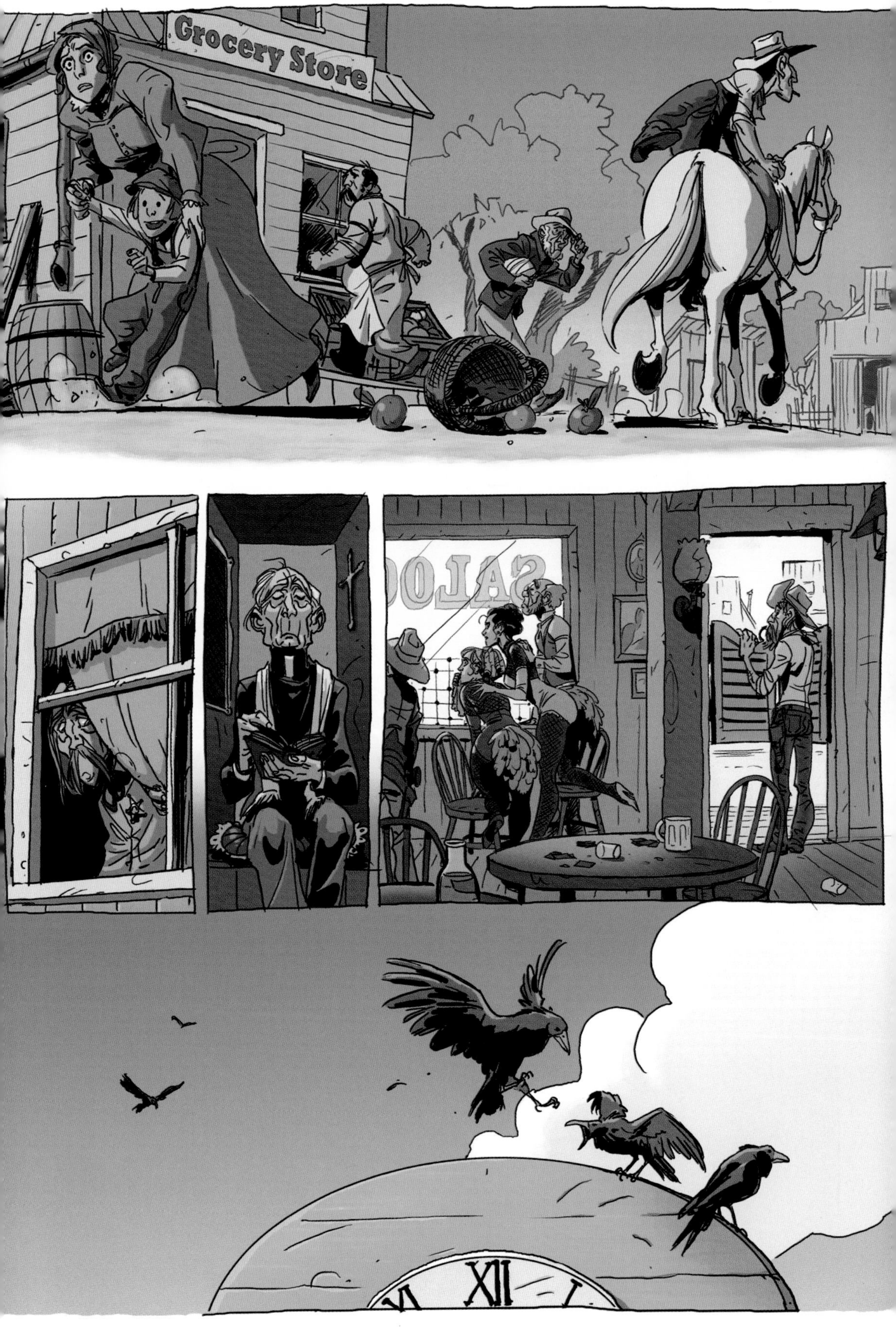
Grocery Store
XII

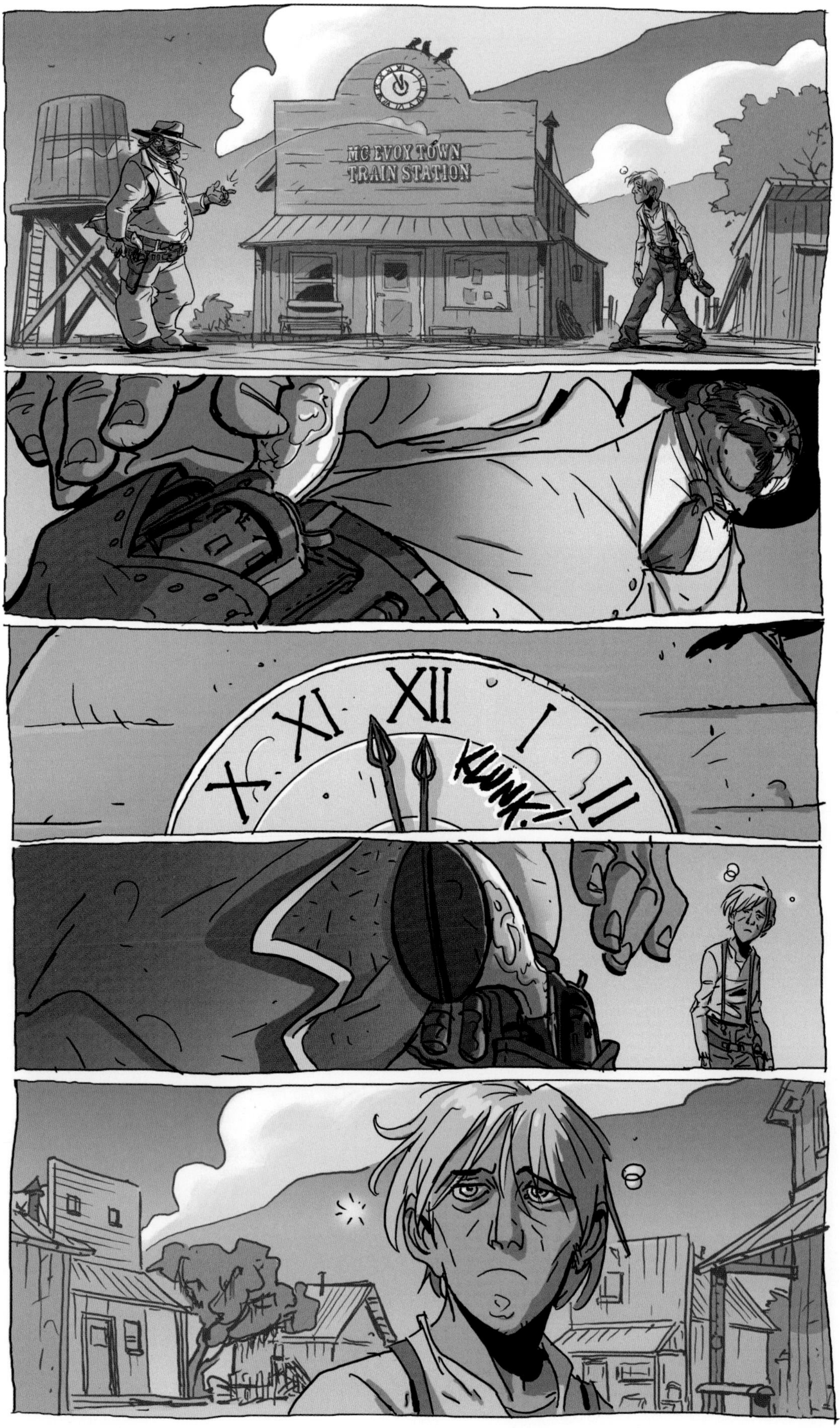
MC EVOY TOWN
TRAIN STATION
KLUNK!

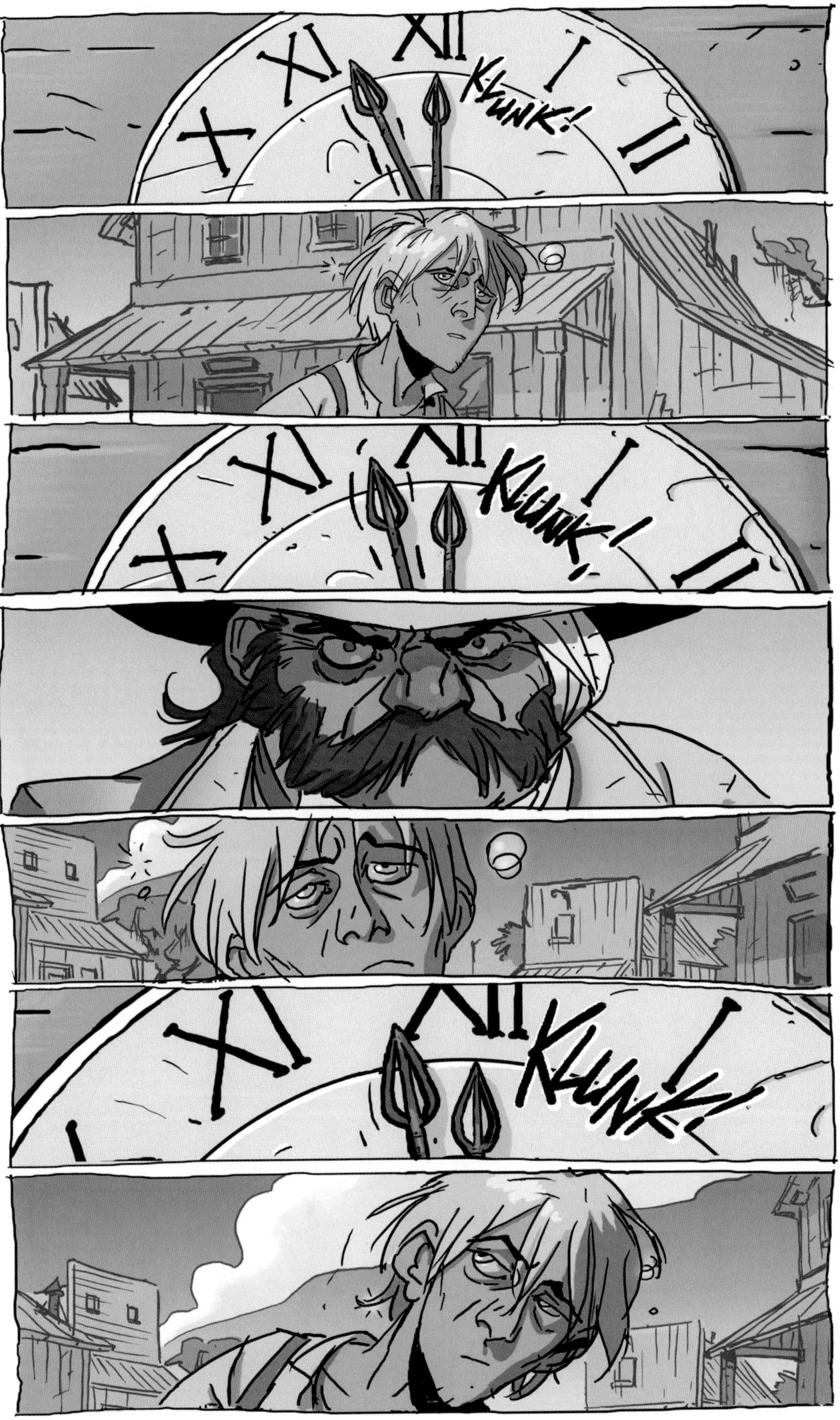
KLUNK!
KLUNK!
KLUNK!

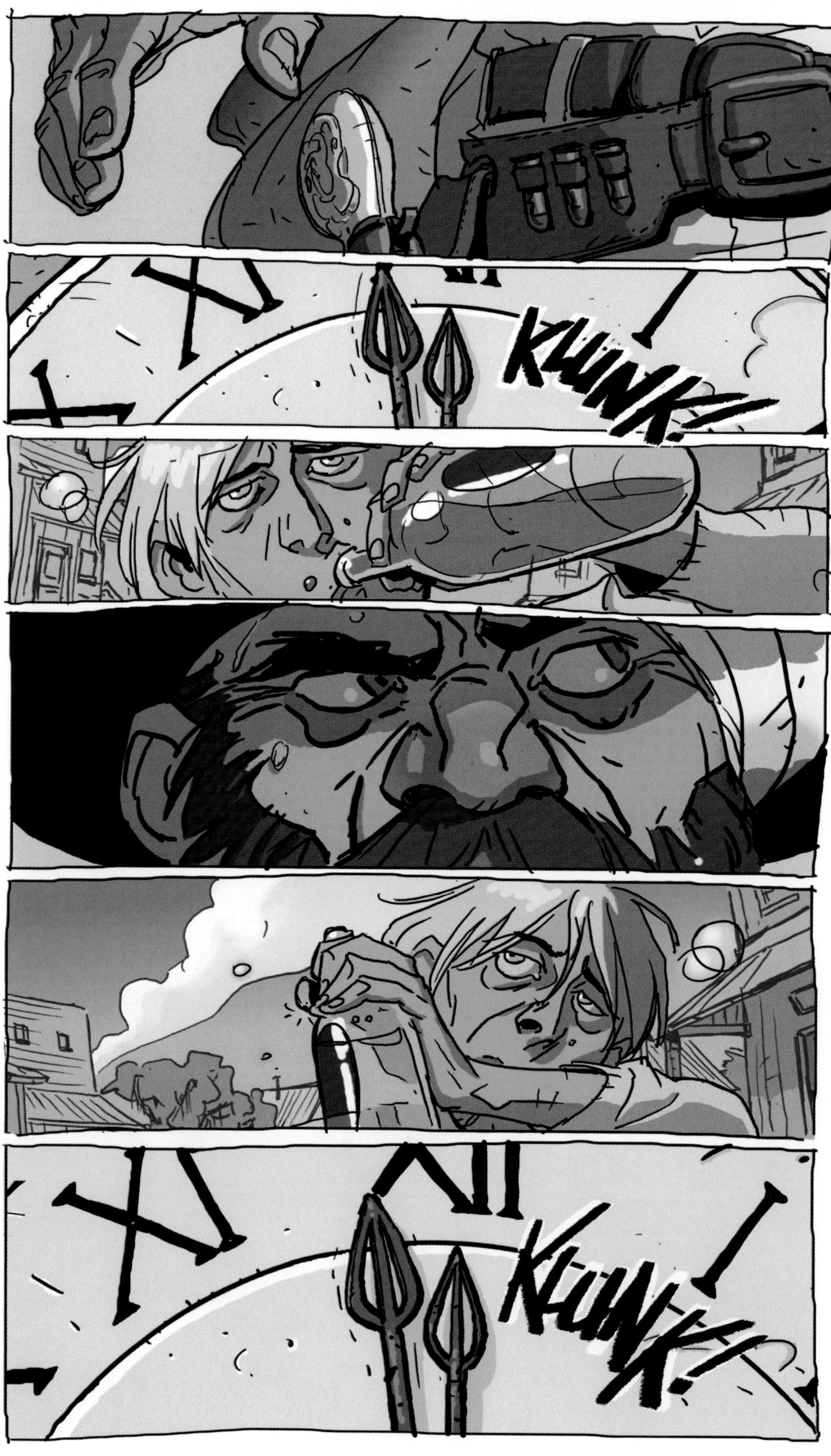
KLUNK!!
KLUNK!!

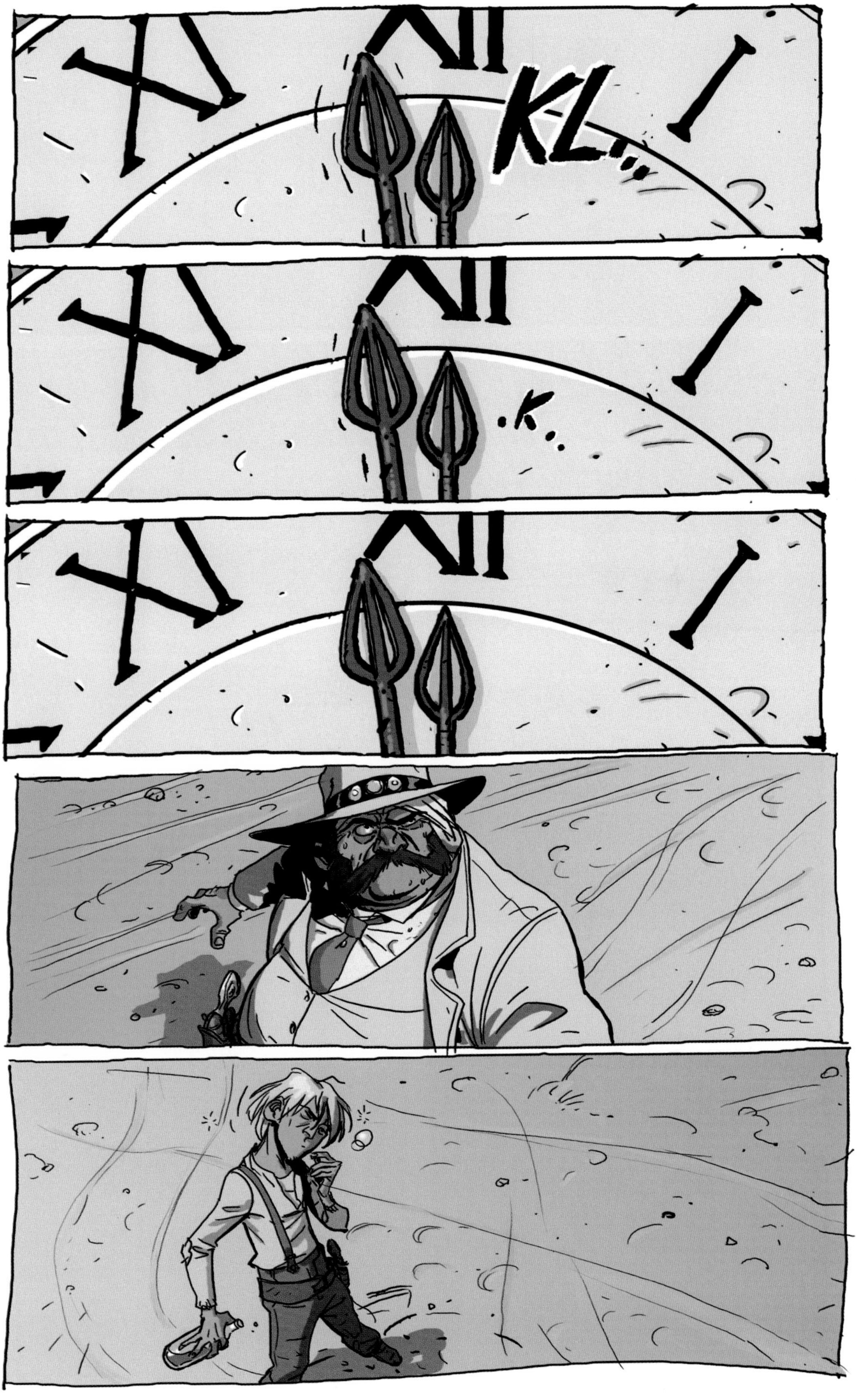
KL..
.K..

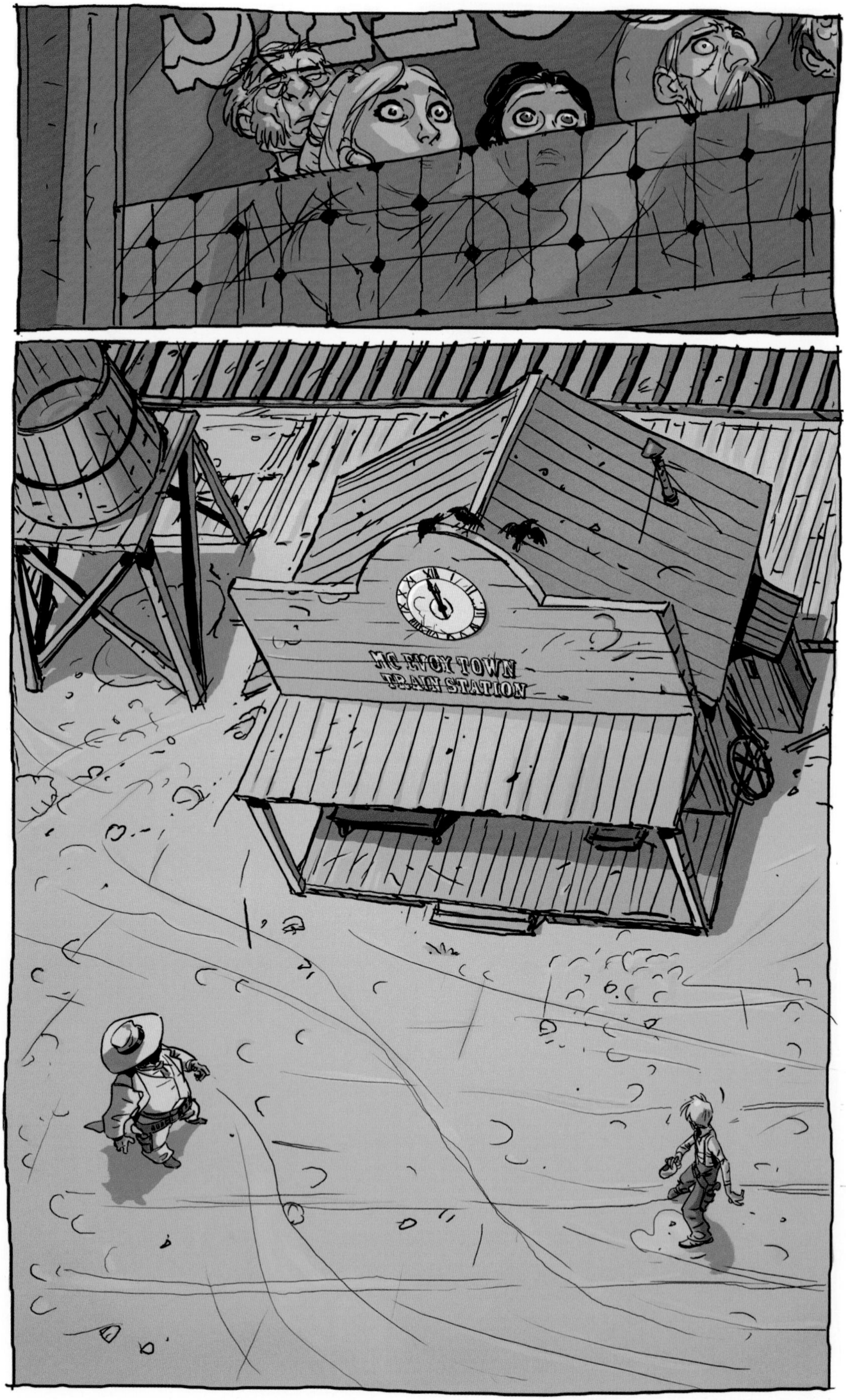
MC EVOY TOWN
TRAIN STATION

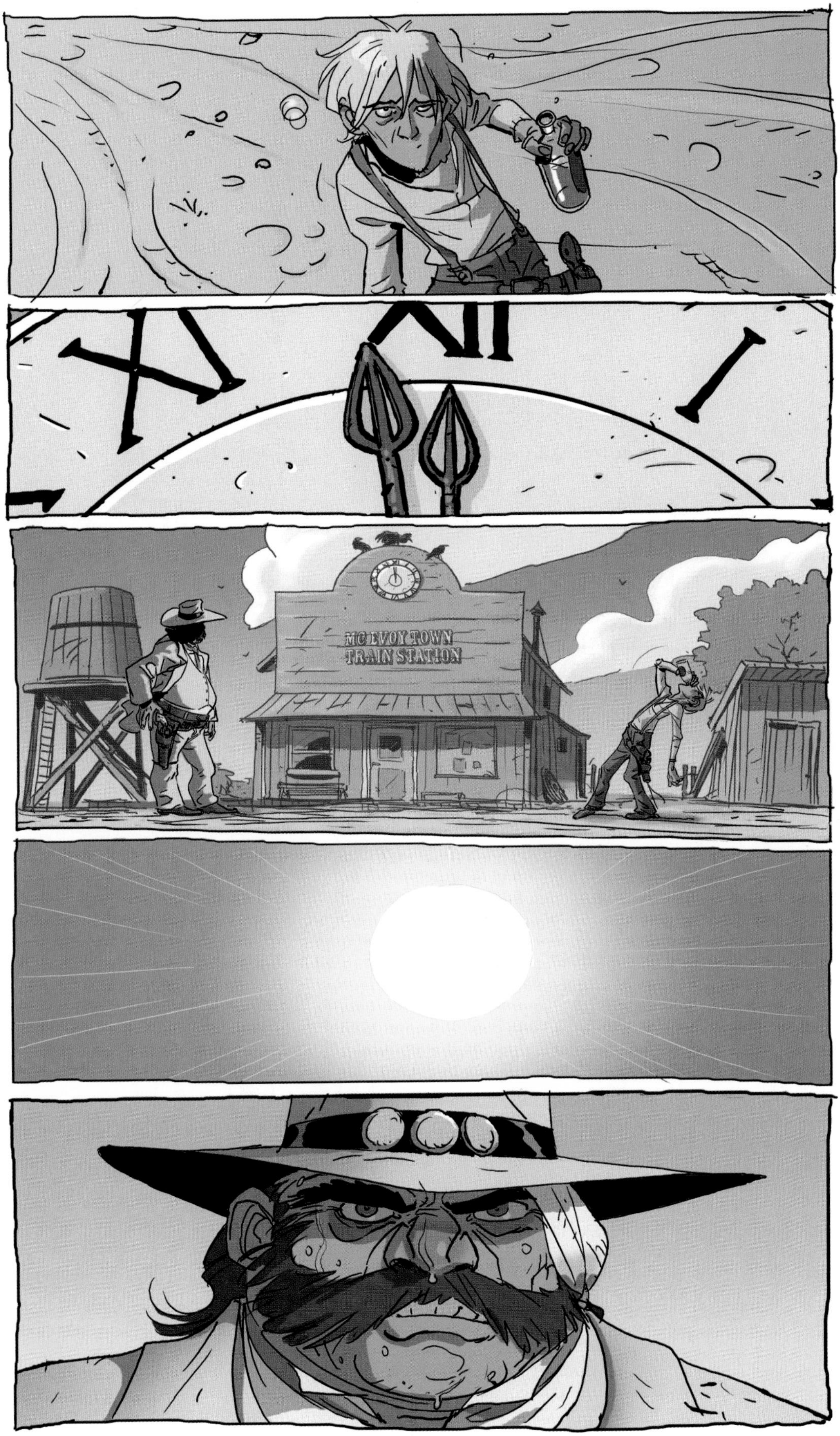
MC EVOY TOWN
TRAIN STATION

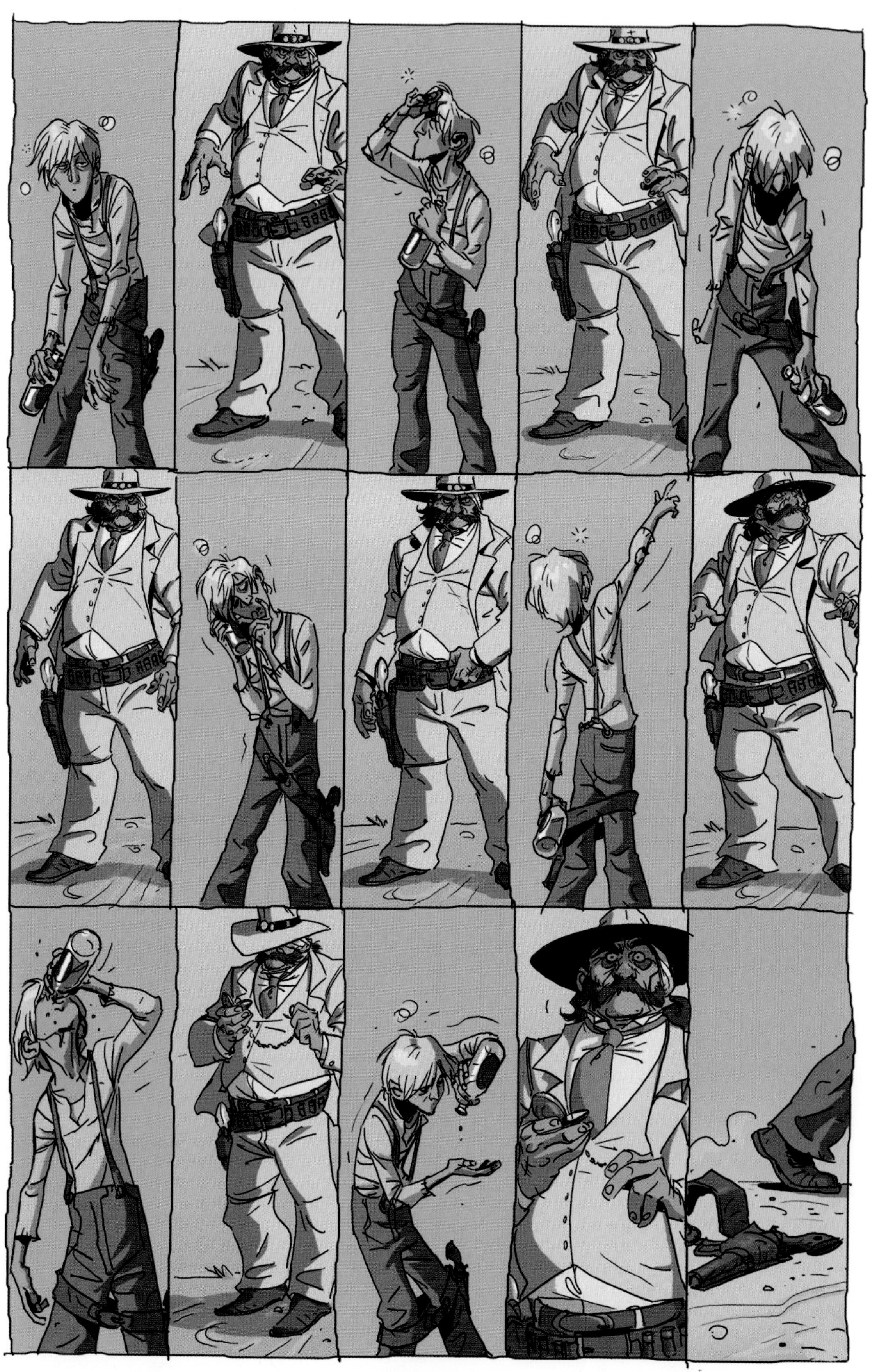

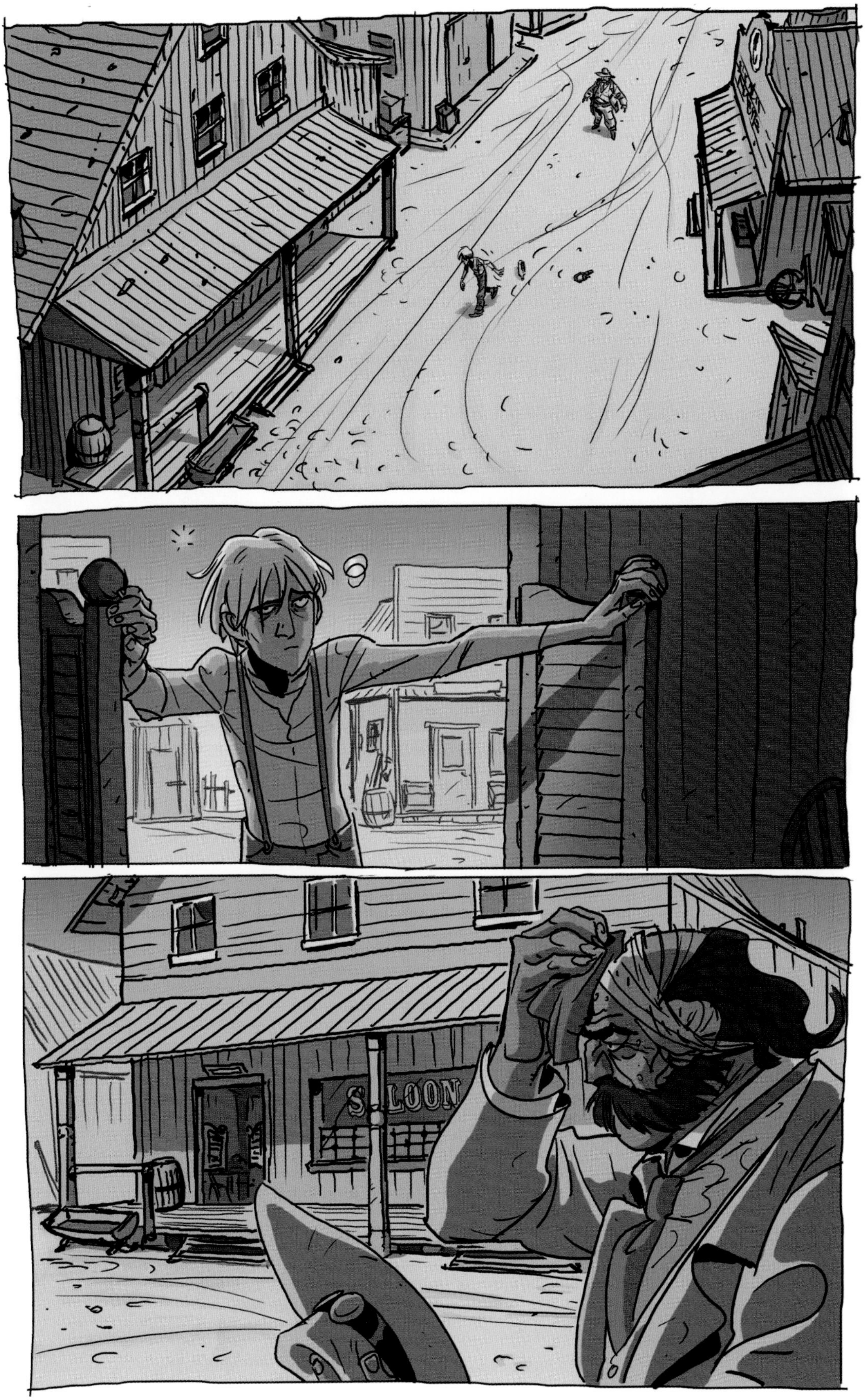
S LOON

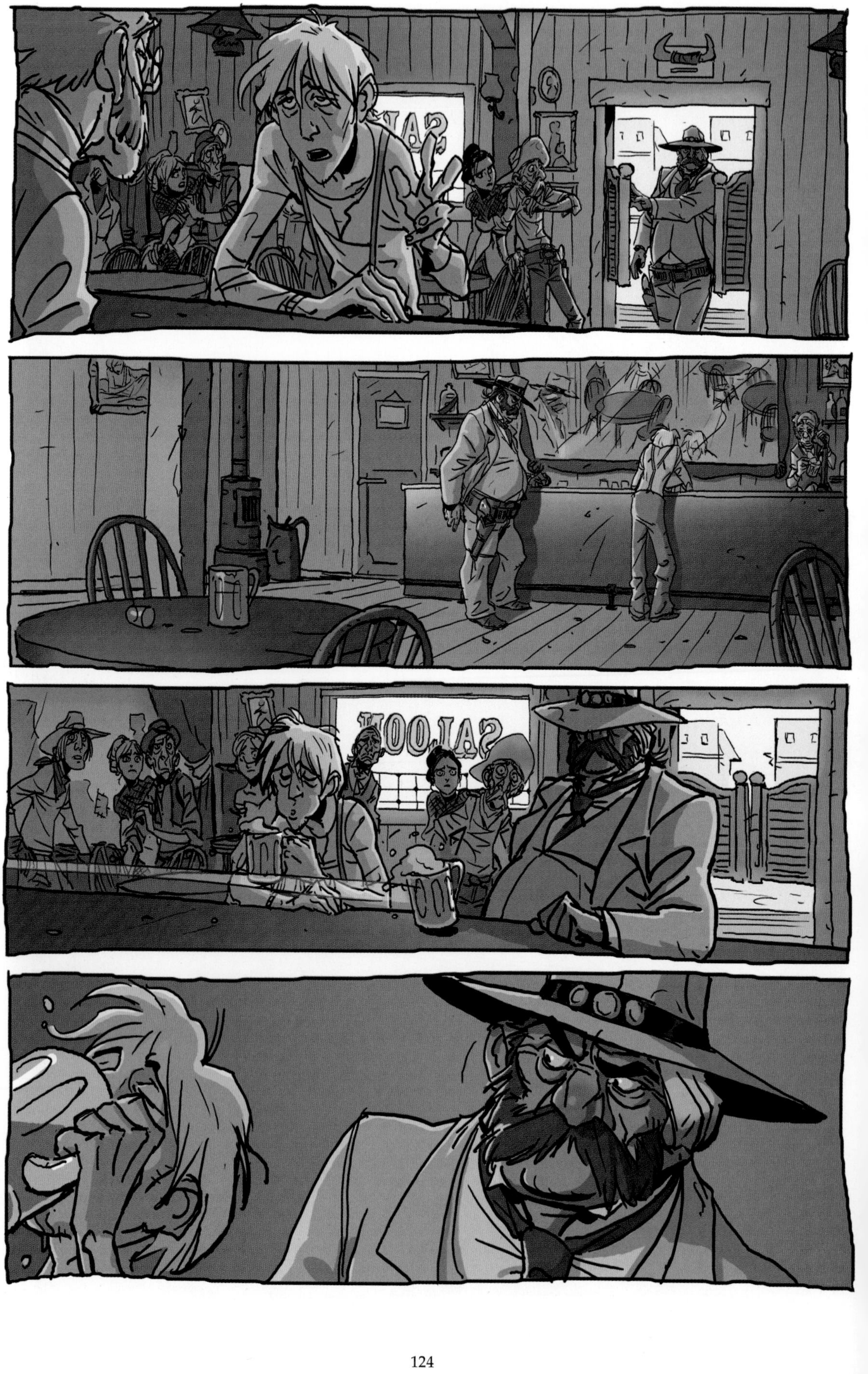

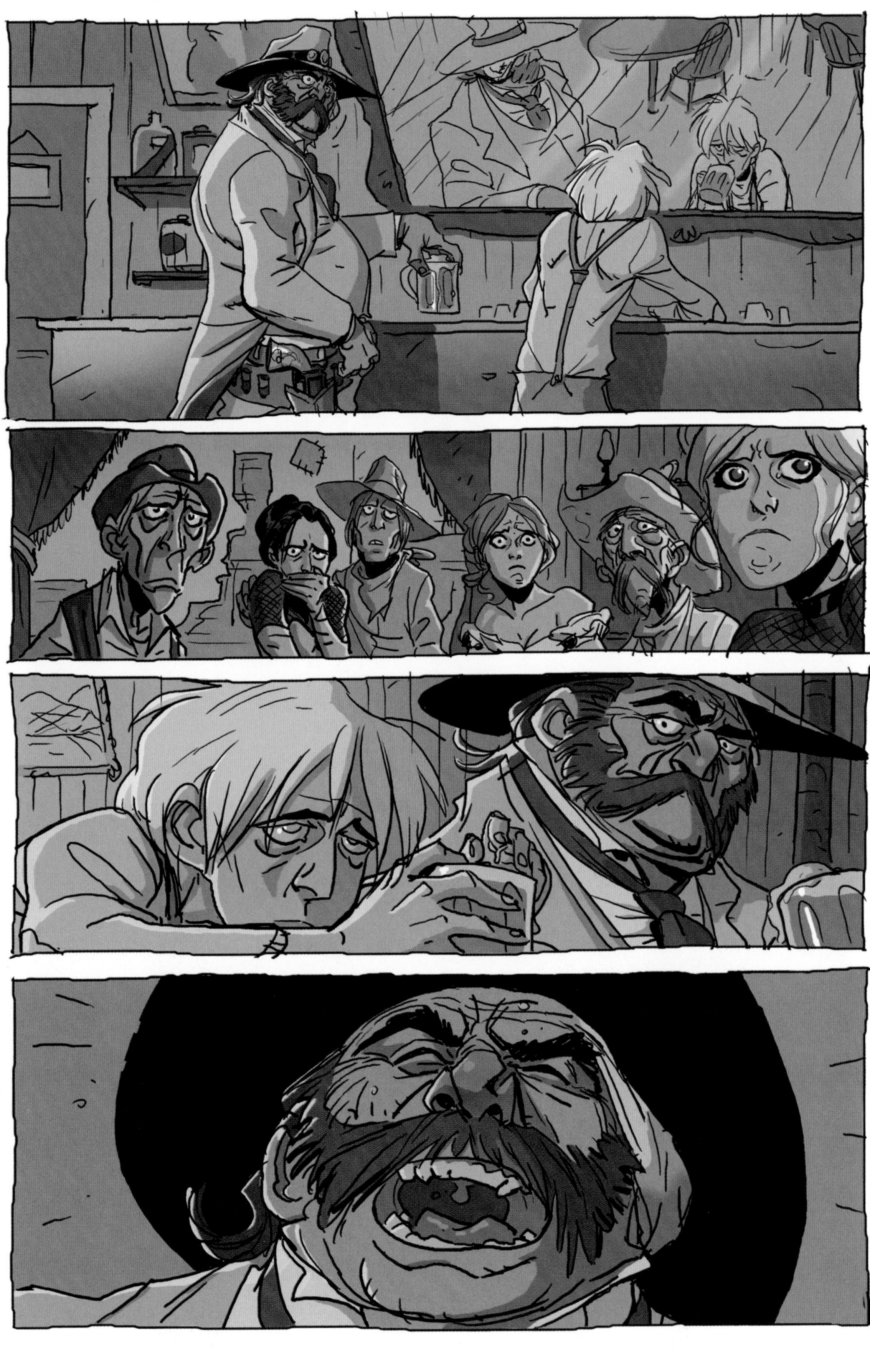

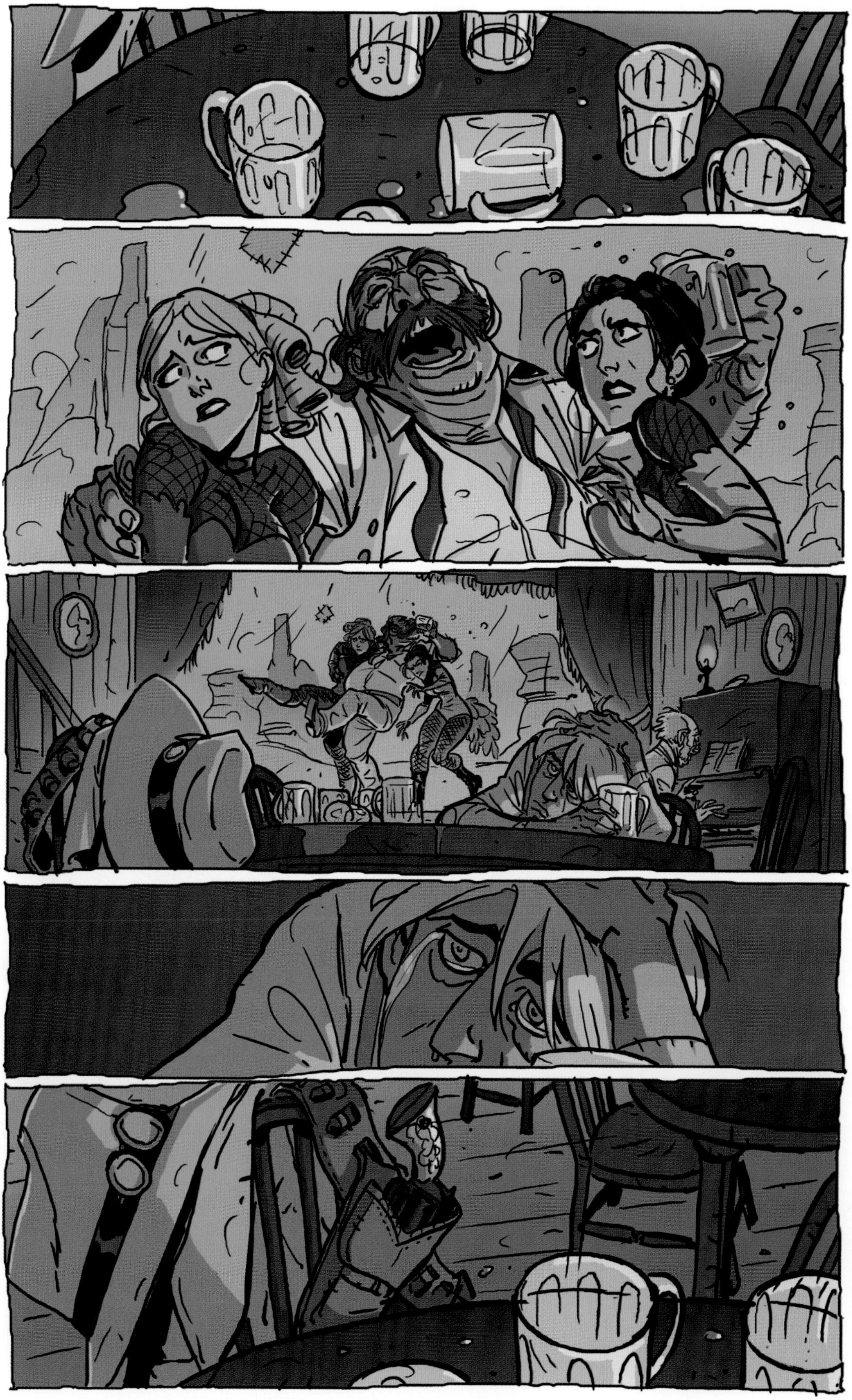

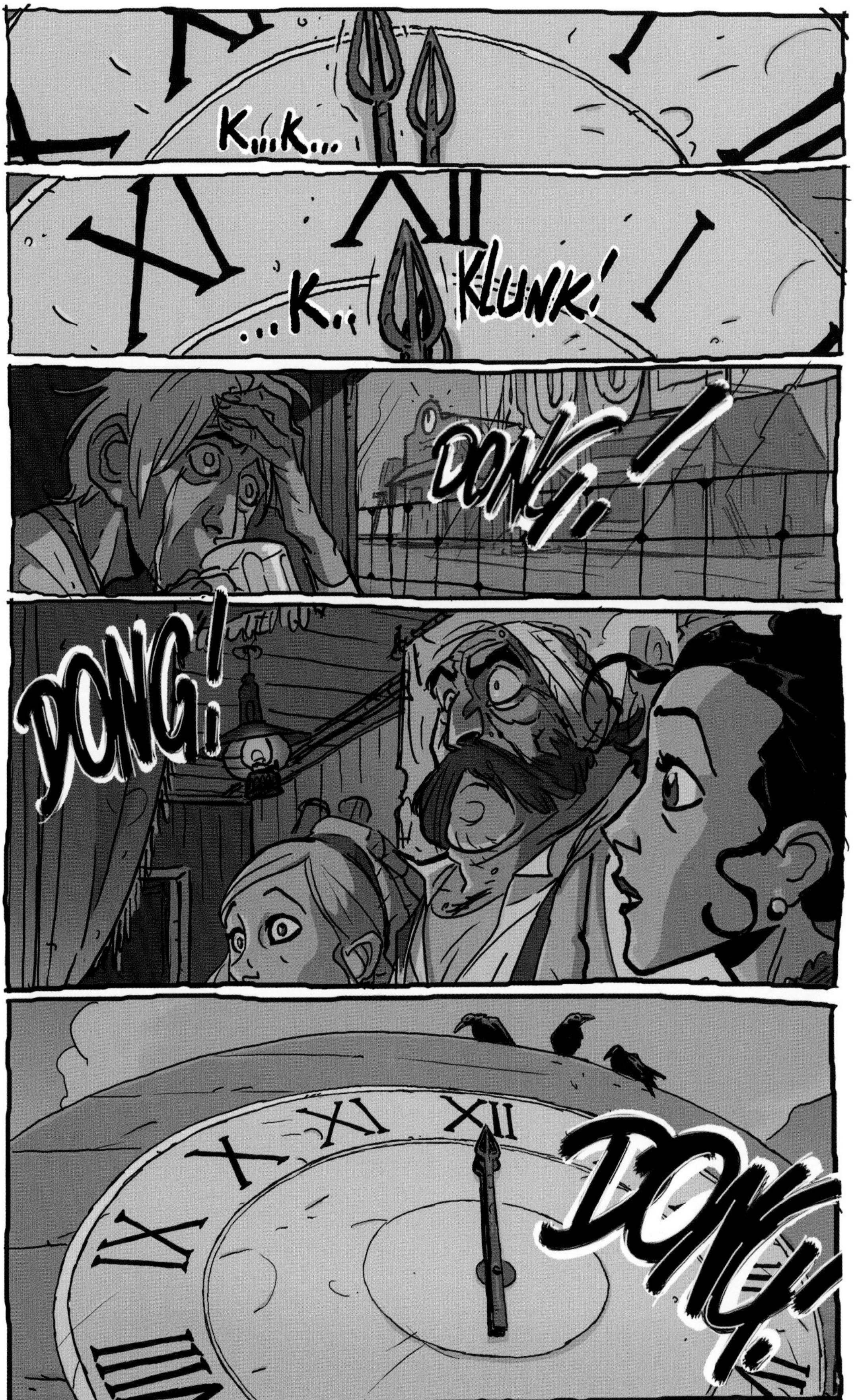

K...K...
...K...
KLUNK!
DONG!
DONG!
DONG!

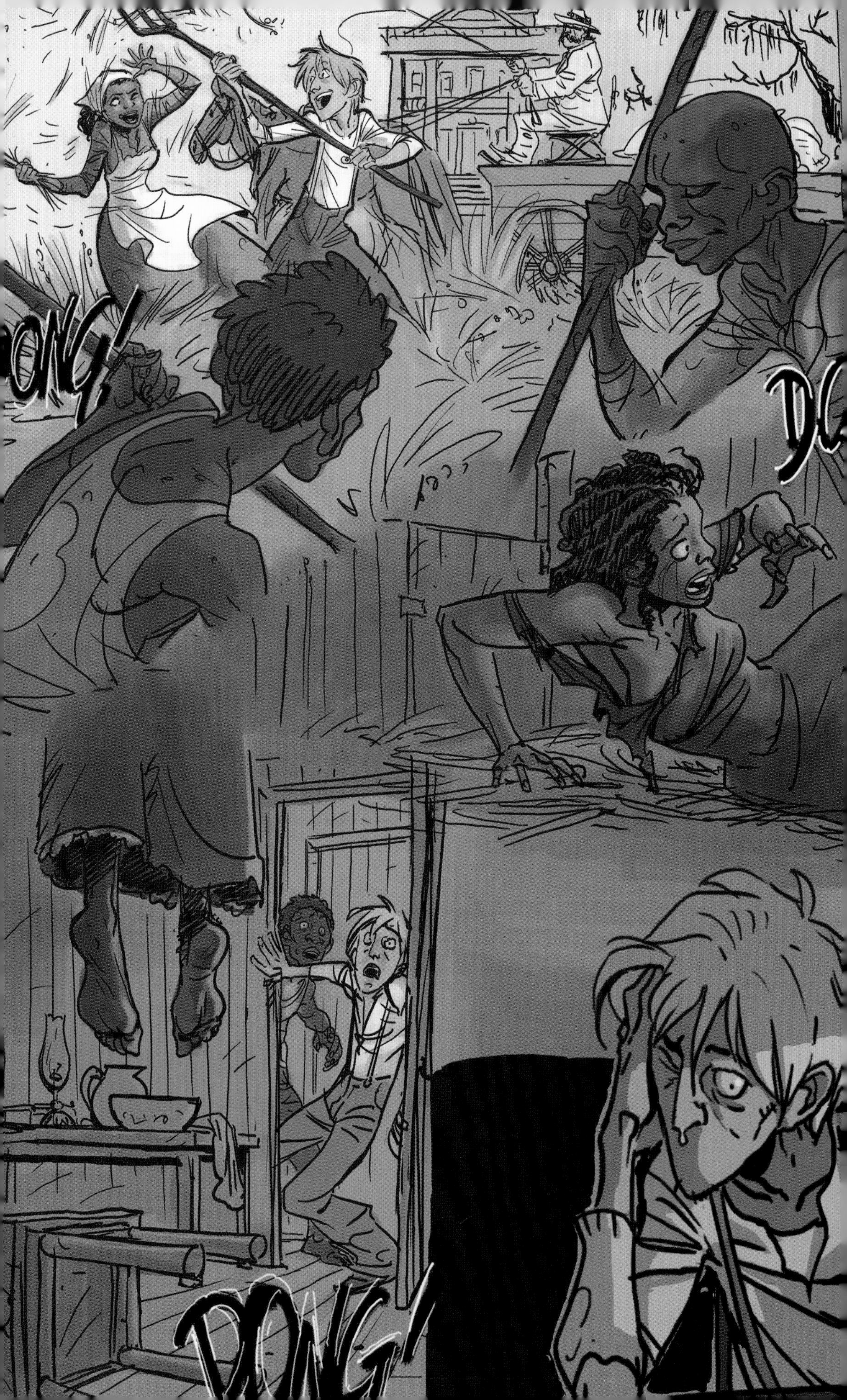
DONG!
DONG!

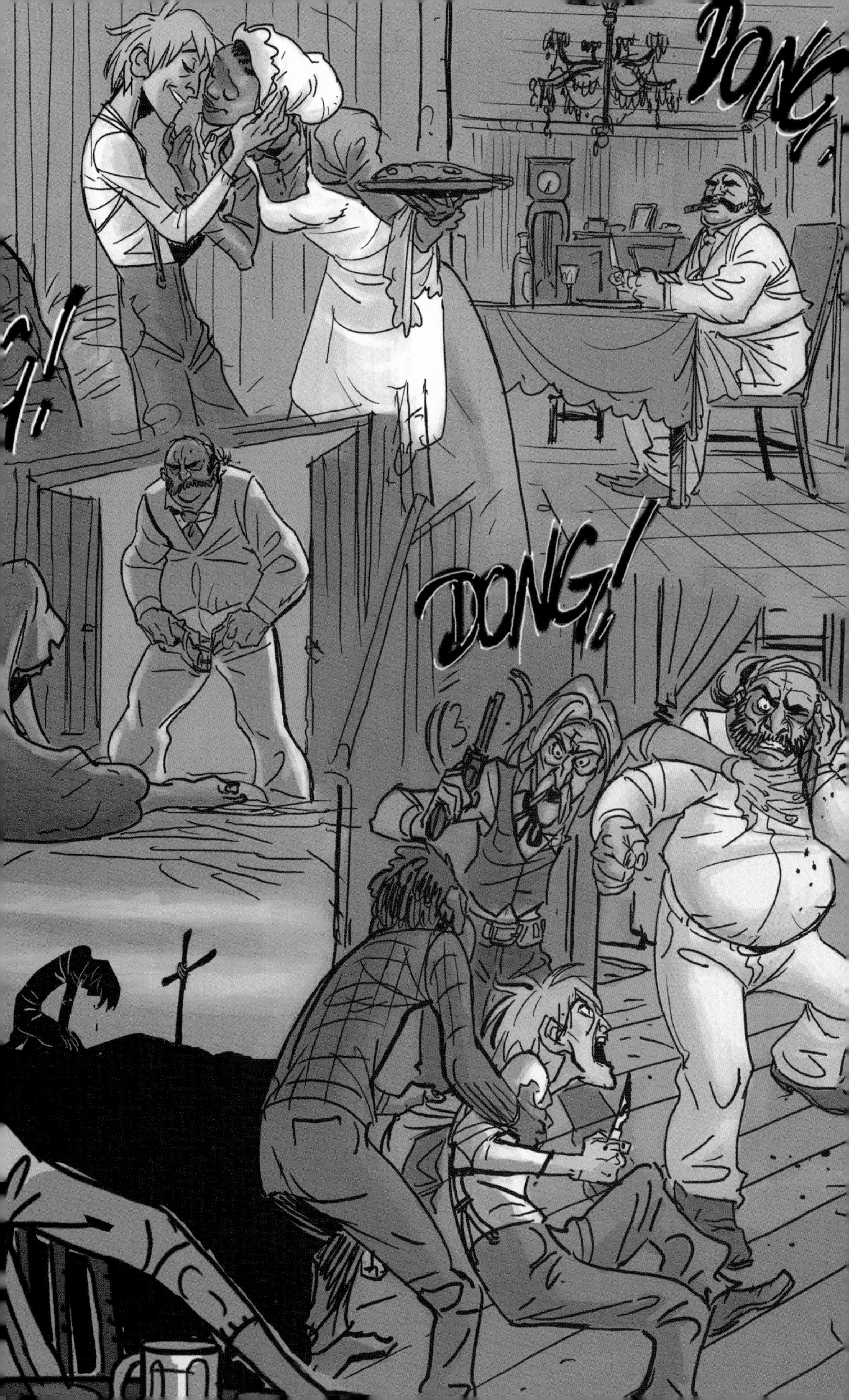
DONG!
DONG!

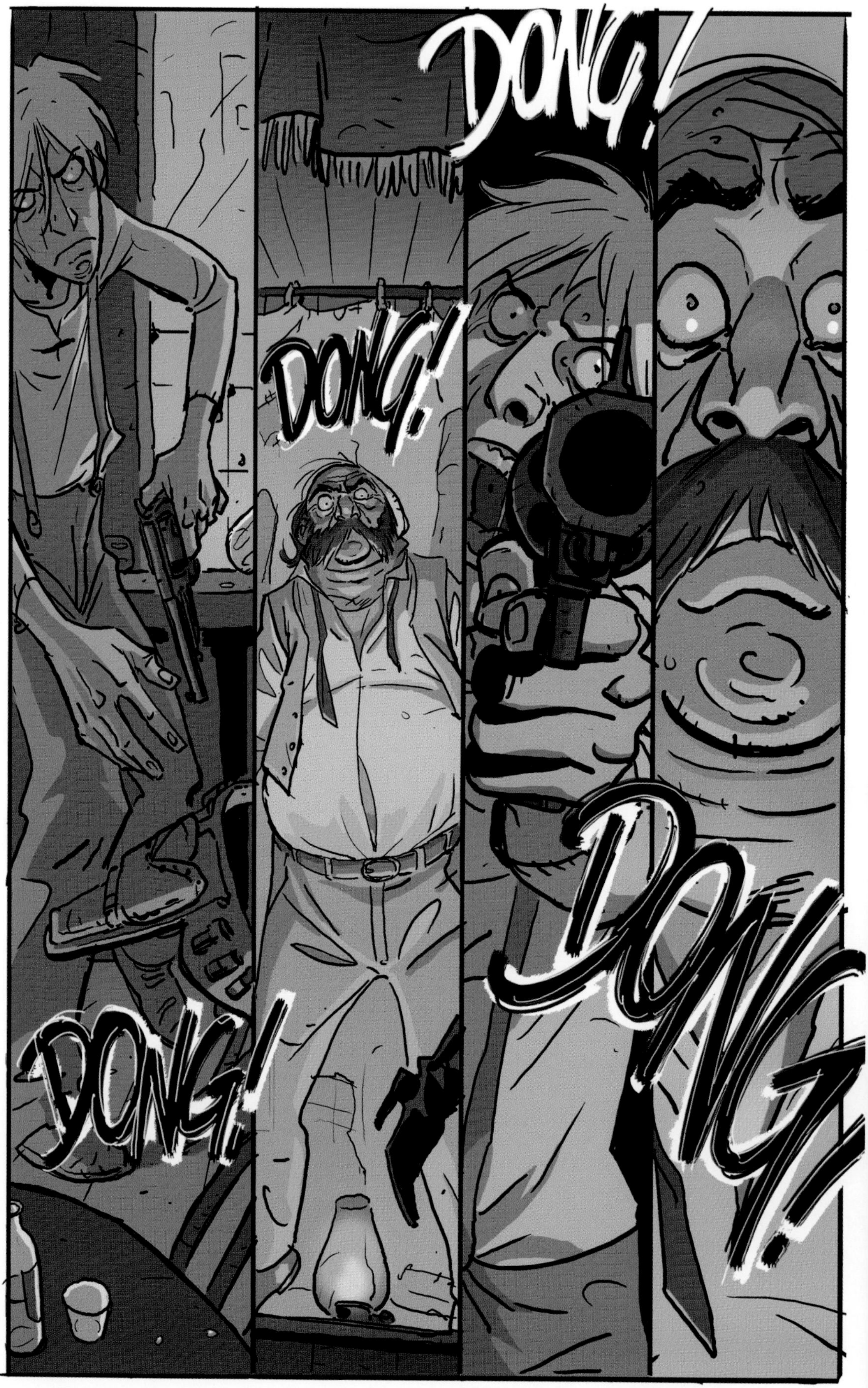
DONG!
DONG!
DONG!
DONG!
DONG!

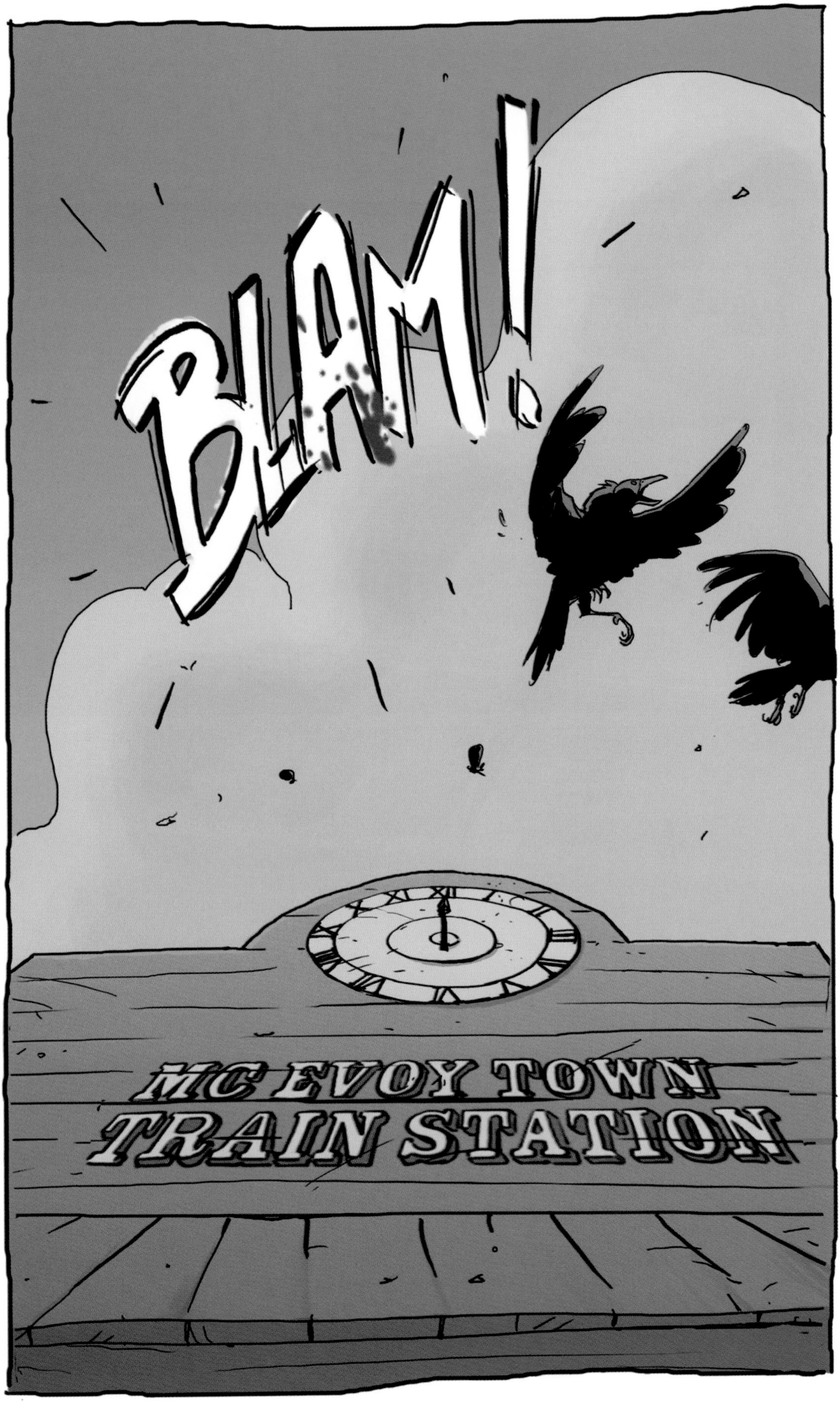
BLAM!
MC EVOY TOWN
TRAIN STATION

epitaph

by Phil Craven

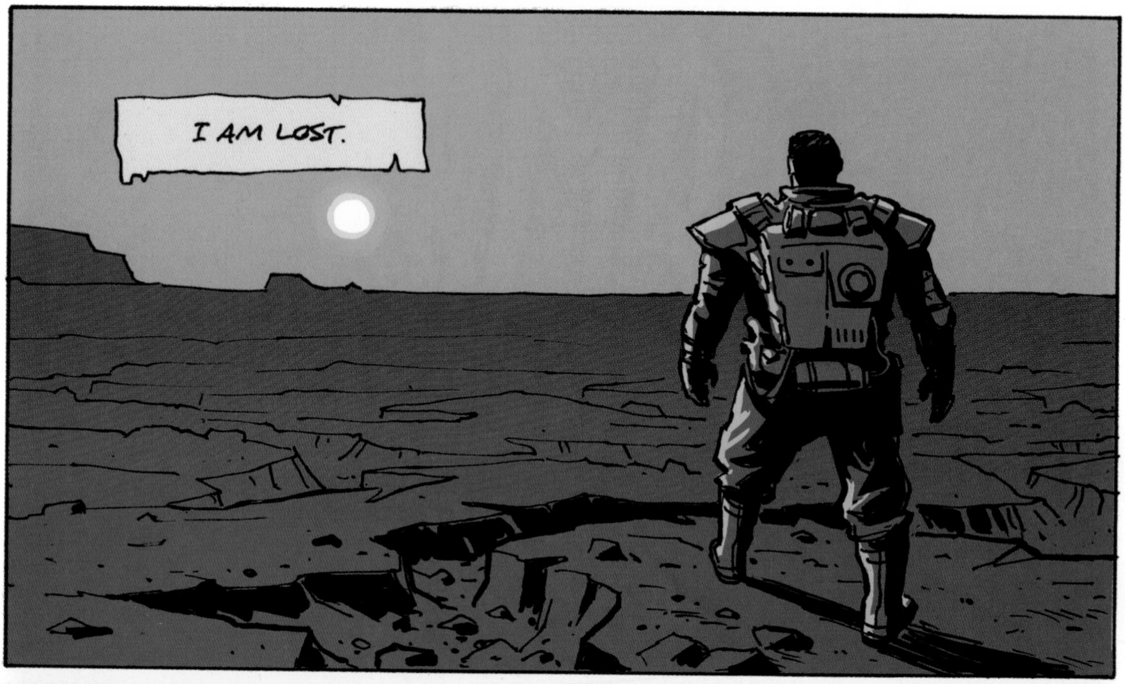
I AM LOST.

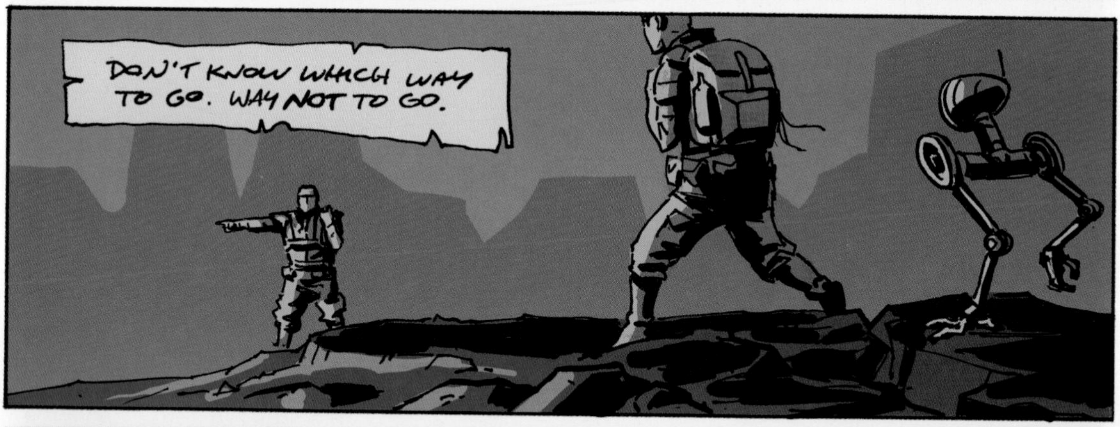
DON'T KNOW WHICH WAY TO GO. WAY NOT TO GO.

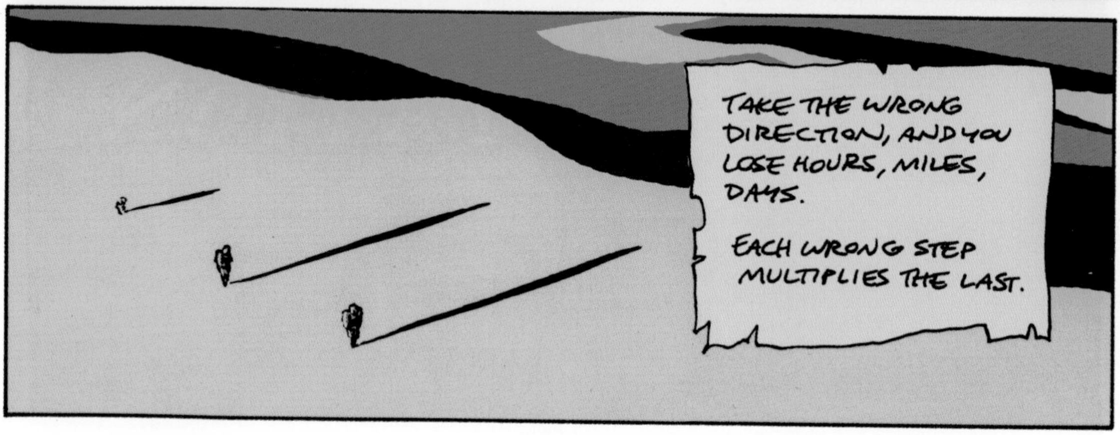
TAKE THE WRONG DIRECTION, AND YOU LOSE HOURS, MILES, DAYS.
EACH WRONG STEP MULTIPLIES THE LAST.

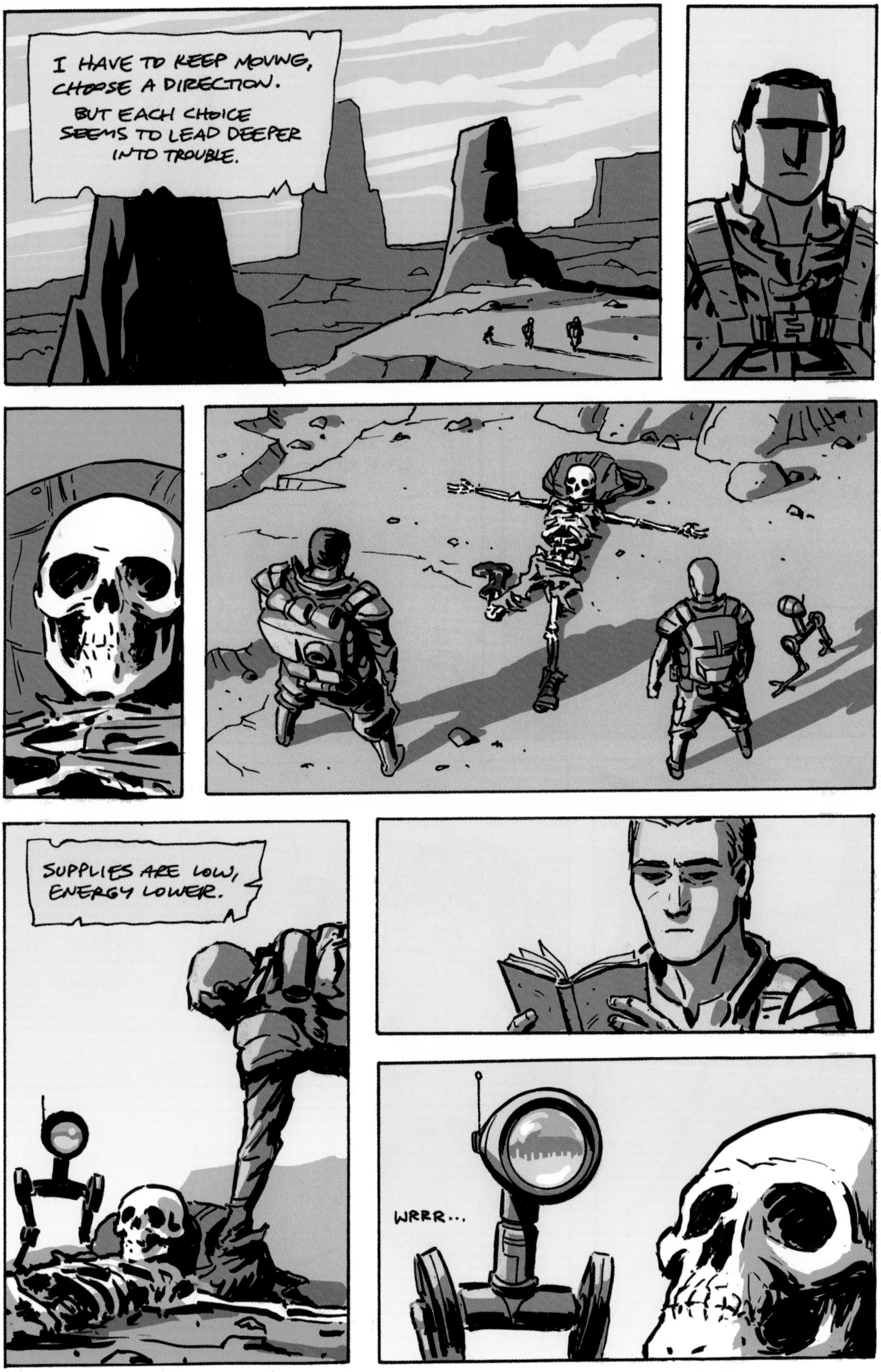
I HAVE TO KEEP MOVING, CHOOSE A DIRECTION.
BUT EACH CHOICE SEEMS TO LEAD DEEPER INTO TROUBLE.
SUPPLIES ARE LOW, ENERGY LOWER.
WRRR...

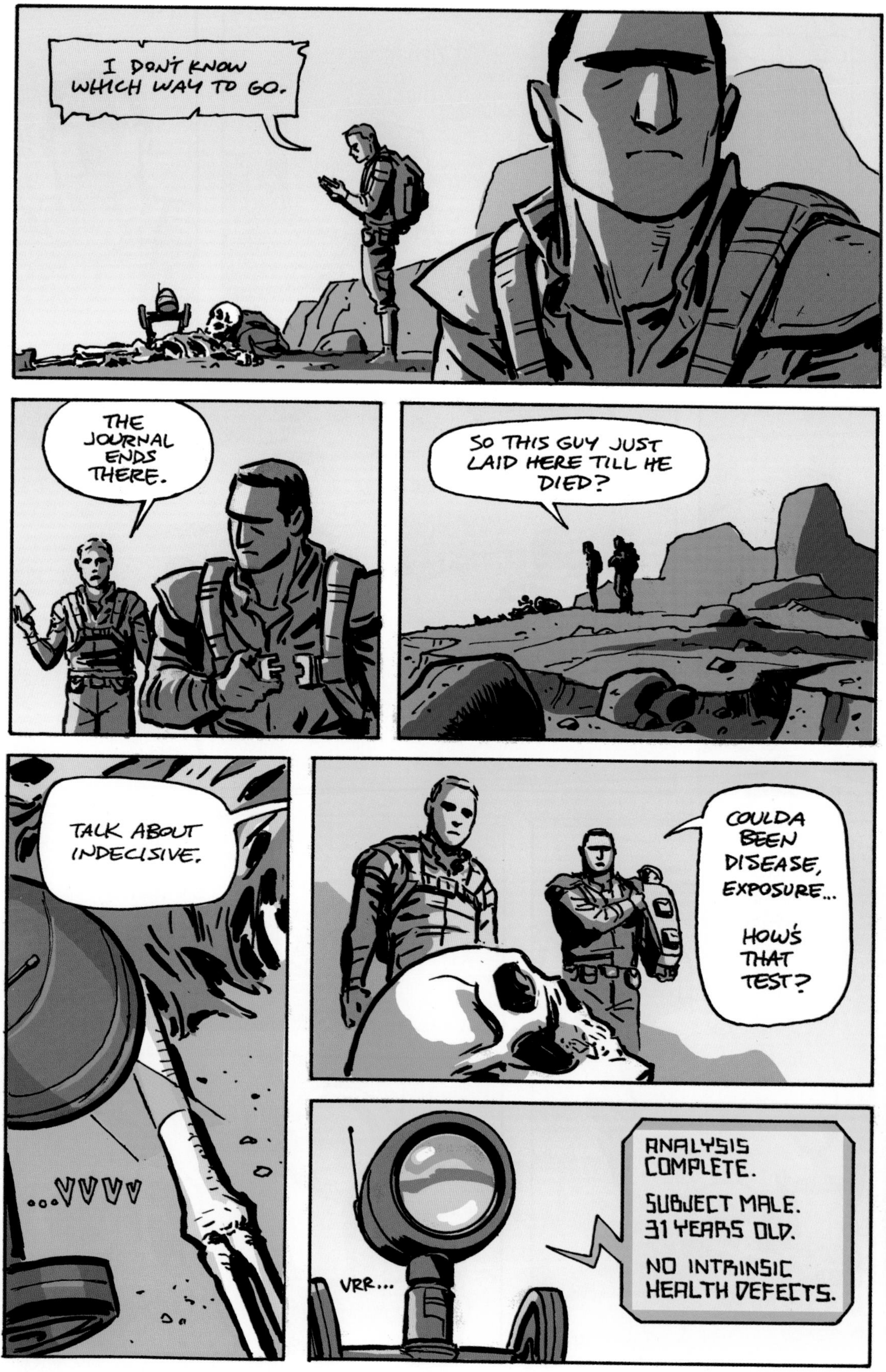
I DON'T KNOW WHICH WAY TO GO.
THE JOURNAL ENDS THERE.
SO THIS GUY JUST LAID HERE TILL HE DIED?
TALK ABOUT INDECISIVE.
...VVVV
COULDA BEEN DISEASE, EXPOSURE...
HOW'S THAT TEST?
VRR...
ANALYSIS COMPLETE.
SUBJECT MALE. 31 YEARS OLD.
NO INTRINSIC HEALTH DEFECTS.

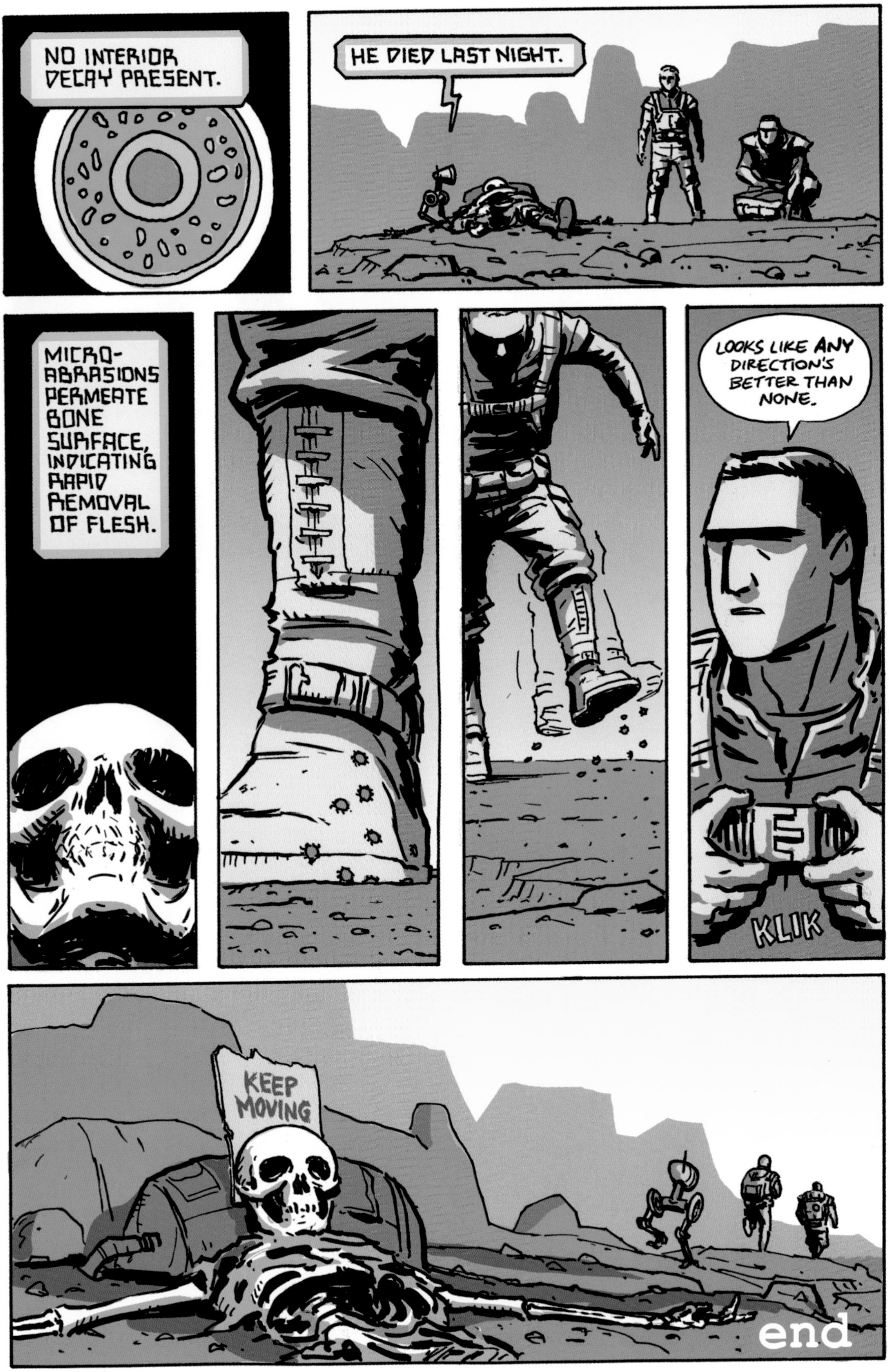
NO INTERIOR DECAY PRESENT.
HE DIED LAST NIGHT.
MICRO-ABRASIONS PERMEATE BONE SURFACE, INDICATING RAPID REMOVAL OF FLESH.
LOOKS LIKE ANY DIRECTION'S BETTER THAN NONE.
KLIK
KEEP MOVING
end

Walters

by Cory Godbey

On July 2, 1982, Larry Walters filled forty-five weather balloons with helium.

He tied the balloons to a lawn chair and rose three miles into the sky.

Larry traveled close to twenty miles before he crash-landed near the Los Angeles airport.

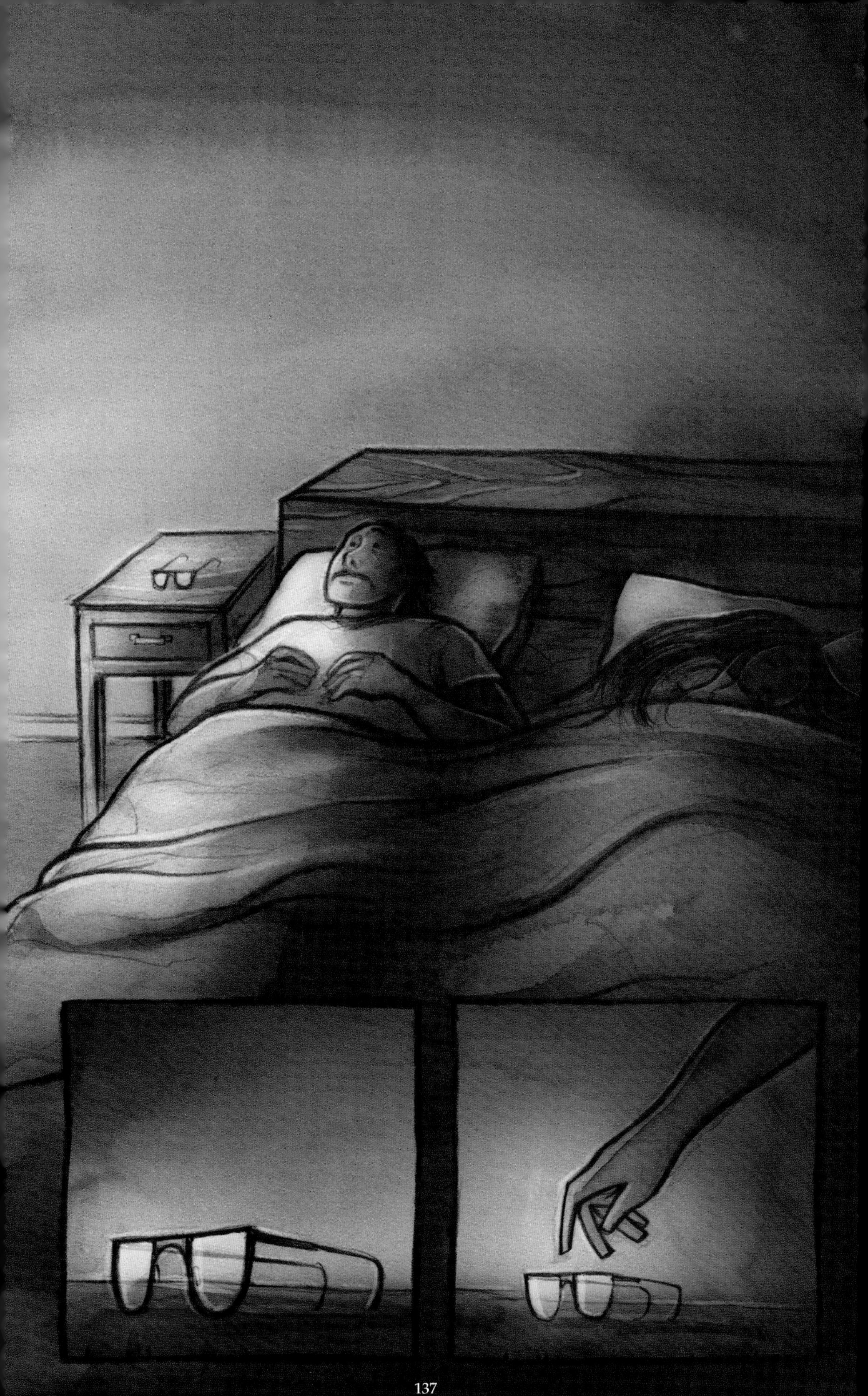

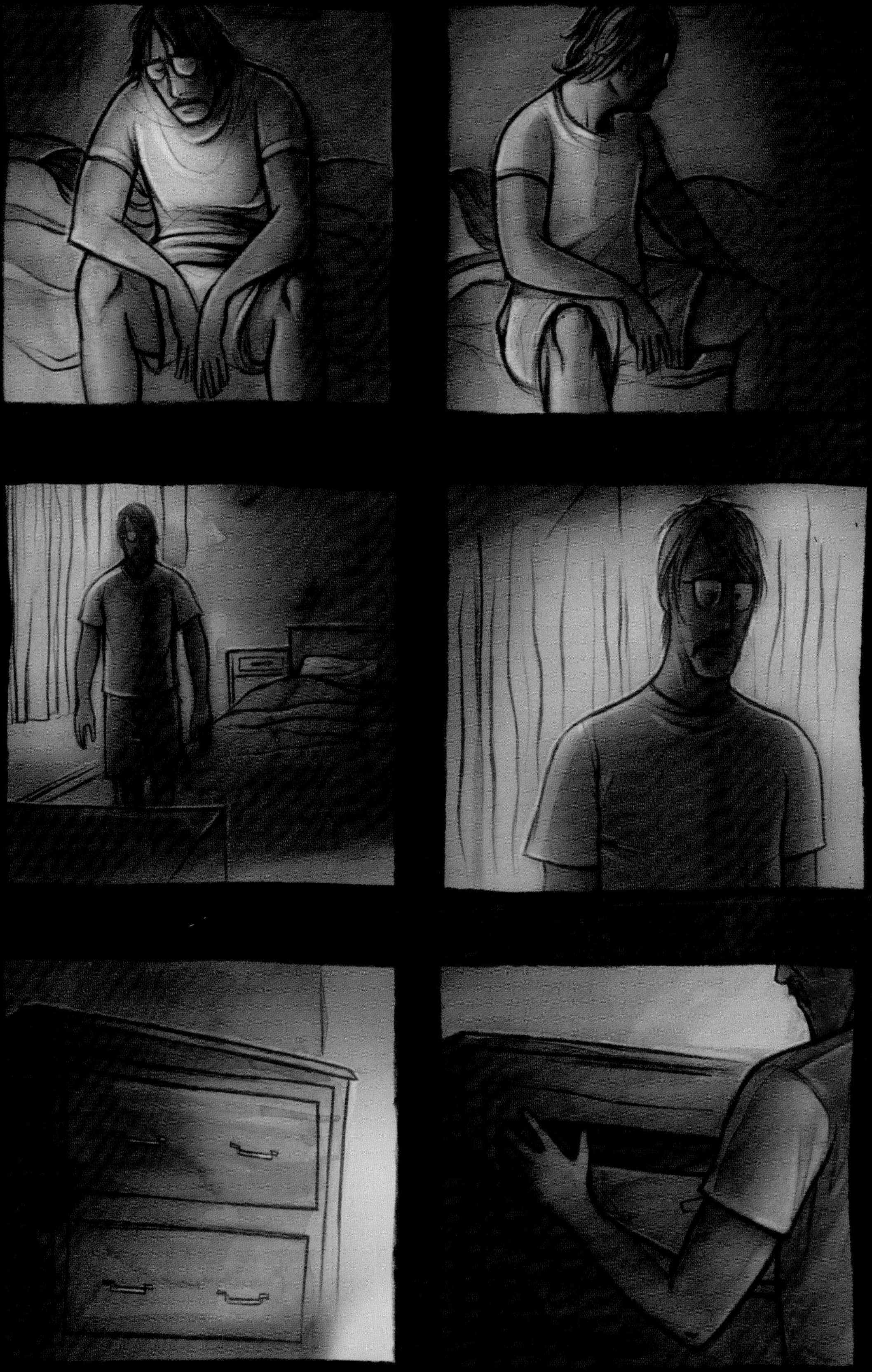

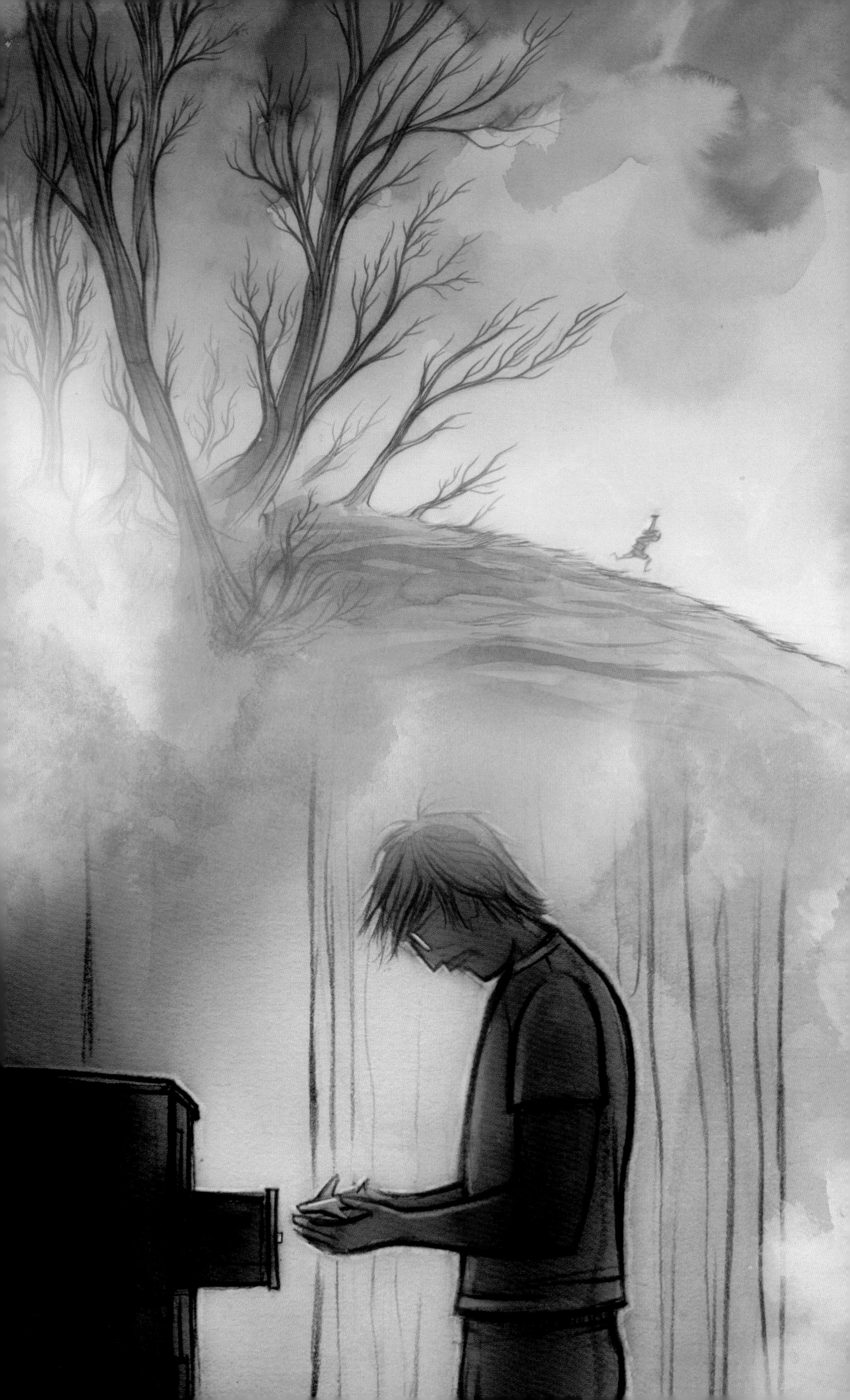

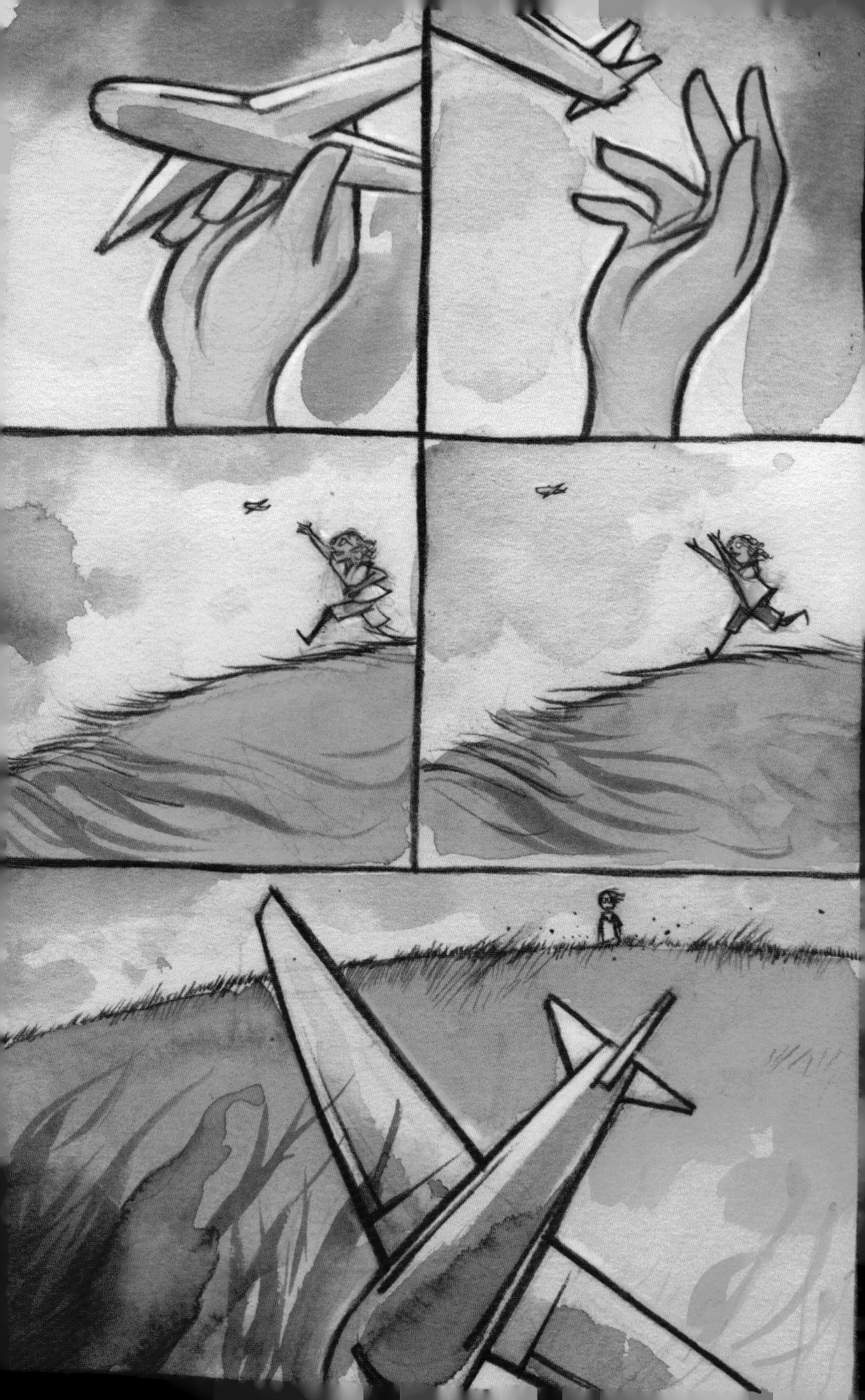

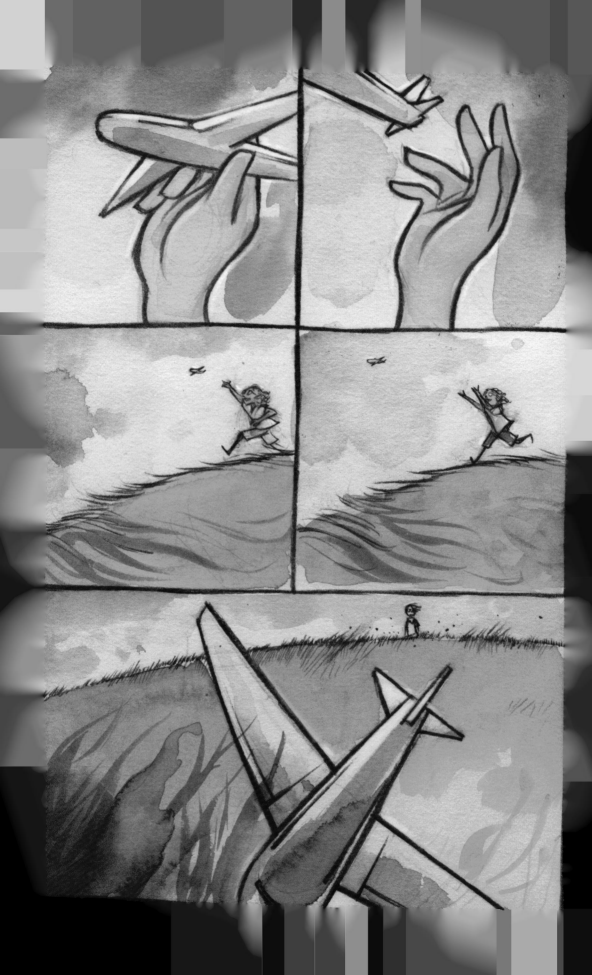

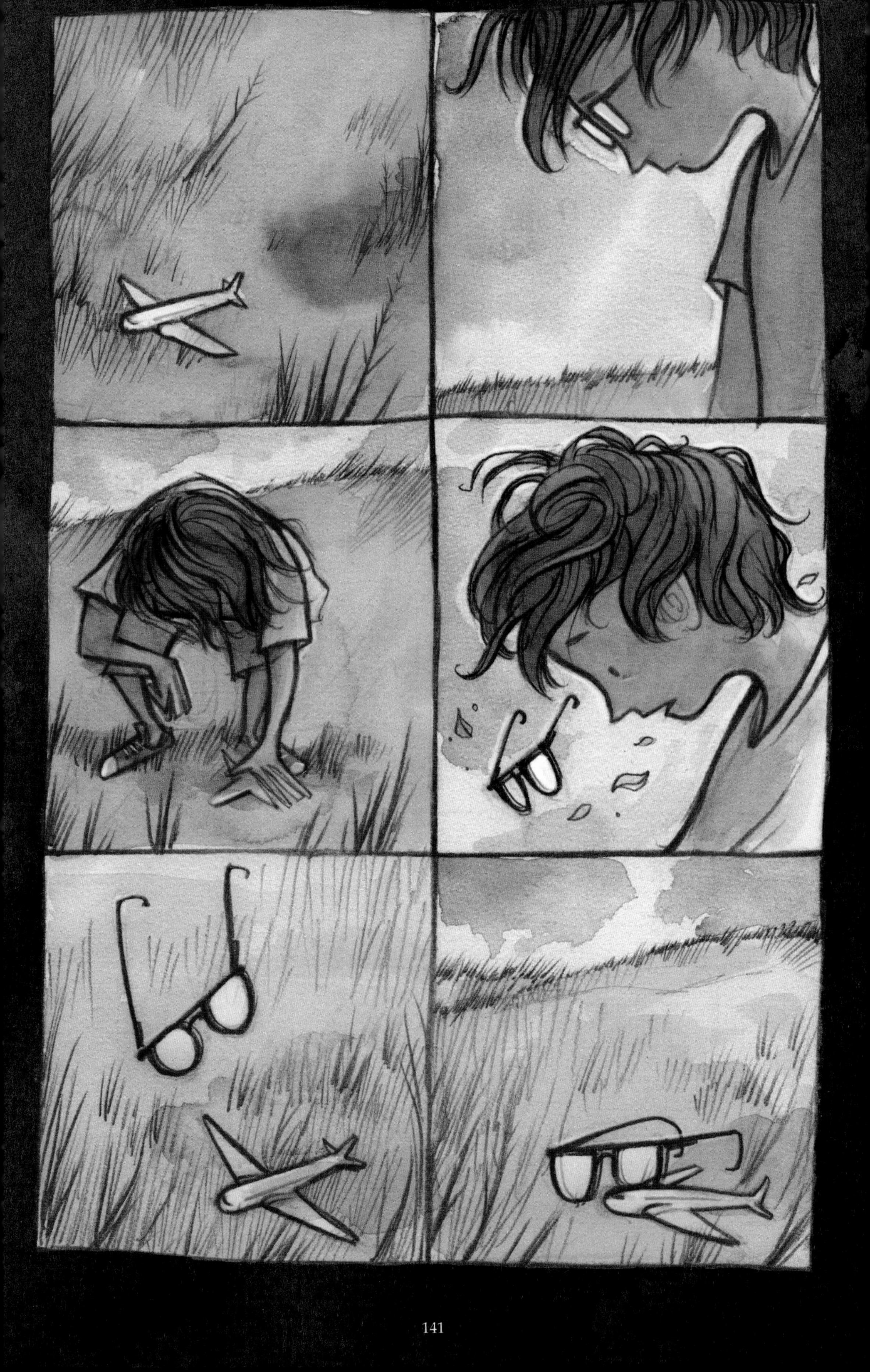

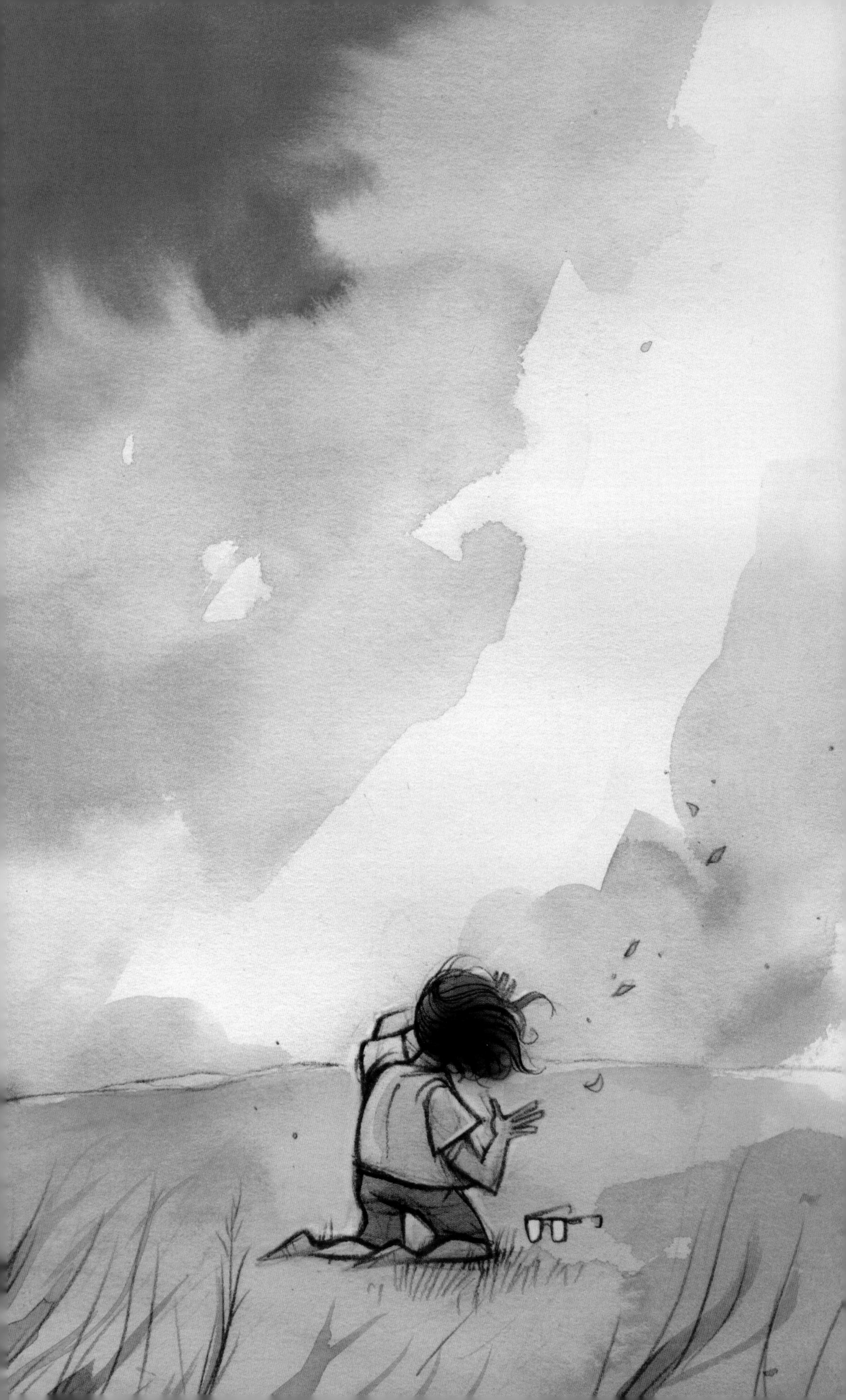

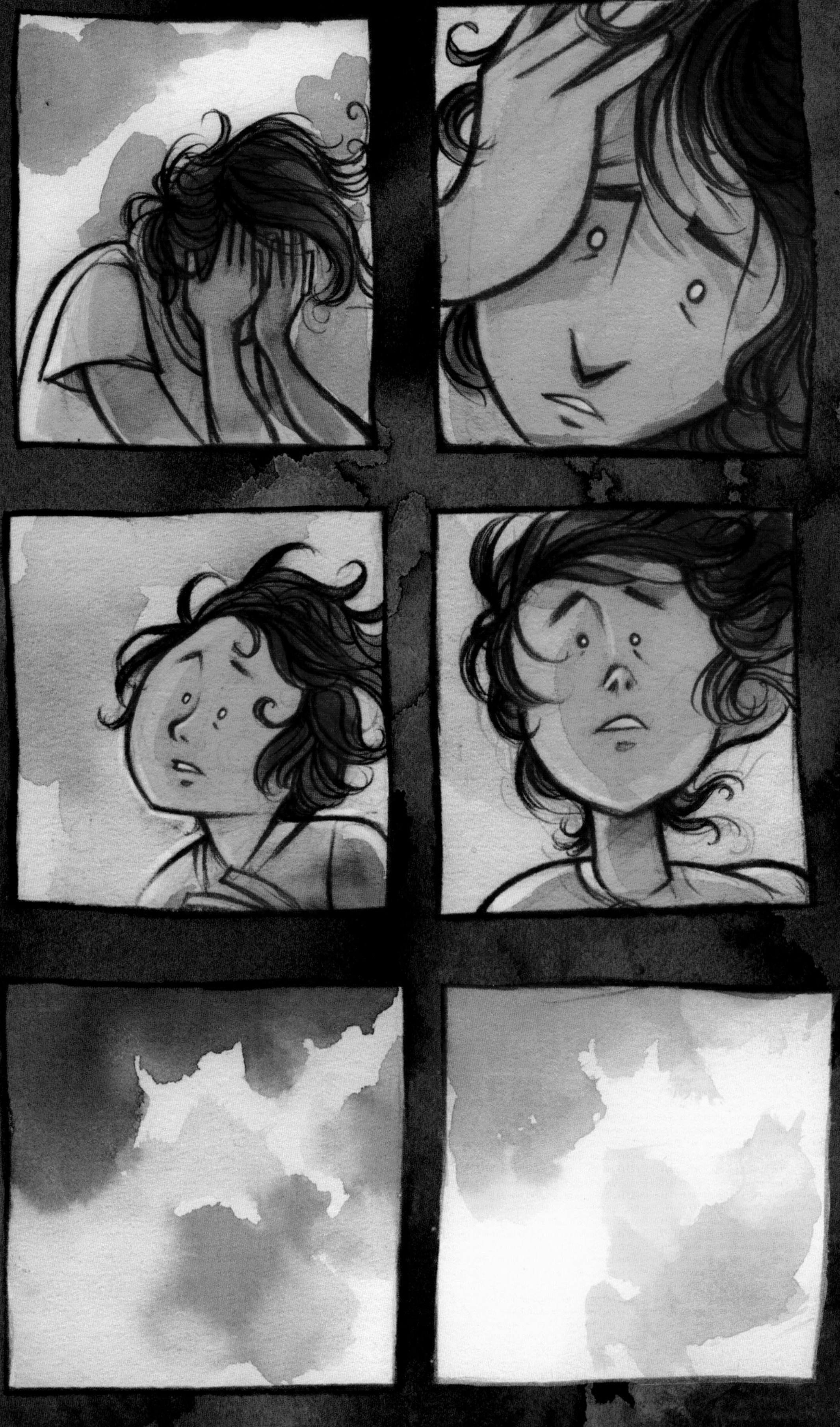

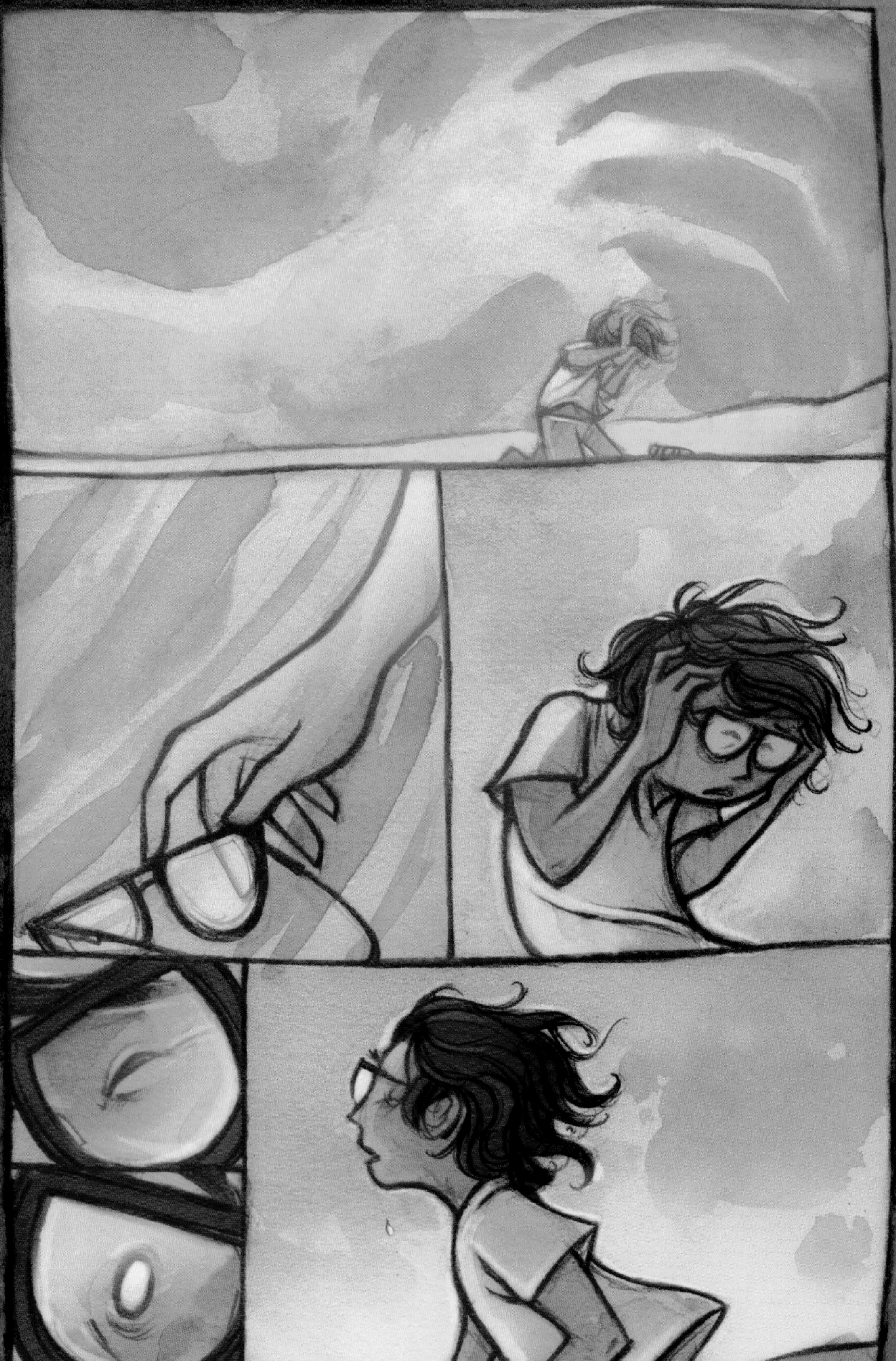

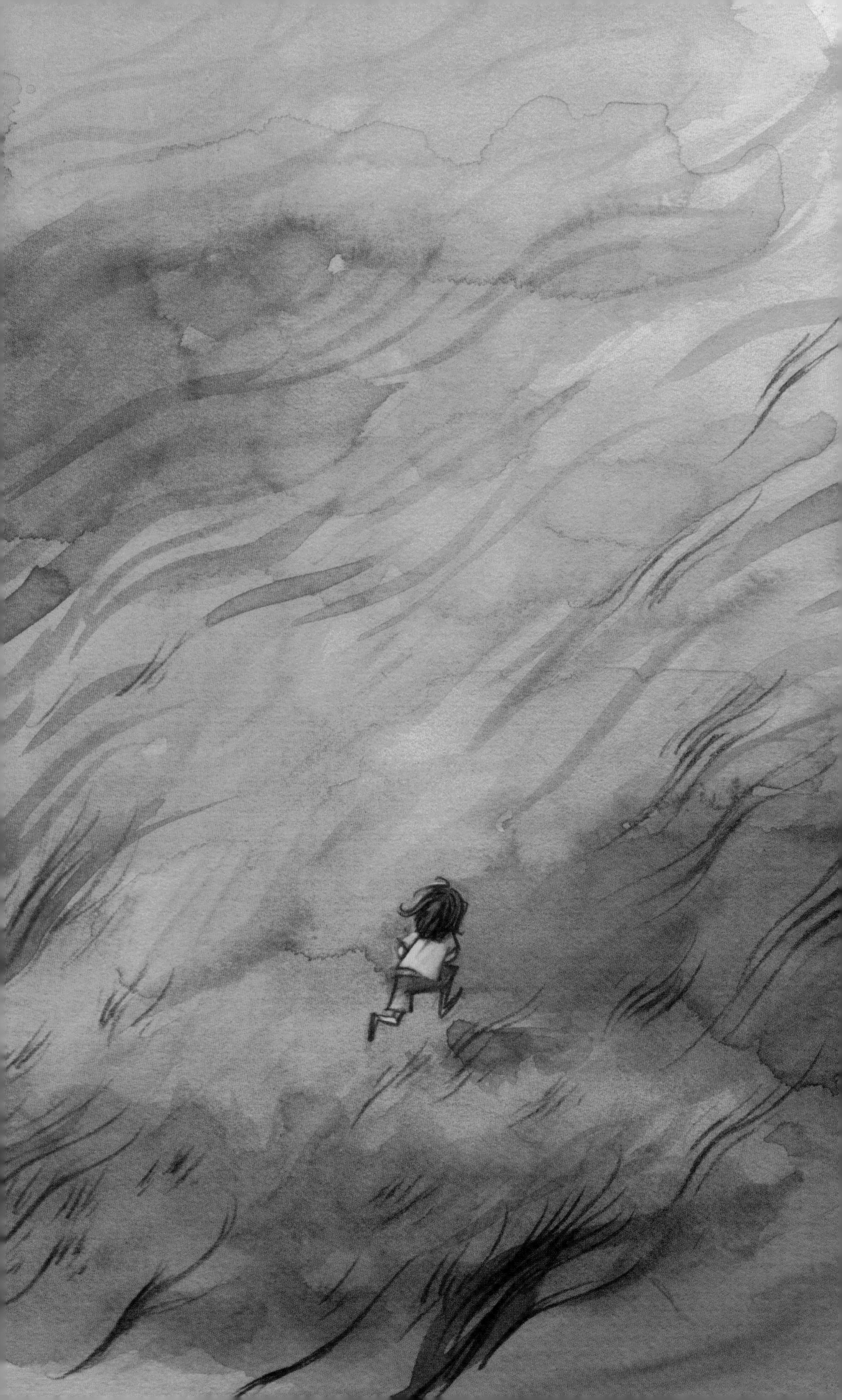

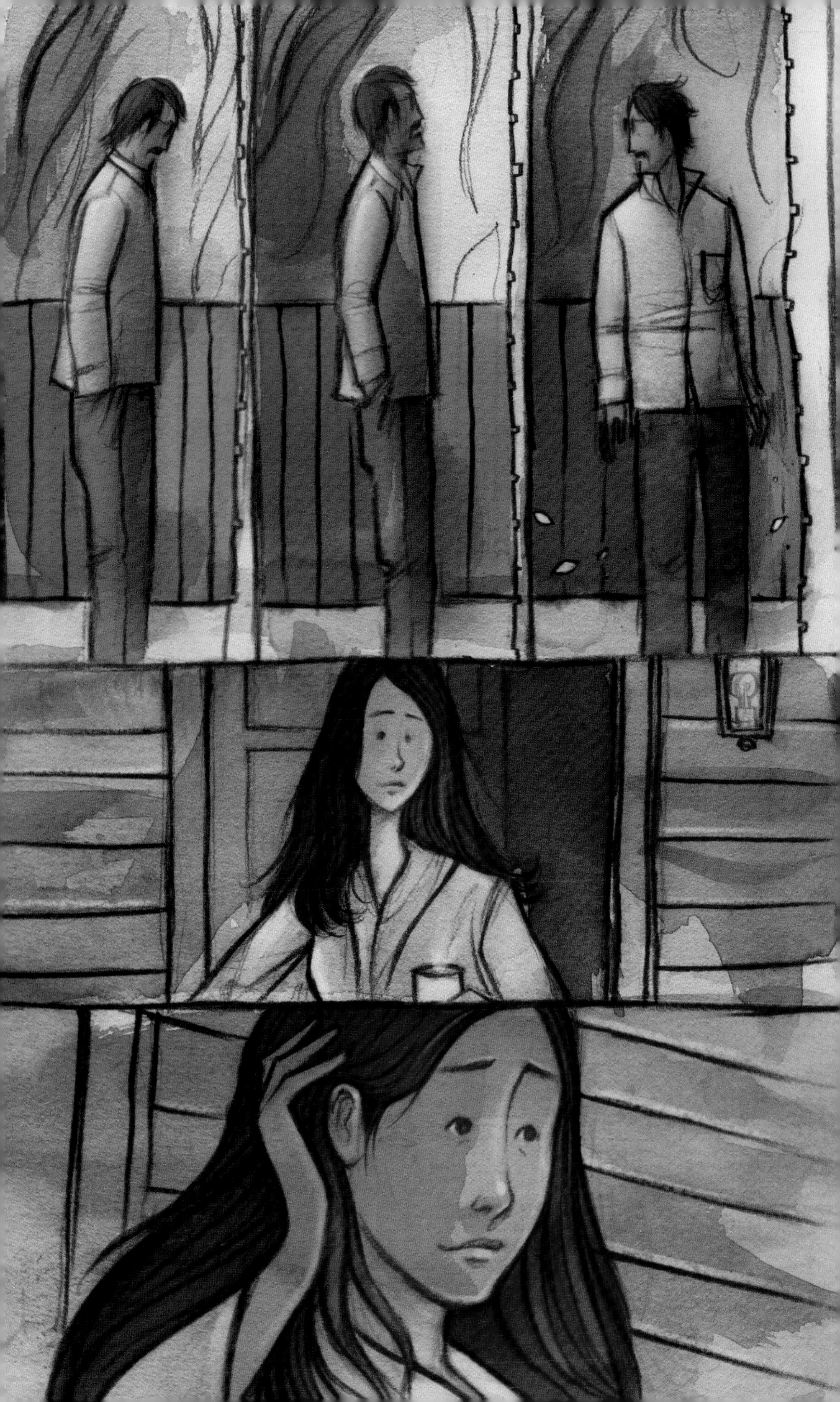

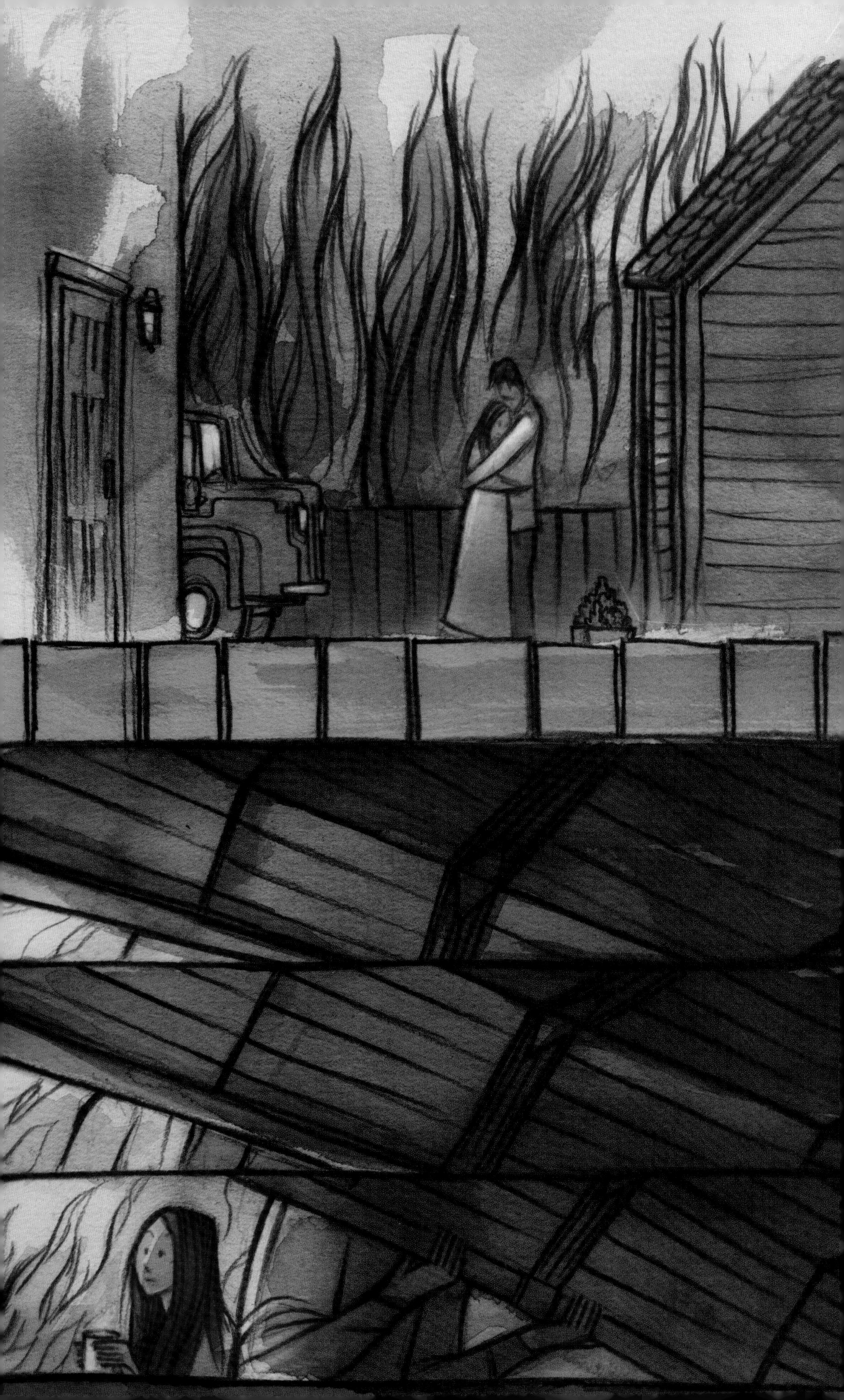

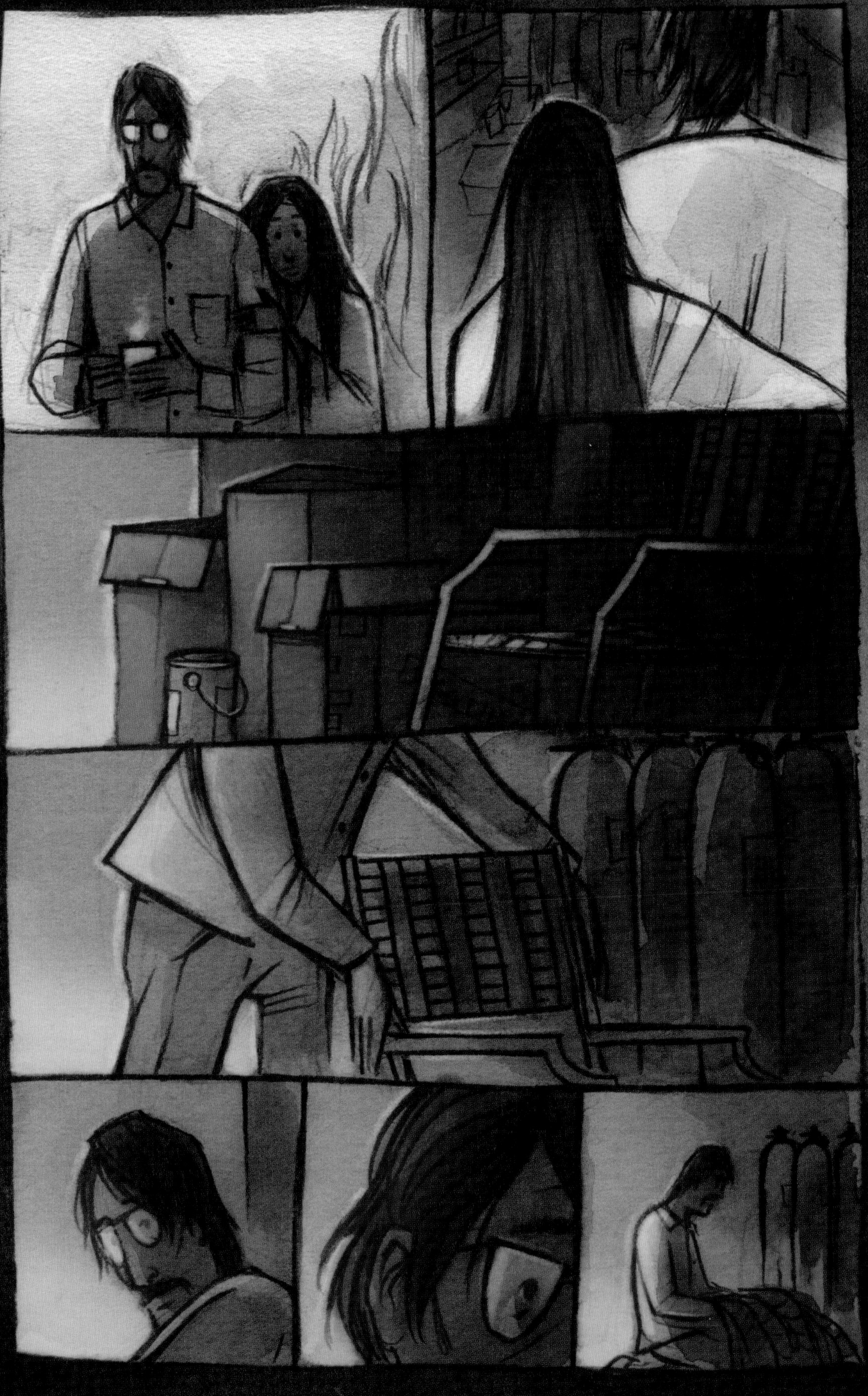

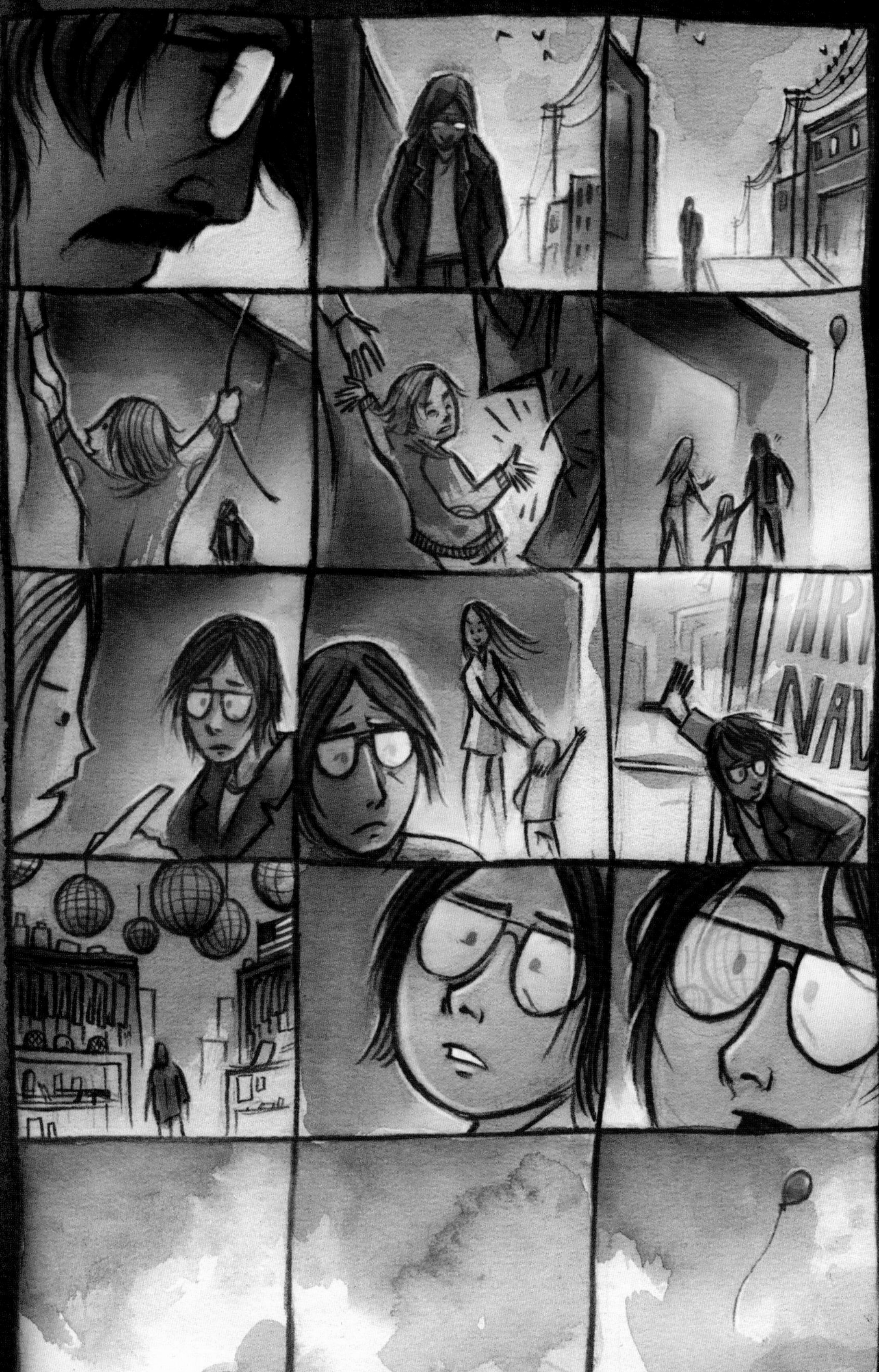

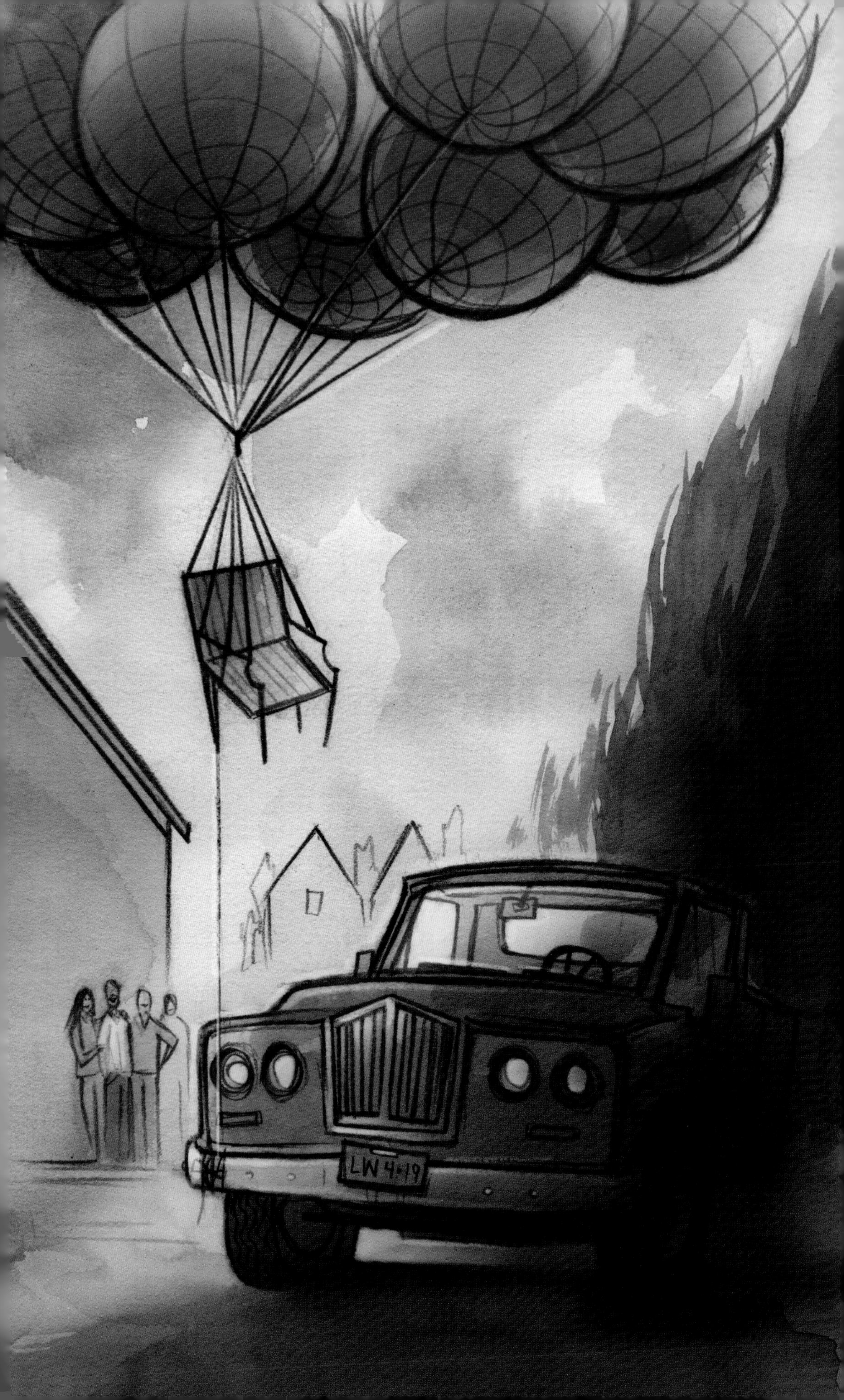
LW 4•19

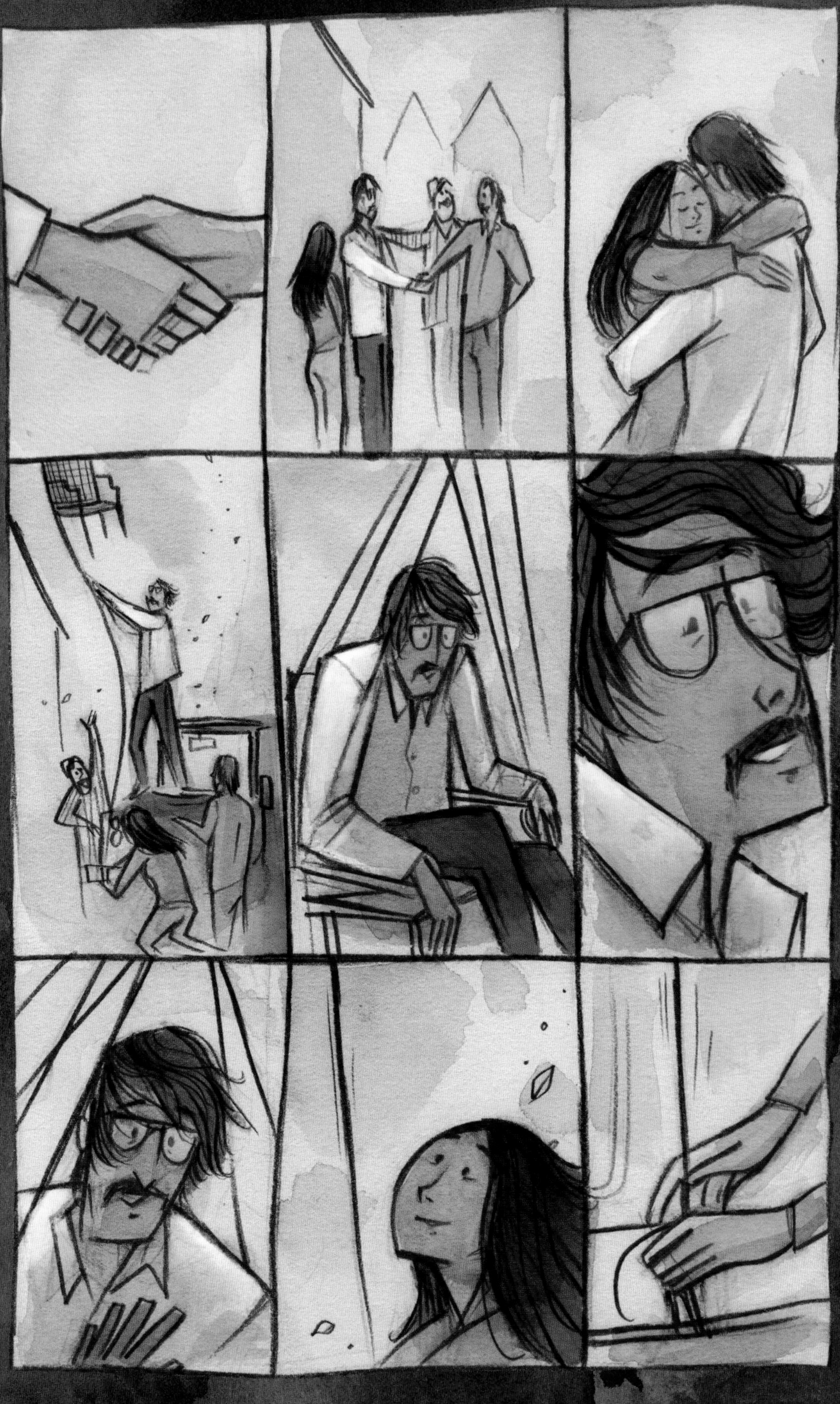

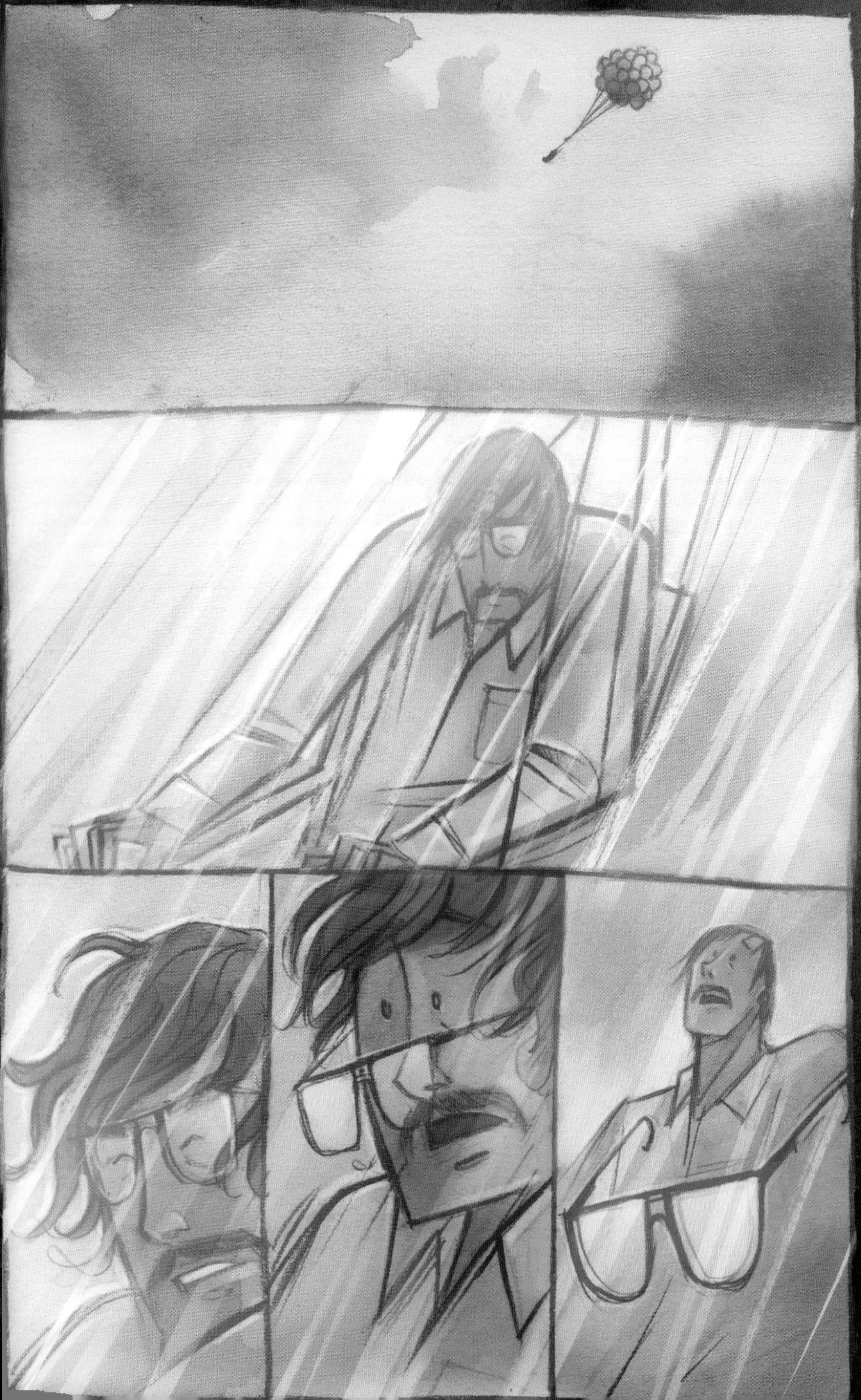

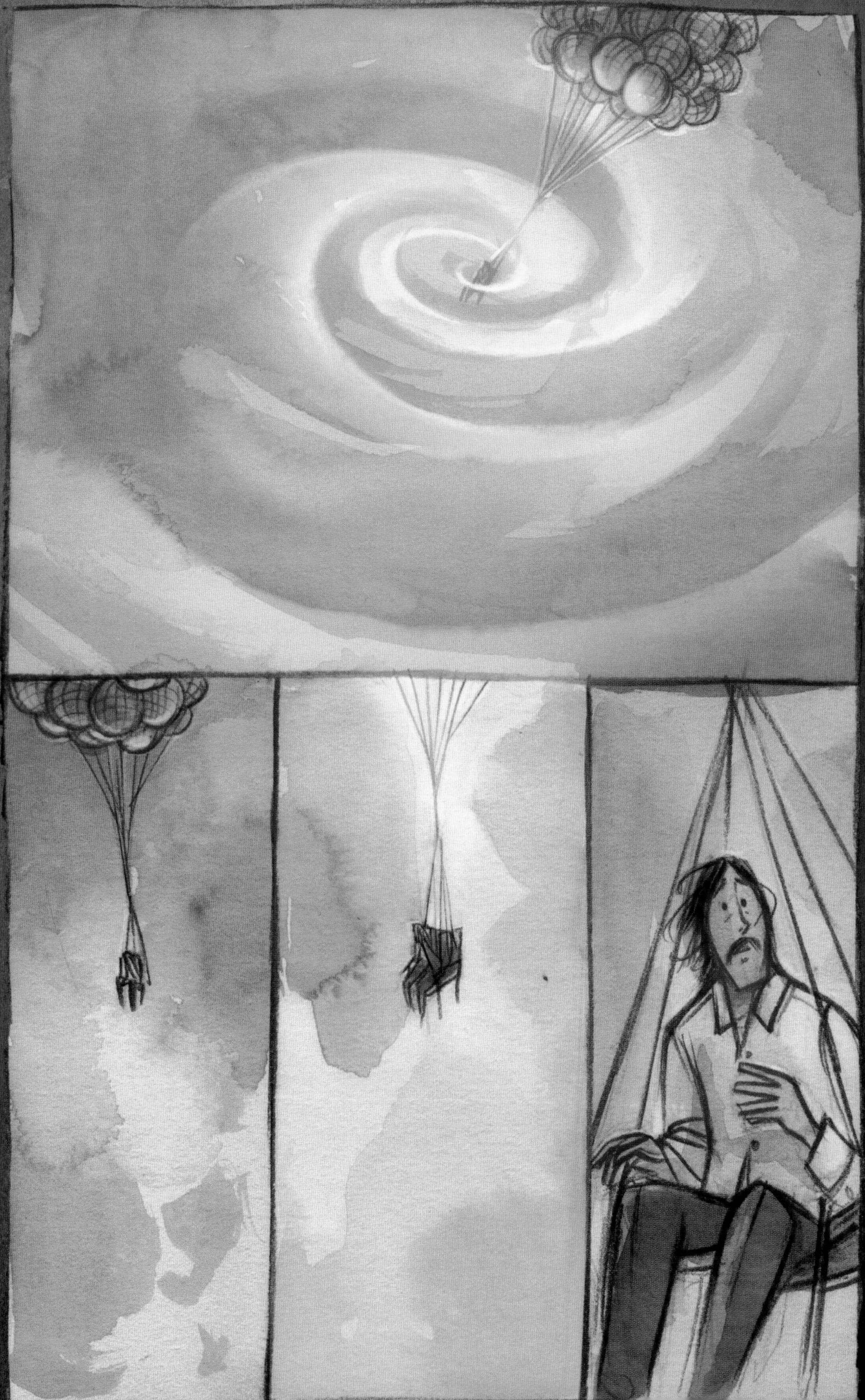

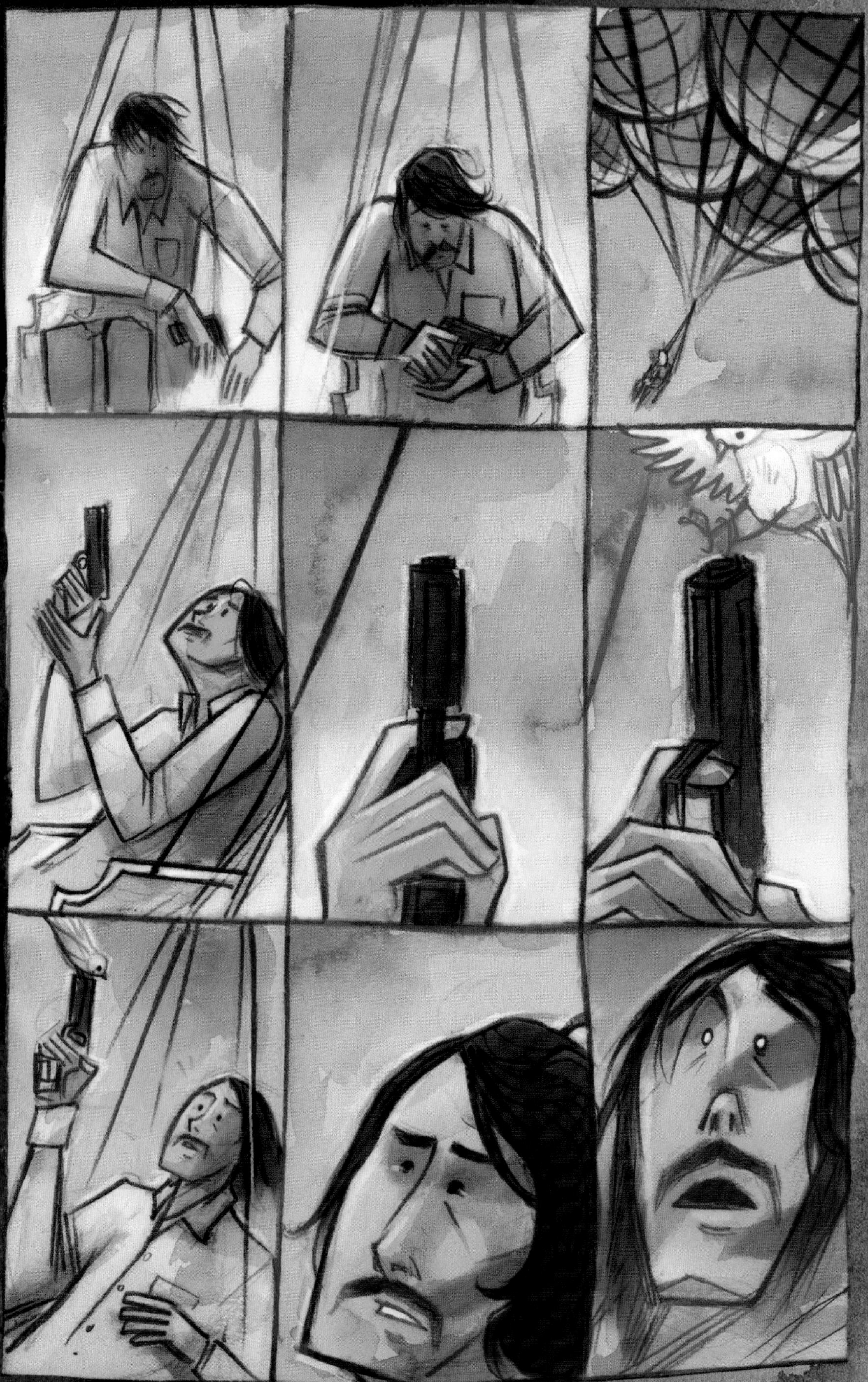

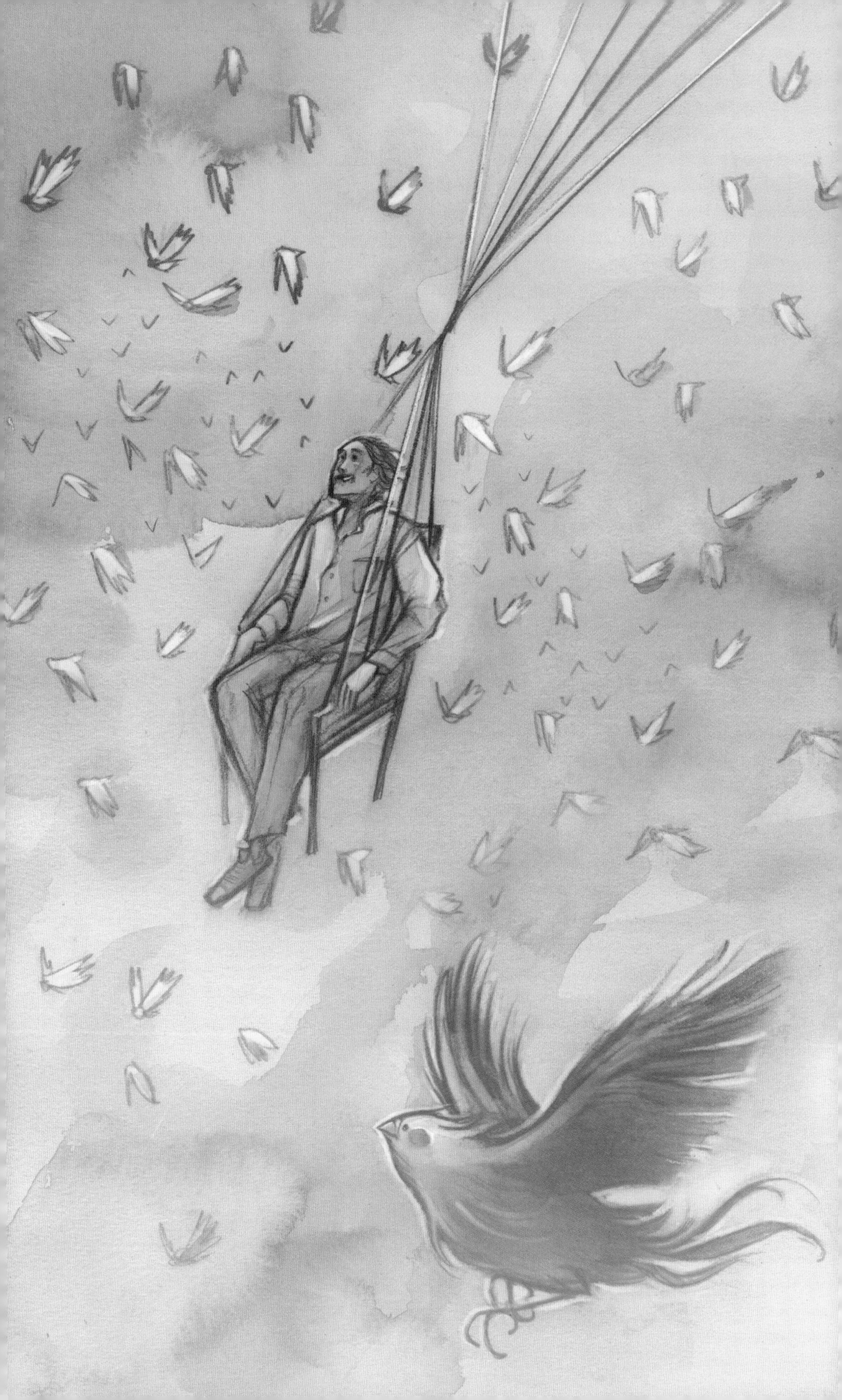

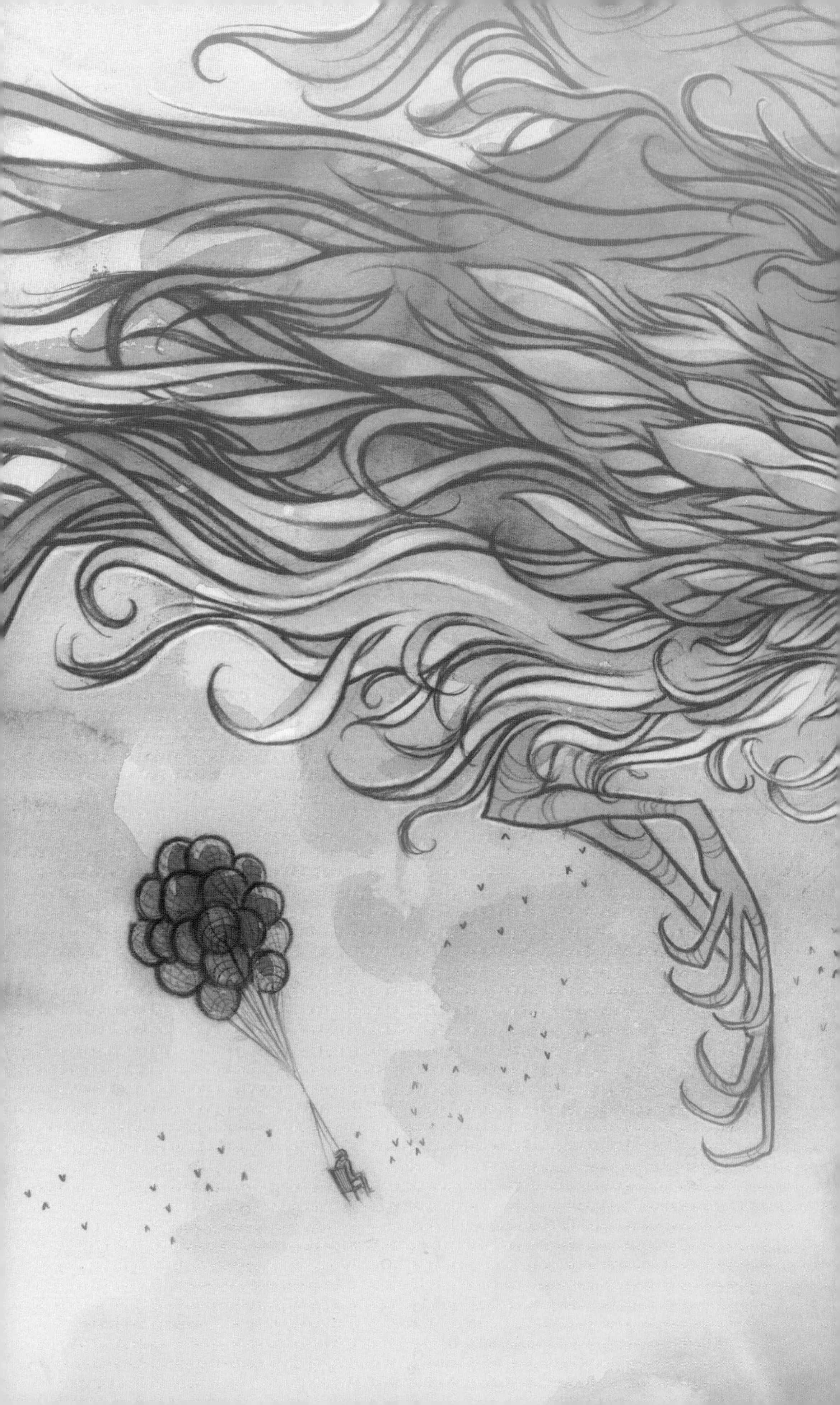

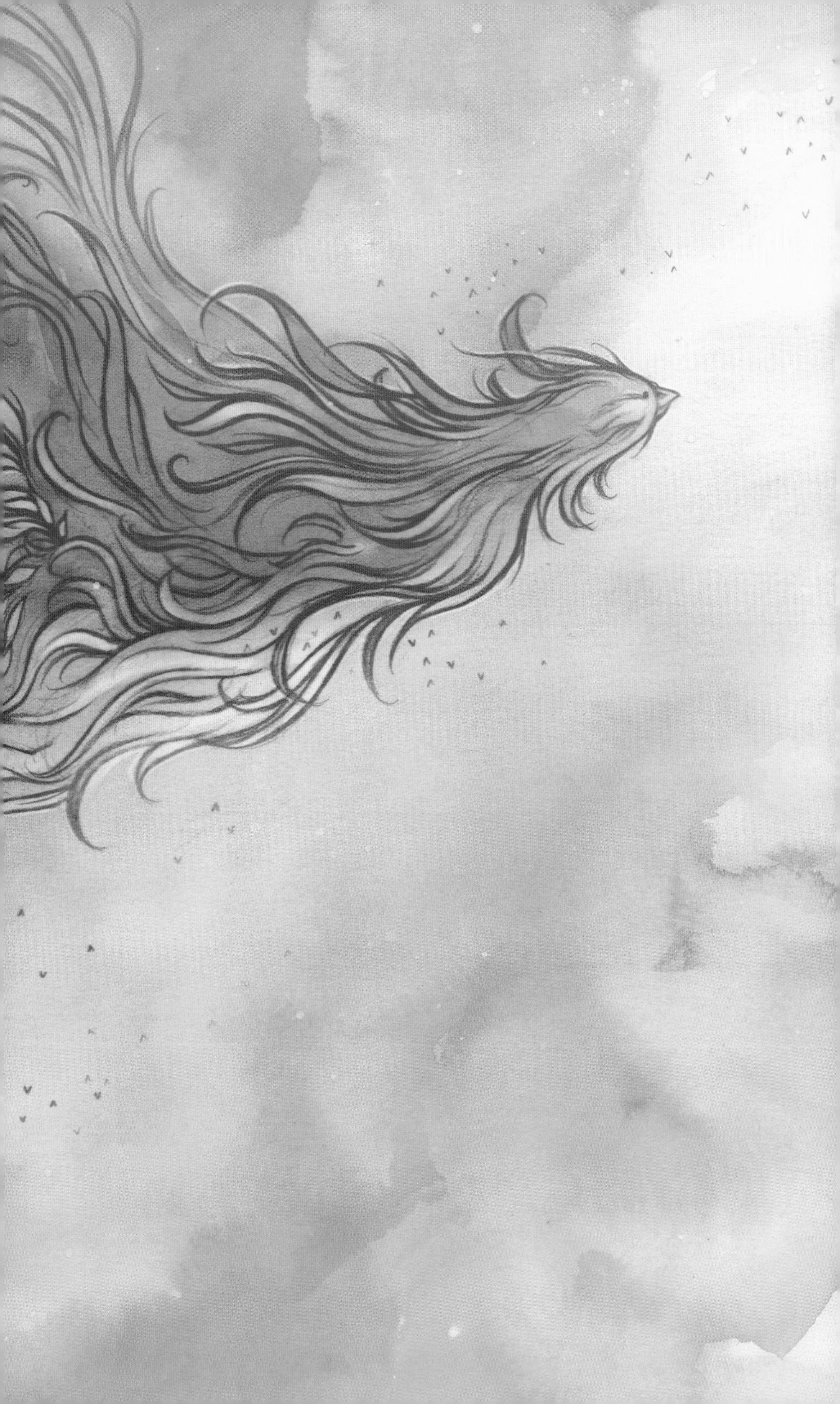

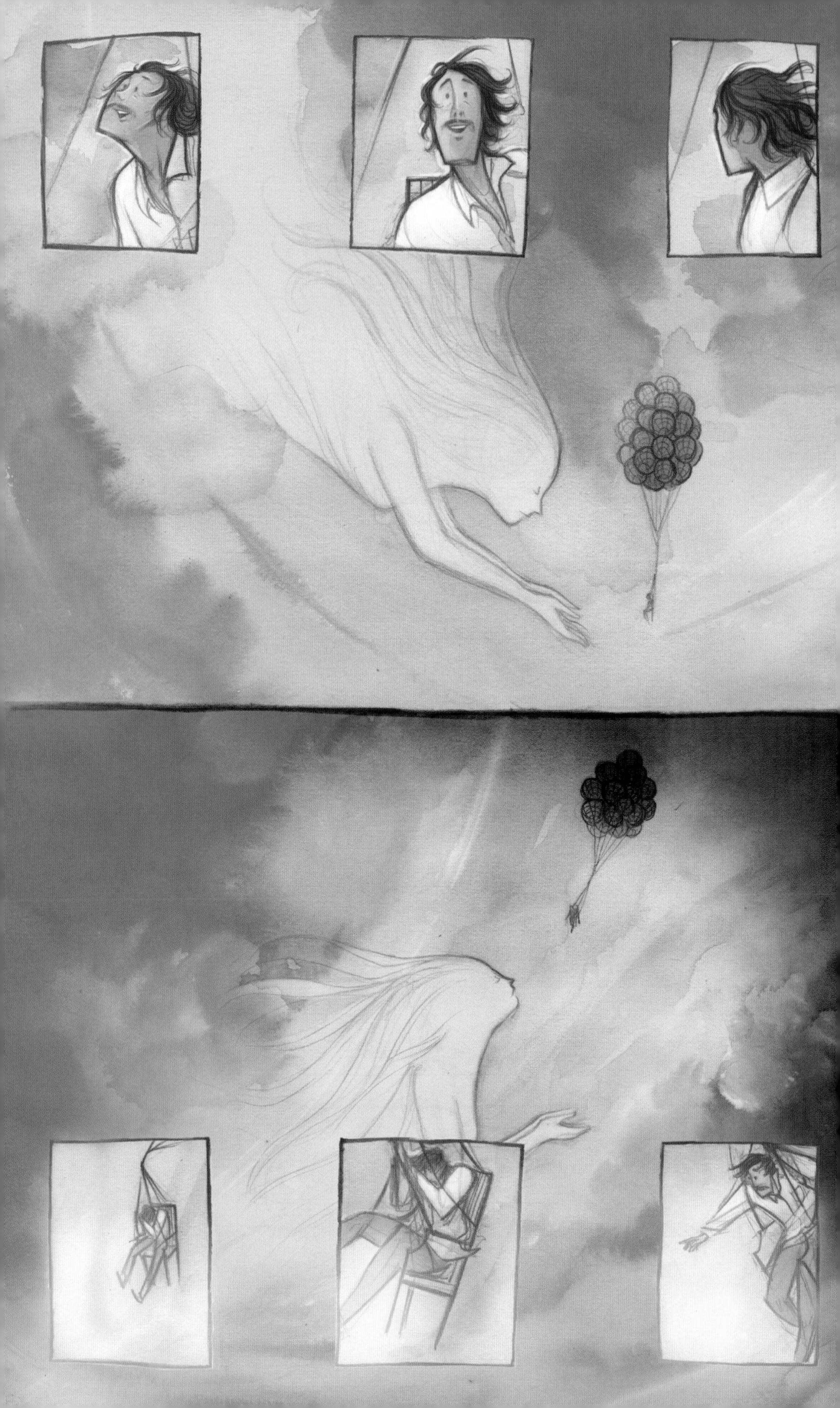

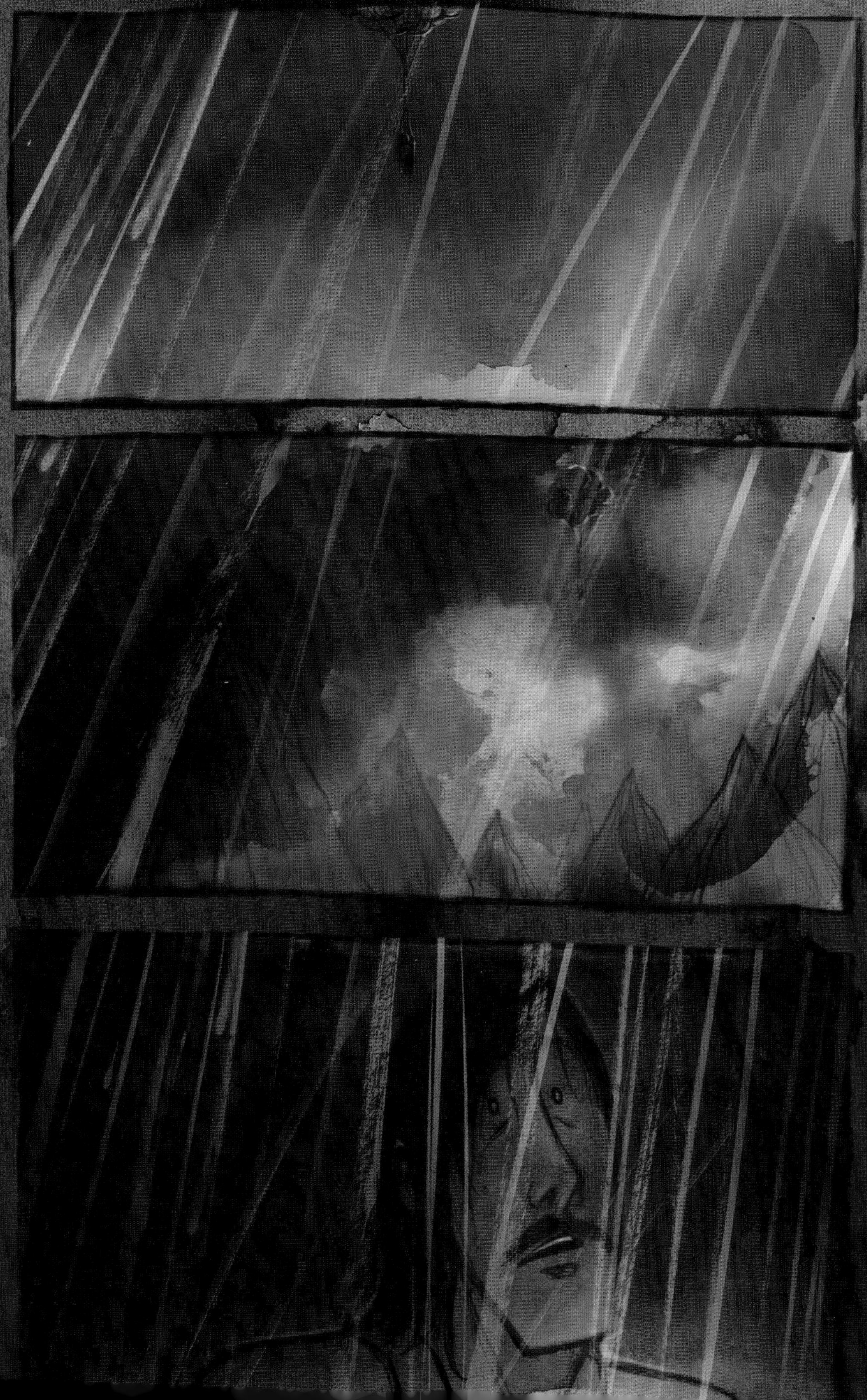

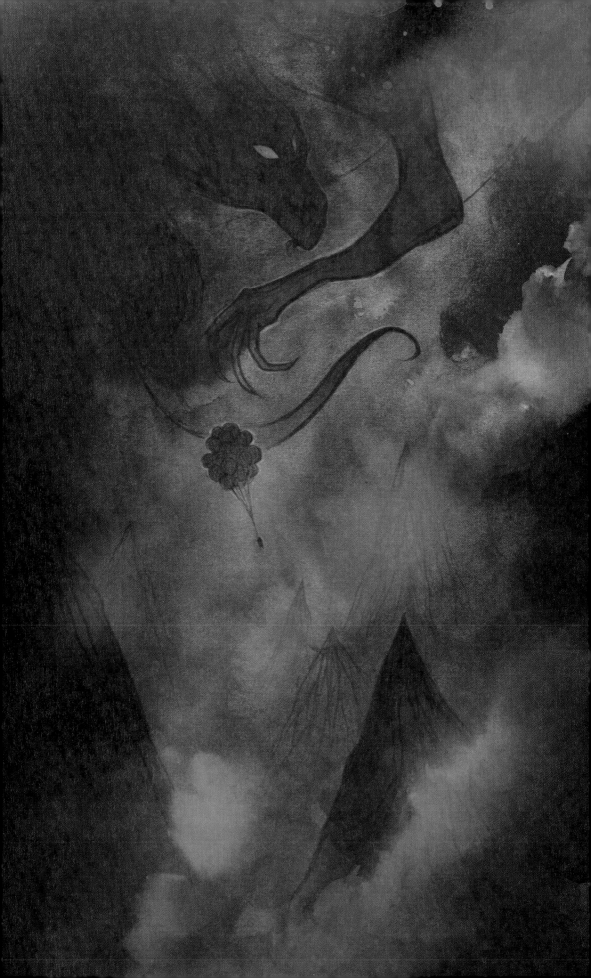

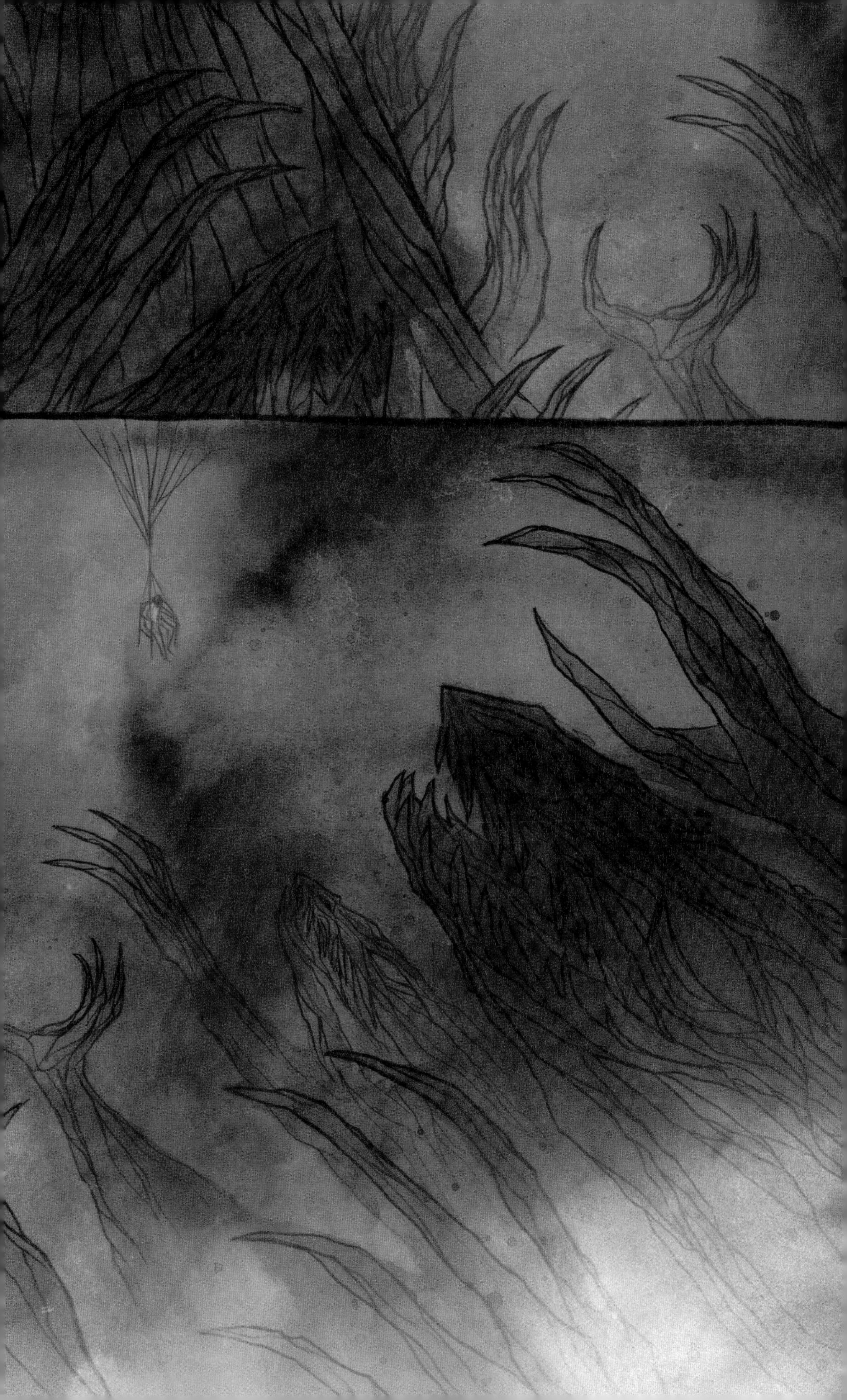

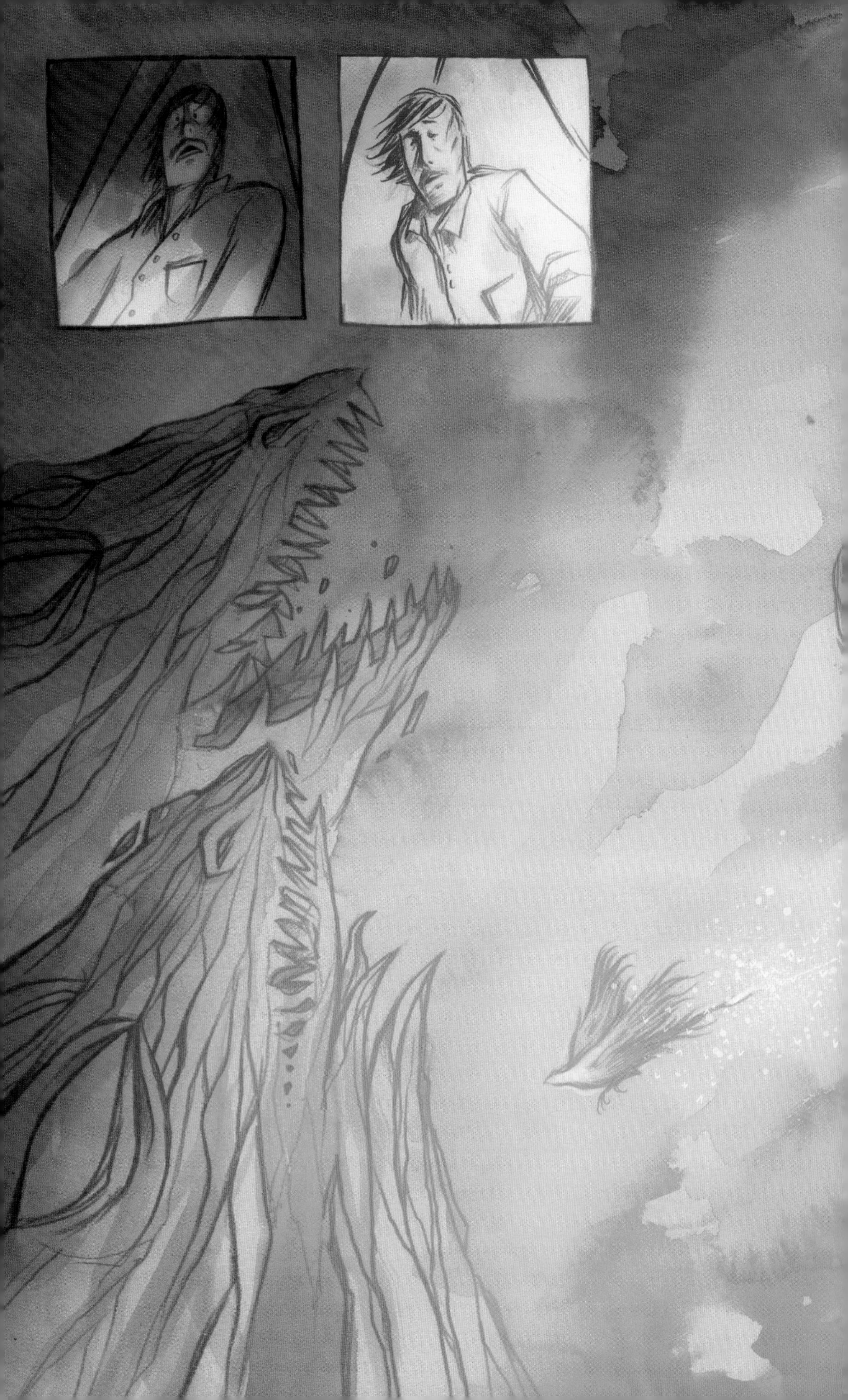

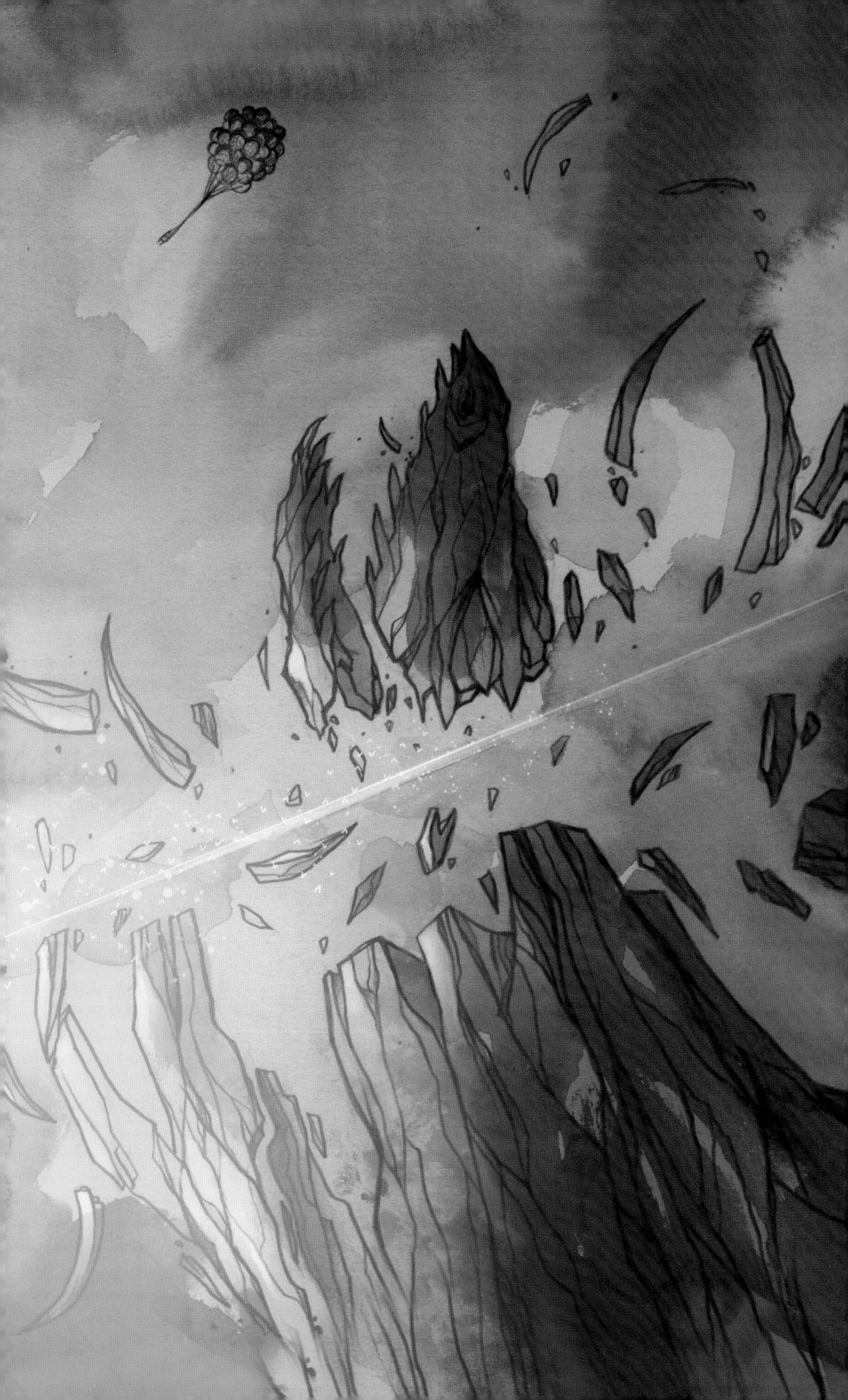

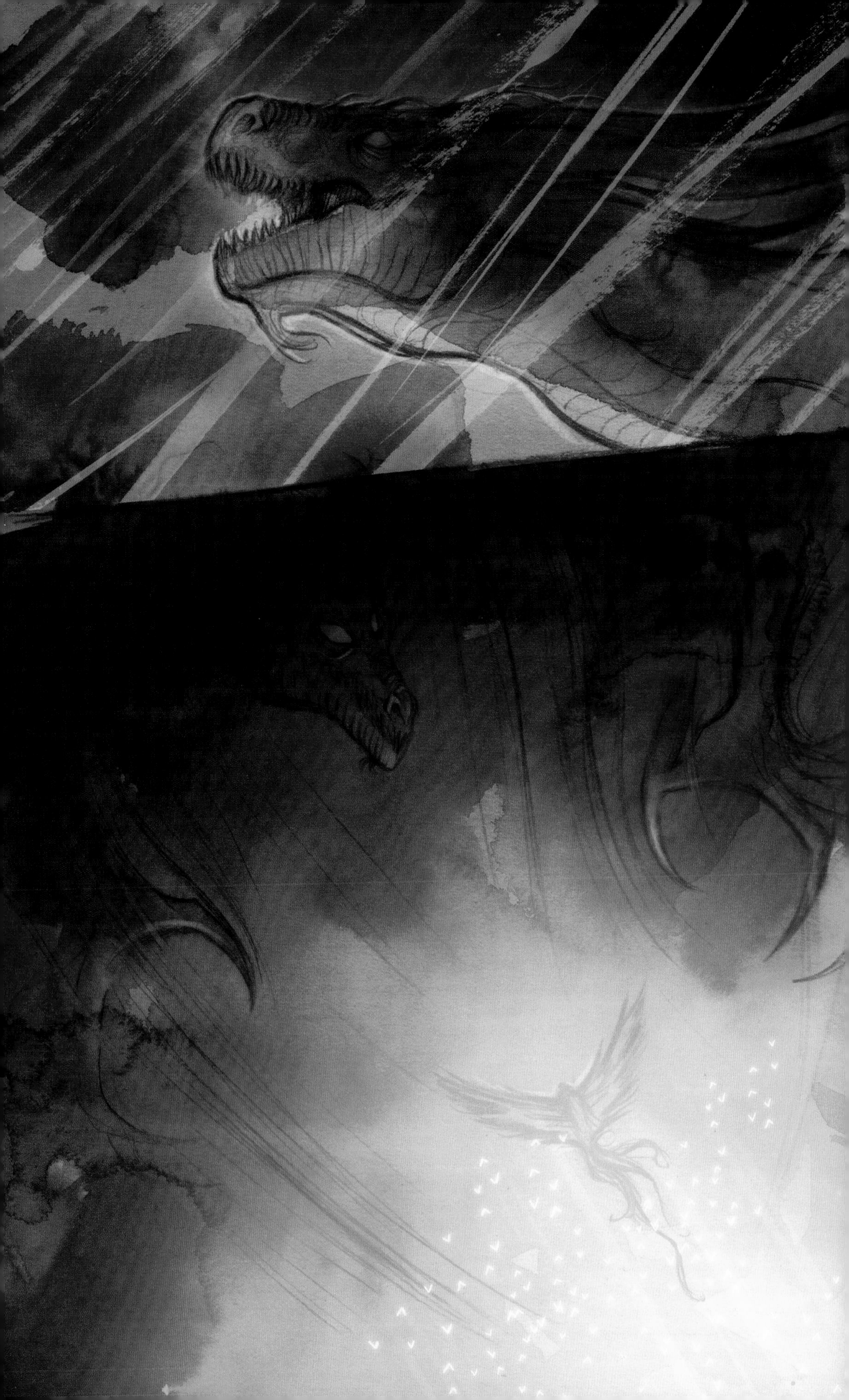

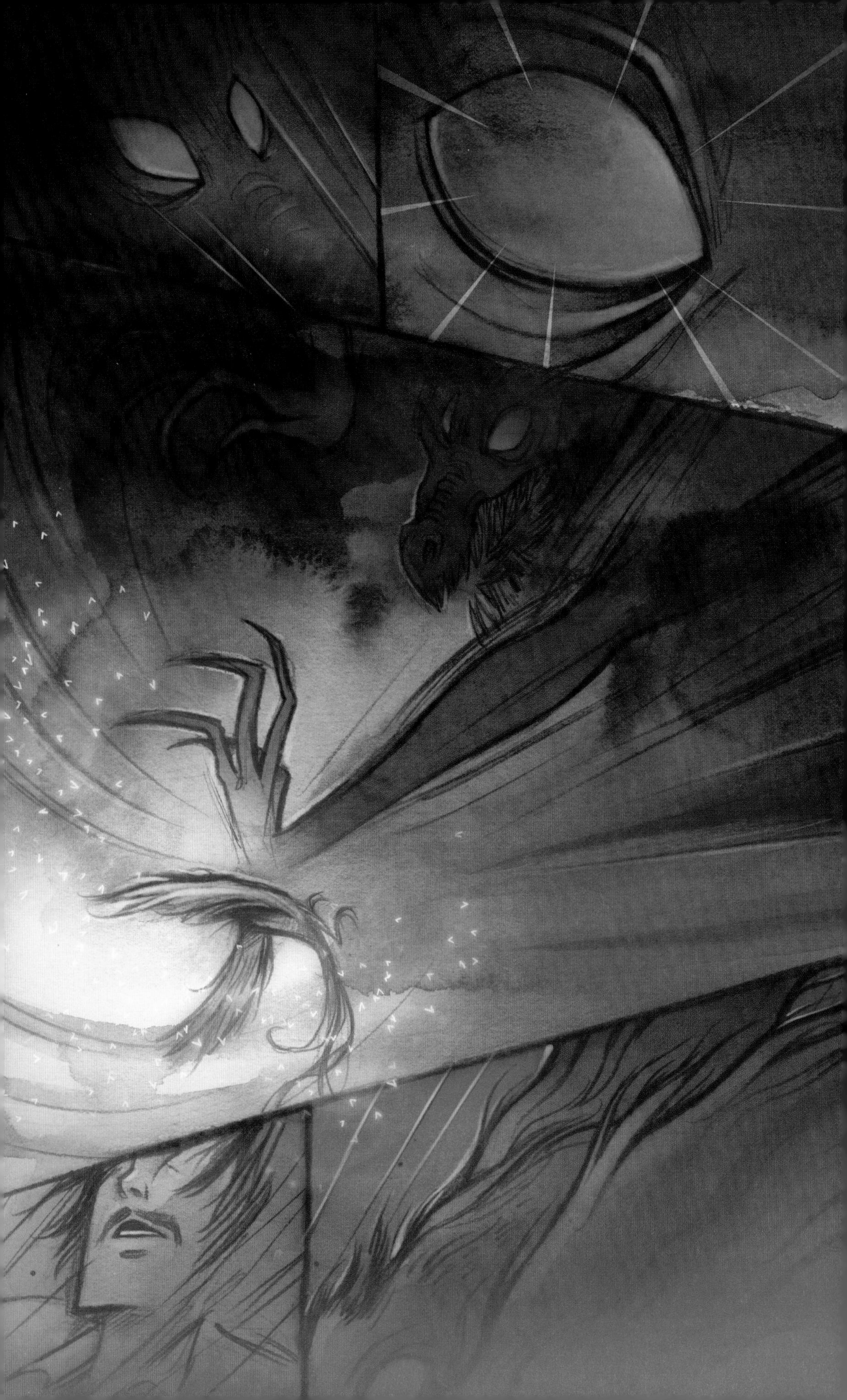

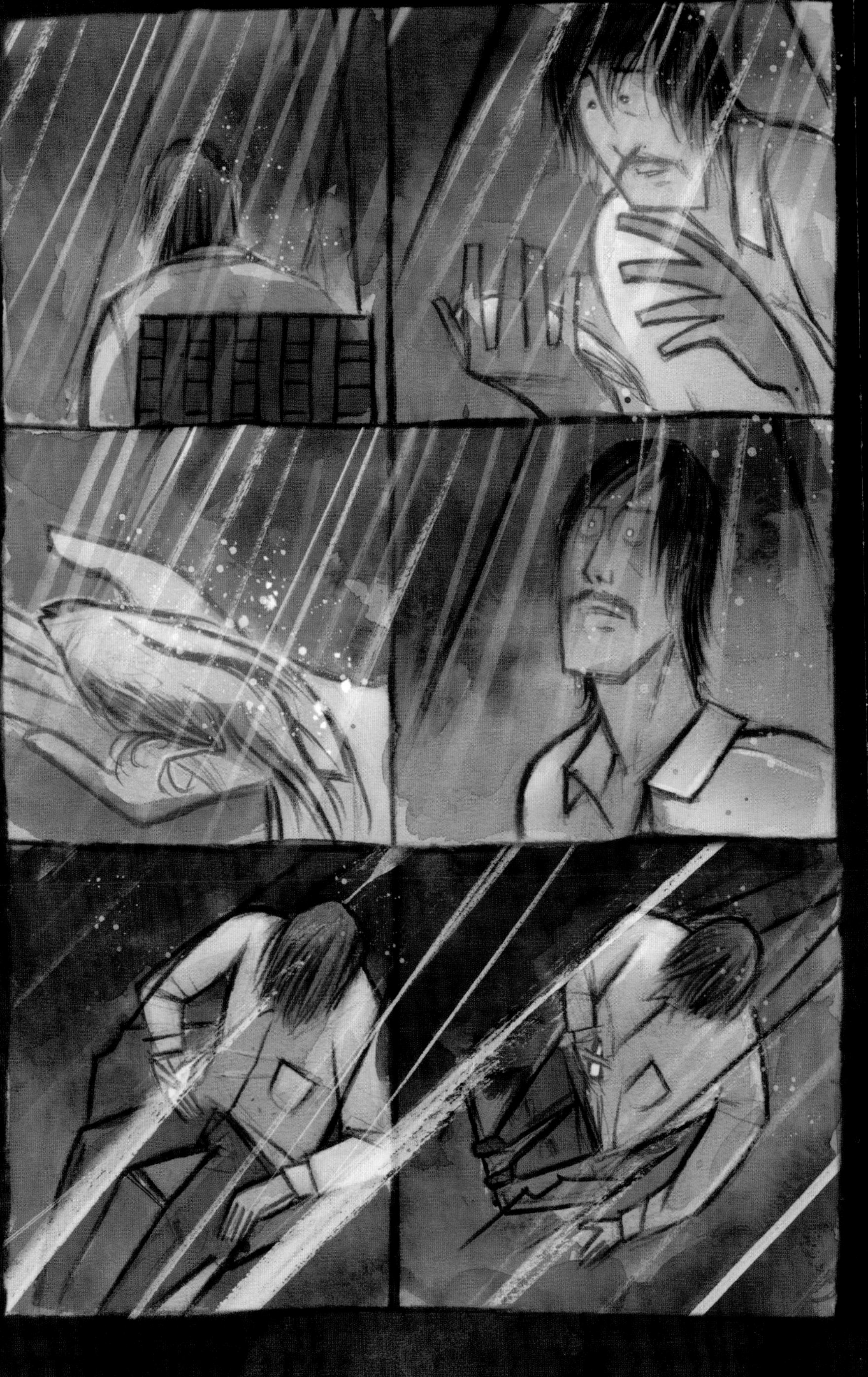

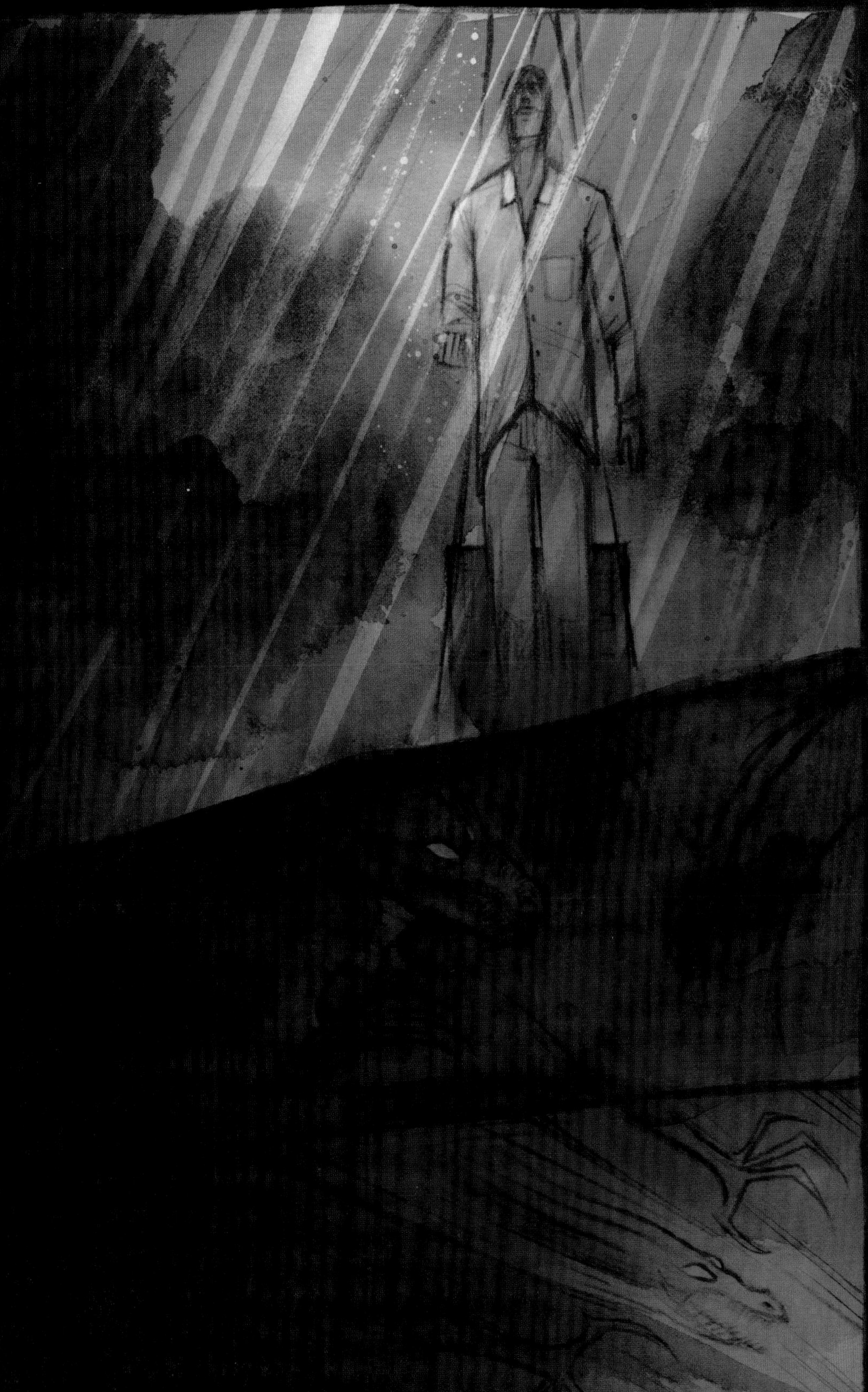

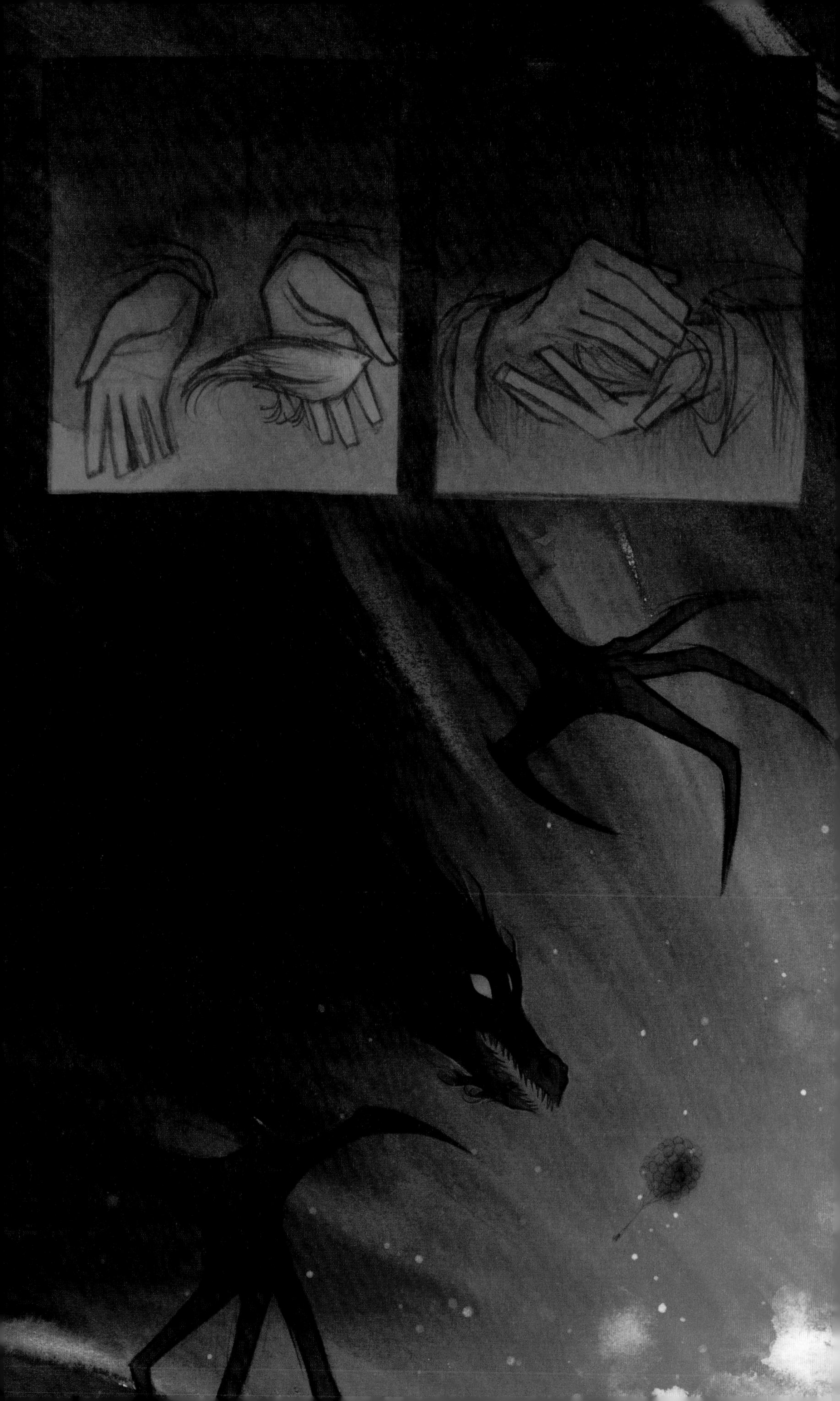

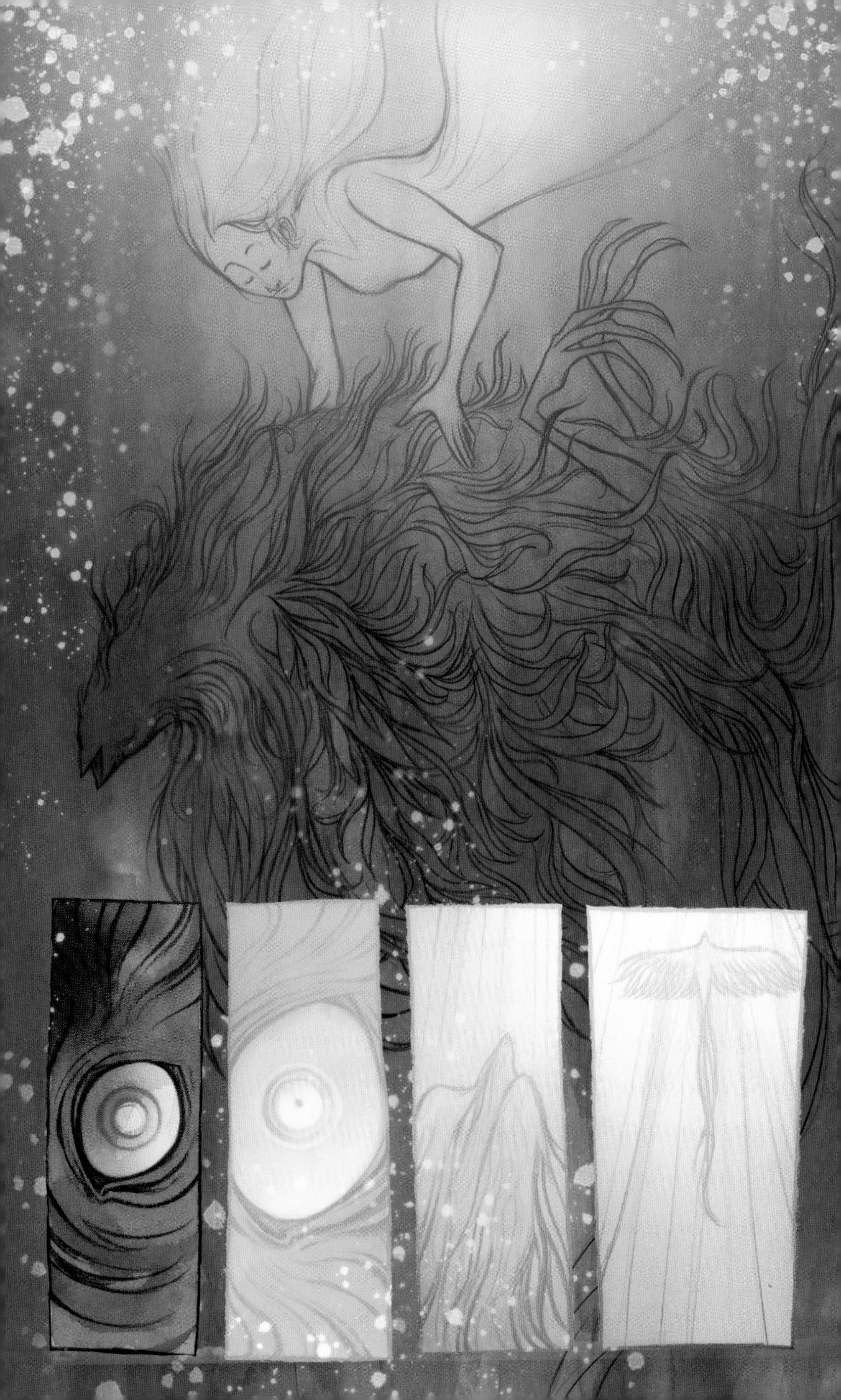

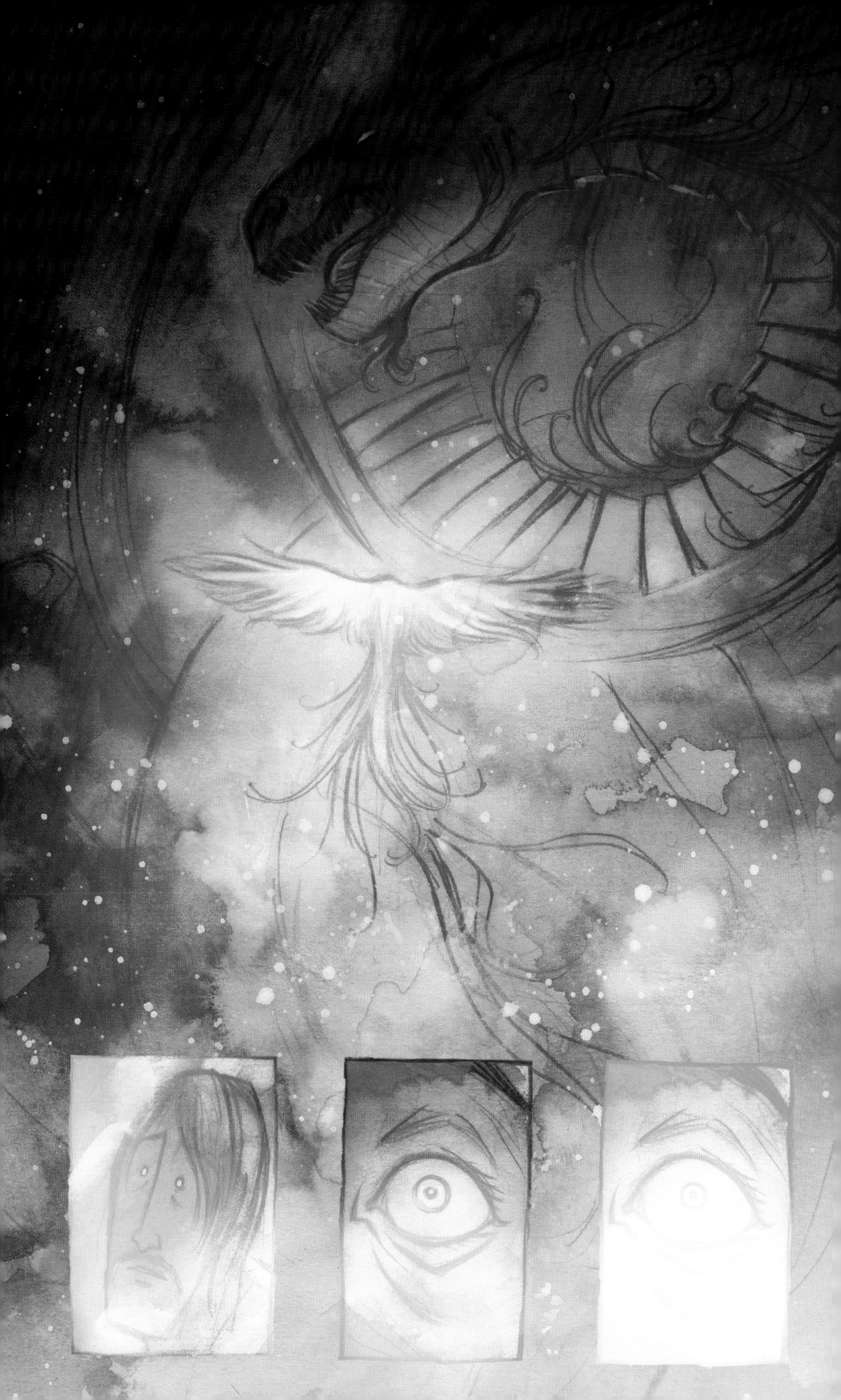

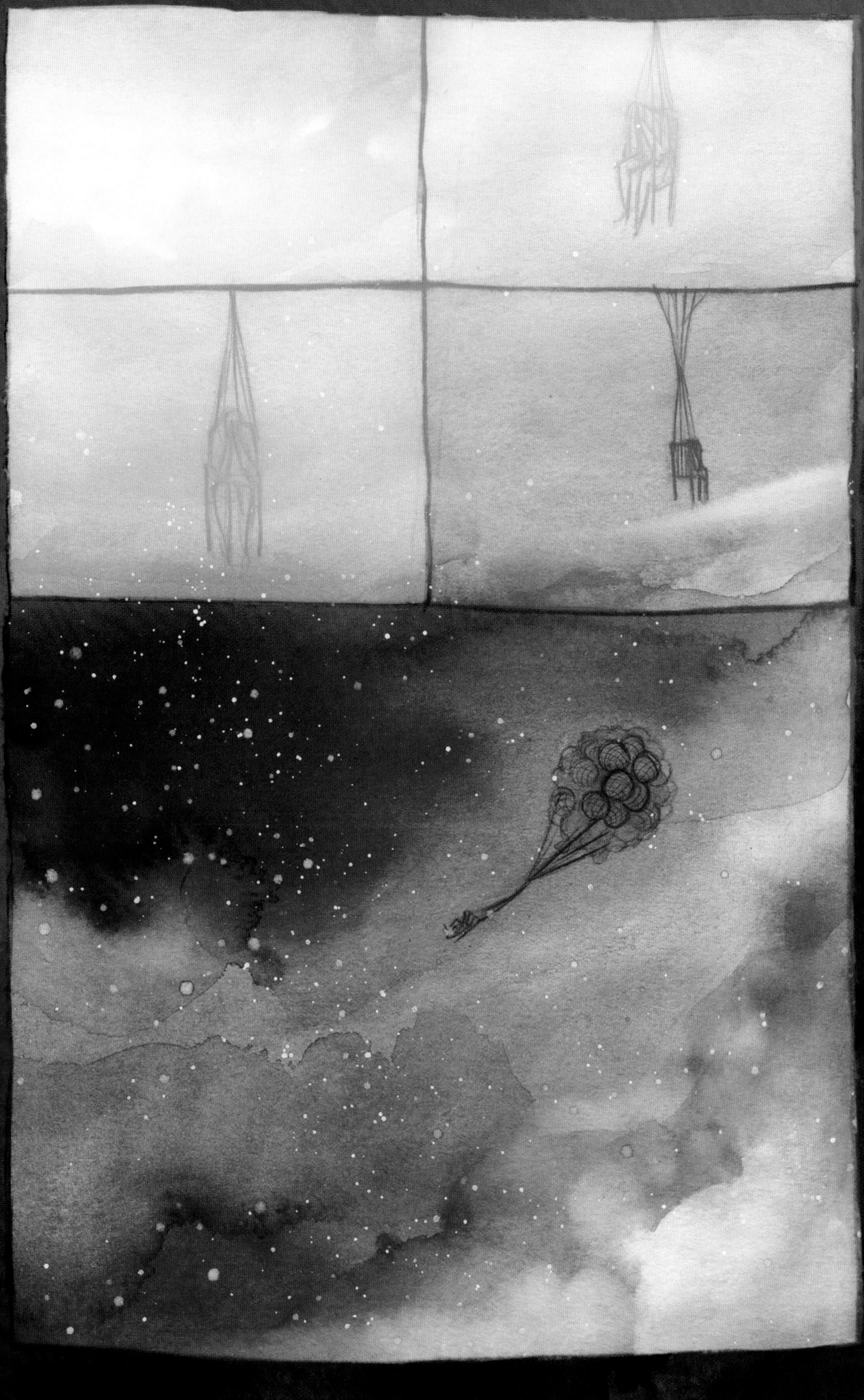

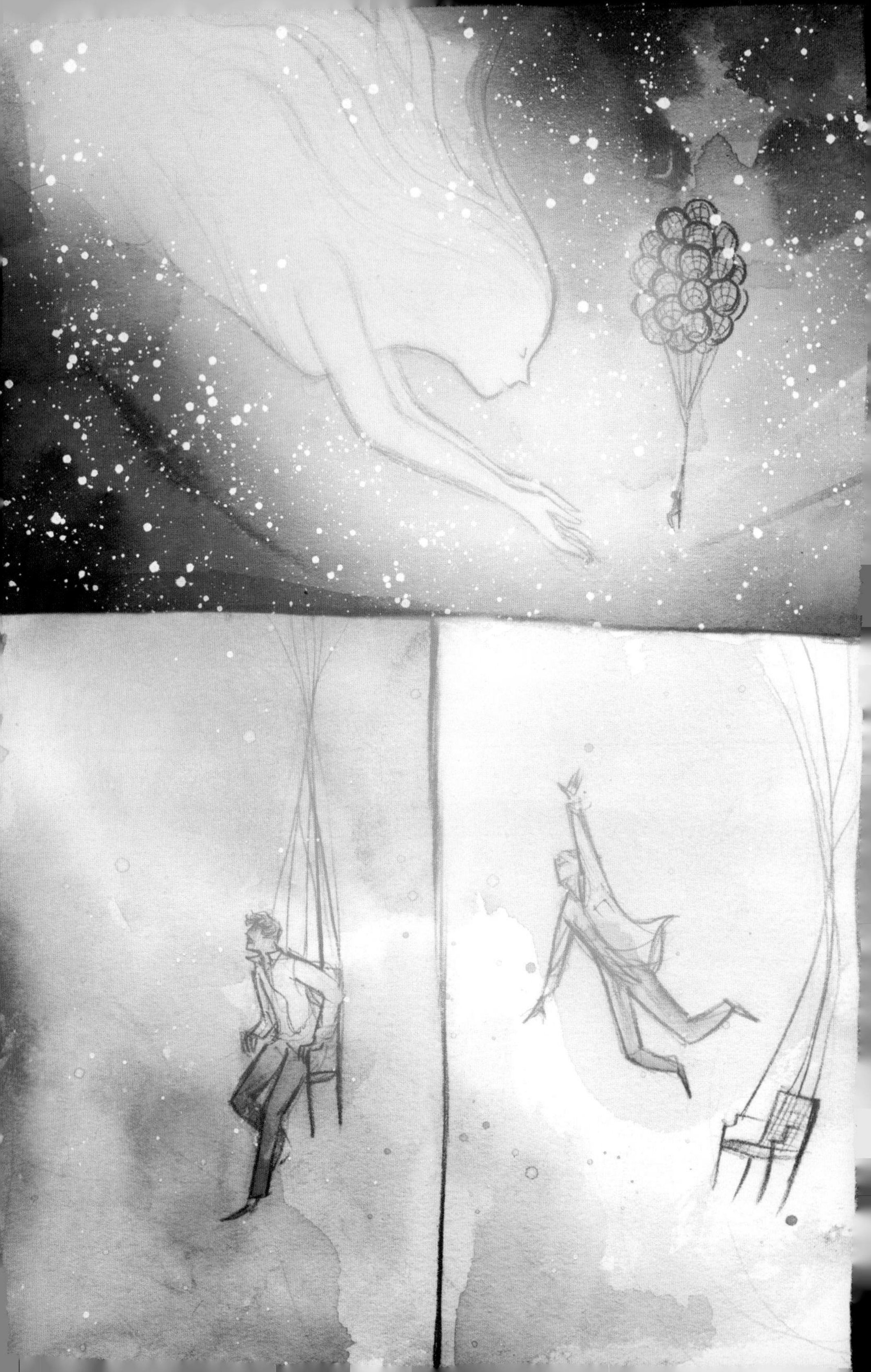

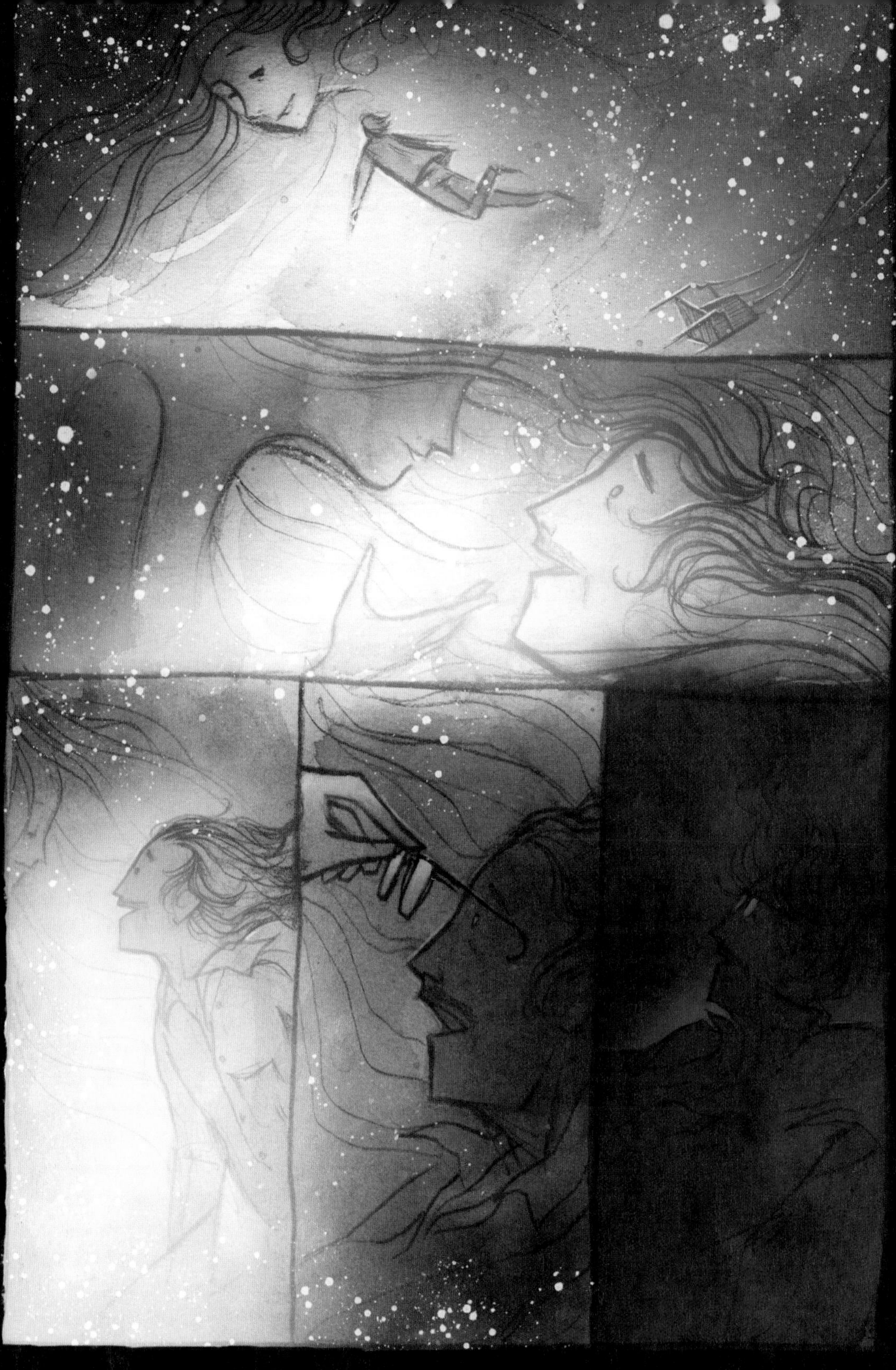

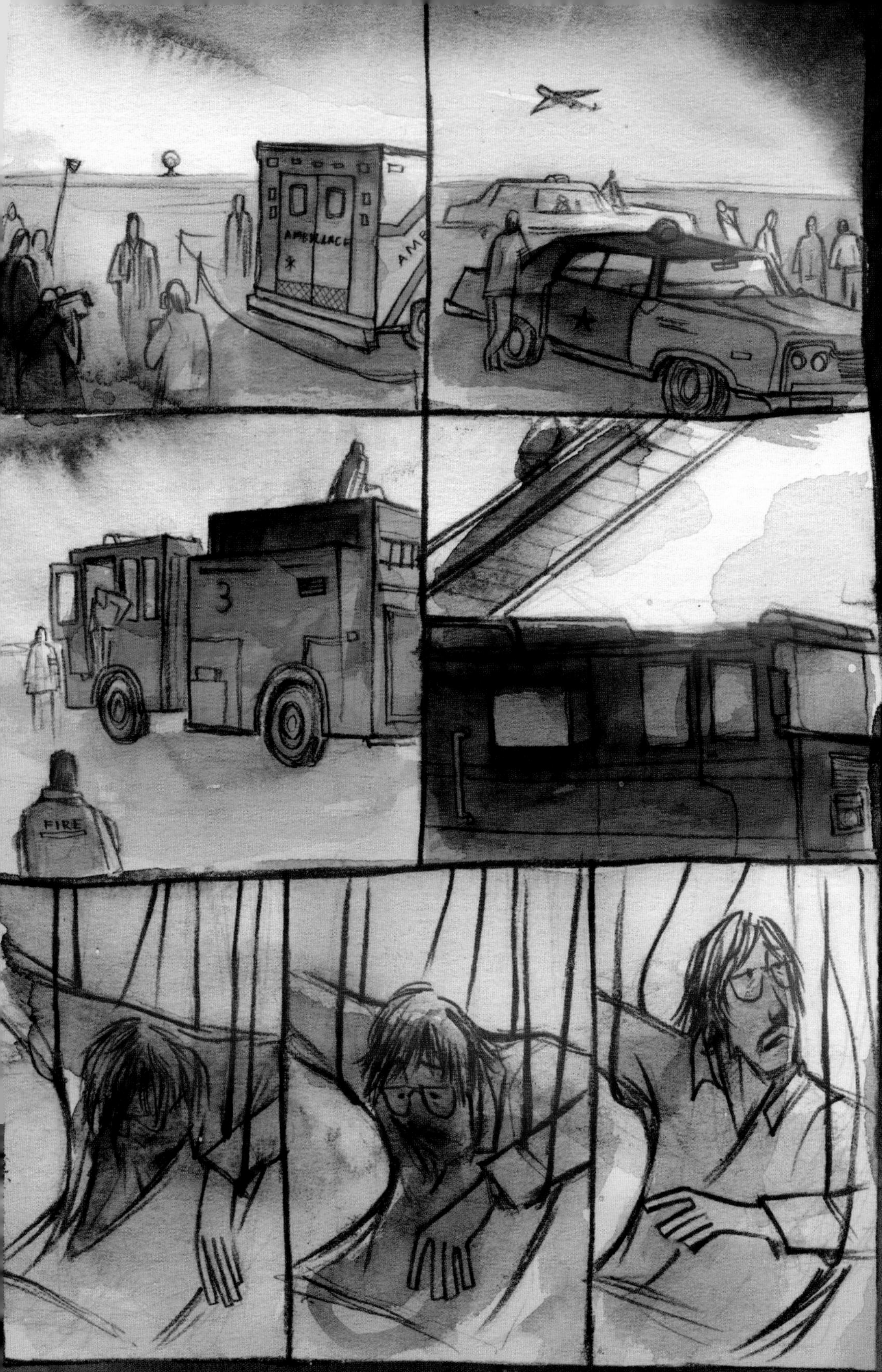
AMB
3
FIRE

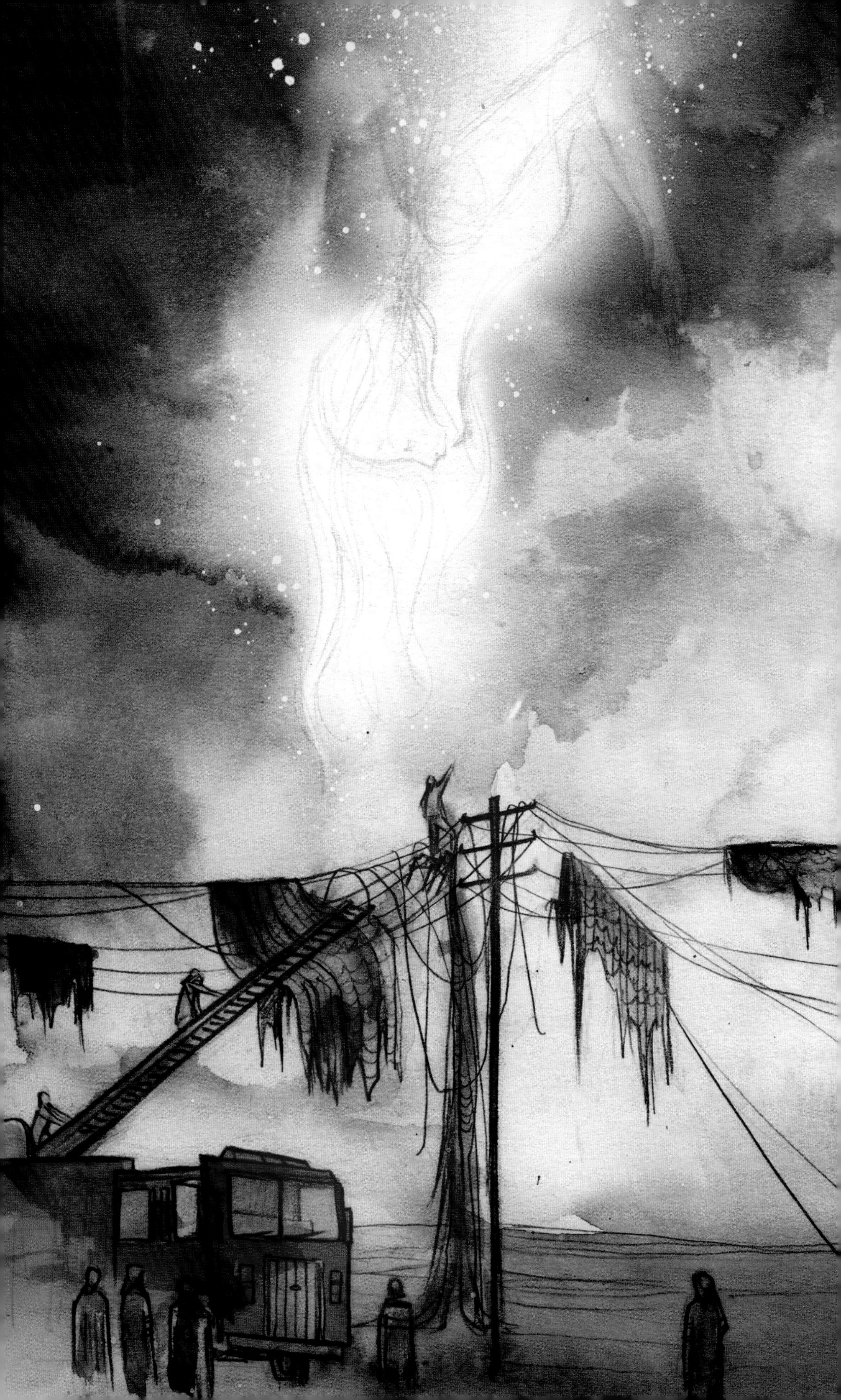

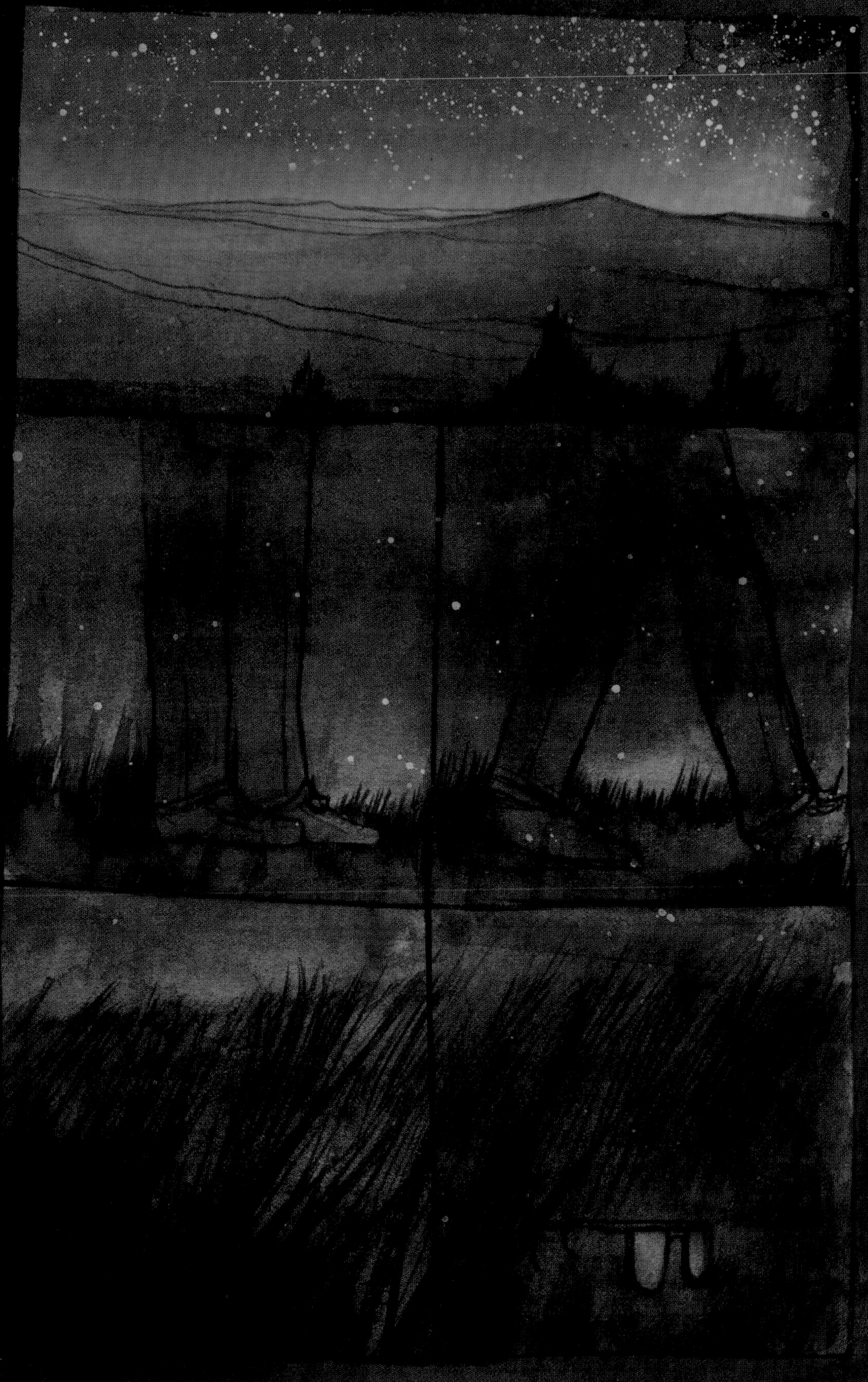

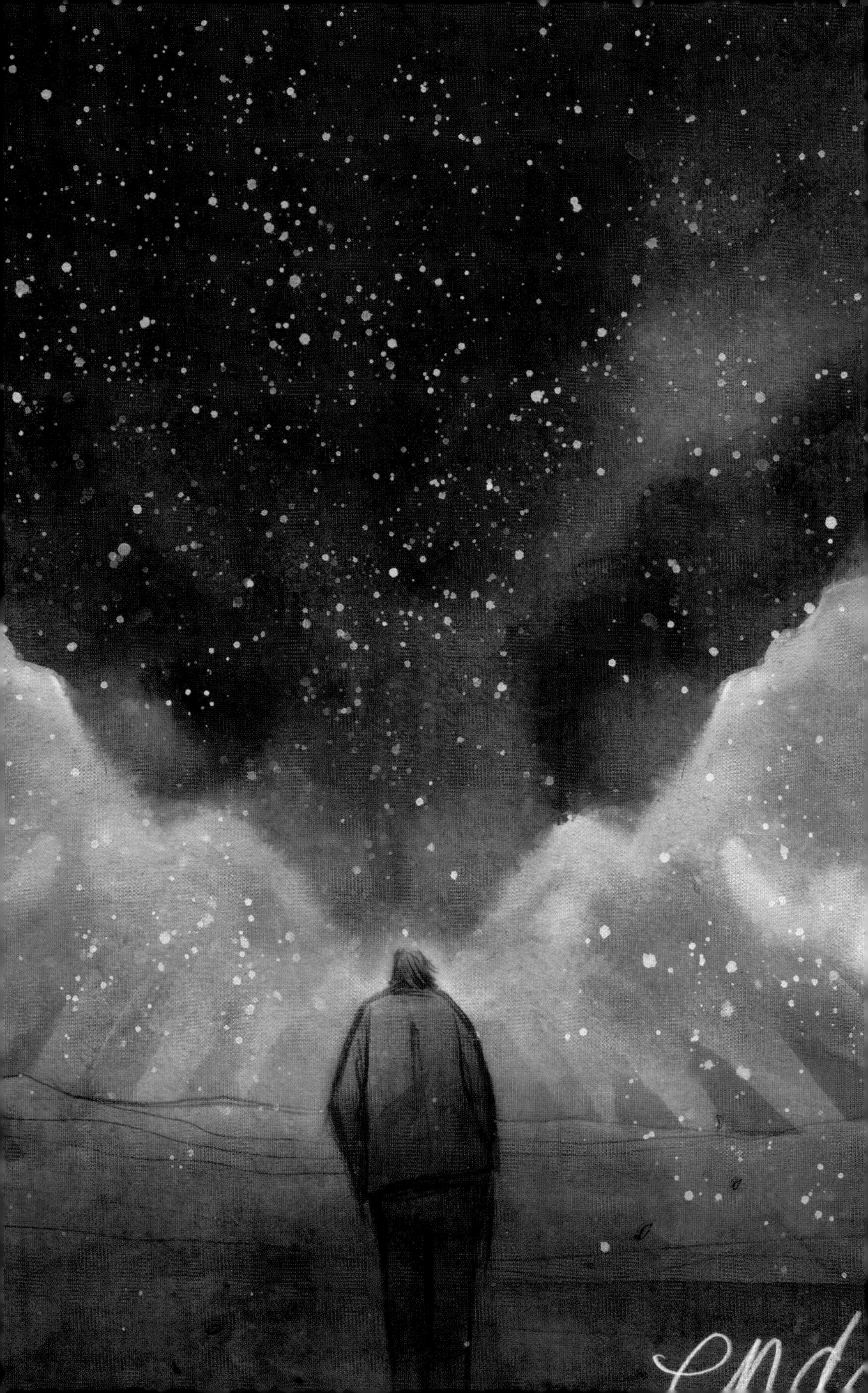

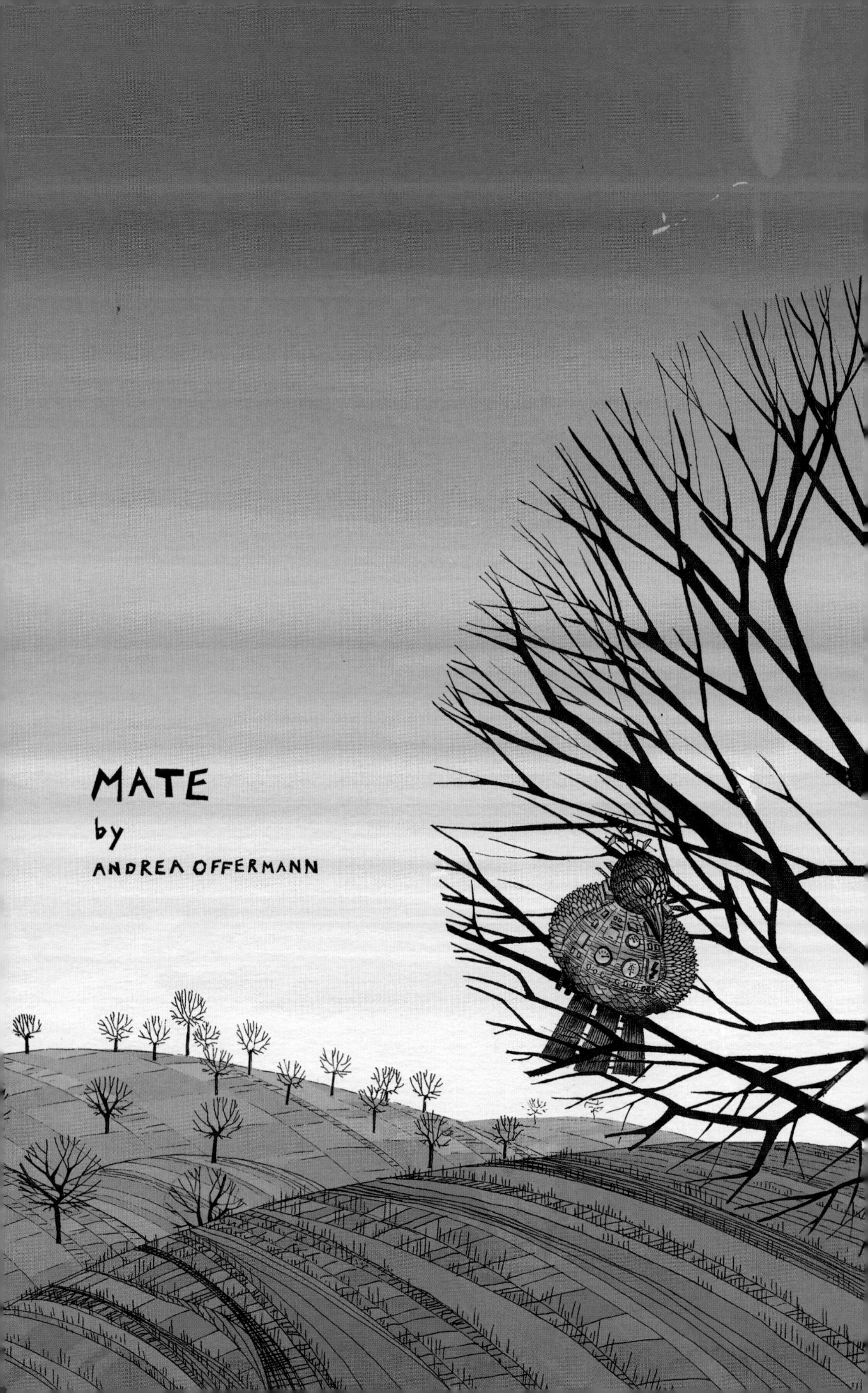
MATE
by
ANDREA OFFERMANN

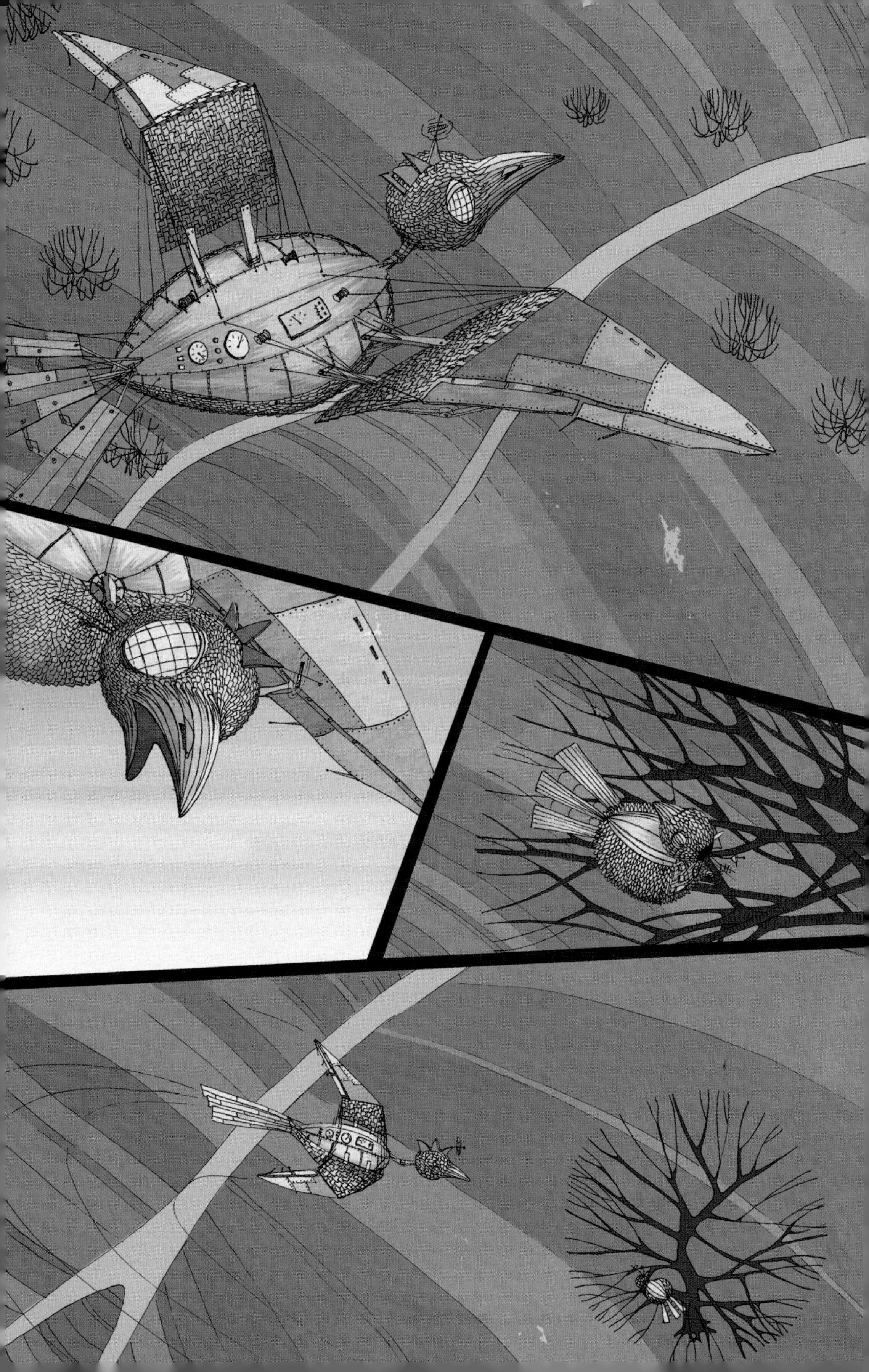

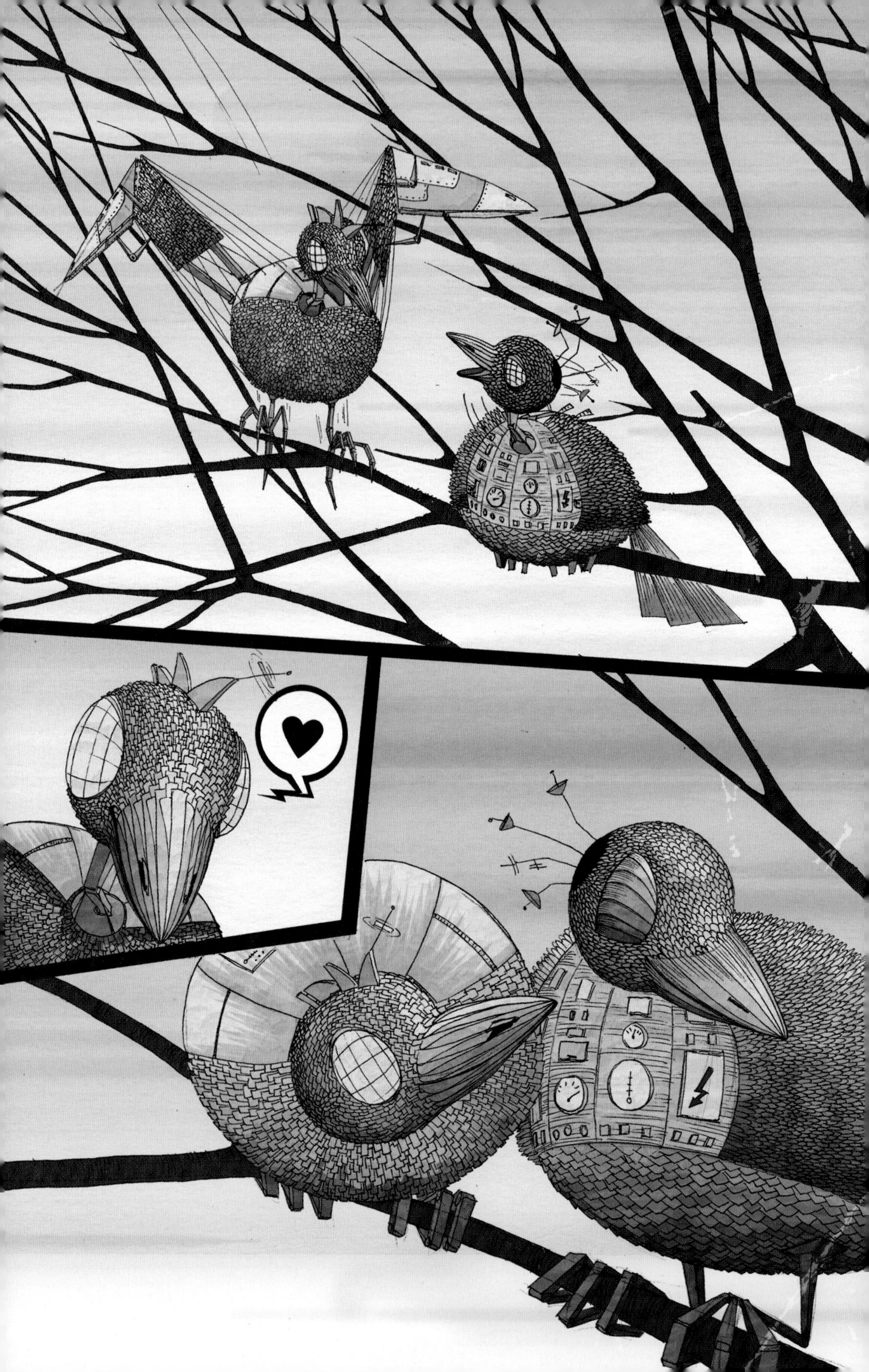

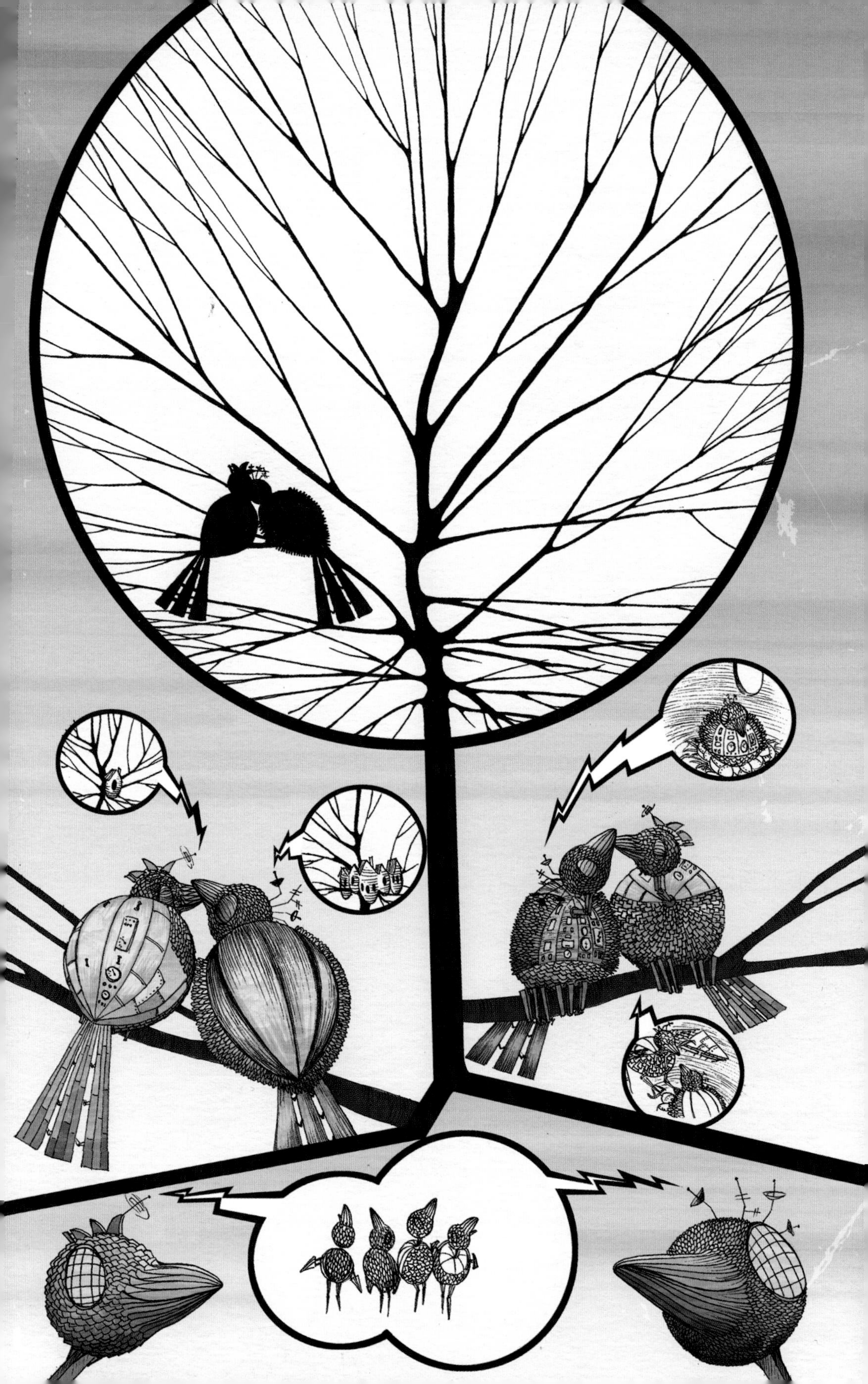

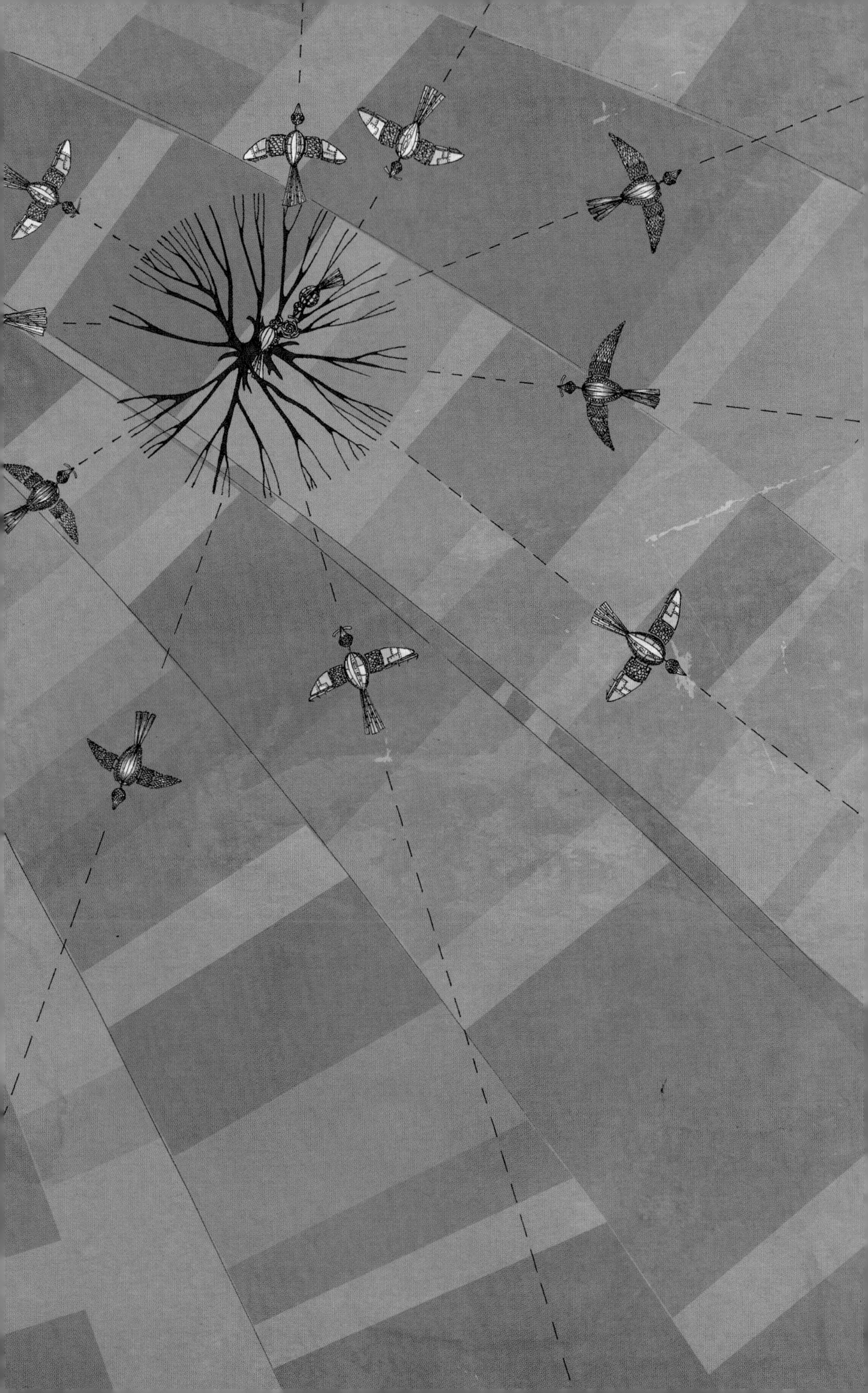

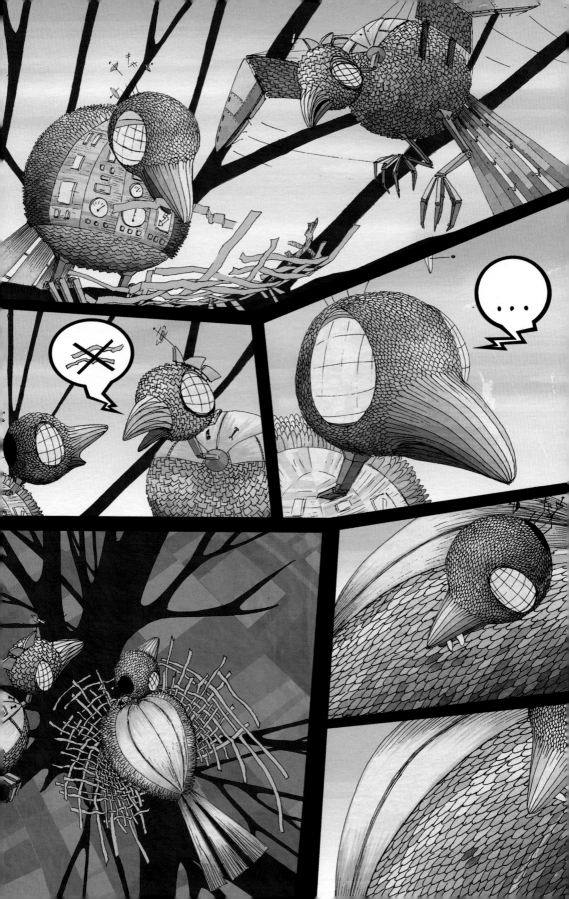

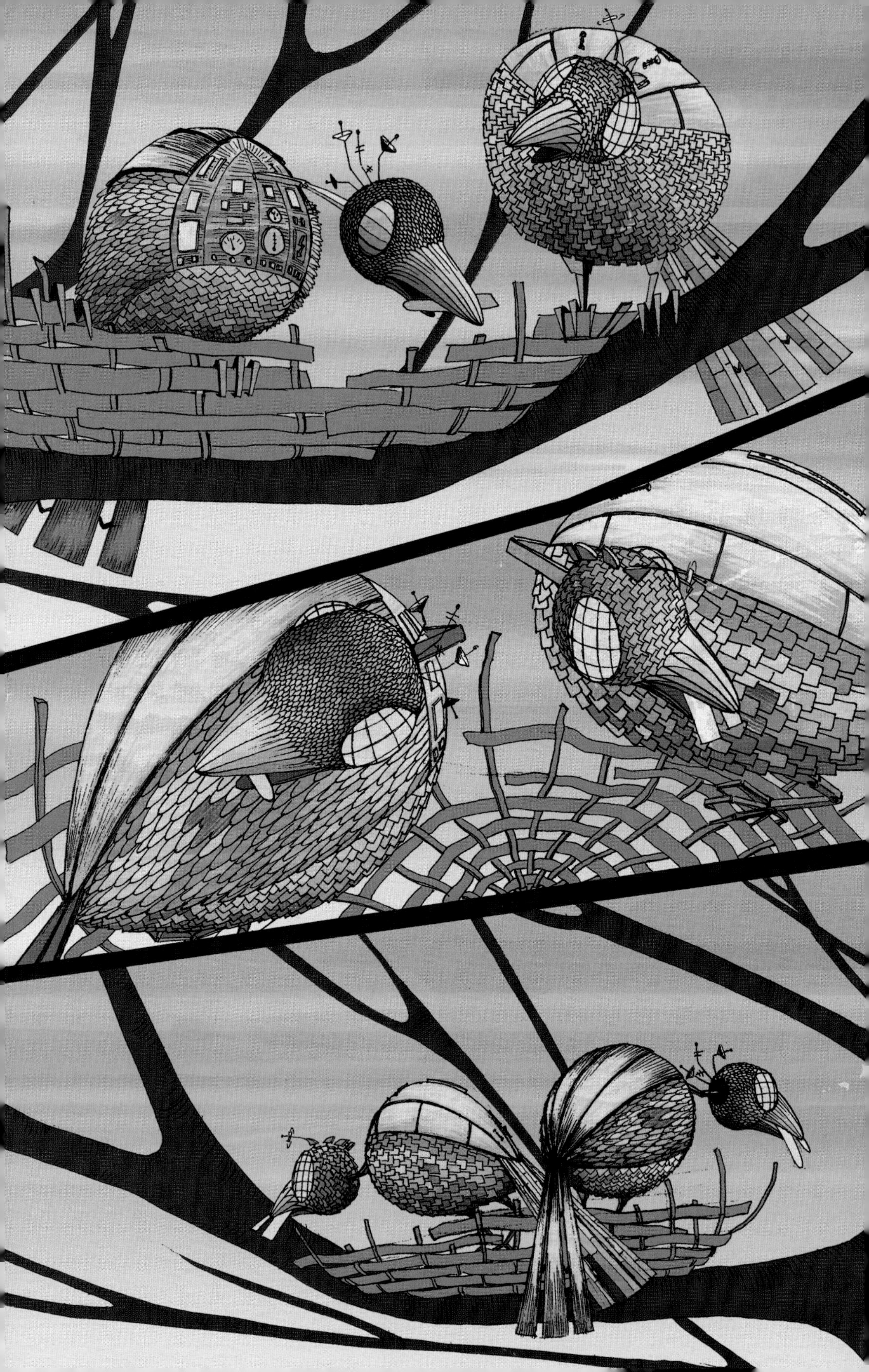

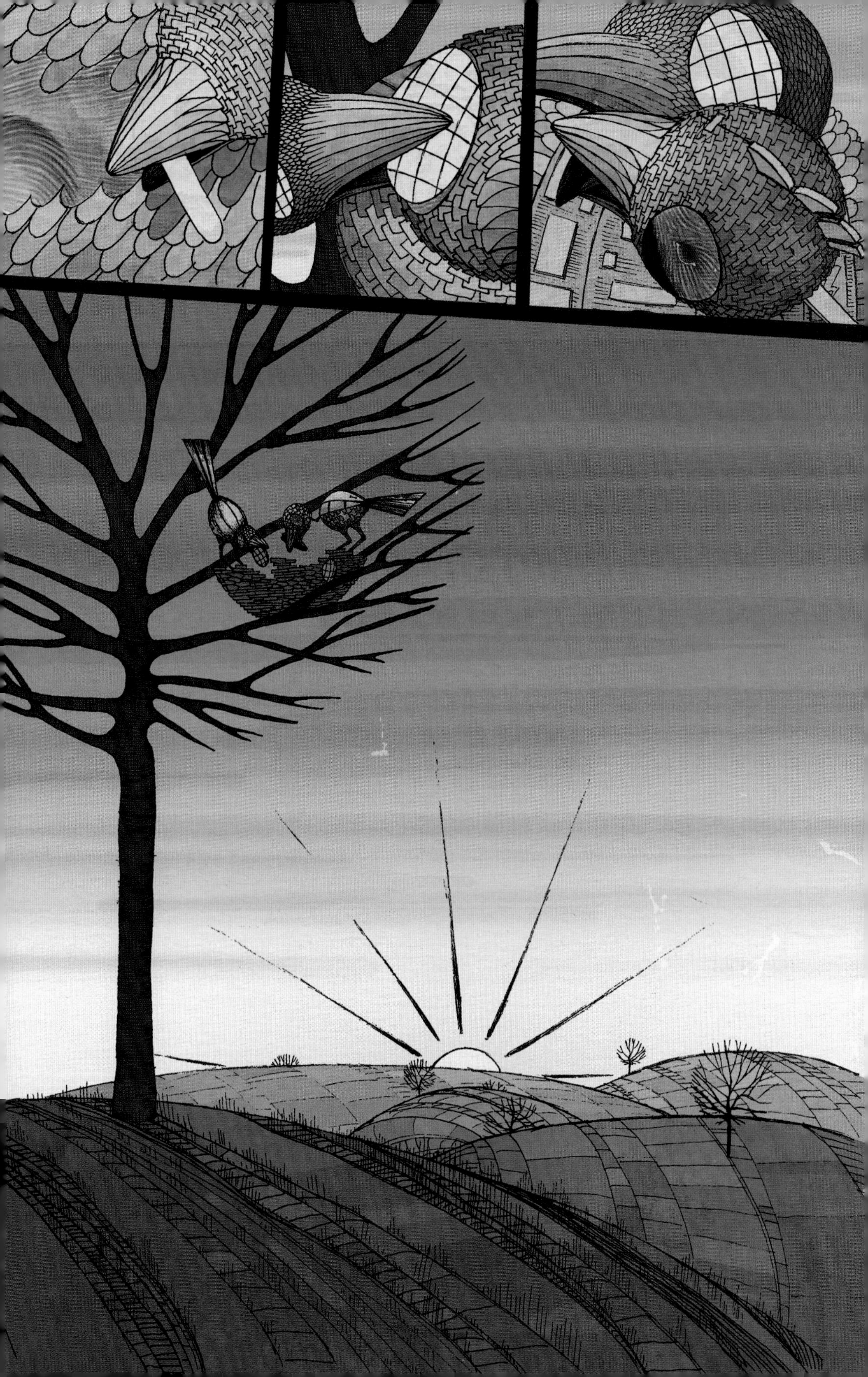

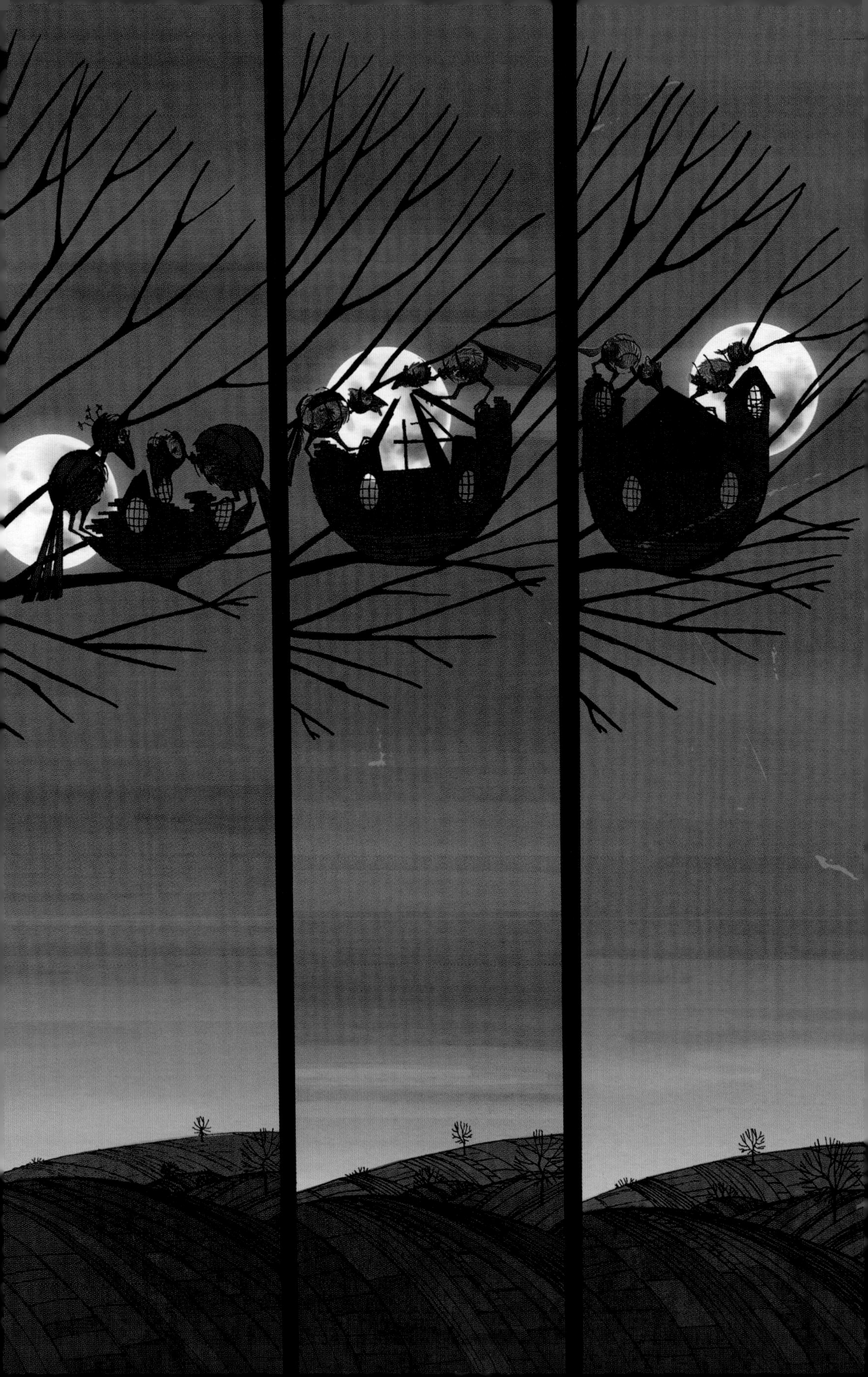

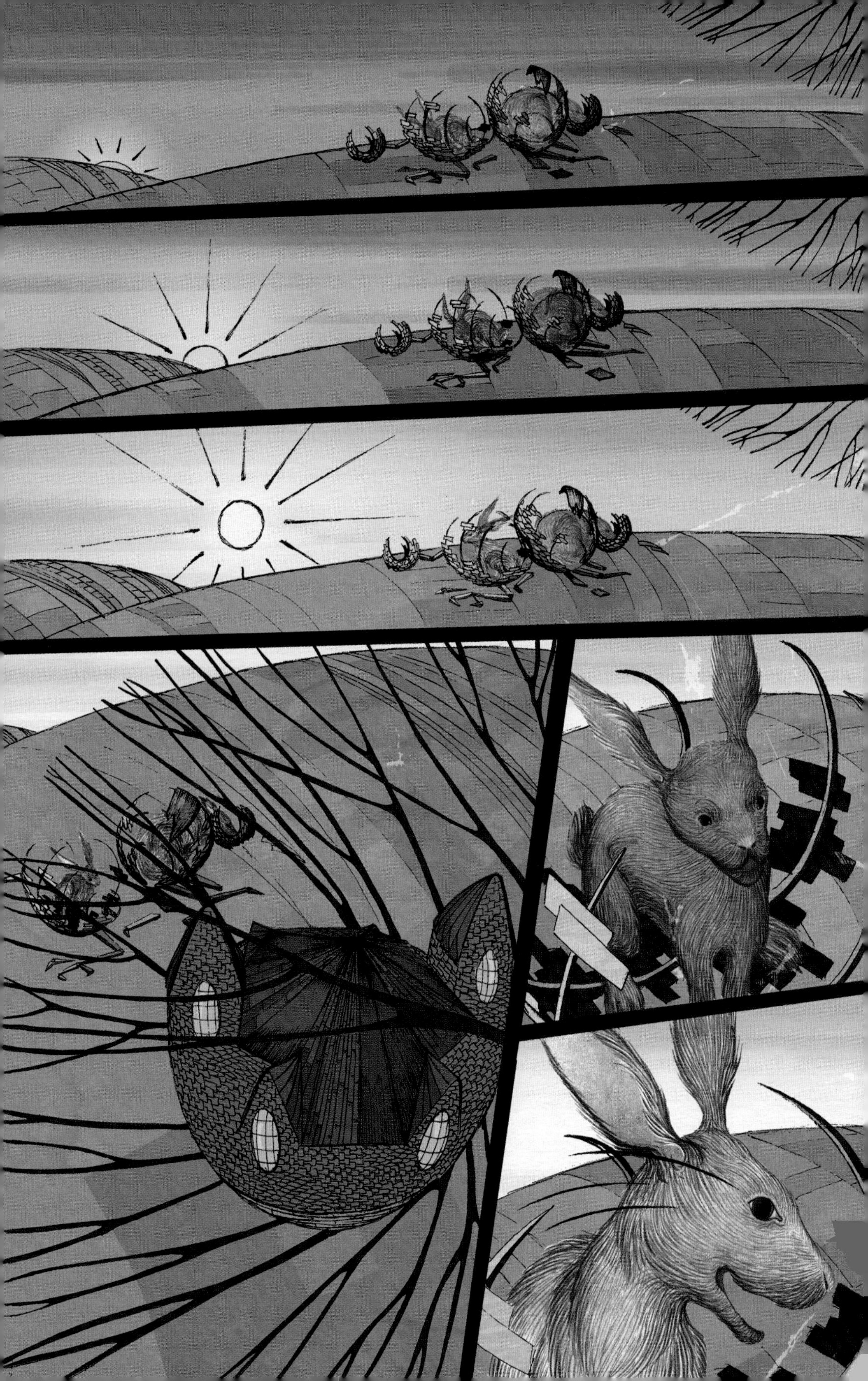

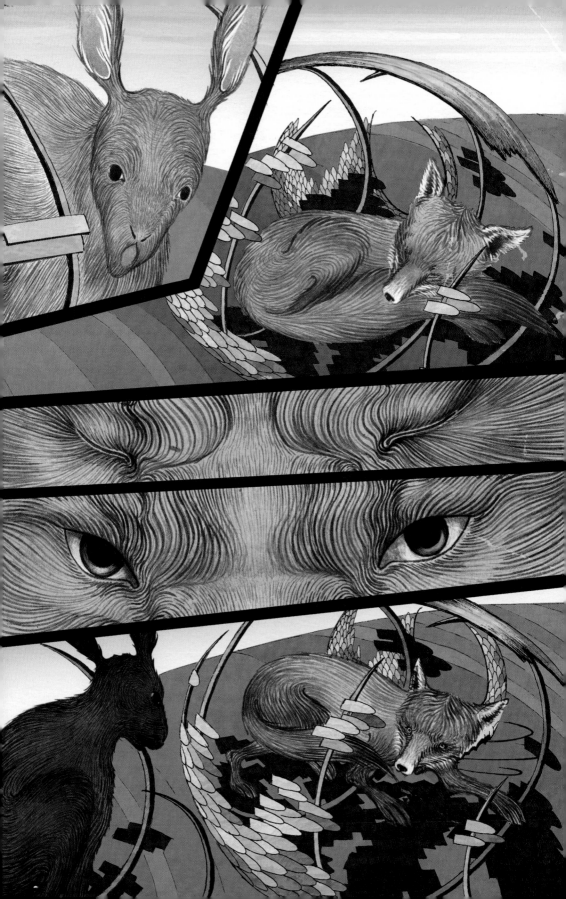

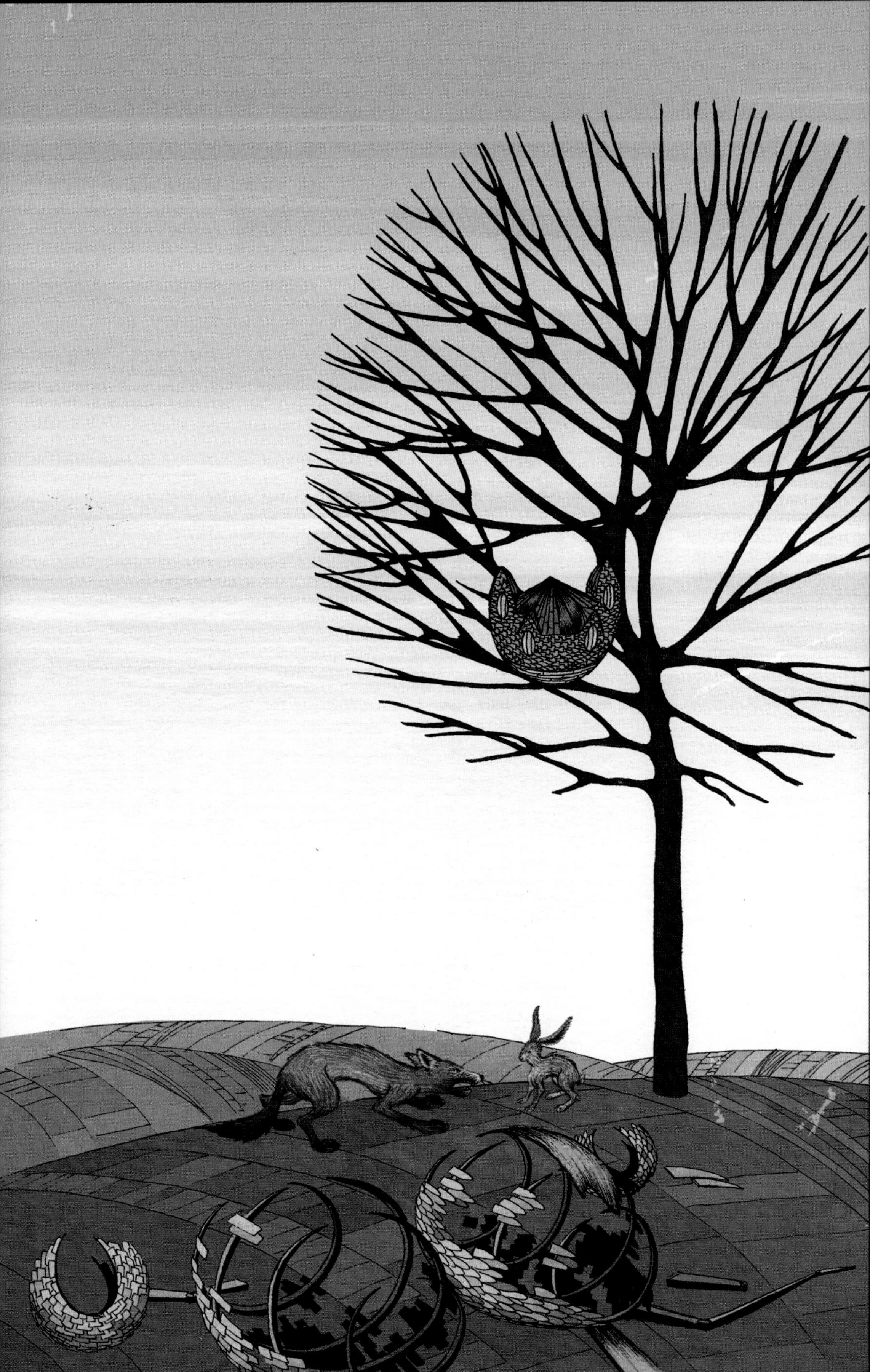

KIDNAPPED

BY: RAD SECHRIST

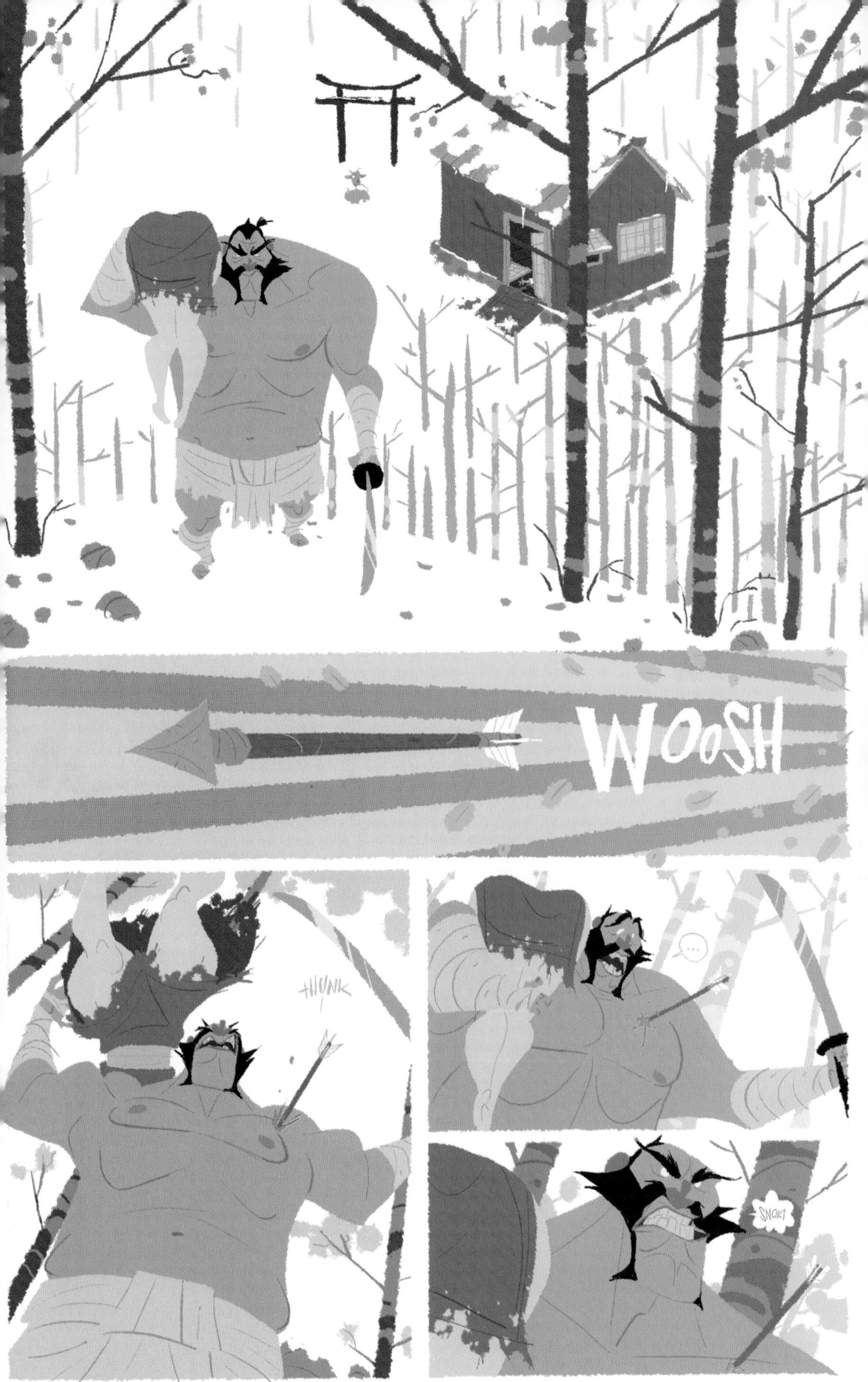
WOOSH
THUNK
...
SNORT

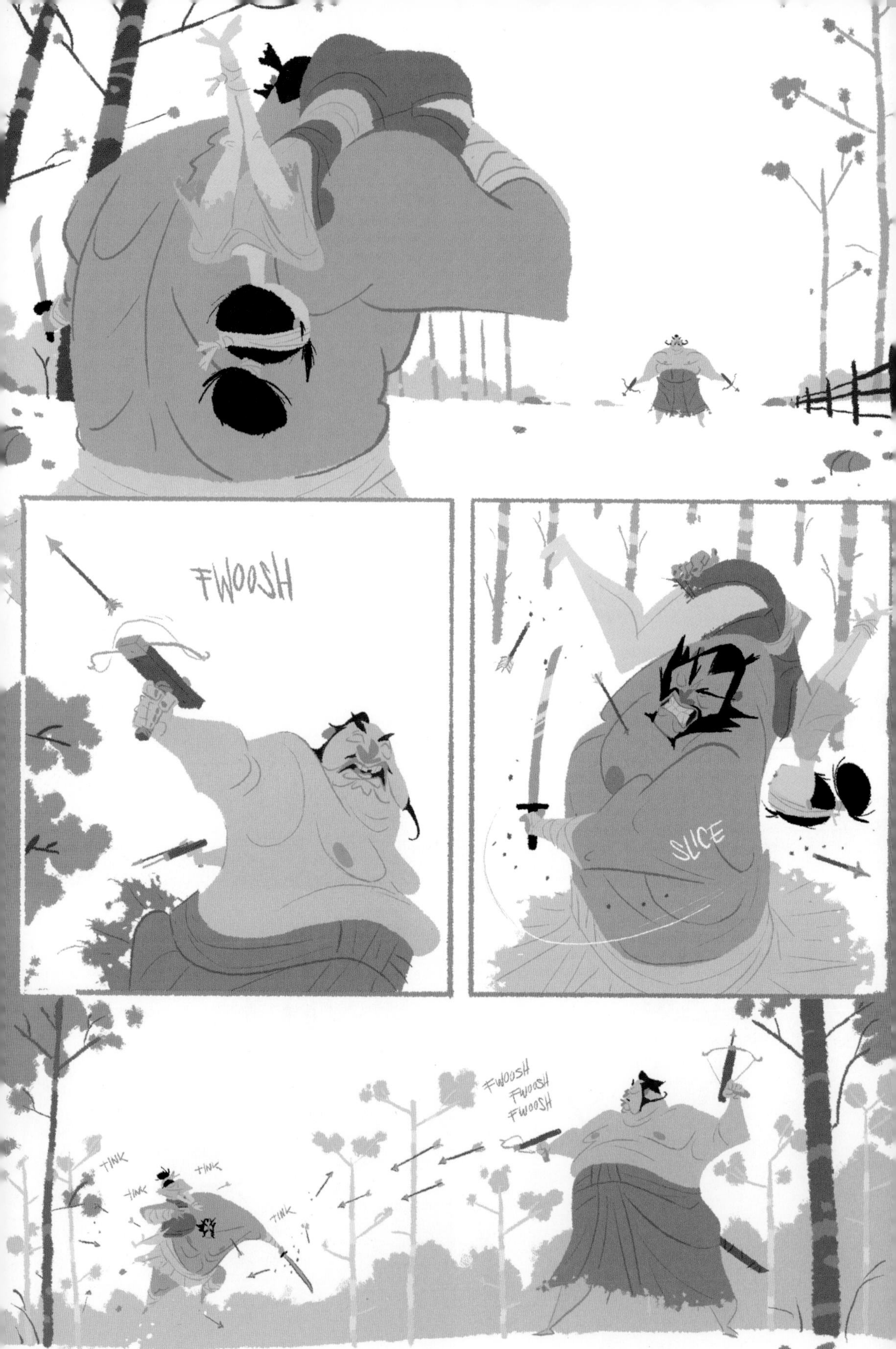
FWOOSH
SLICE
FWOOSH
FWOOSH
FWOOSH
TINK
TINK
TINK
TINK

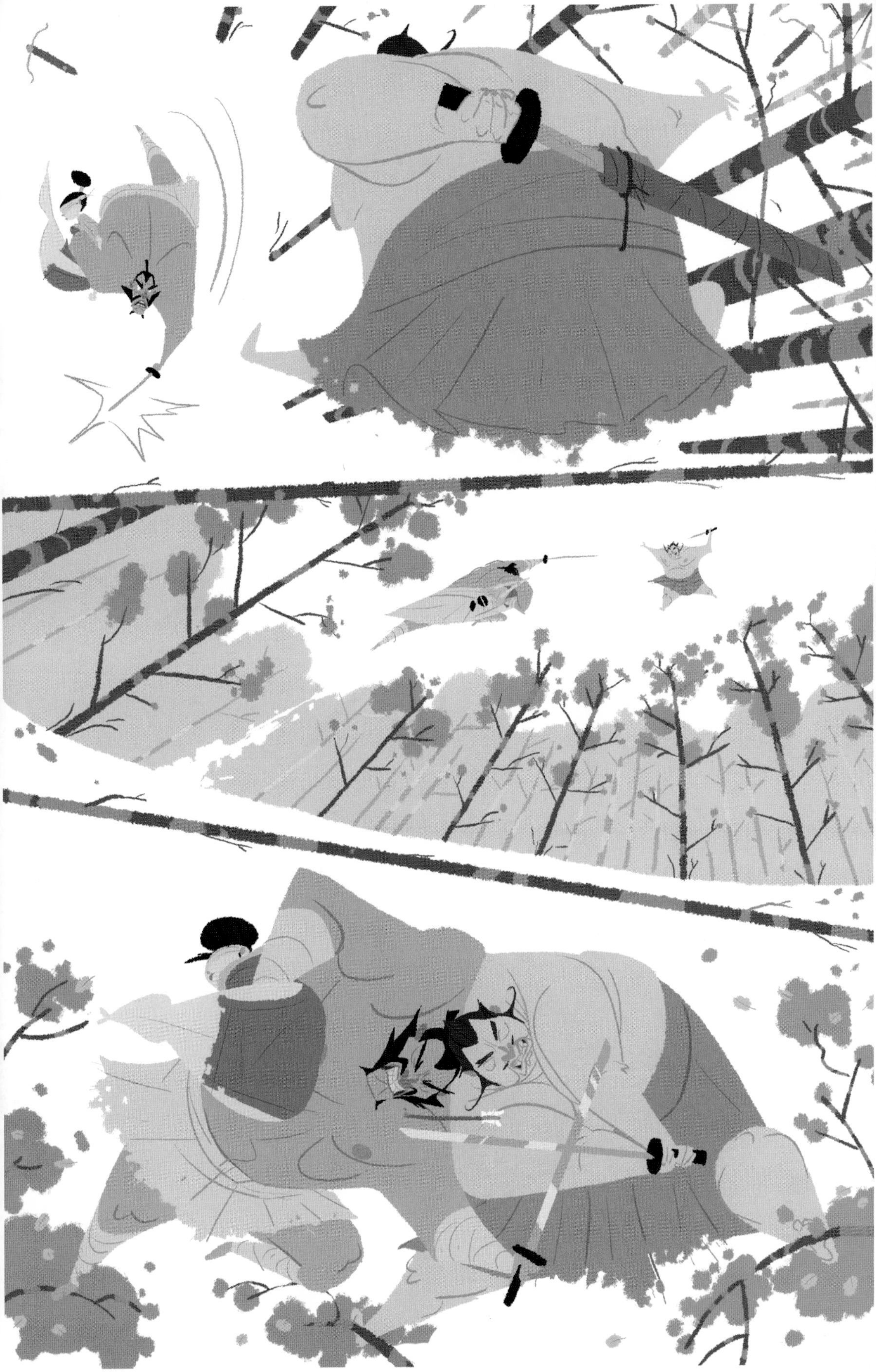

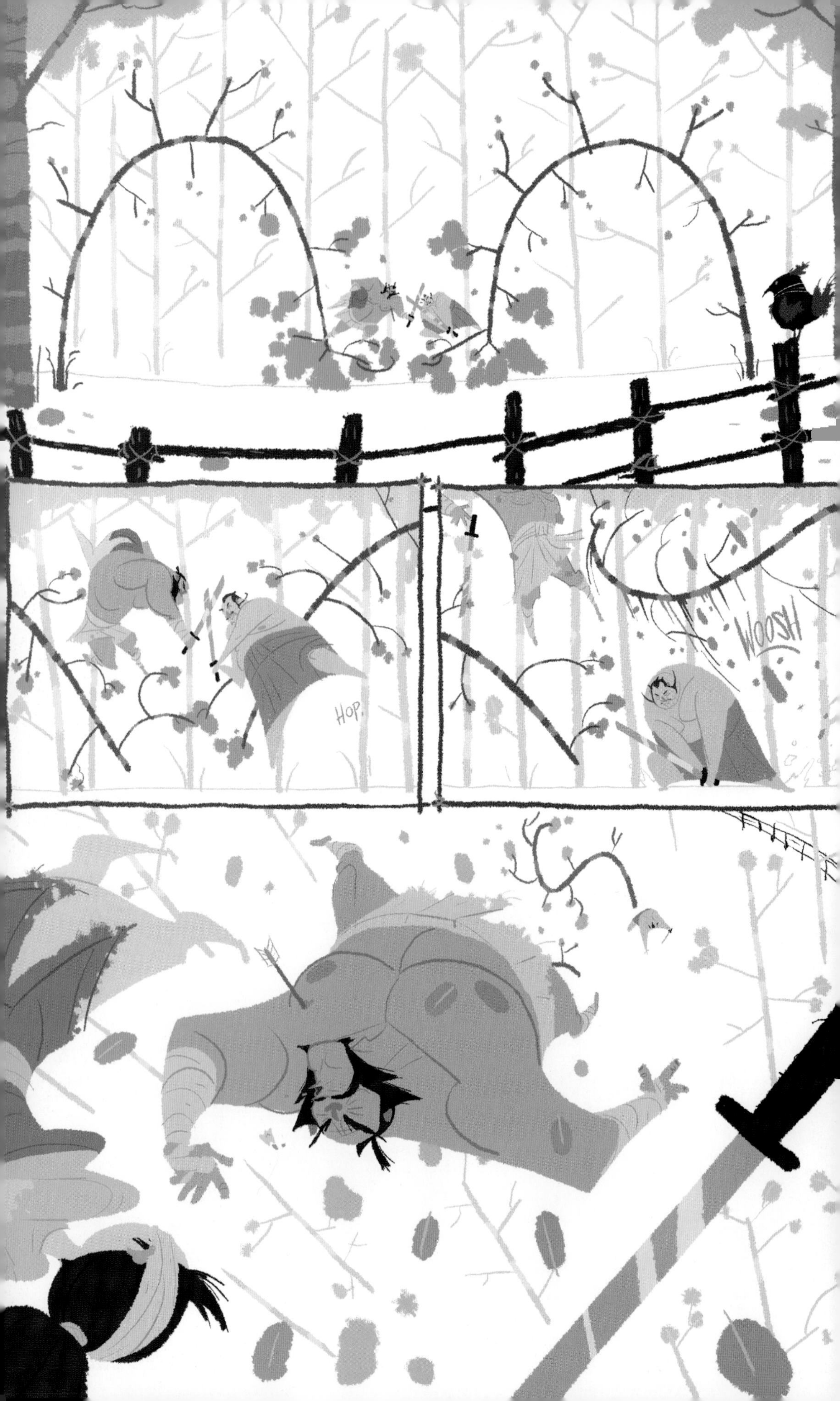
HOP.
WOOSH

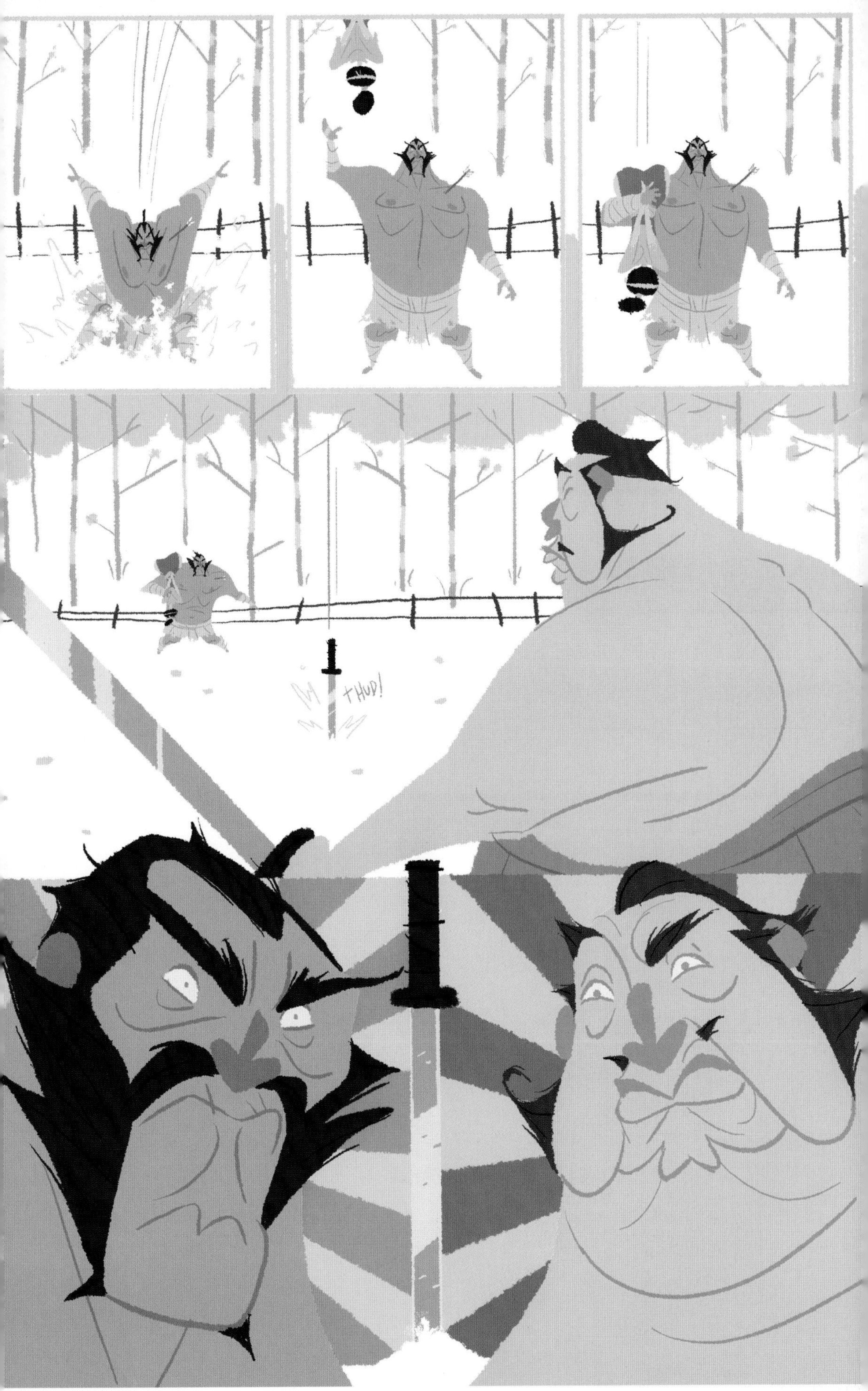
THUD!

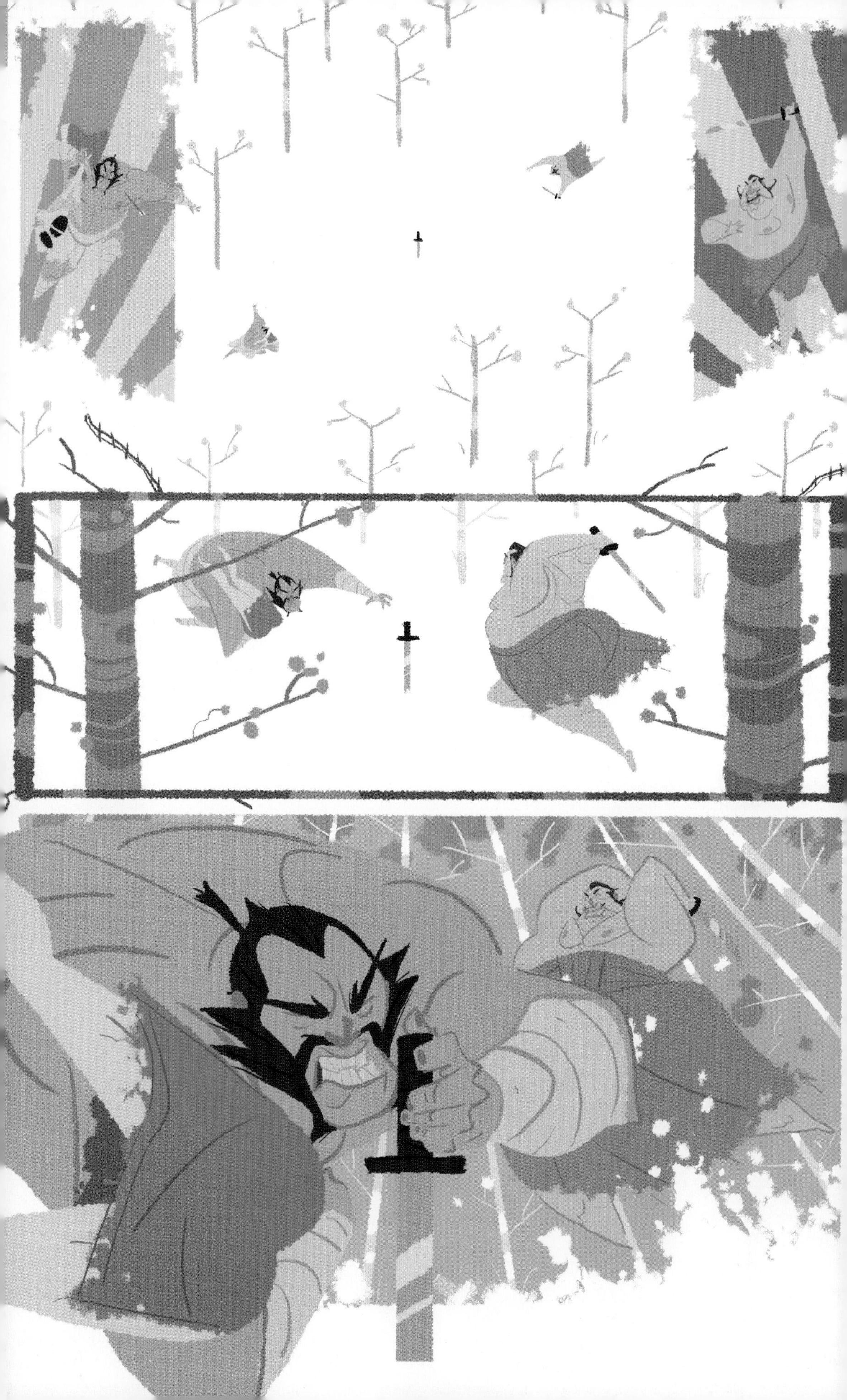

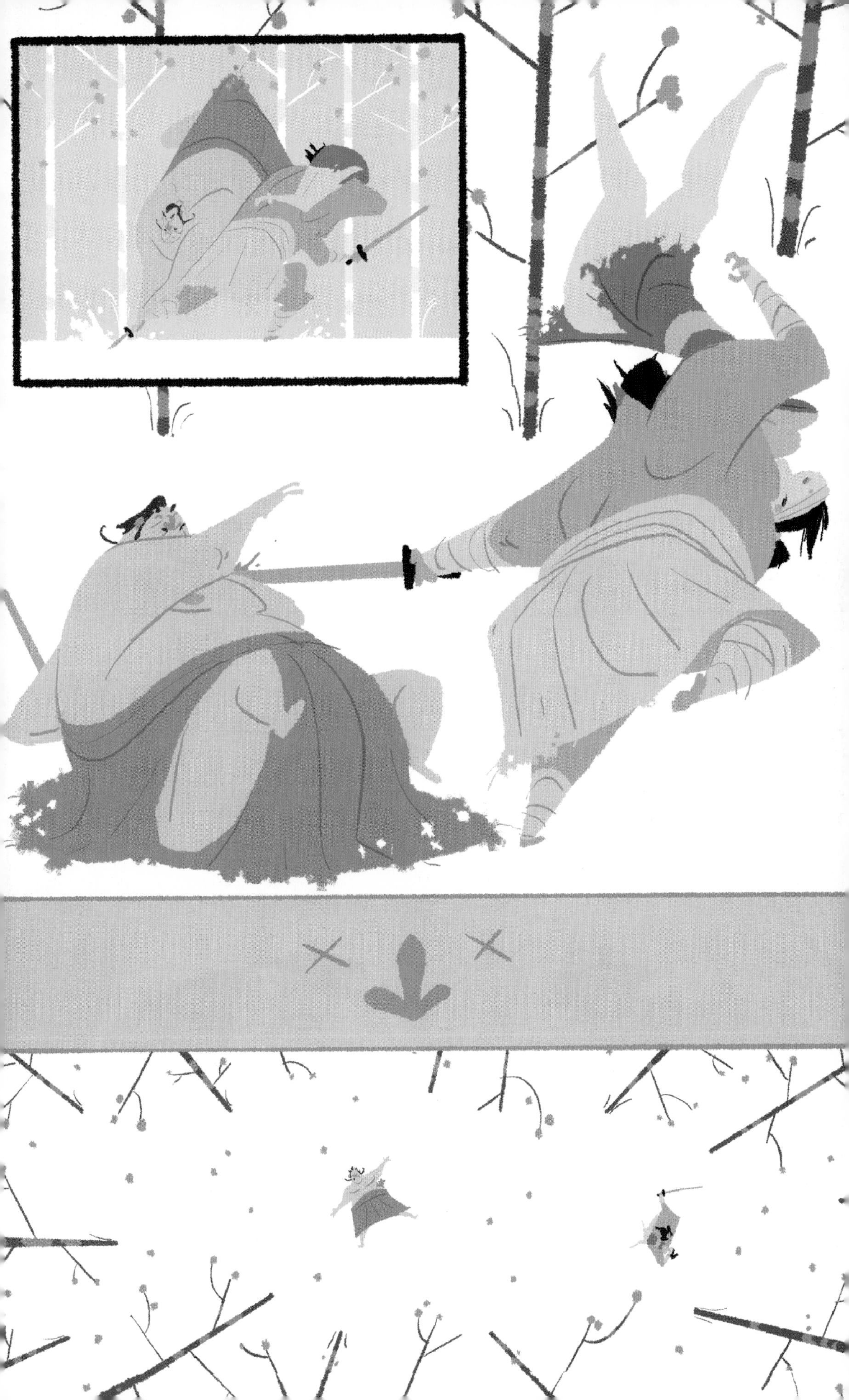

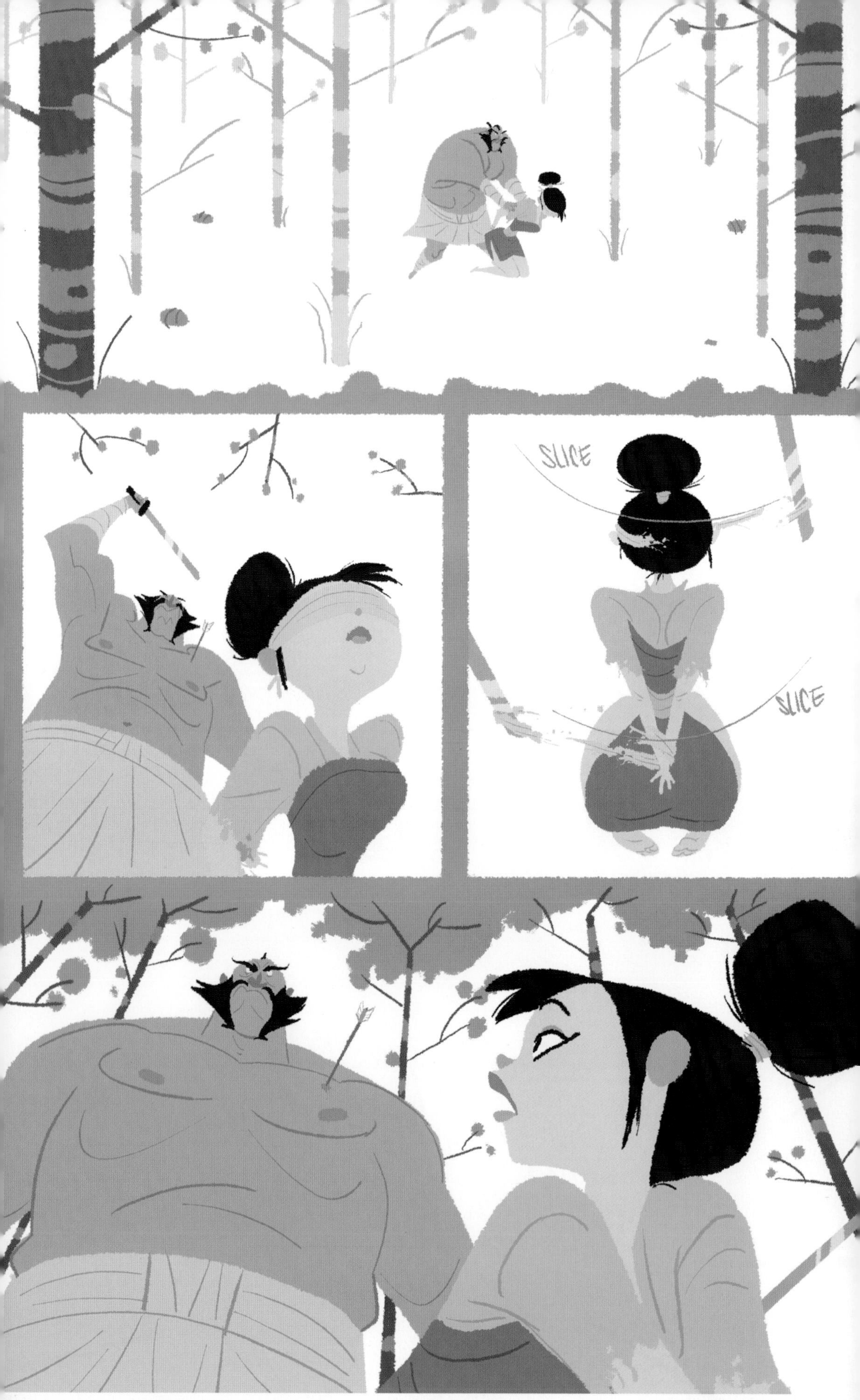
SLICE
SLICE

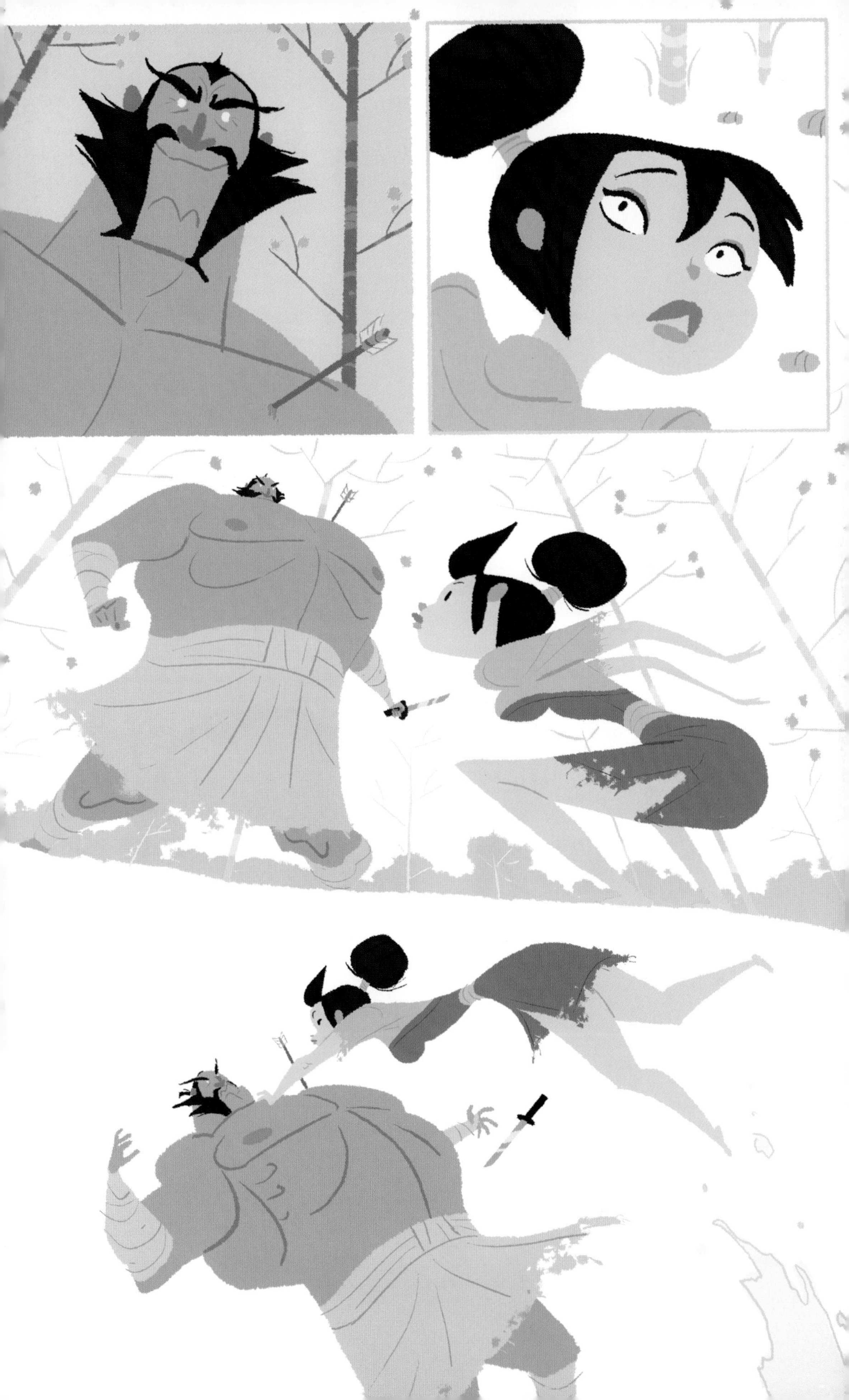

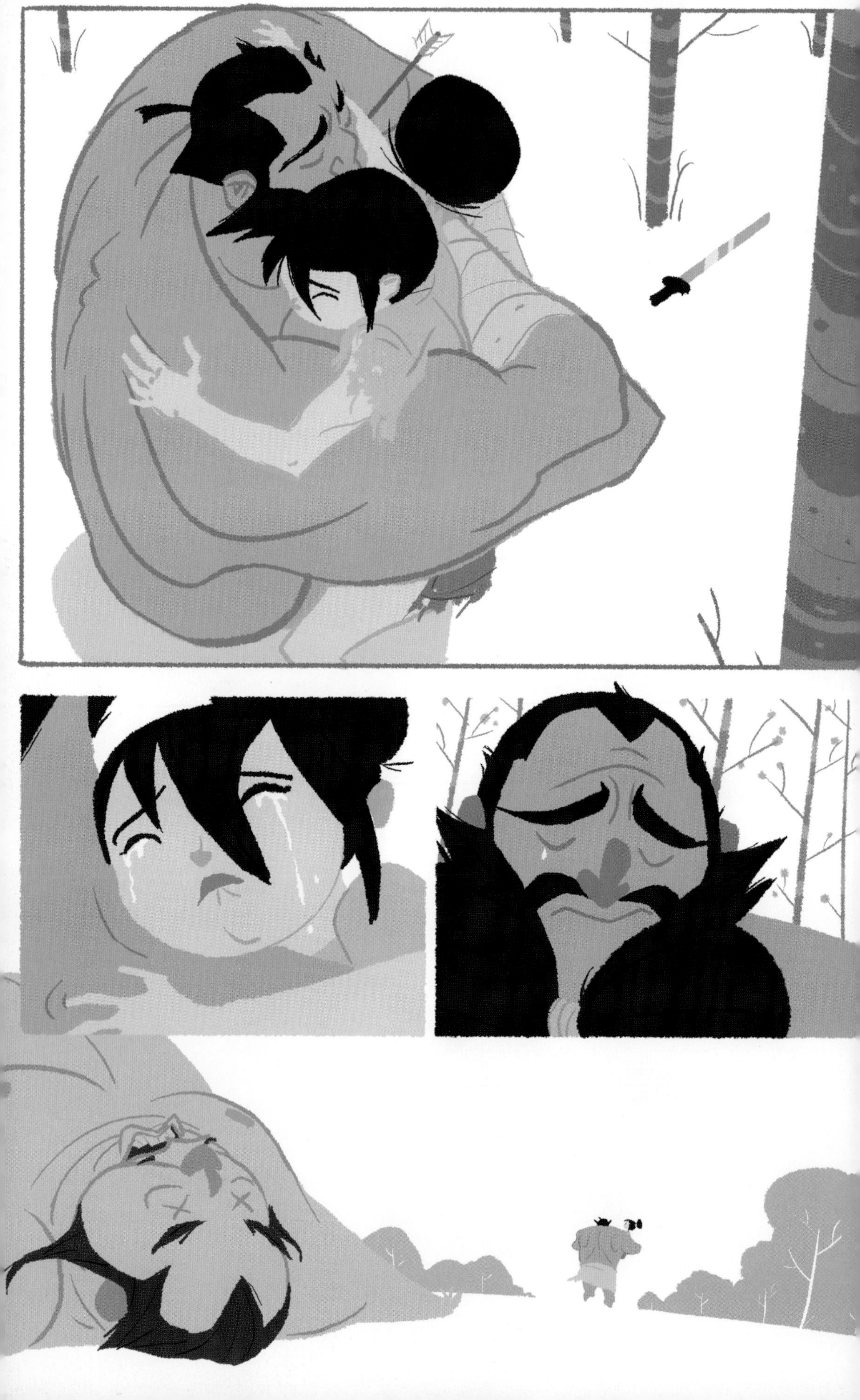

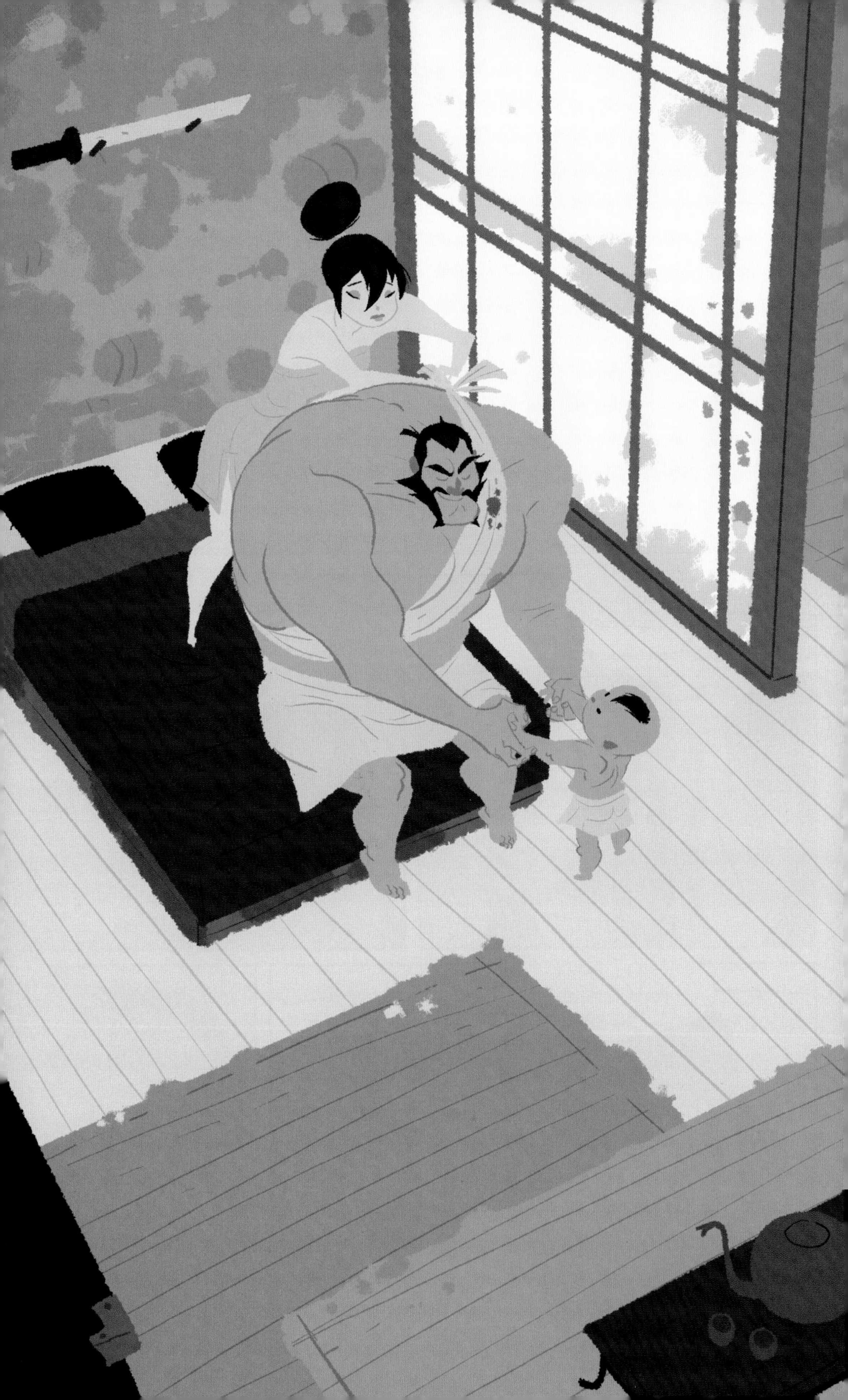

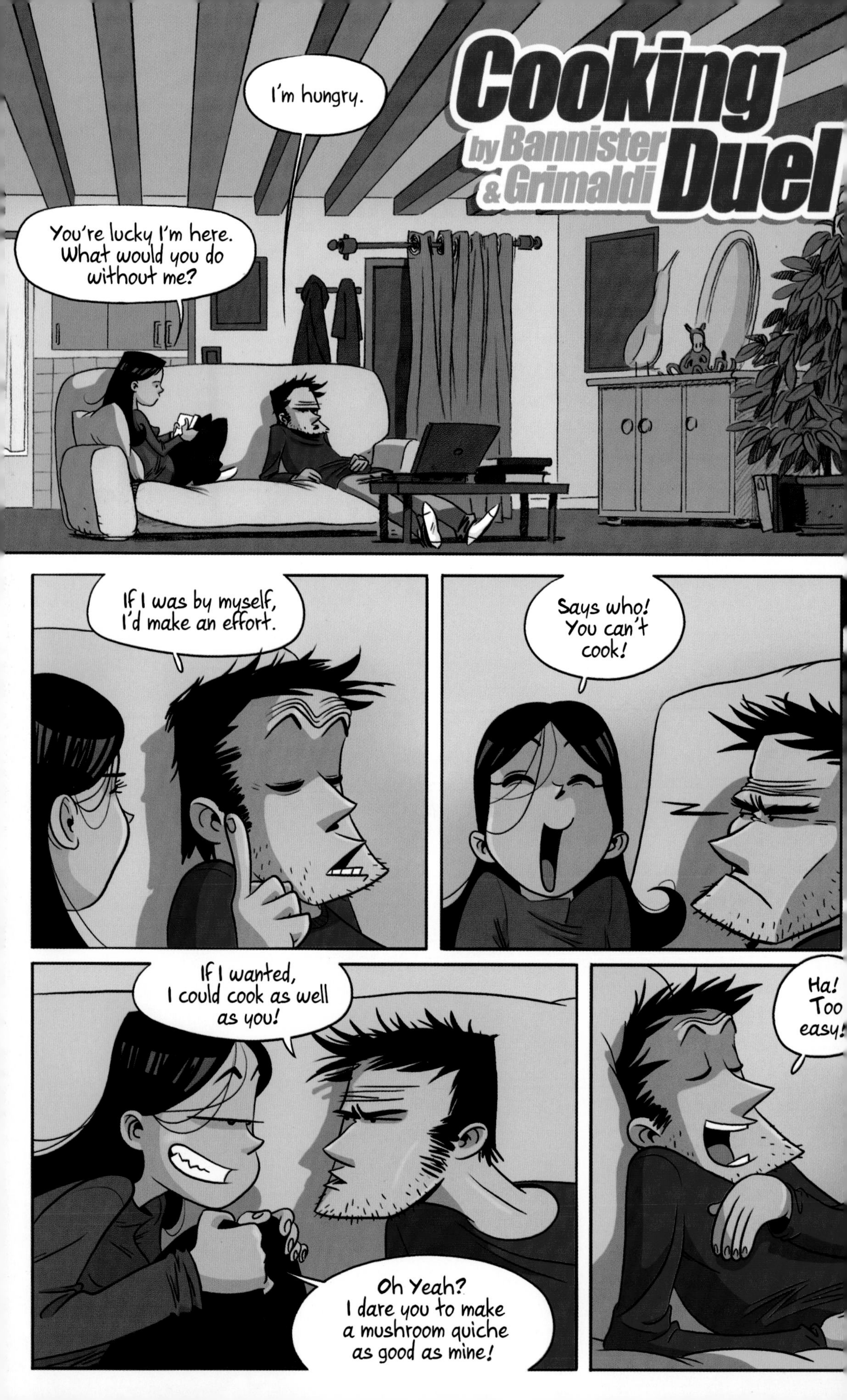
Cooking Duel
by Bannister & Grimaldi
I'm hungry.
You're lucky I'm here. What would you do without me?
If I was by myself, I'd make an effort.
Says who! You can't cook!
If I wanted, I could cook as well as you!
Oh Yeah? I dare you to make a mushroom quiche as good as mine!
Ha! Too easy!

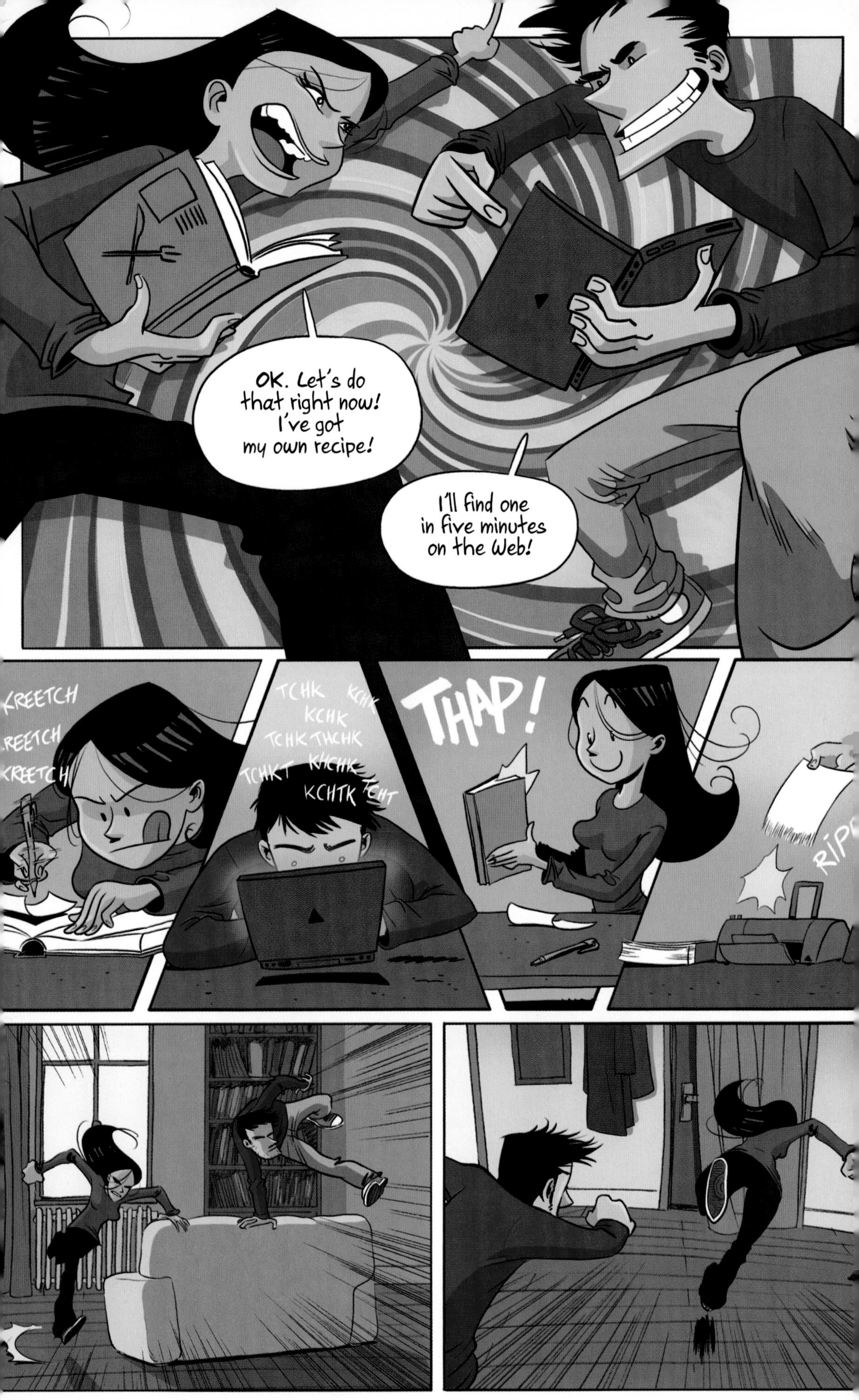
OK. Let's do that right now! I've got my own recipe!
I'll find one in five minutes on the Web!
KREETCH
KREETCH
KREETCH
TCHK KCHK
KCHK
TCHK THCHK
TCHKT KHCHK
KCHTK TCHT
THAP!
RIP

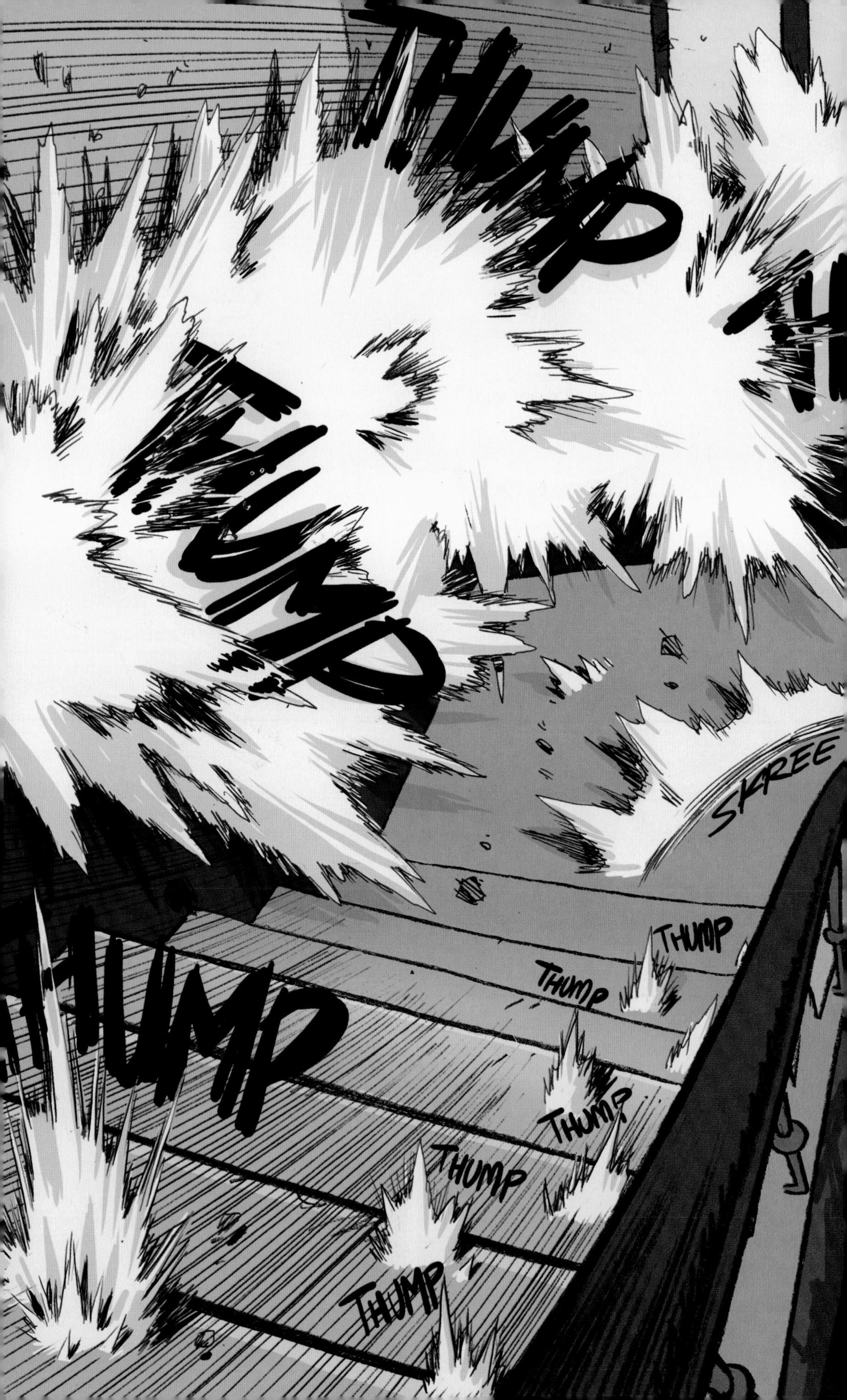
THUMP
THUMP
SKREE
THUMP
THUMP
THUMP
THUMP
THUMP
THUMP

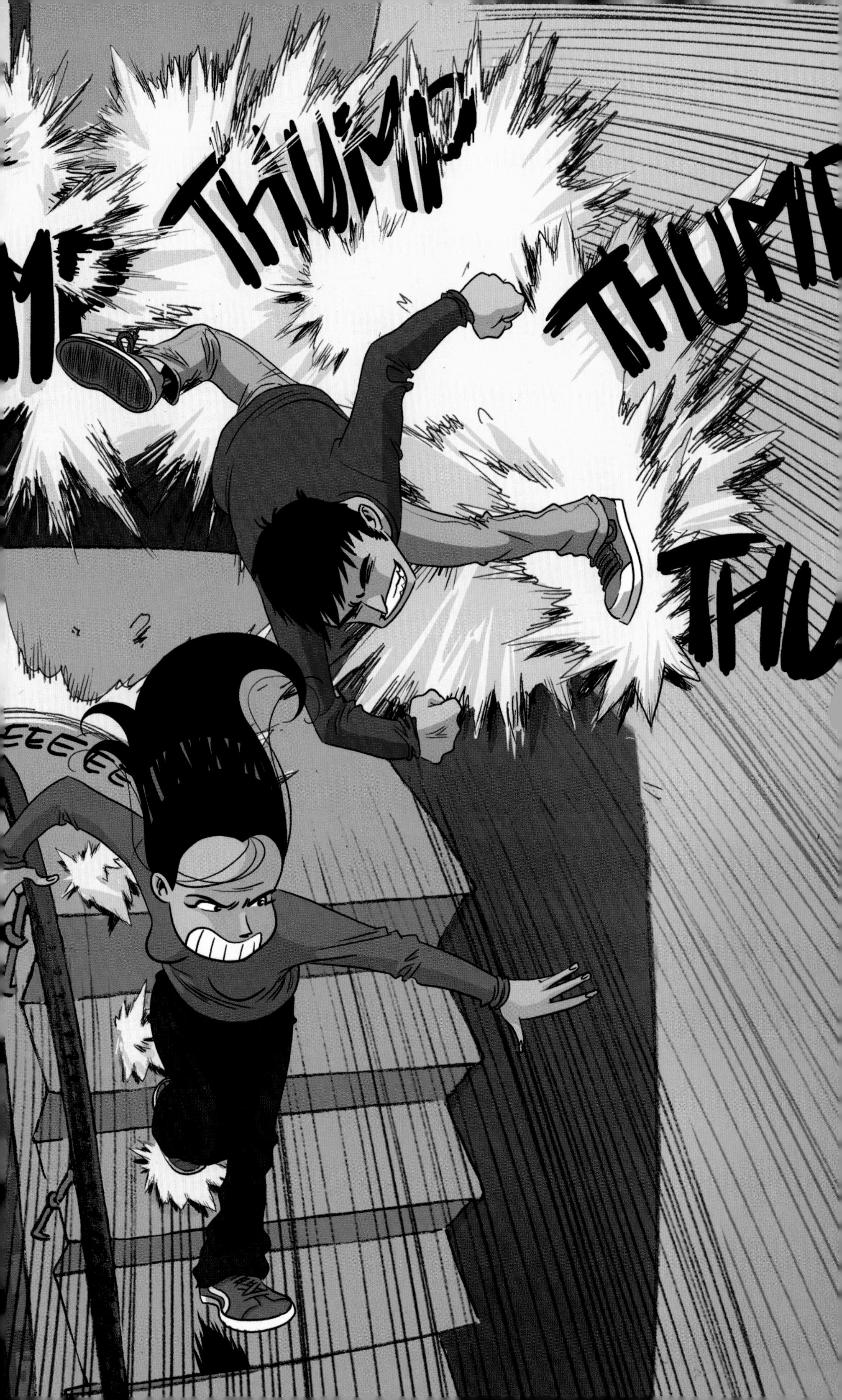

MP
THUMP
THUMP
THU
EEEEEE

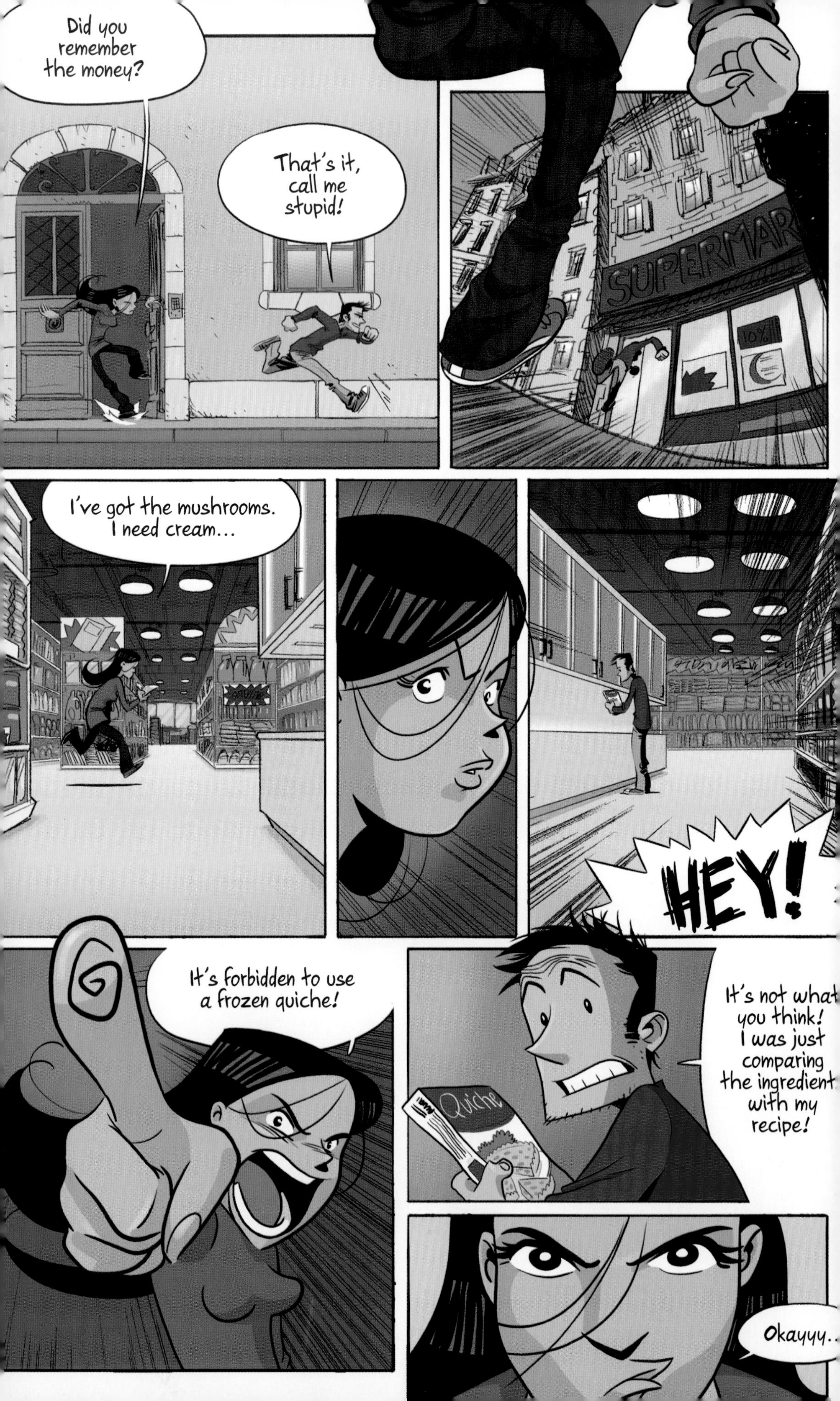

Did you remember the money?
That's it, call me stupid!
SUPERMAR
10%
I've got the mushrooms. I need cream...
HEY!
It's forbidden to use a frozen quiche!
It's not what you think! I was just comparing the ingredient with my recipe!
Quiche
Okayyy...

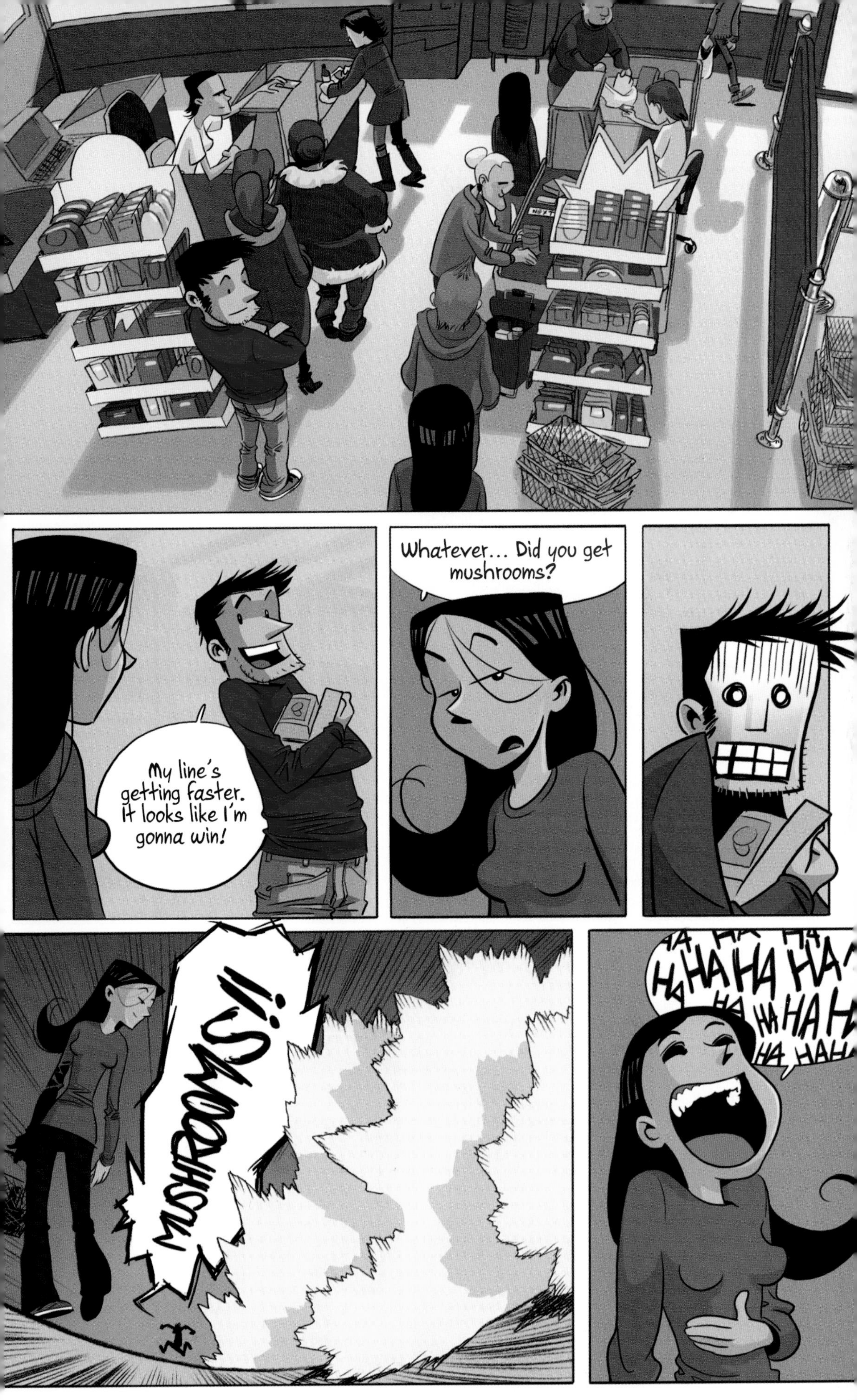

My line's getting faster. It looks like I'm gonna win!
Whatever... Did you get mushrooms?
MUSHROOMS!!
HA HA HA HA HA HA HA HA HA HA

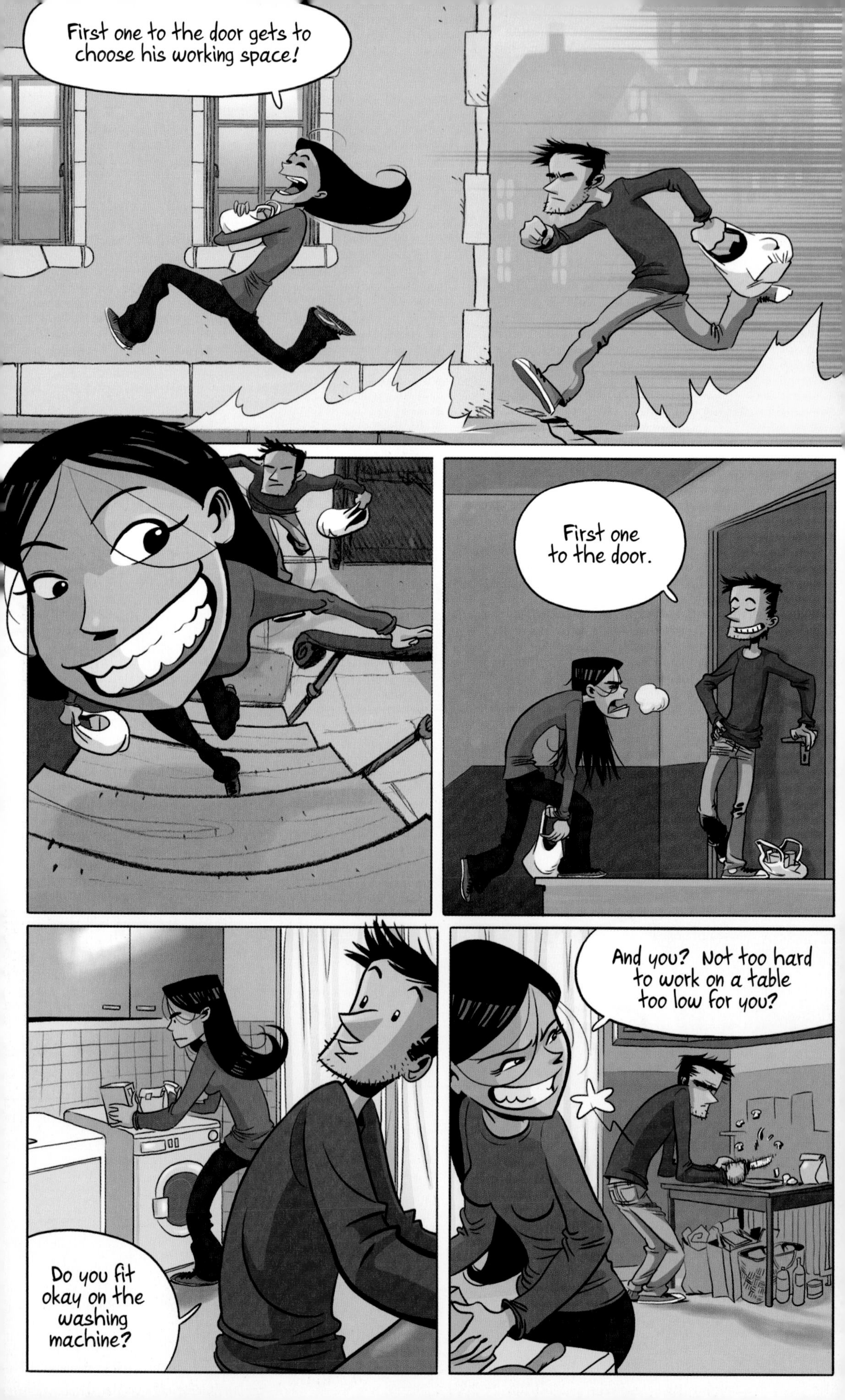
First one to the door gets to choose his working space!
First one to the door.
Do you fit okay on the washing machine?
And you? Not too hard to work on a table too low for you?

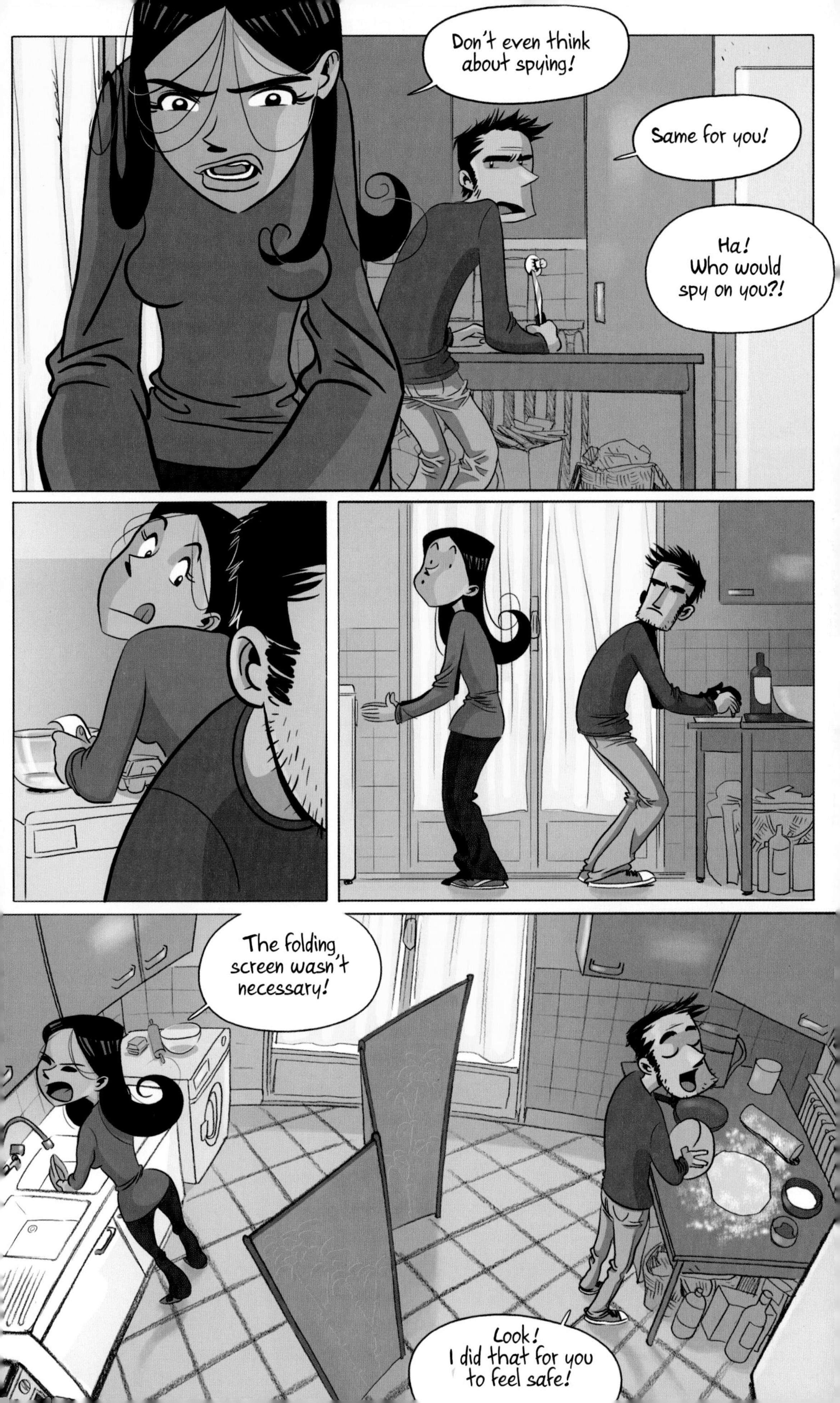
Don't even think about spying!
Same for you!
Ha! Who would spy on you?!
The folding screen wasn't necessary!
Look! I did that for you to feel safe!

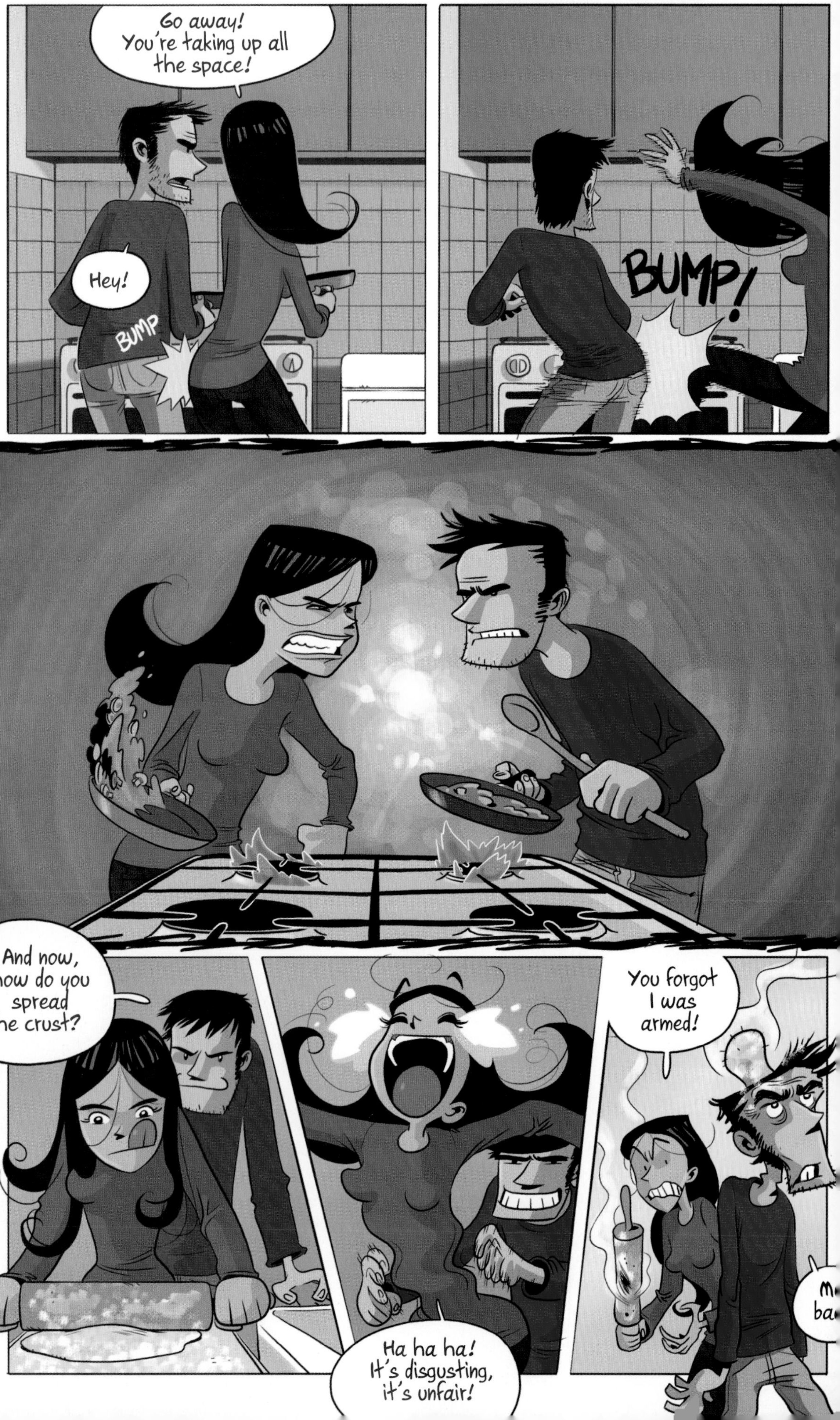

Go away! You're taking up all the space!
Hey!
BUMP
BUMP!
And now, how do you spread the crust?
Ha ha ha! It's disgusting, it's unfair!
You forgot I was armed!

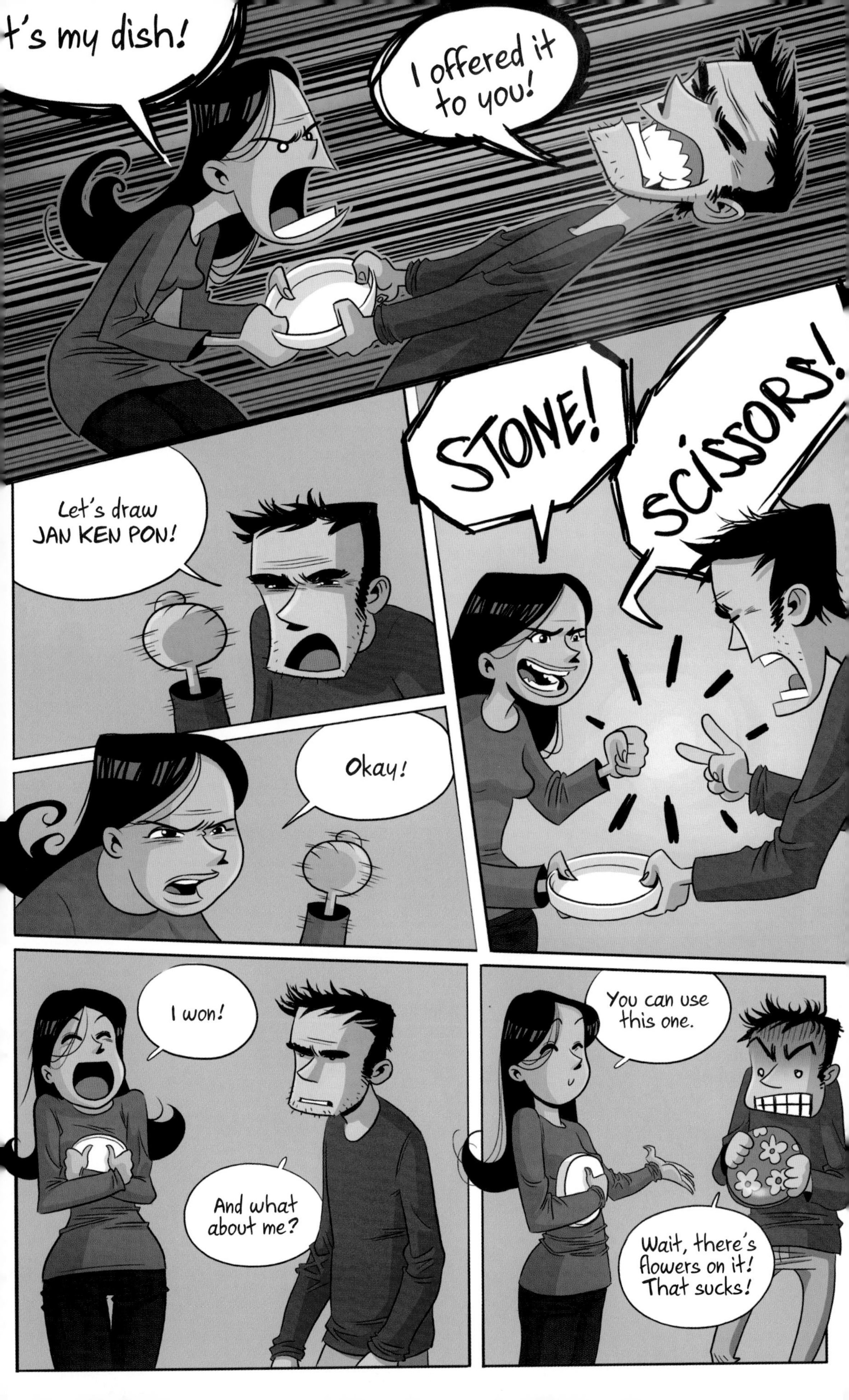
t's my dish!
I offered it to you!
Let's draw JAN KEN PON!
Okay!
STONE!
SCISSORS!
I won!
And what about me?
You can use this one.
Wait, there's flowers on it! That sucks!

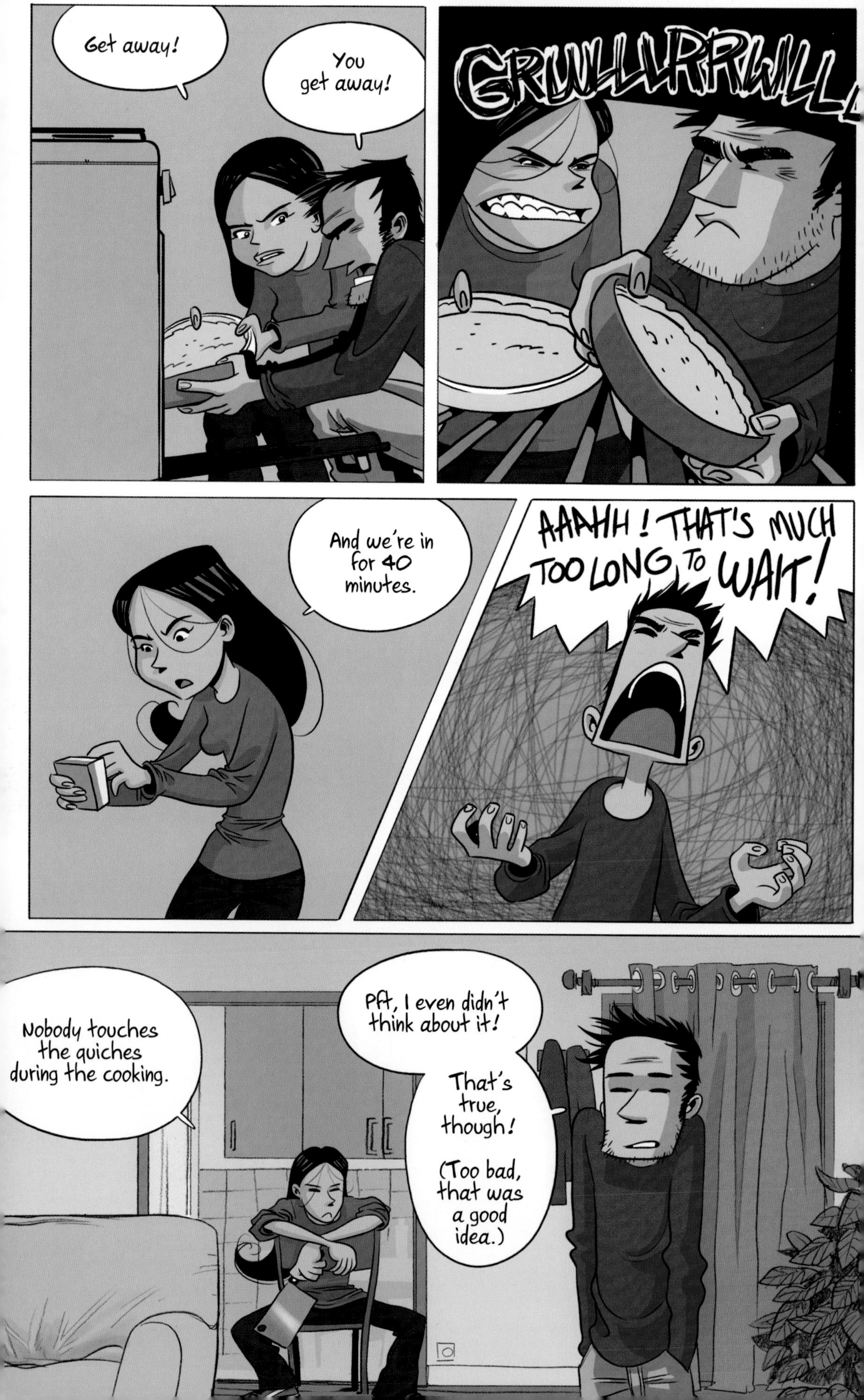
Get away!
You get away!
GRWLLRRWLL
And we're in for 40 minutes.
AAAHH! THAT'S MUCH TOO LONG TO WAIT!
Nobody touches the quiches during the cooking.
Pft, I even didn't think about it!
That's true, though!
(Too bad, that was a good idea.)

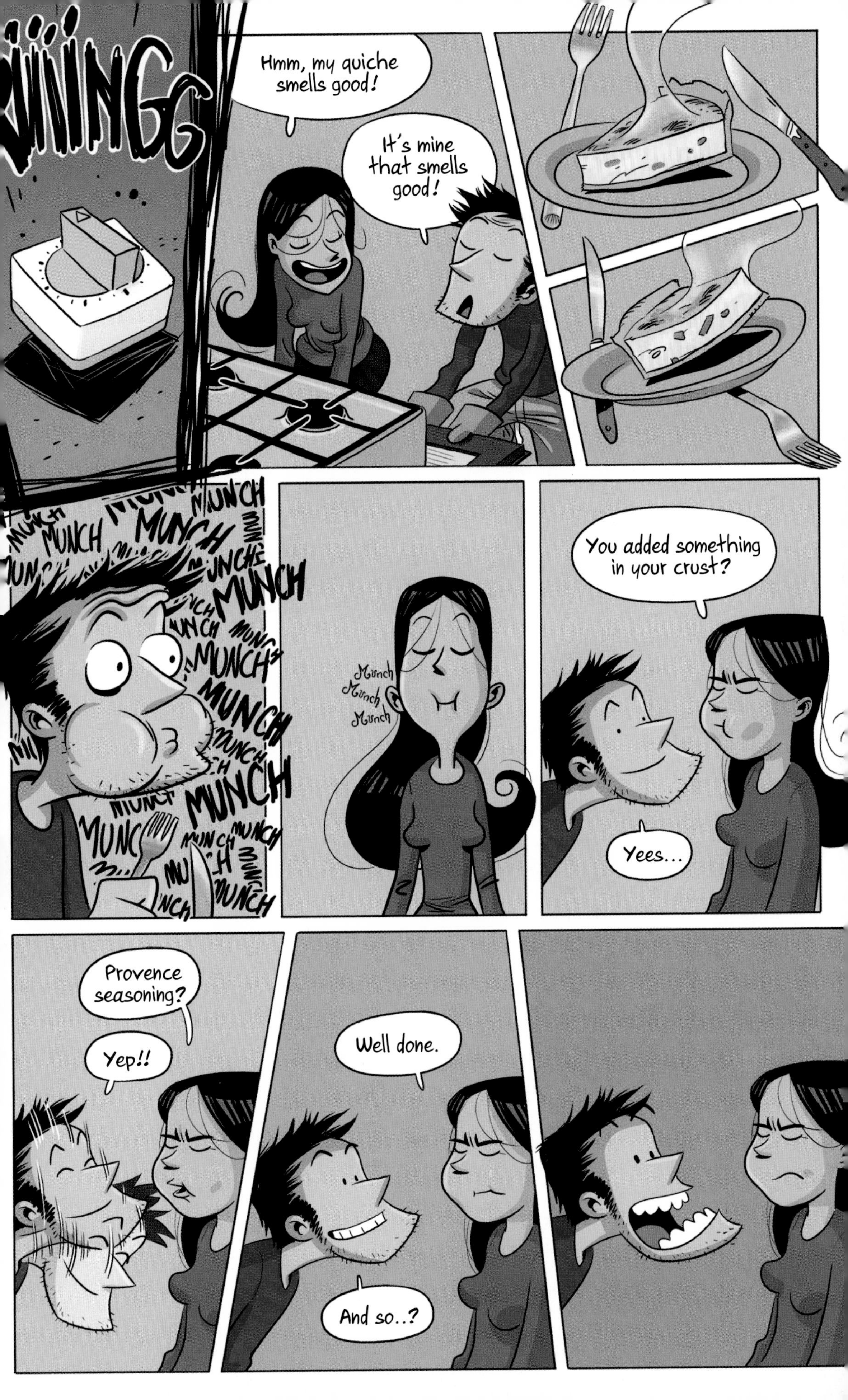
DIIIINGG
Hmm, my quiche smells good!
It's mine that smells good!
MUNCH MUNCH MUNCH
Munch Munch Munch
You added something in your crust?
Yees...
Provence seasoning?
Yep!!
Well done.
And so..?

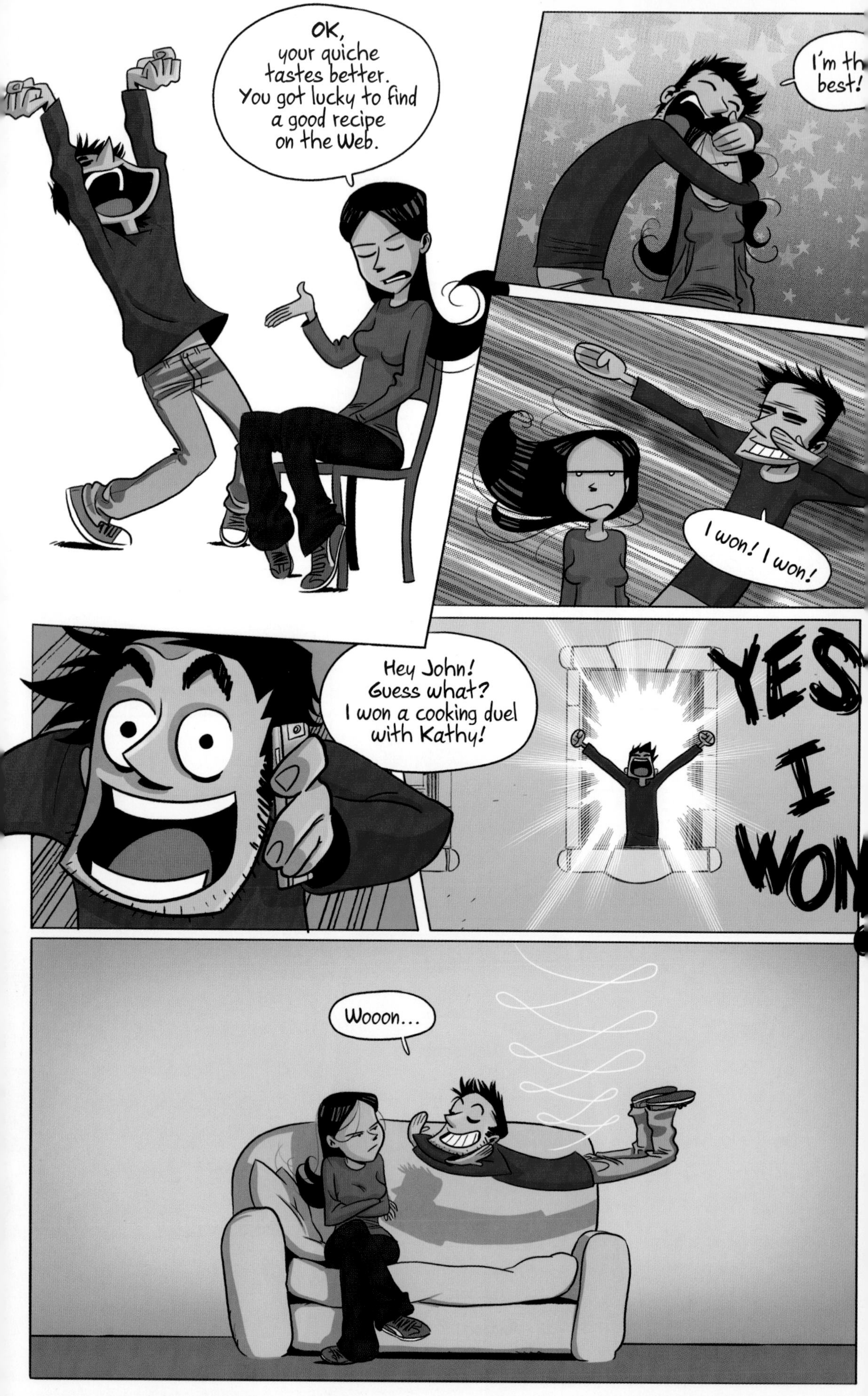
OK,
your quiche tastes better. You got lucky to find a good recipe on the Web.
I'm th
best!
I won! I won!
Hey John! Guess what? I won a cooking duel with Kathy!
YES
I
WON
Wooon...

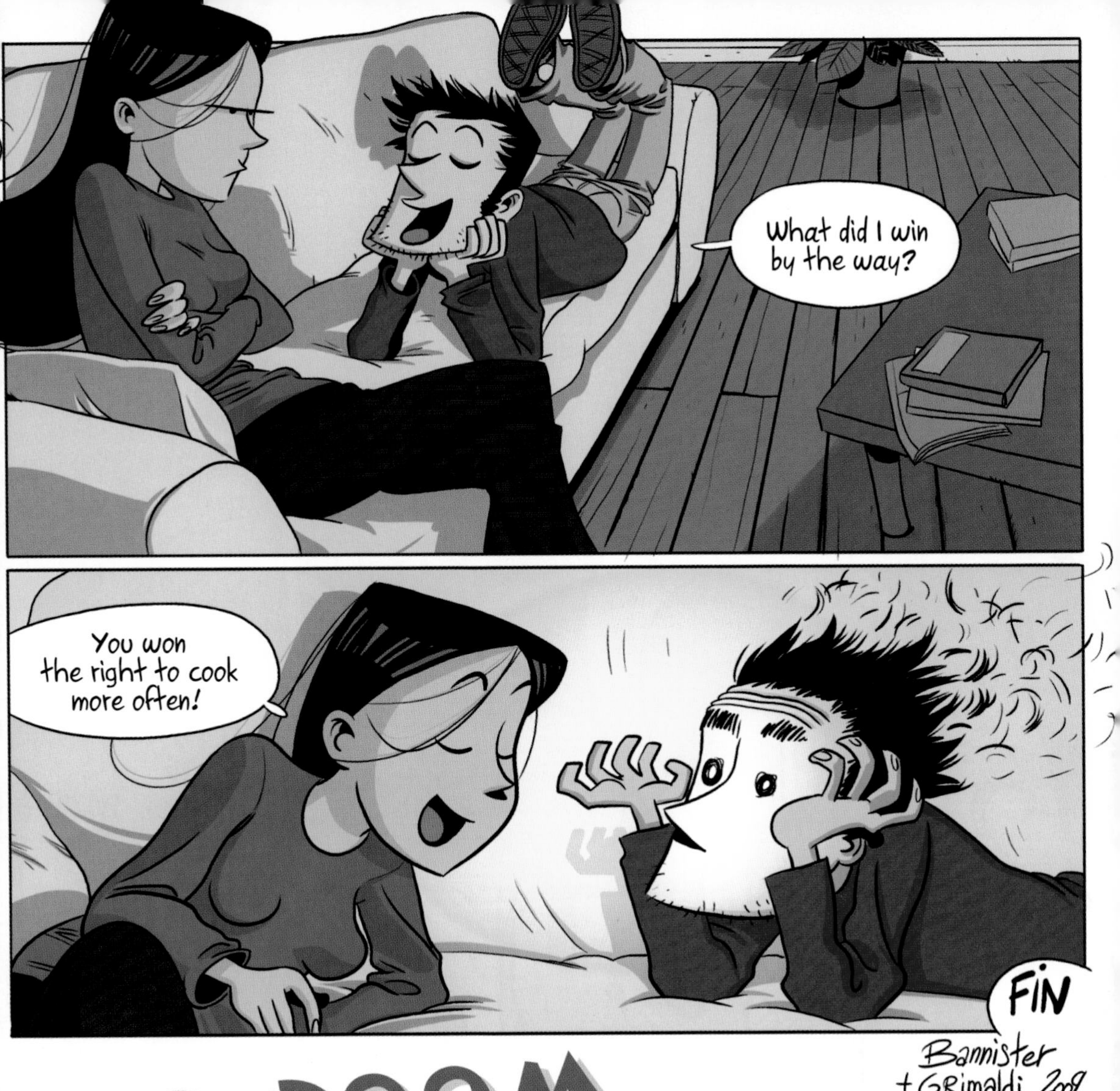

What did I win by the way?
You won the right to cook more often!
FIN
Bannister + GRimaldi 2009

MUSHROOM QUICHE

iNGREDiENTS

CRUST :
1 3/4 cups of flour
3 tbsp olive oil + 1 tsp to oil the pan
1 tsp herbes de Provence
pinch of salt
1/2 cup water (approximately)

FiLLiNG :
1 tbsp olive oil
1 pound mushrooms
3 big eggs
3 tbsp heavy cream (or soy cream)
1 cup grated cheese (your choice)
salt and pepper

1. THE CRUST :

In a large mixing bowl add 1 3/4 cups flour, 3 tbsp olive oil, herbes de Provence, and a pinch of salt. Slowly add water to mixture while stirring together with your hand (note: use just enough water so your dough has a good workable texture). Next, dust a clean flat surface with flour so when you roll out your dough it will not stick. Roll out dough so it will fill your tart pan. Lightly oil the tart pan before pressing in dough. Once pressed into the pan, lightly puncture dough twelve times with a fork. Leave the pan in your fridge while you complete the filling.

Now is a good time to preheat your oven to 410°F.

2. THE FiLLiNG :

Heat up 1 tbsp of olive oil in a pan and saute the mushrooms. Next, break 3 eggs in a bowl, and whisk them together with 3 tbsp of cream. Season mixture with salt and pepper.

Grate 1 cup of good cheese.

Take the tart pan from the fridge. Spread the mushrooms into the pan and then add the egg/cream mixture. Top with the grated cheese.

Put the pan into the oven and bake for 40 minutes until eggs set. (Keep an eye on your quiche. The baking time will vary with each oven.)

SERVE WiTH A SiDE SALAD OF YOUR CHOiCE.

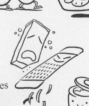

BON APPETiT !

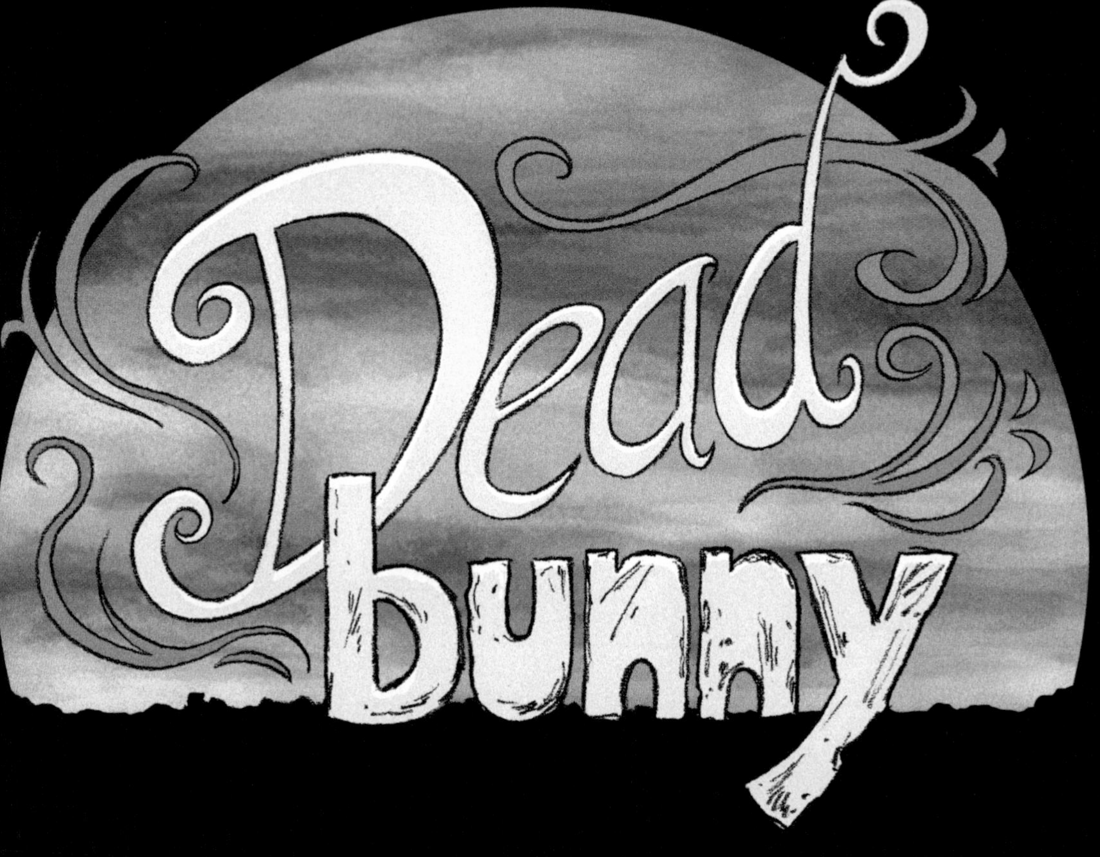
Dead
bunny

Written by

Nikki Damon

Art by

Justin Ridge

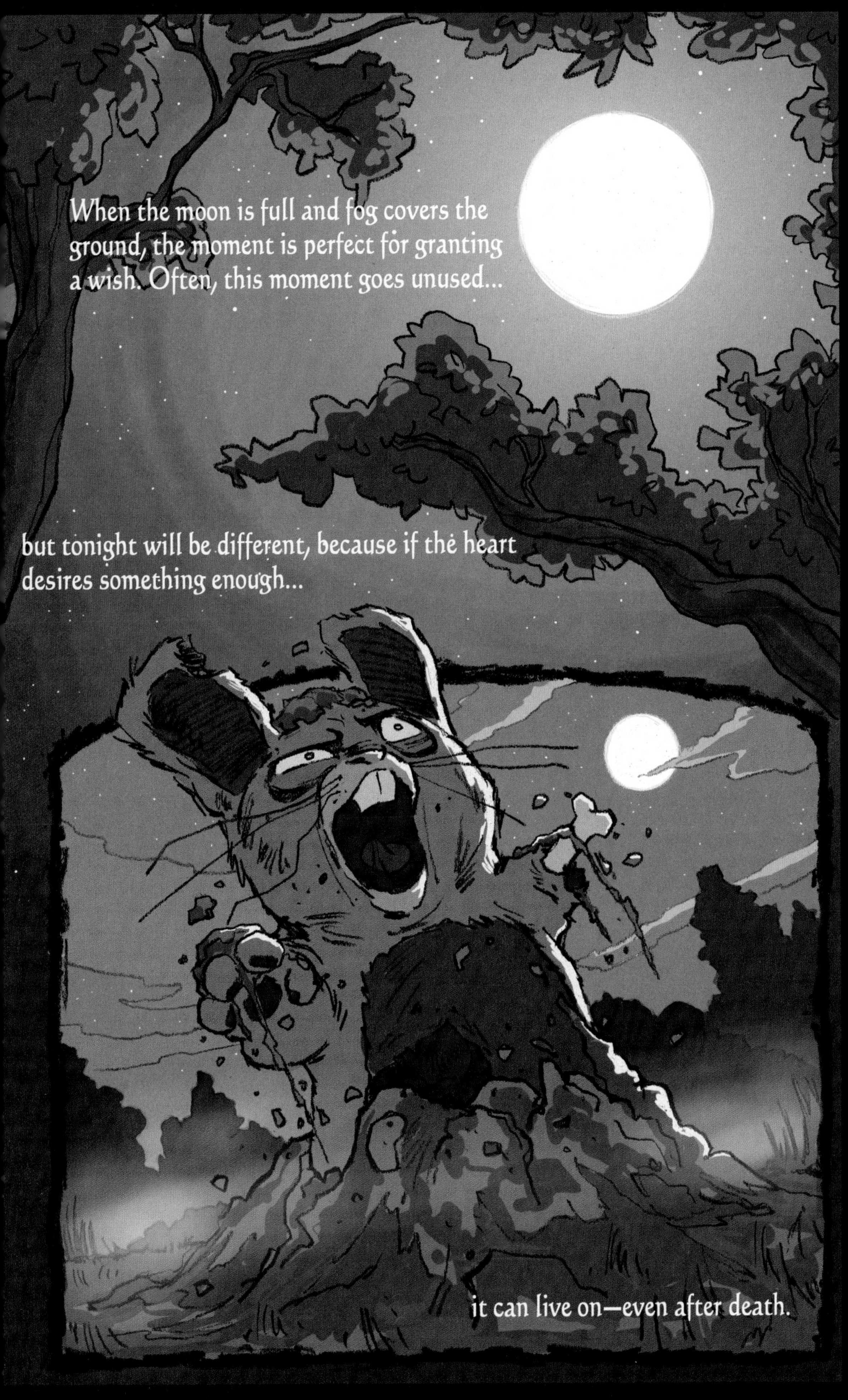
When the moon is full and fog covers the ground, the moment is perfect for granting a wish. Often, this moment goes unused...
but tonight will be different, because if the heart desires something enough...
it can live on—even after death.

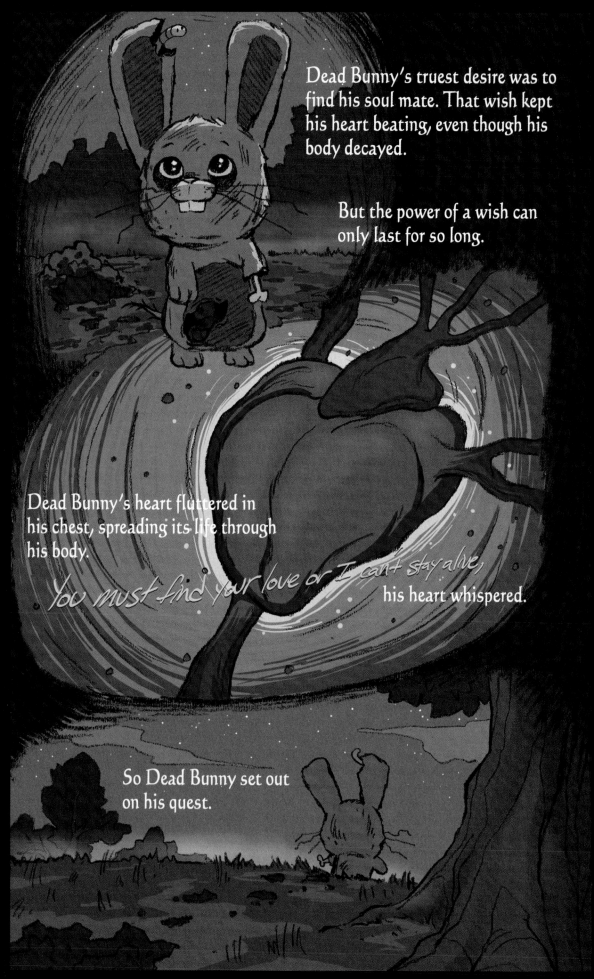

Dead Bunny's truest desire was to find his soul mate. That wish kept his heart beating, even though his body decayed.

But the power of a wish can only last for so long.

Dead Bunny's heart fluttered in his chest, spreading its life through his body.

You must find your love or I can't stay alive, his heart whispered.

So Dead Bunny set out on his quest.

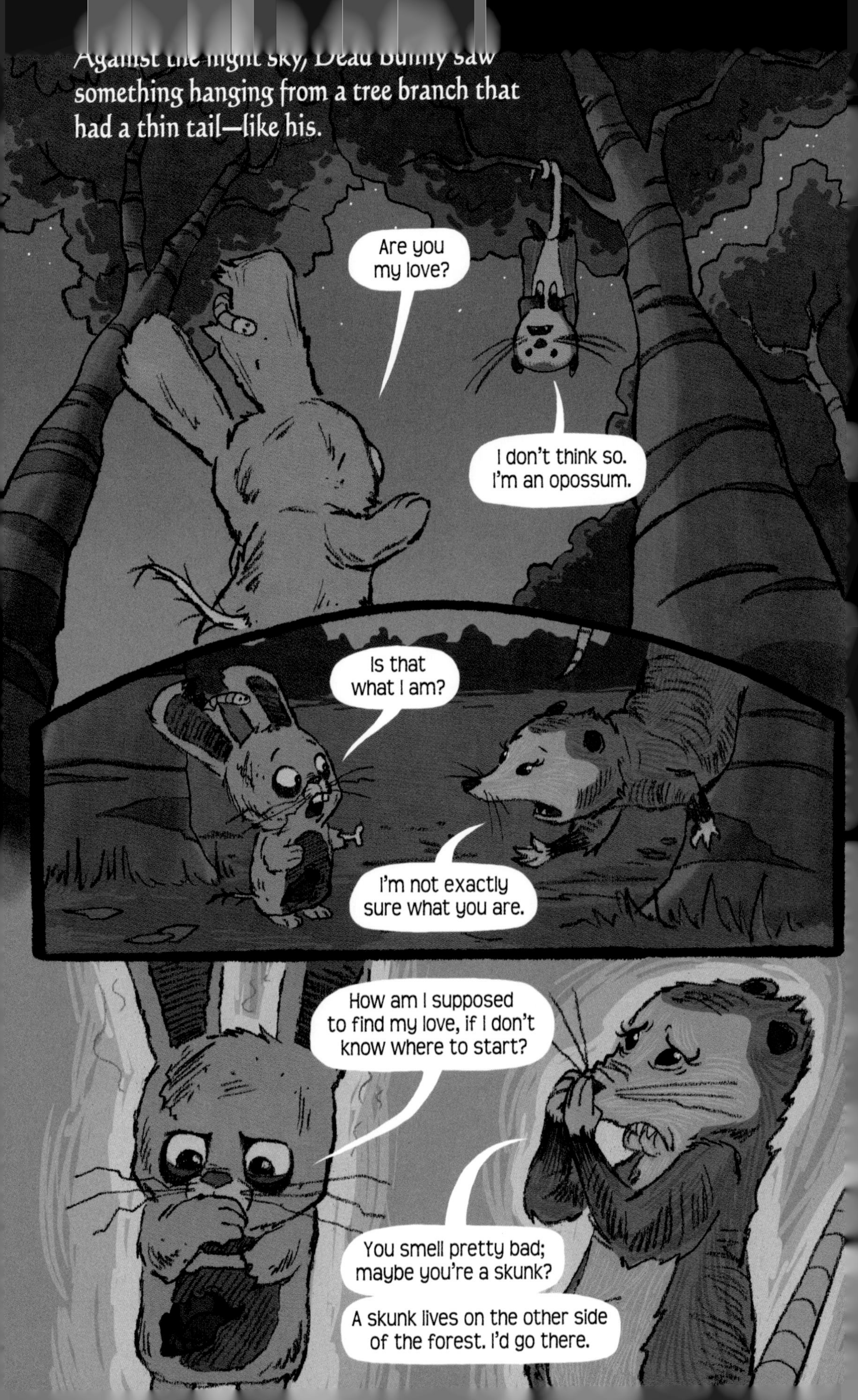
Against the night sky, Dead Bunny saw something hanging from a tree branch that had a thin tail—like his.
Are you my love?
I don't think so. I'm an opossum.
Is that what I am?
I'm not exactly sure what you are.
How am I supposed to find my love, if I don't know where to start?
You smell pretty bad; maybe you're a skunk?
A skunk lives on the other side of the forest. I'd go there.

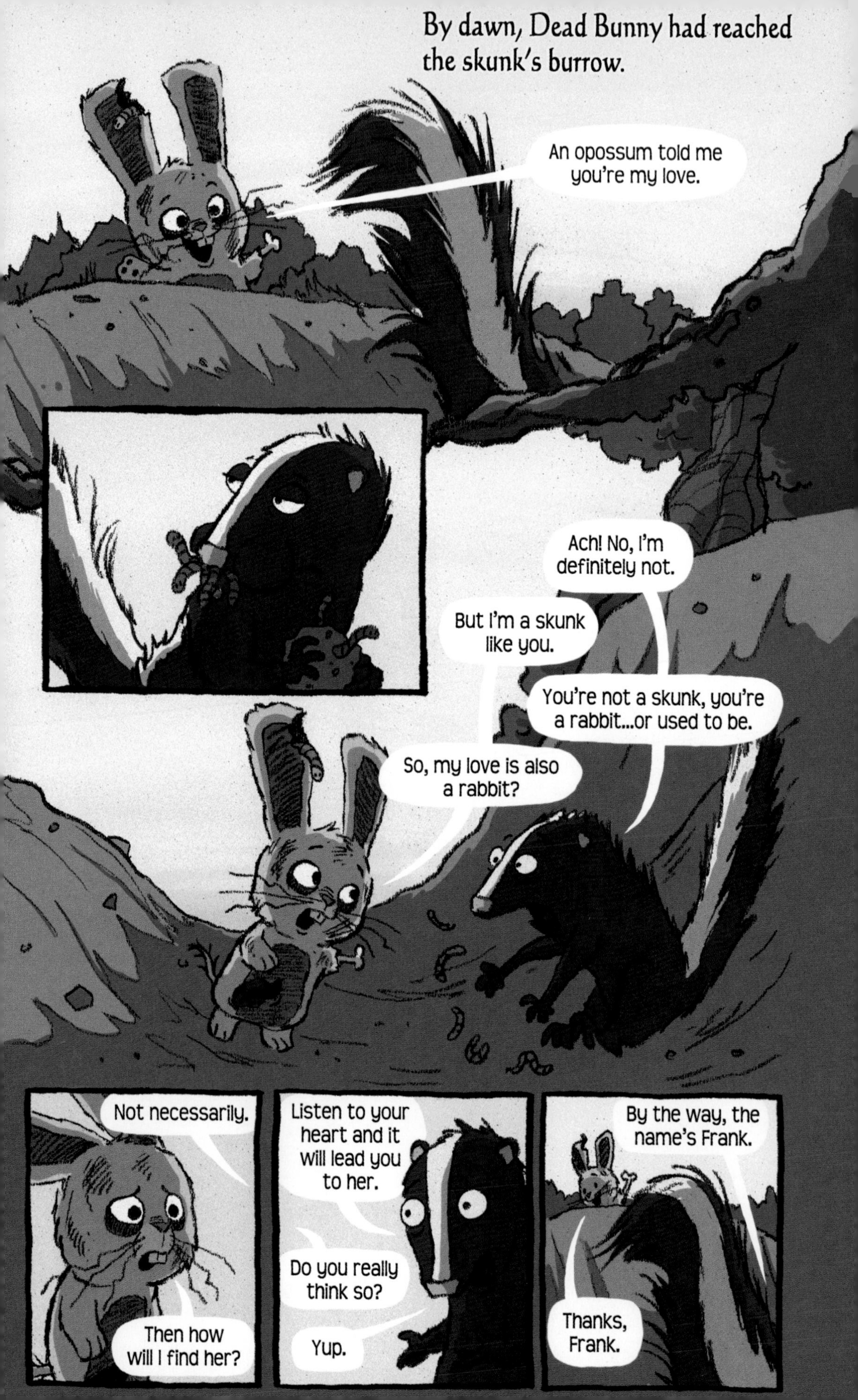
By dawn, Dead Bunny had reached the skunk's burrow.
An opossum told me you're my love.
Ach! No, I'm definitely not.
But I'm a skunk like you.
You're not a skunk, you're a rabbit...or used to be.
So, my love is also a rabbit?
Not necessarily.
Then how will I find her?
Listen to your heart and it will lead you to her.
Do you really think so?
Yup.
By the way, the name's Frank.
Thanks, Frank.

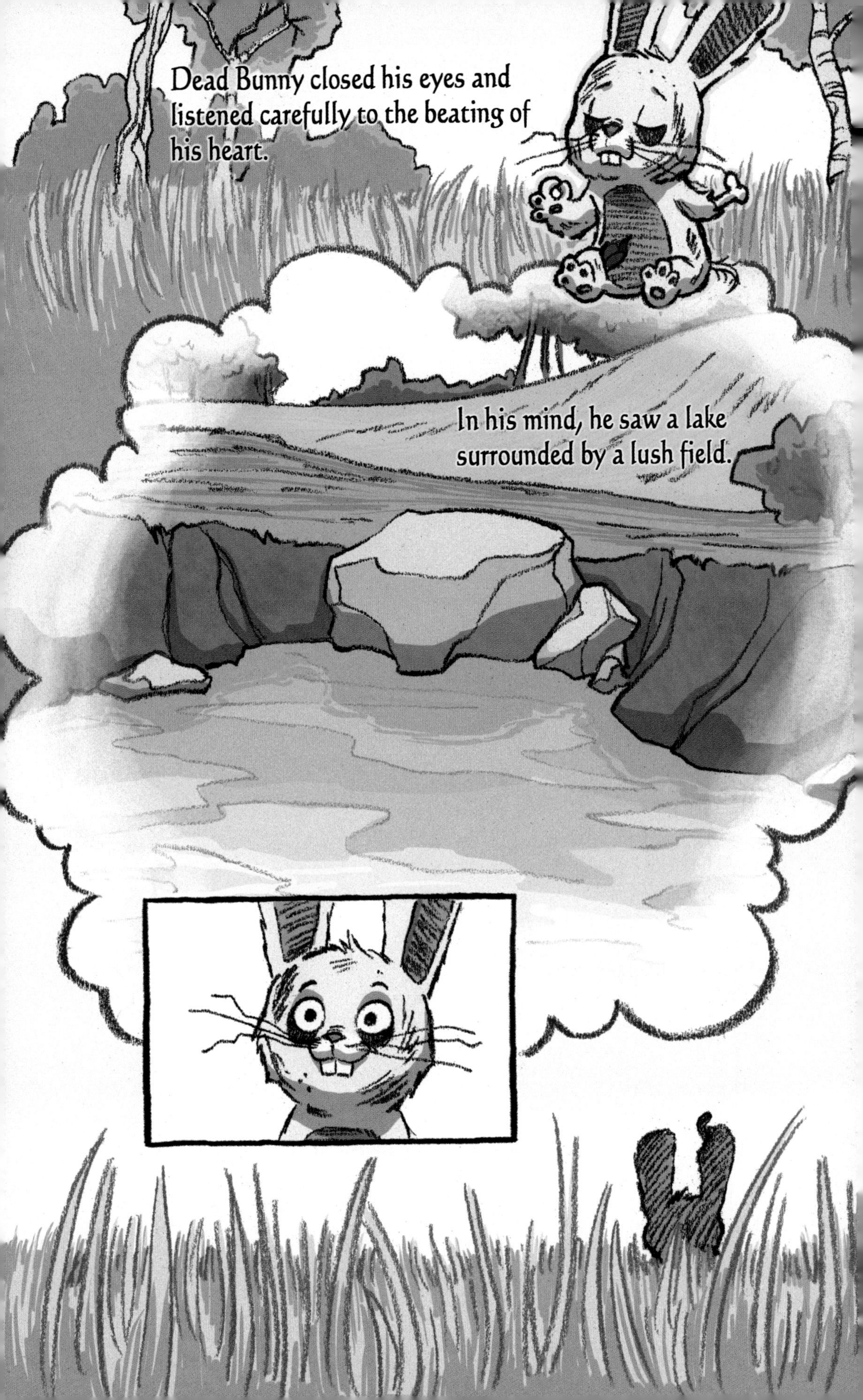
Dead Bunny closed his eyes and listened carefully to the beating of his heart.
In his mind, he saw a lake surrounded by a lush field.

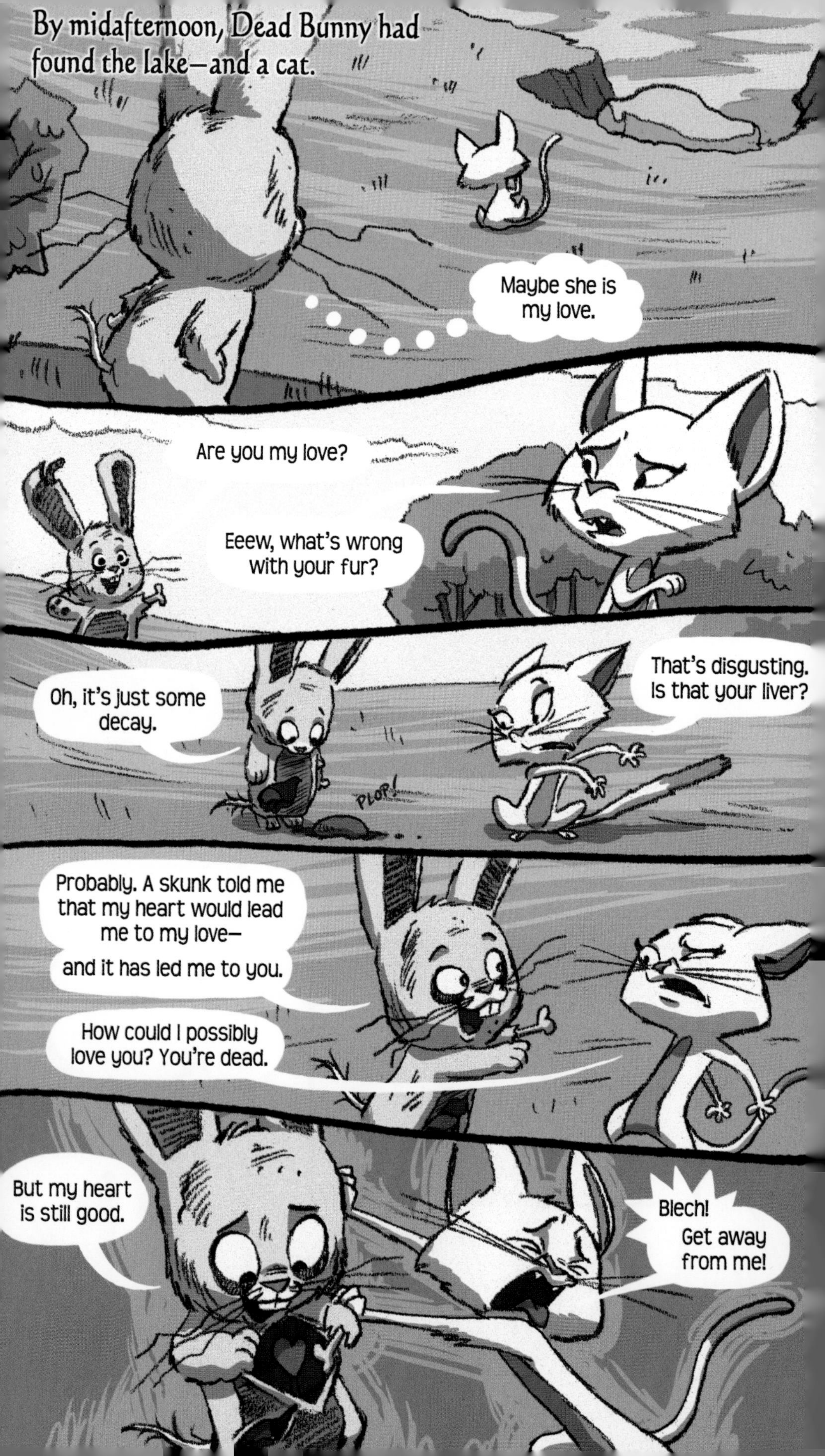
By midafternoon, Dead Bunny had found the lake—and a cat.
Maybe she is my love.
Are you my love?
Eeew, what's wrong with your fur?
Oh, it's just some decay.
That's disgusting. Is that your liver?
PLOP!
Probably. A skunk told me that my heart would lead me to my love—
and it has led me to you.
How could I possibly love you? You're dead.
But my heart is still good.
Blech!
Get away from me!

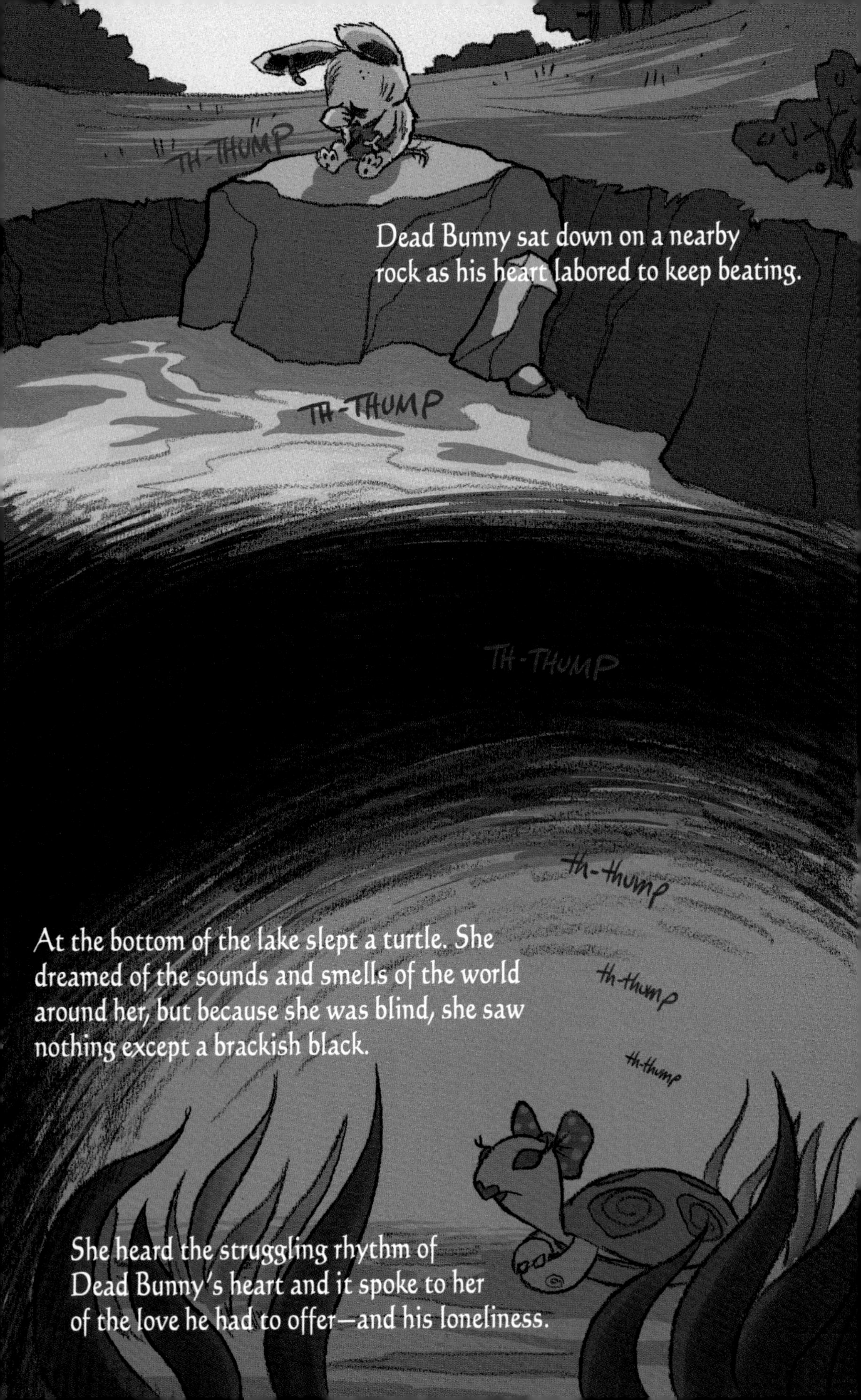
TH-THUMP
TH-THUMP
TH-THUMP
th-thump
th-thump
th-thump

Dead Bunny sat down on a nearby rock as his heart labored to keep beating.

At the bottom of the lake slept a turtle. She dreamed of the sounds and smells of the world around her, but because she was blind, she saw nothing except a brackish black.

She heard the struggling rhythm of Dead Bunny's heart and it spoke to her of the love he had to offer—and his loneliness.

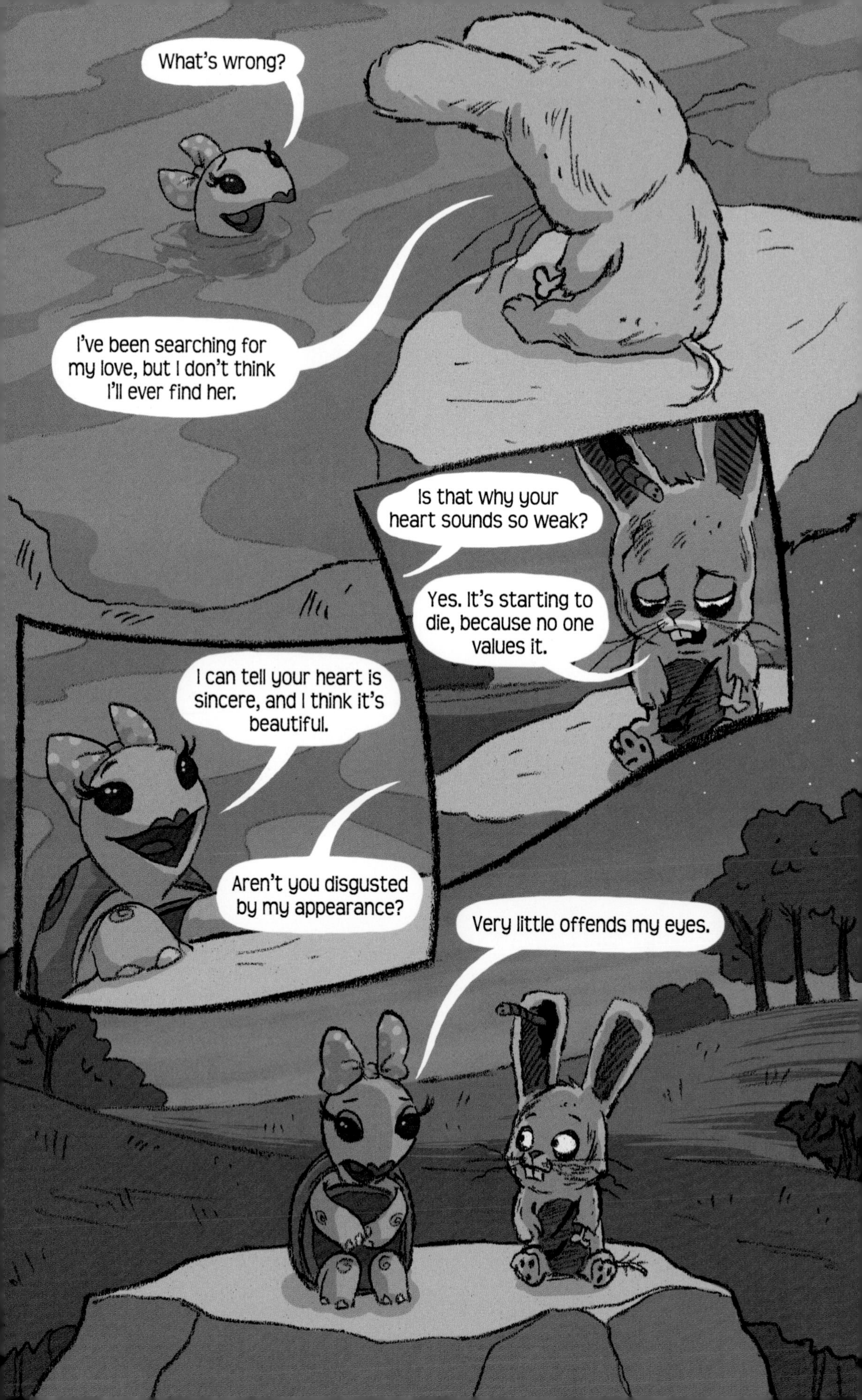

What's wrong?
I've been searching for my love, but I don't think I'll ever find her.
Is that why your heart sounds so weak?
Yes. It's starting to die, because no one values it.
I can tell your heart is sincere, and I think it's beautiful.
Aren't you disgusted by my appearance?
Very little offends my eyes.

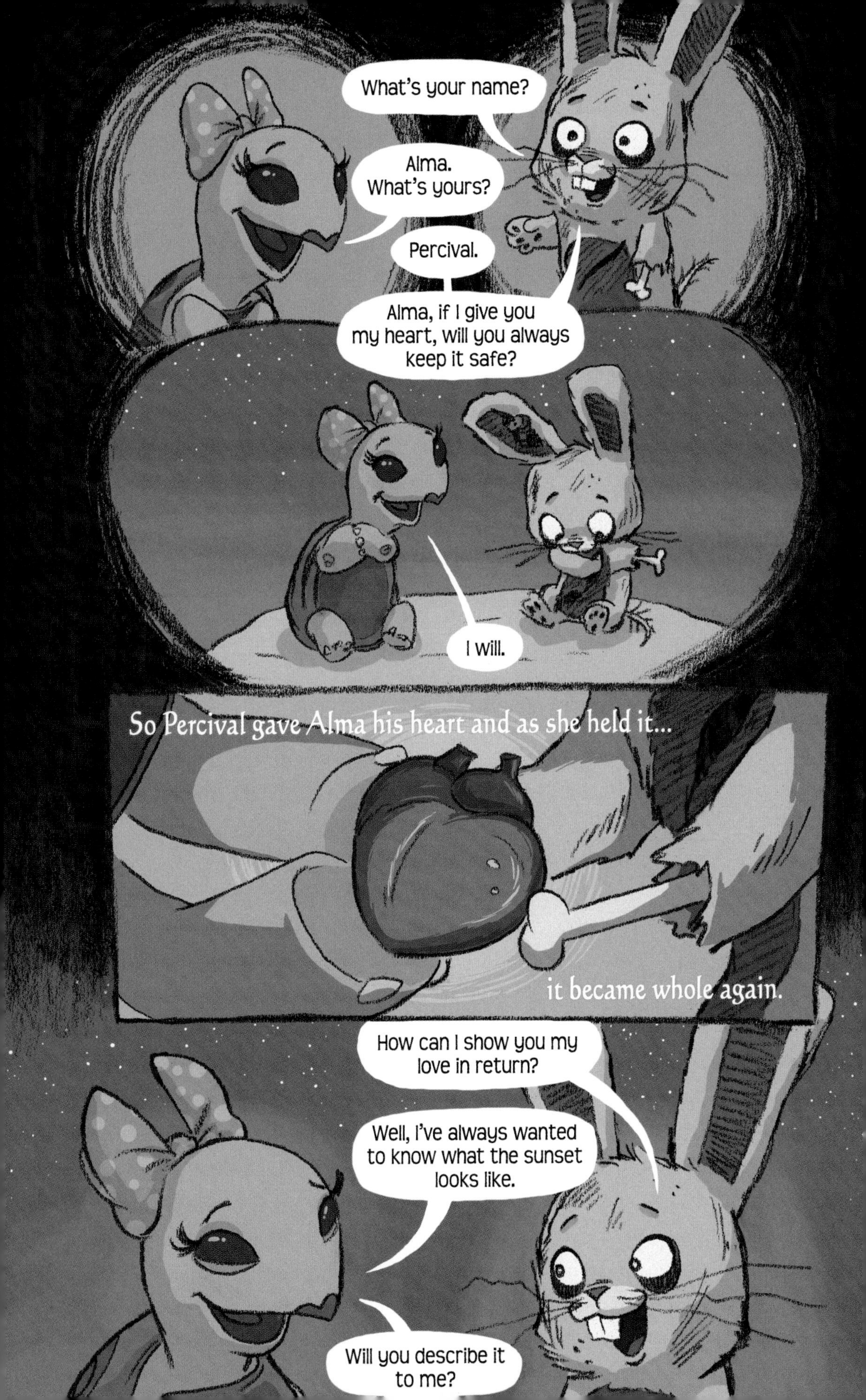
What's your name?
Alma.
What's yours?
Percival.
Alma, if I give you my heart, will you always keep it safe?
I will.
So Percival gave Alma his heart and as she held it...
it became whole again.
How can I show you my love in return?
Well, I've always wanted to know what the sunset looks like.
Will you describe it to me?

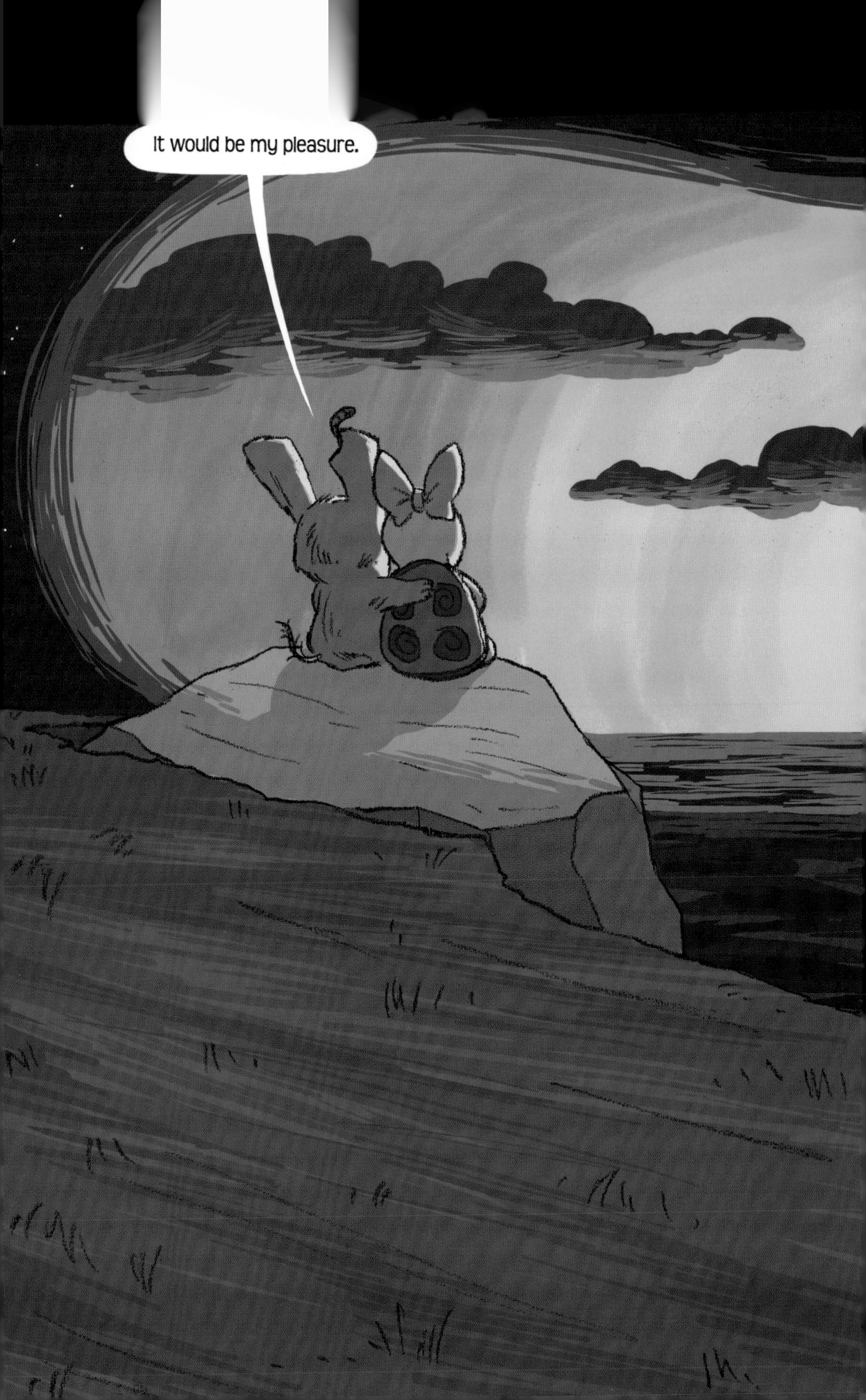
It would be my pleasure.

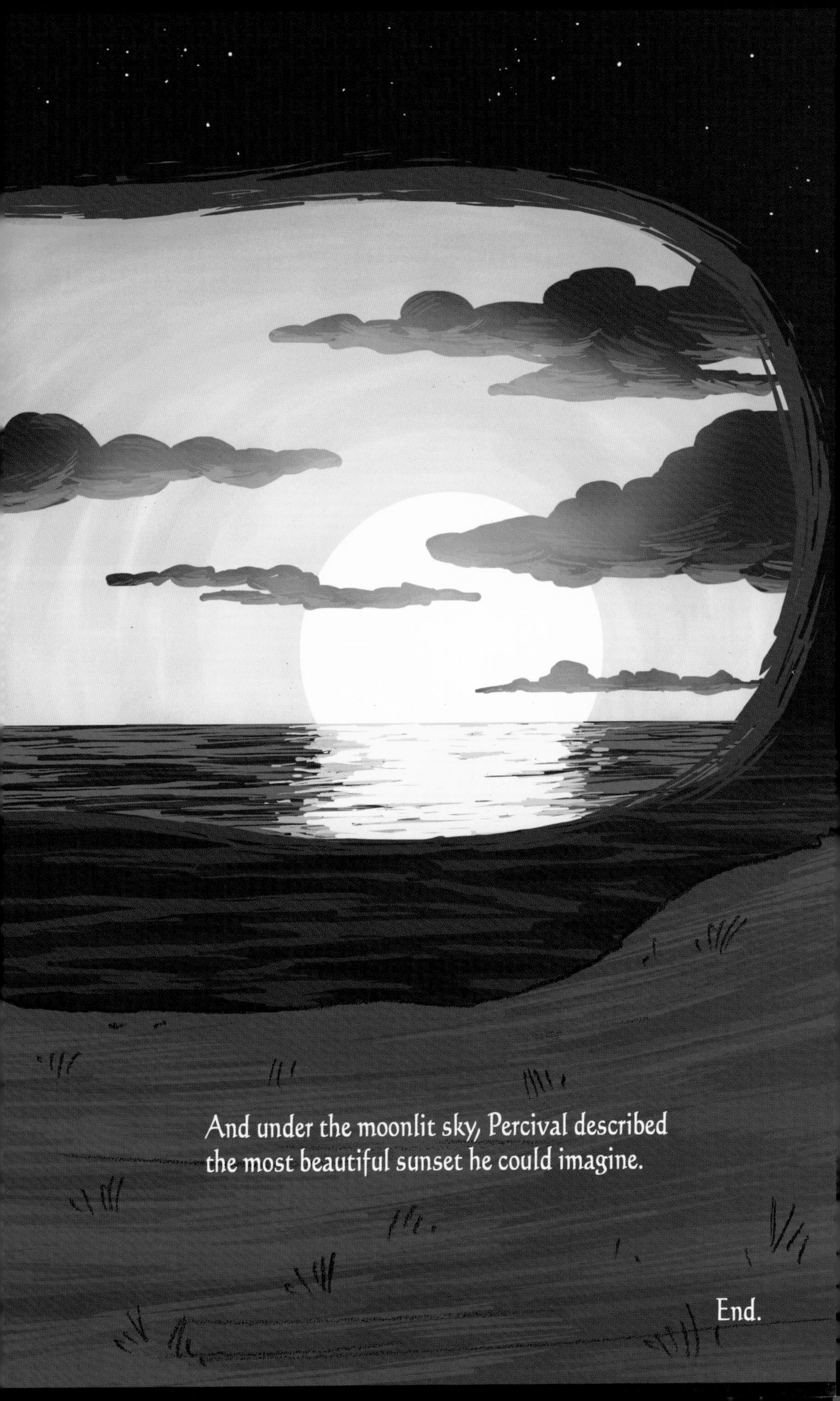
And under the moonlit sky, Percival described the most beautiful sunset he could imagine.
End.

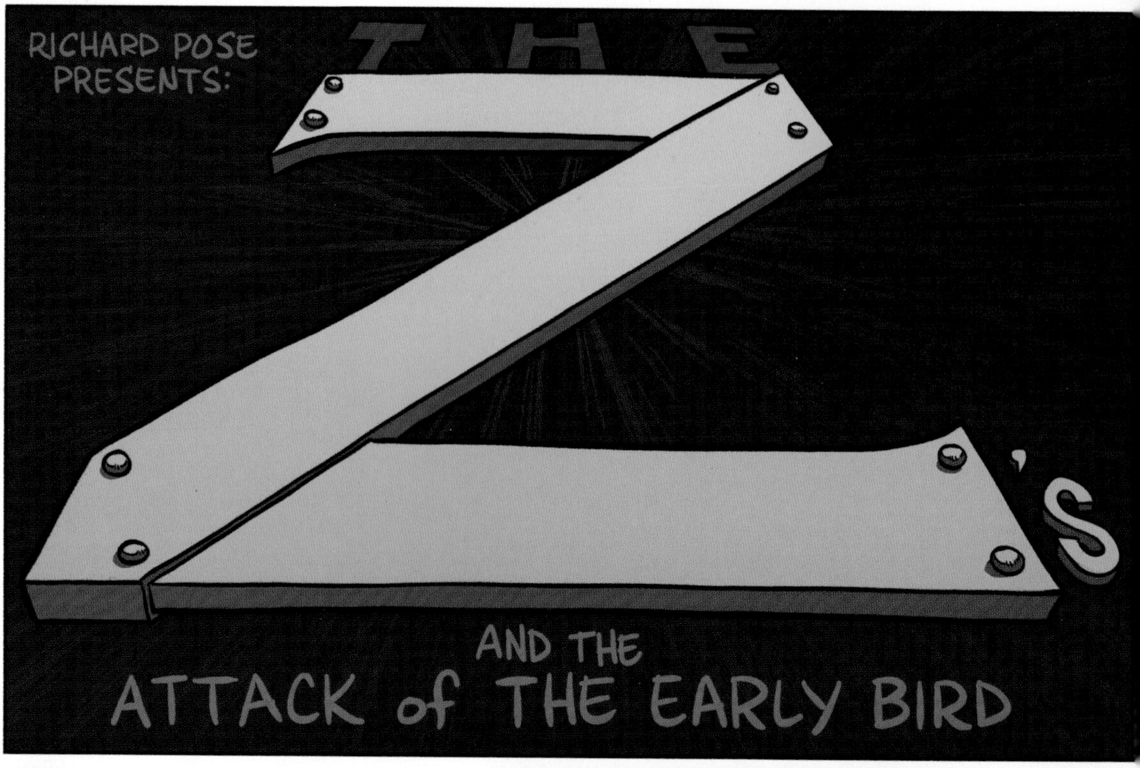
RICHARD POSE
PRESENTS:
THE Z'S
AND THE
ATTACK of THE EARLY BIRD

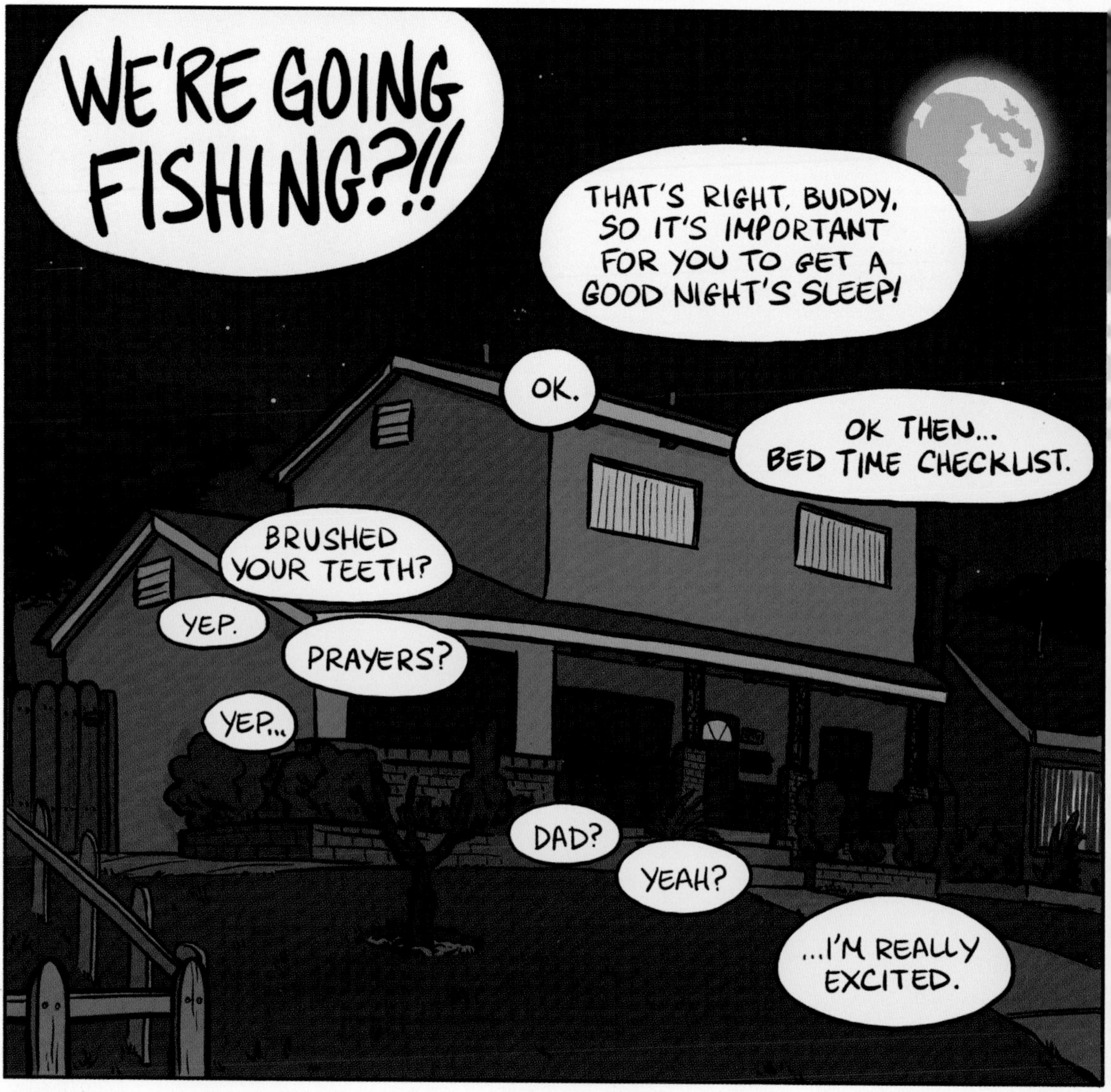
WE'RE GOING FISHING?!!
THAT'S RIGHT, BUDDY. SO IT'S IMPORTANT FOR YOU TO GET A GOOD NIGHT'S SLEEP!
OK.
OK THEN... BED TIME CHECKLIST.
BRUSHED YOUR TEETH?
YEP.
PRAYERS?
YEP...
DAD?
YEAH?
...I'M REALLY EXCITED.

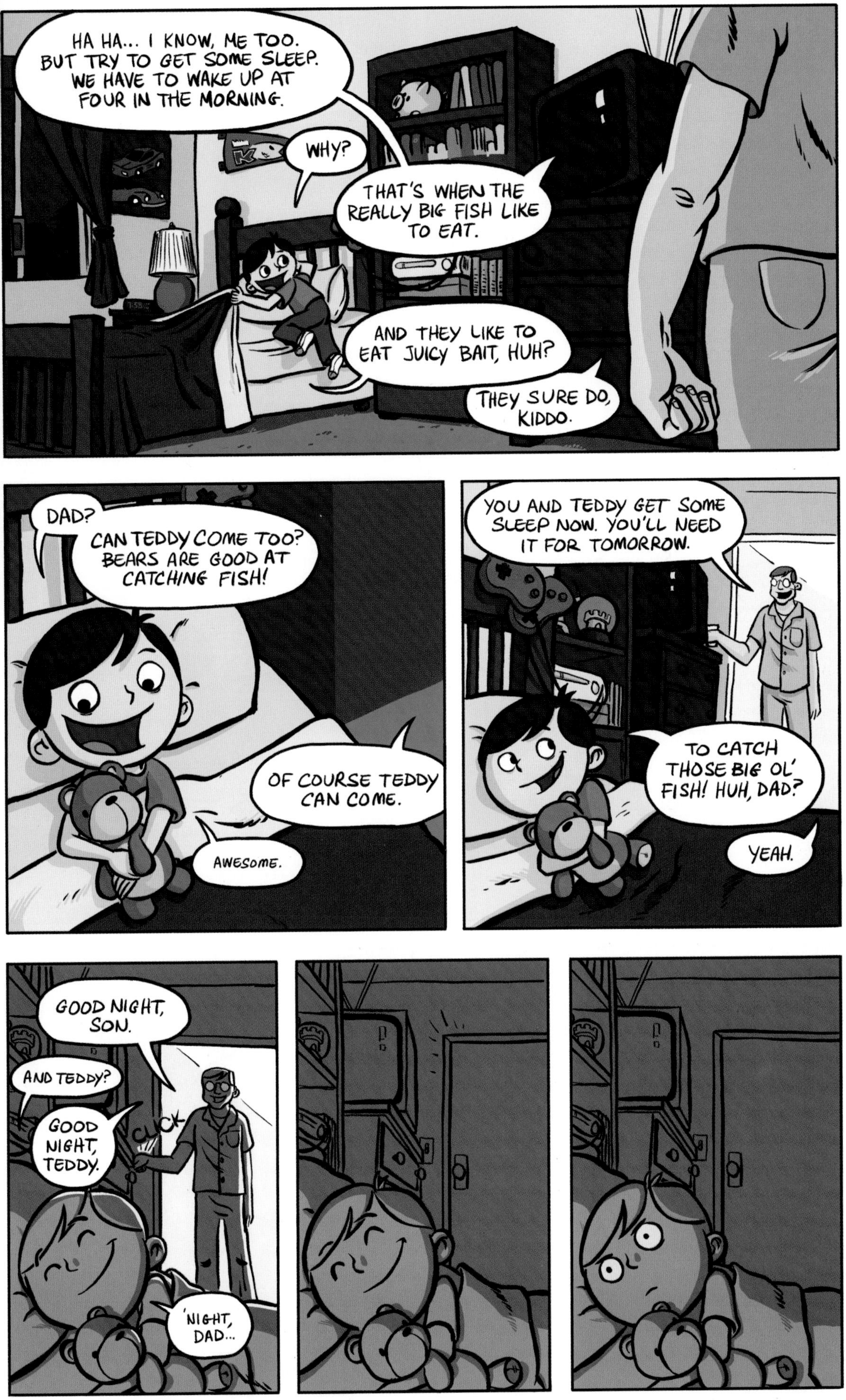
HA HA... I KNOW, ME TOO. BUT TRY TO GET SOME SLEEP. WE HAVE TO WAKE UP AT FOUR IN THE MORNING.
WHY?
THAT'S WHEN THE REALLY BIG FISH LIKE TO EAT.
AND THEY LIKE TO EAT JUICY BAIT, HUH?
THEY SURE DO, KIDDO.
DAD?
CAN TEDDY COME TOO? BEARS ARE GOOD AT CATCHING FISH!
OF COURSE TEDDY CAN COME.
AWESOME.
YOU AND TEDDY GET SOME SLEEP NOW. YOU'LL NEED IT FOR TOMORROW.
TO CATCH THOSE BIG OL' FISH! HUH, DAD?
YEAH.
GOOD NIGHT, SON.
AND TEDDY?
GOOD NIGHT, TEDDY.
CLICK
'NIGHT, DAD...

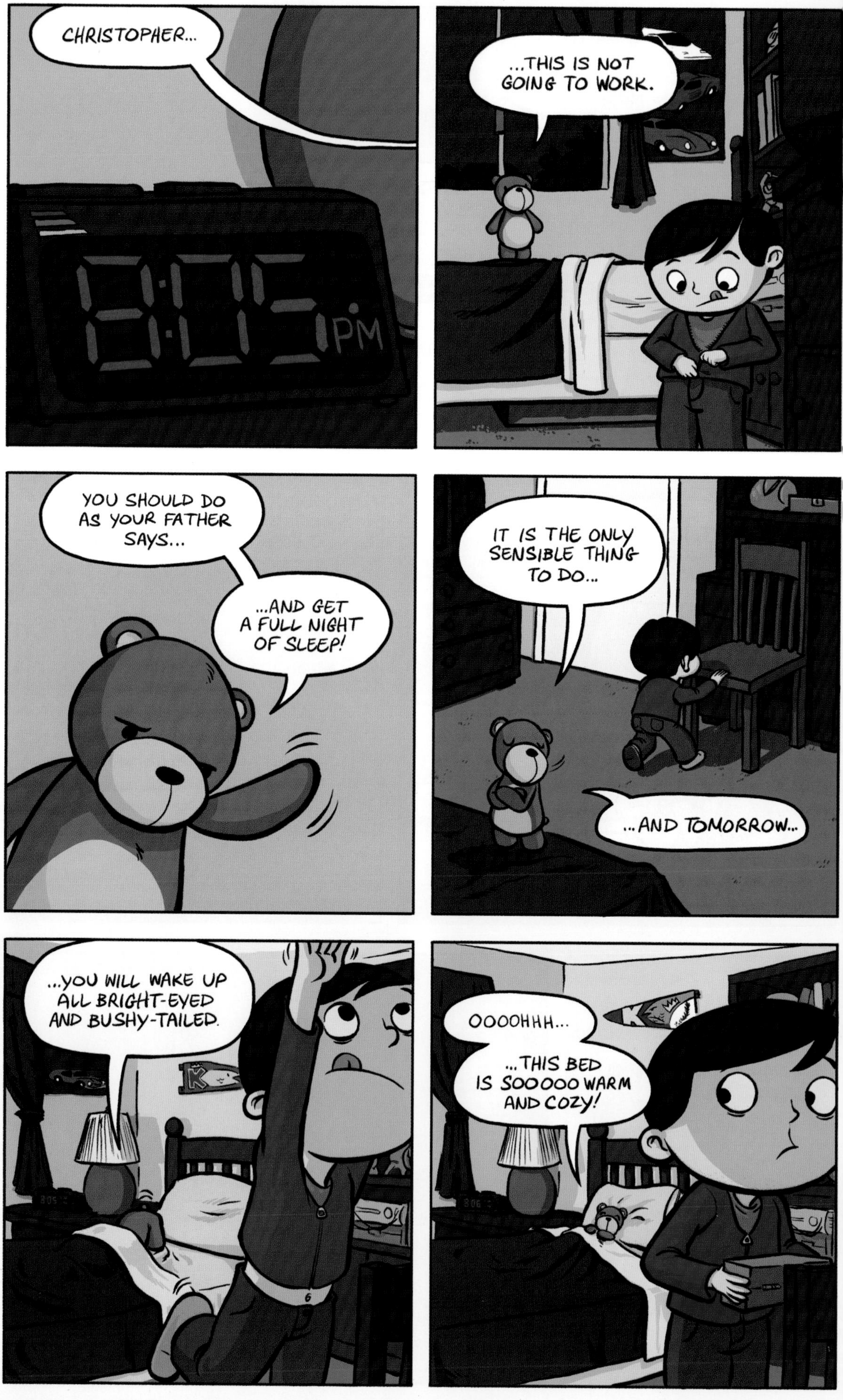
CHRISTOPHER...
8:05 PM
...THIS IS NOT GOING TO WORK.
YOU SHOULD DO AS YOUR FATHER SAYS...
...AND GET A FULL NIGHT OF SLEEP!
IT IS THE ONLY SENSIBLE THING TO DO...
...AND TOMORROW...
...YOU WILL WAKE UP ALL BRIGHT-EYED AND BUSHY-TAILED.
OOOOHHH...
...THIS BED IS SOOOOO WARM AND COZY!

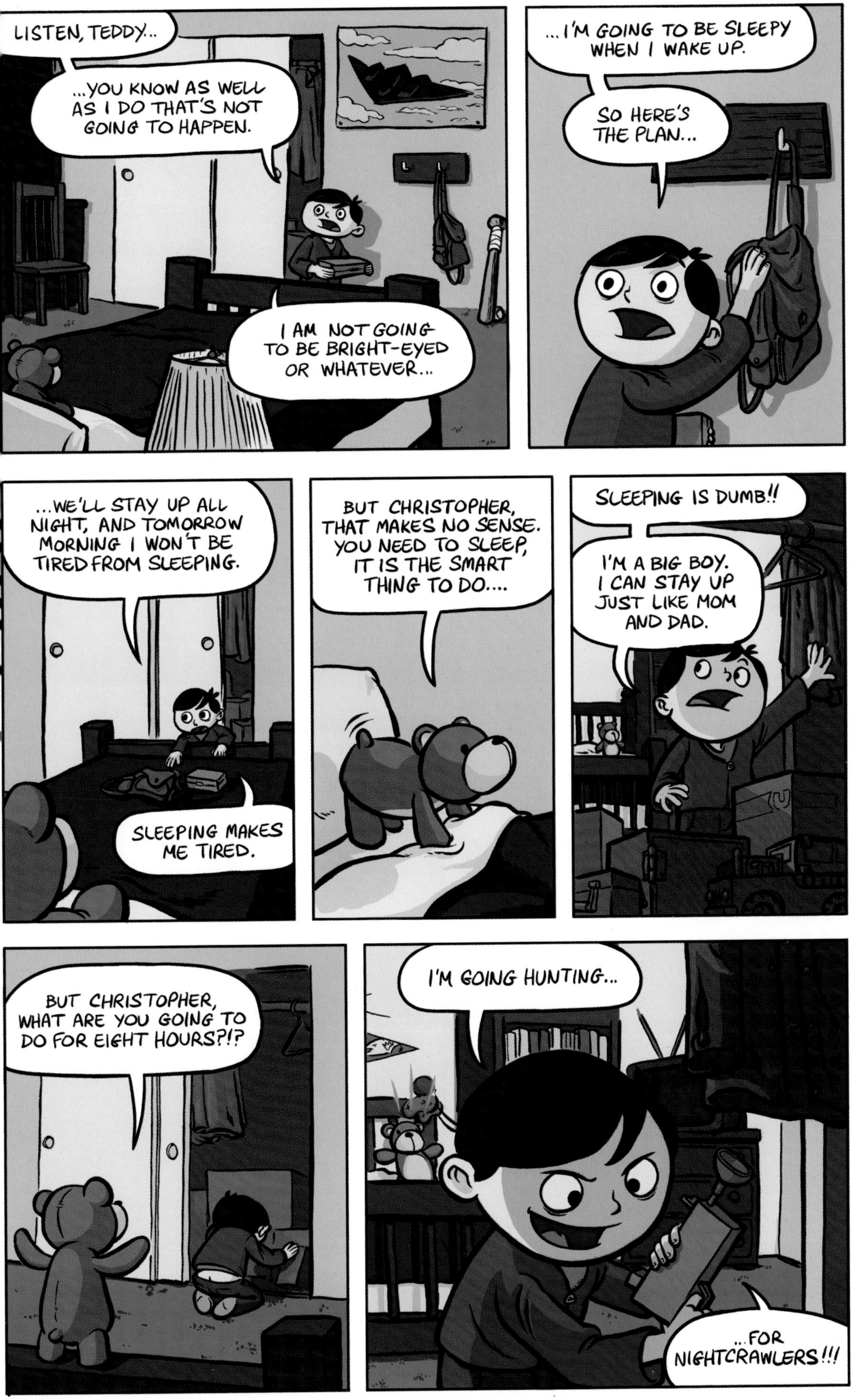
LISTEN, TEDDY...
...YOU KNOW AS WELL AS I DO THAT'S NOT GOING TO HAPPEN.
I AM NOT GOING TO BE BRIGHT-EYED OR WHATEVER...
...I'M GOING TO BE SLEEPY WHEN I WAKE UP.
SO HERE'S THE PLAN...
...WE'LL STAY UP ALL NIGHT, AND TOMORROW MORNING I WON'T BE TIRED FROM SLEEPING.
SLEEPING MAKES ME TIRED.
BUT CHRISTOPHER, THAT MAKES NO SENSE. YOU NEED TO SLEEP, IT IS THE SMART THING TO DO....
SLEEPING IS DUMB!!
I'M A BIG BOY. I CAN STAY UP JUST LIKE MOM AND DAD.
BUT CHRISTOPHER, WHAT ARE YOU GOING TO DO FOR EIGHT HOURS?!?
I'M GOING HUNTING...
...FOR NIGHTCRAWLERS!!!

DAD AND I ARE GOING TO NEED JUICY BAIT TO CATCH THOSE BIG OL' FISH!

I AM JUICY!

I BET!

IT IS A NOBLE GOAL TO HELP YOUR FATHER...

YUM

...BUT CHRISTOPHER, WHAT ABOUT **THE Z'S!!!**

YOU KNOW THEY WILL CATCH UP TO YOU EVENTUALLY!

TEDDY, YOU WORRY TOO MUCH!

BaaaaaaaaaaaAAAA

Baaaaaaaaaaaaaaaa

GRAB THE GEAR AND HOP IN, TEDDY!!

OK, READY.

GOOD...

...LET'S GO!

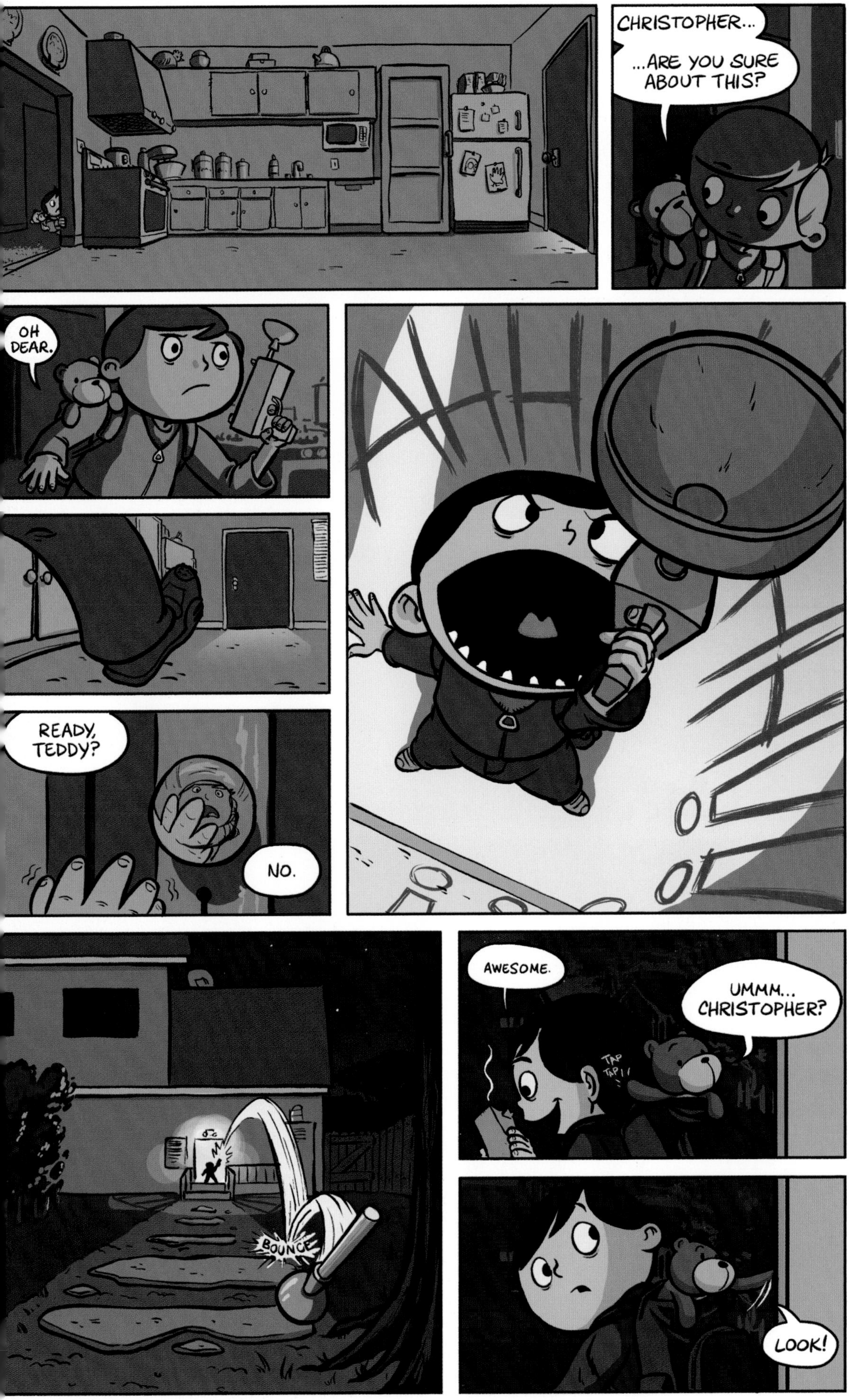
CHRISTOPHER...
...ARE YOU SURE ABOUT THIS?
OH DEAR.
READY, TEDDY?
NO.
BOUNCE
AWESOME.
UMMM... CHRISTOPHER?
TAP TAP!!
LOOK!

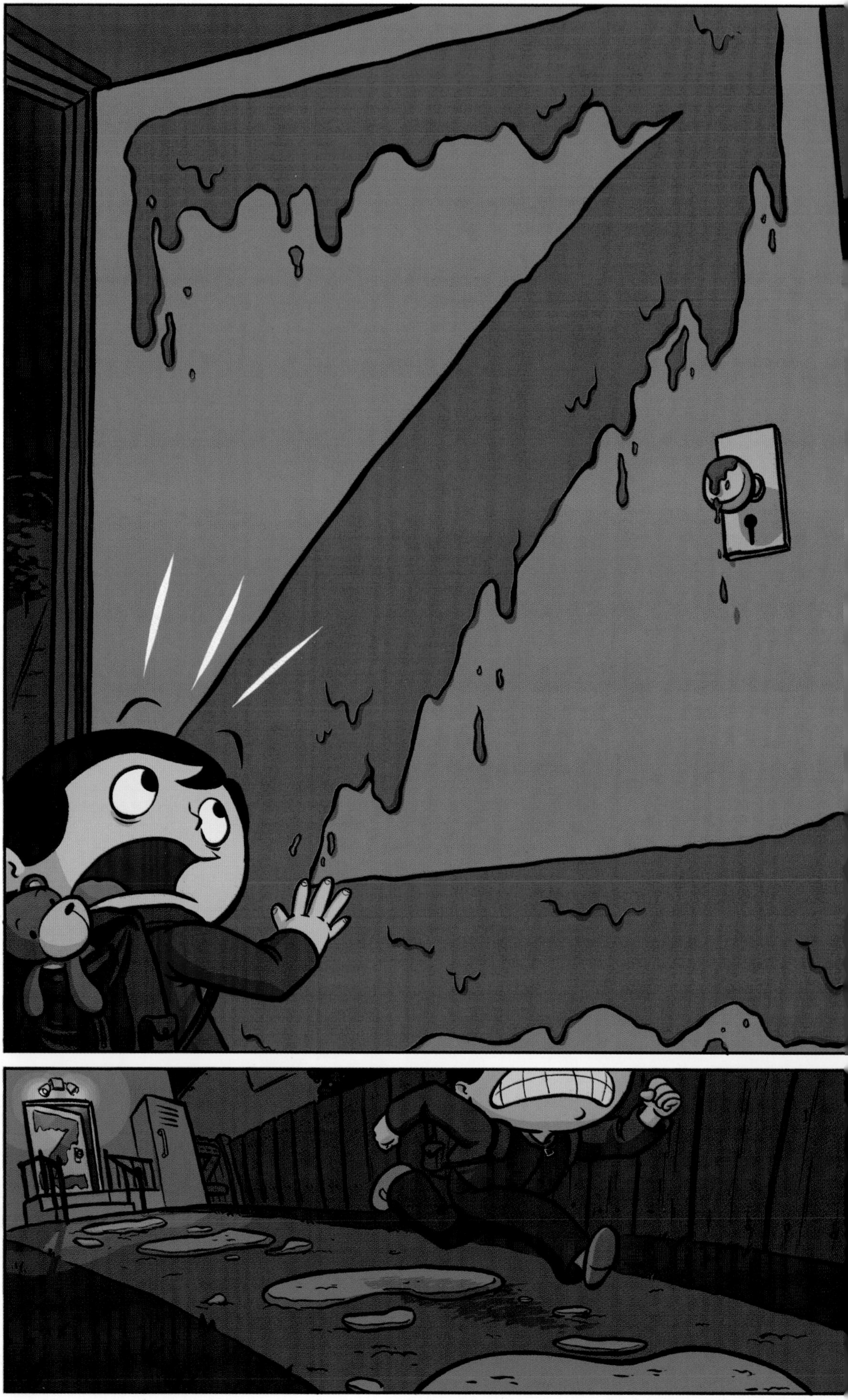

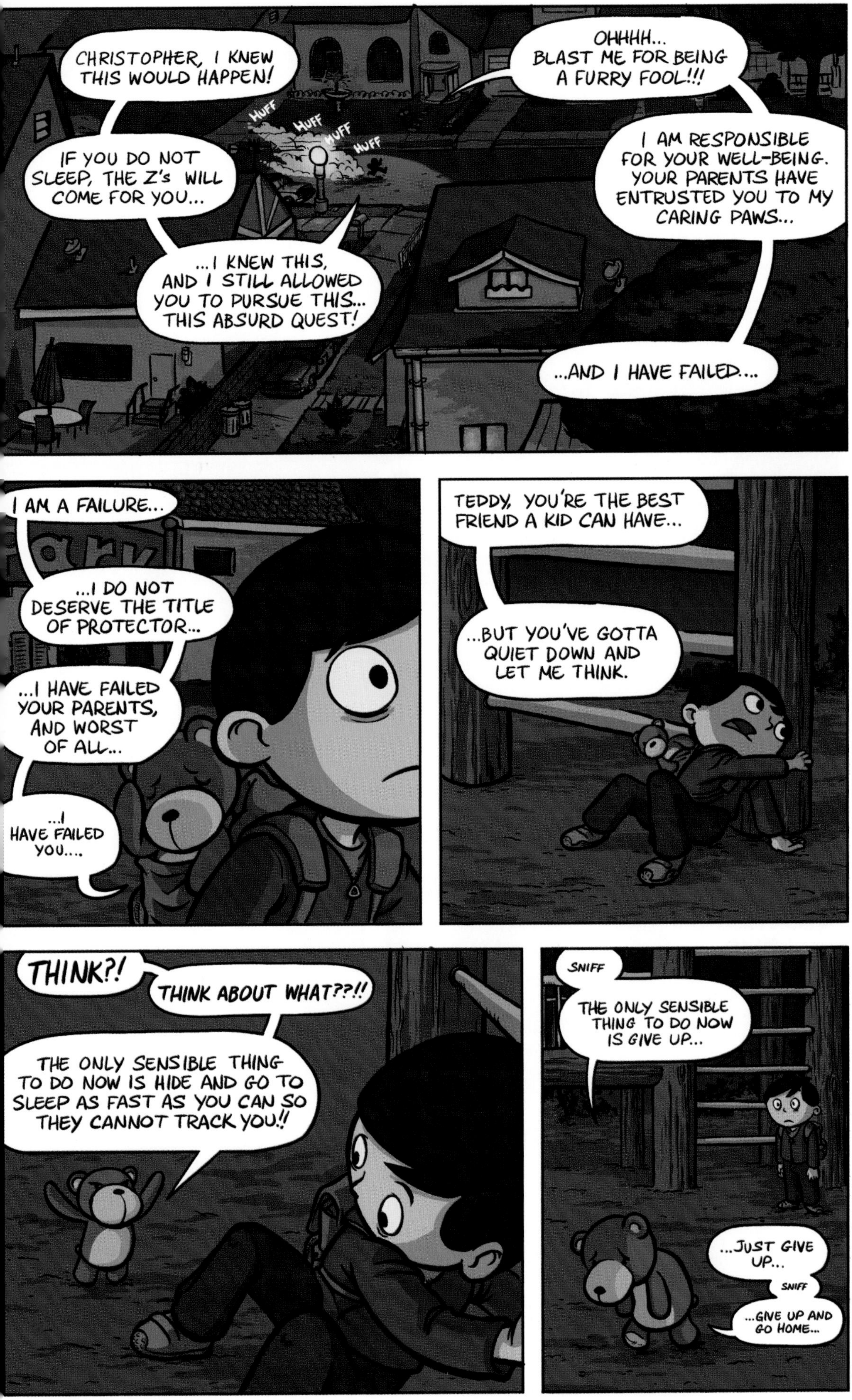
CHRISTOPHER, I KNEW THIS WOULD HAPPEN!
IF YOU DO NOT SLEEP, THE Z's WILL COME FOR YOU...
...I KNEW THIS, AND I STILL ALLOWED YOU TO PURSUE THIS... THIS ABSURD QUEST!
HUFF HUFF HUFF HUFF
OHHHH... BLAST ME FOR BEING A FURRY FOOL!!!
I AM RESPONSIBLE FOR YOUR WELL-BEING. YOUR PARENTS HAVE ENTRUSTED YOU TO MY CARING PAWS...
...AND I HAVE FAILED....
I AM A FAILURE...
...I DO NOT DESERVE THE TITLE OF PROTECTOR...
...I HAVE FAILED YOUR PARENTS, AND WORST OF ALL...
...I HAVE FAILED YOU....
TEDDY, YOU'RE THE BEST FRIEND A KID CAN HAVE...
...BUT YOU'VE GOTTA QUIET DOWN AND LET ME THINK.
THINK?!
THINK ABOUT WHAT??!!
THE ONLY SENSIBLE THING TO DO NOW IS HIDE AND GO TO SLEEP AS FAST AS YOU CAN SO THEY CANNOT TRACK YOU!!
SNIFF
THE ONLY SENSIBLE THING TO DO NOW IS GIVE UP...
...JUST GIVE UP...
SNIFF
...GIVE UP AND GO HOME...

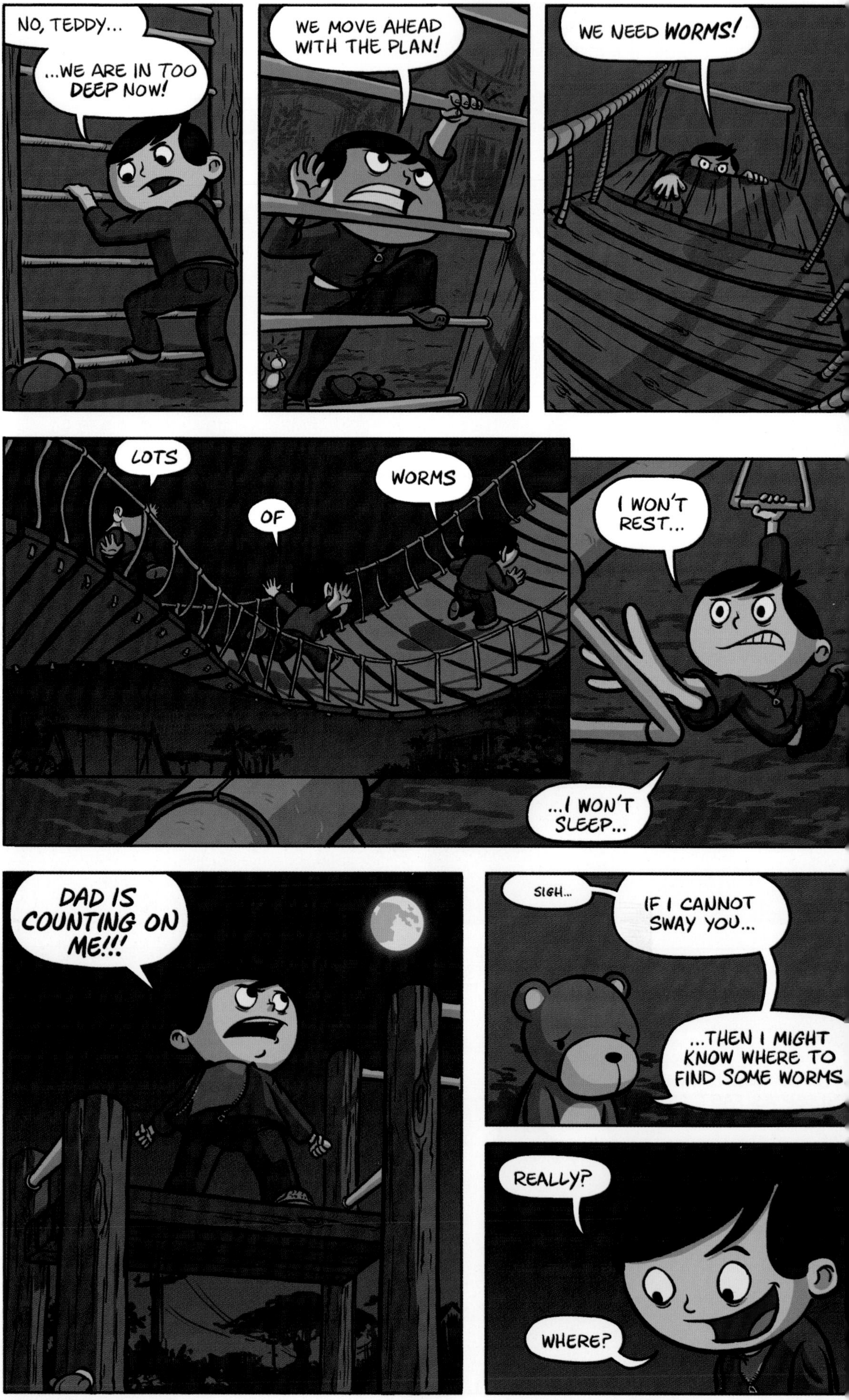

NO, TEDDY...
...WE ARE IN TOO DEEP NOW!
WE MOVE AHEAD WITH THE PLAN!
WE NEED WORMS!
LOTS
OF
WORMS
I WON'T REST...
...I WON'T SLEEP...
DAD IS COUNTING ON ME!!!
SIGH...
IF I CANNOT SWAY YOU...
...THEN I MIGHT KNOW WHERE TO FIND SOME WORMS
REALLY?
WHERE?

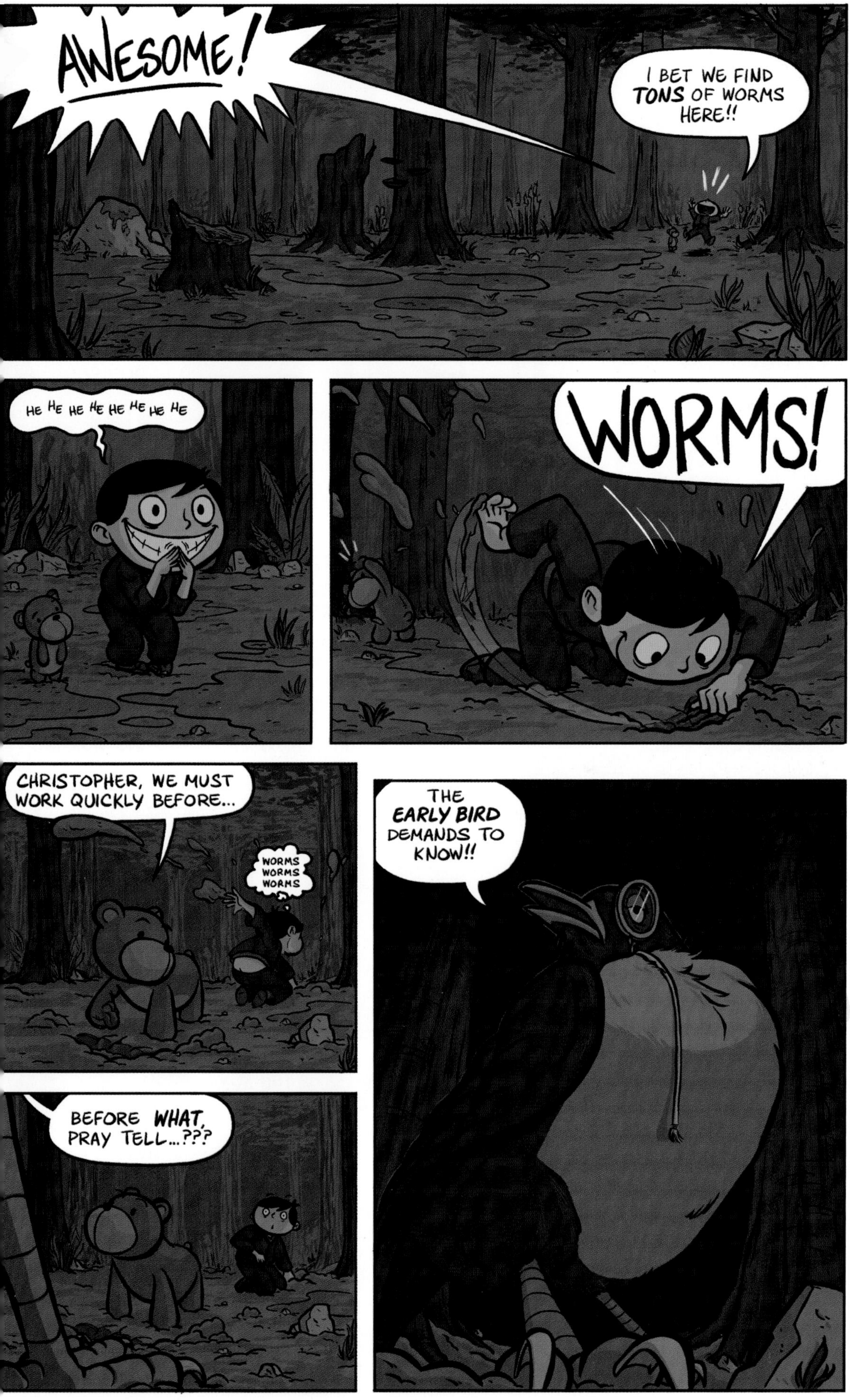
AWESOME!
I BET WE FIND TONS OF WORMS HERE!!
HE HE HE HE HE HE HE HE
WORMS!
CHRISTOPHER, WE MUST WORK QUICKLY BEFORE...
WORMS WORMS WORMS
BEFORE WHAT, PRAY TELL...???
THE EARLY BIRD DEMANDS TO KNOW!!

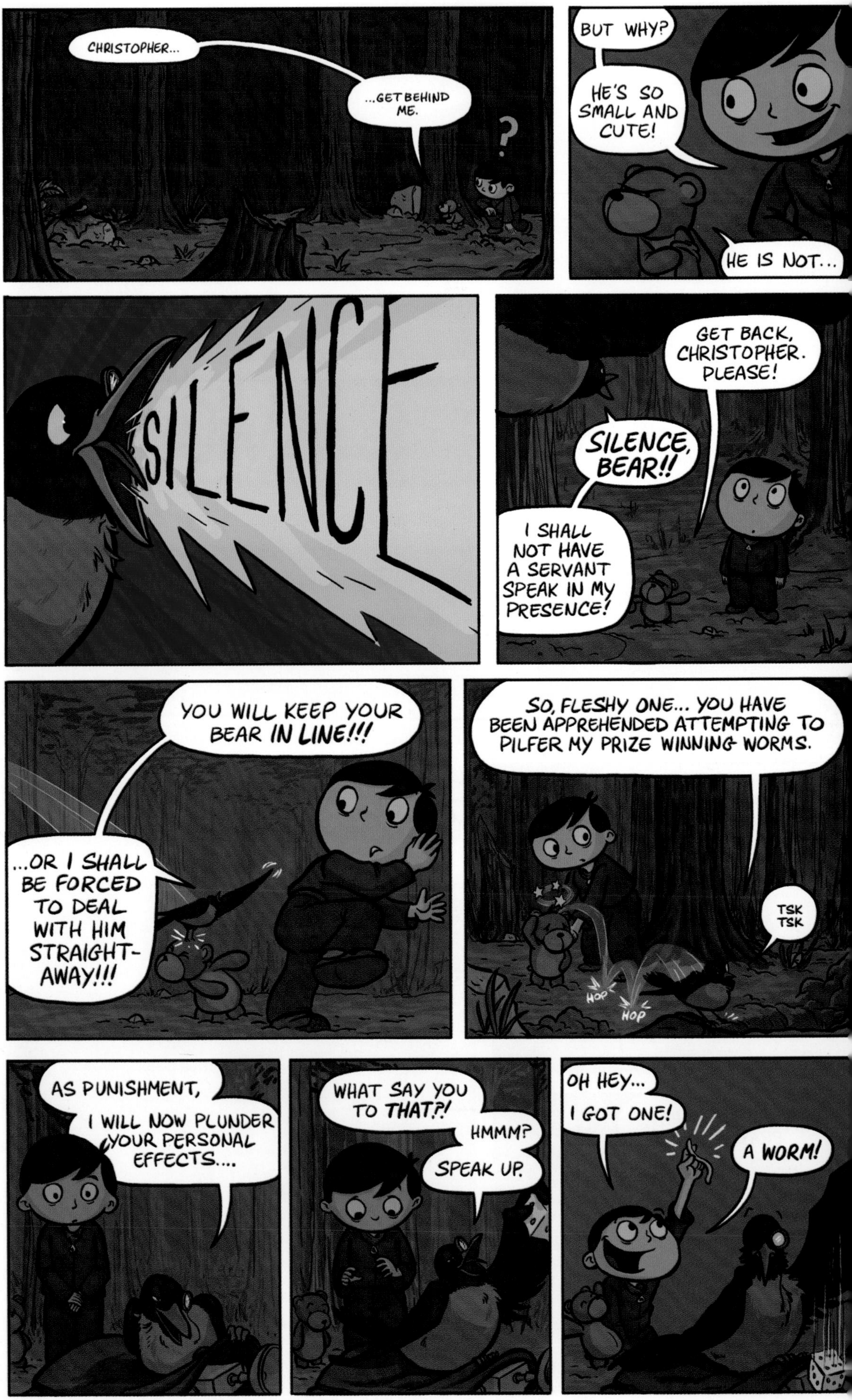
CHRISTOPHER...
...GET BEHIND ME.
?
BUT WHY?
HE'S SO SMALL AND CUTE!
HE IS NOT...
SILENCE
GET BACK, CHRISTOPHER. PLEASE!
SILENCE, BEAR!!
I SHALL NOT HAVE A SERVANT SPEAK IN MY PRESENCE!
YOU WILL KEEP YOUR BEAR IN LINE!!!
...OR I SHALL BE FORCED TO DEAL WITH HIM STRAIGHT-AWAY!!!
SO, FLESHY ONE... YOU HAVE BEEN APPREHENDED ATTEMPTING TO PILFER MY PRIZE WINNING WORMS.
TSK TSK
HOP
HOP
AS PUNISHMENT,
I WILL NOW PLUNDER YOUR PERSONAL EFFECTS....
WHAT SAY YOU TO THAT?!
HMMM?
SPEAK UP.
OH HEY...
I GOT ONE!
A WORM!

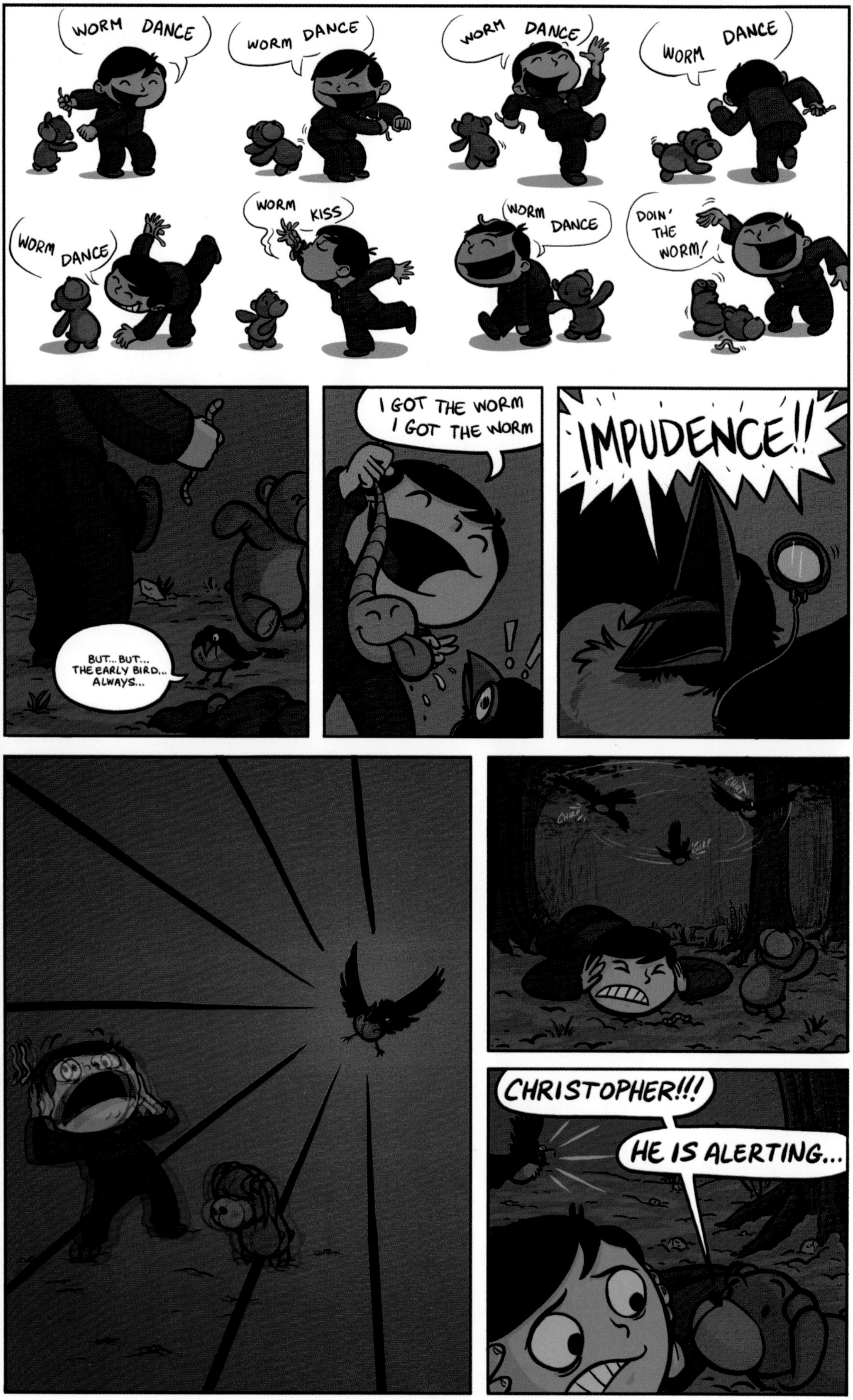
WORM DANCE
WORM DANCE
WORM DANCE
WORM DANCE
WORM DANCE
WORM KISS
WORM DANCE
DOIN' THE WORM!
BUT... BUT... THE EARLY BIRD... ALWAYS...
I GOT THE WORM
I GOT THE WORM
IMPUDENCE!!
CHRISTOPHER!!!
HE IS ALERTING...

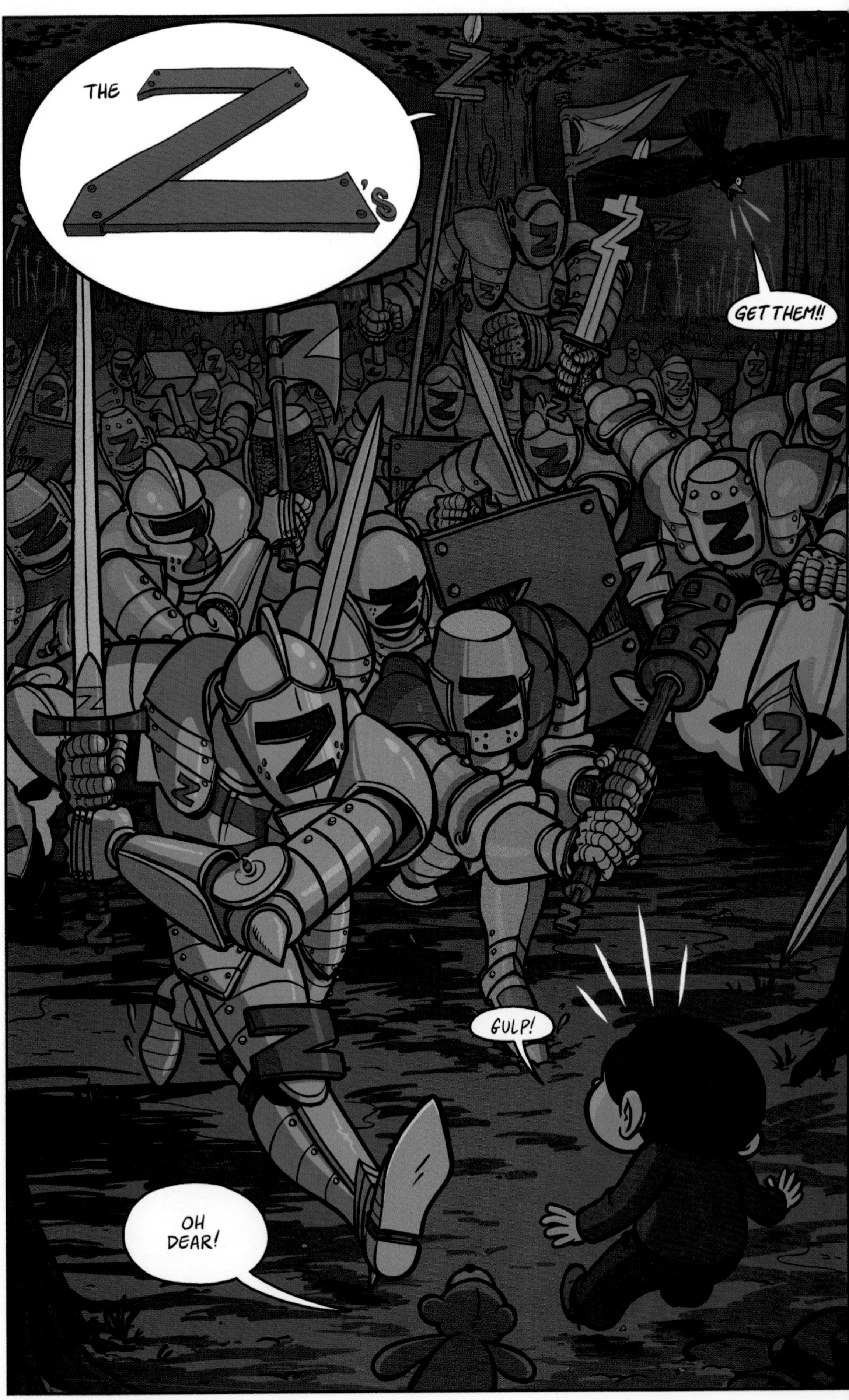
THE Z'S
GET THEM!!
GULP!
OH DEAR!

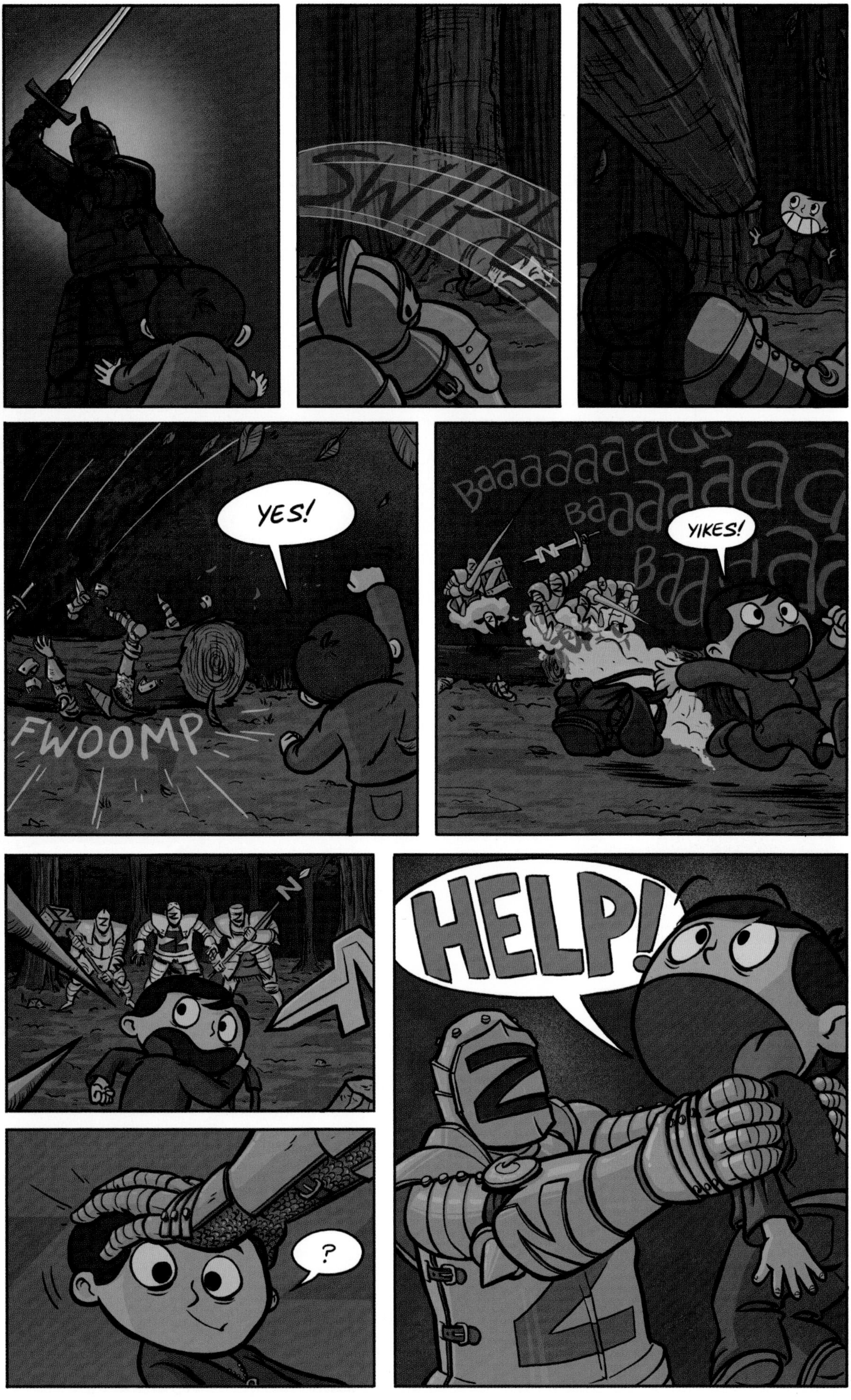

SWIP
YES!
FWOOMP
Baaaaaaaaa
Baaaaaaaa
Baaaaa
YIKES!
HELP!
?

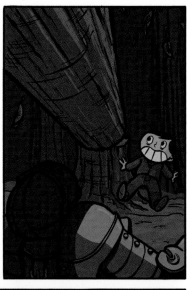

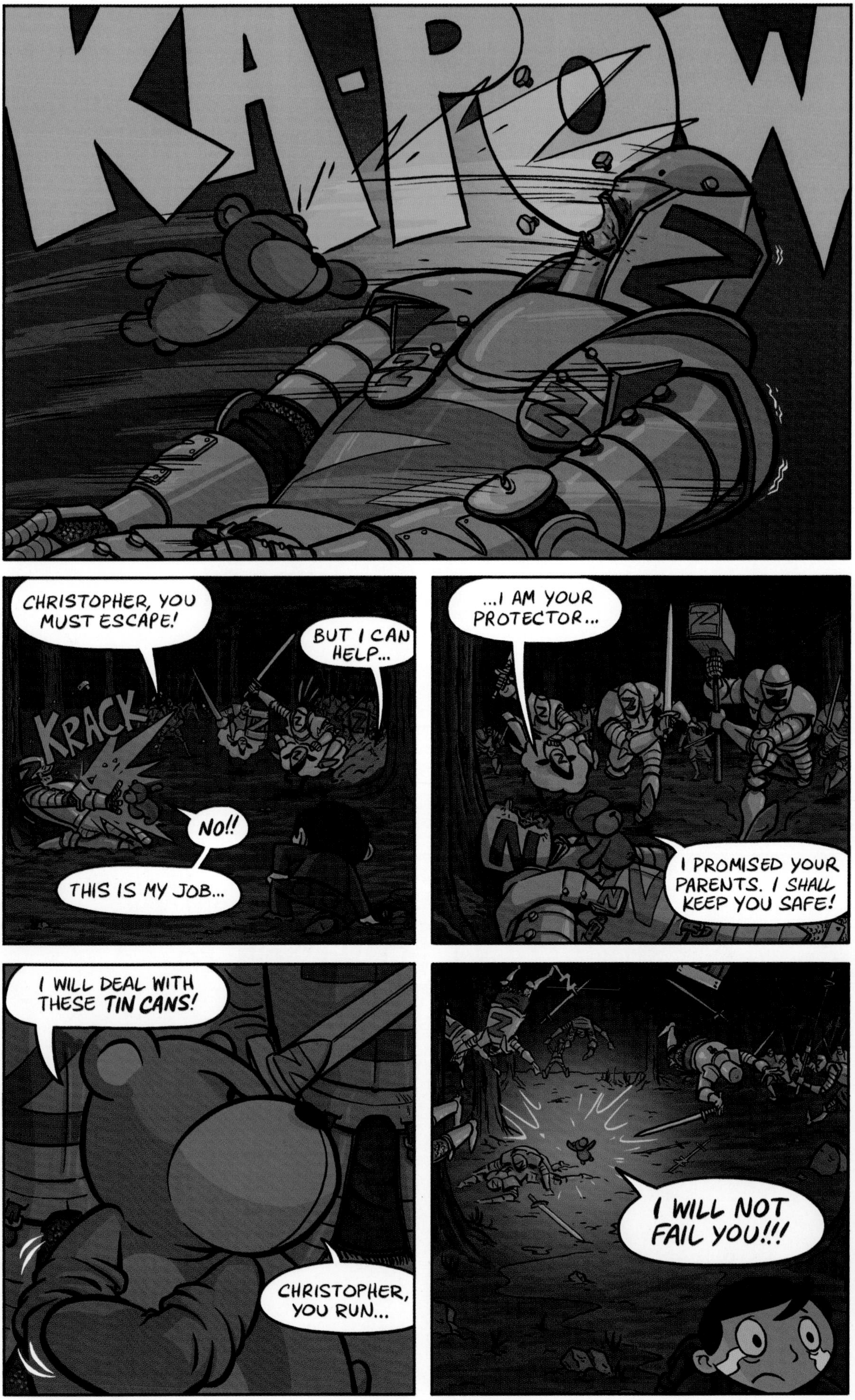
KA-POW
CHRISTOPHER, YOU MUST ESCAPE!
BUT I CAN HELP...
KRACK
NO!!
THIS IS MY JOB...
...I AM YOUR PROTECTOR...
I PROMISED YOUR PARENTS. I SHALL KEEP YOU SAFE!
I WILL DEAL WITH THESE TIN CANS!
CHRISTOPHER, YOU RUN...
I WILL NOT FAIL YOU!!!

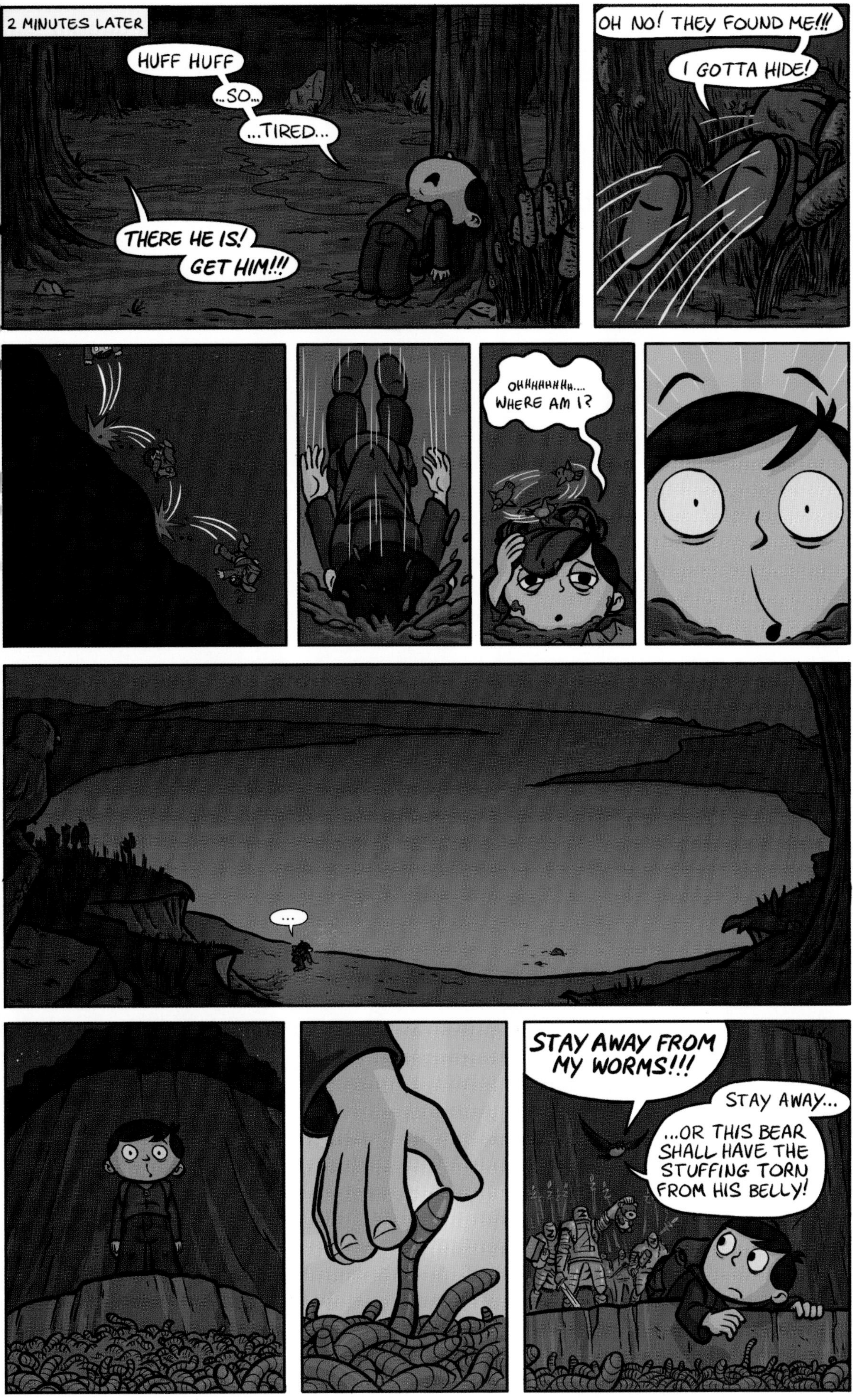
2 MINUTES LATER
HUFF HUFF
...SO...
...TIRED...
THERE HE IS! GET HIM!!!
OH NO! THEY FOUND ME!!!
I GOTTA HIDE!
OHHHHHHHH.... WHERE AM I?
...
STAY AWAY FROM MY WORMS!!!
STAY AWAY...
...OR THIS BEAR SHALL HAVE THE STUFFING TORN FROM HIS BELLY!

TEDDY!!
LEAVE HIM ALONE OR...
CLICK
PLUNK
POP
ACK!
OOF!
WE FIND THIS VERY AMUSING.
HELP!
YOU WANTED WORMS, AND NOW YOU HAVE ALL THE WORMS YOU CAN HANDLE...
I SHALL LAUGH AT YOU NOW... CHIRP-HA CHIRP-HA CHIRP-HA
...THE Z's ARE UPON ME!!
CHIRP-HA
CHIRP-HA
CHIRP-HA
CHIRP-HA
CHIRP-HA
HELP!

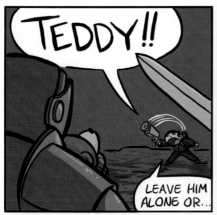

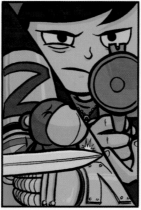

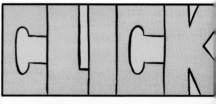

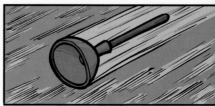

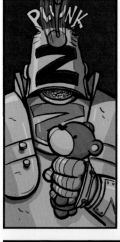

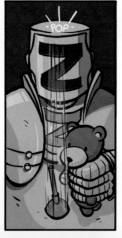

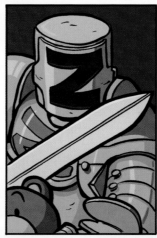

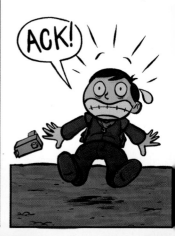

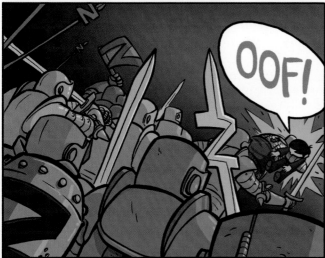

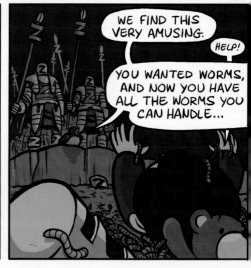

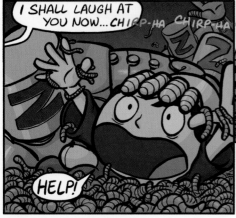

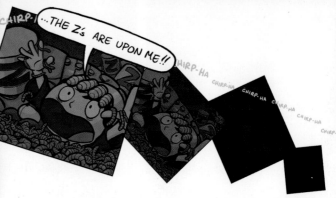

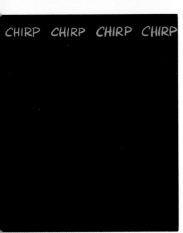

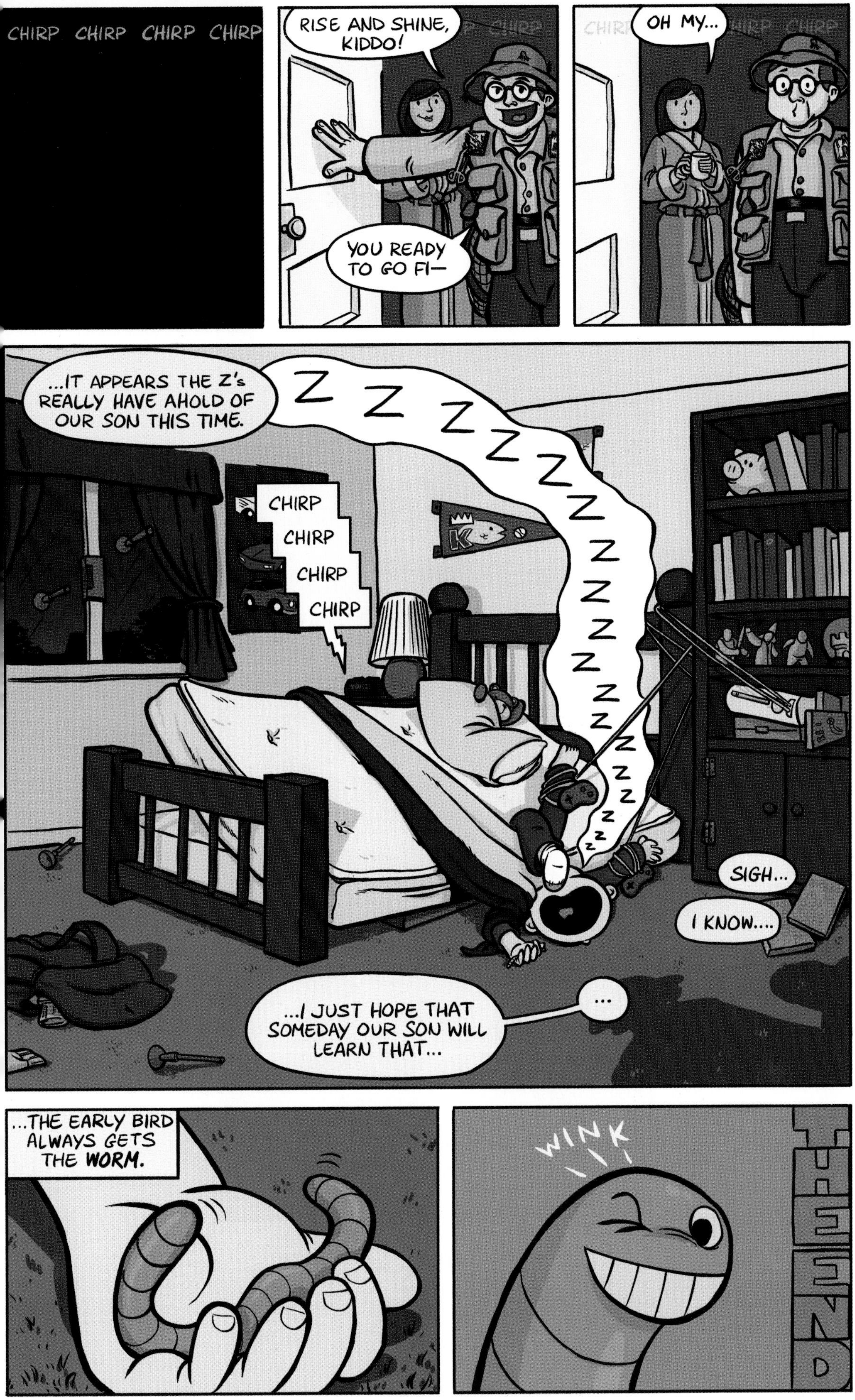
CHIRP CHIRP CHIRP CHIRP
RISE AND SHINE, KIDDO!
YOU READY TO GO FI—
OH MY...
...IT APPEARS THE Z's REALLY HAVE AHOLD OF OUR SON THIS TIME.
CHIRP
CHIRP
CHIRP
CHIRP
SIGH...
I KNOW....
...I JUST HOPE THAT SOMEDAY OUR SON WILL LEARN THAT...
...
...THE EARLY BIRD ALWAYS GETS THE **WORM.**
WINK
THE END

JELLABY

Hide and Seek

96...
97...
98...

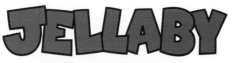

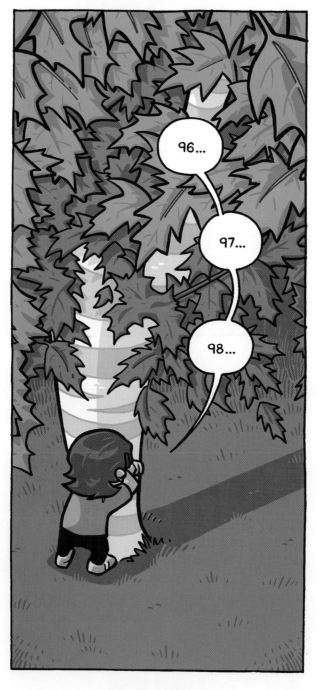

Kean Soo

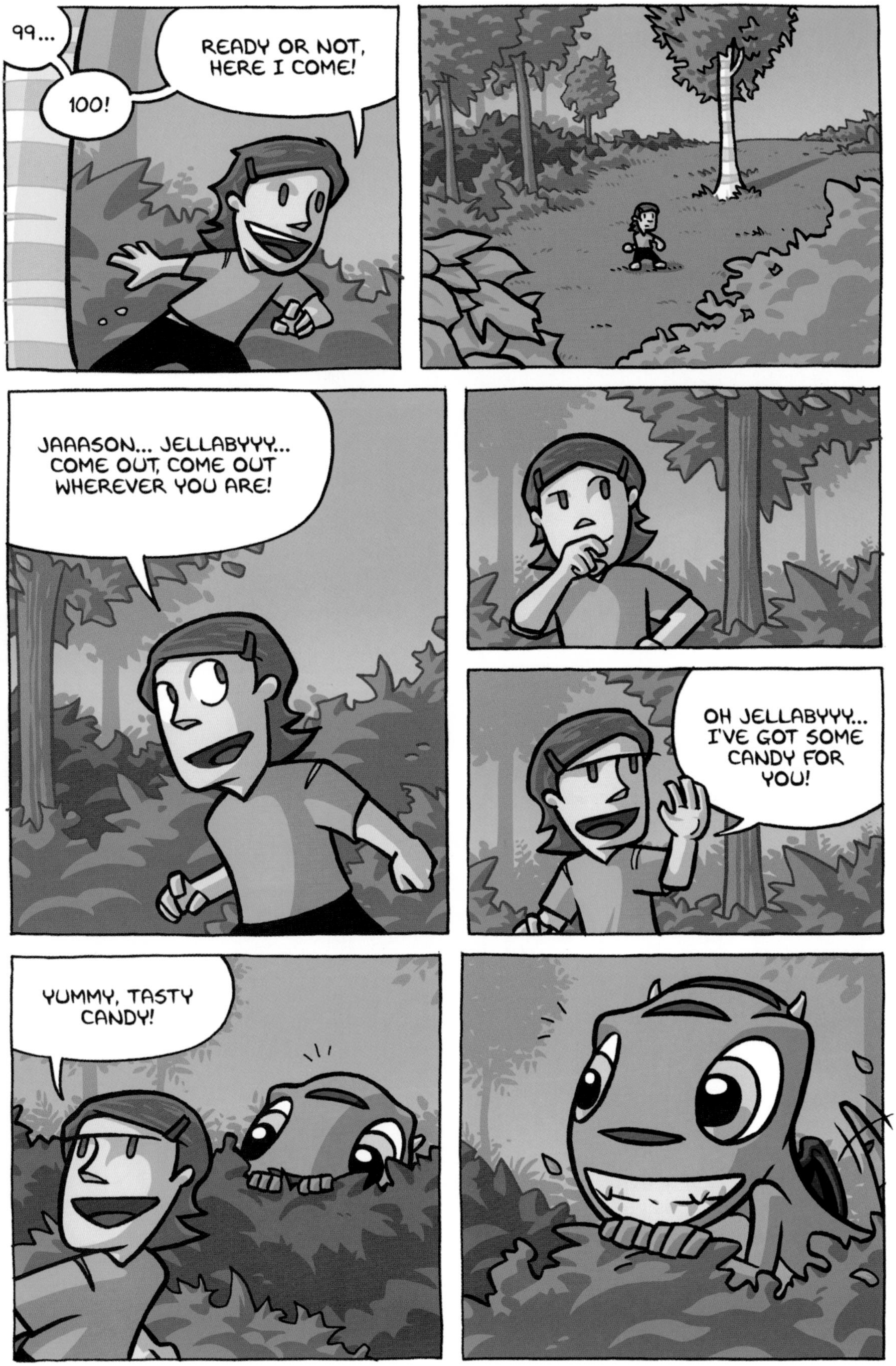
99...
100!
READY OR NOT, HERE I COME!
JAAASON... JELLABYYY... COME OUT, COME OUT WHEREVER YOU ARE!
OH JELLABYYY... I'VE GOT SOME CANDY FOR YOU!
YUMMY, TASTY CANDY!

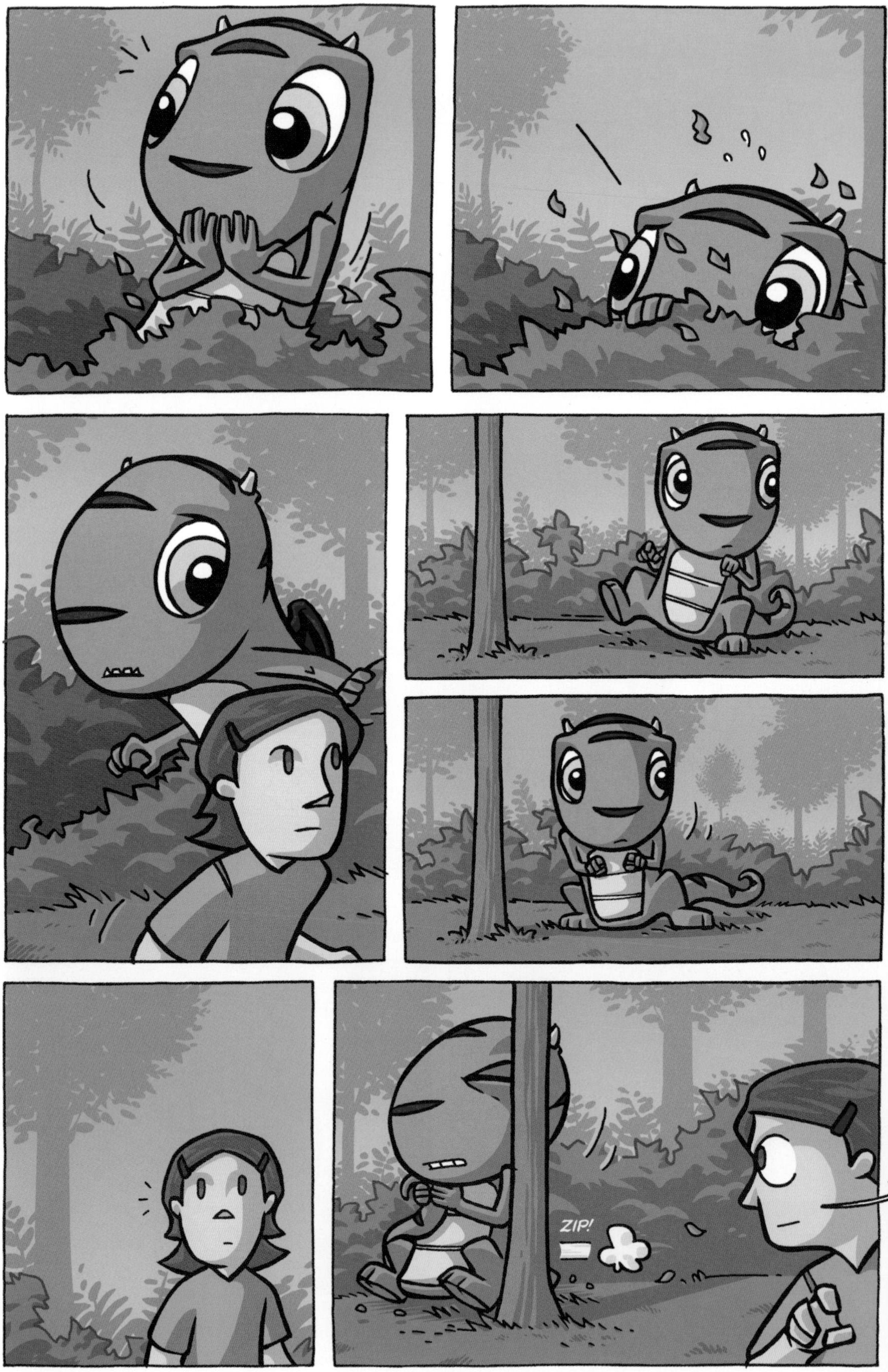
ZIP!

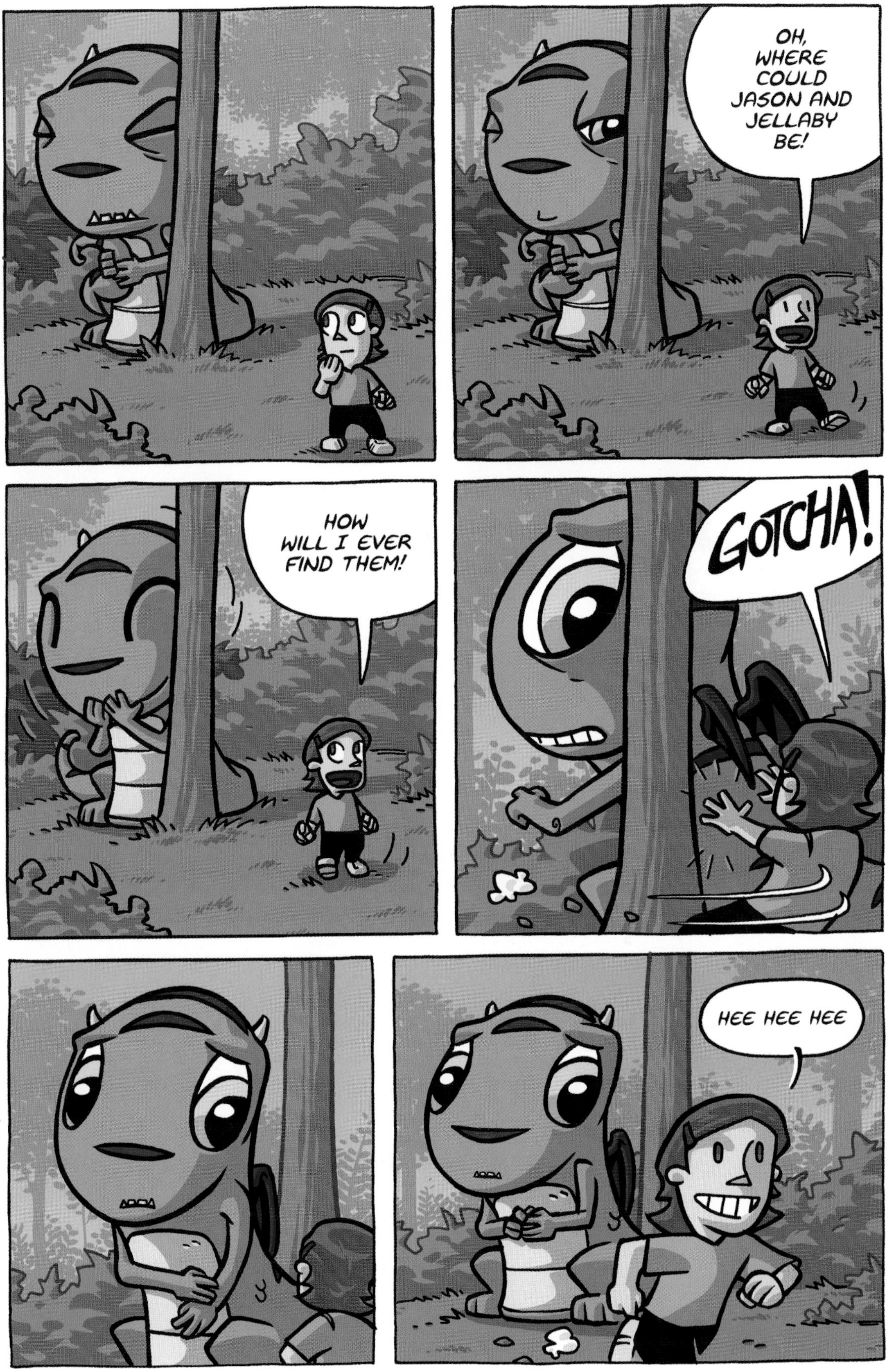
OH, WHERE COULD JASON AND JELLABY BE!
HOW WILL I EVER FIND THEM!
GOTCHA!
HEE HEE HEE

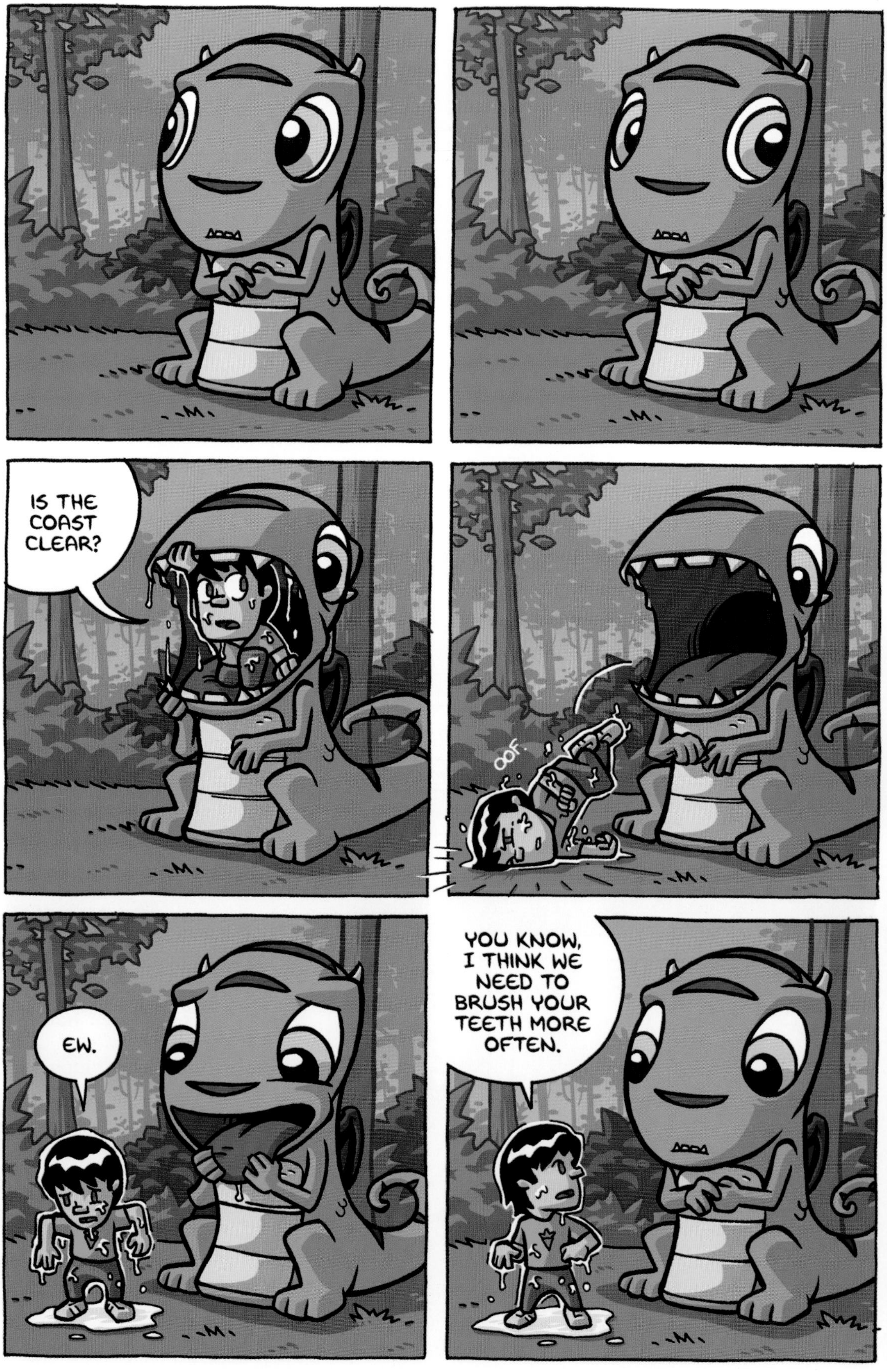
IS THE COAST CLEAR?
OOF.
EW.
YOU KNOW, I THINK WE NEED TO BRUSH YOUR TEETH MORE OFTEN.

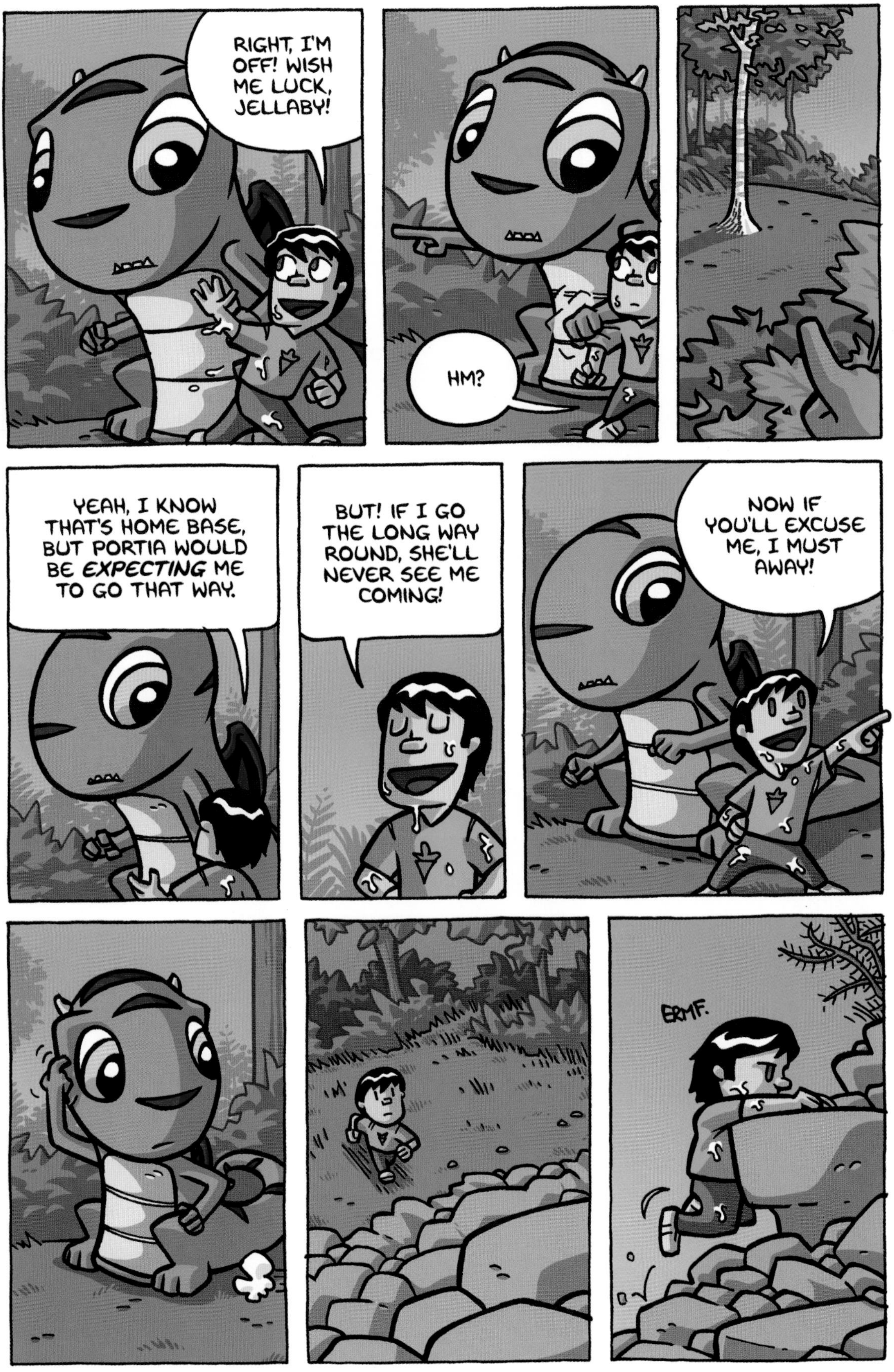
RIGHT, I'M OFF! WISH ME LUCK, JELLABY!
HM?
YEAH, I KNOW THAT'S HOME BASE, BUT PORTIA WOULD BE *EXPECTING* ME TO GO THAT WAY.
BUT! IF I GO THE LONG WAY ROUND, SHE'LL NEVER SEE ME COMING!
NOW IF YOU'LL EXCUSE ME, I MUST AWAY!
ERMF.

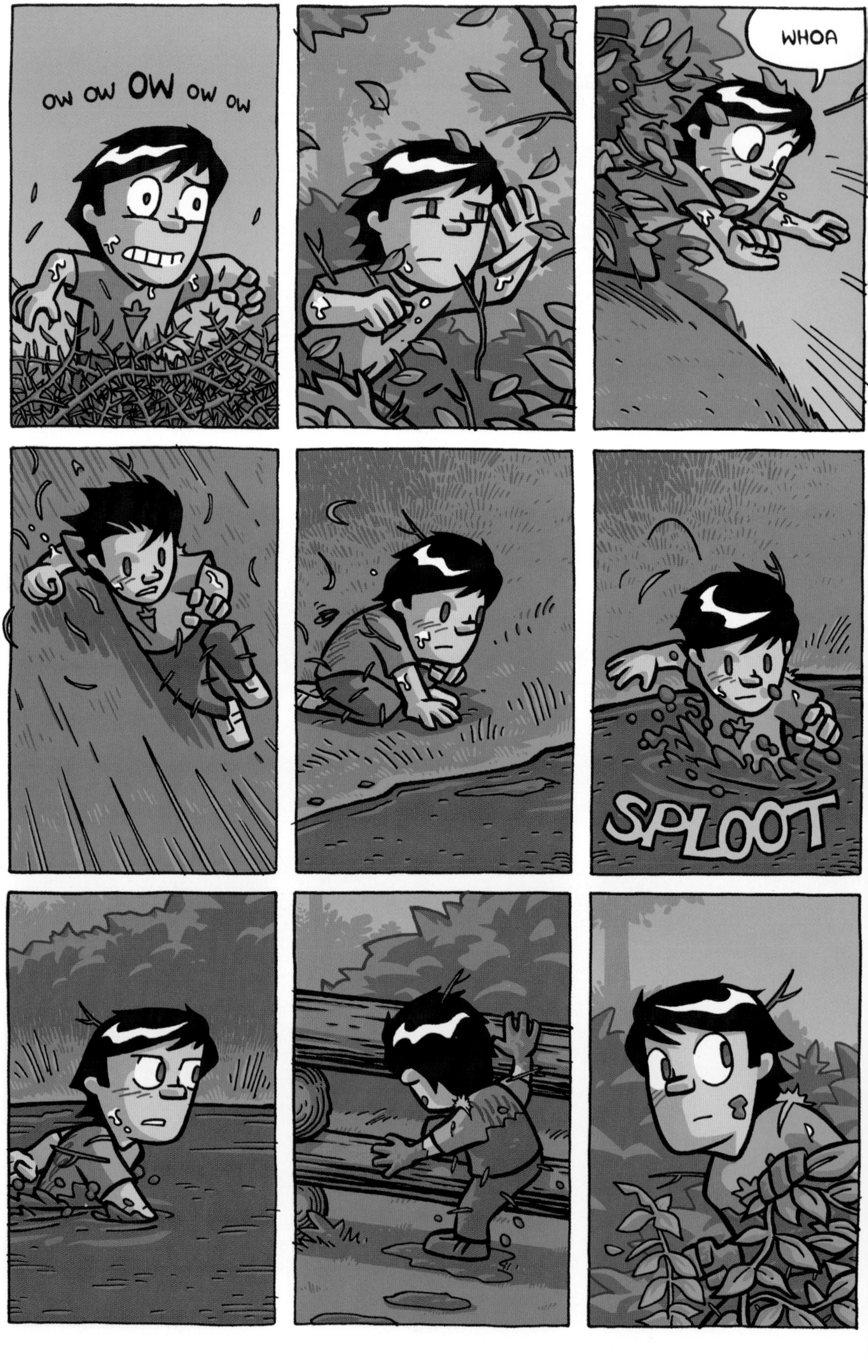
OW OW OW OW OW
WHOA
SPLOOT

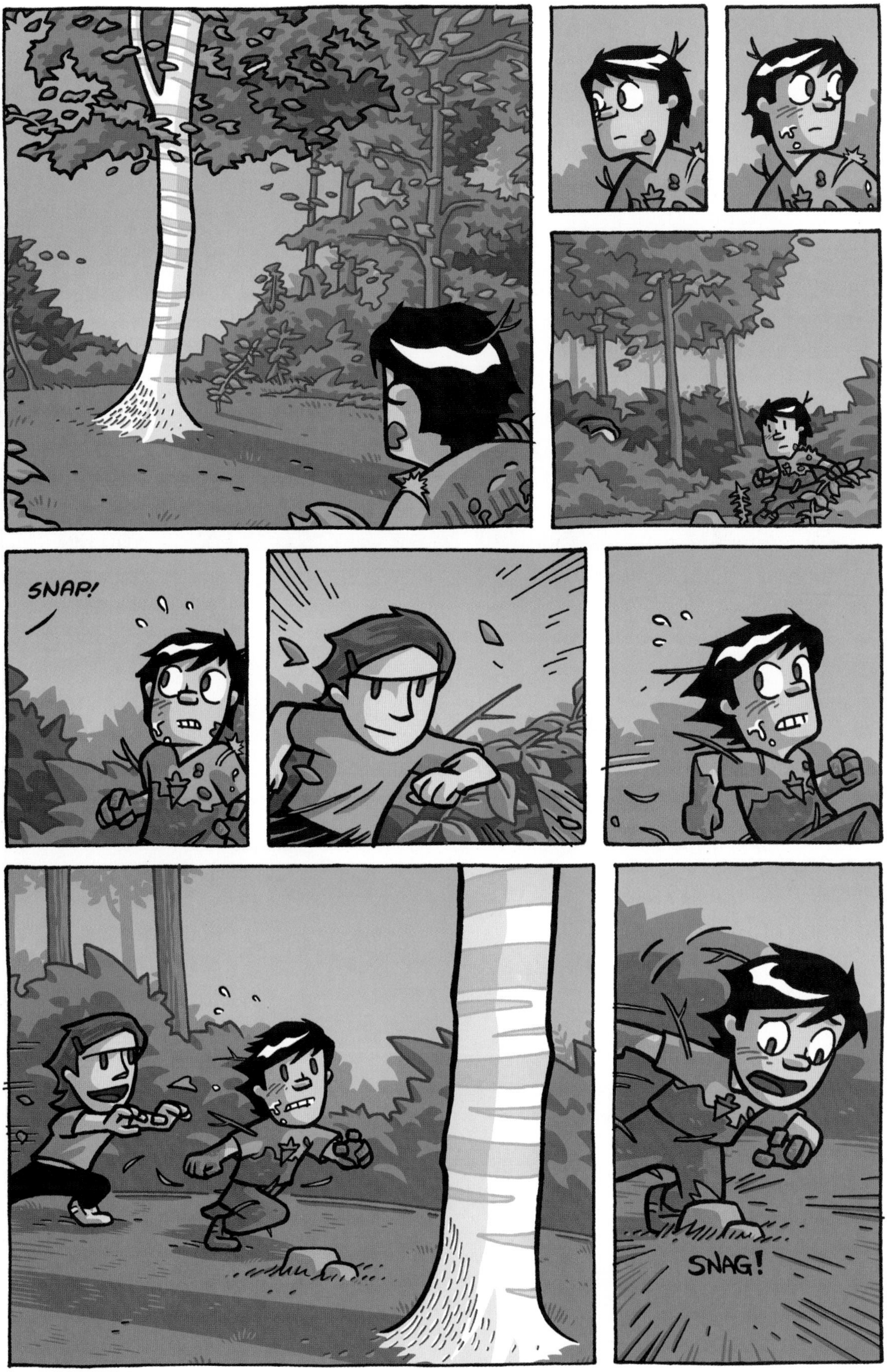
SNAP!
SNAG!

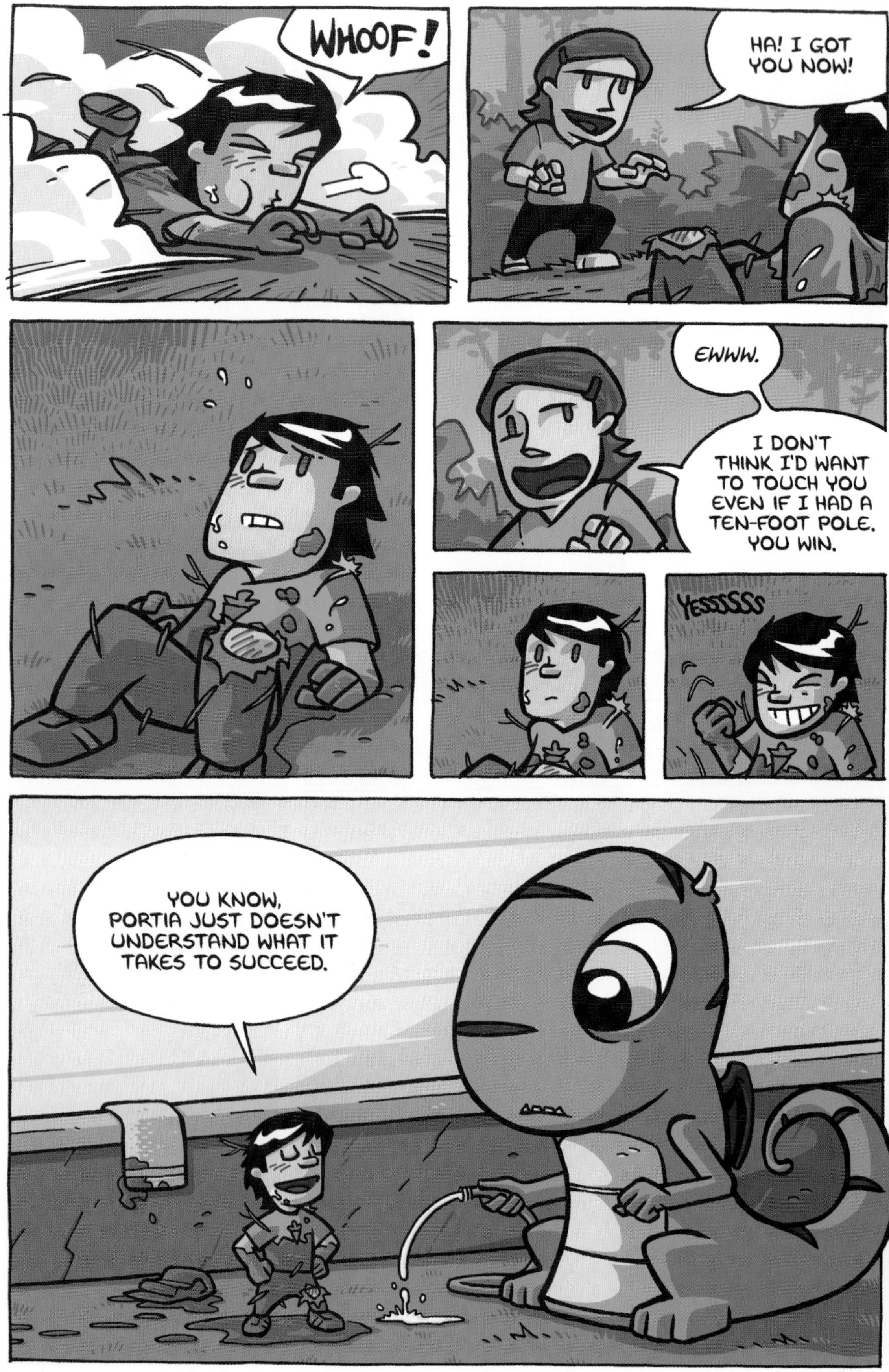
WHOOF!
HA! I GOT YOU NOW!
EWWW.
I DON'T THINK I'D WANT TO TOUCH YOU EVEN IF I HAD A TEN-FOOT POLE. YOU WIN.
YESSSSSS
YOU KNOW, PORTIA JUST DOESN'T UNDERSTAND WHAT IT TAKES TO SUCCEED.

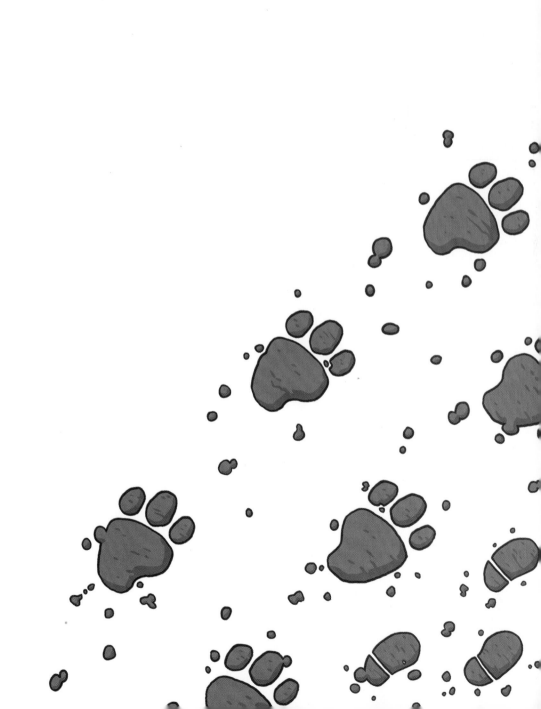

Fish N Chips "Even the Smallest Creatures..." by: Steve Hamaker

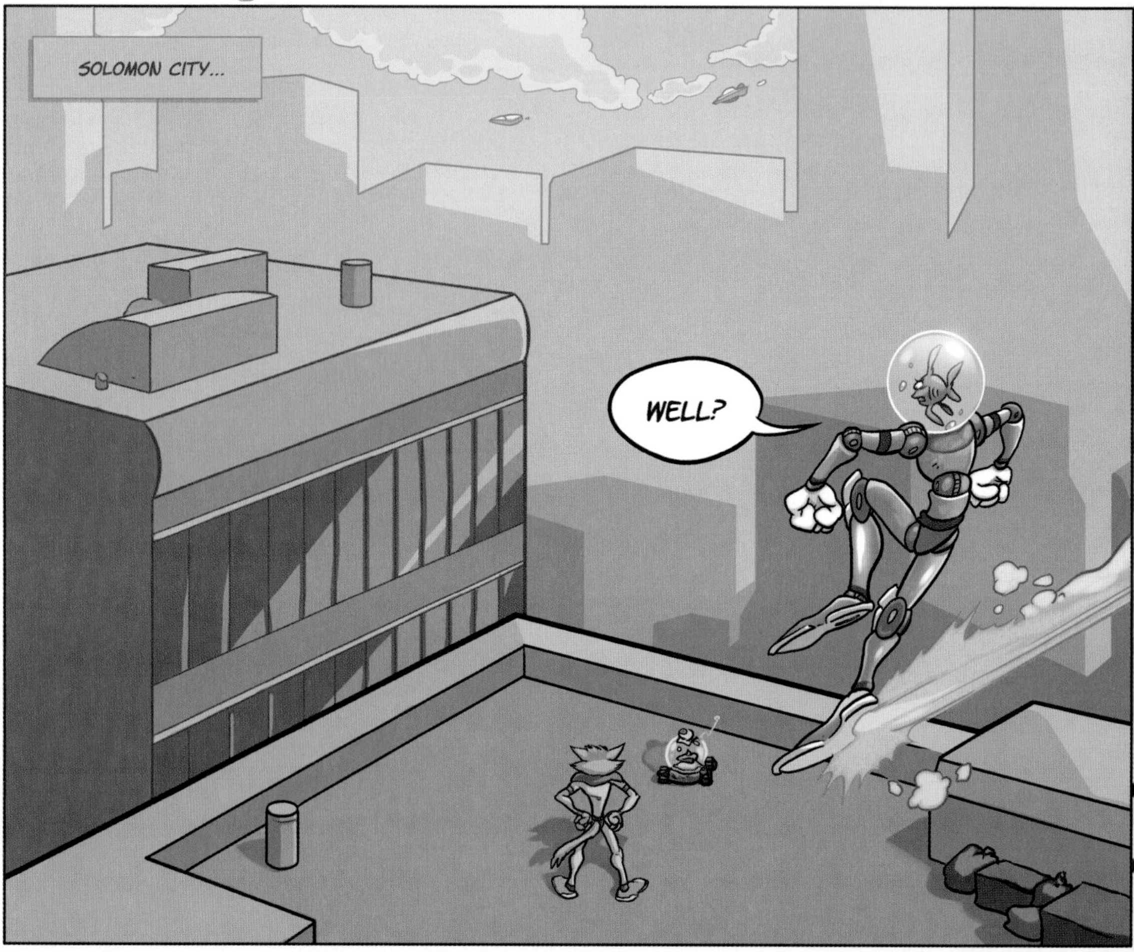
SOLOMON CITY...
WELL?

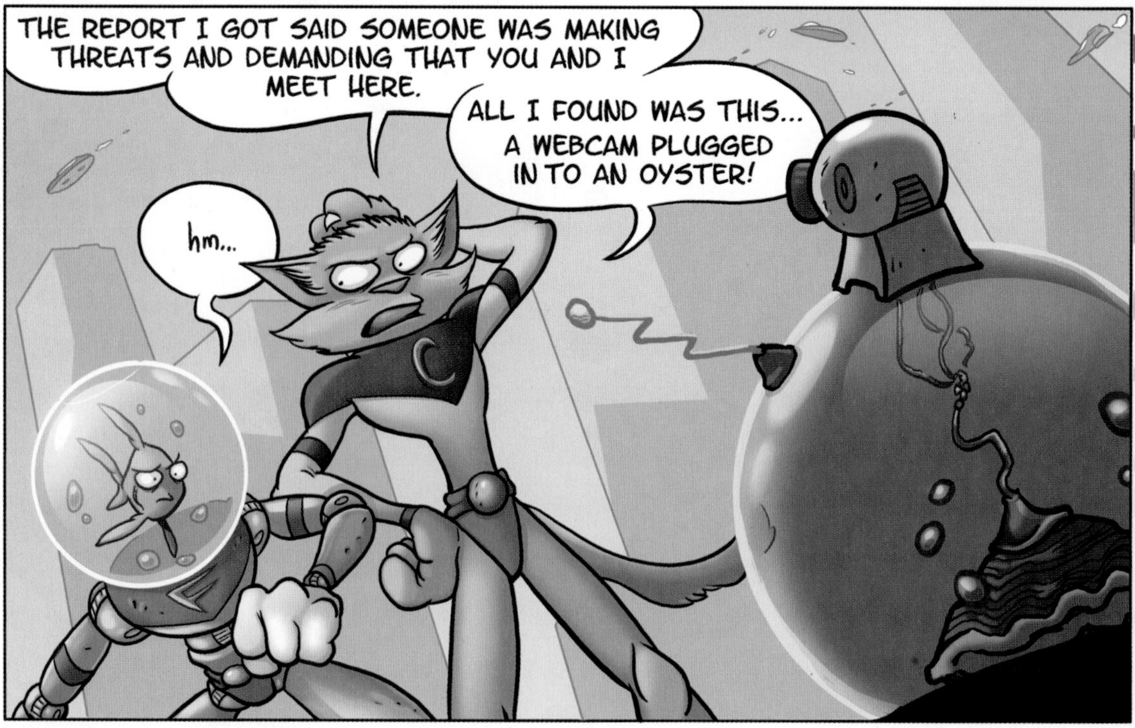
THE REPORT I GOT SAID SOMEONE WAS MAKING THREATS AND DEMANDING THAT YOU AND I MEET HERE.
ALL I FOUND WAS THIS... A WEBCAM PLUGGED IN TO AN OYSTER!
hm...

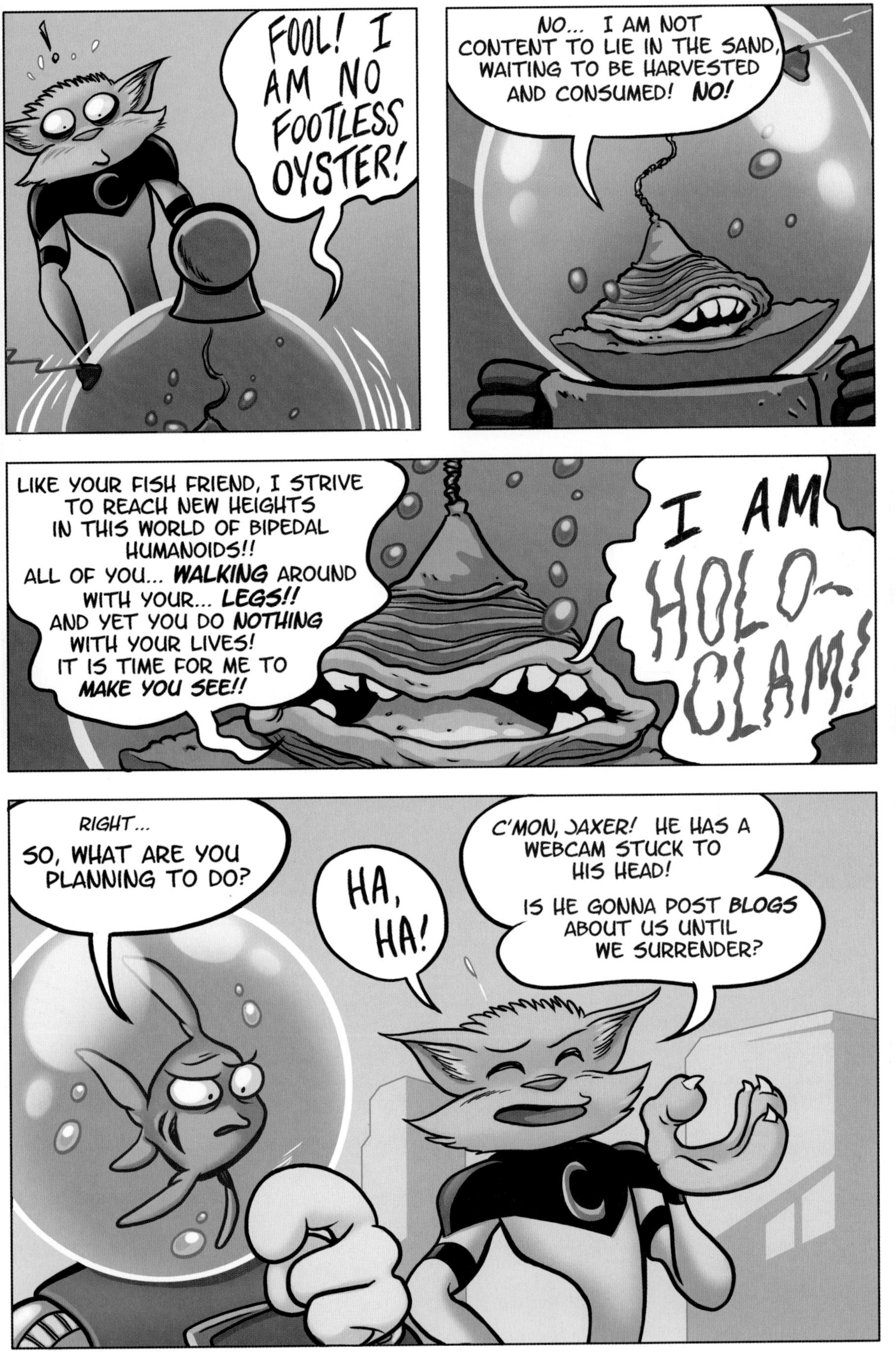

!
FOOL! I AM NO FOOTLESS OYSTER!
NO... I AM NOT CONTENT TO LIE IN THE SAND, WAITING TO BE HARVESTED AND CONSUMED! NO!
LIKE YOUR FISH FRIEND, I STRIVE TO REACH NEW HEIGHTS IN THIS WORLD OF BIPEDAL HUMANOIDS!! ALL OF YOU... WALKING AROUND WITH YOUR... LEGS!! AND YET YOU DO NOTHING WITH YOUR LIVES! IT IS TIME FOR ME TO MAKE YOU SEE!!
I AM HOLO-CLAM!
RIGHT... SO, WHAT ARE YOU PLANNING TO DO?
HA, HA!
C'MON, JAXER! HE HAS A WEBCAM STUCK TO HIS HEAD!
IS HE GONNA POST BLOGS ABOUT US UNTIL WE SURRENDER?

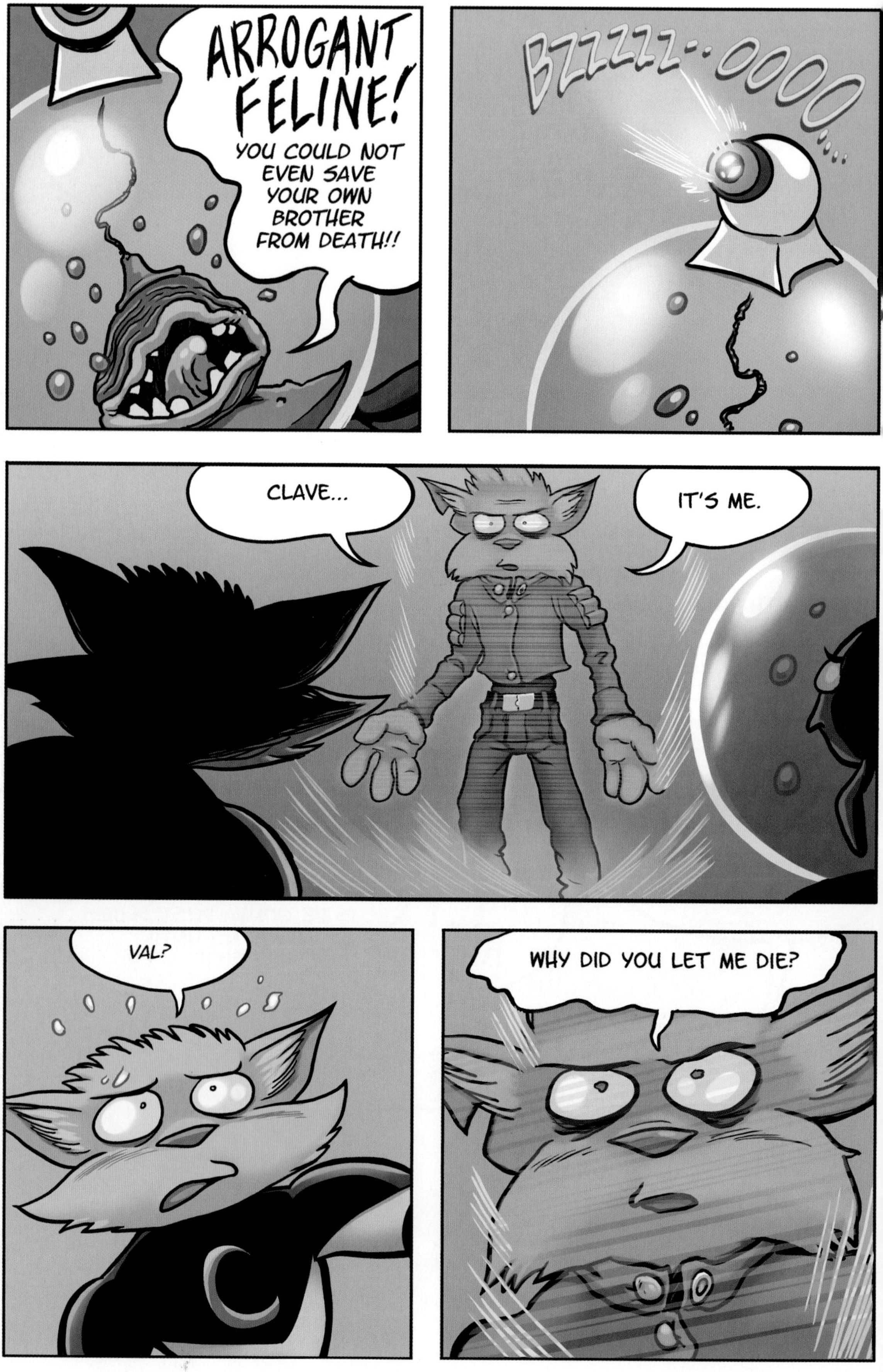
ARROGANT FELINE!
YOU COULD NOT EVEN SAVE YOUR OWN BROTHER FROM DEATH!!
BZZZZZ··OOOO···
CLAVE...
IT'S ME.
VAL?
WHY DID YOU LET ME DIE?

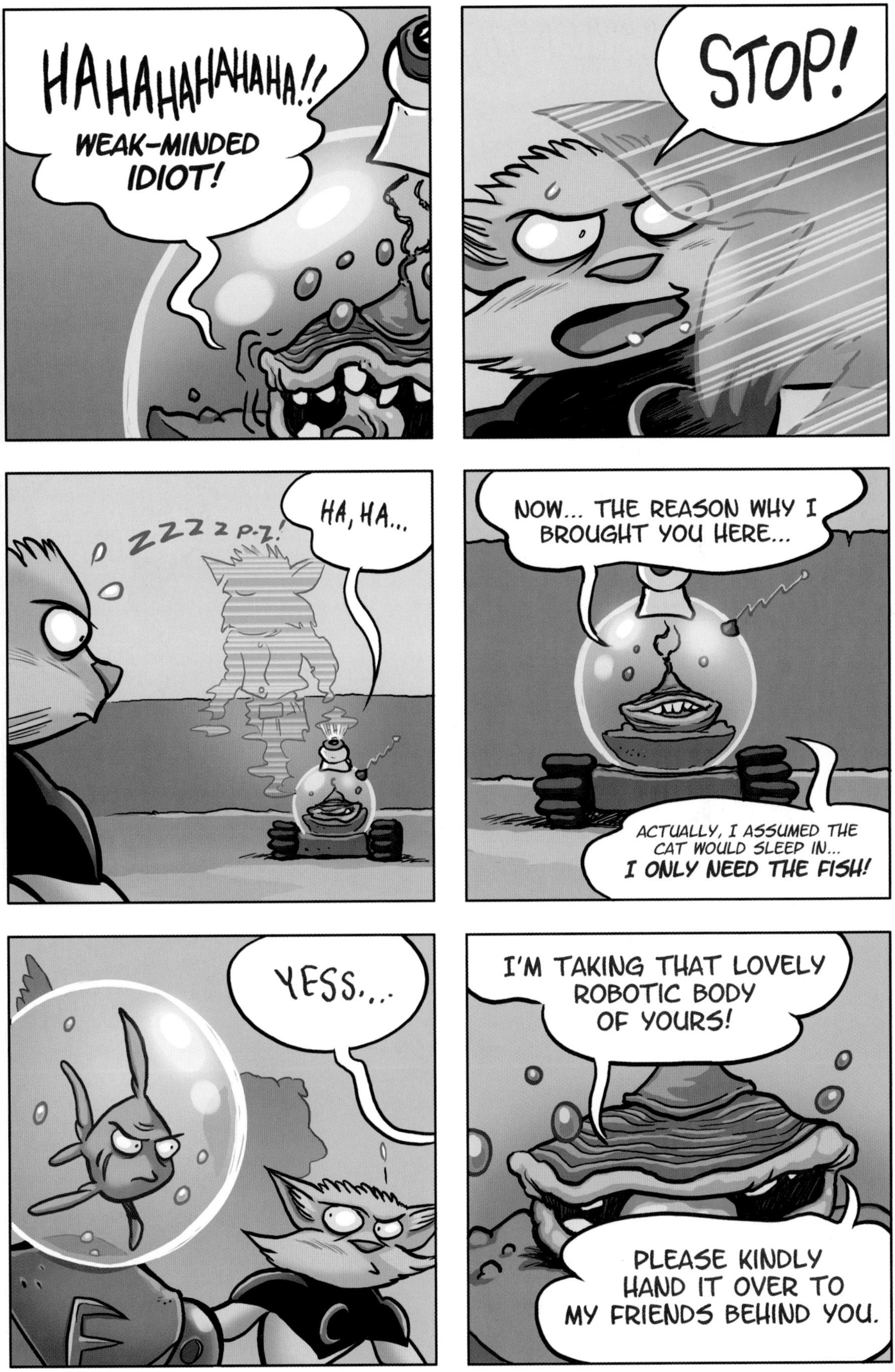
HAHAHAHAHAHA!!!
WEAK-MINDED IDIOT!
STOP!
ZZZZZ P-Z!
HA, HA...
NOW... THE REASON WHY I BROUGHT YOU HERE...
ACTUALLY, I ASSUMED THE CAT WOULD SLEEP IN... I ONLY NEED THE FISH!
YESS...
I'M TAKING THAT LOVELY ROBOTIC BODY OF YOURS!
PLEASE KINDLY HAND IT OVER TO MY FRIENDS BEHIND YOU.

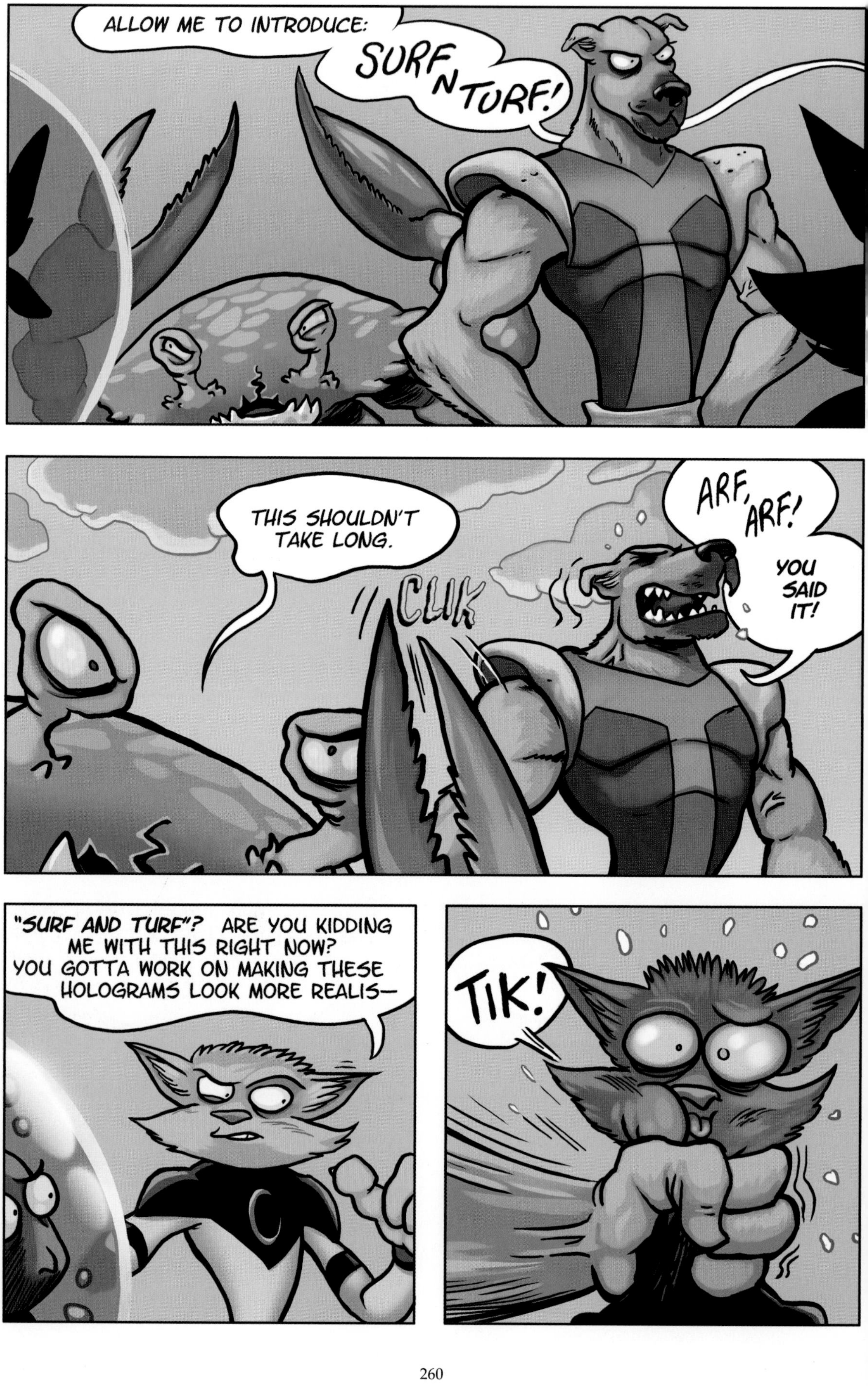
ALLOW ME TO INTRODUCE:
SURF N TURF!
THIS SHOULDN'T TAKE LONG.
CLIK
ARF, ARF!
YOU SAID IT!
"SURF AND TURF"? ARE YOU KIDDING ME WITH THIS RIGHT NOW? YOU GOTTA WORK ON MAKING THESE HOLOGRAMS LOOK MORE REALIS—
TIK!

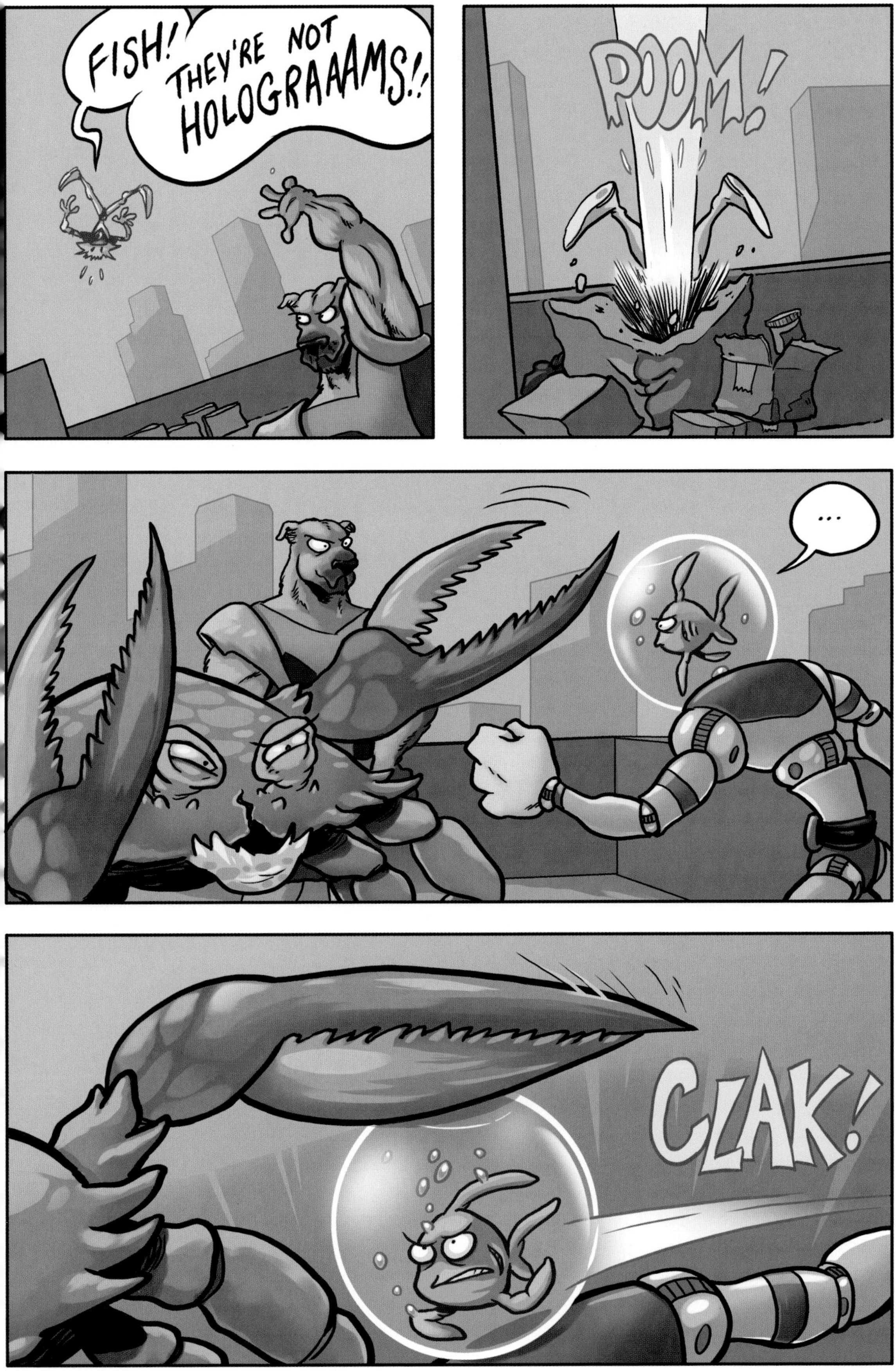
FISH! THEY'RE NOT HOLOGRAAAMS!!
POOM!
...
CLAK!

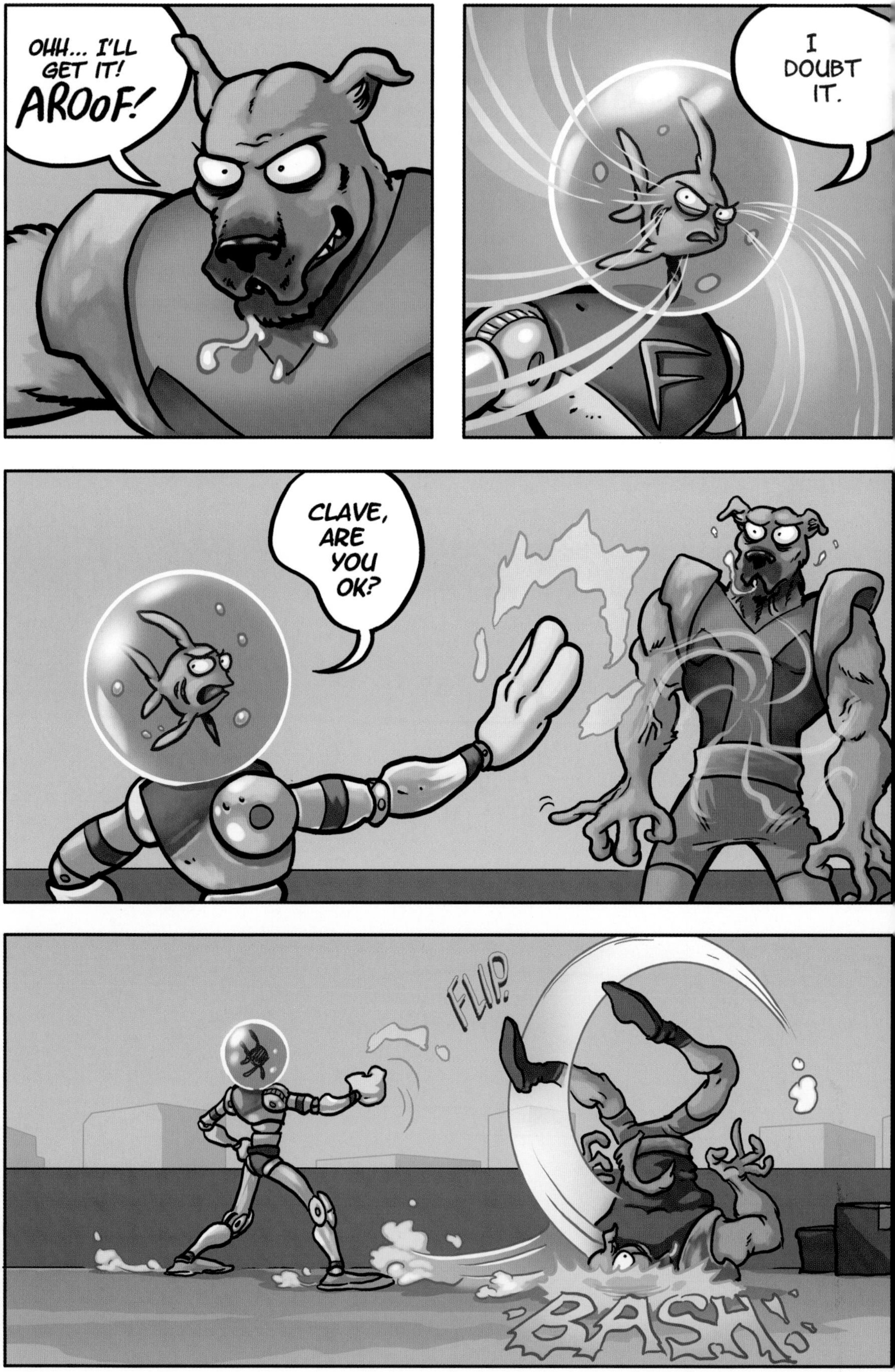
OHH... I'LL GET IT! AROOF!
I DOUBT IT.
CLAVE, ARE YOU OK?
FLIP!
BASH!

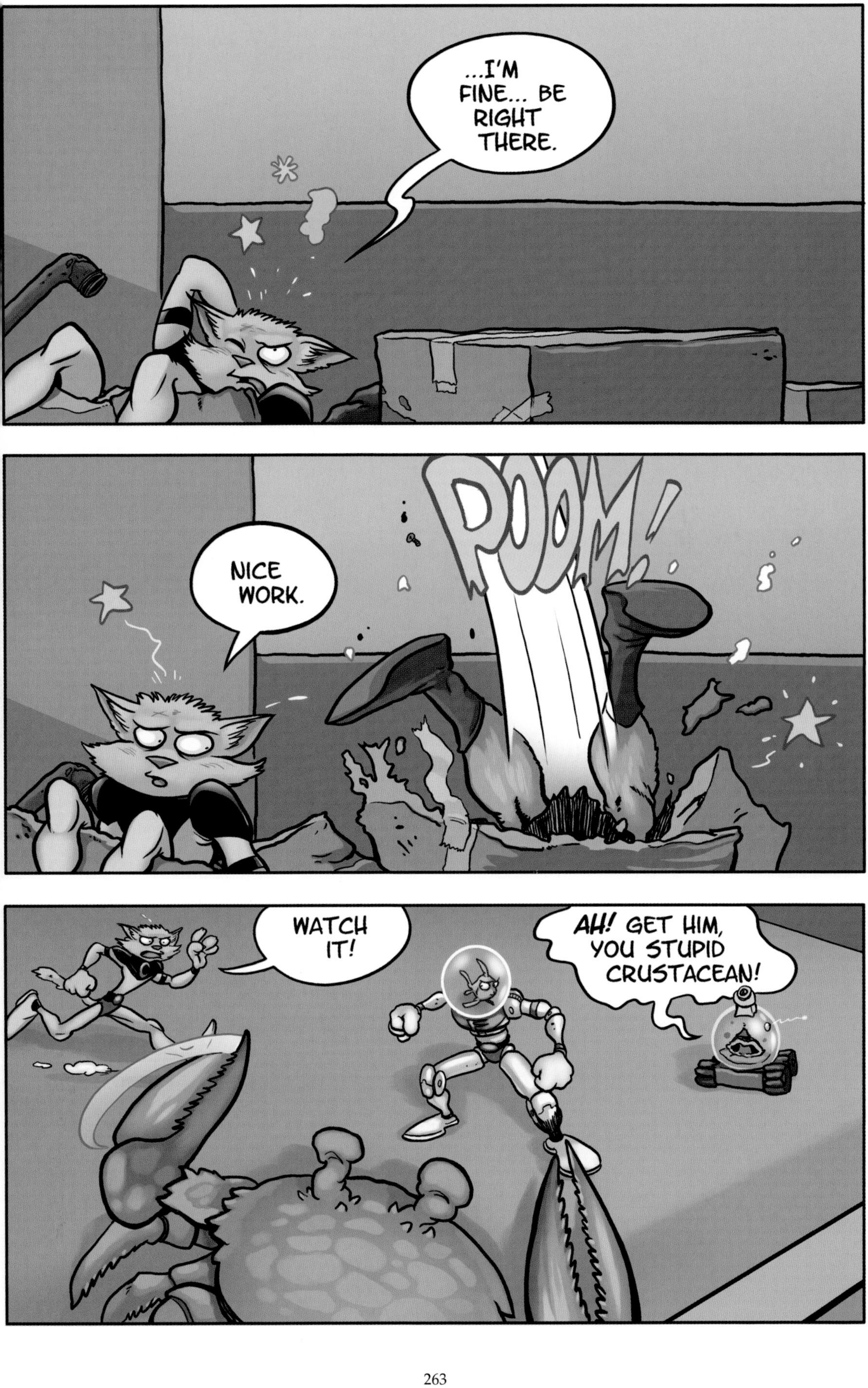
...I'M FINE... BE RIGHT THERE.
NICE WORK.
POOM!
WATCH IT!
AH! GET HIM, YOU STUPID CRUSTACEAN!

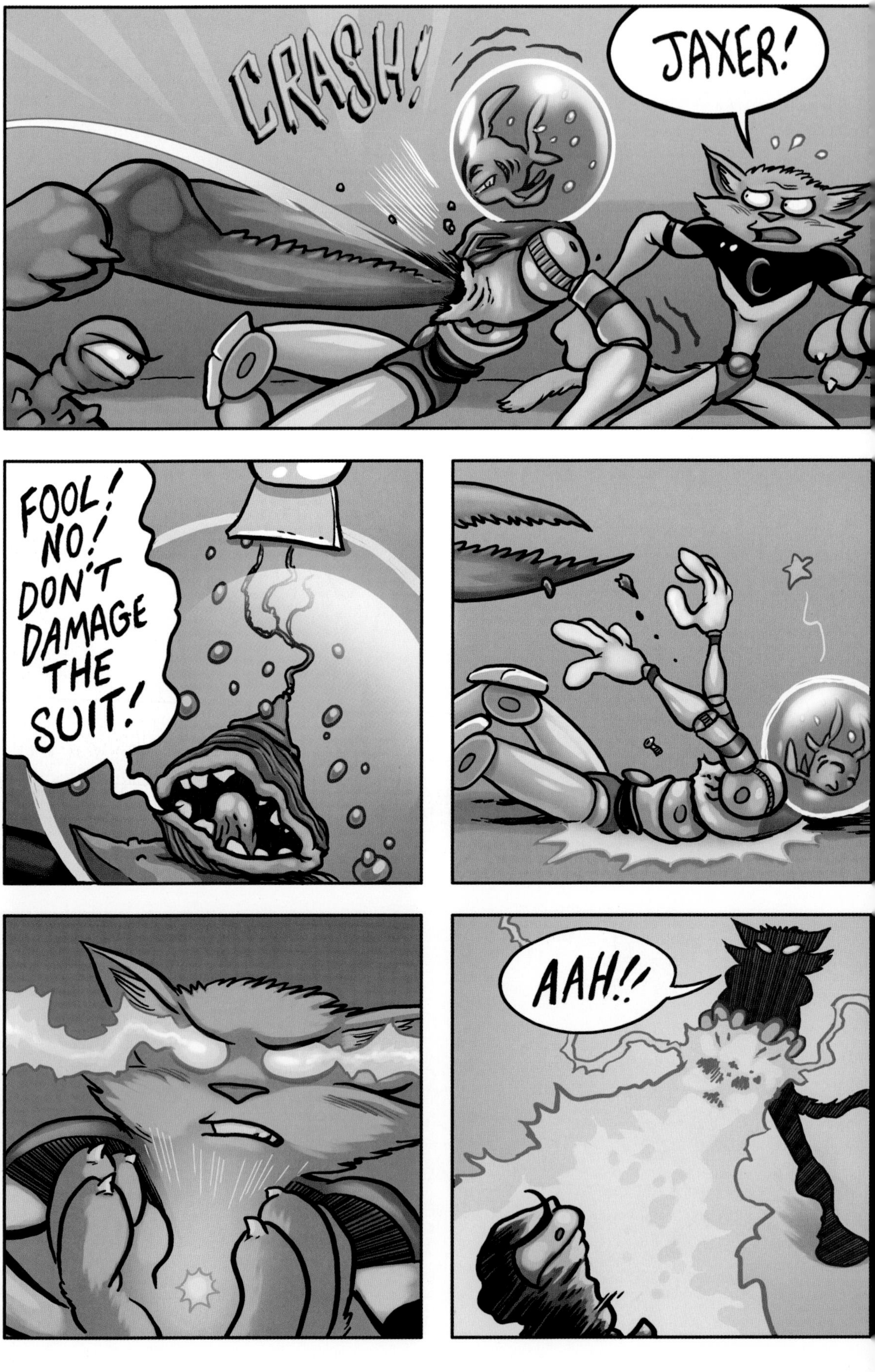
CRASH!
JAXER!
FOOL! NO! DON'T DAMAGE THE SUIT!
AAH!!

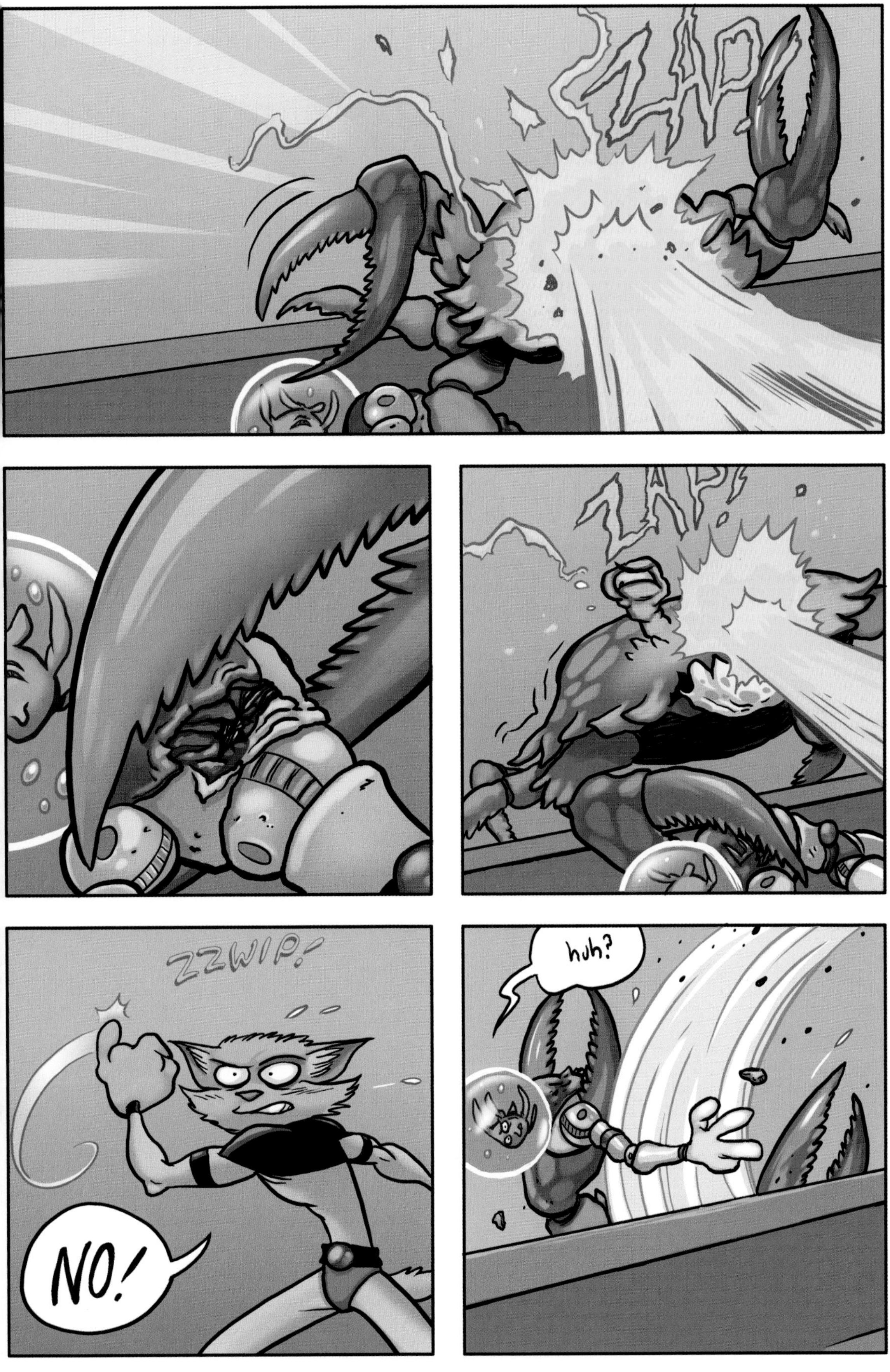
ZAP!
ZAP!
ZZWIP!
NO!
huh?

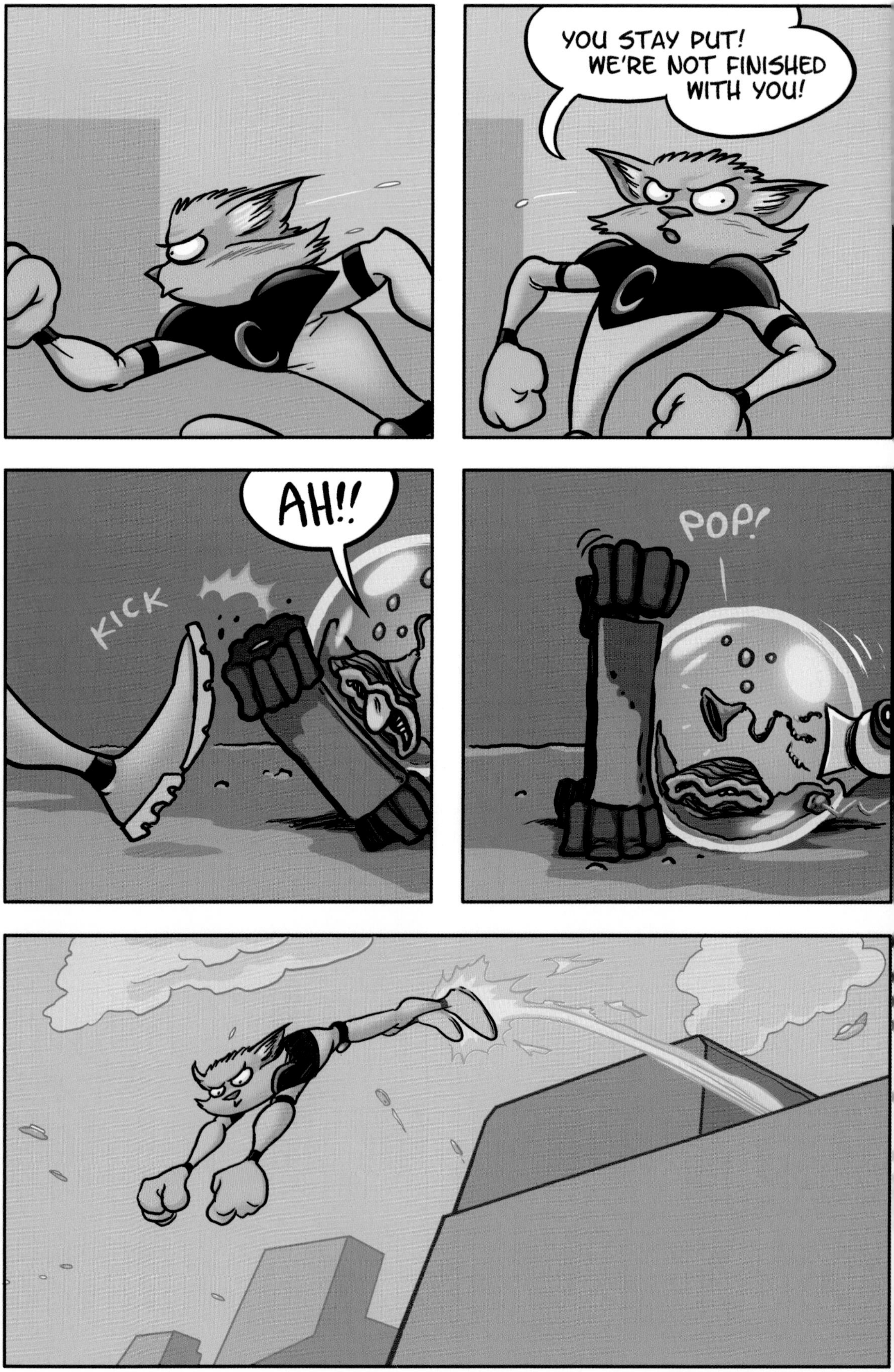
YOU STAY PUT! WE'RE NOT FINISHED WITH YOU!
AH!!
KICK
POP!

CAN YOU BREAK LOOSE?
NO! THE SUIT IS BROKEN!!
POP YOUR LID!
WHAT? NO!

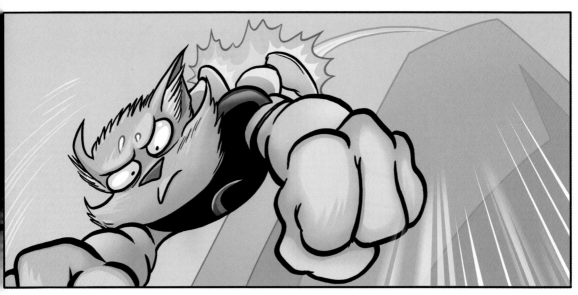

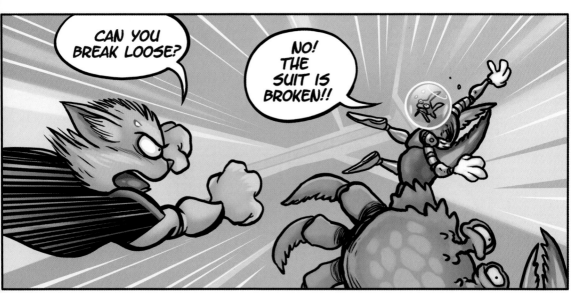

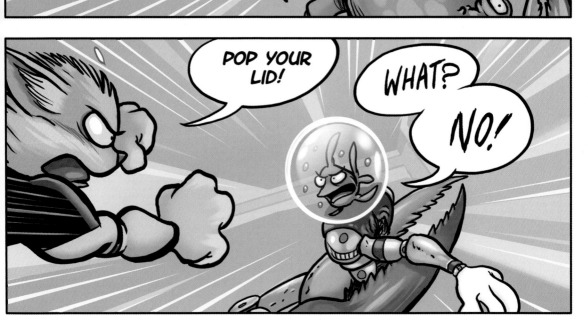

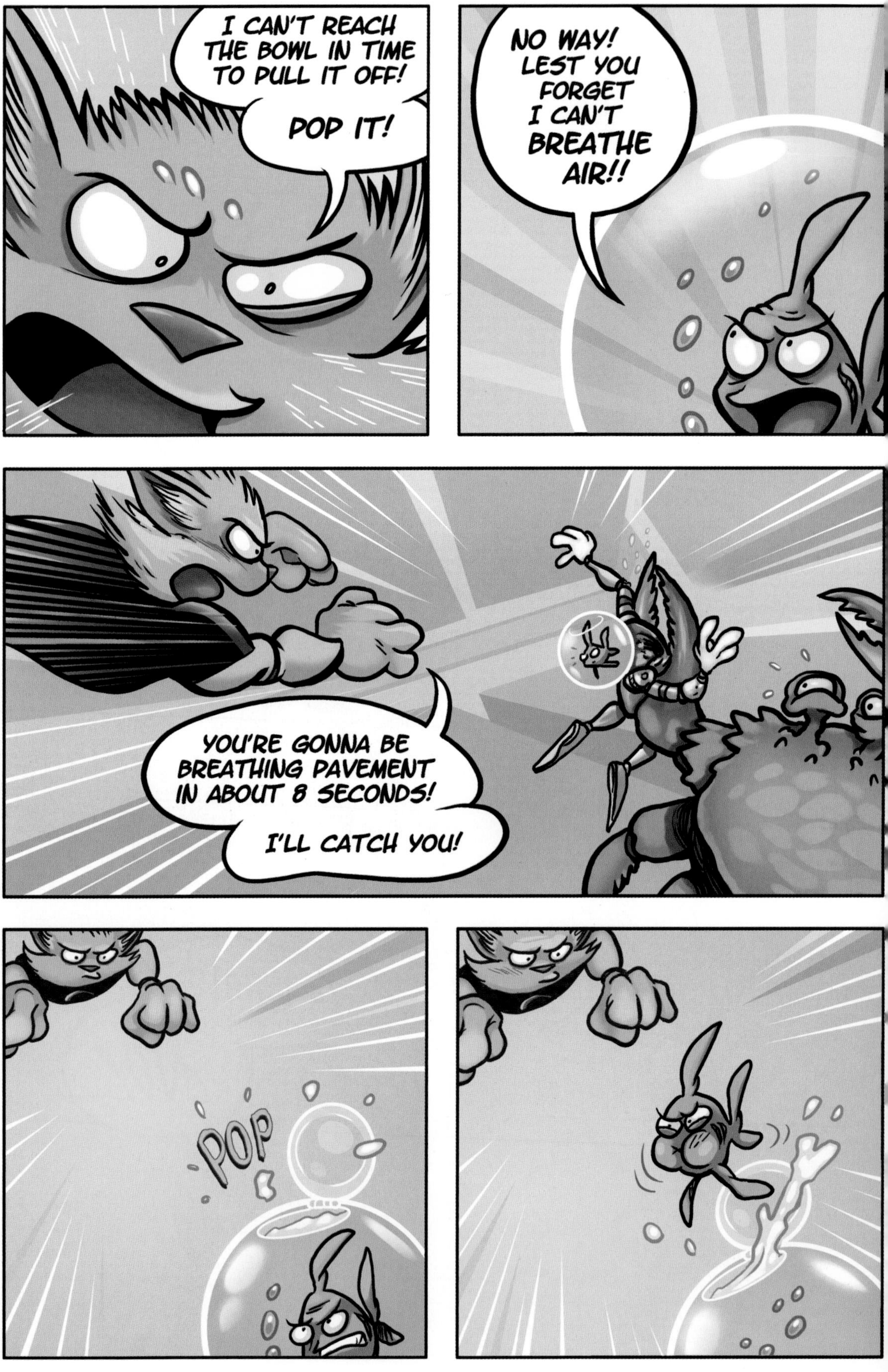
I CAN'T REACH THE BOWL IN TIME TO PULL IT OFF!
POP IT!
NO WAY! LEST YOU FORGET I CAN'T BREATHE AIR!!
YOU'RE GONNA BE BREATHING PAVEMENT IN ABOUT 8 SECONDS!
I'LL CATCH YOU!
POP

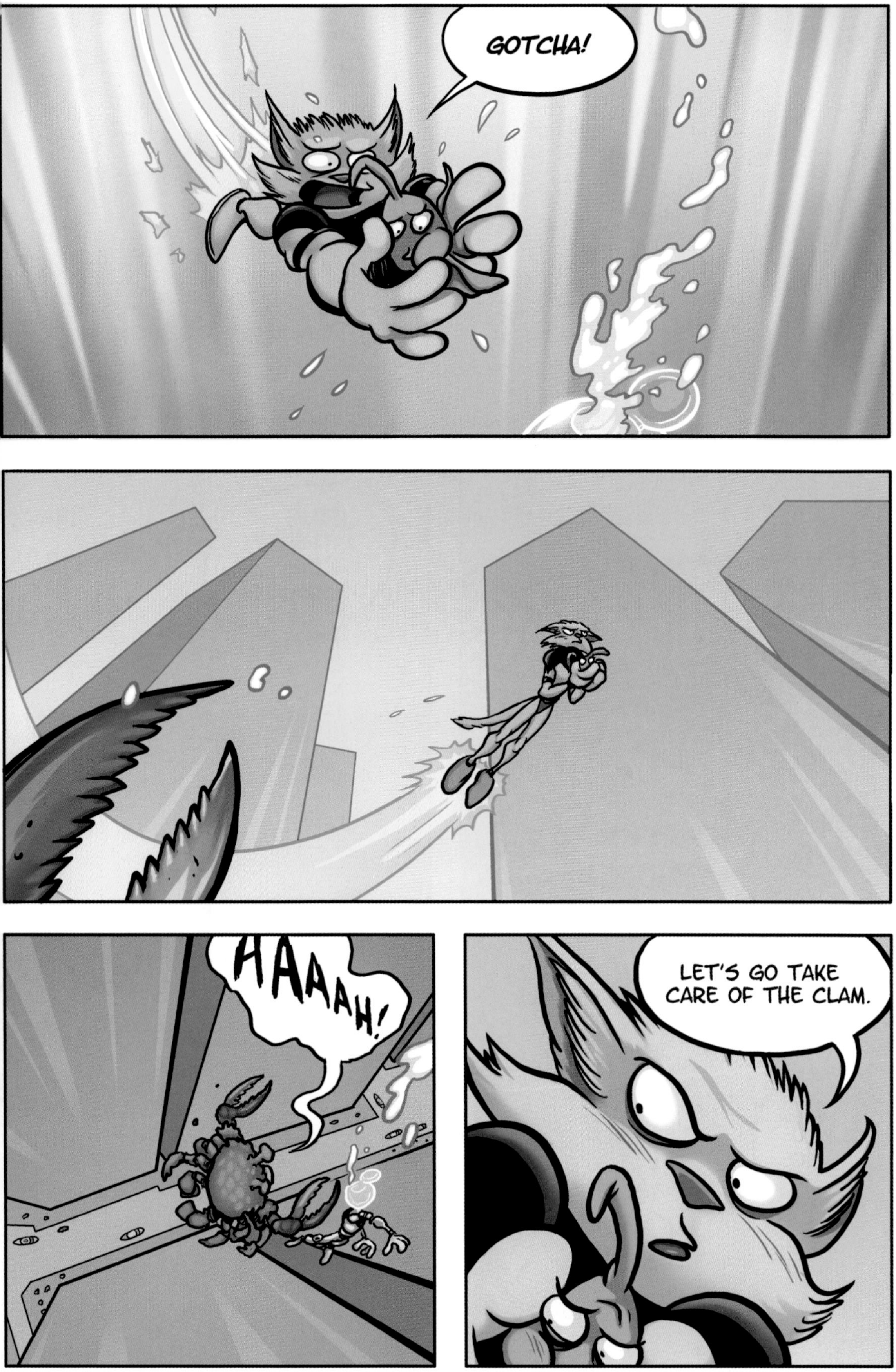
GOTCHA!
HAAAAH!
LET'S GO TAKE CARE OF THE CLAM.

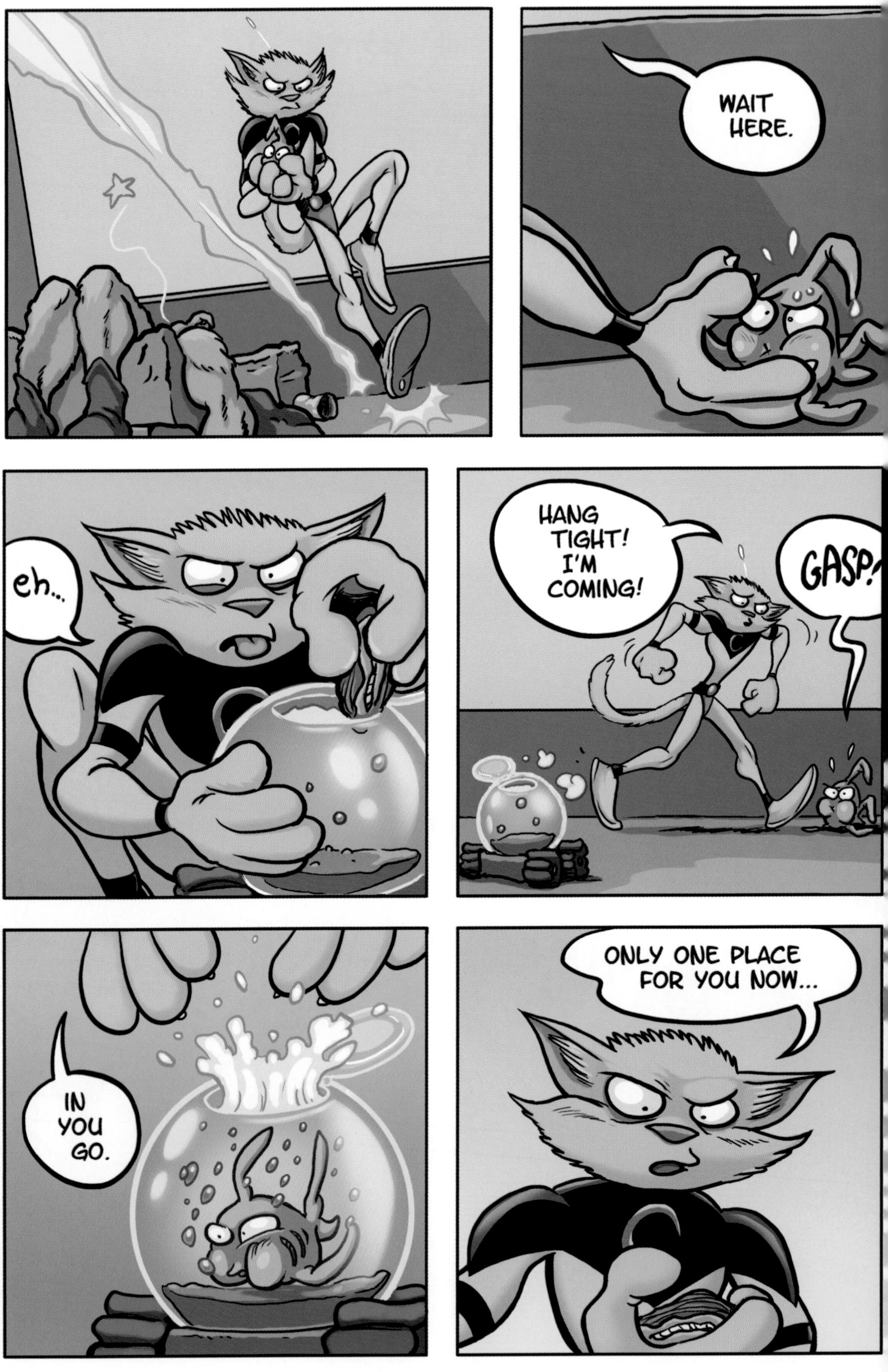
WAIT HERE.
eh...
HANG TIGHT! I'M COMING!
GASP!
IN YOU GO.
ONLY ONE PLACE FOR YOU NOW...

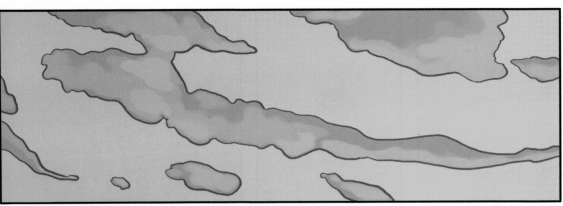

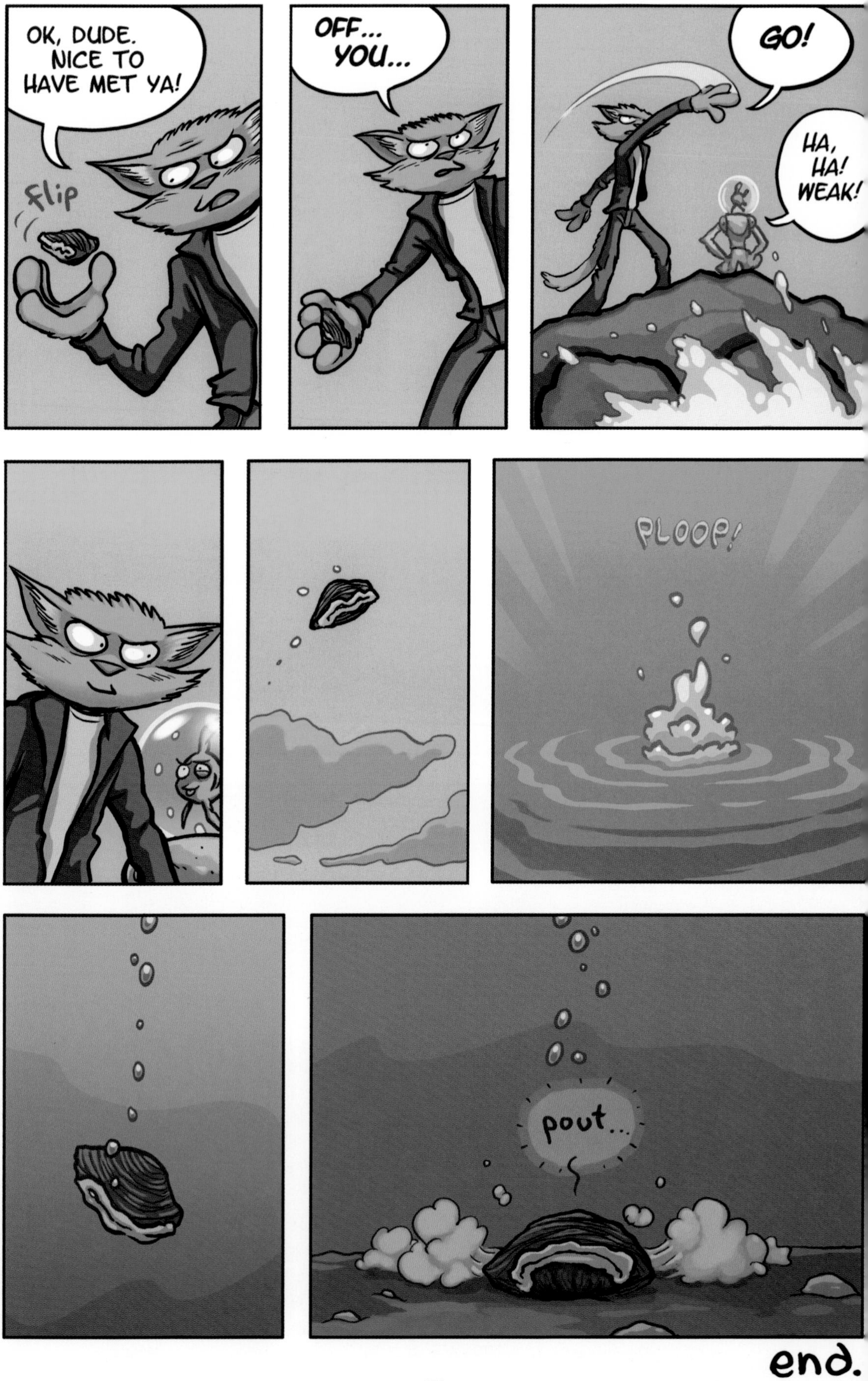
OK, DUDE.
NICE TO
HAVE MET YA!
Flip
OFF...
YOU...
GO!
HA,
HA!
WEAK!
PLOOP!
pout...
end.

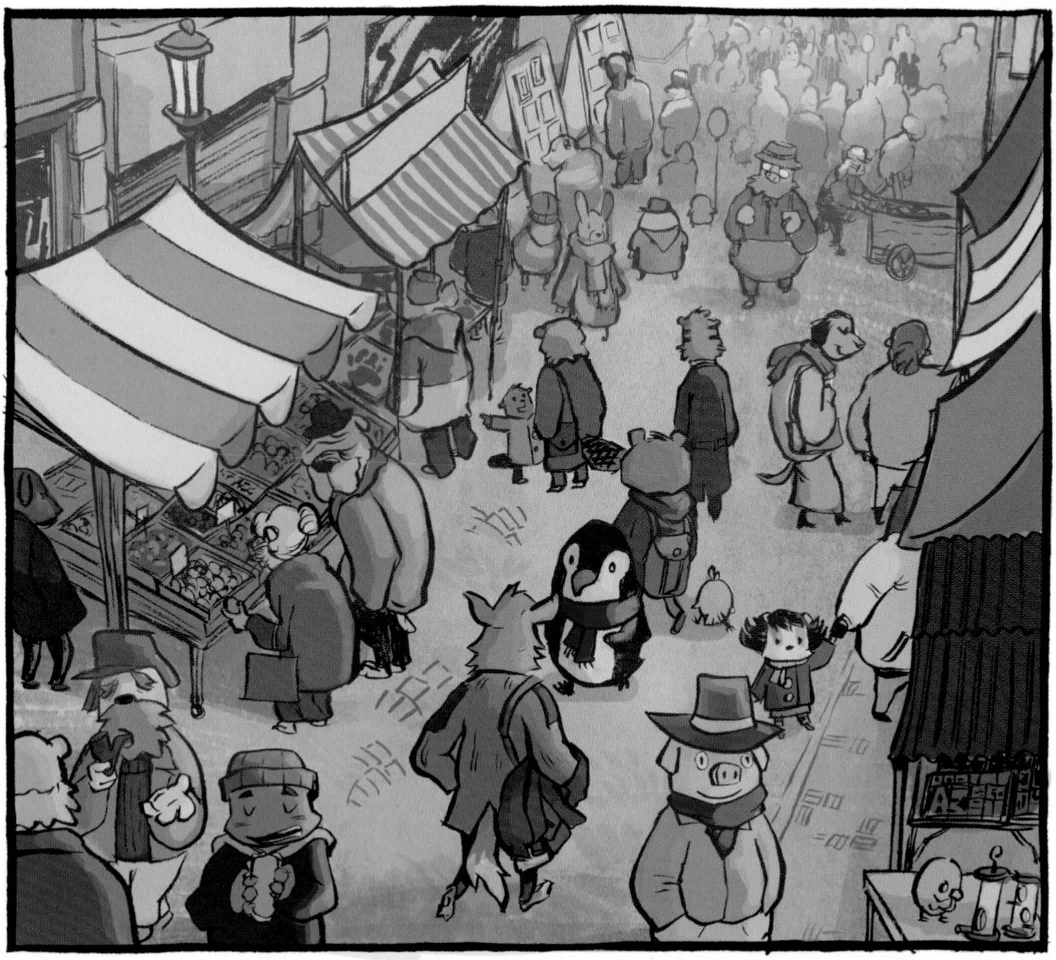

long-winded

by Mike Dutton

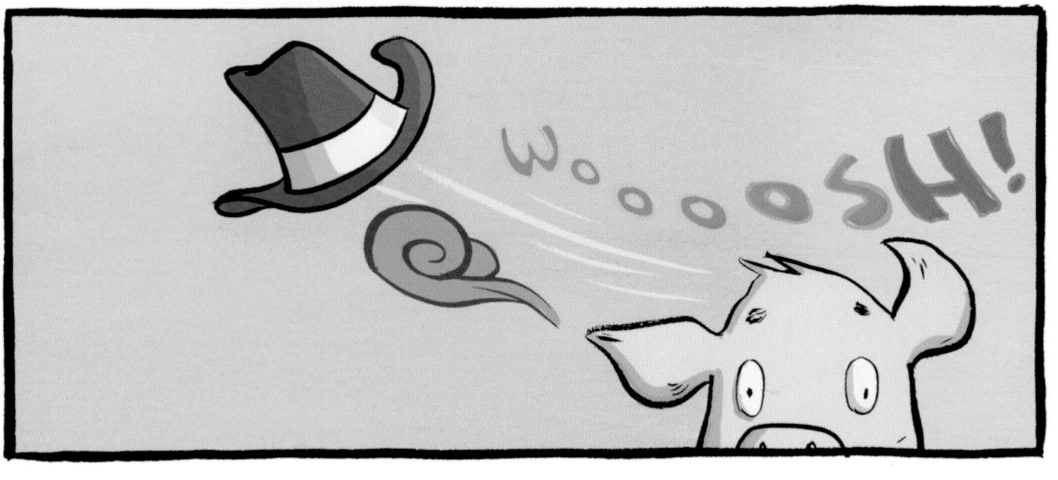
WOOOOSH!

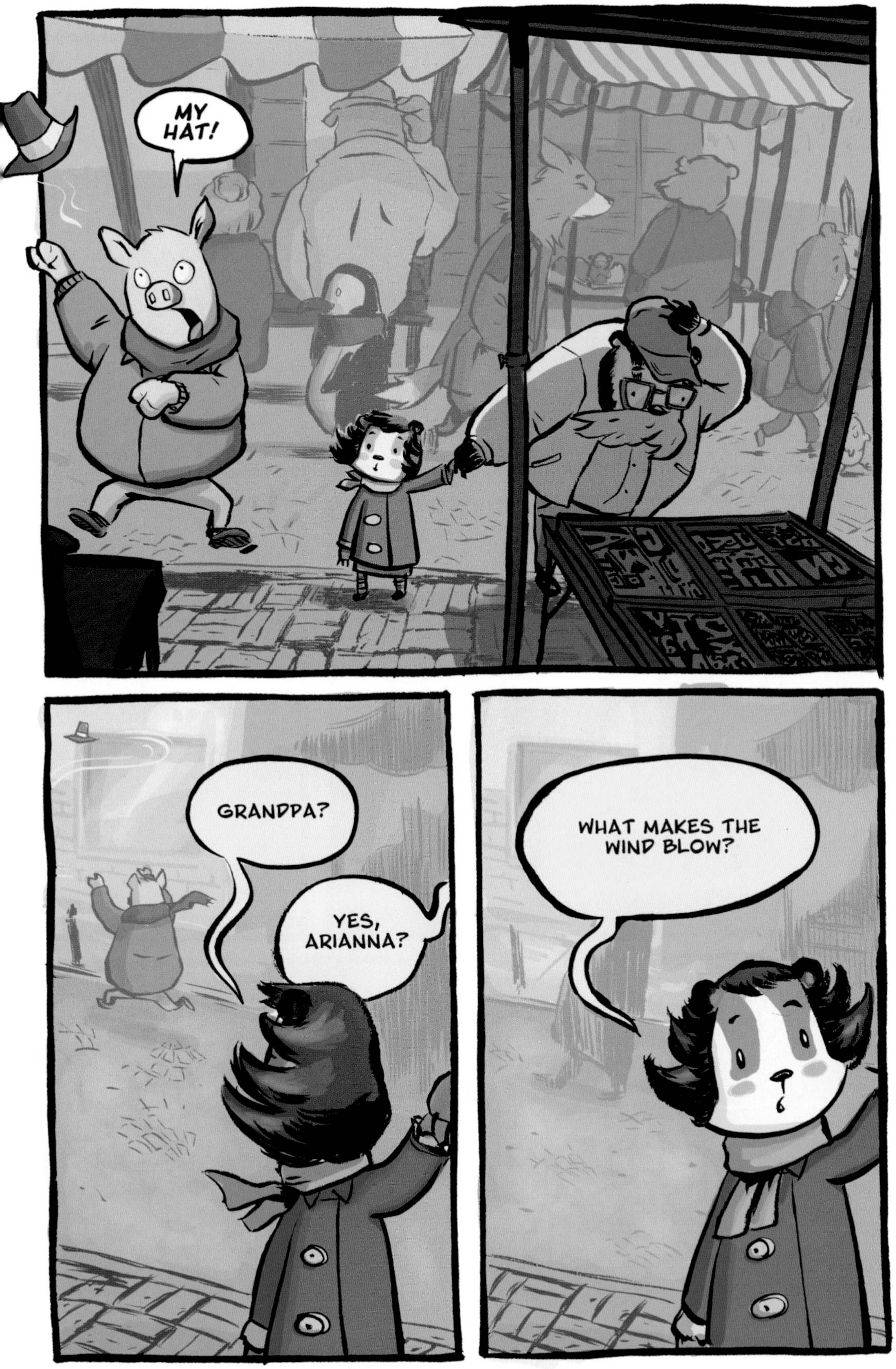
MY HAT!
GRANDPA?
YES, ARIANNA?
WHAT MAKES THE WIND BLOW?

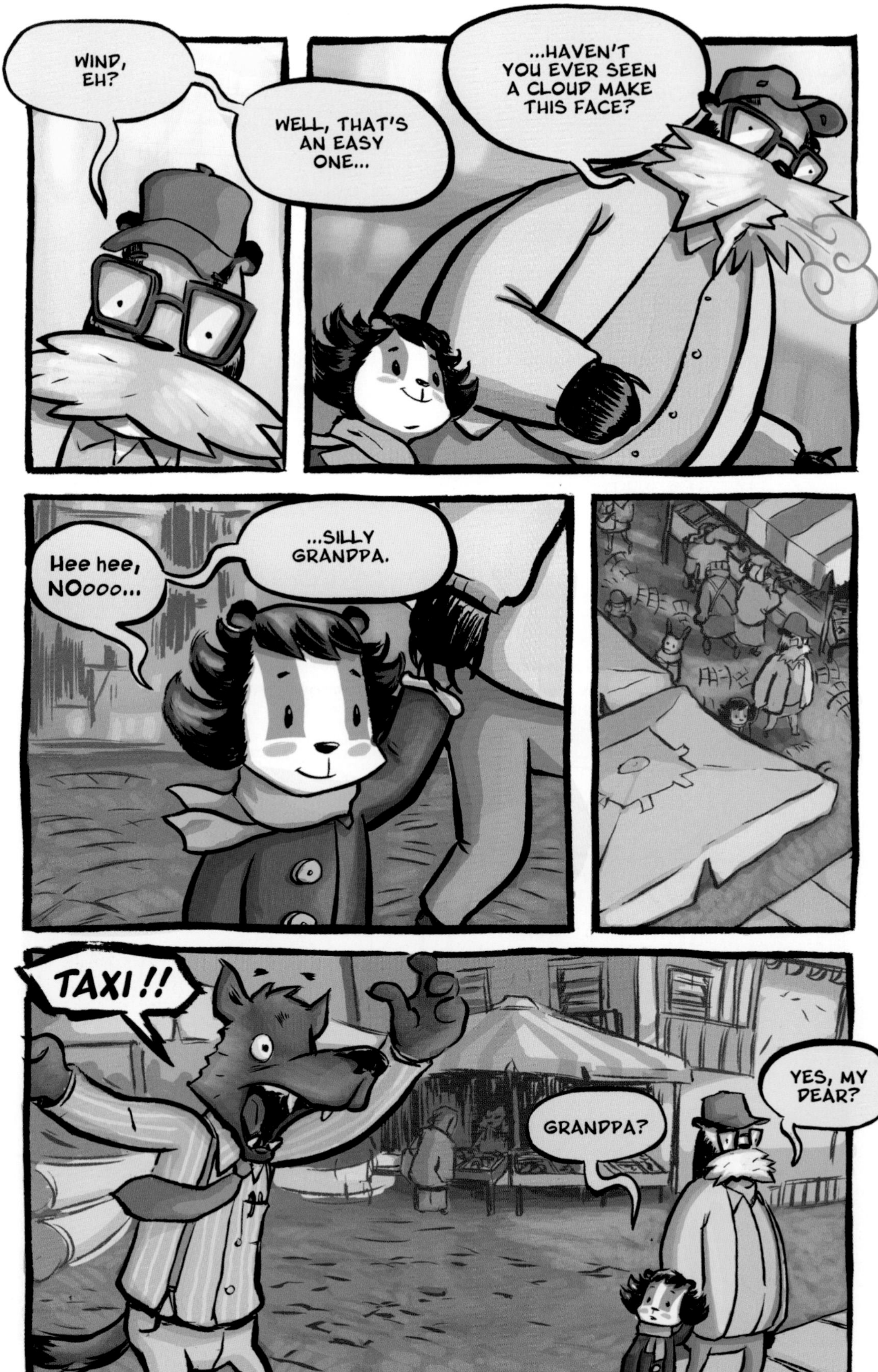
WIND, EH?
WELL, THAT'S AN EASY ONE...
...HAVEN'T YOU EVER SEEN A CLOUD MAKE THIS FACE?
Hee hee, NOooo...
...SILLY GRANDPA.
TAXI!!
GRANDPA?
YES, MY DEAR?

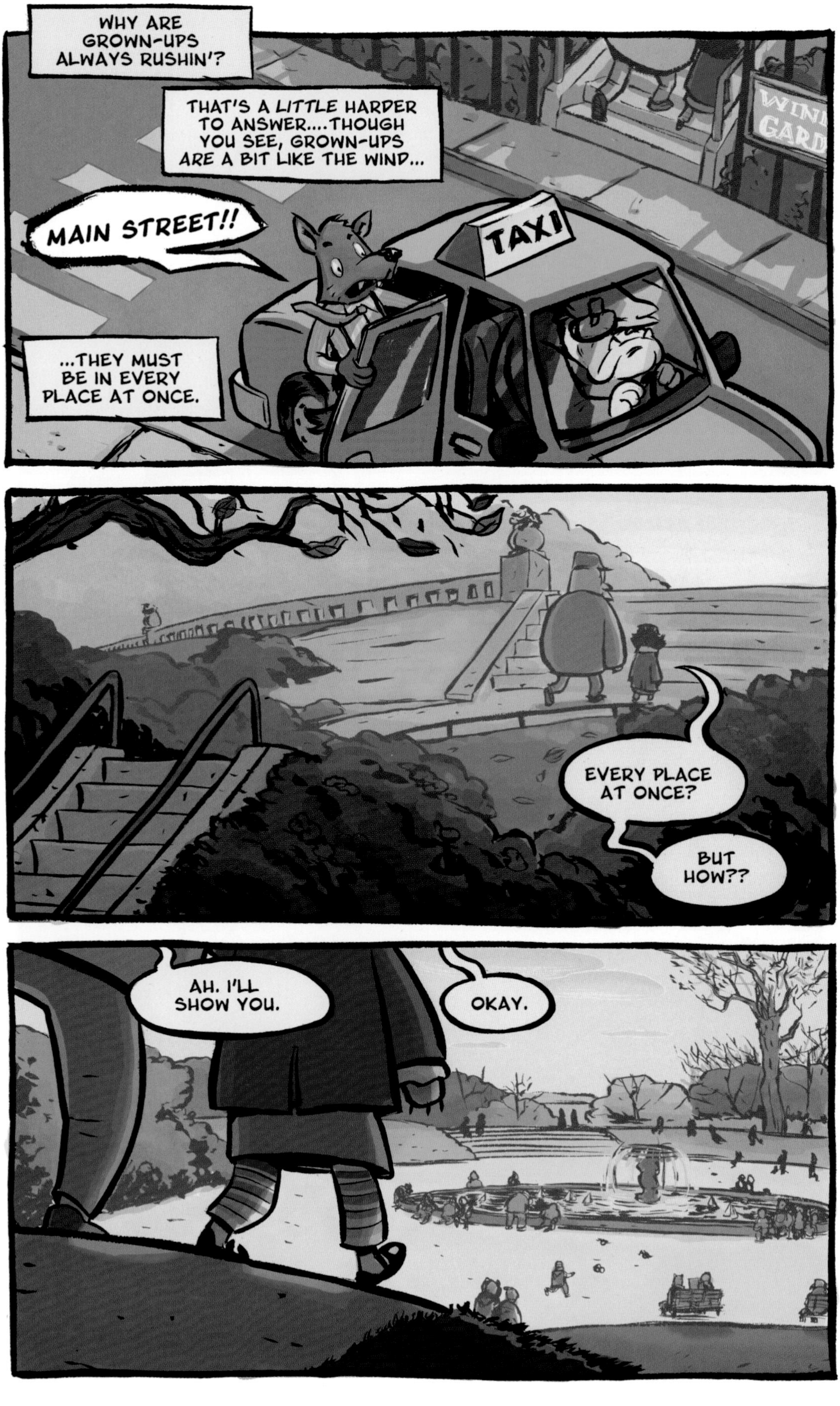
WHY ARE GROWN-UPS ALWAYS RUSHIN'?
THAT'S A *LITTLE* HARDER TO ANSWER....THOUGH YOU SEE, GROWN-UPS ARE A BIT LIKE THE WIND...
MAIN STREET!!
TAXI
...THEY MUST BE IN EVERY PLACE AT ONCE.
EVERY PLACE AT ONCE?
BUT HOW??
AH. I'LL SHOW YOU.
OKAY.

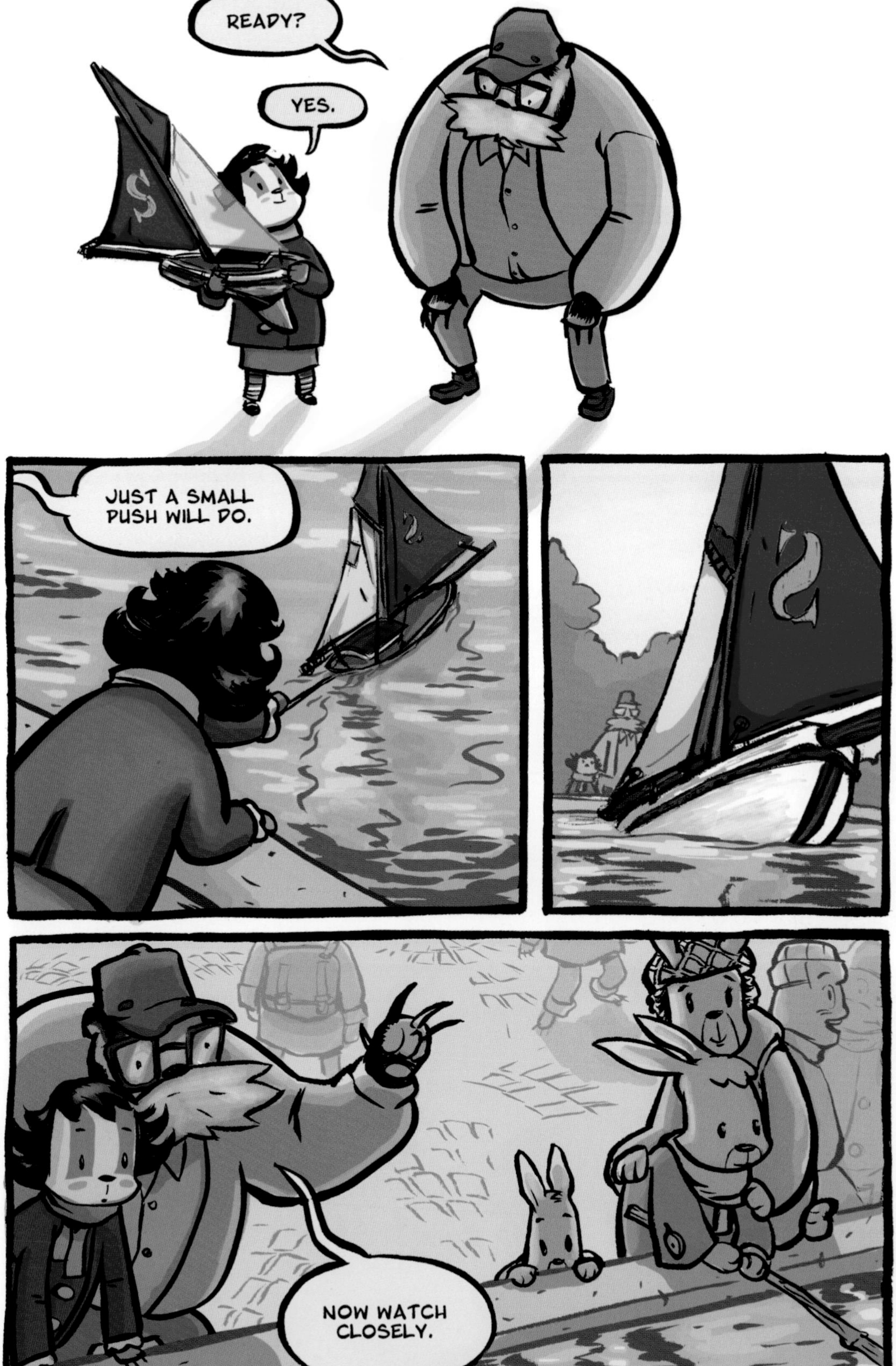
READY?
YES.
JUST A SMALL PUSH WILL DO.
NOW WATCH CLOSELY.

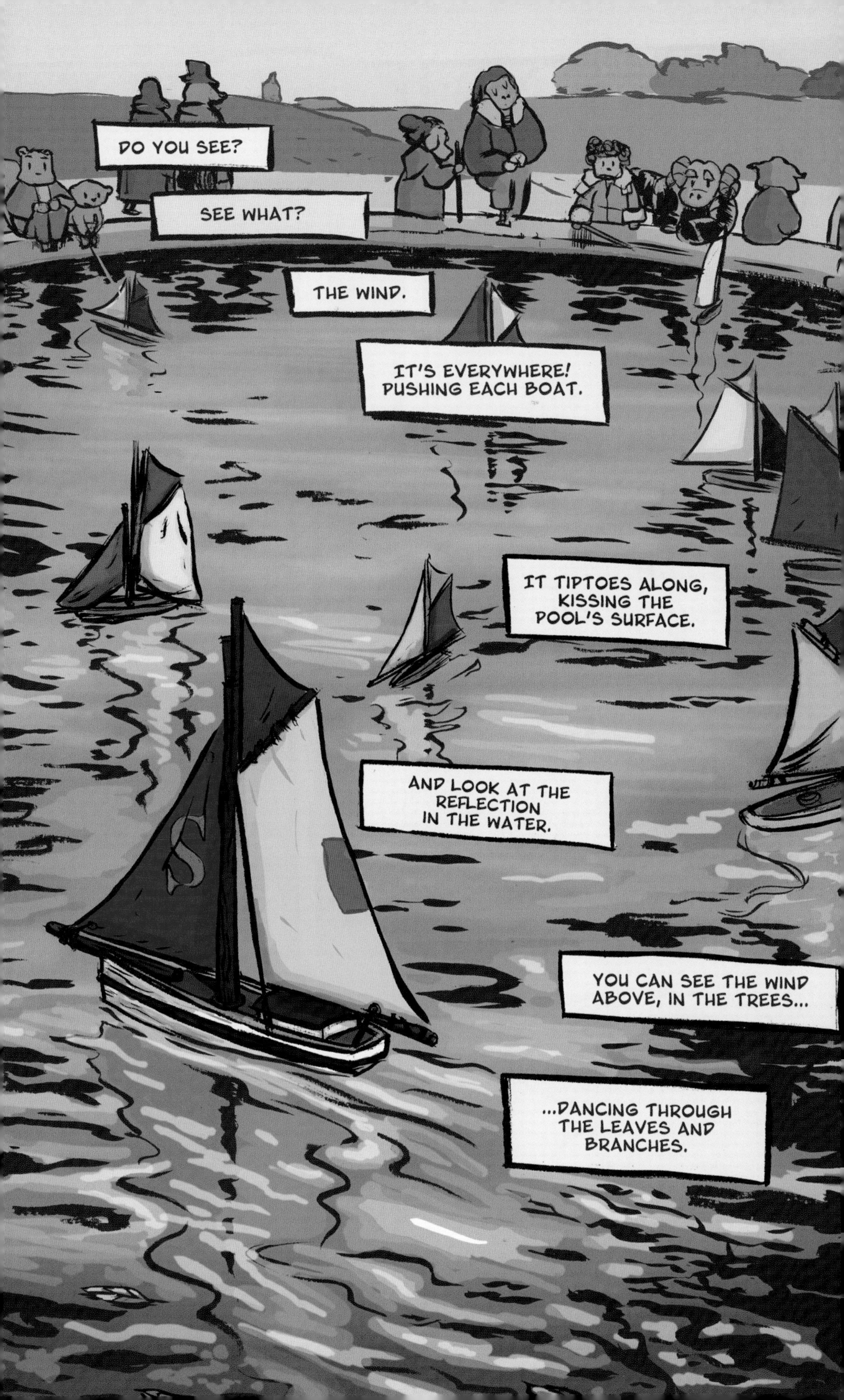
DO YOU SEE?
SEE WHAT?
THE WIND.
IT'S EVERYWHERE! PUSHING EACH BOAT.
IT TIPTOES ALONG, KISSING THE POOL'S SURFACE.
AND LOOK AT THE REFLECTION IN THE WATER.
YOU CAN SEE THE WIND ABOVE, IN THE TREES...
...DANCING THROUGH THE LEAVES AND BRANCHES.

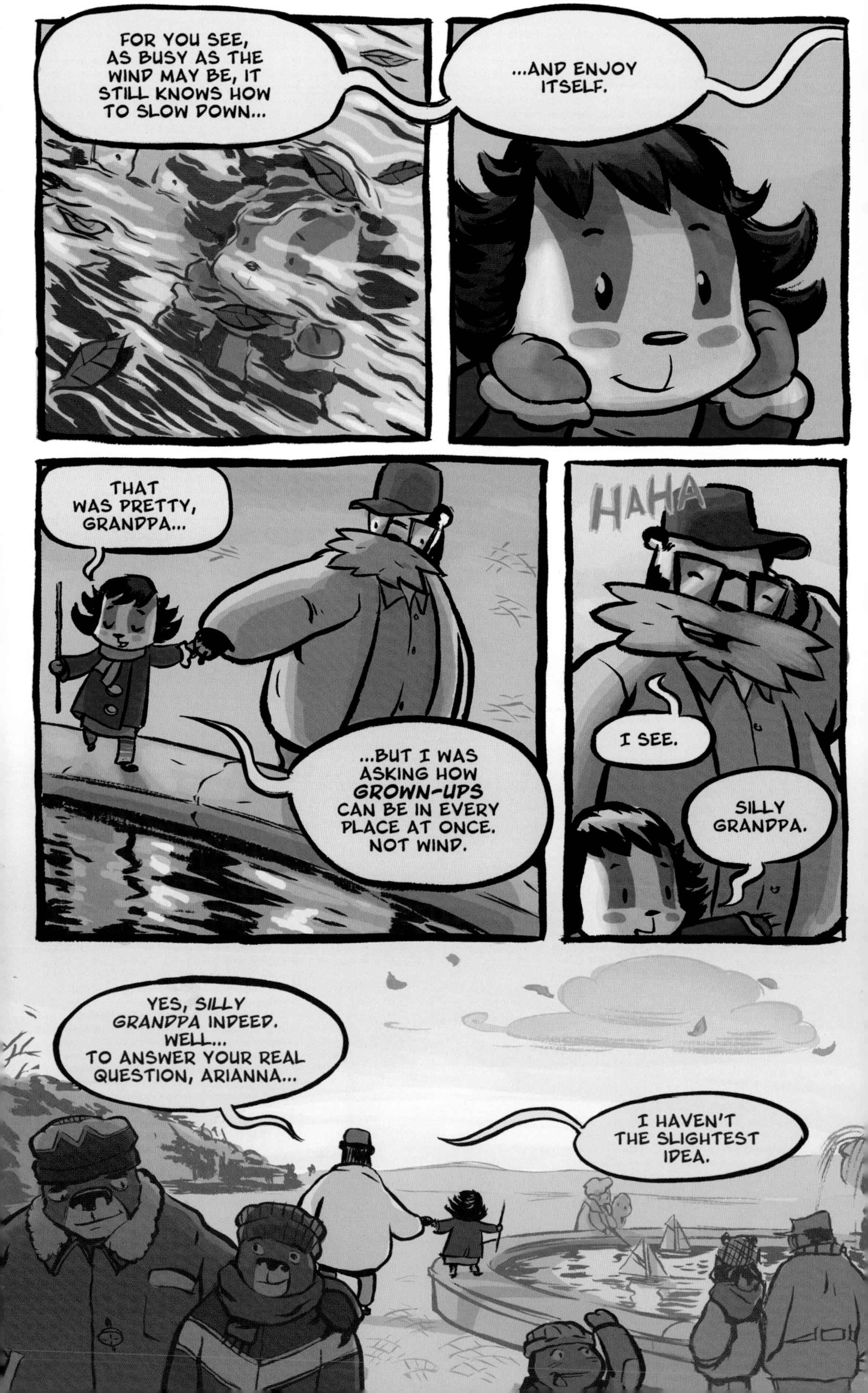
FOR YOU SEE, AS BUSY AS THE WIND MAY BE, IT STILL KNOWS HOW TO SLOW DOWN...
...AND ENJOY ITSELF.
THAT WAS PRETTY, GRANDPA...
...BUT I WAS ASKING HOW GROWN-UPS CAN BE IN EVERY PLACE AT ONCE. NOT WIND.
HAHA
I SEE.
SILLY GRANDPA.
YES, SILLY GRANDPA INDEED. WELL... TO ANSWER YOUR REAL QUESTION, ARIANNA...
I HAVEN'T THE SLIGHTEST IDEA.

FLIGHT: VOLUME SIX CONTRIBUTORS

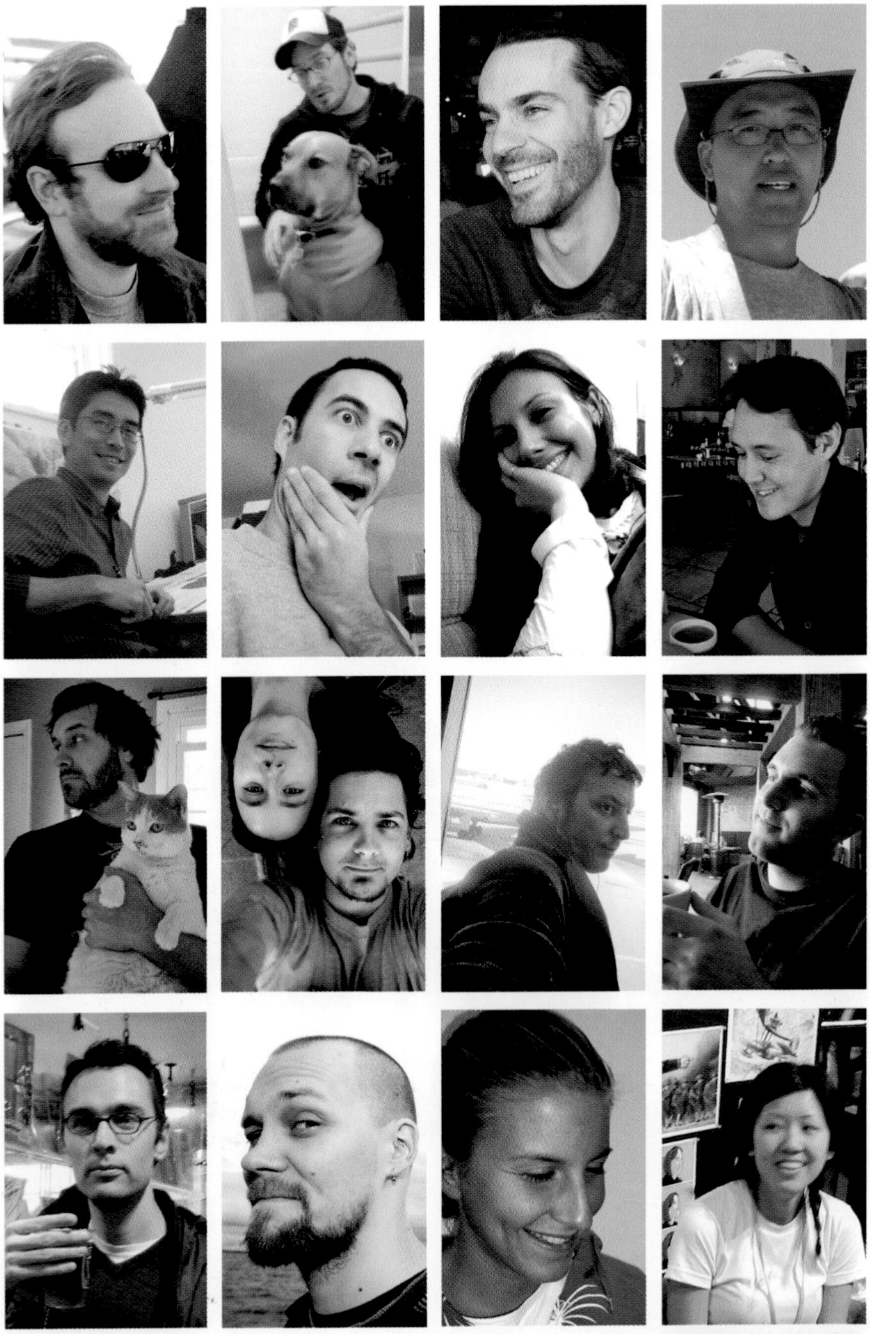

Flight: Volume Six Contributors

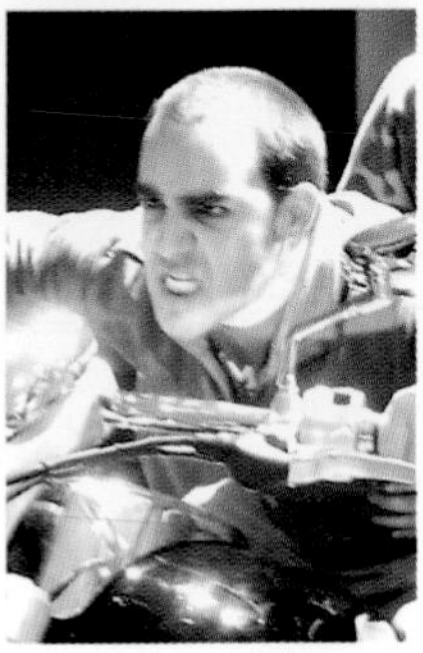

(from left to right)
Top Row: Michel Gagné, Steve Hamaker, Phil Craven, Kean Soo
2nd Row: Kazu Kibuishi, Justin Ridge, Nikki Damon, Mike Dutton
3rd Row: Cory Godbey, Bannister and Grimaldi, Rodolphe Guenoden, Rad Sechrist
4th Row: Graham Annable, JP Ahonen, Andrea Offermann, Catia Chien
Bottom Row: Richard Pose

Ahonen currently lives in Tampere, Finland, the bullet capital of the world. By day, JP draws comics and illustrations for a living, and by night, well…he continues drawing. JP wishes to thank Teem Matinlauri for his help with coloring this volume's story and would like to state that neither of them have bullets. You can find their work at www.jpahonen.com and www.tempesthole.com.

Graham Annable is a cartoonist presently living in Oregon. His work can be found in comics, film, and illustration. Discover all things grickle at www.grickle.com.

Bannister and **Grimaldi** live in France and make comics for a living. Bannister is coauthor of the award-winning series *Les enfants d'ailleurs* (published in the U.S. as *The Elsewhere Chronicles*). Grimaldi is a naturalist painter and colorist, and she works together with Bannister on their comic series for preschoolers, *Toss & Ilda*. www.bannister.fr
http://elsewherechronicles.com   www.titoss.com

Katia Chien is an avid painter who works from her studio in Southern California. She recently illustrated the children's book *The Sea Serpent and Me* by Dashka Slater, and she produces work for various galleries and comic book anthologies.

Phil Craven is a storyboard artist at DreamWorks Animation, where he works with awesome, talented, and inspiring friends.

Nikki Damon likes writing and comics almost as much as she likes peanut butter. This is her first story for *Flight*.

Mike Dutton has been an illustrator for most of his life. He once drew the entire Sunday funnies in the second grade, though none of the jokes were funny. In fact, his teacher found them to be quite rude and his parents were asked to pay a visit. He has since gone on to make all kinds of art: kids' books, video game backgrounds, landscape paintings, and quite possibly a portrait of your dog. Mike lives in Berkeley, California with his lovely wife, Alex, whom he wishes to thank for all her support. He's still learning to be funny, but thinks you might enjoy his online comic, *One Swoop Fell* (www.oneswoopfell.com). You can find more of his art and ramblings at www.DuttonArt.net.

Michel Gagné was born in Québec, Canada, and has had a highly successful career drawing characters and special effects for animated and live-action feature films such as *The Iron Giant* and *Osmosis Jones*. His independant short film *Prelude to Eden* is a favorite among animation students and teachers and has played at festivals throughout the world. Michel and his wife created Gagné International Press in 1998, and he has been writing, illustrating, and publishing books and comics ever since. www.gagneint.com

Cory Godbey lives in South Carolina with his wife, Erin Elizabeth, and their cats, Harrell, Whittington, and James. Cory writes, illustrates, and animates for Portland Studios. He enjoys lively accordion music, pasta, and when it rains at night. www.corygodbey.com

Rodolphe Guenoden has been working in the animation industry as an animator and storyboard artist for twenty years, and loves the sanctuary that comics has always represented for him—both as a reader of comics, ever since he could read, and as a try-to-doer, ever since Kazu encouraged him to. He is ever so freaking thankful for his wife, Benedicte, and sons, Lucas and Eliott, for always being so supportive and understanding of the long hours and trauma…and the cat never complained either. He is now working on his first full-length French graphic novel with an amazing script by Wilfrid Lupano. www.rodguen.com

Steve Hamaker is the colorist for Jeff Smith's *Bone* graphic novel series, published by Scholastic Books. In his free time he enjoys drawing comics, playing video games, and watching cartoons while eating burritos. www.steve-hamaker.com

Kazu Kibuishi is the editor and art director of the *Flight* comics anthology series. He is also the creator of the *Amulet* graphic novel series published by Scholastic, the acclaimed graphic novel *Daisy Kutter,* and the popular webcomic *Copper.* He is married to writer Amy Kim Kibuishi and they live and work together in Alhambra, California.

Andrea Offermann was tired of all the rain and dreary weather in Germany and migrated to California to taste some sun. There she also stumbled over a great art school and learned to appreciate great images and storytelling. Now back in Germany she makes sure to migrate to California at least once a year for gallery shows, conferences, and more sun.

Richard Pose is a freelance artist living in Los Angeles. He is single and enjoys baseball, *Halo,* and sunsets…Ladies, he's a catch! So catch more of his art at www.richardpose.com.

Justin Ridge is a native of smoggy California and has worked on several animated television shows including *Avatar: The Last Airbender, Star Wars: Clone Wars,* and most recently *The Cleveland Show.* You can see some of his silly art at www.justinridge.com.

Rad Sechrist draws all day and loves it. He draws at work, for DreamWorks Animation. He draws for fun everywhere, all the time. Look, he is drawing now! radfordsechrist.blogspot.com

Kean Soo is the author of the *Jellaby* series of graphic novels. His second book, *Jellaby: Monster in the City,* was published by Hyperion Books for Children in the spring of 2009. Like his titular creation, Kean will eat just about anything that crosses his path. www.secret-friendsociety.com

LET YOUR IMAGINATION TAKE FLIGHT!

Savor the work of today's top illustrators—
complete your FLIGHT library today.

Available from Villard Books everywhere books or comics are sold

www.villard.com | The Random House Publishing Group